Bartolomeo Cristofori and the Invention of the Piano

This is the first comprehensive study of the life and work of Bartolomeo Cristofori, the Paduan-born harpsichord maker and contemporary of Antonio Stradivari, who is credited with having invented the pianoforte around the year 1700 while working in the Medici court in Florence. Through thorough analysis of documents preserved in the state archive of Florence, Pollens has reconstructed, in unprecedented technical detail, Cristofori's working life between his arrival in Florence in 1688 and his death in 1732. This book will be of interest to pianists, historians of the piano, musicologists, museum curators and conservators, as well as keyboard instrument makers, restorers, and tuners.

Trained as a violin and keyboard instrument maker, Stewart Pollens served as the conservator of musical instruments at The Metropolitan Museum of Art between 1976 and 2006, and is presently the Director of Violin Advisor, LLC. He is the author of numerous scholarly articles and award-winning publications on musical instrument history including *The Early Pianoforte* (Cambridge, 1995), *Stradivari* (Cambridge, 2010), and the *Manual of Musical Instrument Conservation* (Cambridge, 2015).

Portrait of a lost oil painting of Bartolomeo Cristofori inscribed ATE/1726.

Bartolomeo Cristofori and the Invention of the Piano

STEWART POLLENS

CAMBRIDGE
UNIVERSITY PRESS

University Printing House, Cambridge CB2 8BS, United Kingdom

One Liberty Plaza, 20th Floor, New York, NY 10006, USA

477 Williamstown Road, Port Melbourne, VIC 3207, Australia

4843/24, 2nd Floor, Ansari Road, Daryaganj, Delhi – 110002, India

79 Anson Road, #06-04/06, Singapore 079906

Cambridge University Press is part of the University of Cambridge.

It furthers the University's mission by disseminating knowledge in the pursuit of education, learning and research at the highest international levels of excellence.

www.cambridge.org
Information on this title: www.cambridge.org/9781107096578
DOI: 10.1017/9781316156292

© Stewart Pollens 2017

This publication is in copyright. Subject to statutory exception and to the provisions of relevant collective licensing agreements, no reproduction of any part may take place without the written permission of Cambridge University Press.

First published 2017

Printed in the United Kingdom by TJ International Ltd. Padstow Cornwall

A catalogue record for this publication is available from the British Library

Library of Congress Cataloging-in-Publication data
Names: Pollens, Stewart.
Title: Bartolomeo Cristofori and the invention of the piano / Stewart Pollens.
Description: Cambridge ; New York, NY : Cambridge University Press, 2017. | Includes bibliographical references and index.
Identifiers: LCCN 2016052048 | ISBN 9781107096578
Subjects: LCSH: Cristofori, Bartolomeo, 1655-1732. | Musical instrument makers – Italy – Biography. | Piano – History – 18th century.
Classification: LCC ML424.C67 P65   2017 | DDC 786.2/19092 [B] – dc23
LC record available at https://lccn.loc.gov/2016052048

ISBN 978-1-107-09657-8 Hardback

Cambridge University Press has no responsibility for the persistence or accuracy of URLs for external or third-party internet websites referred to in this publication, and does not guarantee that any content on such websites is, or will remain, accurate or appropriate.

Contents

List of Figures   *page* [vi]
List of Tables   [xv]

Introduction   [1]

1 Bartolomeo Cristofori in Padua   [8]

2 Cristofori in Florence   [16]

3 Cristofori's Extant Instruments   [79]

4 Musical Life in Florence in Cristofori's Time   [212]

5 Cristofori's Influence   [243]

Conclusion   [343]

Appendix 1 Scipione Maffei's notes made in connection with his interview with Bartolomeo Cristofori   [350]

Appendix 2 Scipione Maffei's "Nuova invenzione d'un Gravecembalo col piano, e forte" in the *Giornale de' letterati d'Italia* 5 (Venice, 1711)   [356]

Bibliography   [363]
Index   [378]

Figures

Frontispiece: Portrait of a lost oil painting of Bartolomeo Cristofori inscribed ATE/1726.

1.1 Map of Padua marked with the approximate location of Bartolomeo Cristofori's residence, engraving, P. Mortier, from *Les villes de Venetie* (Amsterdam, 1704). Collection of the author. *page* [10]

2.1 Earliest record of Bartolomeo Cristofori in Florence, April 30, 1688. Payment by the Medici court of 12 *scudi* for provisions. Courtesy of the Archivio di Stato, Florence. [17]

2.2 Map of Florence, *c.* 1730 showing approximate location of Cristofori's residence at Canto agli Alberti. Map by Giuseppe Papini. Collection of the author. [23]

2.3 Cristofori's first bill to the Medici court, for the construction of a new spinet, dated August 15, 1690. Courtesy of the Archivio di Stato, Florence. [34]

2.4 (a), (b) The "oval" spinet made by Cristofori, dated 1690, listed in the 1700 Medici inventory of musical instruments. Courtesy of the Archivio di Stato, Florence. [37]

2.5 The *spinettone* for the orchestra as listed in the 1700 Medici musical instrument inventory. Courtesy of the Archivio di Stato, Florence. [44]

2.6 (a), (b) The "oval" spinet made by Cristofori, dated 1693, as listed in the 1700 Medici musical instrument inventory. Courtesy of the Archivio di Stato, Florence. [50]

2.7 Title of 1716 Medici musical instrument inventory. Courtesy of the Archivio di Stato, Florence. [64]

2.8 Cristofori's signature at the end of the 1716 Medici musical instrument inventory. Courtesy of the Archivio di Stato, Florence. [65]

2.9 "ATE/1726" monogram on portrait of Cristofori as transcribed by Georg Schünemann. [76]

3.1 Cristofori's ebony harpsichord. Photograph courtesy of the Conservatorio di Musica "Luigi Cherubini" di Firenze. [82]

List of Figures vii

3.2 Plan view of Cristofori's ebony harpsichord. Photograph courtesy of the Conservatorio di Musica "Luigi Cherubini" di Firenze.   [83]

3.3 Schematic drawing of the bridge, nut, soundboard ribs (solid lines), case braces, and belly rail (dashed lines) of the ebony harpsichord.   [85]

3.4 Cristofori's oval spinet of 1690. Photograph courtesy of the Conservatorio di Musica "Luigi Cherubini" di Firenze.   [88]

3.5 Cristofori's oval spinet of 1693. Photograph courtesy of the Grassi Museum für Musikinstrumente der Universität Leipzig.   [88]

3.6 Plan view of the 1690 oval spinet. Photograph courtesy of the Conservatorio di Musica "Luigi Cherubini" di Firenze.   [89]

3.7 X-ray plan view of Cristofori's oval spinet of 1693. Courtesy of the Opificio delle Pietre Dure, Florence.   [92]

3.8 Cristofori's *spinettone*. Photograph courtesy of the Grassi Museum für Musikinstrumente der Universität Leipzig.   [94]

3.9 Cristofori's harpsichord of 1722. Photograph courtesy of the Grassi Museum für Musikinstrumente der Universität Leipzig.   [101]

3.10 Schematic drawing of the bridge, nut, soundboard ribs, cutoff bar (solid lines), case braces, and belly rail (dashed lines) of Cristofori's 1722 harpsichord.   [103]

3.11 Plan view of Cristofori's 1722 harpsichord. Photograph courtesy of the Grassi Museum für Musikinstrumente der Universität Leipzig.   [104]

3.12 Cristofori's 1726 harpsichord. Photograph courtesy of the Grassi Museum für Musikinstrumente der Universität Leipzig.   [106]

3.13 Plan view of Cristofori's 1726 harpsichord. Photograph courtesy of the Grassi Museum für Musikinstrumente der Universität Leipzig.   [107]

3.14 Schematic drawing of the bridges, 2′ and 4′ hitchpin rails, nuts, soundboard ribs, cutoff bar (solid lines), case braces, and belly rail (dashed lines) of Cristofori's 1726 harpsichord.   [108]

3.15 Cristofori's clavichord. Photograph courtesy of the Grassi Museum für Musikinstrumente der Universität Leipzig.   [114]

3.16 Plan view of Cristofori's clavichord. Photograph courtesy of the Grassi Museum für Musikinstrumente der Universität Leipzig.   [115]

3.17 Medici musical instrument inventory of 1700: "Arpicimbalo di Bartolomeo Cristofori di nuova inventione, che fa' il piano, e il forte." Courtesy of the Archivio di Stato, Florence.   [120]

3.18 Engraving of Cristofori's hammer action from the *Giornale de' letterati d'Italia* (Venice, 1711).   [123]

3.19 Engraving of Cristofori's hammer action from Maffei's *Rime e prose* (Venice, 1719).   [124]

3.20 Cristofori piano of 1720. The Metropolitan Museum of Art, Crosby Brown Collection, 1889. Photograph courtesy of The Metropolitan Museum of Art.   [130]

3.21 Cristofori piano of 1722. Museo Nazionale degli Strumenti Musicali, Rome.   [131]

3.22 Cristofori piano of 1726. Grassi Museum für Musikinstrumente der Universität Leipzig.   [132]

3.23 Accidental key lever from the 1726 Cristofori piano.   [133]

3.24 Detail of the escapement mechanism from the 1726 Cristofori piano.   [133]

3.25 Detail of the escapement jack from the 1726 Cristofori piano.   [134]

3.26 Hammer from the 1722 Cristofori piano.   [135]

3.27 Hammer from the 1720 Cristofori piano.   [136]

3.28 Hammer from the 1726 Cristofori piano.   [137]

3.29 Detail from the lost portrait of Cristofori dated 1726 showing him holding a drawing of one of his hammer actions.   [137]

3.30 Georg Schünemann's schematic recreation of the hammer action depicted in the lost portrait of Cristofori. Georg Schünemann, "Ein Bildnis Bartolomeo Cristoforis," *Zeitschrift für Musikwissenschaft* 16/11–12 (November–December, 1934).   [137]

3.31 Hammer rack of 1722 Cristofori piano showing the wood spacers located between the hammers.   [139]

3.32 Dampers from the 1726 Cristofori piano. The narrow one is from the treble, the wider one from the bass.   [141]

3.33 Detail of the 1726 Cristofori piano showing the inverted wrestplank.   [143]

3.34 (a), (b) Section of the wrestplank from the 1720 Cristofori piano removed during the 1938 restoration.   [145]

3.35 Gap spacer running from wrestplank to belly rail of the 1726 Cristofori piano.   [146]

3.36 X-ray of the 1720 Cristofori piano showing the gap between the inner and outer bentsides. X-ray courtesy of the Objects Conservation Department, The Metropolitan Museum of Art.   [147]

List of Figures

3.37 Schematic drawing of a cross-section of the 1720 Cristofori piano case showing the hitchpin rail suspended over the soundboard, the internal bentside that supports the soundboard, and a case brace that bypasses the internal bentside and "plugs" into the heavy liner. [147]
3.38 (a), (b) Interior views of the 1720 Cristofori piano. [148]
3.39 Detail of interior of 1720 Cristofori piano showing a case brace. [149]
3.40 Schematic drawing of the bridge, nut, soundboard ribs, cutoff bar (solid lines), case braces, and belly rail (dashed lines) of the 1726 Cristofori piano. [149]
3.41 (a), (b) Interior views of the 1722 Cristofori piano. Photographs courtesy of the Museo Nazionale degli Strumenti Musicali, Rome. [150]
3.42 Acoustic holes in the belly rail of the 1720 Cristofori piano. [152]
3.43 Detail of bass bridge of the 1722 Cristofori piano. [155]
3.44 Plan view of the 1720 Cristofori piano showing present non-original position of the bridge, which veers away from the bentside. [162]
3.45 Fragment of the original soundboard that was removed from the 1720 Cristofori piano in the 1938 restoration. [164]
3.46 Reconstruction of a hammer for the 1720 Cristofori piano made by the author showing the original shape of the hammer butt, the leather bushing for the pivot rod, and the cylindrical hammer head. [166]
3.47 The "Gatti-Kraus" Cristofori piano action. Museo degli Strumenti Musicali del Conservatorio "Luigi Cherubini" di Firenze. [167]
3.48 Two key levers from the Gatti-Kraus action showing score lines on one key and their absence on the other. [172]
3.49 Two escapement jacks from the Gatti-Kraus action showing discrepancies in workmanship and tool marks. [174]
3.50 Two escapement mechanisms from the Gatti-Kraus action showing discrepancies in workmanship and tool marks. [175]
3.51 Two hammer heads from the Gatti-Kraus action showing discrepancies in workmanship. [175]
3.52 Two dampers from the Gatti-Kraus action showing discrepancies in workmanship. [176]
3.53 Schematic drawing of Cristofori's hammer action. [178]
3.54 Pianoforte/harpsichord by Giovanni Ferrini, Florence, 1746; collection of Luigi Ferdinando Tagliavini, Bologna. [184]
3.55 Jack from the pianoforte/harpsichord by Giovanni Ferrini. [186]

List of Figures

3.56 Damper from the pianoforte/harpsichord by Giovanni Ferrini. The dampers dog-leg and operate from both the harpsichord and piano keyboards. [187]

3.57 Detail of key lever from the piano keyboard of Ferrini's pianoforte/harpsichord showing the vertically attenuated escapement jack and the cutout area that allows the intermediate levers to sit lower and more compactly. [188]

3.58 Hammer from the Ferrini pianoforte/harpsichord. The wooden core of the cylindrical hammer head shown here is not original and was removed during a recent restoration. [189]

3.59 Detail of the bottom of the Ferrini pianoforte/harpsichord showing kerf-bending of the molding and case side – a wood-bending technique employed by Cristofori and used in most of his instruments. [190]

3.60 Keywell bracket of the Ferrini pianoforte/harpsichord. The design of the upper section is derived from Cristofori's bracket. [191]

3.61 Schematic drawing of the Ferrini pianoforte/harpsichord. Nut, bridge, soundboard ribs, and cutoff bar are solid lines; case braces are dashed lines. [192]

3.62 Posts with metal pins used as the "nut" of Ferrrini's pianoforte/harpsichord. Because the strings pass under the pins, the pins prevent the strings from lifting during impact from the hammers. [193]

3.63 Ferrini *cembalo traverso*, Florence, 1731. Museo Clemente Rospigliosi, Pistoia. [195]

3.64 Detail of keyboard and stop mechanism of Ferrini *cembalo traverso*. [196]

3.65 Detail of the treble sections of the 4′ and 8′ bridges of the Ferrini *cembalo traverso*. [197]

3.66 *Cembalo traverso* attributed to Giovanni Solfanelli, 1704. Photograph courtesy of the Smithsonian Institution, National Museum of American History, Washington, DC. [198]

3.67 Plan view of the *cembalo traverso* attributed to Giovanni Solfanelli showing mitered (rather than curved) bridges. Photograph courtesy of the Smithsonian Institution, National Museum of American History, Washington, DC. [199]

3.68 Plan view of a harpsichord by Girolamo Zenti, Rome, 1666. The Metropolitan Museum of Art, Crosby Brown Collection, 89.4.1220. [200]

List of Figures xi

3.69 Detail of Girolamo Zenti harpsichord showing separate parallel bass bridges, two of which (those closest to the main bridge) are likely the work of Giovanni Ferrini, who restored the harpsichord and extended the compass in 1755. Short, parallel bass bridges were sometimes used by Ferrini's master, Bartolomeo Cristofori, for example in the 1726 harpsichord. The Metropolitan Museum of Art, Crosby Brown Collection, 89.4.1220. [202]

3.70 Upright piano by Domenico del Mela, Gagliano, 1739. Photograph courtesy of the Museo degli Strumenti Musicali del Conservatorio "Luigi Cherubini" di Firenze. [204]

3.71 Nameboard inscription of the del Mela upright pianoforte. [205]

3.72 Hammer action of the del Mela upright pianoforte. [207]

3.73 Hammer of the del Mela upright pianoforte. [208]

3.74 Schematic drawing of the Ferrini pianoforte hammer action. [209]

4.1 Engraving of the third floor of the Medici Villa di Pratolino showing the theater and the *platea*, or area for the audience. From Bernardo Sansone Sgrilli's *Descrizione della regia villa, fontane, e fabriche di Pratolino* (Florence, 1742). [217]

4.2 Group portrait of Medici court musicians by Anton Domenico Gabbiani, 1685–1686. Courtesy of the Palazzo Pitti, Appartamenti Monumentali, inventory no. 1890/2805. [223]

4.3 Cover of a manuscript book of keyboard music bearing the Medici arms that is preserved in the Biblioteca del Conservatorio di Musica "Luigi Cherubini" di Firenze, catalog number D.2358. Courtesy of the Biblioteca del Conservatorio di Musica "Luigi Cherubini" di Firenze. [236]

4.4 "Aria alla Francese" from the Medici keyboard book. Courtesy of the Biblioteca del Conservatorio di Musica "Luigi Cherubini" di Firenze. [237]

4.5 Page from Lodovico Giustini's *Sonate da Cimbalo di piano, e forte*, showing dynamic markings. [239]

5.1 Spanish piano attributed to Francisco Pérez Mirabal, Seville, 1745. Collection of the late Bartolomé March, Madrid. [253]

5.2 Third-choir mutation batten (located beyond the damper rack) of Spanish piano; collection of the late Bartolomé March, Madrid. [255]

5.3 Hammer of Spanish piano; collection of the late Bartolomé March, Madrid. [257]

5.4 Hammer of Spanish piano; collection of the Museo Provincial de Bellas Artes, Seville. [258]

List of Figures

5.5 Escapement mechanism of Spanish piano; collection of the Museo Provincial de Bellas Artes, Seville. [259]

5.6 Staple and escapement spring of Spanish piano; collection of the Museo Provincial de Bellas Artes, Seville. [259]

5.7 Back section of key levers of Spanish piano; collection of the Museo Provincial de Bellas Artes, Seville. [260]

5.8 Treble section of soundboard of Spanish piano showing broad hitchpin rail; collection of the Museo Provincial de Bellas Artes, Seville. [262]

5.9 Piano by Henrique Van Casteel. Museu da Música, Lisbon. [263]

5.10 Action frame of the piano by Henrique Van Casteel. [263]

5.11 Detail of key levers of Van Casteel piano showing maker's inscription "Henrique [partially missing] Van Casteel." [264]

5.12 Anonymous Portuguese piano. Private collection, Switzerland. [265]

5.13 Portuguese piano by Antunes. National Music Museum, Vermillion, South Dakota. [266]

5.14 Inscription on a key lever of the Antunes piano. National Music Museum, Vermillion, South Dakota. [266]

5.15 Hammer of the piano by Van Casteel; collection of the Museu da Música, Lisbon. [268]

5.16 Detail of escapement mechanism of the Van Casteel piano; collection of the Museu da Música, Lisbon. [270]

5.17 Detail of escapement mechanism of the Antunes piano; collection of the National Music Museum, Vermillion, South Dakota. [271]

5.18 Schematic drawing of the bridge, nut, soundboard ribs, cutoff bar (solid lines), and case braces (dashed lines) of the anonymous Portuguese piano, private collection, Switzerland. (After a drawing by Christopher Nobbs.) [272]

5.19 Schematic drawing of the bridge, nut, soundboard ribs, cutoff bar (solid lines), and case braces (dashed lines) of the Van Casteel piano, Museu da Música, Lisbon. [273]

5.20 Schematic drawing of the bridge, nut, soundboard ribs, cutoff bar (solid lines), and case braces (dashed lines) of the Antunes piano, National Music Museum, Vermillion, South Dakota. (After a drawing by John Koster.) [274]

5.21 Schematic drawing of Spanish andPortuguese hammer actions. [277]

List of Figures xiii

5.22 Cristofori's hammer action as it appeared in Johann Ulrich König's "Musicalische Merckwürdigkeiten des Marchese, Scipio Maffei," in Johann Mattheson, *Critica Musica* (Hamburg, 1725).   [281]

5.23 Hammer action, Ignace Joseph Senft; Crosby Brown Collection, The Metropolitan Museum of Art. Note the similarity to the drawing of Cristofori's early action pictured in Figure 5.22.   [282]

5.24 Christoph Gottlieb Schröter's first hammer action, from Marpurg's *Kritische Briefe über die Tonkunst* (Berlin, 1763).   [287]

5.25 Christoph Gottlieb Schröter's second hammer action, from Marpurg's *Kritische Briefe über die Tonkunst* (Berlin, 1763).   [287]

5.26 Piano by Gottfried Silbermann, 1746. Stiftung Preußische Schlösser und Gärten Berlin-Brandenburg, Potsdam, Sanssouci.   [294]

5.27 Piano by Gottfried Silbermann, *c.* 1746. Stiftung Preußische Schlösser und Gärten Berlin-Brandenburg, Potsdam, Neues Palais.   [294]

5.28 Escapement mechanism of Gottfried Silbermann piano, 1746; Sanssouci, Potsdam.   [297]

5.29 Escapement jack of Gottfried Silbermann piano, 1746; Sanssouci, Potsdam.   [298]

5.30 Hammer of Gottfried Silbermann piano, 1746; Sanssouci, Potsdam.   [298]

5.31 Keywell of piano by Gottfried Silbermann, *c.* 1746; Neues Palais, Potsdam.   [301]

5.32 X-ray view of Gottfried Silbermann piano, 1749; collection of the Germanisches Nationalmuseum, Nuremberg.   [302]

5.33 Rosette of Gottfried Silbermann piano, *c.* 1746; Neues Palais, Potsdam.   [304]

5.34 Detail of mutation batten showing springs, ivory plates, and adjustment screws. Gottfried Silbermann piano, *c.* 1746; Neues Palais, Potsdam.   [305]

5.35 *Pyramide* piano by Christian Ernst Friederici. Engraving, Johann Christian Müller, Gera, 1745.   [310]

5.36 *Pyramide* piano by Christian Ernst Friederici, *c.* 1745; Frankfurter Goethe-Haus.   [311]

5.37 Soundboard rose of the Friederici *Pyramide* piano; Frankfurter Goethe-Haus.   [314]

5.38 Hammer action of the Friederici *Pyramide* piano; Frankfurter Goethe-Haus.   [315]

5.39 Detail of the escapement lever of the Friederici *Pyramide* piano; Frankfurter Goethe-Haus.   [316]

xiv　　*List of Figures*

5.40　Hammer action of the *Pyramide* piano in the Germanisches Nationalmuseum, Nuremberg.　[317]
5.41　Hammer action of the *Pyramide* piano, Muziekinstrumentenmuseum, Brussels.　[318]
5.42　Schematic drawing of the Gottfried Silbermann hammer action.　[321]
5.43　Schematic drawing of the Friederici *Pyramide* hammer action; Frankfurter Goethe-Haus.　[324]
5.44　Schematic drawing of the Brussels collection *Pyramide*'s hammer action.　[325]
5.45　Schematic drawing of the Nuremberg collection *Pyramide*'s hammer action.　[326]
5.46　Jean-Henri Silbermann piano, detail of the inverted wrestplank. Photograph courtesy of Alan Curtis.　[332]
5.47　Jean-Henri Silbermann piano, detail of hammer showing leathered cylindrical hammer head. Photograph courtesy of Alan Curtis.　[333]
5.48　Jean-Henri Silbermann piano, detail of escapement mechanism; note lack of back check. Photograph courtesy of Alan Curtis.　[334]
5.49　Label in English and French in a late-eighteenth-century Broadwood square piano, providing instructions for regulating the action.　[335]
5.50　Piano by Louis Bas, 1781. National Music Museum, Vermillion, South Dakota.　[335]
5.51　Rose of Louis Bas piano, 1781. National Music Museum, Vermillion, South Dakota.　[336]
5.52　Erard 1821 patent drawing for the repetition action.　[339]
5.53　Superimposition of the 1821 patent drawing of Sébastien Erard's "repetition action" (from Rosamund Harding's *The Pianoforte*) and a version of Maffei's drawing of Cristofori's hammer action. The hammers, intermediate levers, and escapement jacks of the actions are similarly positioned and proportioned.　[341]

Tables

3.1 Measurements of Cristofori's hammer actions.   *page* [178]
3.2 String lengths/striking points of Cristofori's pianos.   [179]
3.3 Wire diameters found in Cristofori's pianos.   [179]
3.4 Case and keyboard measurements of Cristofori's pianos.   [180]
3.5 String lengths/plucking points of *cembali traversi* (*spinettone*).   [199]
3.6 Case measurements of *cembali traversi* (*spinettone*).   [199]
3.7 Comparative measurements of hammer actions of Cristofori and Ferrini pianos.   [209]
3.8 String lengths/striking points/plucking points of del Mela, Ferrini, and Cristofori instruments.   [210]
3.9 String-gauge markings of Ferrini/Cristofori instruments.   [210]
3.10 Case measurements of Ferrini pianoforte/harpsichord.   [211]
3.11 Case measurements of del Mela upright pianoforte.   [211]
5.1 Comparative measurements of hammer actions of Cristofori and Spanish pianos.   [277]
5.2 Comparative measurements of hammer actions of Cristofori and Portuguese pianos.   [278]
5.3 String lengths/striking points of Cristofori and Spanish pianos.   [279]
5.4 String lengths/striking points of Cristofori and Portuguese pianos.   [280]
5.5 String-gauge markings of Portuguese pianos.   [280]
5.6 Case measurements of Portuguese and Spanish pianos.   [280]
5.7 Comparative measurements of hammer actions of Cristofori and Silbermann pianos.   [321]
5.8 String lengths/striking points of Cristofori and Silbermann pianos.   [322]
5.9 String diameters of Silbermann pianos.   [322]
5.10 Cristofori and Silbermann piano-case dimensions.   [323]
5.11 String lengths/striking points of Friederici *Pyramide* pianos.   [323]
5.12 Hammer-action measurements of Friederici *Pyramide* (Frankfurt) and Silbermann pianos.   [324]
5.13 Case and keyboard dimensions of *Pyramide* pianos.   [327]

Introduction

My interest in Bartolomeo Cristofori began in the early 1970s while serving an apprenticeship in harpsichord making with John Challis in New York. I had taken an afternoon off to visit the newly installed André Mertens Galleries of Musical Instruments at The Metropolitan Museum of Art, and as I was examining the harpsichords on exhibit, I heard the most beautiful sounds coming from what I thought was a harpsichord further down the gallery. The instrument that I heard was being played by Edwin Ripin, an associate curator in the Department of Musical Instruments, who was giving a tour to a group of students. As soon as they moved on, I read the instrument's label, and to my amazement discovered that I had not been listening to a harpsichord but to the earliest known piano made by that instrument's inventor, Bartolomeo Cristofori. I vowed then and there that the first instrument I would make upon completing my apprenticeship would be a copy of The Met's Cristofori piano. The instrument that I finally managed to complete was not what one would today call an "exact replica," for I had not been granted direct access to the instrument by the then head of The Metropolitan Museum of Art's Department of Musical Instruments, Laurence Libin, but was only permitted to measure an action model and to consult some general measurements and catalog descriptions in the department's files (by then Edwin Ripin had left the museum, and though I never had the pleasure of meeting him, I did speak with him over the telephone about the Cristofori piano). In 1976, the fortepianist Steven Lubin made an informal recording on my copy that was featured on "The Laughing Cavalier," a classical-music program on WBAI in New York.

Shortly after completing the copy, I began working as the conservator of musical instruments at The Metropolitan Museum of Art and had greater access to the original instrument. Not only did I then learn the error of my ways, but I discovered how the original instrument had been greatly altered in the course of its long history. The changes to its keyboard range, scaling and striking points, as well as to the hammer-action geometry and action parts, were later compounded by an unfortunate restoration carried out at the museum in the late 1930s, in which the original soundboard, bridge, wrestplank, case bottom, and other parts were removed, discarded, and replaced with new ones, thereby rendering the original piano about as inauthentic as my copy! A research grant awarded by the museum provided an opportunity to examine the other two Cristofori pianos, in Rome and Leipzig. This enabled me to compare the hammer actions of the three instruments and to verify the authenticity of various idiosyncratic aspects of case structure that I had discovered in The Metropolitan Museum's piano – notably the use of a secondary internal bentside and a form of structural bracing that isolated the soundboard from the stress-bearing parts of the case. This innovative case design was as remarkable as Cristofori's invention of the escapement mechanism, as it foreshadowed many features of the modern piano, including the ubiquitous cast-iron plate that hovers over the soundboard much like Cristofori's suspended hitchpin rail. In 1984 I published these findings in the *Journal of the American Musical Instrument Society*.

In 1995, Cambridge University Press published my book *The Early Pianoforte* (reissued in paperback in 2009). In that work, Cristofori makes his entry in Chapter 3, as I believed then and still do that Cristofori was not actually the inventor of the piano, but that its history extends back as far as the harpsichord and clavichord. Though the idea of striking strings with hammers or tangents seems to have fallen by the wayside sometime after the mid-fifteenth century, it may have made a brief reappearance in the sixteenth century, as I documented in my study of a sixteenth-century pentagonal spinet by Franciscus Bonafinis that was converted to a tangent-action piano. Nevertheless, Bartolomeo Cristofori is still universally credited with the invention of the piano, and it is clear that his concept of the instrument's pivoted hammer and escapement mechanism, his recognition for the need of greater string tension than in the harpsichord or clavichord, as well as his development of a new form of case construction, led the way to the development of the modern piano. The declaration "inventor," which emblazons Cristofori's nameboard inscriptions, is entirely justified.

While Cristofori's fame derives from the fact that he is widely recognized as the inventor of the pianoforte, his ingenuity is manifest in virtually every other type of instrument he constructed, including clavichords, spinets, and harpsichords. For example, the new form of case structure that he developed for use in his pianos was also employed in his large harpsichords. He was the first keyboard instrument maker to make use of lamination and kerf-bending to decrease stress on delicate sound-producing parts of the instrument. He designed new shapes of cases, such as for his "oval" spinets, a large spinet, termed the *spinettone*, that was specially designed for use in the opera orchestra, and an upright harpsichord whose soundboard was unencumbered by a conventional case. He also developed clever types of stop actions and experimented with unusual string layouts, the double-pinning of bridges and hitchpin rails, and the use of divided bridges in both the bass and treble.

Cristofori worked in the Medici court in Florence between 1688 until his death in 1732. His position there was unique: he worked under the protection of Grand Prince Ferdinando de' Medici and received a monthly stipend, which had never before been granted to an instrument maker. His duties included the general maintenance of the court's growing keyboard collection (which included tuning, adjusting, and major restorations), as well as the construction of new instruments. As someone trained as a harpsichord and organ builder who spent over thirty years working as the conservator of musical instruments at The Metropolitan Museum of Art (an institution that comes about as close to a "royal court" as we have in the United States), I often flattered myself in comparing my position to that of Cristofori, for my duties were similar to his: restoring, tuning, and otherwise maintaining a large collection of fine musical instruments. When I discovered that this distinguished historical figure had often been involved in the ignominious task of carting instruments to and from his workshop and various concert venues in Florence and beyond, I took heart, as I too spent much of my time moving keyboard instruments around the vast museum for concerts, special exhibitions, social events, gallery renovations, and storeroom relocations – so frequently did these moves take place that I often joked that the freight elevator was my office.

In 2010, Cambridge University Press published my book entitled *Stradivari*. Though Antonio Stradivari may be the most famous musical instrument maker of all time, I have always believed that Bartolomeo Cristofori should share the podium with him and that a stand-alone biography was well deserved and long overdue, as there had never been a comprehensive study that integrated biographical information, his work as a harpsichord maker, his invention of the pianoforte, and his official duties as Medici court restorer, tuner and custodian of its collection of musical instruments, with the above placed in the context of musical life in Florence during his years of service there. In writing *Bartolomeo Cristofori and the Invention of the Piano*, it has been my goal to recount Cristofori's life and to describe all of the instruments he is recorded as having made, as well as the few that survive, in a format that is not only readable but also includes sufficient detail to satisfy makers, restorers, and serious historians of early keyboard instruments. In addition to my own archival research and examination and analysis of all his extant instruments, I have attempted to draw together and integrate information derived from doctoral dissertations, obscure *Festschrifts*, conference preprints and proceedings, century-old museum catalogs, and other long-out-of-print publications (often in foreign languages) that deal with Cristofori's life and work, invariably in a piecemeal fashion. I was specially guided by the dissertations and writings of Stefania Gitto, Warren Kirkendale, James Samuel Leve, Giuliana Montanari, Michele Nisoli, Michael Kent O'Brien, Paola Romagnoli, Kirsten Schwarz, Robert Lamar Weaver, and Denzil Wraight, nineteenth-century studies of Cristofori and piano history by Ferdinando Casaglia, Cesare Ponsicchi, and Leto Puliti, and of course Scipione Maffei's 1711 account of the newly invented piano – the first published interview of a musical instrument maker, which stunningly reveals how Cristofori's radical concept of keyboard instrument structure was derived from his understanding of acoustics. More broadly, Maffei's article reveals that musical instrument makers of his time were not simply skilled woodworkers, but were sophisticated individuals with an understanding of performance practice, temperament theory, materials science, and engineering, and who could bring this knowledge to bear in designing their instruments.

The following institutions have kindly made their collections, archives, and services accessible to me over the years: Grassi Museum für Musikinstrumente der Universität Leipzig (formerly the Musikinstrumenten-Museum der Karl-Marx-Universität); Germanisches Nationalmuseum, Nuremberg; Stiftung Preußische Schlösser und Gärten Berlin-Brandenburg (formerly the Staatliche Verwaltung der Schlösser und Gärten, Potsdam); Freies Deutsches Hochstift, Frankfurter Goethe-Haus; Muziekinstrumentenmuseum, Brussels; Museu da Música, Lisbon; Museo Provincial de Bellas Artes, Seville; Museo Nazionale degli Strumenti Musicale, Rome; Museo degli Strumenti Musicali del Conservatorio "Luigi Cherubini" di Firenze; National Music Museum (formerly the Shrine to Music), Vermillion, South Dakota; Accademia Bartolomeo Cristofori, Florence; Archivio di Stato, Florence; Galleria dell'Accademia, Florence; Opificio delle Pietre Diure, Florence; Biblioteca del Conservatorio di Musica "Luigi Cherubini" di Firenze; Archivio Diocesano, Cremona; Biblioteca Capitolare, Verona; Bibliothèque nationale de France; Library of the University of California, Berkeley; The Metropolitan Museum of Art, New York; New York Public Library; and Beinecke Library, Yale University. I would also like to acknowledge Harold Lester and the late Bartolomé March for allowing me to examine their rare Portuguese and Spanish pianofortes,[1] as well as the late Alan Curtis who provided photographs

---

[1] Lester's anonymous Portuguese piano has since been sold to a private collector in Switzerland.

of his Jean-Henri Silbermann piano. Thanks must also go to Donatella DeGiampietro, Michael Latcham, Emanuele Marconi, and Luisa Morales for their generous assistance over the years.

Having gradually come to the realization that a book can never serve as a "virtual" instrument, I have refrained from overburdening readers with minutiae, such as tabulating every string length, plucking point, and striking point – data that the original makers themselves probably never possessed (string lengths, for example, were not plotted string by string, but rather by setting down a few waypoints for the Cs and Fs and allowing the natural fairing of the bridge to take care of those in between). Back in the 1970s, when I made my "copy" of the 1720 Cristofori piano, I believe I was able to capture the spirit of the original using fewer measurements than have been tabulated here.

Readers familiar with my previous work on the topic, *The Early Pianoforte*, will find that some of the material in Chapters 4 through 7 of that book reappears in Chapters 3 and 5 of *Bartolomeo Cristofori*, though a considerable amount of new information has been added in the new work (notably recently discovered biographical material on the Florentine makers del Mela and Ferrini, and possible connections between Cristofori and instrument makers Eugen Casparini, Giovanni Solfanelli and Sébastien Erard). Included in Chapter 3 of *Bartolomeo Cristofori* are technical studies of all his known instruments (including the pianos, harpsichords, spinets, and a clavichord) – the first time all of his instruments have been described and illustrated in a single publication. Some material from *The Early Pianoforte* does not reappear in Chapter 5, such as the discussion of the supposed earliest square piano by Johann Socher, which I dismissed as fraudulently mislabeled in my earlier book, and the full texts and translations of published material relating to the inventive work of Jean Marius and Christoph Gottlieb Schröter, both of whom mistakenly claimed to have developed the hammer action before Cristofori. Chapter 5 of *Bartolomeo Cristofori* thus focuses attention on Cristofori's immediate influence on ultramontane makers, rather than more broadly exploring the early history of the piano. Cambridge University Press has fortunately kept *The Early Pianoforte* in print so that the material, data, and illustrations that I have refrained from including in *Bartolomeo Cristofori* are concurrently available. Throughout *Bartolomeo Cristofori*, the reader will discover new observations and conclusions that supplant those in the earlier work.

I must add that I am indebted to John Challis, the pioneering American harpsichord maker (and innovator in his own right) for giving me my start in the profession of instrument making. His working models of early piano actions crafted after the drawings in Rosamund Harding's *The Pianoforte* initially caused me a great deal of head scratching, though eventually they inspired me to explore and understand the development and workings of the piano. The unknown individuals who need to be gratefully acknowledged are the legions of Medici record keepers and generations of archivists in Florence, Padua, Verona, and other locales who made it possible to look back some 300 years and reconstruct Cristofori's life in vivid detail. And of course, I must thank my wife, Stephanie Chase, for her encouragement, enthusiasm, and patience.

I have often been asked to define and distinguish between the terms "clavier" and "cembalo," as well as "piano," "pianoforte," and "fortepiano." "Clavier" and "cembalo" were (and are) generic terms that may refer to any type of stringed keyboard instrument (i.e., harpsichord, spinet, clavichord, or piano). The term "piano" is actually an unfortunate contraction of "pianoforte," which is derived from the original expression used to indicate Cristofori's new invention: *cembalo che fa piano e forte* (It. "keyboard instrument that makes soft and loud"). I say "unfortunate," because the contraction misses the point entirely: the piano is not only capable of playing softly, but of playing loudly, as well as everything in between. Furthermore, this capability is conveniently placed at the player's fingertips. Dynamic flexibility, which is a feature of most instruments, was not shared by the harpsichord, which in comparison to the newly invented piano was suddenly viewed as being hobbled by its fixed or terraced dynamics.[2] Today, we use the term "fortepiano" to denote wood-framed pianos, specifically those with German- or Viennese-style hammer actions that were made from around 1760 until the adoption of iron framing around the mid-nineteenth century. For some reason, pianos made with English-style hammer actions (be they of English, French, or American manufacture) during this same period are generally referred to as "pianofortes." There is no logic to this distinction, only convention. Throughout this book, I have attempted to retain original spellings when quoting foreign-language texts, even when they are inconsistent (such as *spineta*, *spinetta*, *cembalo*, *cimbalo*, *gravecembalo*, *gravicembalo*, etc.).

All of the instruments described in this book were examined first-hand by the author. Unless otherwise indicated, measurements, photographs, and technical drawings are by the author.

---

[2] The idea that the harpsichord was musically limited by its dynamic inflexibility is disputed in Stewart Pollens, "The Pianoforte in the Performance of Scarlatti's Sonatas," in *Domenico Scarlatti en España: Actas de los Symposia FIMTE 2006–2007* (Garrucha, 2009), pp. 301–311.

Florentine Units

The *braccio* (arm length) used in Florence in Bartolomeo Cristofori's day was approximately equivalent to 551.2 mm. This is at variance with the metric equivalent that is commonly associated with the Florentine *braccio* (583.6 mm); the larger value reflects a change in the length of the *braccio* enacted in 1782. The *braccio* was divided into 2 *palmi* (approximately the width of an outstretched hand) and 20 *soldi* (*soldo* means "coin" or "penny," and was thus approximately equal to the diameter of a coin then in use). The *palmo* is approximately equal to 275.6 mm, and the *soldo* is approximately equal to 27.56 mm.[3]

Florentine unit of weight
    1 *libbra* = 12 *onci* = 0.34 kg[4]
Florentine currency
    1 *scudo* = (approx.) 7 *lire*
    1 *lira* = 20 *soldi*
    1 *soldo* = 12 *denari*

Abbreviations

ASF   Archivio di Stato di Firenze
DP   Depositeria Generale
GM   Guardaroba Medicea

---

[3] Angelo Martini, *Manuale di metrologia* (Turin, 1883), p. 206. Grant O'Brien, "Il percorso di un' idea: dal progetto allo strumento," in *Bartolomeo Cristofori: La spinetta ovale del 1690*, ed. Gabriele Rossi-Rognoni (Florence, 2002), p. 66. See also Stewart Pollens, *The Manual of Musical Instrument Conservation* (Cambridge, 2015), s. v. "historical metrology," and "Historical Metrology in the Service of Organology: Some Caveats," in *Unisonus: Musikinstrumente erforschen, bewahren, sammeln* (Vienna, 2014), pp. 510–537.
[4] Bruno Kisch, *Scales and Weights: A Historical Outline* (New Haven, 1965).

1 | Bartolomeo Cristofori in Padua

Scant information has been uncovered about Bartolomeo Cristofori's early years in his home town of Padua. We know that he was born in Padua on May 4, 1655 and baptized there in the Church of S. Luca on May 6 under the name Bortolomio Christofani.[1] The baptismal record indicates that his father was named Francesco di Christofani, and that his mother's name was Laura. Orthography was inconsistent in the late seventeenth century, so Cristofori's name appears alternately in later official records as "Cristofali," "Cristofani," and "Cristofori," though "Cristofori" was more consistently used in Medici accounts after 1694. Even Cristofori himself was inconsistent in spelling his own name: on bills to court it appears as Bartolomeo Christofori and Bartolomeo Cristofori. Francesco Scipione, Marchese di Maffei (more commonly referred to as Scipione Maffei, 1675–1755), the author of an article on the invention of the piano published in the *Giornale de' letterati d'Italia* in 1711, variously refers to him as "Christofori" (crossed out in the original manuscript notes of his interview conducted in 1709), "Bortolo Cristofali" (as corrected in the same MS), "Bartolommeo Cristofali" (in the article published in 1711), and "Bartolomeo Cristofali" (in the 1719 republication of that article in a compilation of Maffei's writings entitled *Rime e prose*).[2] Niccolò Susier, a Medici court musician and diarist, used the spelling "Bartolomeo Cristofani" and the nickname "Bartolo" in a diary entry marking Cristofori's death dated January 27, 1731.[3] Here the date is given in the *stile fiorentino*, notated *ab incarnatione* (abbreviated *ab. inc.* in this book, when so

---

[1] Padua, archive of the Church of S. Luca, May 6, 1655; Cristofori's baptismal certificate is illustrated in Bruno Brunelli Bonetti, "Bartolomeo Cristofori e il mondo musicale padovano," in *Bartolomeo Cristofori, inventore del pianoforte*, nel terzo centenario dalla nascita (Padua, 1955), p. 31.

[2] Verona, Biblioteca Capitolare, cod. DCCCCLX, fasc. VI, no. I. Scipione Maffei, "Nuova invenzione d'un Gravecembalo col piano, e forte; aggiunte alcune considerazioni sopra gli strumenti musicali," *Giornale de' letterati d'Italia* 5 (Venice, 1711), pp. 144–159; Scipione Maffei, *Rime e prose del Sig. Marchese Scipione Maffei, parte raccolte da varij libri, e parte non più stampate* (Venice, 1719), p. 309; Laura Och, "Bartolomeo Cristofori, Scipione Maffei e la prima descrizione del 'gravicembalo col piano e forte'," *Il Flauto Dolce* 14–15 (1986), pp. 16–23.

[3] Florence, Biblioteca Moreniana, Acquisti diversi 54, ff. 73r, 73v.

specified in cited documents), in which the year began on March 25, the date of the Incarnation; thus, Susier's diary entry was written in 1732 according to the modern calendar. In an anonymous, posthumous tribute to Cristofori written in 1741, he is referred to as "Bartolomeo de Christofani Padovano." From this tribute we also learn that Cristofori was nicknamed "il Burtulo."[4] An anonymous, eighteenth-century musical dictionary refers to him as "Christofori Bartolomeo da Padova."[5]

Various archival records reveal an association between the Cristoforis and the Papafavas, the latter being an old, noble Paduan family. Bartolomeo Cristofori's baptismal certificate documents that his godmother was Lina Pani, a servant of Laura Papafava. Bartolomeo's father's profession was that of a *fattore*, that is, a property agent or administrator, and he worked for the Papafava family in that capacity; in 1662, he also served as best man at Laura Papafava's wedding. Many years later, when Bartolomeo Cristofori was in the employ of Grand Prince Ferdinando de' Medici in Florence, he was either asked or offered to contact Roberto Papafava, then a member of the Accademia Patavina, in order to inquire about engaging the singer Laura Spada for an opera that Ferdinando was staging in Livorno. When Papafava wrote back to Ferdinando on May 30, 1693, he invoked Cristofori's name in connection with that engagement.[6]

The Cristofori family owned parcels of land and houses in a small village outside Padua named Grantorto. This property (much of it was rented out and was thus income generating) had been passed down from generation to generation and ultimately came into the possession of Bartolomeo.[7] In his will, he made provision for his property to pass on to his niece, Laura Pavese (see Chapter 2). A few months after the death of Bartolomeo's father on January 29, 1684, Bartolomeo rented a house behind the city's cathedral in a quarter called the *Drio Domo* (Figure 1.1), which suggests that he was domiciled in his home town until his departure for Florence in 1688.

Surprisingly, no documentation has been discovered in Padua that would indicate that any member of the Cristofori family, including

---

[4] O. Mischiati, "Un elenco romano di cembalari redatto nel 1741," *L'Organo* 10/1 (1972), pp. 105–106.

[5] Bologna, Civico Museo Bibliografico Musicale, H62, miscellaneous writings of Padre Martini, vol. C.

[6] ASF GM 5878, f. 268. Leto Puliti, "Della vita del Ser.mo Ferdinando dei Medici Granprincipe di Toscana e della origine del pianoforte," *Atti dell'Accademia del R. Istituto Musicale di Firenze* 12 (1874), pp. 140–141.

[7] Michele Nisoli, "Bartolomeo Cristofori (1655–1732): Rassegna bibliografica con alcune aggiunte biografiche sugli anni padovani" (Ph.D. diss., University of Florence, 2011), pp. 16–17.

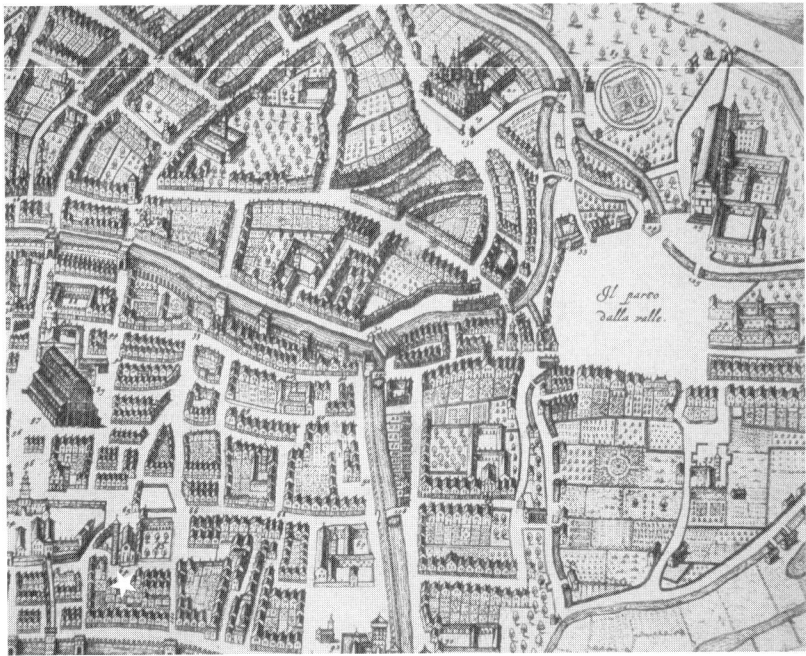

Figure 1.1 Map of Padua marked at bottom left with the approximate location of Bartolomeo Cristofori's residence, engraving, P. Mortier, from *Les villes de Venetie* (Amsterdam, 1704). Collection of the author.

Bartolomeo, was involved in musical instrument making or an associated craft. There has been considerable speculation that Bartolomeo Cristofori was originally trained as a violin maker in Cremona, as a thirteen-year-old Christofaro Bartolomei is listed as a household member in the 1680 census return of the violin maker Nicolò Amati (1596–1684).[8] Because apprentices generally lived in the houses of their masters, we can assume that the above-named individual was serving his apprenticeship in violin making. However, the Christofaro Bartolomei listed in the 1680 Cremonese census return could not have been our Bartolomeo Cristofori, who then would have been twenty-five years old. Furthermore, the census returns of the parish in which Nicolò Amati lived consistently present Christian names first and surnames last; thus, the last name of the apprentice in the Amati shop is "Bartolomei" and not "Christofaro."[9]

---

[8] Cremona, Archivio Diocesano, census returns of the parish of S. Faustino, 1680, Casa Amati.
[9] For a discussion of Cremonese census documents, including the lack of reliability of ages cited in these returns, see Stewart Pollens, *Stradivari* (Cambridge, 2010), pp. 13–15.

Though there are several violoncellos and double basses with printed or handwritten inscriptions indicating that they were made by Bartolomeo Cristofori, these instruments are either stylistically dissimilar to one another or they have been altered in ways that make authentication problematic. This author has examined a refined contrabass (Museo del Conservatorio, Florence) bearing a printed label, and a crude, perhaps recut, contrabass with a handwritten inscription (The Metropolitan Museum of Art, New York). Both instruments could be eighteenth century and Florentine, but they are certainly by different makers. A third contrabass, bearing little resemblance to the other two, is in the collection of the Museo degli Strumenti Musicali in Milan.[10] However, in this author's opinion, none of the handwritten labels of the bowed-string instruments purported to be by Cristofori is in his hand. Furthermore, the wordings "Bartolomeo Cristofori in Firenze 1715 Primo" (contrabass at the Museo del Conservatorio, Florence),[11] "Bartolomeo Cristofori in Firenze 1716" (violoncello, private collection),[12] and "Io Bartolomeo Cristofori fecit in Firenze 1717" (three-string contrabass, The Metropolitan Museum of Art, New York) differ from the inscriptions consistently found on his keyboard instruments, typically "BARTHOLOMÆVS DE CHRISTOPHORIS PATAVINVS FACIEBAT FLORENTIÆ" (1722 and 1726 harpsichords). The wording of the inscription in the much-altered 1717 contrabass, "Io Bartolomeo Cristofori" (I, Bartolomeo Cristofori) is an unlikely way to begin a violin label and would appear to derive from the opening declarations of several of Cristofori's bills submitted to the Medici court; "Bartolomeo Cristofori in Firenze 1715 Primo" would also appear to be a corruption of the wording used in several other bills (see Chapter 2). Transcriptions of these bills were published in Florence in 1876 and would have been accessible to unscrupulous makers and dealers, who likely relabeled a few anonymous violoncellos and contrabasses to exploit the name of this famous instrument maker.[13] Furthermore, there is not a single

---

[10] Natale and Franco Gallini, *Museo degli strumenti musicali: Catalogo* (Milan, 1963), pp. 73–74, pl. 51.

[11] Mario Fabbri, Vinicio Gai, and Leonardo Pinzauti, *Conservatorio di Musica Luigi Cherubini: Antichi strumenti* (Florence, 1980), pp. 69–70; Giuliana Montanari, "Bartolomeo Cristofori: A List and Historical Survey of his Instruments," *Early Music* 19 (1991), p. 392.

[12] John Dilworth, "Two-part Invention," *The Strad* 95/1136 (1985), pp. 668–670; Montanari, ibid., pp. 392–393.

[13] Ferdinando Casaglia, *Per le onoranze a Bartolommeo Cristofori* (Florence, 1876), pp. 17–31.
   This wording was also used by Bartolomeo Cristofori when he signed and certified his 1716 inventory of the Medici's musical instruments; a facsimile of this signature was published by Puliti, *Della vita del Ser.^mo Ferdinando dei Medici*, p. 198.

mention of a bowed-string instrument by Bartolomeo Cristofori in the Medici musical instrument inventories dated 1700, 1716, and 1732, nor is there any indication among the numerous bills and payment records preserved in the Medici Archives that Cristofori was involved in making or restoring such instruments – though there are records that other instrument makers, such as Sabatino Ciampi (Campi, Ciompi, or possibly Cianchi), were paid for work done on string instruments.[14] All of Cristofori's bills (see Chapter 2) are for work on keyboard instruments.[15] This strongly suggests that the Bartolomeo Cristofori who served Grand Prince Ferdinando de' Medici was not involved in the making or restoring of violins, violoncellos, and contrabasses, and the ascription of any bowed-string instrument to Bartolomeo Cristofori of Padua must thus be viewed with suspicion.[16] Unfortunately, no evidence has yet been discovered that Cristofori served a formal apprenticeship in keyboard instrument making or was a member of any craft guild in his home town; nor did he become a guild member when he settled in Florence.

In his biography of the organ builder Gottfried Silbermann, Ernst Flade suggests that there could have been a working relationship between the organ builder Eugen Casparini (true name Johann Caspar; b. Sorau [now Poland], 1623; d. Wiesa, 1706) and Cristofori. Eugen Casparini was the son of an organ builder and mathematician, Adam Caspar. Eugen worked in Venice and Gorizia (in the Friuli region) before settling in Padua around 1669, where he constructed a number of organs, including two for the basilica of S. Giustina: one in 1679 (which included a 16′ *Principal* and 26′ *Fagott* [bassoon stop] of wood) and another in 1681 having 32 stops. Cristofori would have been in his twenties when these organs were constructed and might have taken an interest or perhaps participated in their construction. Previously, Casparini had made a small organ (having six *ripieno* ranks and a wood *Fagott* on a separate wind chest) for the basilica of S. Antonio in 1662. In 1686 Casparini departed Padua for Vienna, where he worked on the court's organs and constructed a *Positiv* (a small,

---

[14] ASF DP 434, f. 38r; 435, f. 30r; 438, ff. 47r, 74r.
[15] ASF GM 1073bis, ff. 2567–2584; Casaglia, *Per le onoranze a Bartolommeo Cristofori*, pp. 17–31.
[16] Notes made during Scipione Maffei's 1709 interview with Cristofori (which deal primarily with the development of the pianoforte) nevertheless reveal that Cristofori did have knowledge of violin acoustics, including an understanding of soundpost adjustment. This should not be viewed as evidence that Cristofori was formally trained as a violin maker, for when Maffei conducted his interview, Cristofori had already been the official court instrument maker for over twenty years and had certainly gained some familiarity with the tonal apparatus of the violin. See Stewart Pollens, *The Early Pianoforte* (Cambridge, 1995; repr. 2009), pp. 232–237.

semi-portable organ) having five registers of paper pipes.[17] Such pipes, made of rolled paper impregnated with glue, were thought to impart a softer, sweeter sound than metal or wood pipes. Organs with paper pipes date back in Italy to the late fifteenth century (one such organ, constructed in 1494 by Lorenzo da Pavia, possibly for Isabella d' Este, is preserved in the Museo Correr in Venice),[18] and such pipes may have been the inspiration for the rolled paper hammer heads that Cristofori used in his 1720 and 1726 pianos (cylinders made of multiple layers of rag paper impregnated with animal hide glue are light in weight and rigid, though springy). Casparini sometimes equipped his organs with "toy stops," such as the drum, which might have provided the impetus for Cristofori's invention of the hammer action later used in his piano. The organ builder Andreas Silbermann (1678–1734) is believed to have worked for Eugen Casparini around 1697 – perhaps this relationship facilitated Gottfried Silbermann's (Andreas' brother, 1683–1753) later familiarity with Cristofori's piano action, which he scrupulously copied in the pianos he made in the 1740s (see Chapter 5). As we shall see in Chapter 2, Cristofori was evidently a capable organ builder, for he constructed a small organ with wooden pipes for the court.

In the sixteenth century, two prominent harpsichord makers were associated with Padua: Franciscus Patavinus (Francesco of Padua, also known as "Il Hongaro" or "l' Ongaro" ["the Hungarian"]), who flourished between 1527 and 1562, and Antonius Patavinus (Antonio of Padua), who flourished around 1550. The Medici musical instrument inventory of 1700 lists a *cimbalo dell'Ongaro* inscribed "Francisci Patavini dicti Ongaro MDLXII" having two registers, principal and octave, and 52 keys of boxwood and ebony having a compass of G–c^3, with the first two sharps split (thus a short-octave compass of BB/GG–c^3). The inventory description further describes it as being removable from a lacquered (*vernici all'indiana*) outer case with painted lid, and having the typical Italianate thin-walled construction of cypress, with case sides inlaid with strips of ebony and garnished with ivory studs; the soundboard of

---

[17] Ernst Flade, *Der Orgelbauer Gottfried Silbermann* (Leipzig, 1952), pp. 1–8; Peter Williams, *The European Organ 1450–1850* (London, 1966), p. 221; *The New Grove Dictionary of Music and Musicians* (London and New York, 1980), s.v. "Casparini."

[18] Marco Tiella, "The Positive Organ of Lorenzo da Pavia (1494)," *The Organ Yearbook* 7 (1976), pp. 4–15; Clifford M. Brown, *Isabella d'Este and Lorenzo da Pavia* (Geneva, 1982), pp. 196–197; Luisa Cervelli, "Un prezioso organo del '400: alla ricerca della sua voce perduta," *Bollettino dei Musei Civici Veneziani* 4 (1969), pp. 21–36; Carlo dell'Acqua, *Lorenzo Gusnasco e i Lingiardi da Pavia* (Milan, 1886).

cypress with four fretworked roses. No harpsichords made in Padua in the latter half of the seventeenth century have come down to us, nor do we know of any harpsichord makers of note living there with whom Cristofori might have apprenticed with. In fact, there are no known keyboard instruments of Cristofori's dated prior to his arrival in Florence, and all of his extant inscribed instruments indicate they were made there (BARTHOLOMÆVS DE CHRISTOPHORIS PATAVINVS FACIEBAT FLORENTIÆ [Bartolomeo Cristofori of Padua made in Florence]). Aside from an uninscribed and undated thin-walled harpsichord attributed to him (the so-called "ebony harpsichord" inventoried by the Medici in 1700 and now in the collection of the Museo degli Strumenti Musicali del Conservatorio "Luigi Cherubini" di Firenze; see Chapter 3) and his two oval spinets (one presently on loan from the Museo Bardini to the Museo degli Strumenti Musicali in Florence and the other in the collection of the Grassi Museum für Musikinstrumente der Universität Leipzig; see Chapter 3), all of his instruments exhibit heavy-walled construction that bears no resemblance to the few Paduan-school harpsichords attributed to the considerably earlier makers of that city who are mentioned above. In any case, we should not assume that their harpsichords were still present in Padua during Cristofori's residence there, and if any of them were, that he was familiar with or had access to them. Thus, we cannot conclude that Cristofori was steeped in what little we know of the Paduan harpsichord-making tradition, and it is entirely possible that he was self-taught.

In Scipione Maffei's notes of his interview with Cristofori made in preparation for his article on the invention of the piano published in 1711, he writes that Cristofori indicated that he did not want to come to Florence, but that Grand Prince Ferdinando replied "*il farò volere io*" (it will be, I wish it). He was evidently induced to relocate by the offer of a generous stipend, the payment of his rent, and the loan of furniture, pots and pans, and other household sundries. As we shall see in Chapter 2, his stipend and perquisites were not considered remuneration for making new instruments, undertaking complex restoration work on valuable keyboard instruments in the court's collection, or even fulfilling mundane tasks such as moving keyboard instruments – for he billed the court separately for those services.

What impelled Grand Prince Ferdinando (then twenty-four years of age) to hire the thirty-two-year-old Cristofori, initially under the title of instrument maker and tuner, remains unclear. Perhaps Cristofori impressed Ferdinando with the idea of a dynamically flexible keyboard instrument fitted with a hammer action and was invited to work out the details and build such an instrument in the Ufizzi workshops with the assistance of its highly skilled court craftsmen. It is also conceivable that Cristofori had already constructed a piano and that Ferdinando somehow encountered and became intrigued by it, though perhaps he was simply impressed by Cristofori's skill as a harpsichord tuner.

As we shall see in the next chapter, Cristofori never billed the Medici court for constructing a pianoforte (which may indicate that he did not build it in Florence, but arrived there with it). The first documentation of such an instrument is an entry in the 1700 Medici musical instrument inventory that describes it as an "Arpicimbalo di Bartolomeo Cristofori di nuova inventione, che fa' il piano, e il forte" (a large keyboard instrument by Bartolomeo Cristofori, of new invention, that makes soft and loud). The date of the inventory is generally associated with the year the piano was invented, but the appellation "new invention" could refer to an instrument made any time after March 17, 1691, *ab. inc.* (1692 by the modern calendar), the date of the previous Medici musical instrument inventory, which does not list such an instrument, or even before Cristofori began working in the Florentine court in 1688. There is, however, one piece of documentary evidence, slender though it is, that he did invent the piano in 1700 (see Chapter 3).

We know that Grand Prince Ferdinando departed Florence on December 18, 1687 to take part in the *Carnivale* in Venice, and that he arrived there with thirty of his courtiers on or around January 17. Along the way, he and his entourage are recorded as having visited Bologna, Vicenza, and Padua. According to a letter posted from Venice on January 17, 1688 by the *abate* Carlo Antonio Gondi, Ferdinando stopped in Padua and left for Venice by boat the following morning after attending mass at the basilica of S. Antonio (for which Casparini had built a small organ in 1662; see above).[19] It is possible that Ferdinando encountered Cristofori during that brief stay, or perhaps the two met in Venice during the protracted carnival season. Ferdinando returned to Florence on March 24, and by April 30 Cristofori was ensconced at the Medici court and variously described in court records as a *strumentaio* (instrument maker) and *buonaccordaio* (keyboard tuner).

[19] Nisoli, *Bartolomeo Cristofori (1655–1732)*, pp. 30–33; Lorenzo Spinelli, "Le esperienze veneziane del principe Ferdinando de' Medici e le influenze sulla politica spettacolare e dinastica toscana (1688–1696)," *Medioevo e Rinascimento* 19/16 (2005), pp. 159–199.

2 | Cristofori in Florence

Arrival in 1688

The earliest documentation we have of Bartolomeo Cristofori's presence in Florence is the record of payment for provisions issued to him by the Medici court on April 30, 1688 (Figure 2.1).

The payment record states: "*e ottanta quattro L. Pag. à Bartolomeo Cristofori Strumentaio che S.A. à fermato e gli à Assegnato L. 84 p. Provisione il Mese e si deve Mettere à rolo porto. detto 12 – –.*"[1] (And eighty-four *lire* paid to Bartolomeo Cristofori musical instrument maker whom His Most Serene Highness has hired and assigned 84 *lire* per month for provisions, and who is admitted to the roll, received by same 12 [*scudi*].) As a point of reference, in 1641 Cardinal Antonio Barberini in Rome paid the harpsichord maker Girolamo Zenti the same annual tuner's fee of 12 *scudi*.[2]

As we have seen in Chapter 1, the circumstances that led to Cristofori's employment in Florence are unknown. The musicologist Leto Puliti speculated that while returning from the Carnival of Venice, Grand Prince Ferdinando de' Medici may have encountered Cristofori in his native Padua.[3] However, if they did meet in Padua, it was more likely that it was prior to Ferdinando's arrival in Venice, rather than after the carnival, for the prince and his retinue are documented as having stopped in Padua on the way to Venice rather than on their return to Florence.[4] It is also possible that they met in Venice during the prince's protracted stay there. We do know that a Florentine harpsichord maker named Antonio Bolgioni (also spelled Bolcioni), who had been serving the Medici court prior to Cristofori's arrival,

---

[1] ASF DP 434, f. 53r. The value of the *lira* floated relative to the *scudo*; this record provides the then current exchange rate of approximately 7 *lire* per *scudo* (1 *lira* = 20 *soldi* = 240 *denari*). Michael Kent O'Brien, "Bartolomeo Cristofori at Court in Late Medici Florence" (Ph.D. diss., The Catholic University of America, 1994), p. 135.
[2] Frederick Hammond, "Some Notes on Giovanni Battista Boni da Cortona, Girolamo Zenti, and Others," *The Galpin Society Journal* 40 (1987), p. 41.
[3] Puliti, *Della vita del Ser.^mo Ferdinando dei Medici*, p. 130.
[4] Nisoli, *Bartolomeo Cristofori (1655–1732)*, pp. 159–199.

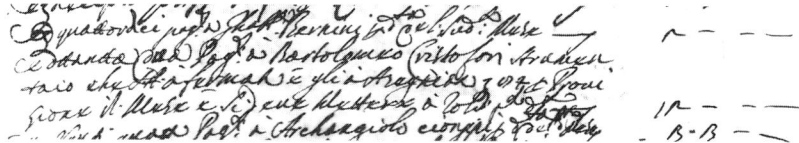

Figure 2.1 Earliest record of Bartolomeo Cristofori in Florence, April 30, 1688. Payment by the Medici court of 12 *scudi* for provisions. Courtesy of the Archivio di Stato, Florence.

passed away in early February of 1688 (he is recorded as having lain in state in the church of S. Maria Nuova on February 3 of that year).[5] A replacement was needed for ongoing musical events, including those held at the Villa di Pratolino, a Medici retreat some twelve kilometers north of Florence (see Chapter 4), as well as those planned for the celebration of Ferdinando's wedding to Violante Beatrice of Bavaria the following year. Bolgioni had been a self-employed instrument maker who was brought in on a freelance basis when instruments needed tuning, adjustment, or repair. Another individual who passed away in early February of 1688 was Giovanni Battista Lassagnini, a member of the Medici court ballet who had served as the *guardaroba della musica* from 1671 (his name appears on the title page of the Medici musical instrument inventory that was compiled posthumously in 1691).[6] This was an administrative post that presumably involved keeping track of the court's musical instruments and scores that were lent to musicians, members of the Medici family, and others involved with the court. Cristofori would ultimately be appointed *custode* of the instrument collection (see below) – perhaps there was something in Cristofori's background (such as a familiarity with the administrative work that his father did) that suggested to Prince Ferdinando that he might be groomed for such a post, though he did not receive that appointment until 1716, three years after Ferdinando's death. While the Medici court had long supported a number of composers and musicians as *stipendiati*, Cristofori's formal position as a recipient of a stipend was unique, as no other instrument maker had ever held such a position in the Medici court. Cristofori received the same payment as many court musicians, and the regular monthly income provided him with a degree of financial security and freedom that most privately employed musical instrument makers did not enjoy.

---

[5] ASF DG 434, f. 47r; Michael Kent O'Brien, "Bartolomeo Cristofori at Court," p. 64.
[6] ASF GM 1005; Vinicio Gai, *Gli strumenti musicali della corte medicea e il Museo del Conservatorio Luigi Cherubini di Firenze, cenni storici e catalogo descrittivo* (Florence and Licosa, 1969), p. 3.

There was certainly no shortage of keyboard instrument makers and tuners residing in Florence at the time of Bolgioni's death who could have serviced the court's instruments, either on a freelance basis or as a salaried technician. Between 1634 and 1697 the Università di Por San Piero e dei Fabbricanti (the craftsmans' guild) listed the following harpsichord makers as matriculants: Luigi Bassilichi (1695), Niccolò Berti (1696), Antonio Bolcioni (1663), Stefano Bolcioni (1634), Agnolo Cigulari (1669), Giuseppe Falconi (1689), Michele Feroci (1680), Agostino Landi (1694), Antonio Migliai (1684), Bartolomeo Pini (1664), Francesco Poggi (1634), Vincenzio Querci (1634), Aurelio Ricevuti (1650), and Giuseppe Zolfanelli (1690 and 1697). Listed separately in the guild rolls for that period are numerous harpsichord tuners: Antonfrancesco Berti (1674), Iacopo Papi (1635), Giovanni Pertici (1665), Agostino Soldini (1636), and Ferdinando Vincenti (1634).[7] In addition to the harpsichord makers and tuners, the guild rolls listed dozens of string instrument makers and four organ builders. Several harpsichord tuners and makers, including Giovanni Pertici and Giovanni Pichileri (the latter was evidently not a guild member), are listed in the Medici accounts as having worked on a freelance basis for the court during Antonio Bolgioni's tenure, though none was selected to replace him as the court's principal keyboard technician.

No keyboard instruments by Cristofori dated prior to his employment in Florence have come to light or are documented (the earliest dated instrument of his is one made in Florence in 1690). In addition to his abilities as an instrument maker, Cristofori appears to have had social connections in the musical world that were useful to the Florentine court. We have learned in Chapter 1, for example, that his name is mentioned in a letter written to Grand Prince Ferdinando on May 30, 1693 by a Paduan nobleman named Roberto Papafava with regard to the engagement of the singer Laura Spada. We must also consider the possibility that Cristofori had been working on the pianoforte prior to his arrival in Florence, and that Ferdinando agreed to sponsor the development of this instrument by offering him funds for provisions, free accommodation with furnishings, and access to the court's workshop facilities, woodworkers, and other artisans. In notes made on the occasion of his visit to the Medici court in 1709 the noted literary figure and editor of the *Giornale de' letterati d'Italia*, Francesco Scipione, Marchese di Maffei (who is generally referred to as Scipione Maffei, 1675–1755), recounted Cristofori's first impressions of life in the Medici court:

---

[7] Puliti, *Della vita del Ser.^{mo} Ferdinando dei Medici*, pp. 168–173.

Che da principio durava fatica ad andare nello stanzone in questo strepito; che fu detto al principe che non voleva rispos'egli "il farò volere io."[8]

(At the beginning it was very tiring for him to be in the large room with this deafening noise; he told the prince that he did not want it so; the latter replied "it will be, I wish it.")

Maffei added that Cristofori was the recipient of a stipend (*stipendiato*), and *che molto ha imparato qua dopo venuto da gli altri... gli da dieci scudi al mese* (that he learned very much from the others after coming here... he [received] ten *scudi* per month). The large, noisy workroom was presumably situated in the Uffizi's Galleria dei Lavori, where over one hundred artisans carried out the work of the court. Oddly, official records indicate that Cristofori received twelve *scudi* per month earmarked for provisions (*provisione*), not ten, as indicated by Maffei.[9]

In Cristofori's early years in Florence, the craft workshops of the Medici court were directed by Diacinto Maria Marmi, who designed and constructed magnificent furniture and architectural woodwork for the Pitti Palace. In 1695 the sculptor Giovanni Battista Foggini took charge and concentrated much of his energies primarily on smaller works, such as marble busts, bronzes, ornamented cabinets, and reliquaries decorated with precious and semi-precious stones. Ferdinando de' Medici was evidently an accomplished musician, having studied counterpoint and harpsichord with Giovanni Francesco Pagliardi, who had been appointed *maestro di cappella* by Ferdinando's father, Grand Duke Cosimo III (1642–1723), around 1670.[10] In addition to his love of music, and especially opera, Ferdinando was a cultivated and enthusiastic patron of painting and the decorative arts. He bought works by Raphael, Andrea del Sarto, and Parmigianino, and commissioned new paintings by artists such as Giuseppe Maria Crespi, Sebastiano Ricci, and Antonio Domenico Gabbiani (see Figure 4.2). In his dealings with painters, Ferdinando often took a collaborative role, suggesting unusual themes and compositional elements.[11] The prince was also fond of ivory carving and turning (he himself was an amateur ivory turner, which at that time was a popular gentleman's avocation) as well as horology – over forty clocks are listed in an immense

---

[8] Verona, Biblioteca Capitolare, cod. DCCCCLX, fasc. VI, n. 1; Och, "Bartolomeo Cristofori, Scipione Maffei e la prima descrizione del 'gravicembalo col piano e forte'," pp. 21–22; Montanari, "Bartolomeo Cristofori: A List and Historical Survey of his Instruments," pp. 384–385.

[9] ASF DG 434, f. 53r.   [10] Kirkendale, *The Court Musicians in Florence*, pp. 417–418.

[11] Francis Haskell, *Patrons and Painters: Art and Society in Baroque Italy* (New York, 1971), pp. 228–241.

inventory of some two hundred pages documenting thousands of personal possessions that was compiled after his death (see below and Chapter 4).[12] Ferdinando's interest in complex mechanical devices of all kinds may have led him to support Cristofori's experimentation with the piano action. Though Cristofori's hammer action made use of an escapement mechanism, there does not appear to be any similarity between the escapement he developed and those employed in other mechanical devices of the period, such as clockworks (including the striking mechanisms of chimes and repeaters), trigger mechanisms of firearms, or trip-hammers used in manufacturing equipment. The inspiration for Cristofori's escapement mechanism is unknown.

Cristofori's second payment for provisions of 12 *scudi* was made on May 6, 1688, though in this account he is referred to as the *bonacordaio* (tuner) rather than as a *strumentaio* (instrument maker).[13] (It should be noted that among the craftsmen listed in the Università di Por San Piero e dei Fabbricanti, a distinction was made between *strumentai* and *buonaccordai*.)[14] A separate entry made on this date is a receipt for the following furniture, linens, silverware, fireplace, and cooking utensils that were provided by the court:[15]

> Two small benches of poplar for the bed.
> Two mattresses of linen, straw, and hair.
> Four mattresses of buckram and wool.
> Two bolsters, matching the first two items.
> A contraption of linen [*trabacca*] stuffed with cotton waste, yellow, worked with eyelets in 4 pieces, the top part in 2 pieces with trimming and turning.[16]
> A frame for it with its screws...
> Two quilts of pink linen.
> Two bed sheets of white wool.

---

[12] ASF GM 1222, ff. 1v–103v; Anna Maria Massinelli and Filippo Tuena, *Treasures of the Medici* (New York, 1992), pp. 180–181.

[13] ASF DG 434, f. 54r.   [14] Puliti, *Della vita del Ser.^mo Ferdinando dei Medici*, pp. 167–173.

[15] ASF GM 903, ff. 129v–130r.

[16] Michael Kent O'Brien interprets the term *trabacca* as a canopy for a bed. Considering the context, this is very likely, though modern Italian dictionaries such as Nicola Zingarelli's *Vocabolario della lingua Italiana*, 12th edition (Bologna, 1998) define it as tent, curtains, awning, hangings, shack, hut, or booth, and *Cassell's Italian Dictionary* (New York, 1967) defines *trabaccolo* as a "trawler, lugger, rickety vehicle, and ramshackle contraption," which seems to capture the spirit of this confusing description. O'Brien, "Bartolomeo Cristofori at Court," p. 184.

Four sheets similar to item number 3 [above].
Four domestic table napkins.
Twelve matching table napkins.
Twelve small plates of tin.
Twelve matching dishes.
Four similar, medium size.
Three spoons and three forks of brass.
Three knives with bone handles.
A table of poplar for the kitchen, with iron feet.
Two sideboards of walnut.
A little table of poplar for the sideboard.
Six stools of walnut with backs.
Eight stools of poplar colored green.
Two heavy candlestick holders of brass.
A basin of copper weighing 9.
A kettle of copper weighing 7.
A cauldron of copper weighing 6.
A jug of copper weighing 7.
A copper bucket with its chain of iron, weighing in total 13.8.
A small kettle of copper weighing 3.3.
A warming pan weighing 5.4.
Two tripods of iron weighing 7.
One fire shovel, and a pair of tongs of iron, weighing 5.
One grill of iron weighing 3.
One ladle and one cooking spoon of iron weighing 2.
One candlestick holder of iron.
One little kitchen chair and small box stained the color of walnut.
Three spoons and three forks of brass.
Three knives with bone handles.
An iron chain for the fireplace.
A cushion for the head with cover of taffeta.
A pillow case of linen.

It is interesting that this list includes only prosaic household items – there are no tools, workbenches, or supplies typically used in the construction or repair of musical instruments. Cristofori either brought these workshop materials with him or acquired whatever he needed in Florence using funds supplied by the court (either through his monthly allotment for provisions or by reimbursement; see below). The unit used in measuring the heavy metal household objects listed above is not indicated but was probably the *libbra* of Florence, which was then about

0.34 kg.[17] One *libbra* equaled 12 *once*. In Cristofori's last will and testament, he instructed the executors of his estate to return these household articles to the Medici court after his death (see below).

Cristofori's Workshop

Cristofori appears to have removed himself from the court workrooms and set up a workshop at his residence by 1690, as bills submitted to the court dating from August of that year often indicate that instruments were moved between his house, where we may presume he worked on them, and the royal residences and theatres where they were used. In Cristofori's last will and testament, he is recorded as having lived in the parish of San Remigio on the Canto agli Alberti (Figure 2.2).

This street is now via de' Benci, not far from the Palazzo Vecchio and Uffizi. In his bills to court (see below), he sought funds for craftsmen and assistants who helped him complete his commissions. These individuals are not named but are variously identified as a cabinet maker (*ebbanista* or *stipetaio*), woodworker (*legnaiolo*), assistant (*lavorante*), and apprentice (*garzone*).[18] Cristofori's principal assistant, Giovanni Ferrini, is named in the first draft of his will, though two members of the del Mela family were bequeathed his tools and instruments in the second and final version (see below and Chapter 5). Cristofori never matriculated in the Università di Por San Piero e dei Fabbricanti, to which many of Florence's instrument makers belonged, presumably because he worked under the direct protection of his patron, Grand Prince Ferdinando de' Medici.

Earliest Work for the Court

As indicated above, Cristofori received his first payment for provisions in April of 1688, and he continued to receive these payments through August of that year (they were generally made on the last day of the month). On September 24, instead of his usual payment of 12 *scudi*, he received 25 *scudi* for services rendered at performances at the Medici villa at Pratolino (see Chapter 4). In this record, Cristofori is listed among eighteen

---

[17] Ronald Edward Zupko, *Italian Weights and Measures from the Middle Ages to the Nineteenth Century* (Philadelphia, 1981), p. 135.
[18] ASF GM 1073bis, no. 325, ff. 2567–2584.

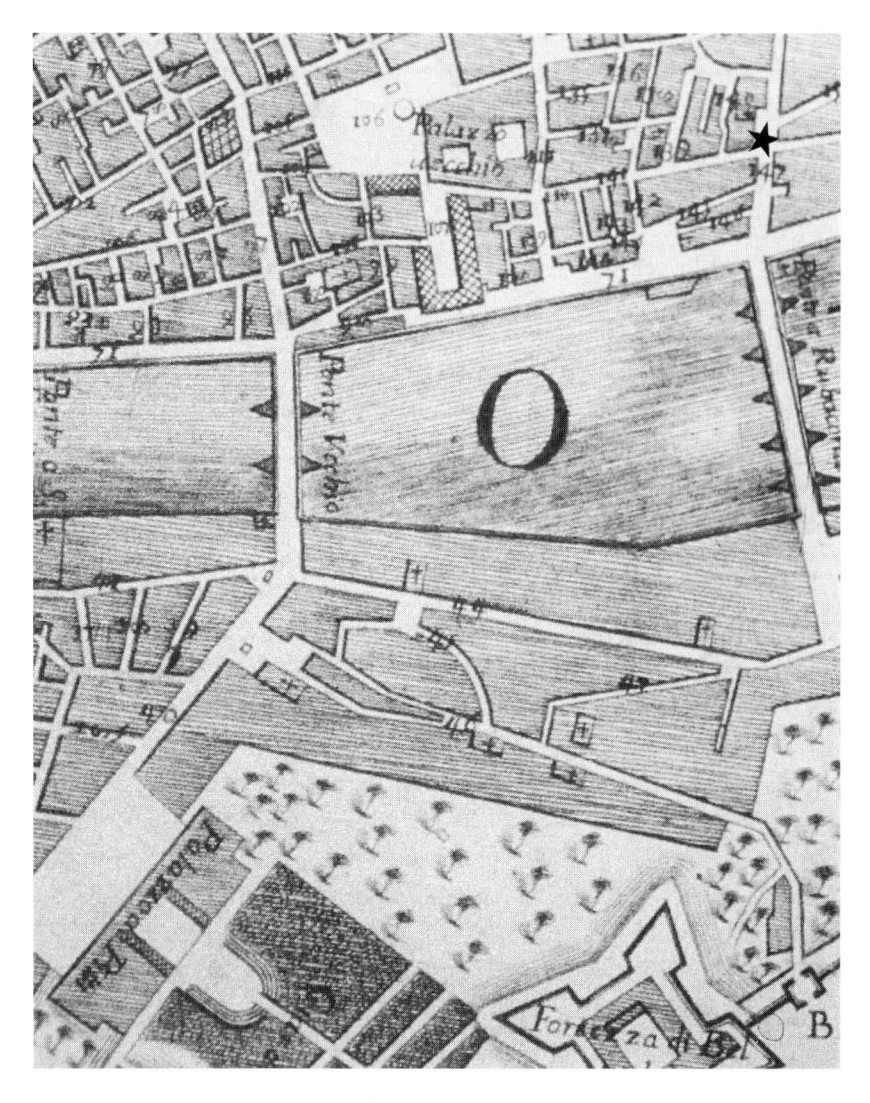

Figure 2.2 Map of Florence, *c.* 1730 showing at top right the approximate location of Cristofori's residence at Canto agli Alberti. Map by Giuseppe Papini. Collection of the author.

singers, musicians, and the composer Giovanni Maria Pagliardi. Pagliardi received 142.6 *scudi*, as did the noted castrato Francesco de Castris, while singers Carlo Antonio Zanardi, Marcantonio da Palermo, and Giuseppe Canavese received 114.6 *scudi*. The instrumentalists were paid between 25 and 50 *scudi*, and the page turner earned 2.6 *scudi*.[19] During the years that

---

[19] ASF DG 434, f. 80r.

Cristofori attended to the keyboard instruments at Pratolino, the cast of singers was sometimes augmented, though the instrumentalists listed in these payment orders usually consisted of two violinists (Martino Bitti and Francesco Assolani), two violists (Bartolommeo Bruschi [or Brischi] and Giovanni Taglia), a cellist or bass viol player (Pietro Salvetti), a theorbist (Giovanni Battista Gigli), and a harpsichordist (Giovanni Fuga). Fuga was sometimes listed as the "second" harpsichordist; in these instances, Pagliardi was assisted by a page turner (Agnolo Berni or Giuseppo Ceroti), which suggests he conducted or led the musicians from the keyboard. Members of this ensemble are depicted in paintings by Anton Domenico Gabbiani, and some of the instruments shown in these paintings can be identified as those described in the Medici inventories (see Figure 4.2).[20]

The October payment for provisions included the missed allotment for September, and in November Cristofori not only received his monthly provision payment but an additional 84 *lire* (equivalent to 12 *scudi*) to cover six months' rent for the house in which he lived and worked.[21] For the month of December, there is a record of the usual 12 *scudi* for provisions, but in January 1689 there were two payments: 13.6 *scudi* for the *buonaccordaio* (tuner) Bartolomeo Cristofoli [*sic*] for the "value and balance of a bill for work done for His Most Serene Highness," paid on the 22nd of that month, followed by the usual provision payment of 12 *scudi* paid on the 31st.[22] This is the first indication that the payments for provisions did not cover certain types of work, the nature of which will become evident in later court documents (see below). Payments appear to have continued through July 1689 (the court records for May and June are missing), though none is recorded for August. On the last day of September, Cristofori was again awarded 25 *scudi* for his participation in musical performances that took place at Pratolino.

Supplemental Billing for Various Tasks

Cristofori's provision payments resumed in October of 1689 (the October 11 payment was for the months of August and September, while the October 31 payment was for that month) and continued in November.[23] In

---

[20] John Walter Hill, "Antonio Veracini in Context: New Perspectives from Documents, Analysis and Style," *Early Music* 18/4 (1990), p. 545.
[21] ASF DG 434, ff. 87v and 94r.   [22] Ibid., ff. 102v, 108r and 109v.
[23] ASF DG 435, ff. 31v, 35v, 45r.

December there was no allotment for that month's provisions, but on the 24th he was granted 12 *scudi* to cover back rent.[24] The missed December provision payment was made up on January 31, 1690, when he received 24 *scudi*.[25] On February 28, the usual payment was made, though the March allotment was missed, only to be recouped in April.[26] In May, June, and July, the monthly 12 *scudi* provision payments were duly issued, and on June 6 he received additional payments of 16.5.15 *scudi*, once again for the "value and balance of a bill," as well as 61..10 *scudi* for a "*cembalo* made for His Most Serene Highness."[27] This last payment record is of considerable interest because it indicates that Cristofori's monthly allotments did not cover the construction of new instruments, and as we shall see from the sequence of supplemental bills submitted by him from August 12, 1690 through August 30, 1698, he was paid separately for mundane tasks such as moving instruments and their stands, as well as for adjusting instruments, undertaking major restorations, and making other new instruments. These supplemental bills typically include detailed itemizations for materials and reimbursement for unnamed woodworkers, apprentices, and others who assisted him, thus providing insight into Cristofori's activities, both as a craftsman and courtier. Regarding the moving of instruments and their stands, for which there are numerous bills, such tasks could not have been performed by a single person, as it would have taken at least two people to lift a keyboard instrument and load it onto a cart or carriage for transport. It is not clear whether Cristofori was physically involved in packing and moving instruments or simply sought funds for reimbursing hired hands. His earliest supplemental bill for moving instruments is as follows:

August 12, 1690 A.D.

Owed to me, Bartolomeo Christofori, by the Chamber of the Most Serene Prince Ferdinando of Tuscany, and first
for having a *cemballo* moved twice to the Piti [sic] Palace from my house L 2 : 13 – 4
And again for taking and bringing back one *cemballo* as above L 1 : 6 – 8
And for loading two instrument stands for Pratolino L 1 : 10 – 0
And for three vulture quills and *aciero* [steel] strings L 1 : 3 – 4
And for removing from Piti [sic] to my house three *cemballi* with their stands L 2 : 13 – 4

---

[24] Ibid., f. 53v.   [25] Ibid., f. 64r.   [26] Ibid., ff. 74v, 94r.
[27] Ibid., ff. 102r, 105r, 114r, 124r.

September 6, 1690

And for moving a *cemballo* from the palace L : 13 – 4

Total   L   10: – –[28]

The task of moving unwieldy yet delicate keyboard instruments between the Pitti Palace and Cristofori's residence would have involved loading them onto hand-drawn or horse-drawn carts and crossing the Arno, either by way of the Ponte Vecchio or more likely the Ponte Rubaconte (now called Ponte alle Grazie), the latter being a more direct route to and from Cristofori's workshop and residence on the Canto agli Alberti and the Pitti Palace. From this bill we deduce that Cristofori was quilling harpsichords (hence the three vulture quills mentioned in the above receipt) as well as replacing broken strings. The wingspans of the species of vultures common to Italy are approximately three times greater than that of the common crow, which was the usual source of quills in countries north of the Alps, and it would take just a few of a vulture's flying feathers to quill a single register of a harpsichord. It is possible that the three feathers for which he sought reimbursement were used to replace plectra in the instruments cited in this particular bill; greater quantities of vulture feathers are listed in later bills. Quilling, voicing, and regulating a harpsichord require a quiet environment, and as Maffei indicated, this was the principal reason Cristofori chose to work at home rather than in the noisy workshops of the court.

The strings that he specified in the August 12, 1690 bill were of *aciero*, or steel, rather than *ferro*, or iron. This is a distinction made in several of his bills, as the wire then used in stringing musical instruments was considerably stronger and less ductile than common iron wire, and thus could be tuned to the requisite pitch and hold its tuning. Though high-carbon steel music wire as we know it today was not developed until around the middle of the nineteenth century, analyses of samples of eighteenth-century ferrous harpsichord wire indicate that it was distinguishable from plain iron: it had negligible carbon content (under 0.007% by weight) but considerably higher phosphorus content (0.1% by weight), which imparted greater tensile strength and reduced ductility. An analysis of a

---

[28] ASF GM 1073bis, no. 325, f. 2569. In this bill for moving instruments on August 12 and September 6 of 1690, as well as subsequent bills submitted by Cristofori for moving instruments, instrument making, and repair, the currency denominations generally used are the *lira*, *soldo*, and *denaro*. Thus, L 2 : 13 – 4 represents 2 *lire*, 13 *soldi*, and 4 *denari*. Some of the bills, such as that of August 15, 1690 for the construction of a new instrument (Figure 2.3), provide a *scudi* equivalent immediately below the *lire* total. In those cases, the numerical figures are preceded by a cursive "S."

sample of modern ingot iron revealed a higher carbon content (0.037%) though less phosphorus (0.008%) than eighteenth-century harpsichord wire, while modern steel music wire has a considerably higher carbon content (0.91%), from which it derives its enormous strength, with comparatively less phosphorus (0.016%) than the early wire.[29] From Cristofori's August 12, 1690 bill and later ones submitted by him, it is clear that he distinguished between steel and iron; while he specified steel (*aciero*) for strings, he employed iron stock (*ferro*), which was more malleable, for making tuning pins.[30] Iron was probably available to him in the form of wrought-iron rods, which had to be cut to length and then hammered flat at the top to fit a tuning wrench.

The Court's Keyboard Instrument Collection

Six musical instrument inventories were compiled in the Medici court between 1640 and 1691. The inventory made in 1670 lists no *cembalo* (a generic term for harpsichord, but generally indicating the large, wing-shaped harpsichord) and three *spinette* (here indicating a smaller version of the harpsichord, either in pentagonal or rectangular form, or perhaps having a bentside),[31] while the one made in 1691 lists two *cembali* and three *spinette*.[32] Cristofori's responsibilities with regard to maintaining the court's keyboard instruments expanded considerably within a few years of his arrival in Florence, as the court's inventory of musical instruments compiled in 1700 lists seventeen *cembali*, fifteen *spinette*, one pianoforte, two *sordini* (clavichords), and two chamber organs. According to the descriptions in the 1700 inventory, several of these keyboard instruments predate the 1691 inventory by a few years or decades, which indicates that the Medici were acquiring both new and second-hand instruments. Many of those listed in 1700 date from the sixteenth century and would have

---

[29] Martha Goodway and Jay Scott Odell, *The Metallurgy of 17th- and 18th-Century Music Wire – The Historical Harpsichord* 2, ed. Howard Schott (Stuyvesant, NY, 1987).

[30] ASF GM 1073bis, no. 325, ff. 2568, 2570, 2573.

[31] The author does not subscribe to the current identification of pentagonally shaped harpsichords as virginals rather than as spinets on the basis of their strings running parallel to the keyboard rather than at an angle to it. In the seventeenth century, well-informed Italian makers and inventory compilers, such as Bartolomeo Cristofori, referred to pentagonal instruments as *spinette*, and the author believes that this is what they should be called in this context. See *The New Grove Dictionary of Musical Instruments* (London and New York, 1984), s.v. "spinet" and "virginal."

[32] Gai, *Gli strumenti musicali della corte medicea*, pp. 4–5; Frederick Hammond, "Musical Instruments at the Medici Court in the Mid-Seventeenth Century," in *Analecta Musicologica* 15: *Studien zur Italienisch-Deutschen Musikgeschichte* 10 (Cologne, 1975), pp. 202–219.

had considerable antiquarian value, for at that time instruments such as harpsichords, lutes, and bowed instruments were thought to improve with age, and a premium was paid for old ones.[33] As we shall see, one of Cristofori's tasks was to maintain and in some cases restore the valuable old keyboard instruments in the Medici collection, the earliest being a two-register (8′ and 4′) *cimbalo* signed Dominicus Pisaurensis M.D.XXXVIII. During the court's keyboard acquisition spree, Cristofori journeyed outside of Florence to collect instruments (see below) and was presumably involved in examining them prior to purchase in order to assess their condition and potential value to the court. He was evidently not the only individual involved in procuring keyboard instruments for the court, for in 1697 Ferdinando sought an "older" harpsichord, and Monsignor Rinaldo degli Albizzi in Cesena sent a report of a spinet, including a sketch of it, back to Luca Casimiro degli Albizzi (who had served as Ferdinando's *maestro di camera* and tutor until 1689) for Ferdinando's approval.[34]

Of the keyboard instruments listed in the 1700 inventory, six were made by Girolamo Zenti, the noted maker from Viterbo (born *c.* 1609–11, died 1667):[35]

cimbalo dated 1659 made in Rome;
cimbalo dated 1656 made in Rome;
cimbalo dated 1653 made in Stockholm;
spinetta dated 1668 made in Paris;
spinetta no date or place of manufacture; and
spinettina no date or place of manufacture.

He principally worked in Rome, but late in his career enjoyed royal patronage in Sweden, England, and France, and made instruments in London as well as Stockholm and Paris. Zenti is recorded as having received payment in 1664 for repairing the harpsichord of Charles II of England, and is thought to have died in Paris while in service to Louis XIV.[36] Regarding the Medici's Zenti harpsichords, one would expect

---

[33] Thomas Mace, *Musick's Monument* (London, 1676; repr. New York, 1966), p. 48. Mace states that old lutes are better than new ones. In Paris during the eighteenth century, great efforts were made to keep sixteenth- and seventeenth-century harpsichords in playing order by extending their compasses and redecorating their cases; see Frank Hubbard, *Three Centuries of Harpsichord Making* (Cambridge, Mass., 1965), pp. 112–114, 247–248.

[34] William C. Holmes, *Opera Observed*: Views of a Florentine Impresario in the Early Eighteenth Century (Chicago, 1993), p. 23n.

[35] Patrizio Barbieri, "Cembalaro, organaro, chittararo e fabbricatore di corde armoniche nella *Polyanthea technica* di Pinaroli (1718–32)," *Ricercare* 1 (1989), pp. 123–210.

[36] Margaret Mabbett, "Italian Musicians in Restoration England (1660–90)," *Music & Letters* 67/3 (1986), p. 246.

all of them to have been made in Rome (two of them – see the list above – bear inscriptions that indicate they were made in Rome), but the 1700 inventory also lists a *cimbalo* that he made in Stockholm, as well as a gold-strung *spinetta* made in Paris (apparently dated as 1668 posthumously, unless the date of Zenti's death as established by Patrizio Barbieri, cited above, is incorrect). The instrument made in Stockholm (inscribed "Hyeronimus de Zentis Romanus faciebat in Civitate Holmie anno Domini 1653," according to the inventory) is no longer believed to be a similarly inscribed instrument in the collection of the Grassi Museum für Musikinstrumente der Universität Leipzig (catalog no. 75) because its disposition and aspects of its case construction and decoration differ.[37] How these two instruments were "repatriated" to Zenti's native Italy is unknown, though the Medici did acquire instruments made in other countries, including Austria (three violins by Jacob Stainer), Germany (an anonymous clavichord and woodwind instruments by Johann Christoph Denner), England (a *violetta* by Christopher Wise), France (the folding harpsichord listed in the 1716 Medici musical instrument inventory was most likely made by Jean Marius; see Chapter 5), and the Low Countries (the 1700 inventory lists sixteen recorders made by Richard Haka of Amsterdam, and the 1716 inventory lists a two manual, three-register harpsichord made in Antwerp).[38] In addition to the Zenti keyboard instruments discussed above, the Medici owned two others made by him: one identified as a *spinetta* and another termed a *spinettina*, though their dates and cities of manufacture are not indicated in the inventories. The diminutive *spinettina* is described in the 1700 inventory as having a case made of solid ebony, a compass of G to C, with keys of ivory and ebony, no moldings, a soundboard of *abeto* (fir or spruce), and as being small enough to rest upon one's stomach when playing it (*per appoggiarsi allo stomaco quando si suona*), presumably while reclining in bed. An instrument now in the collection of The Metropolitan Museum of Art (accession no. 89.4.1227) fits this description perfectly and is signed G°Z[i] on both the top and bottom key levers. Another harpsichord, inscribed HIERONYMVS DE ZENTIS VITERBIENSIS F. ROMAE ANNO. DOM. MDCLVIII, not listed in the Medici inventory, was until recently in the collection of The Metropolitan Museum of Art, but was deemed a fake and de-accessioned.[39]

---

[37] Edwin M. Ripin, "The Surviving Oeuvre of Girolamo Zenti," *Metropolitan Museum Journal* 7 (1973), pp. 78–79.
[38] Pollens, *The Early Pianoforte*, pp. 214–220.
[39] Though legitimate doubts had been raised regarding the authenticity of this harpsichord, it had long been in the museum as part of the Crosby Brown Collection, and had even been on

Listed in the 1700 inventory are five keyboard instruments made by another important Italian maker, Domenico da Pesaro (fl. 1533–1575), including a spinet dated 1562, an undated spinet, and three harpsichords dated 1538, 1550, and 1566. There is also a harpsichord made by Giovanni Antonio Baffo of Venice dated 1575, two harpsichords by the Florentine maker Prete Giuseppe Mondini (otherwise known as "Prete da Imola") dated 1687 and 1688 as well as an undated spinet by him, an undated upright harpsichord by Giuliano Giovannini, a harpsichord dated 1693 and two undated *spinettine* by the Florentine maker Niccolò Berti, an undated spinet by Giovanni Battista Magnelli, a harpsichord by Giuseppe Buoni of Cortona dated 1681, an undated harpsichord by Antonio (last name left blank but possibly Casella), a harpsichord by Franciscus Patavinus (Francesco of Padua, otherwise known as "Il Hongaro" or "l' Ongaro" ["the Hungarian"]) dated 1562, as well as other unsigned keyboard instruments. Two anonymous clavichords are also listed, one specified as German.[40]

Of special interest in the 1700 Medici musical instrument inventory are the seven keyboard instruments made by Bartolomeo Cristofori:

1. A *cimbalo* having an ebony case, two 8′ registers, a GG–c^3 compass, and 53 keys.
2. A *cimbalo* having a cypress case, two 8′ registers, a GG–c^3 compass, and 53 keys.
3. An upright cimbalo, dated 1697, two 8′ registers, a C–c^3 compass, and 49 keys.
4. A *spinetta* having an oval case of rosewood, dated 1690, two 8′ registers, a C–c^3 compass, broken octave, and 47 keys.
5. A *spinetta* having an oval case of cypress, dated 1693, two 8′ registers, a C–c^3 compass, and 49 keys.
6. A *spinettone* for the orchestra with poplar case, two registers (8′ and 4′), a GG–c^3 compass, and 53 keys.
7. An *arpicimbalo* with hammers (pianoforte), compass C–c^3, and 49 keys.

Over the years, Cristofori submitted the following itemized bills for seven new instruments that he made for the Medici:

display for many years. As such, it would have been wise to retain it as a study piece. Another keyboard instrument de-accessioned by then curator Laurence Libin, mistakenly thought to be a fake, turned out to be an early pianoforte by Vincenzo Sodi. John Koster, "Three Grand Pianos in the Florentine Tradition," *Musique, Images, Instruments* 4 (Paris, 1999), pp. 95–116.

[40] ASF GM 1117, ff. 1–118.

1. A *spineta* in 1690.
2. A two-register *cemballo* of cypress in 1692.
3. A two-register *cemballo* designated for the theater in 1692.
4. A two-register *spineta* in 1693.
5. An organ in 1693.
6. A two-register *cembalo rito in piedi* (an upright harpsichord) in 1697.
7. A large two-register *cembalo* with a compass extending down to GG in 1698.

Unfortunately, there is not always a correspondence between the bills, payment records, and inventories. For example, there is no bill for the harpsichord that Cristofori made for the Medici in 1690, though there is a record that he was paid for one in June of that year, nor are there bills for the undated ebony harpsichord or the newly invented pianoforte that appear in the 1700 inventory; however, the two oval spinets, the *spinettone* for orchestra, and the upright harpsichord that are alluded to in his bills are presumably the instruments that are similarly described in that inventory. No bills or records of payment have been discovered for four undated single-register *cembali* that first appear in the 1716 Medici musical instrument inventory. Though Cristofori's two oval spinets and the pianoforte that are listed in 1700 are missing from the 1716 inventory, there is documentation that at least one of the oval spinets and the pianoforte were still in the Medici collection through at least 1713 and 1714, respectively (see below and Chapter 4). The 1732 inventory made shortly after Cristofori's death does not include any instruments of his made subsequently to those listed in 1716.

The Medici Musical Instrument Inventories

Of the two musical instrument inventories compiled during Cristofori's tenure in the Medici court, the author of the earlier inventory dated 1700 is unknown, as the title page is apparently missing, while the 1716 inventory was drawn up by Cristofori and dated September 23 of that year. One might assume that Cristofori was responsible for the earlier inventory, because by that date he was entirely familiar with the Medici collection, and the inventory's entries include the type of technical detail that would have been of interest to an instrument maker and that Cristofori would have been competent to describe. For example, its author employs the proper terminology for the parts of the instruments and includes details about the keyboard range, such as the distinction between *in sesta* (lit. "at the sixth," indicating short-octave compasses beginning at C/E or GG/BB, in which the lowest key is tuned down an octave from a note a sixth above it) and *ottava stesa* ("stretched octave," or "full octave"), as well as the presence or absence of *spezzati* ("split sharps").[41] Also described are the number of registers and the working of stop mechanisms, including the position of springs and location of stop knobs; the proper names of obscure woods and other materials are also identified. However, in a memorandum dated October 2, 1716 submitted by court harpsichordist Giovanni Fuga to Grand Prince Ferdinando in response to the prince's inquiry regarding the whereabouts of certain instruments that had been borrowed by court musicians, Fuga replied that he would need to refer to "his" inventory in order to refresh his memory regarding their location, though he did recall that *cemballetti* by Undeo and Pesaro, as well as several stringed instruments and an oboe, had been borrowed by Signor Martino (court violinist Martino Bitti was sometimes referred to in this way) and Signor Salvetti (another court stringed-instrument player).[42] From Fuga's response, it is unclear whether he was the author of the 1700 inventory or simply that he did not have his copy of it at hand. (This memorandum is appended to the earlier 1700 inventory, rather than to the one compiled in 1716, and includes additional entries regarding instruments borrowed by the Medici family and court musicians; see below.) Stylistic and handwriting distinctions between the 1700 and 1716 inventories would

---

[41] In the "short-octave" arrangement implied by the term *in sesta*, such as a 45-note keyboard with an apparent range of E–c^3, the low E would be tuned down to C, and the two lowest "accidental" keys would be tuned to D and E. Another arrangement, such as a 54-note keyboard with an apparent range of BB–f^3, would have the BB tuned down to GG, and the two lowest accidental keys tuned to AA and BB. "Split sharps" may connote the so-called "broken octave," in which the lowest accidental keys are divided, most often into two separate keys. An example would be a keyboard with the low E, again tuned down to C, with the front part of the first accidental tuned to D, and the back part tuned to F#, while the front of the second accidental would be tuned to E and the back to G#. The rationale for the short-octave keyboard was to increase the range of the keyboard in the bass without widening the keyboard and case of the instrument unduly. Though the keyboard was kept narrow with the broken-octave arrangement, the backs of the extra keys had to be splayed to accommodate the extra strings and jacks, so the case would have to be made somewhat wider. "Split sharps" could also refer to the division of accidentals throughout the keyboard range to provide non-enharmonic keys, for example, g#/a^b and d#/e^b, to facilitate meantone tuning. The term *ottava stesa* (literally "stretched octave") suggests a full complement of keys (including accidentals) extending throughout the keyboard range, as opposed to the short octave, where accidentals are missing. Some authors translate this term as "full octave," though a number of the instruments described in the Medici inventories as having *ottava stesa* do not have a full complement of keys: for example, 53-note keyboards having compasses of GG–c^3 are obviously missing a key, probably the lowest accidental.

[42] ASF GM 1117, f. 1A.

indicate that they were compiled by different people. For example, Cristofori's 1716 inventory is surprisingly uninformative with regard to technical details and focuses instead upon superficial decorative aspects of the sort that would enable someone unfamiliar with the mechanics of keyboard instruments to quickly identify them. The disparity between the two inventories is also evident in the descriptions of woodwind and plucked stringed instruments – while the 1700 inventory identifies the makers' names (including such prominent figures as Richard Haka, Johann Christoph Denner, Magno Dieffopruchar, Matheus Buechenberg, and Magno Longo), the 1716 inventory neglects to do so – perhaps an indication of its keyboard-centric compiler. Nevertheless, comparisons between the 1700 and 1716 inventories are revealing, and it is interesting to find concordances between Cristofori's bills and the inventory entries, which will be explored below.

Bill for the Construction of a New Spinet

Cristofori submitted a bill (Figure 2.3) just three days after the August 12th bill cited above:

August 15, 1690 A.D.

> The Chamber of the Most Serene Prince Ferdinando of Tuscany owes me, Bartolomeo Christofori for a *spineta* made at new expense by the same, and first
> For getting *ebano* [ebony], *abbete* [fir or spruce],[43] and *albero* [poplar][44] sawn up L 12 – 10
> For a pound-and-a-half of *colla di pesce* [fish glue] L 12 – –
> For *colla ordinaria* [ordinary glue] and *aqua vita* [distilled ethyl alcohol][45] L 5 – –

---

[43] *Abbete* (*abete*) is likely *Abies alba* (Silver fir, which grows in Italy) or *Picea abies* (Norway spruce, which grows in the alpine region; sometimes referred to as "spruce fir").

[44] Modern dictionaries define the word *albero* as "wood," though Filippo Baldinucci's *Vocabolario toscano dell'arte del disegno* (Florence, 1631) also indicates that it can refer to poplar (*Populus alba*). Poplar grows in Italy, and this light-colored, soft, close textured wood was widely used in Italian keyboard construction, especially for case braces, stands, and outer cases that were intended to be painted.

[45] *Aqua vita* is incorrectly transcribed as *aqua reica* and mistranslated as *aqua regia* in Giuliana Montanari, "Le spinette ovali e la collezione di strumenti a penna del Granprincipe Ferdinando de' Medici," in *Bartolomeo Cristofori: La spinetta ovale del 1690*, pp. 32–43. *Aqua regia* is a highly corrosive mixture of nitric and hydrochloric acids that is uniquely capable of dissolving gold and platinum – a reagent that would have been of little use to Cristofori. The term in the bill is *aqua vita*, or distilled alcohol, which could have been used to make spirit varnish or used as a cleaning solvent.

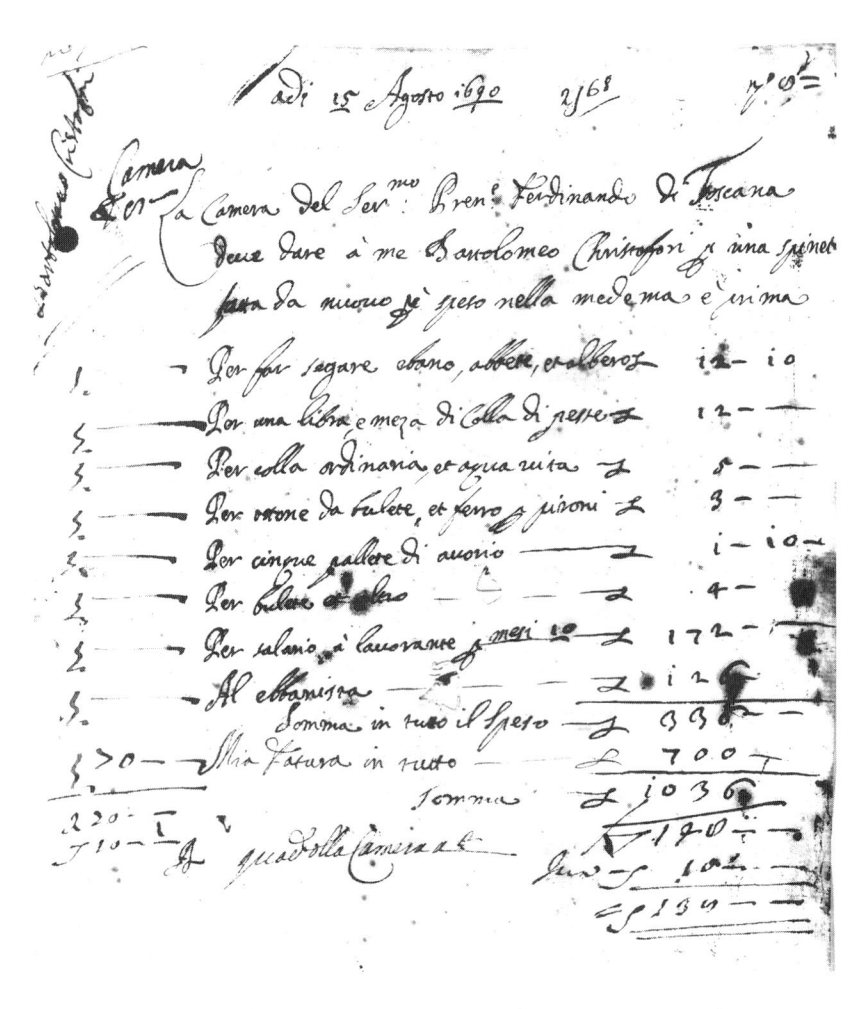

Figure 2.3 Cristofori's first bill to the Medici court, for the construction of a new spinet, dated August 15, 1690. Courtesy of the Archivio di Stato, Florence.

> For brass tacks and *ferro* [iron] for [tuning] pins L 3 – –
> For five pieces of ivory L 1 – 10 –
> For tacks, etc. L 4 –
> For salary and labor for ten months L 172 – –
> For the *ebbanista* [cabinet maker] L 126 –
>
> Sum total of expenses   L 336 –
> My labor in total   L 700 –
> Total   L 1036[46]

[46] ASF GM 1073bis, no. 325, f. 2568.

This bill for a *spineta* is the earliest one for a new instrument by Cristofori that has come to light. He was evidently paid in installments for this rather expensive instrument (1036 *lire* was then equivalent to the price of six new Stradivari violins),[47] for there is no record of a payment made to him in full, though in addition to his monthly stipends and rent payments dating from August, 1690 to the end of the year, he received two supplemental payments of 29 and 25 *scudi*, with the notations *pagati a Bartolommeo Cristofori per acconto di suo avere porto d.to* and *pagati a Bartolommeo Cristofori strumentaio per a bon conto di suo avere porto d.to* (loosely, "paid to Bartolomeo Cristofori, instrument maker, on good account for what is owed him, received by same").[48]

A badly damaged oval spinet signed by Cristofori and dated 1690 was recently "rediscovered" in storage at the Museo Bardini in Florence (it is now on loan to the Museo degli Strumenti Musicali del Conservatorio "Luigi Cherubini" and presently on exhibit at the Galleria dell'Accademia in Florence; see Chapter 3). It is believed by some to be the instrument referred to in the above bill.[49] However, a study conducted by scientists, curators, and instrument makers published in 2002 indicates that the case veneer of this oval spinet is African rosewood (*Dalbergia baroni*), rather than ebony (*Diospyros* sp.), which might be inferred from the bill (which lists *ebano*, rather than commonly used Italian terms for rosewood, such as *palissandro* and *jacaranda*); furthermore, the glue used in laminating the case veneer to the poplar core is casein, not the fish glue or "ordinary" glue (animal hide glue) that is listed in his bill (for ramifications regarding the use of various glues, see Chapter 3), and the spinet's soundboard is of cypress, though that wood is not mentioned in this particular bill, as it is in other bills submitted by Cristofori.[50] Materials listed in the bill that are consistent with those used in the construction of the 1690 spinet include brass tacks (analysis of the oval spinet's hitchpins indicates they are made of brass), *albero* (poplar has been identified as the core wood used to make the veneered case sides), *abbete* (fir has been identified as a wood used in interior case construction of the oval spinet as well as the

---

[47] Carlo Chiesa and Duane Rosengard, *The Stradivari Legacy* (London, 1998), p. 93. In one version of Stradivari's will, he bequeaths six of his violins valued at 1000 Cremonese *lire* to his son Omobono.

[48] ASF DG 435, 173r and 183r.

[49] Montanari, "Le spinette ovali," in *Bartolomeo Cristofori: La spinetta ovale del 1690*, pp. 32–43.

[50] Marco Fioravanti and Francesca Ciattini, "Le specie legnose," in *Bartolomeo Cristofori: La spinetta ovale del 1690*, pp. 87–90; Giancarlo Lanterna and Maria Rizzi, "Adesivi ed elementi metallici," ibid., pp. 91–93.

plank of wood that serves as a lower jack guide), and ivory (which has been identified as the material used to make the natural key coverings). It is possible that the small quantity of ebony referred to in the bill was used to fashion the accidental keys and the moldings around the soundboard, as those parts are made of that wood in the rediscovered spinet. Though the discrepancy in the identification of the woods suggests that the spinet rediscovered in 2000 may not be the one associated with the August 15, 1690 bill, we should perhaps not rely too heavily upon the identification of exotic woods in early bills and inventories (armed with microscopes and wood identification keys, today's wood anatomists still have a difficult time identifying some of the most common woods).

In the Medici musical instrument inventory of 1700, two spinets by Cristofori are listed: one dated 1690, and another dated 1693 (see below and Chapter 3). The spinet dated 1690 is described as follows in the 1700 Medici musical instrument inventory (Figures 2.4(a) and 2.4(b)):

Una spinetta di Bartolomeo Cristofori di forma ovale, levatora di cassa à due registri principali unisoni, con fondo di cipresso, e rosa traforata nel mezzo, con fascie di sciacarandà, e scorniciatura di Ebano, con filetto d'avorio, con traversa à pirámide, e leggio simile, nel quale vi è un frontone di Ebano, con l'arme Ser.[mo] intarsiata d'avorio, con tastatura d'avorio et ébano, con due primi neri spezzati, che servono d'ottava al fafaut e gisolreut diesis, che comincia a in cisolfaut in sesta e finisce in cisolfaut, con n°. quaranta sette tasti tra bianchi neri e spezzati, con due molle di ferro ne i sodi laterali della tastatura, che servono per registrare con cassetta per d'avanti al piano della tastatura, nel di dentro della quale vi stà scritto Bartholomæus Cristophori Patavinus faciebat Florentiæ M.DCXC, con sua contro cassa di abeto pura, e coperta di cuoio rosso foderata di ermisino cremisi, orlata di nastrino d'oro, con suoi piedi torniti avvolti di pero tinto di nero, e legati con traverse simile, con piano nel quale vi incastra la sud[a] spinetta, con una scorniciatura d'Ebano, che lo circonda tutto.[51]

(A *spinetta* by Bartolomeo Cristofori in the form of an oval, removable from the case, having two registers of principal unisons, with soundboard of cypress wood and a perforated rose in the middle, with sides of jacaranda wood, and moldings of ebony with inlaid strips of ivory, with pyramidal jack rail and music desk similarly inlaid, in which there is a pediment of ebony inlaid with the arms of the Serene [Medici] in ivory, with keys of ivory and ebony, with the two first black [keys] split that serve the octave of F [sharp] and G sharp commencing with C *in sesta* [C/E short octave] and ending with C, with 47 keys between the white, black, and *spezzati* [split sharps], with two iron springs in the end blocks used to move the keyboard

---

[51] ASF GM 1117, ff. 27–28.

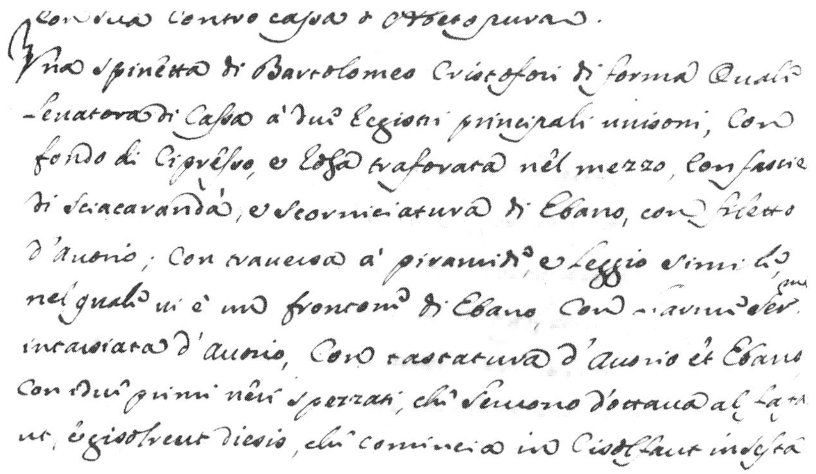

(a) [handwritten Italian text, transcription of the manuscript:]

Con sua Contro cassa ò Coperojuna.
Una spinetta di Bartolomeo Cristofori di forma Ouale
-enatora di Cassa a due Registri principali unisoni, con
fondo di Cipresso, e top traforata nel mezzo, con fascie
di Sciacaranda, e Scorniciatura di Ebano, con filetto
d'auorio; Con tauersa a' piramidi, e leggio simile
nel quale vi è un frontone di Ebano, con tauniolers
incausiata d'auorio, Con tastatura d'auorio et Ebano
Con dui pirui neri spezzati, che Seruono d'octava al Latu
re, è gisoleent diesis, che cominciao in Cisolfaut incipta

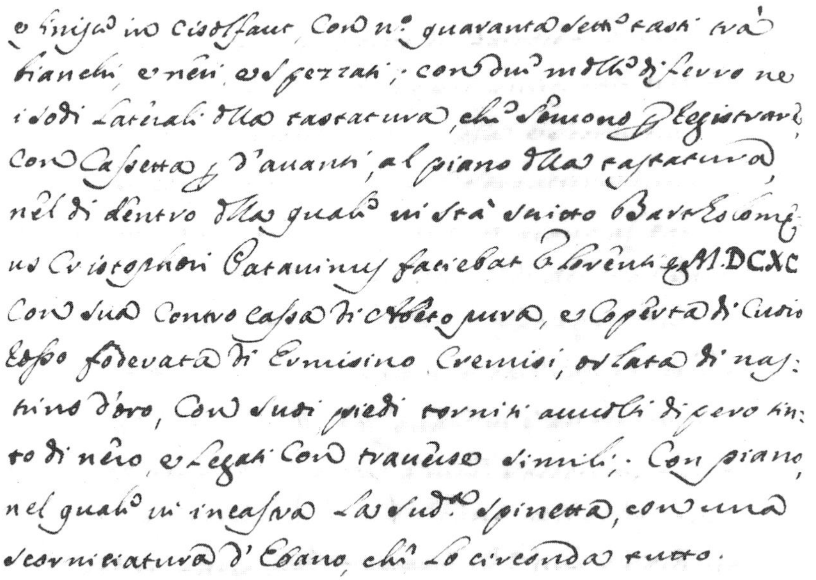

(b)

e finiscano in Cisolfaut, Con n.° quaranta Sette tasti tra
bianchi e neri spezzati, con dui molle di ferro ne
i dui Laterali della tastatura, che Seruono Rgistrare,
con Casseta d'auanti, al piano della tastatura,
nel di dentro della quale vi sta scritto Bartholomé
us Cristophori Patauinus faciebat Florentie MDCXC
Con sua Contro cassa di Abeto puro, e Coperta di Cuoio
Rosso foderata di Ermisino Cremisi, orlata di nas:
trino d'oro, Con suoi piedi torniti auncti di pero tin:
to di nero, e Legati Con trauerso simile; Con piano,
nel quale vi incassa la sud.ª spinetta, con una
Scorniciatura d'Ebano, che lo circonda tutto.

Figure 2.4 (a), (b) The "oval" spinet made by Cristofori, dated 1690, listed in the 1700 Medici inventory of musical instruments. Courtesy of the Archivio di Stato, Florence.

laterally, that serve to adjust the registration, with a small box in front and level with the keys which has written within Bartholomæus Cristophori Patavinus faciebat Florentiæ MDCXC, with its outer case of clear *abeto* [fir or spruce] and cover of red leather, lined with red silk hemmed with gold ribbon, with its turned legs of pear wood stained black joined together with a similar stretcher with a recess for the above-mentioned *spinetta* with a molding of ebony that surrounds it completely.)

This inventory description is entirely consistent with the following features of the recently rediscovered spinet in Florence: the 47-note keyboard, the short-octave compass, the use of split sharps, and the wood used for the case sides, jacaranda. The split sharps provide the D and E of the short octave (the lowest key E is tuned down to C), while the F and G keys are also equipped with their accidentals, F# and G#, which would otherwise be sacrificed in 45-note short-octave keyboards that lack the split sharps. The phrase "*levatora di cassa*" ("removable," or perhaps more accurately "liftable" from its case) refers to one of the two traditional forms of Italian keyboard-instrument design, today termed "inner-outer construction," in which a thin-walled instrument with decorative moldings is placed in an outer protective case. (Another form of construction employing thick-walled cases fitted with thin laminations, moldings, and decorative keyboard brackets in order to provide the illusion that a thin-walled instrument is fitted into an outer case, is referred to as "false inner-outer construction.")[52] The keyboard instruments listed in various Medici inventories, whether "removable" from outer cases or not, were invariably fitted with colorful leather covers, often described as being lined with silk and hemmed with ribbon. These are sometimes termed "*sopra coperta*" (outer cover), though in the 1700 inventory, they are simply termed *coperta* (cover). Because the spines of the thin-walled type of keyboard instrument were quite delicate (typically 4–5 mm in thickness), they could not bear the weight of hinged lids, so lids were attached to their outer cases; in some instances, the undersides of the outer-case lids were decorated with figurative paintings. It is unclear whether the leather covers referred to in the inventories had to be removed in order to gain access to the keyboards and to open the lids, or were tailored in such a way that they remained attached to the instruments, but permitted the keyboards and soundboards to be exposed for playing (see Chapter 4). Thus, while the 1690 bill for a spinet may not refer to the "rediscovered" spinet now on exhibit in Florence, the 1700 Medici musical instrument inventory description is consistent with it.

On December 23, 1690, Cristofori submitted the following bill for sundries:

> I, Bartolome [*sic*] Cristofori claim from the Chamber of the Most Serene Prince Ferdinando of Tuscany, and first
> For vulture feathers, no. 10 L 2 : 10
> For steel strings purchased in Pisa L 2 : 10[53]

---

[52] Hubbard, *Three Centuries of Harpsichord Making*, p. 20, pl. 4.
[53] ASF GM 1073bis, no. 325, f. 2572.

Cristofori's regular 12 *scudi* provision payment was made in January, 1691.[54] Though the February stipend was missed, it was made up in a double payment in March, and he was paid an additional 30.4 *scudi* in partial payment for his outstanding bills.[55] He received his stipends through September, as well as an additional 12 *scudi* in June for six months' rent on his house and 20 *scudi* in July, again in partial payment for the money owed him.[56] On the same sheet of paper as Cristofori's December 23, 1690 bill is another bill dated August 8, 1691 for 25 vulture feathers priced at 7 : 10 *lire*, followed by a bill dated August 16, 1691 for 4 : 13 – 4 *lire* for loading three instrument stands in Florence and unloading them at Pratolino. Following this entry is another dated October 1 in which he bills the court 5 *lire* for loading three stands at Pratolino and returning them to Florence (presumably the same three stands he had delivered to Pratolino in August).[57] This is in addition to the customary payment of 25 *scudi* that he was to receive on October 9 for his work at the villa, which presumably involved tuning and adjusting harpsichords that were used in rehearsals and opera performances.[58]

On October 11, 1691 he submitted bills of 1 *lira* for moving a *cemballo* to the Palazzo Pitti, 21 *lire* for "adjusting a *cemballo* of Cortona" (*racetare il Cemballo del Cortona*) and 4 *lire* for moving two *cemballi* with their stands from via della Pergola and bringing them back to the house.[59] Regarding the *cemballo* of Cortona, Cristofori may be referring to the harpsichord listed in the musical instrument inventory of 1700 that is inscribed "Giuseppe Buoni da Cortona faceva MDCLXXXI." It was of so-called "inner-outer" construction, with a case of cypress having ebony inlay, 8′ and 4′ registers, a soundboard of *abeto* (fir or spruce) without a rose, and a 45-note, C–c^3 short-octave keyboard without split sharps.

The harpsichords moved to via della Pergola were most likely used in performances at the Teatro della Pergola, a large theater founded by the Accademia degli Immobili in 1656 under the patronage of Cardinal Giovanni Carlo de' Medici and officially opened in 1657 (see Chapter 4). It was used for the production of many large-scale operatic works, including those staged in celebration of the wedding of Grand Duke Cosimo III and Marguerite d'Orléans in 1661, and that of Grand Prince Ferdinando de' Medici and Violante Beatrice of Bavaria in 1689.[60] The Teatro della Pergola is still an active concert venue.

---

[54] ASF DG 438, f. 20r.   [55] ASF DG 438, ff. 39v, 42v.
[56] ASF DG 438, ff. 51v, 59r, 65v, 68r, 73v, 78v, 91v, 99v.
[57] ASF GM 1073bis, no. 325, f. 2572.   [58] ASF DG 438, f. 106r.
[59] ASF GM 1072bis, no. 325, f. 2572.
[60] Kirkendale, *The Court Musicians in Florence*, pp. 427–430.

The accounts for November of 1691 are of considerable interest. On November 12, Cristofori received a payment of 80 *scudi* (560 *lire*) in partial payment of the money owed him – this was the largest installment received to date for accumulated bills – and on November 30, he received his provision allotment for October and November, 24 *scudi*.[61] However, on November 13, Medici records indicate that the harpsichord maker Niccolò Berti was paid 2 *scudi* for adjusting (*settare*) Ferdinando's instruments four times in "Bartolo's" absence.[62] This is the first indication, though not the last (see below), that Cristofori did on occasion leave Florence. It is possible that his absence in November of 1691 was due to family events that required his return to Padua, for in June his sister had given birth to twin girls, and his mother was apparently gravely ill, for she died on November 19th.[63] This payment record also provides some indication of the price of "servicing" a keyboard instrument – work that might include tuning, quilling, action regulation, and replacing broken strings.

Cristofori Builds a New Cembalo

In 1692, Cristofori received his usual payments for provisions through March,[64] though on the 15th of that month, he submitted a supplemental bill for a new harpsichord that he had built for the court:

March 15, 1692

For a new *cemballo* with two registers, and first
For locally grown cypress wood and having it sawn up L 14 : –
For all expenses involving the cabinet maker L 114 : –
For the woodworker L 40 : –
For iron pins, brass tacks, glue, etc. L 13 : –
For my work L 350 : –
Total L 531 : 3.4[65]

---

[61] ASF DG 438, ff. 116r, 123r.   [62] Ibid., f. 117r.
[63] Nisoli, *Bartolomeo Cristofori (1655–1732)*, p. 5.   [64] ASF DG 438, ff. 135r, 141r, 147r, 154v.
[65] ASF GM 1073bis, no. 325, f. 2573. The total has been interpreted as 597 : 3.4 in Raymond Russell, *The Harpsichord and Clavichord: An Introductory Study*, 2nd edn., rev. Howard Schott (London, 1973), p. 127, but in fact, in the original the 3.4 has been crossed out, and the 9 and 7 appear to have been overwritten or smeared, and might be interpreted as having been a 3 and a 1, which would be in keeping with the proper arithmetical sum for the figures above; however, at the top of the page is the figure 66. 3. 4, which appears to be the sum carried over from an earlier bill dated 2 April 1692 (ASF GM 1073bis, no. 325, f. 2572). Thus the sum of 597 : 3.4 *lire* represents a running total.

The harpsichord alluded to in the March 15 bill, which would appear to have been made principally of cypress wood, may be the second harpsichord made by Cristofori that is listed in the 1700 Medici musical instrument inventory (the first of his that is listed, also undated, is described as having a solid ebony case and has been identified as the so-called "ebony harpsichord"; see Chapter 3). The inventory description is as follows:

Un Cimbalo di Bartolomeo Cristofori, levatoro di cassa, à due registri principali unisoni, con fondo, e fascie di cipresso, traversa, e scorniciatura simile, con filetto d'Ebano, e piccola rosa traforata nel mezzo, con tastatura di Bossolo, e Ebano senza spezzati, che comincia in gisolreut ottava stesa, e finisce in cisolfaut, con n°. cinquanta tre tasti, tra Bianchi, e neri, lungo B^a. quattro, e un quarto, largo nel d'avanti B^a. uno e soldi nove scarsi, con suo leggio di cipresso filettato d'ebano, e sua contro cassa di abeto pura, con sua coperta di cuoio rosso foderata di taffetà cremisi, orlata di nastrino, oro, e cremisi, con suoi piedi torniti e intagliati, dorati nell'intaglio, e nel liscio neri, intelaiati, e legati per di sopra.[66]

(A *cimbalo* of Bartolomeo Cristofori, removable from the case, of two registers of principal [8′] unisons, with soundboard and case of cypress, jack rail, and moldings similarly inlaid with strips of ebony, and a small perforated rose in the middle [of the soundboard], with keys of boxwood and ebony without split sharps that begin at G *ottava stesa* [stretched octave], and end at C with 53 keys of white and black, length four *braccia* and a quarter [2343 mm], length at the front one *braccia* and a scant nine *soldi* [approx. 799 mm], with a music desk of cypress inlaid with ebony, and its outer case of clear *abeto* [fir or spruce], with its cover of red leather lined with crimson taffeta hemmed with gold and red ribbon, with its legs turned and carved, the carving gilded and glossy black, with moldings and inlays as above.)

Another bill dated March 15 (no year is given, but it appears just above an entry dated April 2, 1692; see below) is for fifteen vulture feathers in the amount of 4 *lire*. These were presumably used in quilling the harpsichord described above.[67]

Cristofori received his usual 12 *scudi* provision payment in March of 1692,[68] though from April, 1692 through August, 1693 there are no monthly provision payments recorded,[69] though he submitted bills for new work in that period:

---

[66] ASF GM 1117, f. 26. [67] ASF GM 1073bis, no. 325, f. 2572. [68] ASF DG 438, f. 154v.
[69] Michael Kent O'Brien suggests that the lack of records of payments during this period may be due to a missing volume in the series of account books. O'Brien, *Bartolomeo Cristofori at Court*, p. 77.

> April 2, 1692, for a music desk of cypress wood sent to the Serene Electress of Hamburg
> L 14 :[70]

Regarding this bill, there does not appear to be any formal connection between the Medici and the city of Hamburg at that time, and a simple music desk would seem to be a rather meager court gift for an electress. However, Grand Duke Cosimo's peregrinations back in 1667–1668 did bring him to Hamburg, and his son Prince Gian Gastone traveled there in 1703–1704, possibly making the acquaintance of George Frideric Handel and extending him an invitation to visit the Medici court, though he did not arrive in Florence until 1706. The wording of the bill appears to be in error, however, as there was no elector or electress of Hamburg as such, though on April 29, 1691 Anna Maria Luisa de' Medici (one of Cosimo's three offspring) married the Elector Palatine Johann Wilhelm II, thereby becoming the Electress Palatine. At the time of their marriage, the Elector Palatine's residence was in Düsseldorf. Perhaps Electress Anna Maria Luisa was in need of a music desk and contacted her father or brother to have one made and shipped to her.

Cristofori Designs a New Form of Spinet for the Theater

Three months later, Cristofori submitted a bill for a new spinet:

First of July 1692 A.D.

> I, Bartolomeo Cristofori claim from the Chamber of the Most Serene Prince Ferdinando of Tuscany for a *cembalo* newly made for the theater, with two registers, and first
> For cypress of Candia and having it sawn up   L 45 : –
> For all expenses of the cabinet maker   L 4 : –
> For a rose of cypress   L 4 : 10
> For expense of a woodworker   L 35 : –
> Expenses for iron pins, brass tacks, red cloth, glue, etc.   L 18 : –
> For my work   L 350 : –
> Total   L 596 : 10[71]
> In addition, for a music desk of cypress inlaid with strips of ebony   L 18 : –
> For another music desk of cypress made for a *cembalo* of the priest from Rome   L 14 : –

---

[70] ASF GM 1073bis, no. 325, f. 2572.   [71] Ibid., f. 2570.

For two music desks for the above-mentioned spinet for the theater, one of cypress, and the other of *abete* [fir or spruce] with their cases of tin-plate L 18 : –

Total   L 646 : 10[72]

On another page of the bill, this L 646 : 10 is brought forward and some additional items are added:

For a stand of *albero* [poplar] for the said *cembalo*   L 21 –
For all sorts of vulture feathers   L 5 –
For carrying the *cembalo* to the palace and for bringing it back home   L 1 – 6 – 8
Total   L 673 : 16 – 8[73]

This *cembalo* for the theater is certainly the *spinettone da orchestra* listed in the 1700 inventory (Figure 2.5):

Un Spinettone da Orchestra di Bartolomeo Cristofori, non levatoro di cassa à due registri, cioè principale, e ottava, con fondo di Cipresso, e rosa in mezzo, con fascie per di fuora di Abeto che servono di cassa al d°. spinettone, e per di dentro impiallacciate di Cipresso, con traversa, et un pianetto, dove sono i pironi et un' altro pianetto, dove si attaccano le corde, tutti scorniciati pur di Cipresso, con tastatura di bossolo et ebano, che comincia in gisolreut, ottava stesa, e finisce in cisolfaut senza spezzati, con n°. cinquanta tre tasti, trà bianchi, e neri, lungo B^a. tre e tre ottavi, largo nel più dal petto alle rene B^a. uno, e soldi tre e mezzo, e nel d'avanti B^a. uno e tre quarti, con due molle di ferro ne i sodi laterali, che servono per registrare, e due bottoncini di Ebano, con una cassettina à mano destra, con suo leggio di Cipresso, e coperchio di Abeto maschiettato, e due toppe, con sua coperta di cuoio giallo, foderata di canavaccio, orlata di nastrino di filaticcio giallo.[74]

(A *spinettone da orchestra* by Bartolomeo Cristofori, not removable from its case, having two registers, that is, the principal and octave, with soundboard of cypress having a rose in the middle, with sides for the outside of *abeto* [fir or spruce] that serves as the case of the said *spinettone* and with the inside veneered in cypress, with the jack rail and flat piece by the tuning pins and another where the strings are attached all framed in cypress, with keys of boxwood and ebony that commence at G *ottava stesa* [stretched octave] and end at C, without split sharps, with 53 keys in white and black, length three *braccia* and three *ottavi* [1860 mm], width from front to back one *braccio* and three-and-a-half *soldi* [648 mm] and in the front one-and-three-quarter *braccia* [965 mm], with two lateral iron springs that operate the registers with two small buttons of ebony, with a small box on the right-hand

---

[72] Ibid.   [73] ASF GM 1073bis, no. 325, f. 2571.   [74] ASF GM 1117, f. 29.

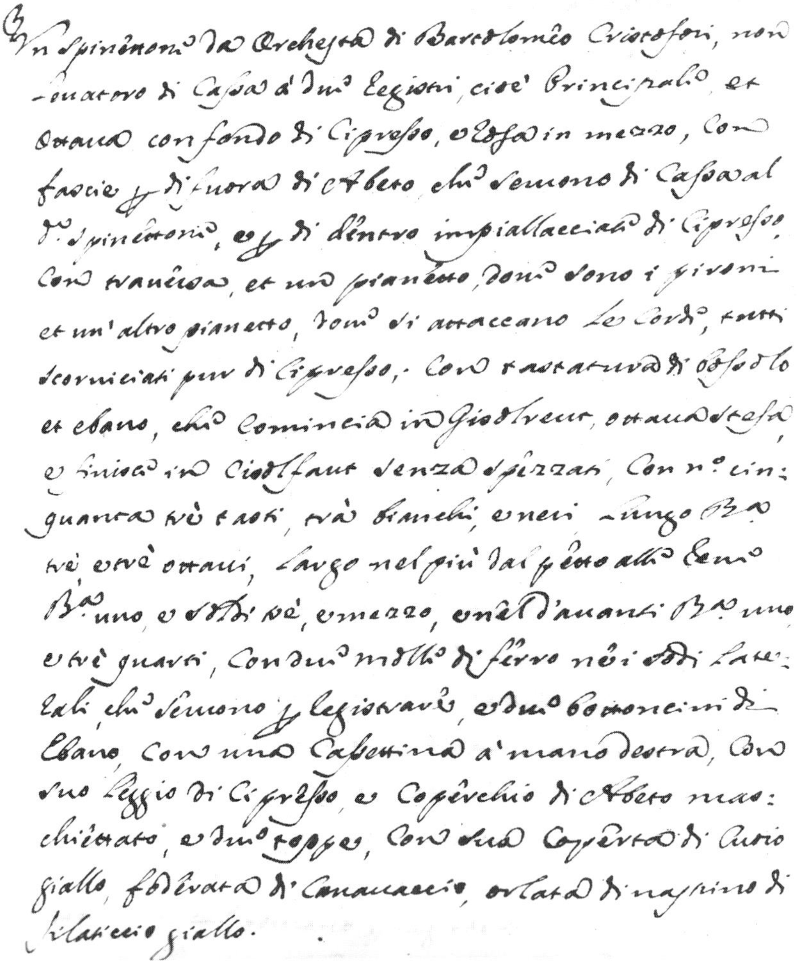

Figure 2.5 The *spinettone* for the orchestra as listed in the 1700 Medici musical instrument inventory. Courtesy of the Archivio di Stato, Florence.

side, with its music desk of cypress and a hinged lid of *abeto* [fir or spruce] and two locks, with its cover of yellow leather lined with coarse linen hemmed with yellow spun ribbon.)

The term *spinettone* implies a large form of *spinetta*, and the inventory description cited above is consistent with an uninscribed spinet attributed to Cristofori, made at a later date, that is presently in the collection of the Grassi Museum für Musikinstrumente der Universität Leipzig (inventory no. 86; see Chapter 3). The Leipzig example, which is aptly termed a *cembalo traverso* in the collection's catalog (1979), is made of the same materials as the instrument described in the inventory, though it is considerably longer (2435 mm).[75]

Cristofori's *spinettoni*, with their long bass strings, use of multiple choirs of strings, and the ability to change registration, had all of the musical resources of a conventional Italian harpsichord. Nevertheless, they were more compact, and if an orchestra were led from this type of keyboard instrument its player could face the orchestral players as well as the front of a stage. The addition of bass notes tuned down to GG mirrored the extended bass strings of *chitarroni*, and such keyboard instruments with extended bass compasses were evidently used interchangeably with *chitarroni*. For example, Mauritio Cazzati's *Correnti, Balletti, Galiarde 3. e 4.*, published in Venice in 1659, includes a part-book designated for *spinetta o chitarrone*. The only possible drawbacks of the *spinettone da orchestra* when compared with a full-size wing-shaped harpsichord were its compressed string band (conventional harpsichords have a string band of approximately the width of the entire keyboard) and reduced soundboard area relative to the conventional harpsichord – features that may have compromised its tone to some degree. It should be pointed out that three of Zenti's spinets described in the 1700 Medici inventory also had compasses extending down to GG.

On August 18 and October 6 of 1692 Cristofori billed the court a total of 4 : 10 *lire* for travelling to Pratolino in order to pack three instrument stands and move them to the theater, including a tip for the movers, and then unloading at his house two pairs of stands that had been returned from Pratolino. On November 28 of that year he billed the court a total of 48 *lire* for the restoration (*restaurare*) of a *spinetina*, which required remaking (*rifarli*) the keyboard and resetting (*rimeter*) the bridges, as well as for strings, cloth, and other work of 15 days."[76] "Remaking" the keyboard might refer to repairing the original keyboard by replacing worn key plates and deteriorated key cloth, or reducing the play or excessive friction in balance-pin mortises and pin racks, though it could also indicate that he made an entirely new keyboard. When restoring spinets for the Medici, Cristofori often "reset" the bridges. There are several reasons

---

[75] The *braccio* (arm length) used in Florence at that time was approximately equivalent to 551.2 mm. This unit was divided into 2 *palmi* (approximately the width of an outstretched hand) and 20 *soldi* (*soldo* means "coin" or "penny," and was thus approximately equal to the diameter of a coin then in use). The *palmo* is approximately equal to 275.6 mm, and the *soldo* is approximately equal to 27.56 mm. Martini, *Manuale di metrologia*, p. 206; Grant O'Brien, "Il percorso di un' idea," in *Bartolomeo Cristofori: La spinetta ovale del 1690*, p. 66.
[76] ASF GM 1073bis, no. 325, f. 2574.

why this might have been necessary: the first is that wood shrinkage or possibly the detachment and springing of the bridges might have caused the jacks and strings to become misaligned (a problem that especially plagues spinets because of the alternating plucking direction of adjacent jacks), which could have been remedied by repositioning the bridges; another possibility is that Cristofori was rescaling keyboard instruments for use at Medici court pitch or for different stringing materials.

Cristofori Constructs an Organ

On February 10, 1693 Cristofori submitted a bill for the following:

> Work for a month-and-a-half
> organ of wood made by me   L 105 : –
> cost of sheep leather   L 1 : 10
> for brass wire and cloth   L 2 : 15
> for green silk ribbon, 20 *braccia*   L 1 : 7
> for an assistant, one month   L 30 :
> for turning certain pipes for the said organ L 1 : 6 – 8
> for glue   L : 18
> Sum L 195 : 6–8[77]

This is the first indication that Cristofori was versed in organ building. The term "organ of wood" probably refers to an organ fitted exclusively with wooden pipes (most organs contain both metal and wood pipes). Wooden pipes are typically square or rectangular in cross section, though the listing for turned pipes might indicate that some were round in cross section, which would have been unusual, though not unheard of. The feet of wooden pipes are generally cylindrical and thus would have been turned on a lathe – perhaps Cristofori was billing the court for those parts. Several organs are listed in the 1713 inventory, entitled: *Inventario dei mobile e masserizie della proprietà del Serenissimo Signor Principe Ferdinando di Gloriosa Ricordanza. Ritrovate doppo la di lui morte nel suo appartamento nel Palazzo de' Pitti, e sono l'appresso cioè* (Inventory of furniture and household effects of the Most Serene Grand Prince Ferdinando of Glorious Memory. Discovered after his death in his apartment in the Pitti Palace, and its environs, that is); one of those listed may be the organ constructed by Cristofori that is referred to in the above bill:

[77] Ibid.

Un organo con canne di cipresso quadre, fermo dentro nella grossezza del muro della camera de' cimbali, con tastatura di cipresso, con un' asse avanti a dette canne tinta di verde rabescata d'oro, fermovi due viticci d'ottone dorato, con suoi mantici et alter applicazione.[78]

(An organ with square pipes of cypress mounted in a wall of the keyboard room, with keyboard of cypress, with a plank in front of the said pipes painted green with arabesques of gold, and gilded brass supports, with its bellows and other appurtenances.)

It is worth noting that this inventory entry makes reference to a special room in the Pitti Palace that housed keyboard instruments.

Cembali with Ottava Bassa and Tiorbino Stops

On February 10, 1693 Cristofori submitted another bill for restoration work:

> For work of 12 days on a *cembalo* by Gierolamo [sic] Zenti with *ottava bassa* in the Chamber of His Serene Highness   L 36 : –
> Expenses for the said *ceamballo*   L – : 15[79]

The term *ottava bassa* (bass octave or octave lower) may be interpreted in different ways: as representing an extension of the keyboard below C (which might provide extra notes for pedals operated by pull-downs, for example) or as a full-compass 16′ stop.[80] The first keyboard instrument listed in the 1700 inventory is a *cimbalo* made by Girolamo Zenti, which is described as having "three registers, that is two principal unisons [8′] and *ottava bassa*... with a compass of 54 keys, commencing at C *ottava stesa* (stretched octave) and ending at F, without split sharps." This must be the harpsichord that Cristofori is referring to in the above restoration bill. In this instance, *ottava stesa* indicates that the keyboard extended down to C with a full complement of accidentals (rather than having a short octave), and Cristofori's use of the term *ottava bassa* must refer to a register of jacks plucking a full choir of strings at 16′ pitch. The second Zenti harpsichord listed in the 1700 inventory has the conventional disposition of "two registers of principal unisons," while the third harpsichord made by him again has three registers, though they are described as "two

---

[78] ASF GM 1222, f. 15.   [79] ASF GM 1073bis, no. 325, f. 2575.
[80] Hammond, "Some Notes on Giovanni Battista Boni da Cortona, Girolamo Zenti, and Others," pp. 41–42.

principal unisons and *tiorbino*." The 1700 Medici inventory also lists two harpsichords made by Giuseppe Mondini that feature this *tiorbino* stop, one dated 1687 and the other dated 1688. The inventory indicates that the Mondini harpsichords also had three registers, with two principal unisons and a *tiorbino*, but most importantly, it states that the *tiorbino* stop was at unison pitch – thus the *tiorbino* stop was not at 16′ pitch. The bass strings of conventional theorbos then extended below C, often to GG, and the Zenti harpsichord featuring the *tiorbino* stop is described in the inventory as having a compass of GG–c^3, with 59 keys, *ottava stesa* (stretched octave), and split sharps, while both Mondini harpsichords are described as having 53-note keyboards extending from G *ottava stesa* (stretched octave; though presumably missing the low G#) to C, *senza spezzati* (without split sharps). Theorbos were generally strung with plain gut (though some were strung with wire), with the lowest strings tuned diatonically (GG, AA, BB, C, etc.). The *tiorbino* register, if strung with gut, might have employed a second bridge and a somewhat longer case, as critically stressed gut strings would have been longer than metal ones; however, there is evidence that longer strings and a second bridge were not necessarily used in harpsichords featuring the *tiorbino* stop.[81] As expected, the three-register Zenti harpsichord with the 16′ *ottava bassa* register described in the 1700 inventory, apparently restored by Cristofori, was considerably longer than the other two harpsichords made by Zenti that are listed in the inventory: it was five *braccia* and eleven *soldi*, which is equivalent to 3059 mm, while his three-register harpsichord with the *tiorbino* register was four *braccia* and nine *soldi* (2452 mm) in length, and his conventional two-register harpsichord was four-and-a-quarter *braccia* (2343 mm) in length. The Mondini harpsichords with the *tiorbino* register were four-and-a-quarter and four-and-a-third *braccia* in length, or 2343 mm and 2389 mm, respectively. It has been suggested that a much altered harpsichord in the Deutsches Museum may be the Zenti harpsichord with *ottava bassa* that is referred to in the Medici inventory.[82] Some years later, Cristofori spent three months restoring yet another harpsichord that may have been equipped with 16′ strings, one made by Giovanni Celestini in 1594 (see below).

The next bill (undated) listed on this page, for the sum of 2 : 3 – 4 *lire*, is "for taking a *cembalo* and its stand of Signor Giosefo Canovese to

---

[81] Grant O'Brien and Francesco Nocerino, "The Tiorbino: An Unrecognised Instrument Type built by Harpsichord Makers with Possible Evidence for a Surviving Instrument," *The Galpin Society Journal* 58 (2005), p. 192.
[82] Denzil Wraight, "A Zenti Harpsichord Rediscovered," *Early Music* 19/1 (1991), pp. 99–102; Hubert Henkel, "Sechszehnfuss-Register im Italienischen Cembalobau," *Das Musikinstrument* 39 (1990), pp. 6–10.

San Firenze and then taking it to my house."⁸³ San Firenze may refer to the Piazza San Firenze near the Palazzo Vecchio. Giosefo Canovese is not listed in the rolls of Medici's salaried musicians, artists, men of letters, or court gentlemen.⁸⁴

On April 1, 1693 Cristofori submitted another bill for restoration work:

> For restoring [*restaurare*] a *spineta* by Domenico da Pesaro involving remaking [*rifarli*] the keyboard, resetting [*rimeteri*] the bridges, the strings, cloths, and quills and other work involving 18 days L 53 : –
> Expenses for the said *spineta* L 5 : –⁸⁵

This bill undoubtedly refers to restoration work carried out on one of the two spinets made by Domenico da Pesaro that are listed in the Medici inventory of 1700. One of these is inscribed with the Latinized form of his name *Dominicus Pisaurensis M.DLXII*, while the other is merely ascribed to *Dom. da Pesaro* and undated. These are described as *levatora di casa* (meaning that the instrument could be lifted from an outer case, or having the so-called "inner-outer" case design), made of cypress, with ebony inlay, and boxwood and ebony keys. The dated spinet is described as lacking split sharps (*senza spezzati*), and having a 50-note keyboard commencing at C *ottava stesa* (stretched octave) and extending to D (considering the number of keys, the keyboard may have lacked c#³). The undated spinet by this maker is described as lacking split sharps and having a 45-note keyboard commencing at C *in sesta* (C/E short octave) and ending at C.

On June 25, 1693 Cristofori billed the court 6: 5 *lire* for twenty-five vulture quills. This bill is followed by an undated one of 13: 10 *lire* for adjusting a keyboard of the organ at Pratolino, work that required three days. There was an additional bill of one *lira* for brass wire and cloth. On August 16, 1693 he billed the court 2 : 6 : 8 *lire* for moving *cemballi* to Pratolino, and then on October 1 of that year, 2 : 10 *lire* for unpacking the stands that had arrived from Pratolino.⁸⁶

The 1693 Oval Spinet
On September 1, 1693 Cristofori submitted the following bill:

> I Bartolomeo Cristofori claim from the Chamber of the Most Serene Grand Prince Ferdinando of Tuscany for one *spineta* having two registers of cypress all inlaid with ebony.

---

[83] ASF GM 1073bis, no. 325, f. 2575.
[84] Kirkendale, *The Court Musicians in Florence*, unpaginated table of Medici courtiers.
[85] ASF GM 1073bis, no. 325, f. 2575.   [86] Ibid.

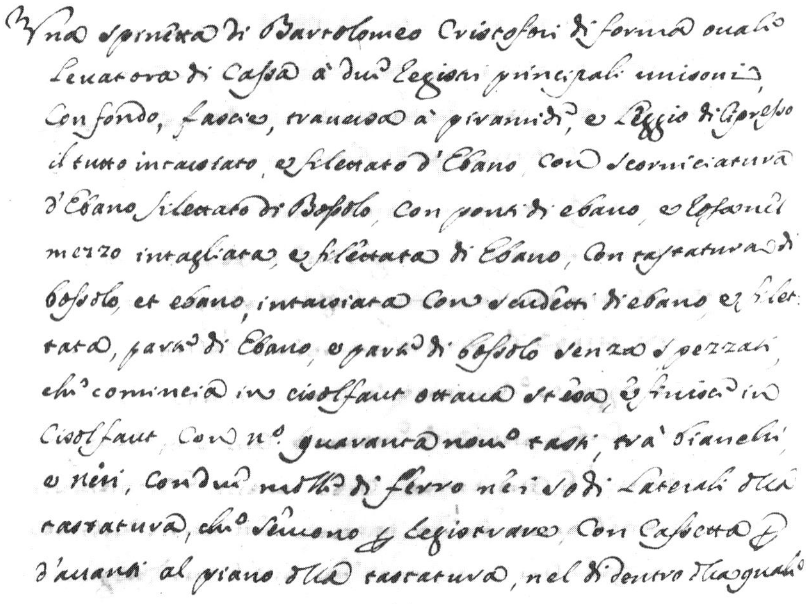

Figure 2.6 (a), (b) The "oval" spinet made by Cristofori, dated 1693, as listed in the 1700 Medici musical instrument inventory. Courtesy of the Archivio di Stato, Florence.

>   the first expense
> for regular cypress and having it sawn up   L 5 : 10
> for a rose of cypress   L 4 : –
> for tuning pins and having them burnished   L 5 : –
> for brass, cloth, kid skin, glue, nails, etc.   L 32 : –
> for the cabinet maker and worker   L 339 : –
> my work   L 800 : –
> Total   L 1185 : 10[87]

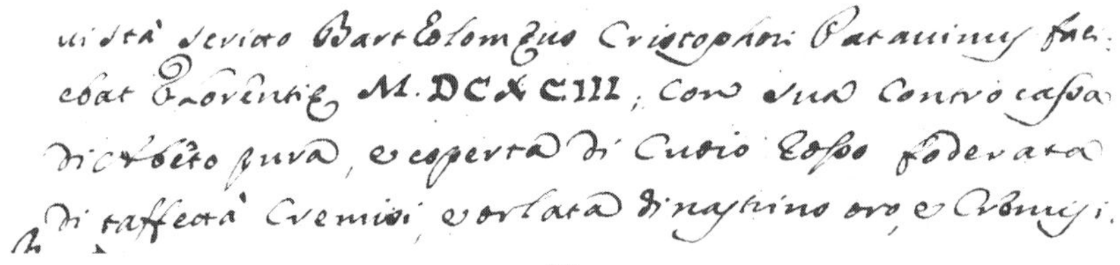

This is most likely the 1693 oval spinet in the 1700 inventory (Figures 2.6(a) and 2.6(b)) that is described as follows:

---

[87] ASF GM 1073bis, no. 325, f. 2577.

Una spinetta di Bartolomeo Cristofori, di forma ovale levatora di cassa à due registri principali unisoni, con fondo, fascie, traversa à pirámide, e leggio di Cipresso, il tutto intarsiato, e filettato d'Ebano, con scorniciatura d'Ebano filettato di Bossolo, con ponti di ébano, e rosa nel mezzo intagliata, e filettata di Ebano, con tastatura di bossolo, et ebano, intarsiata con scudetti di ebano, e filettata, para di Ebano, e para di bossolo, senza spezzati, che comincia in cisolfaut ottava stesa, e finisce in cisolfaut, con nº. quaranta nove tasti, trà bianchi, e neri, con due molle di ferro ne i sodi laterali della tastatura, che servono per registrare, con cassetta per d'avanti al piano della tastatura, nel di dentro della quale, vi sta scritto: Bartholomæus Cristophori Patavinus faciebat Florentiæ M.DCXCIII, con sua contro cassa di Abeto pura, e coperta di cuoio rosso foderata di taffetà cremisi, e orlata di nastrino oro e cremisi.[88]

(A *spinetta* by Bartolomeo Cristofori in the form of an oval, removable from its case, having two registers of principal unisons, with soundboard, sides, pyramidal jack rail, and music desk of cypress all inlaid with strips of ebony, with ebony molding inlaid with boxwood, with ebony bridges and a perforated rose in the middle [of the soundboard] inlaid with ebony, with keyboard of boxwood and ebony inlaid with little ebony shields and inlaid partly with ebony and partly with boxwood, without split sharps, commencing at C *ottava stesa* [stretched octave], and ending at C, with 49 keys in white and black, with two iron springs in the end blocks that serve the registers by lateral movement of the keyboard, with a small box in the front and level with the keyboard that has written on the inside Bartholomæus Cristophori Patavinus faciebat Florentiæ MDCXCIII with its outer case of clear *abeto* [fir or spruce], and cover of red leather lined with crimson taffeta and hemmed in red and gold ribbon.)

This description of the 1693 oval spinet matches the features of the Cristofori spinet that is now in the collection of the Grassi Museum für Musikinstrumente der Universität Leipzig (inventory no. 53; see Chapter 3 and Figure 3.4), and it is presumably the same instrument. Like the other oval spinet made in 1690, it is most unusual in that the bass strings are located in the center of the soundboard and alternate back and forth as one ascends, so that the top strings are positioned at the front and back of the case, somewhat akin to the symmetrical arrangement of façade pipes of many organs. The slots in the soundboard for the jacks form a V (hence the term "pyramidal" jack rail), and the back sections of the key levers alternate from long to short in order to accommodate the positions of the strings. In the bass, the discrepancies in adjacent key lengths are negligible, but as one ascends to the top key, even though the balance points of the alternating keys have been cleverly arranged by the use of two balance rails

---

[88] ASF GM 1117, ff. 28–29.

to provide similar leverage throughout, the lengths of adjacent key levers, and hence their masses, become increasingly disparate and affect the touch to some degree. The stops are activated by sliding the keyboard toward and away from the player (see Chapter 3). The special cabinetry and inlay work of the 1690 and 1693 oval spinets was undoubtedly the work of the anonymous cabinetmaker listed in both of the bills. It is possible that the decorative inlay of the 1693 spinet, a tour de force of design, was executed by Cosimo di Marchionne Maures, an *ebanista* who was on the Medici payroll between 1647 and 1695.[89]

At the time of his death in 1713, Prince Ferdinando had a number of keyboard instruments in his lodgings at the Palazzo Pitti. An inventory made that year (see Chapter 4) describes one of these instruments as follows:

Uno spinettone di cipresso, filattato di ebano, fatto da Bartolommeo Cristofori, con testate d'angolo acuti e tastatura di bossolo et ebano, con cassa d'abeto. Una sopracoperta per detta spinetta di corame, orlata di nastino d'oro e seta, foderata di taffeta rosso.[90]

(A *spinettone* of cypress, inlaid with ebony, made by Bartolommeo Cristofori, with ends angled acutely, and keys of boxwood and ebony, with a case of *abeto* [fir or spruce]. An outer cover of the *spinetta* of leather, hemmed in ribbon of gold and silk, lined with red taffeta.)

The materials listed here are at odds with those of the *spinettone da orchestra* described in the 1700 inventory, and though the phrase *testate d'angolo acuti* might refer to its peculiar angular shape, it could also refer to the pointed ends of the cases of Cristofori's so-called "oval" spinets. The case, cover, and keyboard materials of the *spinettone* described in the 1713 inventory match those of the 1693 oval *spinetta* listed in the 1700 musical instrument inventory, and the elaborate decorative inlay of the oval *spinetta* would have better suited Ferdinando's opulent residence than the spartan case of the *spinettone da orchestra*. The absence of this oval spinet from the 1716 Medici musical instrument inventory is explained by its presence in Prince Ferdinando's private residence.

On September 30, 1693 Cristofori received a double payment for provisions totaling 24 *scudi* covering September and the previous August.[91] On October 6, he billed the court 2 *lire* for unloading two stands at his house that had been sent from Pratolino,[92] and on October 11 he received 25

---

[89] Kirkendale, *The Court Musicians in Florence*, p. 638.   [90] ASF GM 1222, f. 17.
[91] ASF DG 436, f. 22r.   [92] ASF GM 1073bis, no. 325, f. 2574.

scudi for his work at Pratolino.[93] That year's program featured Pagliardi's opera *Attilio Regolo* with libretto by Matteo Noris (see Chapter 4). At the end of October Cristofori received his customary 12 *scudi* payment for provisions.[94]

On November 4, 1693 Cristofori submitted the following bill for restoring a harpsichord:

> For remaking [*refato*] another *cemballo* inlaid with intarsia of ivory, ebony, and *serpentino* old, and first
> For two lengths of planed pear wood   L 8 : –
> For another piece of pear wood   L 1 : 6 – 8
> For iron tuning pins, brass tacks, cloth, glue, four pieces of ebony, tacks, etc.   L 28 : –
> For the cabinetmaker and worker   L 146 :
> My work   L 420 :
> Total   L 603 : 6 – 8[95]

Though the 1700 inventory does not list an instrument of this description, the 1716 inventory includes a harpsichord that is described as follows:

Un Cimbalo con' fondo d'abeto, e tastatura d'avorio, con' tt^i: gli spezzati con' fascie di serpentino intarsiate d'avorio, et ebano con' cassa d'albero copta di corame nero, confitta di bottoncini di ferro.[96]

(A *cembalo* with soundboard of *abeto* [fir or spruce], and keys of ivory, with all the split keys, with sides of *serpentino* inlaid with ivory and ebony, with an outer case of *albero* [poplar] covered with black leather fastened with little iron studs.)

In this instance, the term *serpentino* most likely indicates snakewood (*Piratinera guianensis*); for example, the bows accompanying the Stradivari instruments that are listed in the 1700 Medici musical instrument inventory are described as having been made of *serpentino*, and a number of lutes listed in the 1716 inventory have staves made of this wood.

On November 6, 1693 Cristofori received payment of 12 *scudi* for six months' rent, and on December 16, ducal bankers Montauti (possibly Marchese Bartolommeo Montauti, listed as one of Ferdinando de' Medici's *Maestri di campo* in the *Vita del Gran Principe Ferdinando di Toscana*) and Corboli were reimbursed 103. .9.4 (denomination not given but likely

---

[93] ASF DG 436, f. 27r.   [94] Ibid., f. 34r.
[95] ASF GM 1073bis, no. 325, f. 2577.   [96] ASF GM 1241bis, f. 5.

scudi) for money paid in Venice to Bartolomeo Cristofori.[97] This suggests that Cristofori had been dispatched to Venice to examine and purchase a harpsichord, and received funds there to cover the cost (a payment of a similar amount, 100 *scudi*, was made on May 10, 1695 for a harpsichord purchased for the court in Padua by Cristofori; see below).

No provision payments were made for the first few months of 1694, though on March 31, the court paid Cristofori for his provisions for that month as well as for the previous four months.[98] In April he received his funds for provisions, and in May payment for six months' rent.[99]

A *Spinettina* with Strings of Gold

On May 1, 1694 Cristofori submitted the following bill:

> I Bartolomeo Cristofori claim from the Chamber of the Most Serene Prince Ferdinando of Tuscany for this much work, and first for adjusting a *spinettina* with strings of gold, for work and expenses L 28 : –[100]

There are two *spinette* strung with gold wire listed in the 1700 Medici inventory. One is described as having been made by Girolamo Zenti, the other is anonymous. Because Cristofori has not specified that the *spinetta* he has restored was made by Zenti, the one he worked on was probably the anonymous one that is described in the inventory as follows:

Una spinetta levatora di cassa, à un registro solo, con le corde d'oro, fondo di Abeto, e rosa traforata nel mezzo, con fascie, scorniciatura, e traversa di Ebano, il tutto filettato d'avorio, e nella fascia d'avanti vi sono trè spartini, con fogliami intarsiati d'avorio, con trè perni d'avorio, che reggono un' altra picccola fascia da levare, e porre, con tastatura di bossolo, et Ebano senza spezzati, che comincia in cisolfaut in sesta e finisce in cisolfaut, con n°. quaranta cinque tasti, trà bianchi e neri con sua controcassa foderata per di dentro di tabì verde à onda, e per di fuora di raso verde, guarnita di nastrino d'oro, con bottoncini dorati, e toppa dorata, con coperta di vacchetta rossa orlata di nastro di filaticcio verde, e foderata di frustagno verde con fibbie e cigne per serrarla.[101]

(A *spinetta* [spinet] removable from its case, of one register, with strings of gold, soundboard of *abeto* [fir or spruce] with fretworked rose in the middle, with sides,

---

[97] ASF DG 436, ff. 37v, 49v; Michael Kent O'Brien, *Bartolomeo Cristofori at Court*, p. 77. O'Brien identifies Montauti and Corboli as ducal bankers. *Vita del Gran Principe Ferdinando di Toscana* (Florence, 1887), pp. 60–62.
[98] ASF DG 436, f. 76v. [99] Ibid., ff. 87r, 93r.
[100] ASF GM 1073bis, no. 325, f. 2579.   [101] ASF GM 1117, f. 22.

moldings, and jack rail of ebony all inlaid with strips of ivory, and in the board in front there are three sections with foliate intarsia of ivory with three studs of ivory that support another small board in position, with keys of boxwood and ebony without split sharps that commences at C, *in sesta* [C/E short octave], and ends at C, with 45 keys in white and black, with its outer case covered with green tabby garnished with little gold ribbons, with little gilded buttons and gilded lock, and a cover of red cowhide hemmed with ribbon of green coarse silk lined with green fustian, with buckles and straps for closing.)

According to the *Encyclopaedia Londinensis* (London, 1810), "chords of gold wire in harpsichords yield a sound almost twice as strong as those of brass, while steel wires give a feebler sound than brass, as being less heavy and less ductile."[102] Instruments made for the nobility were sometimes fitted with strings of this precious material.[103] One example was Padre Antonio Soler's *Acordante*, a monochord used for tuning a special temperament devised by Soler, made around 1775 for the *Infante* of Spain.[104]

On June 25, 1694 Cristofori submitted the following bill:

For remaking a *cembalo* having four registers by Celestini
expenses for cypress from Candia [Crete]   L 3 : 10 –
for scarlet cloth   L 4 : 5
for glue and wire of brass   L 2 : 15
assistant for three months   L 117 : –
for the apprentice   L 26 : –
my work   L 250 : –
Total   L 405 : 10[105]

No harpsichord by (Giovanni) Celestini is listed in the inventory of 1700, though a much altered instrument dated 1594 by this maker (who flourished in Venice between 1583 and 1610) was recently discovered.[106] This instrument is currently set up with two registers and a non-original bridge having the profile and double pinning that are characteristic of Cristofori's work. At some point, this harpsichord appears to have been fitted

---

[102] John Wilkes, compiler, *Encyclopaedia Londinensis, or Universal Dictionary of Arts, Sciences, and Literature* (London, 1810), s.v. "chord."
[103] Patrizio Barbieri, "Gold- and Silver-Stringed Musical Instruments: Modern Physics vs. Aristotelianism in the Scientific Revolution," *Journal of the American Musical Instrument Society* 26 (2010), pp. 118–154.
[104] Stewart Pollens, "Soler's Temperament and his *Acordante*," in *Nuevas perspectivas sobre la música para tecla de Antonio Soler* (Series FIMTE, Garrucha, 2016), pp. 17–38.
[105] ASF GM 1073bis, no. 325, f. 2579.
[106] Tony Chinnery, "A Celestini Harpsichord Rediscovered," *Recercare* 11 (1999), pp. 51–73.

with four registers, two at 16′ pitch and two at 8′ pitch, and thus it is conceivable that it is the Celestini harpsichord cited in Cristofori's June 25 bill. Furthermore, there is documentary evidence that Giuseppe Ferrini (the son of Cristofori's assistant Giovanni Ferrini) made repairs on a four-register Celestini harpsichord in 1765 – presumably the same instrument that passed through Cristofori's hands some seventy years earlier. Appended to this June bill is another for 14 *lire* dated July 15 for a music desk, presumably for the above *cembalo*. This is followed by an undated bill of 113 *lire* for the repair of Cristofori's house, as well as for 54 *lire* for four curtains lined with coarse linen.[107] On June 30, Cristofori received his provisions payment for the months of May and June.[108] He evidently returned to Padua around this time, for on July 5, ducal bankers Montauti and Corboli were once again reimbursed, this time for advancing him 40 : 5 : 12 *scudi* (in partial payment of his outstanding bill to the Medici court) while he was in Padua.[109] At the end of July Cristofori received his 12 *scudi* payment for provisions, and though the court missed the August and September payments, they were made up in October.[110]

The next bill that Cristofori submitted was simply dated September 1694:

> Adjusting the two *cembali* of Gierolimo [*sic*; probably Girolamo Zenti] and the organ in the Chamber of His Serene Highness, work of fifteen days with an assistant, in all L 90 : –[111]

On February 10, 1694 Cristofori submitted a bill for:

> Adjusting a *spinet*, that is, remaking the keyboard of ebony, resetting the bridges, all the strings, cloths, and quills, with other work of one month with assistants L 95 : –
> Expenses for the *spinet* L 5 : 10[112]

This was followed on February 25, 1694 with a bill of 6 *lire* for twenty-four vulture quills.[113]

In 1695, Cristofori received his usual monthly provision allotments for the period of January through June.[114] He also received partial payments for past work, including 8 *scudi* installments each month from January through June, as well as six months' back rent.[115] On May 10, he was reimbursed 100 *scudi* for purchasing a *cimbalo* for His Serene

---

[107] ASF GM 1073bis, no. 325, f. 2579. [108] ASF DG 436, f. 102v. [109] Ibid., f. 104v.
[110] Ibid., ff. 111r, 132v. [111] ASF GM 1073bis, no. 325, f. 2579. [112] Ibid., f. 2580.
[113] Ibid. [114] ASF DG 436, ff. 156r, 162r, 169r, 175v, 181v, 188r.
[115] Ibid., ff. 151r, 156v, 164r, 172v, 178v, 183r, 188r.

Highness.[116] Once again, this indicates that Cristofori was involved in securing new (or antique) instruments for the court.

On June 10, 1695 Cristofori submitted a bill for:

> Adjusting a *cembalo* by Domenico da Pesaro purchased by Signora Luzia Coppa, and remaking the keyboard, resetting the bridges, and restoring in all manner, work of a month with two assistants, for 112 *lire*, plus expenses for the said *cembalo* of 3 *lire*, and a music desk of cypress from Candia [Crete] inlaid with ebony strips for the said *cembalo*, 18 *lire*, and for bringing the *cembalo* to my house from the place it was bought, with its *claviorgano*, and for moving the *cembalo* to Pitti, and bringing it again to my house, 3 : 6 – 8 *lire*.[117]

Signora Luzia di Francesco Coppa was a harpsichordist who is listed on the Medici roll books between 1664 and her death in 1699. She is said to have been one of the most talented pupils of Girolamo Frescobaldi (1583–1643), who served the Medici court between 1628 and 1634. She received her appointment from Grand Duke Ferdinando II (1623–1669), the father of Cosimo III.[118] No *claviorgano* is listed in the 1700 inventory, though three are described in the 1716 musical instrument inventory, and others were acquired much later.[119]

On August 14, 1695 Cristofori billed the court – : 10 *lire* for "loading a pair of instrument stands to send to Pratolino," and two days later he billed them 1 : 10 *lire* "for unloading a pair of stands at Pratolino and carrying a *cembalo* to the theater."[120] On October 12, 1695 he received his customary payment of 25 *scudi* for tuning and adjusting harpsichords at Pratolino. Among the works featured that year was Giuseppe Maria Buini's comic opera *L'Ipocondriaco*, with libretto by Villifranchi. On October 26, Cristofori billed the court 15 *lire* for "a case for the *spinet* of *albero* [poplar] to send to Rome to serve Signor Rafaellino, musician."[121] On October 30, Cristofori billed the court 30 *lire* for "expenses for a *spinetina* purchased from Berti the instrument maker by His Serene Highness and delivered to Signor Maestro Pagliardi."[122] As indicated above, Giovanni Maria Pagliardi taught Ferdinando the harpsichord and counterpoint and was later appointed *maestro di cappella* by Grand Duke Cosimo III. He

---

[116] Ibid., f. 177v.   [117] ASF GM 1073bis, no. 325, f. 2580.
[118] Kirkendale, *The Court Musicians in Florence*, pp. 369, 406.
[119] Giuliana Montanari, "Florentine Claviorgans (1492–1900)," *The Galpin Society Journal* 58 (2005), pp. 242–243; and "The Keyboard Instrument Collection of Grand Prince Ferdinando de' Medici at the Time of Alessandro and Domenico Scarlatti's Journeys to Florence, 1702–1705," in *Domenico Scarlatti en España: actas de los Symposia FIMTE, 2006–2007* (Garrucha, 2009), p. 133.
[120] ASF GM 1073bis, no. 325, f. 2580.   [121] Ibid.   [122] Ibid.

composed a number of operas for the Medici, several of which were performed at Pratolino as well as the Pergola theater in Florence (see Chapter 4). Court records indicate that he borrowed a harpsichord from the Medici collection in 1680.[123] Niccolò Berti was a harpsichord maker and member of the Università di Por San Piero e dei Fabbricanti (the guild to which musical instrument makers belonged). Three of his instruments are listed in the 1700 Medici musical instrument inventory: one, dated 1693, is described as a two-register harpsichord of thin-walled case design, having a compass of 53 keys from GG to c^3; the other two as so-called *spinettine compagne* (small companion spinets), again having thin-walled cypress cases, though with short-octave 45-note compasses ranging from C to c^3.[124] Presumably, these small, one-register instruments could be placed on top of full-size harpsichords to serve as secondary keyboards playing at octave pitch, or perhaps they were coupled to the harpsichord's main keyboard, as was done with Flemish and Antwerp-school mother and child virginals. The 1693 harpsichord by Berti and another by Giuseppe Mondini dated 1688 were acquired in the early years of Cristofori's employment as court instrument maker, which indicates that Cristofori was not the only maker supplying newly made harpsichords to the court during his tenure.

On October 12, 1695 Cristofori received his 25 *scudi* for his work at Pratolino and on October 31 belated provision payments for July, August, and September, as well as a partial payment of 8 *scudi* against his accumulated bill for past work.[125] On November 19th, the court issued his provision payment of 12 *scudi* for the previous month, and on the 30th he received the same amount for his provisions for that month, as well as 8 *scudi*, again in partial payment of his outstanding bill to court.[126]

In December of 1695 Cristofori billed the court for the following:

> Expenses for the repair of my house kindly supplied and paid for by His Serene Highness, and first
> for wood and the woodworker L 64 : –
> for two pieces of framing L 30 :
> for eight *libre* [pounds] of wax L 16 :
> nails and ribbon L 5 : –[127]

From January through July of 1696, Cristofori received his provision payments, his six months' rent reimbursement, as well as additional partial payments totaling 56 *scudi* against his outstanding bill.[128] Then in August

---

[123] Kirkendale, *The Court Musicians in Florence*, p. 418. [124] ASF GM 1117, ff. 42, 43.
[125] ASF DG 437, ff. 27v, 28v. [126] Ibid., ff. 33v, 36v. [127] ASF GM 1073bis, no. 325, f. 2581.
[128] ASF DG 437, ff. 52v, 53v, 56r, 62r, 69r, 78v, 79r.

(no date) he submitted a bill of 3 *lire* for remaking the moldings of a *spinetta*, including expenses for an assistant, as well as another undated bill of 14 *lire* for putting in order (*rasetare*) a *cembalo* for one Signor Pucini, which involved three days' work with an assistant and expenses.[129] No musician, artist, man of letters, or gentleman of the court by the name of Pucini (or Puccini) is listed in the Medici rolls.[130] On August 10, Cristofori billed the court 14 *lire* for resetting a patch or possibly repairing a lock (*rasetare una topa*) on a *cembalo* at Pratolino, as well as 1 : 6 – 8 *lire* for packing three *cembali* and loading them for travel there. Then in September of 1696 he billed 2 : 6 – 8 *lire* for expenses at Pratolino for packing and loading the instruments, undoubtedly for their return to Florence.[131] On October 3, the customary payment of 25 *scudi* was issued for his services at Pratolino.[132]

On October 27, 1696 Cristofori billed the court : 10 – *lire* for three ounces of brass wire sent to Poio Caiano.[133] The town of Poggio a Caiano (as it is referred to today) in the province of Prato is the site of another Medici villa that was used as a retreat (in 1674 Cosimo III's estranged wife temporarily resided there before departing for France). On October 30 Cristofori received his payment for provisions for the previous three months, plus six months' rent, and an additional 24 *scudi* in partial payment for work that he had done for the court.[134] The year ended with provision payments made in November and December, with an additional 8 *scudi* in partial payment for outstanding bills.[135]

Cristofori Builds an Upright Harpsichord

On March 30, 1697 Cristofori received a payment for provisions of 36 *scudi* for the months of January, February, and March.[136] On August 10, 1697 he billed the court for the following:

> I Bartolomeo Cristofori claim from the Chamber of the Most Serene Prince Ferdinando of Tuscany for work and expenses, and first
> For an upright harpsichord [*cembalo rito in piedi*], of two registers delivered to the Chamber on the said date.
> For local cypress for the said *cembalo*   L 7 : –
> For iron tuning pins, brass, cloth, glue, and the rest   L 13 : –

---

[129] ASF GM 1073bis, no. 325, f. 2581.
[130] Kirkendale, *The Court Musicians in Florence*, unpaginated table of Medici courtiers.
[131] ASF GM 1073bis, no. 325, f. 2581.   [132] ASF DG 437, f. 93v.
[133] ASF GM 1073bis, no. 325, f. 2581.   [134] ASF DG 437, ff. 100r, 100v.
[135] Ibid., ff. 114v, 117r.   [136] Ibid., f. 136r.

> For the assistant and apprentice   L 170 :
> For my work   L 560 : –[137]
> Additionally,
> For work and expenses for Signor Nicola Onofri at the request of His Serene Highness for fifteen days in June, 1697   L 40 : –
> Expenses in the countryside of Pratolino 1697   L 2 : 12[138]

The two-register upright harpsichord mentioned above is certainly the *Cimbalo in piedi, o' sia ritto di Bartolomeo Cristofori* that is described in the 1700 Medici musical instrument inventory:

Un Cimbalo in piedi, o' sia ritto di Bartolomeo Cristofori levatoro di cassa à due registri principali unisoni senza fascie, con fondo senza rosa, e scorniciatura di Cipresso, con filetto d'Ebano, e serratura d'avanti consistena in tre pezzi, cioé uno in piano al pari della tastatura, nel quale vi è scritto per di dentro Bartholomæus de Cristophoris Patavinus faciebat Florentie M.DCIIIC., l'altro incanalato, che copre il d'avanti l'ordingo de salterelli, nel quale vi è attaccato il leggio, e l'altro serve di traversa à med.[i] salterelli, tutto di Cipresso, con qualche filetto d'Ebano, altro B[a]. tre, e soldi sedici, largo nel d'avanti B[a]. uno, e soldi nove, con tastatura di bossolo, et Ebano senza spezzati, che comincia in cisolfaut ottava stesa, e finisce in cisolfaut con n°. quaranta nove tasti, trà bianchi, e neri, con sua contro cassa d'Abeto pura.[139]

(A *cembalo* standing upright by Bartolomeo Cristofori, removable from its case [the so-called "inner-outer" case design], having two registers of principal unisons, without case sides, with a soundboard lacking a rose, and moldings of cypress with inlaid strips of ebony, and a lock in front consisting of three pieces, that is, one level with the keyboard, inscribed on the front Bartholomæus de Cristophoris Patavinus faciebat Florentiæ MDCIIIC, the other covering the jack mechanism, on which is attached the music desk, and also serving as the jack rail, all of cypress with some inlaid strips of ebony, height three *braccia* and sixteen *soldi*, width of the front one *braccia* and nine *soldi*, with a keyboard of boxwood and ebony without split keys that commences at C *ottava stesa* [stretched octave] and finishes at C with 49 keys of white and black, with its outer case of plain *abeto* [fir or spruce].)

The phrase "without sides" (*senza fascie*) is most unusual, though considering Cristofori's tendency to deviate from tradition, why should we not expect him to come up with another fresh design? It would be possible to construct an upright harpsichord with a panel-like soundboard supported along its back edge by a framework of sufficient strength to support two choirs of strings, especially greatly foreshortened bass strings that the 992 mm overall case height suggests (the height given in the inventory certainly does not include a stand or other support). The width of 799 mm

---

[137] ASF GM 1073bis, no. 325, f. 2582.   [138] Ibid.   [139] ASF GM 1117, f. 27.

is consistent with that of a four-octave keyboard; for example, Cristofori's conventional harpsichord dated 1722 in the Leipzig University collection (inv. no. 84), which has the same four-octave span of C–c^3, has a case width of 802 mm. One of Cristofori's followers, Domenico del Mela, constructed what is believed to be the earliest upright pianoforte in 1739 (now in the collection of the Museo degli Strumenti Musicali del Conservatorio "Luigi Cherubini" di Firenze; catalogue no. 103; see Chapter 3).[140] The soundboard of that peculiar instrument is mounted over the case sides (that is, the case sides do not extend beyond the soundboard as in a conventional harpsichord, or clavicytherium), and its keyboard extends beyond the case. Another upright harpsichord, a South German example dating from around 1480 (Royal College of Music Museum of Instruments; RCM 1), also has a soundboard that is relatively flush with the sides of the case and a keyboard that projects from the case. Though there is no evidence that Cristofori had access to such an early example, perhaps this design is what was meant by the phrase *senza fascie*.

On May 1, 1698, Cristofori submitted a bill for:

> Adjusting a *cembalo* of Gierolimo [sic] Zenti with three stops, work of a month-and-a-half with an assistant   L 164 : –[141]
> For a music desk of cypress tinted black with gilded molding   L 18 : –
> For a new case for the said *cembalo*   L 30 : –[142]

This *cembalo* by Zenti is probably the one with the *ottava bassa* that Cristofori had worked on in 1693 or possibly the one with the *tiorbino* stop (see above).

Cristofori's Last Bill to the Court for Making a New Harpsichord

On July 20, 1698 he billed the court for:

> A new large *cembalo* that extends from G *ottava stesa* [stretched octave], having two registers   L 500 : –
> For a music desk of cypress inlaid with ebony for the said *cembalo*   L 18 : –[143]

This is the last bill submitted by Cristofori for making a new instrument for the court. It is possible that this is the first harpsichord of his that is

---

[140] Pollens, *The Early Pianoforte*, pp. 107–116.   [141] ASF GM 1073bis, no. 325, f. 2582.
[142] Ibid., f. 2583.   [143] Ibid.

listed in the 1700 inventory (see above). At this point, the running bill for Cristofori's work totaled 1522 : 12 *lire*.

Changes in the Court's Billing and Payment Procedure

The bills to court that Cristofori submitted between 1690 and 1698 are recounted in an undated *ristretto* (summary) totaling 1063.2.8.8 *scudi*.[144] Up to and including 1697, 738.5.1.4 *scudi* had been paid, followed by an undated payment of 24 *scudi*. In August of 1698, Cristofori submitted a bill to the Chamber of the Serene Prince Ferdinando of Tuscany for the following:

> August 30, 1698 A.D. for provisions for five months from April 1, 1698 to the above date at a rate of 12 *scudi* per month   L 60 –
> And to cover for rent of the house for one year until April 1698   L 24 – –
> Total   L 84 : – –[145]

Prior to that date, there is no record that Cristofori had ever submitted bills to the court for his provisions and rent – these payments were apparently issued as a matter of course, with notations that he had received the funds. Furthermore, there is no record that he received payment to cover this bill, nor any archival evidence that he received any further regular allotments for provisions and rent. From this point, most of the records of payments he received are for tuning and adjustments, and these payments came out of Grand Duke Cosimo III's treasury rather than from Grand Prince Ferdinando's, as had previous payments. The reason for this is unclear, though Michael Kent O'Brien has proposed that Prince Ferdinando may have lost control over his treasury at this time and thus was unable to continue his monthly payments to Cristofori.[146] Another possibility is that Cristofori's monthly allotments were intended to support the development of the pianoforte, and that once this project was completed the provision payments came to an end. If the fruits of this project were to become the property of the court, this might explain why no bill has ever come to light for the piano's construction, nor a record of payment for one.

Though Grand Duke Cosimo III was evidently disinclined to retain Cristofori as a salaried instrument maker, he continued to pay him on a freelance basis. For example, during the period of June 20, 1704 through

---

[144] ASF GM 1073bis, no. 325, f. 2567.   [145] Ibid., f. 2584.
[146] Michael Kent O'Brien, *Bartolomeo Cristofori at Court*, pp. 87–89, 113.

February 13, 1705 Cristofori was paid 21 *lire* (out of the ducal treasury) for tuning and adjusting *cimbali*.[147] Then on September 3, 1706 he received 15 *lire*, again for tuning and adjustments, followed by payments of 18 *lire* for similar work for the period January 23, 1706 through August 27, 1707, 15 *lire* for the period June 20, 1708 to September 6 of that year, 15 *lire* for the period July 23, 1709 through August 30, 18 *lire* for the period March 23, 1709 (*ab. inc.*) through October 3, 1710, 18 *lire* on August 28, 1711, and 18 *lire* for the periods January 24, 1711 (*ab. inc.*) through August 29, 1712, and January 23, 1712 (*ab. inc.*) through August 30, 1713.[148] These payments represent a deep cut from the regular income that he had previously received, which amounted to about 168 *scudi* (1176 *lire*) per year for provisions and rent alone. Cristofori's patron, Grand Prince Ferdinando, died on October 31, 1713, and after 1713 no payments to Cristofori were recorded until September 23, 1720 when a *ristretto*, or balance that was owed him, was computed to be 300.4.7.4 *scudi*.[149]

Cristofori's Final Bill

On October 12, 1711, Cristofori submitted what appears to be his last itemized bill for work carried out for the court:

> The Chamber of His Serene Highness owes Bartolomeo Cristofori for adjusting an ordinary *cimbalo* by order of Signor Ant. Citerni, gentleman in waiting to the Serene Princess Eleonora, and for replacing all strings, quills, cloth, lengthening the jacks, making a music desk, and restoring the case
> Six days' work with an assistant   L 25 : – –
> Expenses for strings   L 2 : – –
> Cloth, quills, cypress for the music desk, etc.   L 2 : – –
> Total   L 29 : – –[150]

On October 16, 1711 Antonio Citerni borrowed "a *cimbalo* of cypress having one register with a case painted in chiaroscuro, with putti, festoons, and on the inside depicting Apollo and satyrs, with its stand of *albero* [poplar] tinted black," presumably the instrument that Cristofori

---

[147] ASF GM 1025, f. 10v.
[148] Ibid., ff. 10v, 11r, 12r, 12v, 13v, 14r, 14v, 15r, 16r, 17r, 17v, 18r, 19v, 20r. See Chapter 1, pp. 8–9 for an explanation of the Florentine dating system and its notation, abbreviated in this book as *ab. inc.*
[149] ASF GM 1073bis, no. 325, ff. 2567–2584; Michael Kent O'Brien, *Bartolomeo Cristofori at Court*, pp. 85, 176, 189.
[150] ASF GM 1200, no. 392.

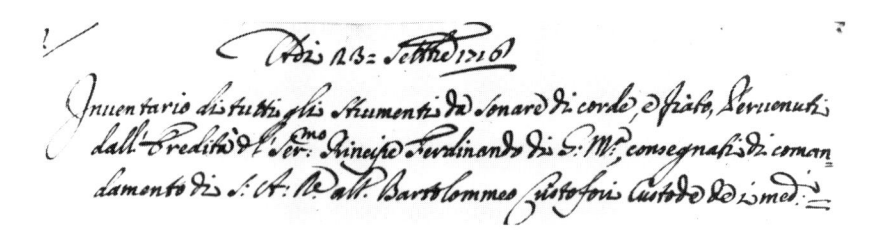

Figure 2.7 Title of 1716 Medici musical instrument inventory. Courtesy of the Archivio di Stato, Florence.

had just adjusted.[151] Princess Eleonora (Gonzaga) had married Prince Francesco Maria de' Medici, the younger brother of Cosimo III, two years earlier. Though Francesco Maria had been a cardinal since 1686, Cosimo persuaded him to leave the church in order to marry in the hope that he would produce male offspring that would continue the Medici line (Cosimo's own offspring, Ferdinando, Gian Gastone, and Anna Maria Luisa had thus far failed to do so; unfortunately, Eleonora's marriage was also without issue, and Francesco died on February 3, 1711). Eleonora evidently played the lute, for an undated loan memorandum associated with the 1700 Medici musical instrument inventory records the following: "Alla Serenissima Principesa Eleonora, un arciliuto con manico di ebano filettato lacco giallo e per di fuori d'incerato nero." (To the Serene Princess Eleonora, an archlute with neck of ebony edged with yellow lace and the outside waxed black.)[152]

Cristofori Appointed Keeper of Medici Instrument Collection

In 1716, Ferdinando's father Cosimo III appointed Cristofori *custode* (keeper) of the musical instrument collection, and he is officially listed on the ducal *ruolo* in August of that year. Though Cristofori drew up an inventory in 1716, there is no record that he was paid for that work or for his responsibilities as keeper. The first page of the 1716 inventory is entitled:

Adi 23: Settbre 1716/Inventario di tutti gli Strumenti da Sonare di corde, e fiato, Pervenuti dall'Eredità del Ser.ᵐᵒ Principe Ferdinando di G: M:ᵃ consegnati di comandamento di S:A:R.ᵉ alt. Bartolommeo Cristofori Custode dei med: (Figure 2.7)

---

[151] ASF GM 1202, f. 6r.
[152] ASF GM 1117, f. 1c; Gai, *Gli strumenti musicale della corte medicea*, p. 22.

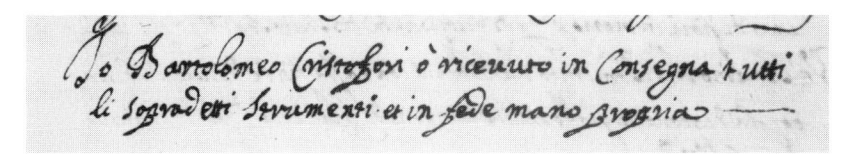

Figure 2.8 Cristofori's signature at the end of the 1716 Medici musical instrument inventory. Courtesy of the Archivio di Stato, Florence.

(September 23, 1716 A.D./Inventory of all string and wind instruments obtained through inheritance from the Most Serene Prince Ferdinando by the G. M.ª [Guardaroba Medicea], consigned by commandment of His Serene Royal Highness to Bartolomeo Cristofori, Custodian, by the same.)

His signature is inscribed on the final page

Io Bartolomeo Cristofori ò ricevuto in Consegna tutti li sopradetti Strumenti et in fede mano propria (Figure 2.8)

(I Bartolomeo Cristofori having received on consignment all of the above-named instruments in trust sign with my own hand)

One of the Medici's most brilliant acquisitions during Cristofori's tenure was a group of five matched instruments (two violins, contralto and tenor violas, and a cello), ordered from Antonio Stradivari by the ducal court in 1684, though not completed until 1690 (Stradivari's actual wood forms and paper patterns used to make the two violas, dated 1690, have survived; the contralto viola's form is inscribed *1690/Forma nova per il Contralto Fatta/Ha Posta per il Ser.ᵐᵒ Gran. Principe/di Firenze* [1690/New form for the contralto made/Especially for the Most Serene Grand Prince of Florence]).[153] In the 1700 inventory, these instruments appear in a single entry as "un concerto di cinque strumenti compagni a quarto corde" (a concerto of five companion instruments of four strings) accompanied by a set of snakewood bows, presumably made by Stradivari as well.[154] This inventory entry even has a hand-drawn rendition of the wood-block seal that Stradivari stamped on his printed labels. The wood forms and patterns used to make the two violas are preserved in the Museo Stradivariano in Cremona.[155] The tenor viola (which miraculously retains most of its

---

[153] Stewart Pollens, *The Violin Forms of Antonio Stradivari* (London, 1992), pp. 10–22, plates 15, 16, 30, 31, 34, and 35; and *Stradivari*, pp. 65, 90–119.
[154] Pollens, *Stradivari*, pp. 131–135.
[155] Andrea Mosconi and Carlo Torresani, *Il Museo stradivariano di Cremona* (Milan, 1987), pp. 77–83; Pollens, *The Violin Forms of Antonio Stradivari*, pp. 10–14, 19–22, plates 15, 16, 30, 31, 34, 35; Pollens, *Stradivari*, pp. 69–72, 75, 82–83, 88–93, 101, 107–110, 116–118, 253–259.

original fittings) and cello are preserved in the collection of the Museo degli Strumenti Musicali del Conservatorio "Luigi Cherubini" di Firenze and are presently exhibited along with Cristofori's ebony harpsichord in the Galleria dell'Accademia. However, in the 1716 inventory compiled by Cristofori, this group of instruments by Stradivari is not listed together but is ignominiously broken up and listed on different pages. No mention is made of the bows. As indicated above, Cristofori failed to identify the makers of the woodwind and plucked-string instruments, though he does provide the names of the violin makers (Antonio and Nicolò Amati, Antonio Stradivari, Jacob Stainer, and Fabrizio Senta).

When did Cristofori Invent the Pianoforte?

The precise date of the piano's invention is unfortunately not revealed in any Florentine court documents. The phrase *di nuova inventione* (of new invention) used in the description of Cristofori's piano in the 1700 Medici musical instrument inventory should not necessarily be interpreted as meaning that the piano was made or invented that year, or even the year leading up to the compilation of the inventory. The previous inventory, compiled in 1691 after the death in 1688 of the keeper of musical instruments, Giovanni Battista Lassagnini, lists but two *cembali* (harpsichords) and three *spinette*, none of which is described as a piano.[156] While it is possible that Cristofori had begun to develop the idea of a keyboard instrument with striking mechanism prior to his invitation to join the Medici court, there is no documentary or physical evidence that this was the case. Thus far, the earliest date that can be placed on the invention is derived from a fragmentary inscription discovered in a copy of Gioseffo Zarlino's *Le istitutioni harmoniche* (Venice, 1558), previously owned by Federigo Meccoli (1635–1710), a keyboard player who joined the Medici *ruolo* sometime between 1664 and 1666 and served until his death.[157] In a margin he wrote the following: "Questi sono gl'andamenti che si possono adattare in su l'Arpi Cimbalo del piano e forte. inventato da M.ro Bartolomeo Christofari Padovano. l'Anno 1700. Cimbalaro del Ser.mo Gran P.pe Ferdinando di Toscana." (These are the ways in which it is possible to play the *Arpicimbalo* with soft and loud invented by Master Bartolomeo

---

[156] Kirkendale, *The Court Musicians in Florence*, p. 383; Gai, *Gli strumenti musicali della corte medicea*, pp. 3–4.
[157] Kirkendale, ibid., p. 407.

Christofari of Padua in the year 1700, harpsichord maker to the Most Serene Grand Prince Ferdinando of Tuscany.)[158] If this inscription is a reliable account (and there is good reason to believe that it is, as Meccoli was evidently acquainted with Cristofori; see below), it confirms the date we have come to associate with the invention of the piano.

In 1964, the musicologist Mario Fabbri published an article alleging that he had discovered an account written by a Florentine musician named Francesco Maria Mannucci (a pupil of the court composer and keyboard tutor of Prince Ferdinando, Giovanni Francesco Pagliardi) that proved Cristofori had perfected his hammer action in 1698.[159] Though Fabbri provided an archival reference for this document, other researchers were unable to locate it, and in 1991 his discovery was deemed fraudulant on stylistic grounds by Carlo Vitali and Antonello Furnari.[160] Thus, the date of the invention of the piano has not been pushed back before the year 1700.

Critical Reception of Cristofori's Pianoforte in Florence

Though Cristofori is credited with inventing the instrument that ultimately eclipsed the harpsichord, he did not live long enough to witness this undoubtedly unintended consequence, nor perhaps could he have even imagined it, as the pianoforte barely survived at the Medici court during his tenure there. Maffei alluded to a lack of universal enthusiasm for the pianoforte when he wrote:

Some professors have not given to this invention all the applause that it merits; first, because they have not understood how much ingenuity was required to overcome the difficulty and what marvelous delicacy of touch was required to carry out the work correctly; second, it has appeared to them that the voice of the instrument, being different from the ordinary, is too soft and dull, an impression produced on first placing the hand on the instrument, given that we are accustomed to the

---

[158] Luisa Cervelli, "Noterelle Cristoforiane," *Quadrivium* 22/1 (1981), p. 98; and *La galleria armonica: catalogo del Museo degli strumenti musicali di Roma* (Rome, 1994), pp. 144–151; Russell, *The Harpsichord and Clavichord*, p. 38f.

[159] Mario Fabbri, "Nuova luce sull'attività fiorentina di Giacomo Antonio Perti, Bartolomeo Cristofori e Giorgio F. Haendel: valore storico e critico di una 'Memoria' di Francesco M. Mannucci," *Chigiana* 21 (1964), pp. 143–190; and "L'alba del pianoforte," in *Dal clavicembalo al pianoforte* (Brescia, 1968), pp. 35–53.

[160] Carlo Vitali and Antonello Furnari, "Händels Italienreise – neue Dokumente, Hypothesen und Interpretationen," *Göttinger Händel-Beiträge im Auftrag der Göttinger Händel-Gesellschaft herausgegeben von Hans Joachim Marx* 4 (Kassel, 1991), pp. 64–65.

silvery sound of other *gravecembali*... There has been further opposition raised that this instrument does not have a powerful tone and is not quite as loud as other *gravecembali*. To this one may answer, first, that it has more power than they give credit, when someone wishes and knows how to produce it, by striking the keys with force; and second, that it is necessary to accept things for what they are, and not consider, as regards one end, something that is designed for another. This is properly a chamber instrument, and it is not adaptable for church music, or for a large orchestra.[161] (See Appendix 2 for the Italian text.)

Though chamber music was composed and performed at the Medici court during Cristofori's time (for example, court violinist Martino Bitti and theorbist Giovanni Gigli composed numerous sonatas and chamber works), the Medici were preoccupied with opera, which then employed relatively small ensembles of musicians that could not be construed as a large orchestra. From the rosters of musicians that took part in operas performed in the Medici villa at Pratolino, the instrumentalists consisted of pairs of violinists and violists, a bass viol player or cellist, a theorbo player, and one or two keyboard players (see Chapter 4); however, there is no indication that Cristofori's piano was used in these performances; rather, it is more likely that his *spinettone* was used.

How Many Instruments did Cristofori Make?

Hubert Henkel estimated that Cristofori constructed between 25 and 30 pianofortes and a total of around 200 keyboard instruments.[162] However, these figures are certainly grossly inflated if we consider the rather close correspondence between the instruments described in the court bills, in its inventories, and those that are still with us. Up through 1698 Cristofori drew a considerable amount of money from the Medici treasury, and with his continued involvement as custodian of the court's collection and his ability to obtain funds (such as the 300 *scudi* that he received from the court in 1720), it would not have been feasible or necessary for him to operate an independent, large-scale manufacturing facility, as is suggested by Henkel's unsubstantiated figures. Considering Cristofori's

---

[161] Pollens, *The Early Pianoforte*, p. 57.
[162] Hubert Henkel, "Cristofori as Harpsichord Maker," *The Historical Harpsichord* 3 (Stuyvesant, NY, 1992), p. 15. In Montanari, "Bartolomeo Cristofori: A List and Historical Survey of his Instruments," pp. 383–396, the author does not distinguish between authentic and misattributed instruments, and thus her tally of Cristofori's output is hugely inflated.

overwhelming court duties, he probably made no more than around two dozen instruments during his career. All told, he submitted bills for constructing seven new instruments (six stringed keyboard instruments and one organ), though of the seven stringed keyboard instruments of his that are listed in the 1700 inventory, only five appear to be associated with these bills; Maffei states that Cristofori had made three pianofortes by 1711, however only one appears in the 1700 inventory; the 1716 inventory lists six instruments by Cristofori, but two of these appear in the earlier inventory and the other four have no bills associated with them. Thus, including the seven late, extant instruments dating from 1719 through 1726 (which are not listed in the 1732 inventory), we arrive at a total of around twenty instruments.[163] By 1729, Cristofori was ill and probably made no instruments through the year of his death (1732).

Curiously, two of the three surviving Cristofori pianofortes are not signed and dated on their nameboards but on their action frames: with the 1720 instrument, one must slide the action out to read the inscription on the hammer rack; while the 1722 pianoforte has an opening cut in the nameboard (where an earlier inscription might have been) so that one can read the inscription on the action frame. Only the 1726 piano is signed and dated on the nameboard. We know that Cristofori completely redesigned his hammer action sometime between Maffei's published description (1711) and the year of his earliest extant pianoforte (1720).[164] It is possible that the two pianos with uninscribed and undated cases were made prior to 1711 and subsequently upgraded with new actions dated 1720 and 1722.

In 1711, Scipione Maffei indicated that Cristofori had made three pianofortes, and in the notes he made from his interview with Cristofori, he stated that two were sold in Florence and one went to Cardinal Pietro Ottoboni in Rome.[165] In a testament dated May 22, 1704, one of Cristofori's keyboard instruments, possibly a pianoforte, was bequeathed by Carlo Antonio Zanardi (1657–1704), a *castrato* from Bologna, to Francesco de Castris (*c.* 1650–1724), another *castrato*, born near Rome – both of

---

[163] The survey by Montanari, ibid., also provides an exaggerated number due to repetition of instruments and the inclusion of those that are falsely attributed to Cristofori.
[164] Pollens, *The Early Pianoforte*, pp. 55–73.
[165] Verona, Biblioteca Capitolare, cod. DCCCCLX, fasc. VI, no. I; Pollens, ibid., pp. 53, 232. The inventory of Cardinal Ottoboni's estate compiled in 1740 lists an organ, fourteen harpsichords, and a spinet. These instruments are well described, but none is listed as a piano. Ralph Kirkpatrick, *Domenico Scarlatti* (Princeton, 1953), p. 360.

whom had been in service to Grand Prince Ferdinando and were among his highest paid musicians.[166] This may account for one of the two pianos sold in Florence as of 1711. On June 17, 1709 Cardinal Ottoboni wrote to Ferdinando: "Il Sig.ʳ Franco di Castris ha sentito il raro Cembalo, che mi ha favorito." (The Signor Fran[ces]co di Castris has heard the rare cembalo with which [you] have favored me.).[167] From the wording of Ottoboni's letter of thanks, the *raro cembalo* (rare keyboard instrument) that he received was probably a piano (certainly a rarity at that time), though it was apparently not de Castris' (de Castris for some reason having been compelled to deliver his own piano to Ottoboni at Ferdinando's request), because he is only reported as having heard it, not as having delivered it (de Castris had been expelled from Florence in 1703, and though his benefactor Zanardi died the following year, it is not known when de Castris came into possession of the instrument he had been bequeathed). Ottoboni's piano is apparently not the one listed in the 1700 Medici musical instrument inventory (though missing from the 1716 inventory), as two loan memoranda associated with the earlier inventory, one dated May 3, 1714 regarding the loan of a *cimbalo* by Cristofori to Prince Gian Gastone, and the second dated July 13 (no borrower's name or year given), indicate that a Cristofori piano was still present at the Florentine court as of the latter date. Unless the piano listed in 1700 was replaced with another, the piano listed in 1700 was not the one given to Ottoboni. The following is the text of these loan memoranda:

Al Serenissimo Principe Gio. Gastone un cimbalo di cipresso, opera di Bartolomeo Cristofori con cassa d'albero e sopra coperta di corame rosso orlata di nastrino d'oro.

(To the Most Serene Prince Gio. Gastone, a *cimbalo* of cypress, work of Bartolomeo Cristofori, with a case of poplar and its outer cover of red leather hemmed with gold ribbon.)

Un cimbalo di cipresso di piano e forte, con tastatura di bossolo, opera di Bartolomeo Cristofori, con suoi piedi d'albero dorati et ombrati e sopra coperta di corame rosso foderata di taffetà verde, guarnita a torno di nastrino d'oro.[168]

---

[166] Carlo Vitali, "Un cantante legrenziano e la biographia Francesco de Castris 'musico politico'," in *Giovanni Legrenzi e la Cappella ducale di San Marco: Atti del convegno internzationale di studi*, ed. Francesco Passadore and Franco Rossi (Florence, 1994), p. 584; and *The New Grove Dictionary of Opera* (London and New York,1992), s.v. Zanardi, Carl'Antonio; Kirkendale, *The Court Musicians in Florence*, p. 446.
[167] ASF GM 5899, fol. 75; Pollens, *The Early Pianoforte*, pp. 53, 232.
[168] ASF GM 1117, f. 1b.

(A keyboard instrument of cypress wood with soft and loud, with a keyboard of boxwood, work of Bartolomeo Cristofori, with its stand of poplar, gilded and shaded, and a cover of red leather lined with green taffeta, trimmed all around with gold ribbon.)

The term "keyboard instrument with soft and loud" was then used (as in the 1700 inventory) to designate the newly invented pianoforte, and the memorandum's cursory description is consistent with the description of the pianoforte listed in the inventory, though the inventory makes no mention of a stand but indicates that the instrument was furnished with an outer case of white wood. Both descriptions of the pianoforte mention a red leather cover lined with green taffeta and hemmed in gold ribbon. Though no borrower's name is given in the second memorandum, it is likely that it is the same individual, Gian Gastone, who borrowed the instrument described immediately above it.

Though there is a lack of bills and payment records for new instruments after 1698, Cristofori evidently continued to make them for the court, as four single-register *cembali* of his are listed in the 1716 musical instrument inventory. Hubert Henkel and Giuliana Montanari both assert that the "three keyboard instruments of one register, work of Bartolommeo Cristofori" and "one keyboard instrument with one stop, work of Bartolommeo Cristofori" listed in the 1716 Medici musical instrument inventory, and the "four keyboard instruments of one register, work of Bartolomeo Cristofori" listed in the 1732 inventory must have been pianofortes, on the grounds that one-register harpsichords are uncommon (despite the fact that such instruments were the subject of a detailed study published by Friedemann Hellwig).[169] However, it seems unlikely that a special instrument such as the newly invented piano would have been described in such a perfunctory manner. Furthermore, in the 1700 inventory, Cristofori's earliest known pianoforte is described as having "due registri principali unisoni" (two registers of principal unisons) – not one register of strings. Cristofori recognized from the outset that his hammers required the resistance of a pair of strings, so it is unlikely that he would have made pianofortes with single courses of strings. A clear distinction between harpsichord and pianoforte is made in a record of a public auction of Medici household items in 1777: one Bastiano Volpini purchased (in addition to a few plucked-string instruments, a psaltery,

---

[169] Montanari, "Bartolomeo Cristofori: A List and Historical Survey of his Instruments," p. 387; Friedemann Hellwig, "The Single-Strung Italian Harpsichord," in *Keyboard Instruments: Studies in Keyboard Organology*, ed. Edwin M. Ripin (Edinburgh, 1971), pp. 27–36.

and a small organ) "quattro cimbali con casse d'albero alla rozza a un registro" (four *cembali* with cases of poplar in the rough having one register) and "un cimbalo a martelli con cassa tinta di rosso, e suo piede a mensola traforato in parte dorato con sopracop[er]ta di corame" (a *cembalo* with hammers with case colored red, and its stand of fretwork brackets in part gilded with a cover of leather).[170] The four *cembali* were most likely the instruments made by Cristofori that are listed in the 1716 and 1732 Medici inventories. The description of the *cimbalo a martelli* in the 1777 auction record is not inconsistent with that of the "Arpicimbalo . . . che fa' il piano, e il forte" listed in the 1700 Medici inventory and the loan document dated July 13, 1714, which supports the proposition that the inventories of 1716 and 1732 simply neglected to include it. If the piano auctioned in 1777 was the same one listed in 1700, it would have been one of the first, if not the first, that Cristofori had built.

Henkel erroneously concludes that "Arpicimbalo di Bartolomeo Cristofori di nuova inventione, che fa' il piano, e il forte" listed in the 1700 Medici inventory is not simply the description of a pianoforte, but that it describes a combined pianoforte/harpsichord, due to his interpretation of the inventory's reference to the instrument's dampers as meaning harpsichord jacks: "salterelli con panno rosso che toccano nelle corde" (jacks with red cloth that touch the strings).[171] What are being described here are certainly dampers, not harpsichord jacks. The term *salterelli* (jumpers) is entirely appropriate in describing the form of damper that is found in the surviving pianos.

The 1720, 1722, and 1726 pianofortes, the 1722 and 1726 harpsichords, the *c.* 1720 *spinettone*, as well as the 1719 clavichord (see Chapter 3), may have been made by Cristofori for private clients, as there is no mention of them in the inventory of 1732 (though it is conceivable that they were made for the court sometime after 1716 and disposed of prior to 1732). Evidence of private ownership of the 1720 pianoforte is cited in Chapter 3. Also entertained in Chapter 3 is the possibility that the 1720 and 1722 pianos were made prior to those dates and refitted with actions of newer design in 1720 and 1722.

The "Gatti-Kraus" Cristofori piano action, which is presently exhibited in Florence at the Galleria dell'Accademia, is at best a reconstruction built around a few original pieces. Its keyboard and action frames do not fit

---

[170] ASF, Magistrato dei Pupilli 3469, 3531. I would like to thank Giuliana Montanari for providing a transcription of these documents.
[171] Henkel, "Cristofori as Harpsichord Maker," p. 2.

together properly, and thus appear to have been built for two instruments that have not survived (see Chapter 3).[172]

Cristofori's Death in 1732

Bartolomeo Cristofori died in Florence on January 27, 1731 *ab. inc.* (1732) at the age of 76 (the official church record inaccurately indicates that he was 80).[173] He was buried in the graveyard of the Church of S. Jacopo fra' Fossi, where he had been a parishioner.[174] The diary of Niccolò Susier (a theorbo player in the Medici court) contains a brief notation marking Cristofori's death:

1731. Adi 27 detto [gennaio] Mori. Bartolomeo Cristofani detto Bartolo Padovano famoso strumentaio del Ser[enissi]mo Gran Principe Ferd[inand]o di Felice Memoria et questo fu un Valente huomo in fabbricare cravicembali, ed anche inventore del Cimbalo del Piano, e Forte che si è fatto conosciere per tutta l'Europa, servitore ne di esso, la Maestà del Re di Portogallo con pagare detti istrumenti p[er] insino 200 Luigi d'oro; et e morto come si e detto d'anni 81.[175]

(1731, 27th [January], Bartolomeo Cristofani, called Bartolo Padovano, died, famous instrument maker to the Most Serene Grand Prince Ferdinando of fond memory, and he was a skillful maker of keyboard instruments, and also the inventor of the pianoforte, that is known through all Europe, and who served His Majesty the King of Portugal [João V], who paid two hundred gold *louis d'or* for the said instruments, and he died, as has been said, at the age of 81 years.)

An anonymous document dated 1741 entitled *Le Maestri più Eccellenti nel far Cembali* (*The most excellent masters in the making of* cembali), preserved in the Biblioteca Apostolica Vaticana, notes: "De nostri Tempi Bartolomeo de Christofani ditto il Burtulo, che hà superato Tutti in questa professione, et è passato all'altra Vita stando al servigio attuale del Gran Duca di Toscana."[176] (In our time, Bartolomeo Cristofori, otherwise known as *il Burtulo*, who has surpassed all in that profession and has passed on to the other life, stood in service to the Grand Duke of Tuscany.)

---

[172] Stewart Pollens, "The Gatti-Kraus Piano Action Ascribed to Bartolomeo Cristofori," *The Galpin Society Journal* 55 (2002), pp. 269–278.
[173] Archivio Curia Arcivescovile di Firenze; Chiesa S. Jacopo fra' Fossi: Registro dei Morti 1634–1793.
[174] Michael Kent O'Brien, *Bartolomeo Cristofori at Court*, p. 5.
[175] Florence, Biblioteca Moreniana, Acquisti diversi 54, fols. 73r, 73v.
[176] Biblioteca Apostolica Vaticana, codice Capponi Lat. 281, parte II, tomo II, carta 269.

From these notices, it is clear that Cristofori was a brilliant and highly industrious craftsman who served the Medici court for some forty-four years and achieved renown during his lifetime as the inventor of the piano. In contrast to his contemporary Antonio Stradivari (*c.* 1644–1737), who ran a family-operated workshop that produced well over 600 instruments, Cristofori's primary responsibility was the maintenance of a large collection of keyboard instruments for a musically active court. Though Stradivari was self-employed and ostensibly free to experiment, he was nonetheless constrained by a rigid violin-making tradition. Stradivari managed to innovate within narrow constraints (for example he vacillated between the traditional shape and a slightly elongated form of his own design known as the "long pattern," as well as with full and flat arching), though he gained an international reputation in his own day not as an innovator but for the extraordinary tonal quality of his instruments as well as their unmatched craftsmanship.[177] On the other hand, Cristofori's monthly salary provided him with financial security and the freedom to develop new forms of harpsichords, spinets, and clavichords, as well as to perfect his pianoforte. Cristofori was not a craftsman in the same sense as Stradivari (the exquisite cabinetry of his oval spinets and the ebony harpsichord was most likely the work of the Medici court *ebbanista* and *legnaiolo* who assisted him); rather, he was a brilliant engineer who was undaunted by an equally staid Italian keyboard tradition.

Provisions of Cristofori's Last Will and Testament

The first version of Cristofori's will was drawn up on January 24, 1728 *ab. inc.* (1729 by the modern calendar; coincidentally this is the same year that Stradivari drew up his will).[178] A codicil was added on February 26, 1729 *ab. inc.* (1730),[179] and the second and final version was completed on March 23, 1729 *ab. inc.* (1730).[180]

The name of Cristofori's principal assistant, Giovanni Ferrini, is revealed in the first will. In that version, drawn up by the notary Christofano Nacchianti, Ferrini was left all of the tools (*tutti gl'arnesi o ferramenti*)

---

[177] Pollens, *Stradivari*, pp. 67–86, 143–164.
[178] ASF Notarile Moderno, 25959, testamenti 1728–1740, 5148/2, ff. 2r–5r. Cristofori's wills, cited here and in footnotes below, are transcribed and translated in full by Michael Kent O'Brien, *Bartolomeo Cristofori at Court*, pp. 191–214.
[179] ASF Notarile Moderno, 23370, testamenti 1728–1733, 5091/8, ff. 34r–35v.
[180] Ibid., ff. 38v–41r.

used in making harpsichords and other instruments "in appreciation for his help, and in compensation for the good and loyal service." The will also stipulates that all the furniture and household items that Cristofori had borrowed from the Guardaroba and from members of the del Mela family be returned. However in the second and final version of the will (see above), drawn up by notary Niccolò Melani, all of his tools and instruments were left to the sister and daughter of the late Giovanni del Mela (rather than Ferrini) in recognition of the assistance they had provided during his illness, as well as 200 *scudi*. At the time the first will was drafted, Cristofori was bedridden, but when the second will was drawn up a year later he was still indisposed, though well enough to sit up. One might presume that the del Mela ladies had provided household and nursing assistance, but the fact that they were bequeathed Cristofori's tools suggests either that they assisted him in the workshop during his protracted illness or that they had a relative who could put the tools to good use, such as Domenico del Mela, the maker of the first upright pianoforte (see Chapter 3).[181] In the final version of Cristofori's will, Giovanni Ferrini was left a perfunctory 5 *scudi*, though by that time he was making instruments on his own (see Chapter 3). Cristofori's will does specify that Ferrini be paid for any outstanding workshop repairs, but that these funds be turned over to his estate. Furthermore, any instruments owned by individuals who had not paid for the repairs were to be legally sequestered in order to protect his estate from suits that might arise from any deterioration or damage that might transpire in the interim.[182]

Cristofori's will indicates that he had always intended to return to his native Padua. He owned property there, and in his will he bequeathed that property, as well as personal possessions (which included furniture, jewelry, gold, silver, and credits), to his niece Laura (the daughter of his sister Lisabetta Cristofori Pavese), with the provision that she pass them on to a daughter, and from her daughter to the next, and so on, until the time came when there were no female heirs in prospect, at which point a son was to be selected by his mother (rather than his father) to inherit the property.[183] Cristofori's bequests to female members of the del Mela family and to his female family members in perpetuity, stand in stark contrast to traditional male primogeniture. Despite Cristofori's

---

[181] Pollens, *The Early Pianoforte*, pp. 107–116.
[182] ASF Notarile Moderno, 25959, testamenti 1728–1733, 5148/2, ff. 3r, 3v; ibid., 23370, testamenti 1728–1733, 5091/8, f. 39v.
[183] Ibid., ff. 39v, 40r.

Figure 2.9 "ATE/1726" monogram on portrait of Cristofori as transcribed by Georg Schünemann.

apparent fondness and concern for women, there is no record that he ever married.

A Portrait of Cristofori

An oil portrait of Cristofori (frontispiece), purportedly painted in 1726, was brought to light in 1934 by the musicologist Georg Schünemann.[184] The painting was unfortunately destroyed in World War II. According to Schünemann, the painting bore the monograph ATE/1726 (Figure 2.9).

According to convention, the enlarged central "T" represents the initial of the painter's surname, though no painter having the initials AET (or any other permutation of the three letters) has been identified as having been associated with the Medici court.

Painted at the age of 71, Cristofori appears remarkably young-looking in his wig and formal court attire. Of great interest is the drawing of the hammer action that he holds in his left hand. Painted below the drawing is his name "BARTHOLOMAEVS CRIST...", which presumably identifies the sitter. Though this painting has been reproduced in many books and articles, the reproductions typically lack clarity. The author was fortunate to examine an original black-and-white photograph of the painting. It was placed on a light box to reveal latent details in the drawing held by Cristofori, and it became clear that the action depicted in the painting is clearly the later version that is found in the extant pianos dated 1720, 1722, and 1726, rather than the earlier design with under-dampers described

---

[184] Georg Schünemann, "Ein Bildnis Bartolomeo Cristoforis," *Zeitschrift für Musikwissenschaft* 16/11–12 (1934), pp. 534–536.

and pictured in Maffei's 1711 article (see Chapter 3). Also evident in the drawing is the non-inverted wrestplank, which is a feature found only in the pianoforte dated 1720.[185] Strangely, the key fronts of the keyboard shown in the lower right corner of the painting lack the arcades one finds in Cristofori's instruments; they look very much like the plain key fronts found on modern pianos, which raises some suspicion about the painting's age.

Summary

Though Cristofori's early years in Padua and his training remain a mystery, Grand Prince Ferdinando de' Medici invited him to Florence, where a salaried position was created for him. During the years that Cristofori worked for the Medici, the number of keyboard instruments in their collection increased significantly, and several court records indicate that he was actively involved in their acquisition. The court's concert schedule kept him busy moving, adjusting, restoring, and building keyboard instruments, yet the stability provided by his position enabled him to develop new types of keyboard instruments, including his *spinettone da orchestra* (which undoubtedly played a major role in opera performances held at the Medici villa at Pratolino) and decorative oval spinets (one of which graced the Grand Prince's private chambers), as well as the piano, which was not fully appreciated at first, though as we shall see, quickly became a favorite of court castrati and ultimately sparked a revolution that toppled the long-reigning harpsichord.

As will be described in the next chapter, Cristofori's pianofortes and certain of his harpsichords employ an important innovation: a double-walled bentside and suspended hitchpin rail that physically isolate the soundboard from the stress-bearing components of the case.[186] Maffei's 1711 article on Cristofori alludes to this novel case design, which was presumably developed to cope with the heavier stringing used in the pianofortes and then later applied in the construction of his harpsichords. The clavichord attributed to Cristofori (Grassi Museum für Musikinstrumente der Universität Leipzig, inventory no. 5433; see Chapter 3) is most unusual

---

[185] Pollens, *The Early Pianoforte*, frontispiece, and pp. 55–56.
[186] Cristofori's case design was first described in Stewart Pollens, "The Pianos of Bartolomeo Cristofori," *Journal of the American Musical Instrument Society* 10 (1984), pp. 32–68. Pollens, *The Early Pianoforte*, pp. 74–79.

in that it is not built in the customary rectangular case but employs an elongated *traverso* case derived from his *spinettone da orchestra*. A unique feature of this clavichord is its set of eight supplementary levers located along the back of the case that are used to extend the reach of the fretted bass key levers (see Chapter 3). The attribution and dating of this unsigned clavichord are supported by an anonymous eighteenth-century music dictionary manuscript that describes two instruments owned by its author and made by Cristofori: a pianoforte dated 1720 (perhaps the pianoforte now in The Metropolitan Museum of Art) and a *sordino con leve inventate dall'autore* (clavichord with levers invented by the maker) dated 1719. The term "with levers" is a perfect description of the supplementary linkages in the clavichord now in Leipzig. In addition, this anonymous dictionary lists several keyboard instruments that were restored by Cristofori: a large harpsichord by Benedetto Floriani dated 1568, a harpsichord by Domenico da Pesaro dated 1537 (which the dictionary author states was subsequently worked on by Giovanni Ferrini), and a clavichord by Domenico da Pesaro dated 1543, which may be a clavichord now in the Leipzig collection.[187] No instruments by Floriani or by Domenico da Pesaro having these dates are listed in the Medici inventories, which suggests that this restoration work was carried out for private clients. Medici documents and other records indicate that court musicians not only borrowed instruments from the *guardaroba* but also had their own instruments worked on by Cristofori. For example, Federigo di Antonio Meccoli, a harpsichordist and organist on the Medici *ruolo* from around 1664 until his death in 1710, is recorded as having borrowed a spinet in 1672 and a harpsichord in 1676, though in his will he left several harpsichords of his own to his sons, including a two-register harpsichord made by Benedetto Floriani that had been readjusted (*riaggiustato*) by Cristofori (possibly the very instrument referred to in the anonymous dictionary cited above).[188] Meccoli's mention of the Cristofori piano in a marginal note made in his copy of Zarlino's *Le istitutioni harmoniche* is the only reference to the piano's invention in the year 1700.

---

[187] Civico Museo Bibliografico di Bologna, Martiniano H. 62, ff. 114–119; Cervelli, "Noterelle Cristoforiane."

[188] ASF GM 822, ff. 12, 15; Kirkendale, *The Court Musicians in Florence*, p. 408.

3 | Cristofori's Extant Instruments

Organological literature is rife with misinformation about Cristofori's extant instruments. For example, one frequently cited article includes virtually every instrument that bears his name or that has ever been ascribed to him with little consideration given to authenticity, and due to formatting redundancy gives a false impression of the number of instruments he made.[1] The major indexes of violin makers, such as William Henley's *Universal Dictionary of Violin and Bow Makers* (Brighton, 1960), Willibald Leo Freiherr von Lütgendorff's *Die Geigen- und Lautenmacher vom Mittelalter bis zur Gegenwart* (Frankfurt, 1913), and René Vannes' *Dictionnaire Universel des Luthiers* (Brussels, 1951) list cellos and double basses ascribed to him, though as indicated in Chapter 1, there is absolutely no documentary evidence that Cristofori ever made bowed-stringed instruments or apprenticed with Nicolò Amati, as is falsely presented by William Henry Hill, Arthur F. Hill, and Alfred Ebsworth Hill in *The Violin-Makers of the Guarneri Family* (London, 1931). Numerous museums, such as the Deutsches Museum in Munich, the Stearns Collection at the University of Michigan, and the Museo degli Strumenti Musicali del Conservatorio "Luigi Cherubini" di Firenze list in their catalogs and other publications inauthentic harpsichords and bowed-string instruments that have been ascribed to Cristofori; for example, from time to time The Metropolitan Museum of Art has exhibited a three-string double-bass attributed to Cristofori, though in the author's opinion that instrument was not made by him. In the previous chapter I reviewed the bills, payment records, and inventories that document Cristofori's work for the Medici court; below I will examine the ten authentic instruments that survive today.

The Harpsichords

As indicated in the previous chapter, the earliest documentation regarding Cristofori's construction of a new keyboard instrument for the Medici is

---

[1] Montanari, "Bartolomeo Cristofori: A List and Historical Survey of his Instruments." It is only with the greatest reluctance that I point out the failings of this article by Montanari, whose later archival research and publications, cited throughout this book, are of the greatest merit.

the court's payment record of June 6, 1689 for a "*cembalo* made for His Most Serene Highness" in the amount of 61.10 *scudi*. There is no record of a bill submitted by Cristofori for this instrument, as there is for many later ones, which is a pity, as his bills typically provide a description of the instrument and an itemized list of materials used in its construction that can assist in identifying it in other court documents, such as the inventories.

The Ebony Harpsichord

An unsigned and undated ebony harpsichord attributed to Cristofori that is now in the collection of the Museo degli Strumenti Musicali del Conservatorio "Luigi Cherubini" di Firenze (inventory no. 1998/101) would appear to be the first of Cristofori's harpsichords that is listed in the 1700 Medici musical instrument inventory:[2]

Un Cimbalo di Bartolomeo Cristofori, levatoro di cassa, a due registri principali unisoni, con fondo di cipresso senza rosa, con fascie ponti traversa salterelli i scorniciatura di ebano filettata d'avorio, con tastatura di avorio et ebano senza spezzati che comincia in gisolreut ottava stesa e finisce in cisolfaut con n. cinquanta tre tasti tra bianchi e neri, lungo braccia quattro e un quarto, largo nel davanti braccia uno e soldi otto, con suo leggio di cipresso, sua contro cassa di abeto pura e sua coperta di cuoio rosso fodorata di taffetà verdi orlata di nastrino d'oro.[3]

(A *cimbalo* by Bartolomeo Cristofori, removable from the case, having two registers of principal [8'] unisons, with a soundboard of cypress without a rose, with sides, bridges, jack rail, jacks, and moldings of ebony with inlaid strips of ivory, with keyboard of ivory and ebony without split sharps that begins at G *ottava stesa* [stretched octave] and ends at C, with 53 keys in white and black, length four and a quarter *braccia* [2343 mm], width of the front one *braccio* and eight *soldi* [772 mm], with a music desk of cypress, with outer case of clear *abeto* [fir or spruce] with its cover of red leather lined with green taffeta hemmed with gold ribbon.)

Such an instrument would have been very expensive to construct, as ebony was a precious imported commodity and was generally used as a veneer, for inlay, or to make moldings, rather than so extravagantly in solid form. According to the inventory, even the original jacks were made of this wood. Strangely, there is no bill or record of payment for this

---

[2] John Henry van der Meer, "Das Florentiner 'Ebenholzcembalo': Eine Arbeit von Bartolomeo Cristofori," in *Festschrift für Gerhard Bott zum 60. Geburtstag*, ed. Ulrich Schneider (Darmstadt, 1987), pp. 227–235.

[3] ASF GM 1117, f. 26.

magnificent instrument. Its original 53-note compass (which lacked the low G#) was subsequently widened by the addition of a high $c\#^3$ and d^3, so it presently does not match the above inventory description. Payment records indicate that the compass enlargement was carried out in 1783 by Giuseppe Ferrini (a son of Cristofori's assistant Giovanni Ferrini); another restoration was undertaken by his brother Filippo Ferrini the following year (see below).[4] Other changes to the ebony harpsichord, that are not documented as having been carried out by the Ferrinis, include the addition of supplemental internal case braces (see below).

These days, we are accustomed to the sight of the ubiquitous "ebonized" grand piano, which in fact is not made of ebony but of a selection of woods, such as maple or spruce for the case, chosen for their acoustical properties and strength, black-polished with shellac or lacquer, or sprayed with a pigmented synthetic finish, in order to resemble ebony (some extravagantly decorated grand pianos made in the past, such as the "Alma Tadema" Steinway made in 1887, were veneered with ebony, but this is a rarity). Thus, at first glance, Cristofori's ebony harpsichord (Figure 3.1) does not impress, but when one considers that its long, elegant case is constructed of solid ebony, one begins to recognize how special this instrument was in its day.

Ebony has always been an exotic and precious material, largely reserved for veneering and inlay work. Even when used to make delicate case moldings, it was often laminated against a backing of less expensive wood. Ebony is quite hard, dense, and brittle, making it somewhat difficult to saw and plane, though it responds well to a sharp cabinet scraper (indeed, finely detailed moldings were formed in ebony and other hardwoods with profiled scrapers), and can take a high polish. In the Baroque period, ebony was often used to make flutes and recorders because it turns well on a lathe, and several of the lutes described in the Medici inventories had backs made of staves of ebony. Occasionally one finds small keyboard instruments made of ebony, such as the diminutive *spinettina* made by Girolamo Zenti that is listed in the 1700 Medici inventory. This is presumably the ebony octave spinet with the initials G^o Z^i inscribed on the top and bottom key levers that is now in The Metropolitan Museum of Art (accession no. 89.4.1227).[5] The cap molding of the case of Cristofori's ebony harpsichord is discreetly inlaid with thin strips of ivory. The key levers are of chestnut,

---

[4] Franca Falletti, Renato Meucci, and Gabriele Rossi-Rognoni, *La musica e i suoi strumenti: La Collezione Granducale del Conservatorio Cherubini*, ed. Franca Falletti (Florence, 2001), pp. 195–197.

[5] Ripin, "The Surviving Oeuvre of Girolamo Zenti," pp. 85–87.

Figure 3.1 Cristofori's ebony harpsichord. Photograph courtesy of the Conservatorio di Musica "Luigi Cherubini" di Firenze.

with natural key tops and arcades of ivory, and accidentals of solid ebony. Ebony was also used to make the jack rail (which, like the cap molding, is inlaid with strips of ivory) and to face the walnut box slide.

As we can see from the inventory description, the bridge, jack rail, and even the jacks were originally made of ebony. Mechanical parts such as jacks were rarely made of this material, as it is difficult to work, and its considerable density would not be conducive to providing light key touch. In Italy, these parts were more often made of the ubiquitous maple, beech, or walnut, all of which are less dense than ebony. We will never know whether Cristofori used ebony for the bridge as an acoustical experiment or simply to suit the whim of his extravagant patron.

The original ebony jacks of the ebony harpsichord were replaced at some point with walnut ones, though this is not specified in the Guardaroba

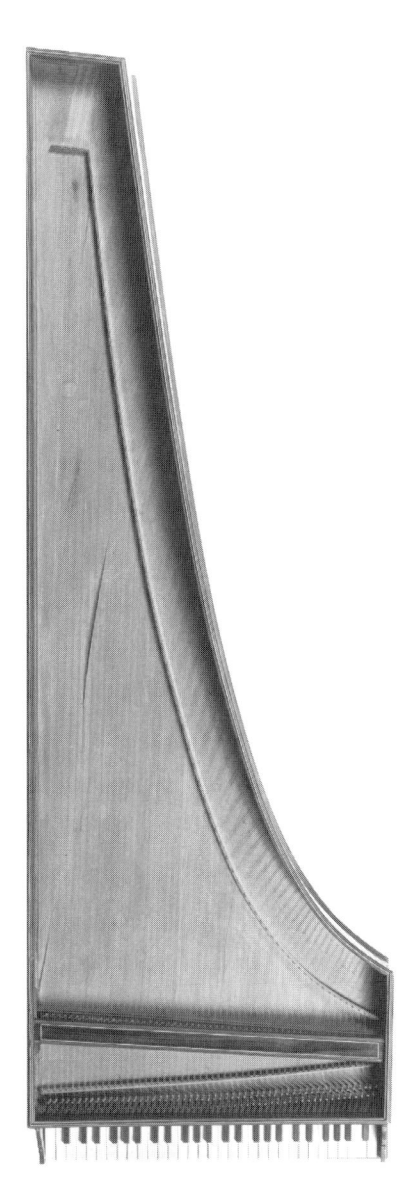

Figure 3.2 Plan view of Cristofori's ebony harpsichord. Photograph courtesy of the Conservatorio di Musica "Luigi Cherubini" di Firenze.

Generale bill for the restoration work carried out in 1783 by Giuseppe Ferrini (see below), nor in the bill for a further restoration carried out by his brother Filippo the following year (see transcriptions of their bills below). A few of the walnut jacks were later replaced with ones made of pear wood. Giuseppe Ferrini's compass extension involved removing the keyboard end blocks in order to make room for two extra keys (Figure 3.2), as well as shifting the entire keyboard to the left (also, the balance pins were moved back around 15 mm).

The present bridge is a replacement, though there is no indication in the bills submitted to the ducal treasury by Giuseppe and Filippo Ferrini that a new bridge was installed. Holes in the soundboard left by earlier positioning pins indicate that the present bridge is not in the original position, though it is not clear whether its position was changed to re-establish the original string lengths when the compass was enlarged or to establish new scaling, as the c^2 length of this instrument is now 265 mm – which is at variance with most of Cristofori's instruments, which have c^2 lengths averaging around 285 mm (see below). The job of extending the compass and shifting the keyboard and bridge is similar to the work carried out by Giovanni Ferrini on the 1666 Girolamo Zenti harpsichord that is now in the collection of The Metropolitan Museum of Art (accession no. 89.4.1220; see below), as well as the unsigned compass extension of the 1720 Cristofori pianoforte, also in the Museum's collection (accession no. 89.4.1219).

Unlike Cristofori's late harpsichords, and pianofortes, which feature thick-walled cases, the ebony harpsichord is of the thin-walled, "inner-outer" type that was commonly used in Italy during the sixteenth and seventeenth centuries. These thin-walled instruments had case sides of cypress that generally ranged around 3 or 4 mm thick, and in keeping with this tradition the case sides of the ebony harpsichord are about 4 mm thick. The description of the ebony harpsichord in the 1700 inventory indicates that its original outer case was of *abeto* (spruce or fir). It was presumably left unfinished, though it was fitted with a red leather cover. Other instruments made by Cristofori for the Medici court also had red, or yellow, leather covers, often lined with silk or another fabric and trimmed with gold ribbon. The outer case and leather cover of the ebony harpsichord are unfortunately lost.

The internal case construction of the ebony harpsichord originally consisted of three diagonal braces running from the bentside to the spine (still present), another diagonal brace that ran from the treble end of the bentside to the bass end of the belly rail (subsequently removed), and a long brace extending from the treble end of the belly rail, running tangentially to the bentside, and intersecting three of the original diagonal braces (also removed; see Figure 3.3).

The original four diagonal braces were oriented perpendicularly to the bentside and were glued to and nailed up through the case bottom. The use of side-to-side braces and the long brace tangentially to the bentside are not typical of seventeenth-century Italian harpsichord construction

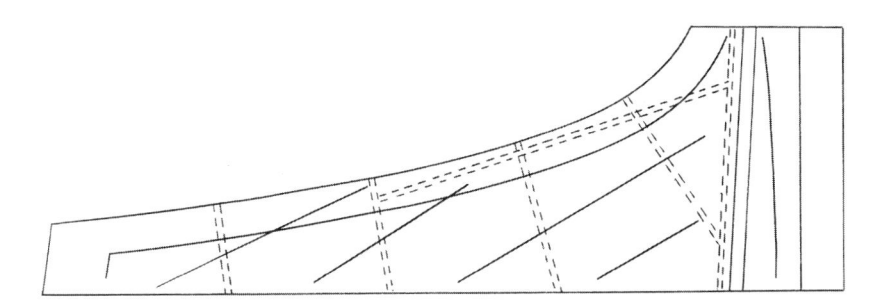

Figure 3.3 Schematic drawing of the bridge, nut, soundboard ribs (solid lines), case braces, and belly rail (dashed lines) of the ebony harpsichord.

(which often employed a series of independent triangular knees abutting the bentside and spine), though they are features shared by all of Cristofori's pianofortes and his later thick-walled harpsichords (see below). The long brace added rigidity to the bentside/cheek joint and was presumably intended to prevent the cheek from twisting upwards due to string tension. In the Italian tradition, the case sides are fitted around the bottom, which in this instance is made of spruce (*Abies alba*). The tail angle is 83°.

Three non-original braces run from bentside to spine, although they are not perpendicular to the bentside but are oriented at a considerable angle to it and the spine. As indicated above, two members of the Ferrini family (Giuseppe and Filippo) did restoration work on this instrument in 1783 and 1784 (see below); however, the payment records for these interventions do not mention the removal of old braces or the addition of new ones. The non-original walnut wrestplank, veneered with cypress, may have been installed in 1784 (see below).[6]

The slab-sawn cypress soundboard has no opening or rose – a trait shared by a number of Cristofori's instruments, including his 1722 and 1726 harpsichords and the three extant pianofortes. The ebony harpsichord's soundboard is approximately 3.3 mm thick, with the grain running nearly parallel to the spine. The soundboard is reinforced by four diagonally oriented ribs, two of which cross under the bridge.

The 8′ registers are disposed as follows:

8′ ←
8′ →

The registers themselves are original, but have been extended to receive the jacks added during the compass extension carried out by Giovanni Ferrini. The registers are the typical Italian box slides of joined up blocks

---

[6] Falletti, Meucci, and Rossi-Rognoni, *La musica e i suoi strumenti*, pp.195–199.

of walnut, though in this instance their upper surfaces are veneered with ebony.

The scaling of the ebony harpsichord (c^2 is presently 265 mm) is somewhat shorter than that found in most of Cristofori's keyboard instruments, which have a c^2 length of around 285 mm (see descriptions of instruments below, as well as the table of comparative string lengths at the end of this chapter), suggesting, perhaps, that this late-seventeenth-century harpsichord was rescaled for a higher pitch in its 1783 restoration. Assuming similar stringing material and tension were employed in the restoration, the present strings would have been pitched between a semitone and a whole tone higher than Cristofori's instruments scale at $c^2 = 285$ mm. The string lengths and plucking points of the longer string of each string pair are set out below, followed by string gauge numbers and case dimensions:

String lengths and plucking points of the ebony harpsichord

Note	String length (mm)	Plucking point (mm)
GG	2110	169
C	1889	161
F	1495	151
c	1034	138
f	799	128
c^1	536	114
f^1	394	104
c^2	265	88
f^2	196	77
c^3	126	60
d^3	109	56

String gauge numbers on the ebony harpsichord

Note	String gauge number
GG	3
BB$^\flat$	4
D	5
G	6
c	7
g	8
d^1	9
c^2	10

Case dimensions of the ebony harpsichord

Case dimensions (mm)	
Length	2497
Width	814
Height	186
Three-octave span	497[7]

Account of the 1783 Restoration of the Ebony Harpsichord

La Guardaroba Generale di S. A. R. deve dare ammè Giuseppe Ferrini q[u]anto appresso per avere accomodato un cimbalo intarsiato di ebano, e avorio consistente la detta accomodatura di averlo rincordato più della metà, rinpergniata di novo tutta la tastiera, e rassettati tutti i tasti, che ammotivo di essere stati i medesimi anticamente impiombati, nel corso di molti anni si sono i detti piombi venuti a incalcinare, e a fato si, che si erano venuti a rompere. Rifatte tutte le fasciature di pelle, e rimpannata del tutto, e rifatte diverse linguette a detti tasti, come ancora ai salterelli rimesse tute le molle, e penne, e aggiuntovi due tasti ne soprani, Cisolfaut diesis, e Desolrè, il tutto la somma il più ristretto L 40 – –.[8]

(The Guardaroba Generale of His Serene Royal Highness shall remit to Giuseppe Ferrini the amount given below for having put in order a *cembalo* inlaid with ebony and ivory, including replacement of more than half the strings, new balance pins for all the keys, resetting all the keys that had become sluggish due to the ancient leads that in the course of many years had become calcified [more likely fouled by the corrosion product lead acetate], and for making those that have broken. Remade all the leather strips, replacing all the cloth, and remaking diverse tongues for the keys, and again for the jacks replacing all of the springs, the quills, and adding two keys in the treble, C#, and D, all for the total sum of 40 *lire*.)

Account of the 1784 Restoration of the Ebony Harpsichord

La Guardaroba Generale di S. A. R. deve dare a me Filippo Ferrini quanto appo: Per avere accomodato un cimbalo con sponde d'ebano, et accomodato il pancone, e rimesso tutte le corde, e rimpannato la tastiera, e rimpennato, e linguette ai saltarelli, e accomodato il leggio, e fatto fare i piedi novi fatto il di 14 Luglio L 35.[9]

(The Guardaroba Generale of His Serene Royal Highness shall remit to me, Filippo Ferrini, the following amount: For having put in order a *cimbalo* with sides of ebony, and putting in order the plank [regluing or possibly replacing the wrestplank],

---

[7] Ibid., p. 199.   [8] Ibid., pp. 197, 199.   [9] Ibid.

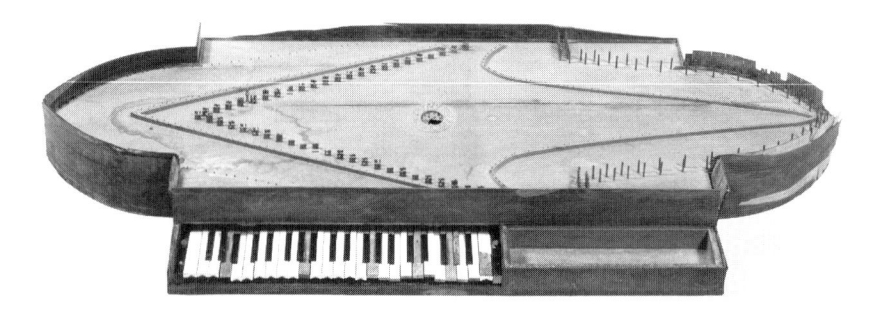

Figure 3.4 Cristofori's oval spinet of 1690. Photograph courtesy of the Conservatorio di Musica "Luigi Cherubini" di Firenze.

replacing all of the strings, replacing the key cloth, re-quilling, replacing tongues of the jacks, and putting in order the music desk, and making new legs, the 14th of July, 35 *lire*.)

The Oval Spinets of 1690 and 1693

There are two spinets with uniquely shaped oval cases – one dated 1690 (Figure 3.4) and another dated 1693 (Figure 3.5).

Both are described in the 1700 Medici musical instrument inventory, and two bills to court submitted by Cristofori appear to refer to these instruments as well (see Chapter 2). The 1690 spinet was recently (2000) "rediscovered" among the treasures of the Bardini collection in Florence and has been entrusted to the Museo degli Strumenti Musicali del Conservatorio "Luigi Cherubini" (inventory no. 3376); it is presently exhibited in the Galleria dell'Accademia in Florence; the 1693 oval spinet is in the Grassi Museum für Musikinstrumente der Universität

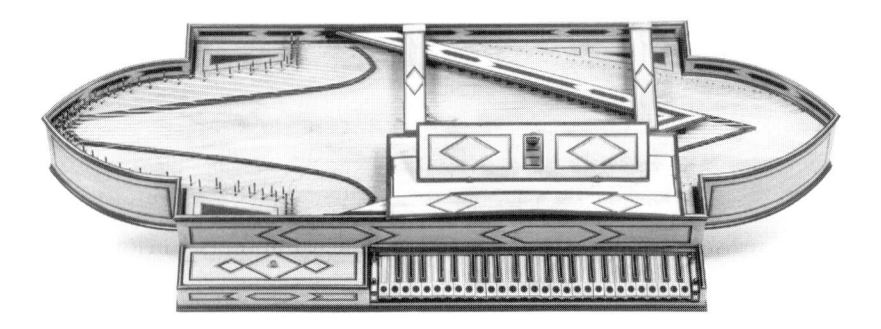

Figure 3.5 Cristofori's oval spinet of 1693. Photograph courtesy of the Grassi Museum für Musikinstrumente der Universität Leipzig.

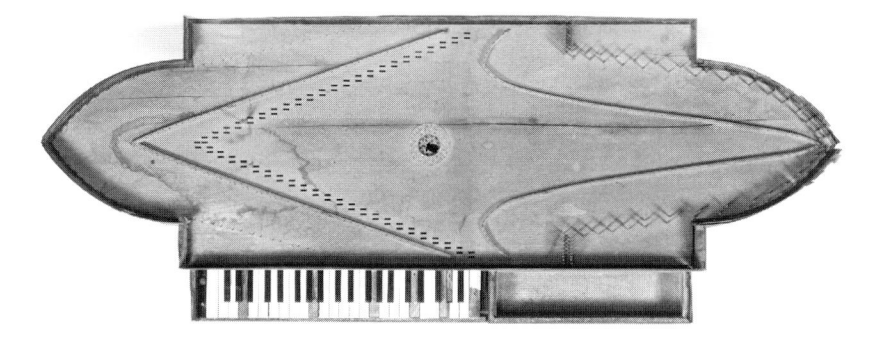

Figure 3.6 Plan view of the 1690 oval spinet. Photograph courtesy of the Conservatorio di Musica "Luigi Cherubini" di Firenze.

Leipzig (catalog no. 53). The 1690 spinet is inscribed inside the storage compartment intended for spare strings and a tuning wrench that is situated to the right of the keyboard: BARTHOLOMÆVS CRISTOPHORI PATAVINVS FACIEBAT/FLORENTIÆ/MDCXC; the 1693 spinet is inscribed in the same location: BARTHOLOMÆVS CRISTOPHORI PATAVINVS/FACIEBAT FLORENTIÆ/MDCXCIII.

These spinets are made of exotic materials and are elaborately decorated: the 1690 spinet is veneered in African rosewood with ebony moldings, while the 1693 spinet is of traditional cypress with elaborate geometric inlays of ebony and boxwood. The key levers of both spinets are of poplar, though Cristofori generally used chestnut – a heavier, coarse-grained wood. The natural keys of the 1690 spinet have one-piece ivory tops (without scribe lines) and ivory arcades in front, the accidentals are of ebony; the 1693 spinet has boxwood naturals with oval inlays of ebony in the heads demarcated by double scribe lines and ebony stringing in the tails, while the accidentals are of ebony with boxwood stringing. Although these spinets share the same general design, their gross measurements and the shapes of their cases differ slightly. Furthermore, the 1690 example has a 47-note C/E–c^3 compass with short octave and split sharps at F#/D and G#/E, while the 1693 spinet features a 49-note compass extending from C/E–c^3. The three-octave span of the 1690 spinet is 496 mm, while that of the 1693 spinet is 497 mm. Both instruments have two 8′ registers with provision for changing registration (see below).

The principal design feature of these two spinets is the unusual arrangement of the strings (Figure 3.6), which run parallel to the long axis of the case, with the lowest bass strings located in the center of the soundboard and the treble strings at the outer edges of the case.

Successive strings alternate back and forth from the central strings creating a symmetrical arrangement. The left bridge consists of two sections oriented in a V shape, while the right bridge consists of two sections shaped like shepherds' crooks. The bridges of the 1690 spinet are of cypress, while those of the 1693 spinet are ebonized (wood unidentified).[10] The mortises for the jacks and the jack rails follow the shape of the left bridge. The 1700 inventory descriptions refer to the jack rails as having a "pyramidal" shape, clearly a reference to their mitered construction that forms a "V" (the jack rail of the 1690 spinet is lost). In order to accommodate the back-and-forth distribution of the strings and their respective jacks, the key levers alternate in length. At the bass end, the difference in length between adjacent key levers is slight, but as one proceeds to the top note, the key lever lengths progressively diverge. Though separate balance rails are used to provide similar leverages for the long and short keys, the key levers' masses and hence their inertias alternate from key to key, which one might expect to render the touch of neighboring keys increasingly disparate as one ascends from bass to treble, though this does not appear to be the case. The key frames are of spruce or fir while the balance rails are of walnut.

The case structure of these instruments is complex owing to the arched projections at either end of what is essentially a rectangular case. As is typical of Italian keyboard construction, the sides are built around the bottom, which in both of these instruments is of fir or spruce. The bottom of the 1690 spinet is about 10 mm thick, while that of the 1693 spinet is about 9 mm thick. What is especially atypical about the construction of these instruments – as well as most other keyboard instruments made by Cristofori – is the use of lamination to form certain parts of the case. In the 1690 spinet, the curved case sides are formed from a core of vertically grained poplar with outer laminations of horizontally grained African rosewood having a composite thickness of around 3.5 mm. The curved case sides of the 1693 spinet consist of two laminated layers of horizontally grained cypress totaling 3.0 mm to 3.5 mm in thickness. The straight case sides are made of solid planks of wood: 3.0–3.5 mm thick African rosewood for the 1690 spinet and 4.0–4.5 mm thick cypress for the 1693 spinet. There

---

[10] After comparing the bridges of the extant oval spinets, Kerstin Schwartz and Tony Chinnery concluded that the bridges of the 1693 spinet are not authentic due to differences in workmanship and the fact that they do not show evidence of having had pins for two top notes that were added and later removed. Tony Chinnery and Kerstin Schwarz, "La creazione di un nuovo strumento: la spinetta ovale vista da un costruttore," in *Bartolomeo Cristofori: La spinetta ovale del 1690*, pp. 44–60, at pp. 48–51, 60.

is very little internal framing: aside from inner case walls that serve as the soundboard liner, there are two front-to-back braces at the juncture of the arched extensions where they join the rectangular section of the case, two blocks that support the ends of the two-piece walnut wrestplank (located on the right side of the case) where they extend past the arched extension into the rectangular section of the case, and blocks supporting the right-hand corners of a lower "soundboard" of fir, which is mortised to serve as a lower guide for the jacks. Two angled hitchpin rails (located on the left side of the case) extend from the spine and front case sides to the arched extension of the case. In the 1690 spinet, the hitchpin rails terminate at the juncture of the left arched case extension and the rectangular portion of the case, while in the 1693 spinet the hitchpin rails extend past this juncture and abut the centers of the curved walls of the arched case extensions. In both spinets the soundboard liners that are glued against the curved walls of the left arched case extension carry the hitchpins for the lowest notes. The walls of the arched extensions are reinforced internally by vertically grained blocks of wood. All corner joints of the case are simply mitered – a weak form of construction considering the narrow gluing surfaces of the thin case walls. The 1693 spinet lacks front and back inner case-wall laminations found in the 1690 example.[11]

The soundboards of both oval spinets are made of slab-sawn cypress with central roses constructed of thin layers of cypress backed with paper. The rose of the 1690 spinet consists of two sections, an upper part glued to the top of the soundboard that frames a lower part glued to the lower surface of the soundboard beneath the circular opening. The rose of the 1693 spinet is additionally surrounded by an inlaid six-pointed star made of ebony and boxwood. The soundboard of the 1690 spinet averages about 4.5 mm in thickness, though it is thinned to about 3.5 mm in the treble areas. An X-ray photograph of the 1690 spinet reveals three ribs reinforcing the soundboard and one rib glued to the underside of a thin lower plank that is mortised for the jacks, while an X-ray photograph of the 1693 spinet (Figure 3.7) reveals seven or possibly eight ribs; however, their distribution between the soundboard and lower plank is unclear. The ribs are oriented roughly perpendicularly to the soundboard grain.

Similar in construction to the box slides traditionally found in Italian harpsichords (as well as the fixed registers of some English bentside spinets), the registers of both spinets are built up of grooved blocks

---

[11] Chinnery and Schwarz, ibid., pp. 45–59.

Figure 3.7 X-ray plan view of Cristofori's oval spinet of 1693. Courtesy of the Opificio delle Pietre Dure, Florence.

(walnut in the 1690 spinet). To make the registers, grooves were planed into a plank, which was then sawn apart into separate blocks. The resulting blocks were then glued up so that the grooves formed pairs of mortises for the jacks. The box slides of both spinets are glued to the undersides of the soundboards and serve as the upper guides for the jacks. Mortises cut in the lower "soundboard" serve as lower guides. Though the registers themselves are fixed, Cristofori cleverly arranged for changes in registration by shifting the keyboard. In the 1690 spinet, a register is "on" when leather-covered blocks of wood mounted on the back sections of the key levers are aligned under and lift the jacks when the keys are played; a register is "off" when the keyboard is shifted so that the jacks rest on fixed slips of wood that project from the key frame and fit through slots in the backs of the keys (these slips also serve as rear guides for the key levers). In the 1690 spinet, when the keyboard is pulled toward the player, only the jacks for the longer strings of each 8′ pair are activated; when the keyboard is fully pushed back, only the jacks for the shorter strings of each pair are used; and when the keyboard is locked by a spring-loaded detent in the halfway position, the jacks of both registers are played simultaneously. Knobs on the keyboard end blocks are used to shift the keyboard back and forth. The shorter strings of the string pairs are played by the close-plucking jacks. The stop action differs in the 1693 oval spinet: when the keyboard is pulled toward the player, the longer-scaled 8′ strings are disengaged and the shorter 8′ strings are in play; when the keyboard is shoved in, both 8′ registers are used. Thus, in this instrument, there is apparently no provision for playing the longer 8′ strings as a solo stop. It is possible that the awkward stop actions of these spinets, which require both hands to push and pull the keyboard (rather than the simple flick of a stop lever), were primarily used to isolate registers for the purpose of tuning rather than to provide changes of registration in the course of playing.

Throughout his career, Cristofori experimented with the design of jacks. The ebony harpsichord and the 1690 oval spinet have jacks of conventional design with brass leaf springs. As noted above, the ebony harpsichord originally had jacks made of ebony that were later replaced with walnut ones. The original jacks of the 1690 oval spinet are of pear wood with beech tongues. The jacks of the 1693 oval spinet are unusually constructed of three strips of walnut – the two outer strips run the full length, while the center strip is shorter to provide the opening for the tongue (the tongues of these jacks are replacements). This may have been intended as a labor-saving design, as it was not necessary to mark, saw, and chisel out the slot, which had to be accurately done to ensure a good fit for the tongue.

The string lengths and plucking points for the longer string of each string pair are set out below, followed by case dimensions:

String lengths and plucking points of the oval spinets

Note	1690 oval spinet (mm)	1693 oval spinet (mm)
C	1561/143	1576/160
F	1540/151	1465/152
C	1095/141	1110/143
F	851/137	871/131
c^1	564/123	568/122
f^1	426/111	428/110
c^2	287/96	288/98
f^2	217/84	224/88
c^3	143/70[12]	141/71[13]

Case dimensions of the oval spinets

Case dimensions (mm)	1690 oval spinet	1693 oval spinet
Length	1827	1820
Width	683	711
Height	171[14]	176[15]

---

[12] Measurements from Grant O'Brien, "Il percorso di un' idea," in *Bartolomeo Cristofori: La spinetta ovale del 1690*, p. 75.

[13] Measurements from Hubert Henkel, *Musikinstrumenten-Museum der Karl-Marx-Universität Leipzig, Katalog, Band 2: Kielinstrumente* (Leipzig, 1979), p. 35.

[14] Measurements from Tony Chinnery, "The Measurements," in *Bartolomeo Cristofori: La spinetta ovale del 1690*, p. 83.

[15] Measurements from Henkel, *Musikinstrumenten-Museum*, p. 36.

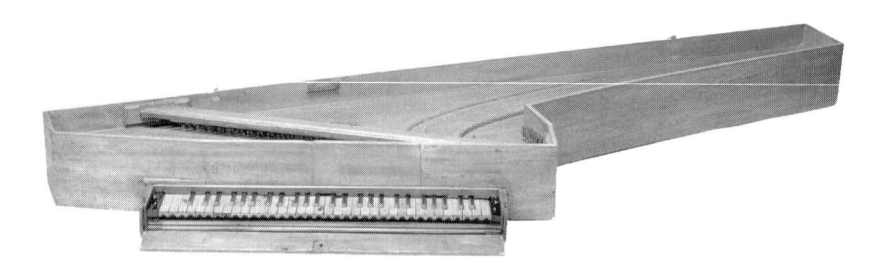

Figure 3.8 Cristofori's *spinettone*. Photograph courtesy of the Grassi Museum für Musikinstrumente der Universität Leipzig.

Spinettone

The presently uninscribed *spinettone* dated *c.* 1720 in the catalog of the Grassi Museum für Musikinstrumente der Universität Leipzig (formerly the Karl-Marx-Universität; inventory no. 86; Figure 3.8) would appear to be similar to the instrument variously referred to as the *spinettone da orchestra* in the Medici musical instrument inventory of 1700 and as the *spinettone da teatro* in the Medici musical instrument inventory of 1716 (see Chapter 2).[16]

The instrument listed in the inventories is certainly the instrument termed *cembalo nuovo per teatro* (new cembalo for the theater) in Cristofori's bill to court dated July 1, 1692, though Medici court inventories (at least one of which was compiled by Cristofori) generally distinguished between *cembalo* (denoting the long, wing-shaped harpsichord with strings running perpendicular to the keyboard) and *spinetto* (having various shapes, though with strings running parallel to the keyboard). The bill to court indicates that the *cembalo* built especially for use in the theater had two registers, that cypress wood was used in its construction, that it had a soundboard rose of cypress, and a music desk of cypress inlaid with ebony. The inventory of 1700 indicates that the *spinettone da orchestra* had two registers and specifies that one register was at principal (8′) pitch and the other at octave (4′) pitch, that the soundboard was of cypress, the case sides were of *abeto* (fir or spruce) with the inside veneered with cypress, and the compass was GG–c^3. We can surmise from the description that registration changes were made by shifting the keyboard, as the inventory mentions the use of two ebony buttons and iron springs in the stop action. Both the 1700 and 1716 inventories indicate

[16] Henkel, ibid., pp. 91–93.

that the *spinettone* had a yellow leather cover. These archival sources make no reference to an unusually shaped case, but the 1700 inventory indicates that it was 3 *braccia* and 3 *ottavi* in length, or about 1860 mm. The Leipzig example, which is presumed to have been made at a later date, is even larger – 2435 mm in length – and it has among the longest bass strings of any of Cristofori's extant keyboard instruments, including his full-size harpsichords and other instruments that have compasses extending down to FF. From a casual glance at the list of string lengths given below, the Leipzig *spinettone* would appear to have longer scaling than Cristofori's other extant instruments, as its c^2 is 335 mm in length rather than his average of about 285 mm; however, the *spinettone*'s 4′ and 8′ bridges are divided at c^2 in order to provide lengthier scaling for just the top octave. While the division may signify a transition from brass to steel wire, there may be another explanation for this feature (see below).

The compass of the Leipzig instrument was originally FF, GG, AA, BB♭, BB–c^3, but it was extended in the treble to f^3 (chromatic) in the course of a restoration that is dated and signed 1795/GCR (in this compass enlargement the FF, GG, AA, BB♭, and BB notes were retained).[17] The original batten located just behind the keyboard (which presumably bore Cristofori's inscription) was replaced with a longer, blank one at that time. As indicated above, the original compass – with the FF# and GG# omitted – was employed in other instruments made by Cristofori, including the 1720 pianoforte and the 1719 clavichord. The Leipzig instrument has an 8′ stop and a 4′ stop, which can be engaged separately or in combination by shifting the keyboard forward and backward by grasping two small knobs mounted on the left and right key blocks.[18] The stop mechanism is similar to that of the *spinettone* described in the 1700 inventory. Two other *spinettoni* having this general shape and configuration, though not made by Cristofori, are presently in the collections of the National Museum of American History, Smithsonian Institution, and the Museo "Clemente Rospigliosi" in Pistoia (see Chapter 5). The Smithsonian example unfortunately does not have its original nameboard, and thus the maker's name and date are lost. On the basis of the molding profiles, Denzil Wraight attributed the Smithsonian example to Giuseppe or Giovanni Solfanelli, a maker active in Pisa around 1721–30.[19] The lowest key bears an inscription that appears to read GS/1704, which supports Wraight's attribution, though no working relationship between Cristofori and Solfanelli has

---

[17] Ibid., p. 91. [18] Henkel, ibid., pp. 91–93; and "Cristofori as Harpsichord Maker."
[19] Denzil Wraight, "Cristofori's Instruments," *Early Music* 20/4 (1992), p. 701.

been established. The example in Pistoia is inscribed by Giovanni Ferrini (Cristofori's assistant; see below) and dated 1731.[20]

The key frame of the Leipzig example is of chestnut with a cypress balance rail, and was originally 829 mm wide though widened to 900 mm as a result of the compass extension, and originally 445 mm deep in the bass and 278 mm deep in the treble, though now 264 mm deep as a result of the compass extension. The key levers are of chestnut, with boxwood natural keys, accidentals made of stained boxwood with ebony slips, and arcaded key fronts (the soundboard rose appears to have been constructed of seven circular ornaments that were made with the same rotating cutter used to make the key-front arcades). Because the lateral positions of both the 8′ and 4′ jacks are fixed, registration changes are made by shifting the keyboard toward or away from the player, which causes leathered platforms or grooves in the key levers to come into alignment with the rows of jacks, thereby engaging or disengaging them. In the middle position, both registers are engaged; when the keyboard is pulled towards the player, only the 8′ is in use; when pushed in, only the 4′ jacks play. This is similar to the system employed in the oval spinets described above. As indicated with regard to the oval spinets, this system of engaging and disengaging registers is awkward and requires the use of both hands; presumably it was primarily employed to isolate choirs of strings in order to facilitate tuning.

Most of the jacks are original. They are of fruitwood and are unusually constructed in that the slots for the tongues are not open at the top, like the tines of a fork, but were formed by drilling two holes and cutting away the material in between to form an opening for the tongue. Another difference is the position of the brass leaf springs, which are mounted in front of the tongues rather than behind them, as was the custom. This is a feature found in the jacks of other spinets and harpsichords made by Cristofori. The rationale for this design change is that the spring does not have to be carefully arched to clear the pivot point so that it can press the tongue forward from behind. In Cristofori's system, the spring presses on the part of the tongue that extends below the pivot point. The jacks are gouged out so that the mounting points of the springs are

---

[20] Stewart Pollens, "Three Keyboard Instruments Signed by Cristofori's Assistant, Giovanni Ferrini," *The Galpin Society Journal* 44 (1991), pp. 80–82. The initials on the lowest key of the Smithsonian's *cembalo traverso* were previously reported to me as "GF," which would have been consistent with those of Giovanni Ferrini, though it is clearly "GS" (see Chapter 5).

recessed to prevent the springs from interfering with the up and down motion of the jacks. The tongues, which are mortised for leather, are not original. At some point fourteen pedal pull-downs were installed; the pedals activated the keys FF, GG, AA, BB♭, BB, C, D, E, F, G, G#, A, B♭, and B.

The case of the *spinettone* is constructed in the thick-walled, "false inner-outer" style that Cristofori used in the clavichord, as well as in his large harpsichords, and pianofortes, described below. The bottom is of poplar, about 12 mm thick, with the sides built around it in typical Italian fashion. The poplar case sides are about 13 mm to 13.5 mm thick and are simply butt joined at the corners. The case wall behind the keyboard consists of four mitered sections that form a slight convex arc (Figure 3.8). The keyboard projects from the front of the case, and a wedge of wood fills in a gap behind the back of the bass keys where the convex wall of the case veers away from them. The belly rail is of poplar, and there are four case buttresses, three running diagonally from the right side of the case to the spine, and another running diagonally from the belly rail to the spine. The main section of the wrestplank is glued to the underside of the soundboard just behind the front board; the lower surface of the wrestplank has a lamination of poplar. The tuning pins are arranged in three rows, two staggered rows for the 8′ and one row for the 4′. Both the 8′ and 4′ tuning pins sit behind the 8′ and 4′ maple nuts, so openings have been made in the 8′ nut to allow the 4′ strings to pass through to their nut. The 8′ nut tapers in width from 8.8 mm to 8.5 mm and in height from 14.5 mm to 10.5 mm. The 4′ nut tapers in width from 8 mm to 7.5 mm and in height from 7.5 mm to 5.8 mm. The positions of the tuning pins and hitchpins for the top eighteen 8′ strings are switched: the tuning pins are situated along the right case wall, while the corresponding hitchpins are mounted to the right of the staggered 8′ tuning pins located on the wrestplank. The bottom octave of 8′ hitchpins are mounted on a rail about 11 mm high that stands free of the soundboard (similar to the suspended hitchpin rails of the pianofortes and full-size harpsichords; see below), and the remainder of the 8′ hitchpins project from a molding that runs along the edge of the soundboard. The 4′ hitchpins pass through the soundboard into a hitchpin rail glued below.

The soundboard is of cypress, around 2.5 mm thick to the right of the rose and about 3.5 mm thick at the perimeter of the rose opening (the rose consists of an arrangement of seven circular ornaments that appear to have been made with the keyboard arcade cutter). There are three soundboard ribs, one to the left of the rose and two to the right. These are oriented diagonally and parallel to one another. The rib at the extreme right passes twice under the hook of the 4′ bridge and is nearly tangent to the 4′ hitchpin rail. The bridges are of maple. The dimensions of the main 8′ bridge taper from bass to treble: in width from 8.5 mm to 7.8 mm and in height from 12.8 mm to 10.5 mm. There are three small, independent bridges in the bass that are mounted parallel to the main bridge: the lowest carries the string for FF, the second carries the strings for GG and AA, and the third carries the strings for BB$^\flat$ and BB. The main bridge is double pinned up to G. The 4′ bridge is 7.5 mm wide and ranges in height from 7.5 mm to 6 mm. At b^1, both the nuts and bridges for the 8′ and 4′ strings terminate, and short sections carry the remainder of the treble strings (c^2–c^3 as well as the later strings up to f^3). These short sections are set back to provide longer string lengths, though it is unclear whether this denotes a change from brass to steel wire or that Cristofori took advantage of the phenomenon termed "tensile pickup," which refers to the increased strength that wire develops as it is drawn through a succession of dies. Whatever the reason, by dividing the bridges, Cristofori was able to move the treble bridges away from the edge of the soundboard and the 4′ hitchpin rail, and onto a more acoustically active area. The length of c^1 is 557 mm (equivalent to a c^2 of 278.5 mm), which most keyboard historians believe implies the use of brass wire, though the actual c^2 on the set back bridge and nut is 335 mm in length, which would signify the use of iron or steel wire. This system of setting back the bridges and nuts in the treble is also used in the 2′ stop of the 1726 harpsichord (see below). The following string gauge numbers are written in ink on the *spinettone*'s wrestplank:

String gauge numbers on the *spinettone*

Pin	String gauge number
F	5
B$^\flat$	6
g	7
b	8
g^1	9
e^2	10

Presumably larger gauges were used below F, but the numbers are not visible.

String lengths/plucking points are as follows:

String lengths and plucking points of the *spinettone*

Note	8′ register (mm)	4′ register (mm)
FF	2045/170	1355/106
C	1965/174	1054/111
F	1622/163	818/100
c	1106/149	551/86
f	858/136	417/81
c^1	557/124	276/67
f^1	424/106	211/57
c^2	335/112	165/53
f^2	258/89	129/51
c^3	166/73	82/41
f^3*	112/60	69/51

* Not original, see above.

The lid and hinges appear to be original, which suggests that this instrument was not originally fitted into a separate lidded outer case. Its plain undecorated case is typical of a number of Cristofori's keyboard instruments, especially those of the so-called "false inner-outer," or thick-walled type. The 1700 inventory descriptions of Cristofori's instruments generally include colorful leather covers lined with expensive fabric and hemmed with decorative ribbon – clearly a method of disguising their rough deal cabinetry. Unfortunately, none of these leather covers has survived, though such a cover may be depicted in a group musician's portrait painted by Anton Domenico Gabbiani (Chapter 4, Figure 4.2), which suggests that they were tailored in such a way that the keyboards and soundboards were exposed for playing. Though Cristofori was capable of constructing keyboard instruments exhibiting the most elegant cabinetry design (the veneer and inlay work of the 1693 oval spinet was undoubtedly carried out by a specialized assistant, as is suggested by the surviving court bill), his pianofortes, 1722 and 1726 harpsichords, the clavichord of 1719, and the *spinettone da orchestra* were apparently conceived as "working" instruments rather than as palace showpieces. Perhaps it was considered an unnecessary expense to employ precious woods in or to superficially decorate utilitarian instruments, especially those that were intended to be carted back and forth from palace to villa, or that were destined for the opera orchestra. It is also possible that the cases of these instruments were left in a rough, unfinished state because they were intended to be placed in decorative outer cases (see below). Michael Kent O'Brien has discovered records of payments made to various painters and a gilder who were engaged to decorate harpsichord cases for the Medici between 1681 and 1683 (i.e., before Cristofori's presence in Florence), though there is no indication in the 1700 and 1716 Medici musical instrument inventories that Cristofori's instruments were painted (with the exception of the turned stand of the 1690 oval *spinetta*, which was tinted black). In the early 1680s, decorative covers were made by leatherworkers Giovanni Maria del Brano and Domenico Ghonelli.[21]

Cristofori's *spinettone* was evidently designed for use in the opera orchestra. The compact case (see measurements below) and uncompromised bass string lengths would have made it highly suitable for use by the orchestra leader, who could conduct from the keyboard while facing the stage and orchestra members. This example (which is tentatively dated at *c.* 1720) is not listed in the 1700, 1716, or 1732 Medici musical instrument inventories; thus, it may have been made for a private client or perhaps it was situated in one of the Medici villas and eluded *guardaroba* compilers.

Case dimensions of the *spinettone*

Case dimensions	
Length	2435 mm
Width	550 mm/675 mm*
Depth (without lid)	202 mm

* Measured from front to spine excluding keyboard console/present width including the extended keyboard console.

1722 Harpsichord

This instrument (Figure 3.9) is inscribed in ink on the nameboard: BARTHOLOMÆVS DE CHRISTOPHORIS PATAVINVS FACIEBAT FLORENTIÆ MDCCXXII.

It is not listed in the 1732 Medici musical instrument inventory, so like the *spinettone* above, it may have been made for a private client or was somehow overlooked by that inventory's compiler, Pietro Mazzetti.

---

[21] Michael Kent O'Brien, *Bartolomeo Cristofori at Court*, p. 62.

Figure 3.9 Cristofori's harpsichord of 1722. Photograph courtesy of the Grassi Museum für Musikinstrumente der Universität Leipzig.

In 1878 the 1722 harpsichord came into the hands of Baron Alessandro Kraus in Florence. His musical instrument collection was subsequently acquired by Wilhelm Heyer in Cologne in 1908, and finally by the university collection in Leipzig in 1926 (the 1722 harpsichord is inventory no. 84).

This four-octave instrument has a compass of C–c^3. The key levers are of chestnut with boxwood naturals, arcaded key fronts, and accidentals of stained pear capped with slips of ebony. The three-octave span is 490 mm. There are two 8′ registers disposed as follows:

8′ ←
8′ →

The registers are operated by dowel-like levers projecting from holes drilled in the moveable upper slides, which are constructed in the manner of traditional Italian box slides, though these are not as tall. Here, Cristofori employed a fixed lower guide for the jacks that projects from the underside of the walnut wrestplank (which is laminated on its upper surface with 3 mm thick cypress and on its lower surface with 8 mm thick fir or spruce) and extends to the poplar belly rail, which is approximately 14 mm thick. All but four of the jacks are original. They are of fruitwood (possibly plum) and of conventional design except for the brass leaf springs, which are mounted in front of the tongues and push back on the sections of the tongues that extend below the pivot point, which is characteristic of Cristofori's jacks. The tongues are not original and are mortised for leather.

The case is constructed in the thick-walled, "false inner-outer" style, with 12.5–13.5 mm thick poplar case sides built around a bottom of spruce or fir, about 12 mm thick. The case walls are simply butt joined. Like the 1726 harpsichord and the three extant pianofortes (see below), a series of vertical reinforcements are glued to the external surfaces of the cheek, bentside, and spine; these align with several of the internal case braces to add extra support. The lockboard slips into grooves in the vertical support pieces located at the front of the cheek and spine, as well as into a groove in a batten that projects below the front edge of the case bottom. At the lower edge of the case there is a molding having a simple rectangular profile. In all, the vertical supports and rudimentary molding give the case a rather ugly, packing-crate appearance that is shared by Cristofori's 1726 harpsichord and the three surviving pianos. A two-piece lid is attached to hinges that are riveted to the spine of the case (in a manner similar to the fixings of the hinges of the 1726 harpsichord and the pianos; see below), so Cristofori apparently did not intend to enclose this instrument in a lidded decorative outer case. Perhaps it was originally fitted with a colorful leather cover, as were other instruments of his that are listed in the Medici inventories. At present, the case is crudely painted, with artwork which is probably not original.

The plain external appearance of this instrument belies its complex and sophisticated internal construction, which appears to have been adapted from a structure first developed for Cristofori's pianofortes. The 1720 pianoforte preserved in The Metropolitan Museum of Art is the earliest dated instrument of his that incorporates this new case design, but it is alluded to in Scipione Maffei's description of Cristofori's newly invented pianoforte published in 1711 (see full text below). As is described in greater detail in the descriptions of the pianofortes below, the

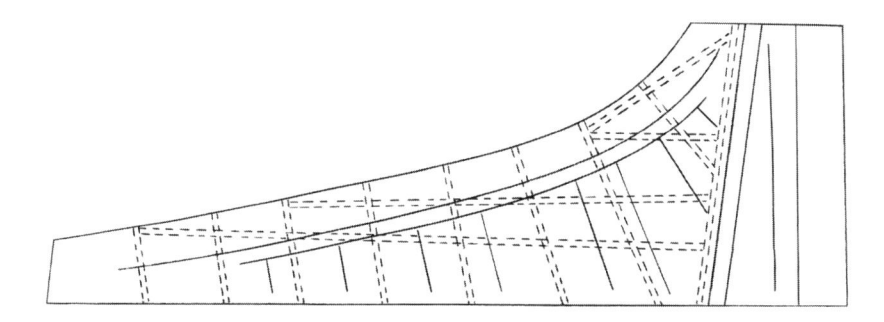

Figure 3.10 Schematic drawing of the bridge, nut, soundboard ribs, cutoff bar (solid lines), case braces and belly rail (dashed lines) of Cristofori's 1722 harpsichord.

soundboard is not mounted directly on a liner glued to the case's bentside (as in conventional harpsichord construction), but is glued to a thinner internal bentside and a delicate liner that run parallel to the outer bentside. The hitchpin rail, which in this instrument is narrower than those used in the pianofortes, is glued atop a massive bentside liner and is suspended over the soundboard, thereby concealing the gap between the edge of the soundboard and the outer case. Thus, the strings are supported by the outer case that is reinforced by the heavy bentside liner, while the soundboard is physically isolated from these stress-bearing parts and is mounted on a more acoustically active bentside that is about as thick as that of a conventional Italian thin-walled, "inner-outer" harpsichord.

The internal case structure consists of eight diagonal braces that run from the bentside to the belly rail and spine, three longitudinal braces that run from the belly rail to the diagonal braces where they meet the bentside, and another brace that extends from the juncture of the belly rail and cheekpiece liner, runs tangentially to the internal bentside, and terminates at the second diagonal brace (Figure 3.10).

From the belly rail and spine, the diagonal braces taper and pass through oversize apertures in the internal bentside, at which point dowel-like extensions of the braces fit into holes drilled in the outer bentside's liner. The layout of the internal bracing is similar to that of the pianoforte made the same year (see below).

The cypress soundboard has no sound hole or rose (Figure 3.11); however, the belly rail has three 34 mm diameter holes bored in it, which serve the same acoustical function as an aperture in the soundboard (see discussion of the 1720 piano below).

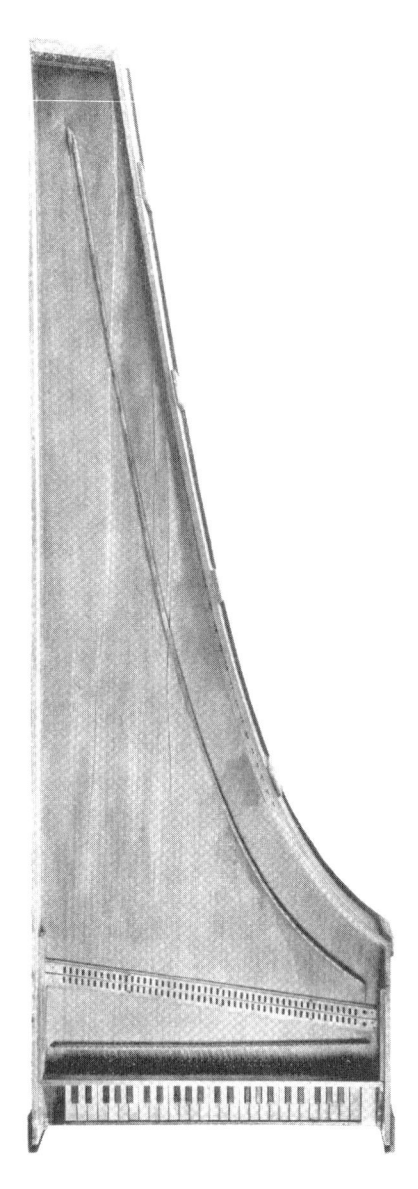

Figure 3.11 Plan view of Cristofori's 1722 harpsichord. Photograph courtesy of the Grassi Museum für Musikinstrumente der Universität Leipzig.

There is a curved cutoff bar and nine diagonally oriented ribs running from the belly rail and spine up to the cutoff bar (Figure 3.10). The maple bridge tapers from 9 mm to 6.8 mm in width and from 12.5 mm to 10.5 mm in height. The nut, also of maple, tapers from 9 mm to 7.8 mm in width and is 11 mm in height throughout its length.

The string lengths/plucking points are set out below:

String lengths and plucking points of the 1722 harpsichord

Note	8′ register (mm)	4′ register (mm)
C	1981/165	1970/147
F	1619/156	1563/139
c	1131/145	1084/127
f	849/134	814/117
c^1	569/120	545/102
f^1	427/109	408/91
c^2	285/93	273/76
f^2	215/81	206/65
c^3	141/65	133/48

The following gauge numbers are written in ink on the wrestplank:

String gauge numbers on the 1722 harpsichord

Note	String gauge number
D	5
G#	6
f#	7
$b^\flat$	8
$f\#^1$	9
$e^{\flat 2}$	10

Case measurements (excluding moldings and lid) are as follows:

Case measurements of the 1722 harpsichord

Length	2400 mm
Width	802 mm
Height	196 mm
Three-octave span	493 mm

1726 Harpsichord

This instrument, inscribed BARTHOLOMÆVS DE CHRISTOPHORIS PATAVINVS FACIEBAT FLORENTIÆ MDCCXXVI, is the most complex of Cristofori's surviving harpsichords in that it incorporates 8′, 4′, and 2′ registers (Figures 3.12 and 3.13).

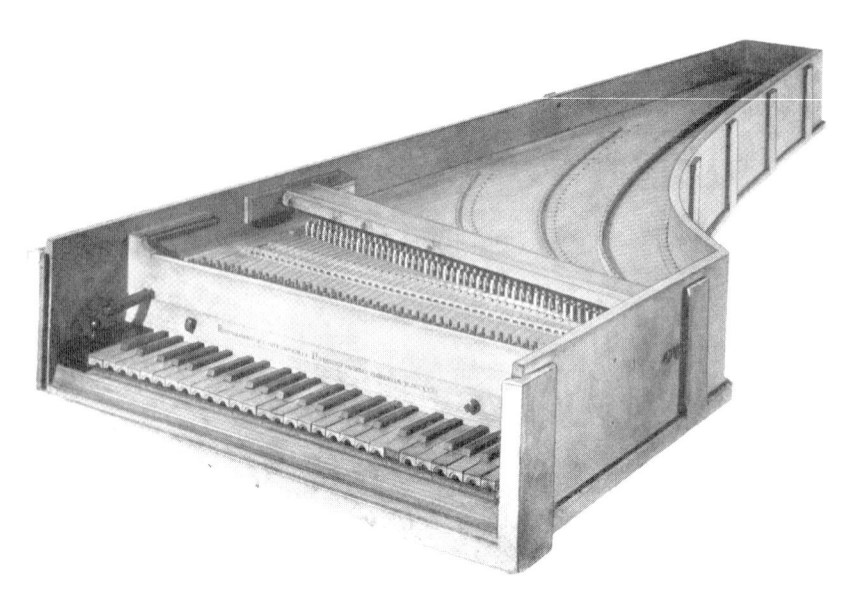

Figure 3.12 Cristofori's 1726 harpsichord. Photograph courtesy of the Grassi Museum für Musikinstrumente der Universität Leipzig.

The 2′ register is most uncommon – notable historic examples include the 1740 Hieronymus Albrecht Hass three-manual harpsichord, formerly in the collection of the late Rafael Puyana, and the 1760 Johann Adolph Hass two-manual harpsichord in the Yale collection – though both were made in Germany after Cristofori's death. In Chapter 2, we learned that Cristofori was involved in restoring harpsichords with 16′ stops, but a 16′ stop presents fewer design problems than the incorporation of a 2′ stop because the strings of the latter's top two octaves would be so short that there would be insufficient room for the jack slides, and its bridge would sit so close to the edge of the soundboard that vibration of the soundboard would be seriously impeded. As we shall see, Cristofori rose to the challenge and introduced a brilliant design that enabled him to incorporate this stop successfully. The compass is C–c^3 (49 keys).

Like in the 1722 harpsichord described above, the case construction of the 1726 harpsichord is of the thick-walled type, with a thin internal bentside supporting the soundboard, the 8′ hitchpin rail being glued atop a massive bentside liner and suspended over the soundboard, thereby isolating the soundboard from the stress-bearing parts of the case. Unlike in the 1722 harpsichord, which has a narrow hitchpin rail from the top to the bottom string, the hitchpin rail of the 1726 harpsichord widens

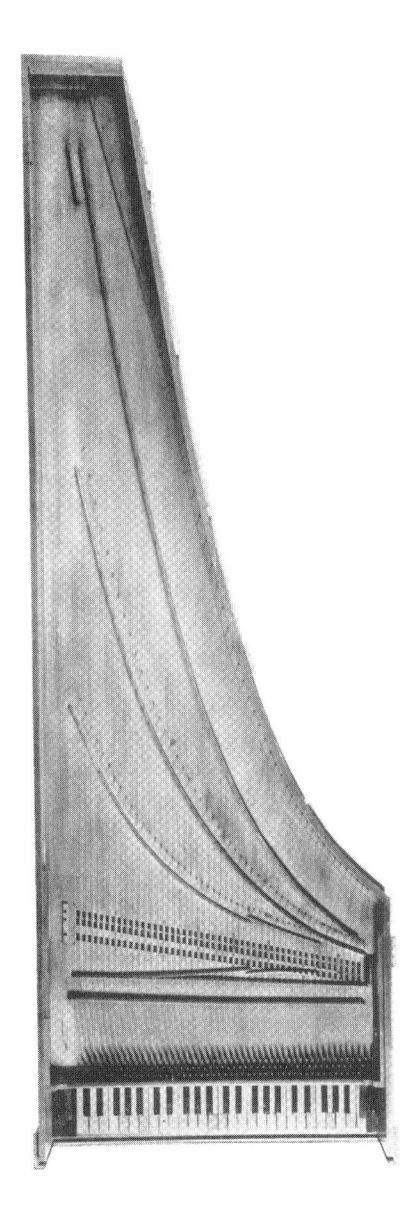

Figure 3.13 Plan view of Cristofori's 1726 harpsichord. Photograph courtesy of the Grassi Museum für Musikinstrumente der Universität Leipzig.

progressively starting an octave below middle C. The case also employs a series of vertical supports glued to its outer surfaces, as well as a similar system of internal diagonal braces (in this instance ten braces are used rather than the eight found in the 1722 harpsichord) that run from bentside to belly rail and spine, plus three lengthwise braces that run from belly rail to bentside and tail, and another segmented brace that runs roughly parallel

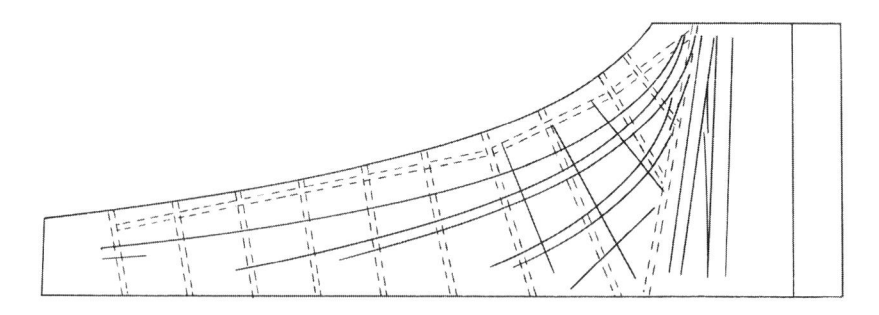

Figure 3.14 Schematic drawing of the bridges, 2′ and 4′ hitchpin rails, nuts, soundboard ribs, cutoff bar (solid lines), case braces, and belly rail (dashed lines) of Cristofori's 1726 harpsichord.

to the bentside and links all of the diagonal braces rather than just two as in the earlier harpsichord (Figure 3.14).

Unlike in the 1722 harpsichord, whose wrestplank extends to the registers, the 1726 harpsichord's walnut wrestplank is only about 60 mm wide, yet this narrow plank supports three rows of tuning pins and the combined string tension of all three choirs of strings. Glued over this narrow wrestplank is an extension of the soundboard that serves as an acoustically active platform for the 8′, 4′, and 2′ nuts. Oversize rectangular apertures cut in the soundboard admit the jacks, while moveable upper registers are mounted directly below these cutouts; a fixed lower jack guide is also used to align the jacks. The lower jack guide extends from the underside of the wrestplank to the belly rail, thereby forming a secondary sound-box for the three nuts. The original jacks are of pear (about half have been replaced, as have all of the tongues, which are mortised for leather plectra) and are constructed like those of the *spinettone* described above in that they have bored and chiseled-out openings for the tongues rather than slots open at the top; they also have their brass leaf springs mounted in front of the tongues rather than behind them, a feature of Cristofori's jacks.

The soundboard is of cypress and has three diagonal ribs extending beneath the 8′, 4′, and 2′ bridges (see Figure 3.14). The soundboard is about 2.5–3.5 mm thick. There are 4′ and 2′ hitchpin rails glued on the underside of the soundboard and a short diagonal cutoff bar is glued to the underside of the soundboard to the left of the 2′ bridge.

The registers are arranged as follows:

2′ ←
8′ ←
4′ →

The 8′ register is divided at c (an octave below middle C), and there are openings in the spine and cheek for operating the slides to effect registration changes. There are also two hand-operated levers passing through the front board into the key well. Parts of this stop mechanism are missing or were never completed (notably, projections on the slides that would have been engaged by the hand levers, as well as a pivot pin for the left-hand stop lever), which makes it difficult to determine precisely how these hand levers operated, though each would seem to have moved (or was intended to move) several of the registers simultaneously.[22] This mechanism must have been installed when the decorative outer case now associated with this instrument was constructed, as the outer case obstructs the original stop knobs that project from the spine and cheekpiece of the instrument proper. Because of this obstruction and the fact that the 1726 harpsichord has lid hinges riveted to its spine (in the manner of Cristofori's other harpsichords, and pianofortes), the lidded outer case is clearly a later accretion. Though much has been made of this outer case (as well as the matching case of the 1726 pianoforte) in recent publications, in my opinion these outer cases are not authentic and probably date from the mid-to-late eighteenth century at the very earliest.[23] Grotesque stands were recently fabricated to replace the non-original legs lost in World War II (the lost legs are pictured in the old Heyer catalog of 1910).[24]

One of the most interesting features of this harpsichord is the scaling of the 2′ stop. The bottom seven notes of the 2′ (from C to F# on the keyboard) run from the 4′ nut to an independent 2′ bridge; from G to f¹ (on the keyboard) the strings run from a separate 2′ nut (that gradually veers away

---

[22] David Sutherland, "Bartolomeo Cristofori's Paired Cembalos of 1726," *Journal of the American Musical Instrument Society* 26 (2000), pp. 36–43; Henkel, *Musikinstrumenten-Museum*, p. 89, and "Cristofori as Harpsichord Maker," pp. 21–23.

[23] Sutherland, ibid., pp. 5–56; Rainer Behrends, "Zum Stil und zu den Vorlagen für die Lackdekorationen des Cembalos und des Hammerklavieres von Bartolomeo Cristofori aus dem Jahre 1726," *Scripta Artium* 2 (Leipzig: Fall, 2001), pp. 7–12; Irmela Breidenstein, "Dass nichts in der Welt, das ewig dauret ... Zur Lackfassung der Instrumentenkästen und ihrer Restaurierung," ibid., pp. 13–17; Klaus Gernhardt, "Ergänzende Bemerkungen zu den Kästen des Hammerflügels (Inv.-Nr. 170) und des Cembalos (Inv.-Nr. 85)," ibid., pp. 19–22. The 1726 harpsichord and 1726 piano are not the only instruments that might be considered to be "paired" on the basis of date – Cristofori also made a harpsichord and piano in the year 1722. These two instruments, which have had different provenances and presently reside in different museums, lack matching outer cases.

[24] Georg Kinsky, *Musikhistorisches Museum von Wilhelm Heyer in Cöln*, 4 vols. (Cologne, 1910–1916), vol. I (1910), p. 171.

from the 4′ nut) to the 2′ bridge; and from f#^{1} to f^2 (on the keyboard) the strings are mounted on a separate nut and bridge that are positioned fore and aft of the main 2′ nut and bridge. This may have been done so that these short sections of nut and bridge could be mounted on more acoustically active regions of their respective soundboards. From f#^{2} to c^3 the strings of this stop "break" (in organ parlance) back to 4′ pitch and are mounted on the main 4′ nut and bridge. There were several reasons for the reversion to 4′ pitch: one would have been the extreme shortness of the 2′ strings, which led to the gradual incursion of the 2′ nut over the 4′ jack guide (this was cleverly accomplished with tab-like extensions to the nut that fit between the 4′ jacks), though it would have been extremely problematic to continue this system up to the top notes. Another reason for the "break" to 4′ pitch at this point might be that 2′ strings of such short length would have been extremely difficult to tune and voice, and most likely virtually inaudible.

These days, it is the consensus among keyboard historians that short-scale harpsichords (such as most of Cristofori's harpsichords [his pianofortes have similar short scaling], which have c^2 string lengths of about 285 mm) were strung with brass wire, while long-scale instruments (having c^2 lengths above around 290 mm) were strung in iron or steel wire. The divided bridge and nut of the 2′ stop of Cristofori's 1726 harpsichord as well as the divided 8′ and 4′ bridges and nuts of his *spinettone* (see above) might appear to provide evidence of a transition from brass to steel, though it is also possible that Cristofori did not switch from one type of wire to another but merely took advantage of the phenomenon known as "tensile pickup," in which both steel and brass wire becomes progressively stronger (by a factor of two or three times above its nominal tensile strength) as it is drawn down through successive dies. This alone might have enabled him to reposition the nut and bridge for the upper notes without changing stringing material.

Regarding original stringing materials, two bills for restoration work submitted in 1765 by Giovanni Ferrini to the ducal court in Florence may shed some light on the subject. One of these bills was for removing all of the steel strings from a two-register harpsichord and replacing them with brass ("un cembalo addue registri si è cavate tutte le corde perché erono di acciaro, e si sono rimesse tutte di ottone"), while the other was for removing the steel strings of a small octave harpsichord and replacing them with brass ("un cimbalino ottavino se è cavate le corde di acciaro, e rimessi di ottone").[25] Neither of these bills indicates that the instruments had their bridges reset or replaced in the course of restoration (as is often indicated in the bills Cristofori submitted to court; see Chapter 2). So what was Ferrini's rationale for replacing steel wire with brass in these two instruments? Had they been improperly strung or restrung with the wrong type of wire? Had the pitch changed since these instruments were constructed? Or was Ferrini's replacement of iron strings with brass simply a matter of individual preference for the sound of brass rather than a technical correction? It should be pointed out that all of Cristofori's extant instruments were discovered strung primarily in iron or steel, with brass found in the bass. This is even true of the 1690 oval spinet – an instrument that is believed to have been in original condition when it was "rediscovered" in 2000.[26] The c^2 string length of 285 mm (Cristofori's average) is at the nexus of brass and iron scaling – presumably one could go either way. The author believes that Cristofori used "steel" (he specified *aciero* [steel] as opposed to *ferro* [iron] wire in his bills – see Chapter 2) through most of the compass, and brass (*ottone*) in the bass.

String lengths/plucking points are as follows:

String lengths and plucking points of the 1726 harpsichord

Note	8′ register (mm)	4′ register (mm)	2′ register (mm)
C	1857/168	1109/86	569/138
F	1618/159	837/78	428/128
c	1128/146	565/67	285/109
f	854/136	427/58	214/94
c^1	571/123	286/47	142/72
f^1	427/112	215/40	104/55
c^2	286/94	141/31	83/41
f^2	215/84	104/24	62/30
c^3	144/68	69/12	72/44

[25] Pierluigi Ferrari and Giuliana Montanari, "Giovanni, Giuseppe e Filippo Ferrini cembalari della corte del Granducato di Toscana – uno studio documentario," in *Musicus Perfectus – studi in onore di L. F. Tagliavini "prattico e specolativo"*, ed. Pio Pellizzari (Bologna, 1995), pp. 29–47.

[26] *Bartolomeo Cristofori: La spinetta ovale del 1690*, ed. Gabriele Rossi-Rognoni (Florence, 2002), pp. 14–15. Though metallurgical analysis was carried out at the Opificio delle Pietre Dure in Florence on the brass wire fragments of the 1690 spinet, the ferrous-alloy wire samples were ignored or not reported because their presence conflicted with the current theory that brass wire was used exclusively in short-scaled harpsichords – despite the fact that the 1690 spinet was deemed in "original condition." Even their diameters were not tabulated. Giancarlo Lanterna and Maria Rizzi, "The Adhesives and the Metallic Parts," ibid., pp. 91–94.

The following string gauge numbers are written in ink on the wrest-plank:

String gauge numbers on the 1726 harpsichord

Note	String gauge number
8'	
D	5
G#	6
e^b	7
b^b	8
f#^{1}	9
e^{b2}	10
4'	
B	8
G	9
e^1	10
d^2	11
2'	
E^b	8
A	9
E	10
c^1	11

Case measurements are as follows:

Case measurements of the 1726 harpsichord

Length (excluding molding)	2423 mm
Width (excluding molding)	803 mm
Height	212 mm

The 1719 Clavichord

An unsigned clavichord came on the market in Florence around 1914 when it was offered by a dealer (probably the notorious Leopoldo Franciolini) to a friend of Arnold Dolmetsch, Herbert Horne, who on May 3 of that year wrote to his sister Beatrice:

You can tell Dolmetsch, if you think fit, that a dealer here has a 16th cent. Italian clavichord for sale. Dolmetsch used to say that Italian clavichords were of the greatest rarity and that he would much like to find one. This is the first that I have come across in all these years. It is made on a wholly different plan from that D. made for me. It is shaped somewhat like a spinette; but with the keyboard to the left, and the soundboard to the right. The mechanism, however, is very complicated, with a second set of tangents working cross-wise. The instrument has no outer case. It is well, but very plainly made. No painting or decoration, except a little moulding or two. The soundboard is cracked in two places, and one or two keys are missing. Otherwise it is still pretty sound, and as far as I can judge could be easily restored. The dealer only asks *lire* 300. I think I could get it packed for *lire* 250, but not less. As prices go here, now this is very little. For that, D would have to pay carriage.[27]

Horne acquired the clavichord and noted in another letter dated May 13 that it lacked a lid, which had evidently slid off its hinges and was misplaced, and had "a curious framed piece, attached, which appears to belong to the instrument" but whose function he could not determine. The clavichord was sent to Dolmetsch for repair, and upon examining it he replied to Horne on June 6:

It is very interesting – The movements you did not understand are a very clever contrivance to get two notes on each string in the bass, which could not be done in the usual "gebunden" way on account of the length of the semitone – The whole construction of the instrument is reversed: it is like the English spinet where the bass strings are at the back instead of at the front as in the Italian instruments. I had never seen or heard of a clavichord made on that plan. I will restore it, and it might have an extraordinary tone.[28]

On the underside of the left wrestplank there is a label that reads:

RESTORED AT JESSES WORKSHOP
HASLEMERE
SURREY

"Jesses" was the name of the country house in Haslemere, Surrey, where the Dolmetsch family moved in 1917, and where a workshop for the construction and restoration of instruments was established.

Arnold Dolmetsch sold the clavichord to Hugh Gough, a former pupil of his, and when Gough emigrated to the United States in 1959 he took the clavichord with him. Gough sold it to a New Yorker, Stephen Barrell, in 1987, who put it on the market in Amsterdam in 1992, at which time it was purchased by Harm Vellguth of Hamburg. In 1993 Vellguth sent the

---

[27] Margaret Campbell, *Dolmetsch: The Man and His Work* (Seattle, 1975), p. 195.
[28] Ibid., p. 196.

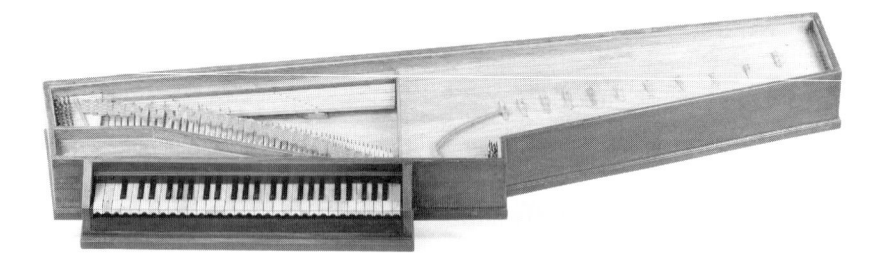

Figure 3.15 Cristofori's clavichord. Photograph courtesy of the Grassi Museum für Musikinstrumente der Universität Leipzig.

clavichord to J. C. Neupert for restoration.[29] Afterwards, it was acquired by the Musikinstrumenten-Museum der Universität Leipzig (now the Grassi Museum).

As indicated in Chapter 2, this clavichord's attribution to Bartolomeo Cristofori and dating (1719) are supported by an account in an anonymous eighteenth-century music dictionary manuscript that describes two instruments made by Cristofori, one of which was a *sordino con leve inventate dall'autore* (clavichord with levers invented by the maker) dated 1719. The term *con leve* (with levers) is a perfect description of the unusual key mechanism of the clavichord that is now in the collection of the Grassi Museum für Musikinstrumente der Universität Leipzig (inventory no. 5433).

The clavichord (Figure 3.15) is most unusual in that it is not built in the customary rectangular case, as was noted by Dolmetsch, but employs an elongated *traverso* case similar to Cristofori's *spinettone* (see above).

Like in the *spinettone*, the bass strings of this clavichord are located toward the back of the case, rather than the front as in most clavichords. Another unique feature of Cristofori's clavichord is the set of eight supplementary pivoted levers located at the back of the case, used to extend the reach of the fretted bass key levers (Figure 3.16).

Rather than employing one continuous bridge as was customary, this clavichord uses eleven short bridges mounted parallel to one another to carry the paired strings of the bottom twenty notes. The rest of the string pairs pass over a conventional curved bridge. The inspiration for using a series of independent bridges oriented in this fashion may have come from some early clavichords, such as those made by Domenico da Pesaro.

---

[29] Wolf Dieter Neupert kindly sent me his unpublished restoration report dated 1994, from which I have gathered technical information.

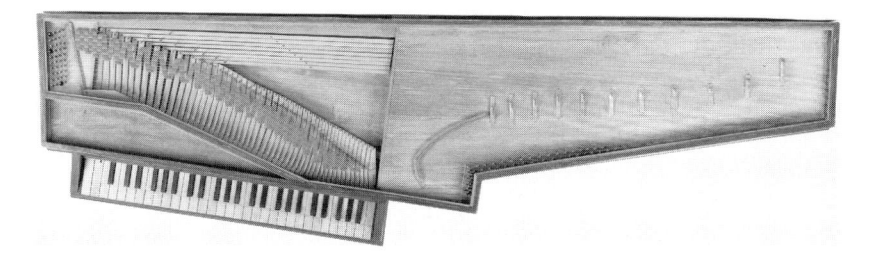

Figure 3.16 Plan view of Cristofori's clavichord. Photograph courtesy of the Grassi Museum für Musikinstrumente der Universität Leipzig.

The anonymous manuscript dictionary cited above lists several keyboard instruments that were restored by Cristofori, including a clavichord by da Pesaro dated 1543. This may be the clavichord having the same date that is now in the collection of the Grassi Museum für Musikinstrumente der Universität Leipzig (inventory no. 1), which features a sequence of independent bridges mounted parallel to one another rather than one continuous bridge.[30] A clavichord by Domenico da Pesaro, mounted on an organ, is listed in the 1716 Medici inventory, but no date is given, nor is it described in sufficient detail to determine the bridge layout.

Cristofori's 1719 clavichord has a 54-note compass of FF, GG, AA to c^3 – the same compass that the 1720 pianoforte and Universität Leipzig's *cembalo traverso* originally had (both of those instruments have had their compass altered to C–f^3 later in the eighteenth century; see below).[31] The natural keys are of boxwood with boxwood arcades, the accidentals are of ebony. The three-octave span is 310 mm – somewhat longer than Cristofori's other keyboards – though this may be due to the fact that the key levers were replaced by Dolmetsch (with the exception of three, all of the original boxwood key platings were transferred to the new keys). The clavichord is unfretted through most of its range, but the following bass notes are fretted as follows: FF–GG, AA–BB$^\flat$, BB–C, C#–D, E$^\flat$–E, F–F#, G–G#, A–B$^\flat$. Because of the extreme length of the bass strings of the extended compass, the brass tangents (8 mm wide in the bass, 6 mm wide in the treble, 0.95 mm thick) for the adjacent notes would have required very wide spacing and thus drastically cranked keys (for this reason, most seventeenth- and eighteenth-century clavichords did not employ fretting for the lowest bass notes). Instead, the tangents of Cristofori's fretted notes

---

[30] Civico Museo Bibliografico di Bologna, Martiniano H. 62, ff. 114–119; Cervelli, "Noterelle Cristoforiane."
[31] Pollens, *The Early Pianoforte*, p. 90.

are mounted on long pivoted levers (about 510 mm in length), which are lifted by their respective keys. This is a very clever system, and entirely in keeping with Cristofori's novel approach to keyboard design: in addition to the acoustical advantage of employing bass strings of unusually great length, the pair-wise fretting of the lowest notes greatly reduces string tension on the case. Though the provenance of this instrument may extend back to the infamous Florentine dealer Leopoldo Franciolini (who is known to have made and sold many fake instruments), Franciolini would not have been sufficiently competent to design and construct a clavichord exhibiting such ingenuity, and if he had bothered to copy Cristofori's construction techniques (such as in scaling, molding profiles, case design, and construction details), why would he neglect to add a false inscription, which he frequently placed on his fabrications?

Unfortunately, many of the original parts were missing when the clavichord was acquired by Horne in 1914, and others were replaced by Dolmetsch during his restoration. The non-original parts include the case bottom, lid, hinges, left and right wrestplanks, and key levers. It is possible that the soundboard ribs, which run diagonally across the soundboard and cross under the bridge, are replacements, as may be the internal structural braces.

The case is of the "false inner-outer" design with 14 mm thick mitered case sides of poplar with cypress moldings glued along the inside to create the visual effect of an inner case. In the Italian fashion, the sides are built around the bottom – which has been replaced with 13.5 mm thick spruce (see the table below for overall case dimensions). The 16 mm thick walnut belly rail has three, 17 mm diameter holes bored in it. In Cristofori's discussions with Scipione Maffei in preparation for the article published by Maffei in the *Giornale de' letterati d'Italia* in 1711 (see below and a full transcription of his notes in Appendix 1), Cristofori indicated that the sound-box of a keyboard instrument requires an opening for acoustical purposes, but that this opening does not have to be in the soundboard, as was traditional. While Cristofori's oval spinets (described above) and the c. 1720 *cembalo traverso* in Leipzig (described below) do have openings and decorative roses in their soundboards, his pianofortes and harpsichords dated 1722 and 1726 employ simple openings in their belly rails rather than in their soundboards, to achieve the same acoustical effect of lowering the Helmholtz resonance of the air chamber below the soundboard. The bottom of the clavichord is presently reinforced beneath the keyboard area by two strips of wood, one around 14 mm thick and 53 mm wide, the other about 14 mm thick and 58 mm wide. In the soundboard area, there are three diagonal braces running along the bottom from the spine to the right-front case wall, and a fourth brace again attached to the bottom reinforcing the right-front corner; these are screwed to the bottom and were presumably installed by Dolmetsch, perhaps in the same position as originals. The outer surface of the case is now crudely painted, which is certainly not original work.

The cypress soundboard is presently fitted with three ribs that are positioned diagonally at roughly the same angle as the case braces noted above. It ranges in thickness from between 2.4 mm and 2.8 mm at the tail to about 3.3 mm along the right case wall. At the left side of the case there is a mock sound-box covered by a "soundboard" of cypress 3.5 mm thick fitted with a nut. It is unlikely that this served a useful acoustical function, as it only would have supported the vibrations of the non-speaking portion of the strings, which would have been out of tune with the speaking lengths and muted with the traditional cloth listing. The bridge supporting the upper twenty-six courses of strings is made of walnut and is 12.5 mm high and 11 mm wide. The individual bridges supporting the bottom twenty courses range in height from 12. 5 mm at the transition from the main bridge to 15.5 mm for the lowest strings. The courses are divided up among the independent bridges in the following way:

Division of courses among independent bridges in the 1719 clavichord

Bridge number	Number of courses
1 (lowest strings)	3
2	2
3–6	1
7–10	2
11	3

Curiously, the fretting system does not coincide with the distribution of courses among the individual bridges. One might expect the course for the first set of fretted notes, FF and GG, to be pinned to its own independent bridge, that for the next set of fretted notes, AA and AA# (or BB♭), to be pinned to the second bridge, and so on. It is unclear why eleven bridges are used to support twenty courses when ten bridges might have been used, with each bridge supporting two courses and the lowest eight bridges used for the sixteen double-fretted bass notes.

The string lengths in the 1719 clavichord are as follows:

Principal string lengths

Note	String length (mm)
FF	1861
C	1697
F	1471
c	1009
f	813
c^1	567
f^1	431
c^2	282
f^2	209
c^3	135[32]

Lengths of fretted notes

Fretted pair	String length (mm)
FF–GG	1861/1675
AA–BB♭	1825/1734
BB–C	1789/1697
C#–D	1660/1566
E♭–E	1620/1515
F–F#	1471/1389
G–G#	1334/1257
A–B♭	1210/1141

Lengths of remaining unfretted notes on individual bridges

Note	String length (mm)
B	1101
c	1009
c#	997
d	903

As we shall see in Chapter 4, Cristofori apparently attempted to explain fifth-comma meantone temperament to Scipione Maffei (see below and

---

[32] String measurements kindly supplied by Wolf Dieter Neupert.

Appendix 1). Writing in 1666, the theorist Lemmi Rossi indicated that this particular temperament was then in common use, and thus it may have been the tuning that Cristofori preferred.[33] Unfortunately, an analysis of the fretting system of the 1719 clavichord failed to identify any paired semitones that can be associated with fifth-comma meantone, nor with sixth-comma, quarter-comma, or third-comma meantone.[34] Calculations of the lengths of paired notes were also made for just, Pythagorean, and equal temperament, but the only match that could be found was for the FF–GG fretted pair, which strangely agreed with the 10:9 ratio of a minor tone rather than the required 9:8 ratio of a major tone. Considering Cristofori's sophistication as a maker and apparent knowledge of temperament, the flawed fretting that one presently finds is very likely due to improper placement, or perhaps even rearrangement, of the independent bridges (which most certainly came loose from the soundboard over the course of time). Furthermore, it is not even clear whether the eleven independent bridges are original.

Case dimensions of the 1719 clavichord

Case dimensions	
Length	2178 mm
Width	595 mm
Depth	189 mm

The Pianofortes

The earliest formal documentation we have of Cristofori's invention of the piano is found in the Medici musical instrument inventory of 1700, which lists:

Un Arpicimbalo di Bartolomeo Cristofori di nuova inventione, che fa' il piano, e il forte, à due registri principali unisoni, con fondo di Cipresso senza rosa, con fascie e scorniciatura mezza tonda simile, con filetto d' Ebano, con alcuni salterelli con panno rosso, che toccano nelle corde, et alcuni martelli, che fanno il piano, et il forte, e tutto l'ordingo vien serrato, e coperto da un piano di cipresso filettato di Ebano, con tastatura di Bossolo et Ebano senza spezzati, che comincia in cisolfaut ottava stesa, e finisce in cisolfaut, con n°. quaranta nove tasti, trè bianchi, e neri,

---

[33] Lemmi Rossi, *Sistema musico* (Perugia, 1666), p. 58.
[34] The author's method of determining a fretted clavichord's temperament is explained in his *Manual of Musical Instrument Conservation*, s.v. "clavichord maintenance."

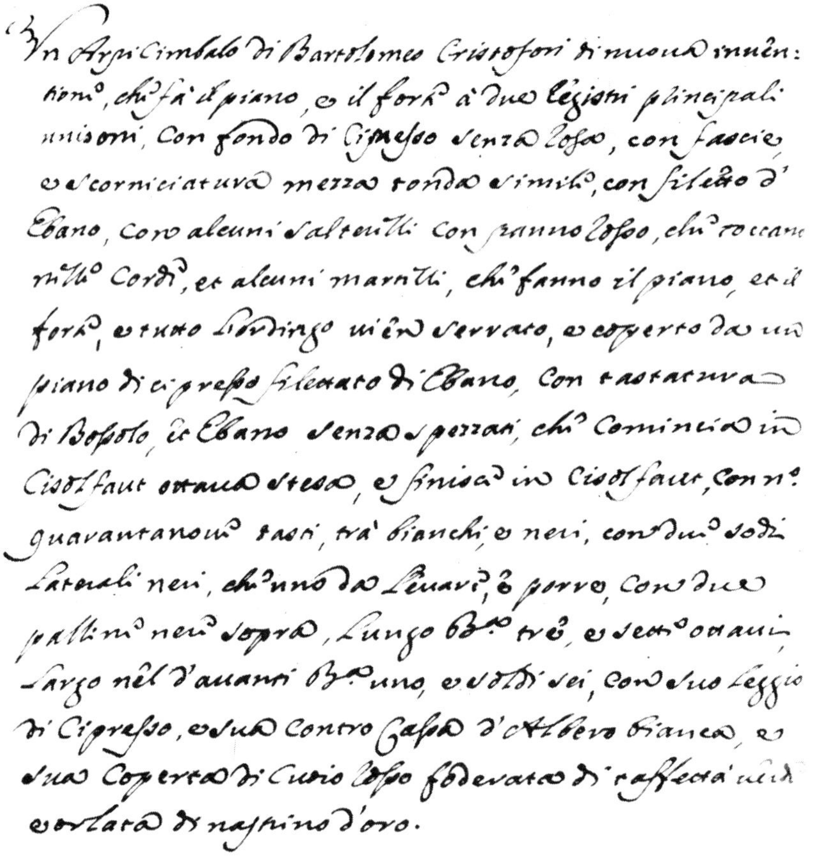

Figure 3.17 Medici musical instrument inventory of 1700: "Arpicimbalo di Bartolomeo Cristofori di nuova inventione, che fa' il piano, e il forte." Courtesy of the Archivio di Stato, Florence.

con due sodi laterali neri, che uno da levare, e porre, con due palline nere sopra, lungo B[a]. tre, e sette ottavi largo nel d'avanti B[a]. uno, e soldi sei, con suo leggio di Cipresso, e sua contro Cassa d'Albero bianca, e sua Coperta di cuoio rosso foderata di taffetta' verde e orlata di nastrino d'oro.[35] (Figure 3.17)

(A large *cembalo* by Bartolomeo Cristofori, of new invention, that makes soft and loud, of two registers at principal unison pitch, with soundboard of cypress without a rose, with sides and half-round moldings similarly inlaid with strips of ebony, with some jacks with red cloth that touch the strings [dampers], and some hammers that make the soft and the loud, and the entire mechanism enclosed and covered by a plank of cypress inlaid with strips of ebony, with keys of boxwood and ebony

---

[35] ASF, Guardaroba Medicea, 1117, fol. 30.

without split sharps that commence at C *ottava stesa* [stretched octave] and finish at C, with 49 keys in black and white, with two black knobs on either side for removing and replacing [the keyboard and action], three *braccia* and seven *ottavi* in length, and in the front one *braccia* and six *soldi*, with its music desk of cypress, and its outer case of white wood, and its cover of red leather lined with green taffeta and hemmed with gold ribbon.)

Unfortunately, this historic piano, possibly the first one made by Cristofori, has apparently not survived.[36] In Scipione Maffei's article entitled "Nuova invenzione d'un gravecembalo col piano, e forte; aggiunte alcune considerazioni sopra gli strumenti musicali" published in 1711 in the *Giornale de' letterati d'Italia* (Appendix 2), the author indicates that as of that date Cristofori had made three pianos.[37] In notes made in connection with the writing of that article, Maffei states that of these three pianos, two were sold in Florence and one was given to Cardinal Ottoboni in Rome (i.e., it was a gift from Grand Prince Ferdinando de' Medici to Ottoboni; see below and Appendix 1).[38]

Scipione Maffei's Interview with Cristofori

Before examining the three extant pianofortes, which date from 1720, 1722, and 1726, we should first review Scipione Maffei's 1711 article, which describes Cristofori's newly invented pianoforte in its earliest form and provides insight into the maker's principles of design and understanding of acoustics. This oft-cited article was in fact anonymous in this first incarnation, though as one of the general editors of the *Giornale de' letterati d'Italia* (along with Apostolo Zeno and Antonio Valisnieri, whom we shall encounter in Chapter 4 as librettists of several operas performed

---

[36] In 2014, the Accademia Bartolomeo Cristofori in Florence published an announcement that on May 3 of that year they would be holding the following event: "Buon Compleanno Bartolomeo Cristofori festa per i 25 anni di vita dell'Accademia: Una giornata con musica e conversazione, con la partecipazione di tutti gli strumenti musicali dell'Accademia, la visita speciale del primo fortepiano costruito da Cristofori..." After ascertaining that the Accademia was not borrowing the 1720 Cristofori piano from The Metropolitan Museum of Art (which in any event should not be construed as "del primo fortepiano costruito da Cristofori" (the first piano constructed by Cristofori), I made several inquiries of the Accademia's staff and others in Florence before I was informed that an earlier Cristofori piano had not been discovered, and that the "special visit" referred to in the invitation was Kerstin Schwarz's copy of the 1726 piano in Leipzig. The author still holds out hope that an earlier Cristofori piano, possibly the one listed in the 1700 inventory, will someday surface.

[37] Scipione Maffei, "Nuova invenzione d'un gravecembalo col piano, e forte."

[38] Verona, Biblioteca Capitolare, cod. DCCCCLX, fasc. VI, no. 1; Och, "Bartolomeo Cristofori, Scipione Maffei e la prima descrizione del 'gravicembalo col piano e forte.'"

under the aegis of Grand Prince Ferdinando de' Medici), Maffei (and his associates) undoubtedly made numerous anonymous contributions to the publication (for example, the eulogy for Grand Prince Ferdinando, published in the *Giornale* in 1714, is an anonymous editorial entry).[39] In 1719, however, the authorship of the 1711 article was established when Maffei republished it in a compilation of his writings entitled *Rime e prose*.[40] The 1719 publication replicates the original virtually word for word (two notable deviations being the spelling of *gravecembalo*, which became *gravicembalo*, and Bartolommeo, which was changed to Bartolomeo).[41] We know that two years before the publication of his article on Cristofori's piano, Maffei visited Florence, for in a letter to Ferdinando dated October 19, 1709, Apostolo Zeno mentions in passing that Maffei was then in Florence.[42] Presumably Maffei and Cristofori met on that occasion. The fact that a distinguished literary figure such as Maffei undertook the remarkable challenge of describing a new and complex mechanical device provides some indication of the intense interest provoked by Cristofori's new invention. However, doubts have recently been expressed regarding the true authorship of the article – that the hammer and escapement mechanism would have been too complex for Maffei to describe and illustrate, and that the description must have been written by Cristofori himself (even though Maffei stipulates that the inventor had been incapable of a coherent description of his own invention; see below). It has even been suggested that Maffei plagiarized Cristofori's writing,[43] though this is grossly unjust, for in notes that he made in connection with his interview of Cristofori (see Appendix 1), Maffei indicates that he intended to seek advice in a follow-up visit to Florence by having "Cavalier Albisi, a relative of Buonarroti, describe the *cembalo* and note all the terminology," and he adds a reminder "to have the instrument maker submit a report noting the substance of the invention, wherein lies its strengths

---

[39] *Giornale de' letterati d'Italia* 17 (Venice, 1714), pp. 1–27.

[40] Scipione Maffei, *Rime e prose*.

[41] Denzil Wraight, "Differences between Maffei's Article on Cristofori's Piano in its 1711 and 1719 Versions, their Subsequent Transmission and the Implications," www.denzilwraight.com (2015).

[42] ASF, Archivio Mediceo, file 5900, p. 589; Puliti, *Della vita del Ser.^{mo} Ferdinando dei Medici*, pp. 150–151.

[43] Laura Och, "Bartolomeo Cristofori, Scipione Maffei e la prima descrizione del 'gravicembalo col piano e forte'," p. 19; and "Interessi e conoscenze musicali di Scipione Maffei," in proceedings of the conference *Scipione Maffei nell'Europa del Settecento, Verona, 23–25 settembre 1996*, ed. Gian Paolo Romagnani (1998), pp. 551–577; Wraight, "Differences between Maffei's Article on Cristofori's Piano in its 1711 and 1719 Versions," p. 10.

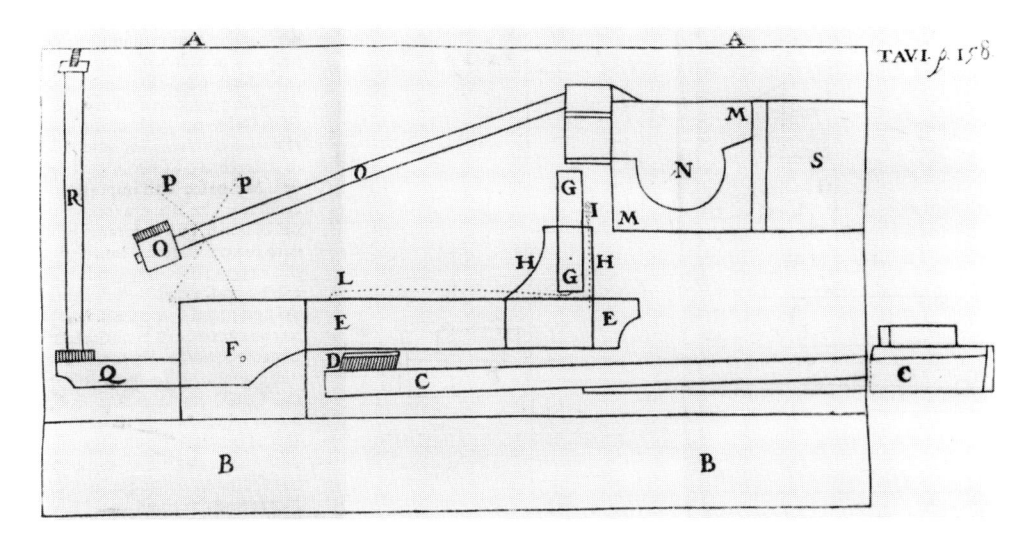

Figure 3.18 Engraving of Cristofori's hammer action from the *Giornale de' letterati d'Italia* (Venice, 1711).

and wherein its greatest difficulties." (Marchese Luca degli Albizzi had been Prince Ferdinando's tutor and served as his *maestro di camera* up through 1689; Buonarroti was very likely Filippo Buonarroti, who later became a minister under Grand Duke Gian Gastone.[44]) Clearly, Cristofori collaborated with Maffei in writing the article: he explained how his piano action worked and apparently discussed general keyboard instrument design, acoustics, and temperament, and even offered suggestions on how to eliminate squeaks in Maffei's own harpsichord.

Regarding the "drawings" that accompany the 1711 and 1719 articles, we should keep in mind that these printed versions are engravings patterned after a lost original sketch that was presumably supplied by Cristofori. There are minute differences between the 1711 and 1719 engravings (Figures 3.18 and 3.19), the most significant being what appears to be a pivot point on the "tongue" represented in the 1719 drawing, which is not present on the 1711 drawing.

However, we should not read too much into this, as the presence or absence of a tiny dot may be a printing artifact rather than a refinement or correction provided by Maffei or Cristofori (Cristofori, in fact, did not use a pivoted tongue, otherwise termed an escapement jack, in any of his three surviving pianos). In any case, it is unlikely that Maffei reached out

---

[44] Eulogy published in the *Giornale de' letterati d'Italia* 17 (Venice, 1714), p. 3; Harold Acton, *The Last Medici* (London, 1980), p. 305.

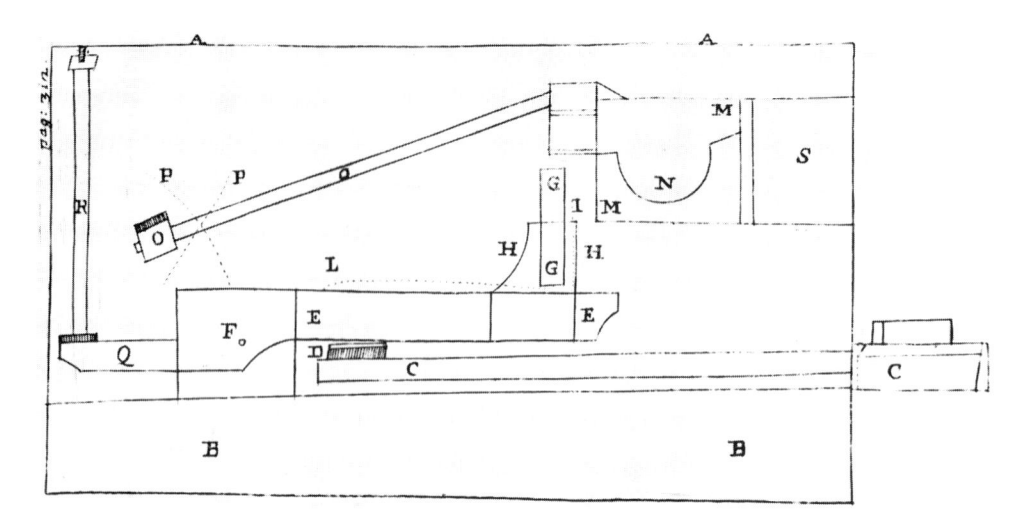

Figure 3.19 Engraving of Cristofori's hammer action from Maffei's *Rime e prose* (Venice, 1719).

to Cristofori for an update when he elected to include his article on the invention of the piano in the 1719 compilation of his writings, and by that time Cristofori was most likely in the process of supplanting his earlier action with an improved version that is found in the piano made in 1720.

Below is a translation of Maffei's account published in 1711 (see Appendix 2 for the original Italian text):

If the value of an invention should be measured by its novelty, and by its complexity, that which we have before us to give an account of is certainly not inferior to any other that has been seen for some time. It is known to whoever loves music, that one of the principal sources from which the skillful in this art draw the secret of singularly delighting those who listen, is the *piano* and the *forte*, whether in statement and repetitions, or when with artful degrees diminishing the voice little by little, one then suddenly returns to full power, an artifice used frequently and to marvelous effect in the grand concerts in Rome to the incredible delight of those who enjoy the perfection of the art. Now, of this diversity and alteration of voice, in which are excellent, among others, bowed instruments, the harpsichord is entirely deprived, and the idea of constructing it so that it might have this gift would be deemed by whosoever it might to be a vain endeavor. Nevertheless, such a bold invention has been no less happily conceived than executed in Florence, by Signor Bartolommeo Cristofali, Padovano, *cembalista* in the employ of the Most Serene Prince of Tuscany. He has already made three of the usual size of other harpsichords, and they have all succeeded perfectly. Producing greater or lesser sound on them depends upon the diverse force with which the player presses the keys, from the regulation of which one comes to hear not only the *piano* and *forte*, but also the diminishing and diversity of the note as would be the case in the violoncello. Some professors have not given to this invention all the applause that it merits; first, because they have not understood how much ingenuity was required to overcome the difficulty, and it has appeared to them that the voice of the instrument, being different from the ordinary, is too soft and dull; an impression produced on first placing the hand on the instrument, given that we are accustomed to the silvery sound of other *gravecembali*; but the ear quickly adapts itself to it, and becomes so charmed that one never tires of it, and the common *gravecembali* no longer please; and we must add that it sounds even more sweet at some distance. There has been further opposition raised that this instrument does not have a powerful tone, and is not quite so loud as other *gravecembali*. To this one may answer, first, that it has more power than they give credit, when someone wishes and knows how to produce it, striking the keys with force; and secondly, that it is necessary to accept things for what they are, and not to consider, as regards one end, something which is designed for another. This is properly a chamber instrument, and it is not adaptable for church music, or for a large orchestra. How many instruments are there, used in such occasions, that are not held as being among the most delightful? It is certain that to accompany a singer, and to support an instrument, or even for a moderate ensemble, it succeeds perfectly; though this is not its principal intention, but, that is, rather to be heard alone, like the lute, the harp, the six-stringed viol, and other most sweet instruments. But truly, the major opposition that has been raised against this new instrument is the general lack of knowledge at first of how to approach playing it, because it is not enough to play perfectly the ordinary instruments with a keyboard, but being a new instrument, it requires a person who to understand its strengths, has made a particular study of it, so as to regulate the strength of the varied pressure which should be given to the keys, and the graceful diminishing, at the [right] time and place, and to choose pieces suited to it, and delicate ones, and especially to separate and make the parts progress, and to make heard the subjects in various places.

But turning to the particular structure of this instrument, if the maker who invented it had known as well how to describe it as he knew perfectly how to build it, it would not be difficult to explain the artifice to the reader: but as he has not succeeded in that, thus, I have judged it impossible to represent it so that one can understand the idea and the skill which another has brought to the task, since I no longer have the instrument before my eyes, but only some notes made while examining it and a rough preliminary design spread out before me.

We will say, then, in the first place, that instead of the usual jacks [*salterelli*] that sound with the quills [*penna*], here there is a row of little hammers [*martelletti*] that strike the string from below, the tops of which, by which they strike, are covered with buckskin. Every hammer has the end inserted into a circular butt [*rotella*] that renders it moveable, and those butts are partially embedded, and strung together, in a rack [*pettina*]. Near the butt, and under the shank of the hammer, there is a support or projecting part, that, receiving a blow from below, raises the hammer, and pushes it to strike the string, with that measure of impulse, and that degree of force given by the hand; and hence the sound is greater or less at the pleasure of the player. Also it is easy to make it strike with much force, because the hammer receives the blow near its pivot, which is to say, near the center of the path through which it moves, and therefore even a slight touch will make it move through a circle. That which gives the blow to the hammer under the extremity of the aforementioned projection is a little tongue [*linguetta*] of wood, placed upon a lever that meets the key, and that is raised by it when it is pressed by the player. This little tongue, however, does not rest upon the lever, but is slightly raised and strung on two thin jawbone-shaped pieces that are placed for this purpose one on each side. But as it was necessary that the hammer, having struck the string, should instantly quit it, detaching itself from it, although the key was still under the finger of the player, and as it was necessary that the said hammer should quickly remain free to return to its place, therefore the little tongue that strikes it is moveable, and so connected that it moves up and strikes firmly, but having struck the blow, it immediately disengages, that is, it moves on; and, when entirely free, it descends, yields and returns, replacing itself under the hammer.

The maker produced this effect with a brass wire spring that is fastened to the lever, and which, distending, strikes a point under the tongue, and doing this with some force, it pushes it and holds it pressed against another brass wire that stands upright and firm on the opposite side. By this firm support given to the tongue, by the spring which is under it, and also by the balance of the whole, it becomes at once firm, and then flexible, as is required. In order that the hammers, in falling back after the blow, should not rebound and strike the string a second time, they are made to fall and rest upon crossed little cords of silk, which receive them without noise. But because, in instruments of this type, it is necessary to suppress, that is to stop, the sound, which by continuing would confuse the notes that follow, for which purpose spinets have cloth at the ends of the jacks, since it is also necessary in this new instrument to deaden it entirely and quickly, therefore each of the aforesaid levers has a little tail-piece, and on these tail-pieces is placed a row or rather a register of jacks, which from their use might be called dampers [*spegnitoi*]. When the keys are at rest, these touch the string with cloth, which they have on their top, and they prevent the vibration which would be caused by the vibration of other struck [strings]; but when the key is pressed, and the point of the lever is raised, the tail-piece is consequently lowered, and with it the damper, so as to leave the string free to sound, which then dies down as soon as the key is released, with the damper rising again to touch the string. However, in order to understand more clearly every movement of this mechanism, and its internal contrivance, take the diagram [Figure 3.18] and observe item by item its make-up.

Explanation of the Diagram

A. String.
B. Frame, or bed of the keyboard.

C. Ordinary key, or first lever, which at its extremity raises the second.
D. Block mounted on the key.
E. Second lever, on each side of which is attached a jawbone-shaped piece that supports the little tongue.
F. Pivot of the second lever.
G. Moveable tongue, which when raised by the second lever, hits and forces up the hammer.
H. Thin jawbone-shaped pieces between which the tongue is pivoted.
I. Fixed brass wire pressed together at the top, which keeps the tongue firm.
L. Spring of brass wire that passes under the tongue and presses it against the fixed wire that is behind it.
M. Rack, in which all the hammer butts rest.
N. Circular part of the hammer, which rests in the rack.
O. Hammer, which when propelled upward by the tongue strikes the string with the buckskin which it has on top.
P. Crossed cords of silk, upon which the hammer shanks rest.
Q. Back of the second lever, lowered when the key is pressed.
R. Register of jacks, or dampers, that, when the key is pressed, are lowered, and leave the string free, and then returning quickly to their place, stop the sound.
S. Part of the frame to strengthen the hammer rack.

After all this, it should be observed that the plank in which the pegs, or iron pins, are fixed that hold the strings, and which, in other *gravecembali*, is under the strings themselves, is above here, and the pins come through it, and the strings are attached to them below, there being more need of space underneath to admit the whole of the mechanism of the key action. The strings are thicker than the ordinary, and, in order that their tension may not injure the soundboard, they are not fastened to this, but somewhat higher. In all points of contact, which is to say wherever any rattle might occur, it is prevented by leather and by cloth, especially in the holes through which the pivots pass, and with singular skill he has placed buckskin everywhere, and the pivot passes through it. This invention has also been effected by the maker in another form, since he has built another *gravecembalo* with soft and loud, in a different and somewhat simpler shape, but nevertheless, the first has been more applauded.

Since this ingenious man is also excellent in the manufacture of ordinary *gravecembali*, it is worth noting that he does not agree with the modern makers, who, for the most part, build them not only without a rose, but even without any other escape for the sound in the whole case. Not that he thinks it necessary to make the hole so large as the roses made by older [makers], nor does he think it desirable to make the opening in that part which is susceptible to attracting dust; but he prefers to make two small apertures in the front, or the front enclosure, which stay concealed and protected from it. He asserts that such an aperture is necessary in some part of the instrument because, when played on, the soundboard ought to vibrate and yield; and that it does so is known by the trembling of anything you may place upon it when someone plays; but, if the body had no opening, given this the air within cannot yield and escape, but remaining harsh and fixed, the soundboard does not move, and hence the sound emerges somewhat dull and short, and not resonant. When, however, a hole is made, you will rather see the soundboard give more, and the string remain higher, and you will hear a stronger tone; and by placing the finger close to the aforesaid opening, when someone plays, you will feel a breeze and the air escaping. On this subject, we do not want to neglect to say that, in the case of drawing illumination from the investigations of natural philosophy into the inclinations and effects of air and of motion, a great source, yet one until now more or less unrecognized, of discoveries and knowledge concerning this could be observing closely the various and wonderful effects of air set in motion by musical instruments; by examining their construction, and reflecting upon the cause of their perfection or imperfection, and how to alter their construction; as for instance, the variations of sound that occur in instruments with a soundpost, which are those played with a bow, if one slightly changes its position, then the string becomes more sonorous or else duller; also, the alteration and diversity of sounds which instruments gain from different sizes, and especially *gravecembali*, given that their soundboard can be thicker or thinner, and so on, concerning a thousand other considerations. It must not be forgotten that as it is the universal opinion that new *gravecembali* are always imperfect, and that they acquire perfection only by age, this maker claims that he can make them in such a manner that they immediately give a sound no less sonorous than old instruments. He asserts that the lack of resonance in new [instruments] arises principally from the property of elasticity, which is retained by the bentside and the bridge; for while these apply force upon the soundboard to retain their shape, the sound remains imperfect, and if this elasticity were to be entirely taken from them before putting them into operation, this defect would immediately be removed, as he finds by practical experience. The good quality of the wood will also contribute, wherefore Pesaro began to make use of old chests that he found in the granaries of Venice and Padua, which were for the most part of cypress wood from Candia [Crete] or Cyprus.

It will not here be disagreeable to lovers of music if one says something of another rare harpsichord, which is still found in Florence, in the hands of Signor Casini, a most esteemed *maestro di cappella*. This has five keyboards – that is, five entire sets of keys, one stepped above the other – and may be called a perfect instrument, since every note is divided into its five *quinti*; hence, one can circulate, and run through all the keys without hitting any dissonance at all, and always finding all the accompaniments perfect, as its owner makes heard, who plays it to perfection.

Ordinary *gravecembali*, like all instruments with keyboards, are very imperfect; because, since the notes are not divided in their parts, there are many strings that do not have a perfect fifth, and one is obliged to employ the same keys for a sharp and for a flat; to avoid in part this defect, one sees some old spinets, chiefly those by Undeo [Donatus or Hieronymus Undeus of Bergamo, fl. 1592–1632], with some of the black keys split and divided in two, the reason for which many professors do not understand; and it is truly because, for example, there is at least a fifth of a tone difference between *Gesolreut* and *Alamirè*, there is a necessity for two strings.

However, despite the aforementioned imperfection of the *gravecembalo* or theorbo, which cannot be tuned perfectly with a violin, when they are used in concert, the ear does not notice it; and similarly it arises that one does not compose using many black notes, and only proceeds sparingly, and by some masters, only when a false and unpleasant note suits the words, or harshness is to be expressed by the voice. This imperfection in instruments that have keys is also the cause of our often perceiving, when we hear them played, that when the piece is displaced, as Florentine dialect has it, or transposed in common parlance, then falling on those notes which do not have the fifth, the falseness of the sound offends the ear. It will not happen thus with the violin, because not having a keyboard, [the strings] can be stopped wherever necessary, and in whatever key produce the perfect notes. Therefore, the *gravecembalo* of which we speak, besides the delight of perfect intonation, may be useful in many speculations on the theory of music; nor should it be believed that its tuning is too difficult, for it really is easier, given that it always proceeds through perfect fifths; whereas with ordinary instruments, one must pay attention to making the fifth lower, and the fourth and major third higher, with many other requirements.

Keyboard Ranges of the Three Pianofortes

The compass of the 1720 piano (The Metropolitan Museum of Art, New York; Figure 3.20) was originally 54 keys, FF, GG, AA–c^3 (later altered to C–f^3; see discussion below).

The pianos of 1722 (Museo Nazionale degli Strumenti Musicali, Rome; Figure 3.21) and 1726 (Grassi Museum für Musikinstrumente der Universität Leipzig; Figure 3.22) have 49-note compasses of C–c^3.

The key levers of three of the four surviving actions (including the Gatti-Kraus action; see below) are of chestnut, while those of the 1722 piano are of walnut. The key levers of the 1722 and 1726 pianos are about the same length, though the levers of the 1720 piano are considerably longer, which is due to the greater depth of that piano's wrestplank, which includes a broad, supporting structure mounted behind the tuning pins (see discussion below). Natural keys in all of the surviving Cristofori pianos are boxwood; accidentals are black-stained pear with ebony slips. Natural key coverings of the 1720 piano are 120 mm long, and accidentals

Figure 3.20 Cristofori piano of 1720. The Metropolitan Museum of Art, Crosby Brown Collection, 1889. Photograph courtesy of The Metropolitan Museum of Art.

80 mm long; the original score lines have been worn or scraped off. The 1722 natural key coverings are also 120 mm long; accidentals are 81 mm long; and natural keys have double score lines, spaced at 3.5 mm. The 1726 natural key coverings are 116 mm long, with accidentals 77 mm in length; natural keys have double score lines spaced at 3.3 mm. Cristofori's keys have wide D-tails (approximately 16 mm in width), a characteristic feature of Italian keyboards. The three-octave spans of the Cristofori pianos are as follows: 1720 piano, 496 mm; 1722 piano, 497 mm; and 1726 piano, 491 mm.

The Hammer Actions

Maffei admits that the hammer action was difficult to understand and describe, and that he was writing from memory with the assistance of some notes (perhaps those that are preserved in the Biblioteca Capitolare in Verona and transcribed in Appendix 1) and a rough diagram (*un disegno rozzamente*) of the hammer action that was most likely supplied by Cristofori. These are important points, as Scipione Maffei was a man of

The Pianofortes 131

Figure 3.21 Cristofori piano of 1722. Museo Nazionale degli Strumenti Musicali, Rome.

letters, not an instrument maker or musician, and the workings of such a complex mechanical device would have been difficult enough for a harpsichord maker to grasp. Maffei alludes to the fact that Cristofori had been unable to describe the mechanism clearly, though this remark should not be construed as evidence that Cristofori was inarticulate, as mechanical devices, especially new and complex ones, do not lend themselves readily to description. We know that Cristofori was literate, as he evidently made out numerous bills to court and composed the 1716 Medici musical instrument inventory that bears the following inscription: "Io Bartolommeo Cristofori ò ricevuto in Consegna tutti li sopradetti strumenti et in

Figure 3.22 Cristofori piano of 1726. Grassi Museum für Musikinstrumente der Universität Leipzig.

fede mano propria" (I Bartolomeo Cristofori have received in consignment all of the above-named instruments and in faith signed in my own hand) (see Figure 2.8). However, it should be noted that the handwriting of the bills and inventory (with the exception of his signature and closing declaration cited above) clearly do not match – perhaps one or all of these documents are transcriptions of rough notes or dictations taken down by a scribe or notary. Aside from a few unclear aspects of the action diagram accompanying Maffei's article (such as the sketchy connection between the hammer shank and the *rotella*, the lack of pivot points for the hammer and key lever, and the vague system of suspending the *linguetta mobile*), the design presented by Maffei in 1711 would appear to be functional if we take into consideration similarities between the parts represented in these engravings and their analogs in the later, extant actions. The structure

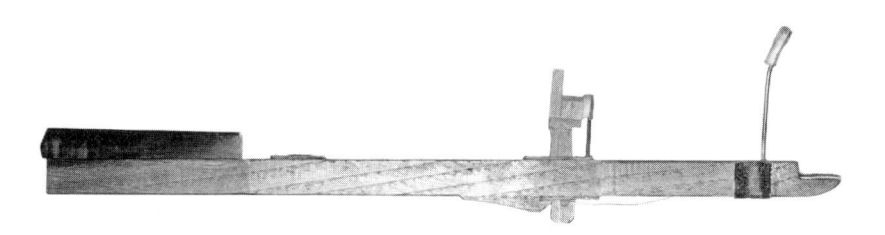

Figure 3.23 Accidental key lever from the 1726 Cristofori piano.

and orientation of the levers and escapement parts are reasonably clear and it seems safe to assume that Maffei's memory and understanding of the mechanism, aided by a sketch of the action, are reasonably accurate. As indicated above, Maffei's description differs in a number of important ways from the four known surviving actions (dating from 1720–1726; see discussion below), so a major redesign of the action was most likely underway in the years that had ensued between 1711 and 1719.

The major differences between the action pictured by Maffei and those of the surviving pianos of 1720, 1722, and 1726 involve the position and size of the secondary, or intermediate, lever (marked *seconda leva*, Q and E in Maffei's article; see Figure 3.18) and the location of the tongue, otherwise known as the escapement jack. In Maffei's drawing, a cumbersome, pivoted secondary lever is lifted by the back of the key lever (*tasto ordinario*, or *prima leva*, C), and a spring-assisted tongue (*linguetta mobile*, G) is supported by a jaw-bone shaped extension of that lever (*ganasce sottili*, H). In the surviving actions the escapement jacks are positioned in mortises at the back ends of the key levers rather than on the secondary levers (Figures 3.23, 3.24, and 3.25).

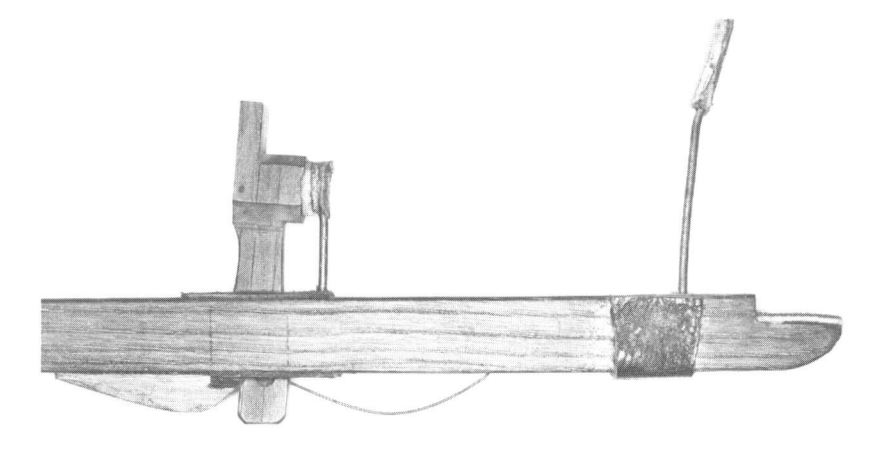

Figure 3.24 Detail of the escapement mechanism from the 1726 Cristofori piano.

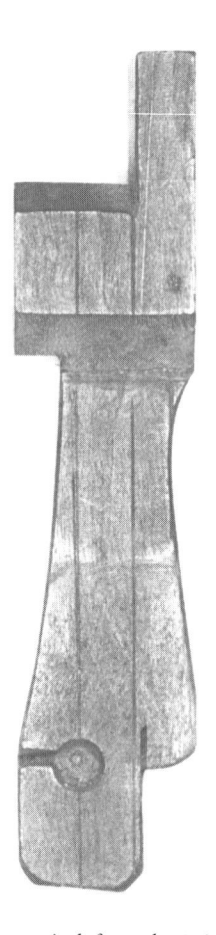

Figure 3.25 Detail of the escapement jack from the 1726 Cristofori piano.

In both types of actions, the tongues, or escapement jacks, move freely, though they are lightly pressed against padded stops by brass wire springs, as is described and depicted by Maffei (*filo fermo d'ottone schiacciato in cima, che tien ferma la linguetta*, I, and *molla di fil d'ottone*, L). In the actions found in the three surviving pianos, the massive secondary levers have been replaced by intermediate levers consisting of slender strips of wood that are hinged to a rail at their distal ends. In these actions, the escapement jack lifts the intermediate lever, which in turn raises the hammer, whereas in Maffei's drawing, the tongue mounted on the intermediate lever lifts the hammer directly. The chief purpose of the secondary lever in both Maffei's drawing and the later surviving actions is to increase hammer speed and displacement relative to the key lever. In the 1720 pianoforte action, for example, the intermediate lever effectively doubles the speed and distance the hammer travels. In the

Figure 3.26 Hammer from the 1722 Cristofori piano.

final tally, about 7 mm of key dip is converted to 31–35 mm of hammer travel.

The tongue in Maffei's drawing and the escapement jack in the surviving actions work in a similar fashion: as the key is pressed, the tongue or jack causes the hammer to rise almost up to the strings; at that point, the rotational displacement of the key lever causes the jack to disengage from the hammer in the 1711 action, or from a small block glued to the underside of the intermediate lever in the later, surviving actions; the hammer then continues up to strike the strings by momentum. The light pressure of the wire spring permits the tongue or jack to slip free, or "escape," as the back section of the key lever continues to travel a bit further, thereby providing a comfortable "after-touch." Most important is the fact that the escapement permits the hammer to fall away from the strings immediately after impact. When the key is released, the jack springs back to its original position and re-engages the hammer (in the 1711 action) or the intermediate lever (in the surviving actions). In both the original and later designs, precise regulation is achieved by adjusting the position of the tongue or jack. This is accomplished by pushing back and forth on the stop (which consists of a small leather pad supported by a thin brass rod [approx. 1.5 mm dia. in the 1720 piano]) with a probe or hook. The intermediate levers of the 1720 Cristofori piano have carved indentations that facilitate insertion of an adjustment tool; those of the 1722 and 1726 pianos are narrower and do not require the indentations.

The hammer pictured in Maffei's 1711 article consists of three parts: the head and shaft (*martello*, both parts labeled O), and butt (*rotella del martello*, labeled N; Figure 3.18). The 1711 hammer head is very much like that found in the 1722 piano (Figure 3.26), in that it is of one piece with a flat striking surface.

Maffei indicates that Cristofori's hammer head is covered with *dante* (buckskin). The 1722 hammer is covered with a thick layer of soft, tawed leather (perhaps buck or sheepskin), with its flesh side out. The hammer heads of the 1720 piano (Figure 3.27) and the 1726 piano (Figure 3.28) are of two parts.

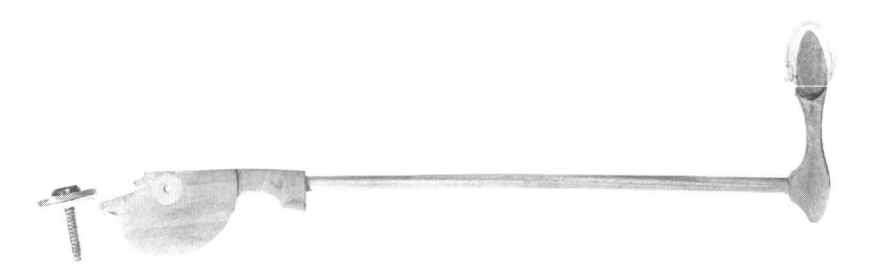

Figure 3.27 Hammer from the 1720 Cristofori piano.

The upper sections of the 1726 hammer heads are hollow cylinders of diagonally rolled and glued paper (about 7 turns, 1.2 mm thick) covered with a single layer of soft white leather. The 1720 hammers presumably once had paper cylinders, but prior to Leto Puliti's description of the action in 1874 (see discussion of Cesare Ponsicchi's 1875 restoration, below), the cylinders were replaced by solid pieces of wood of ovoid section, which in turn were covered with multiple layers of leather.[45] Clearly, it was Cristofori's intention to move away from the incisive tone produced by the narrow quill of the harpsichord towards a more mellow sound (i.e., one having attenuated upper harmonics) made by a soft, broad striking surface. His hammer heads, particularly those consisting of cylinders of glue-impregnated paper topped with soft leather, were clearly designed to imitate the effect produced by fingertips on lute or theorbo strings.

A lost portrait of Bartolomeo Cristofori painted in 1726 (see frontispiece and Chapter 2) depicts him holding a drawing of one of his hammer actions (Figure 3.29).

The musicologist Georg Schünemann examined this painting in 1934 and published a drawing (Figure 3.30) that would appear to be an accurate representation of the action in the painting.[46]

---

[45] A description and drawing of the 1720 piano action in its contemporary configuration (with solid wood hammer heads) was published in 1874 by Leto Puliti: "Allegato F.: Descrizione di un clavicembalo a piano e forte fabbricato in Firenze nell'anno 1720," *Atti dell'Accademia del R. Istituto Musicale di Firenze* 12 (Florence, 1874), pp. 207–216, pl. 2.

[46] Under magnification and transmitted light, the author examined an original 1934 photograph of the painting. Although the hammer head could not be seen in the photograph (it falls into a shaded area), other details, such as the non-inverted wrestplank, key frame, and parts of the action frame could be clearly delineated. The drawing by Schünemann thus appears to be an accurate schematic rendering of the action in the painting. Schünemann, "Ein Bildnis Bartolomeo Cristoforis."

Figure 3.28 Hammer from the 1726 Cristofori piano.

Figure 3.29 Detail from the lost portrait of Cristofori dated 1726 showing him holding a drawing of one of his hammer actions.

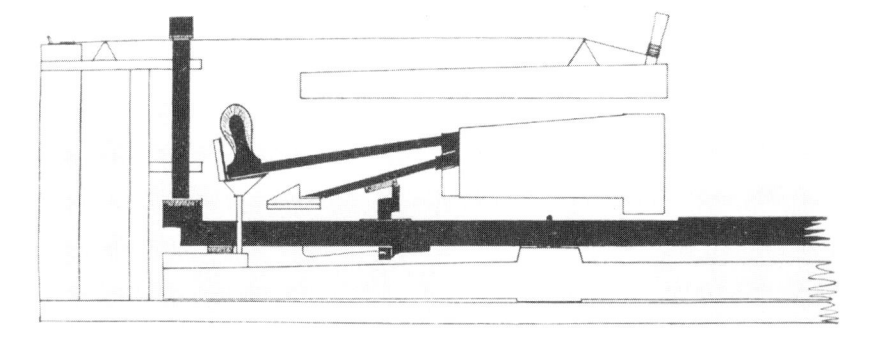

Figure 3.30 Georg Schünemann's schematic recreation of the hammer action depicted in the lost portrait of Cristofori. Georg Schünemann, "Ein Bildnis Bartolomeo Cristoforis," *Zeitschrift für Musikwissenschaft* 16/11–12 (November–December, 1934).

The hammer in Schünemann's drawing appears to be of solid wood with, presumably, a covering of leather. (Surviving photographic reproductions of this painting that have been examined by the author lack sufficient clarity to verify the minute details of Schünemann's reconstruction.)

Maffei states that the hammers were "strung together," suggesting that either wire or a gut cord rather than a metal rod was used to suspend the hammers. All of the hammers of the surviving pianos originally pivoted from metal rods (approx. 1.7 mm dia.) inserted from either end of the action frame. The rods pass through pierced leather bearings in the hammer butts. In the 1720 piano, the bearing consists of two leather disks pressed and glued into a flat-bottomed hole. A conical chamfer on the opposite side of the butt helps guide the pivot rod through the hole when assembling or reassembling the action (for example, after repair). The pivot rods were later removed from the 1720 action and individual leather hinges were installed (again, this modification preceded Leto Puliti's 1874 description and action drawing, which clearly depicts the leather hinges, brass retaining plates, and hand-made brass screws that are still in place today). These individual hinges (most certainly inspired by late-eighteenth- or early-nineteenth-century English and French pianos) may have been installed during an early restoration to facilitate subsequent repairs, as each hammer could be removed separately. With the original system of pivot rods, all of the hammers between the middle and broken one would fall free as the pivot rod was withdrawn. The butts of the 1726 hammers have a semicircular profile (Figure 3.28). The section of the butt behind the pivot rod serves to counterbalance the weight of the shank and hammer head. The butts of the 1720 and 1722 pianos have been cut back somewhat, presumably to lighten the hammer (Figures 3.26 and 3.27).

The hammers pictured in Maffei's drawing pivot from a support rack (*pettine* M, S). The actions of the surviving pianos have a hammer support that consists of a series of wood spacers glued to a platform (Figure 3.31). In this design, each of the spacers must have an accurately positioned hole to guide the pivoting rods.

In the action described by Maffei, the hammers fall back into a network of crossed silk cords (*incrociatura di cordoncini di seta*, P; Figure 3.18) after striking the strings. This delicate (and undoubtedly troublesome) system is not found in the later actions. In the surviving actions, the hammers are actively caught by back checks, which are mounted at the back ends of the key levers (Figure 3.24). The check consists of a brass rod (approx. 1.7 mm dia.), flattened at the top and having a padded upper section of

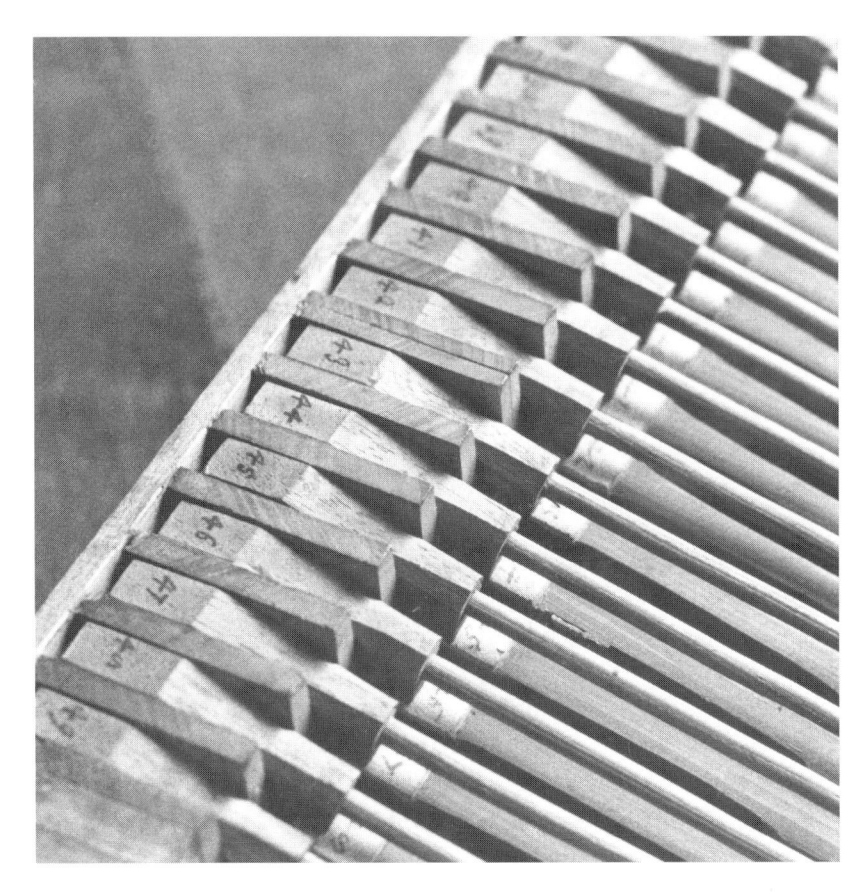

Figure 3.31 Hammer rack of 1722 Cristofori piano showing the wood spacers located between the hammers.

leather. In the 1722 and 1726 instruments, the top section consists of two layers of leather, whereas a single, slit, piece of leather is used in the 1720 piano. This clever device (which is still employed in the modern piano action) plays an important role in controlling the hammer's descent after impact: after the hammer strikes the strings, the back end of the key lever continues to rotate towards the rebounding hammer, and the hammer is thus intercepted by the check; when the key is released, the check releases and the hammer falls free. The primary purpose of catching the hammer is to prevent it from rebounding uncontrollably and possibly re-striking the strings, though by briefly interrupting the hammer's descent, the check also facilitates re-engagement of the escapement mechanism. The back check must be carefully adjusted (by bending the brass rod back and forth) so that it catches the hammer fairly high up. If the check is set too close to the hammer, it may snag the hammer on its ascent. The leather pads in the action of the 1722 piano appear to be original, as they are all of the same, yellow-dyed stock.

The action of 1720 differs in some minor ways from those of 1722 and 1726. In the 1720 action, a shaped wood block mounted below the key forms an extension of the mortise for the escapement jack. The jacks of the 1720 piano are thus longer than those of the other pianos, as they extend considerably below the key (see below). A small block of wood glued to the underside of the shaped piece acts as a bearing point for the jack, and a pad of leather is glued into a notch in this block to prevent the jack from rattling. On the far end of the shaped block is a projection for mounting the brass wire spring. In the 1722 and 1726 actions a smaller, wedge-shaped piece serves as a bearing point for the jack. This piece is also notched and fitted with a leather pad to prevent noise. In these three actions, leather guides are glued above and below the mortise in the key to guide the jack and prevent it from making noise. Because the wedge-shaped piece does not extend beyond the mortise in these actions, the brass wire spring extends directly from the underside of the key lever. Different methods were devised to hook the spring to the escapement jack. In the 1720 action, a slot was cut up through the bottom and a cut made about half way across one side of the jack to a depth sufficient to meet the vertical slot. A small hole was drilled and a wood pin inserted. The spring was inserted through the transverse cut and comes to rest against the wood pin. In the 1722 jack, a hole was drilled through the jack and a saw or knife cut made across the jack, tangent to the hole. A notch was then made in the center of the lower edge created by this cut; the spring rests in this notch. Figure 3.25 shows the escapement jack of the 1726 action. One can observe the flat-bottomed hole and slot. A small notch made in the slot supports the spring.

Another difference between the action depicted in Maffei's articles and the surviving actions can be seen in the damper action. According to Maffei, the damper (*salterello*) rests on the back end of the large secondary lever and retracts from the strings when the key is pressed. The dampers of the surviving actions operate like harpsichord jacks: the damper "jacks" rest on the back end of the key, and the damping material (soft leather in the four surviving actions) is lifted off the strings when the key is pressed. The damper jacks in the four surviving actions are racked in double, leathered guides and are positioned between the bichords. Those of the 1720 piano are of pear and have one or two vertical slits that hold soft leather dampers. The 1722 dampers are of similar design, though they

Figure 3.32 Dampers from the 1726 Cristofori piano. The narrow one is from the treble, the wider one from the bass.

are made of walnut. The 1726 damper jacks have single horizontal slits that permit ribbons of leather to pass through. The leather is stretched up and glued along the sides of wood blocks mounted on the top of the jack (Figure 3.32).

In all of the surviving pianos, the damper jacks are wider in the bass than in the treble, giving the bass dampers more mass to help dampen the heavier strings. There is no provision for raising all of the dampers simultaneously during play. The damper racks can be removed from the piano for repair by unscrewing threaded wooden knobs located at the ends of the racks.

Though the gap spacers of the pianos with inverted wrestplanks interrupt the strike line of the hammers somewhat, they are positioned above the strings (rather than between them), and thus they permit an *una corda* shift. However, the wrestplank design of the 1720 piano (see below) prevents this, as the system of ten struts running across the gap to the belly rail would interfere with a shifting motion. *Una corda* in the 1722 and 1726 actions is operated by grasping the turned knobs on the keyboard end blocks and sliding the entire keyboard and action. It is likely that the *una corda* mechanism was primarily used to isolate one of the strings of each pair to facilitate tuning (that is, the entire keyboard and action was shifted so that the hammers struck only one string of each pair for tuning, and then shifted back so that the second set of strings could be tuned in unison with the first set). We should keep in mind that the "tuning wedge" (which is used by modern piano tuners to isolate strings for tuning) was unknown to harpsichord tuners, who manipulated stop actions to isolate choirs of strings for tuning. Furthermore, it does not make sense that an *una corda* mechanism would have been installed for the purpose of reducing the volume in an instrument that featured dynamic flexibility, and especially one that was inherently soft-voiced.

Case Construction

Generally speaking, the overall layout of the cases, soundboards, bridges, and nuts of Cristofori's 1722 and 1726 pianos is remarkably similar to that of his harpsichords of the same dates. A noticeable exception is that the strike line of the pianos is nearly perpendicular to the spine (which tends to maintain a fairly consistent string length to striking point ratio – around 15:1 in the bass ranging to around 18:1 in the treble of the 1722 piano, for example – whereas Cristofori's harpsichord registers are oriented at a considerable angle, which produces a much wider range of ratios – for the 8′, around 12:1 in the bass diminishing to around 2:1 in the treble of the 1722 harpsichord). The moderately angled strike line in the 1720 and 1726 pianos is due to the progressive lengthening of the hammer shanks from bass to treble. The shanks of the 1722 piano and the *c.* 1725 Gatti-Kraus action are essentially equal in length throughout the instrument's compass (see Table 3.1).

The unusual case design hinted at by Maffei can be better understood by examining Cristofori's three surviving pianos, which appear to confirm the description in Maffei's text. He states that "it should be observed

Figure 3.33 Detail of the 1726 Cristofori piano showing the inverted wrestplank.

that the plank in which the pegs, or iron pins, are fixed that hold the strings, and which, in other harpsichords is under the strings themselves, is above here, and the pins come through it, and the strings are attached to them below." The reason given for this unusual wrestplank orientation is that it provided room for the hammer action. The pianos of 1722 and 1726 do have their wrestplanks in this "inverted" position. In these two instruments, the tuning pins (approx. 4.5–5 mm dia.) pass through the plank (see Figure 3.33) and the strings are wrapped around the parts of the pins that extend below the plank.

In this configuration, the nut is glued to the underside of the wrestplank and consists of a narrow wooden molding with an inlaid brass rod that serves as a bearing for the strings. There are no nut pins to align the strings; instead, the strings pass through thin saw cuts. Cristofori probably developed this clever system to prevent the strings from lifting off the nut during the impact of the hammers. Another advantage of the inverted wrestplank is that it does not pose an obstacle for the hammers; thus, the hammer heads can be kept small and light.

The pianoforte of 1720, on the other hand, has its wrestplank in the conventional orientation, with a pinned nut mounted on its upper surface. This wrestplank consists of two principal sections: an unusually thin

(15 mm) plank of maple veneered with cypress wood that bears the tapered tuning pins; glued and nailed atop this lower piece, and behind the tuning pins, is a stout, trapezoidal plank of poplar that serves to stiffen the entire structure (very much like the yoke found in later English and Viennese grands). Oddly, the grain of the lower section runs in the direction of the strings (and perpendicularly to the heavy plank attached above). The lower section of the wrestplank tapers to 5.5 mm at the gap, and ten gap spacers, ingeniously carved out of the maple plank, extend to the belly rail. Despite the fact that the wrestplank tapers considerably, the hammer heads of the 1720 piano still need to be considerably taller than those of the 1722 and 1726 pianos so that the shanks can clear the wrestplank and nut (see Figures 3.26, 3.27, and 3.28). Surprisingly, the action drawing in the 1726 portrait of Cristofori depicts a wrestplank in the non-inverted orientation with the nut on top. Assuming that this lost portrait was authentic and the date of the inscription is correct, the drawing suggests that Cristofori vacillated between the inverted and non-inverted designs, for he would appear to have abandoned the non-inverted wrestplank by 1722.

The unfortunate choice of grain direction of the lower section of the 1720 wrestplank, compounded by the stout, trapezoidal cross-grained reinforcement that was nailed and glued to it, made it vulnerable to cracks formed by cross-grain shrinkage. In a section of the original wrestplank (Figures 3.34(a) and 3.34(b)) that was removed in the 1938 restoration, one can see the extreme taper, vestiges of the carved gap spacers, and the nail holes used to fasten the upper reinforcement in place.

In that restoration, the original cypress veneer and reinforcement were unglued and reattached to a new lower section, and a new nut was installed in place of the original (see discussion below). Unfortunately, cracks soon developed in the new wrestplank, which had to be reinforced with butterfly-shaped inserts. The more massive, inverted wrestplanks of the 1722 and 1726 pianos also have gap spacers (six in number); however, these arch downward to the belly rail (Figure 3.35) and do not interfere with the strike line.

Maffei states that "the strings are thicker than the ordinary, and, in order that their tension may not injure the soundboard, they are not fastened to this, but somewhat higher." While this description is vague, the three surviving pianos have an unusual hitchpin rail that conforms to Maffei's description. This rail is unusually wide and is suspended over the

The Pianofortes 145

(a)

(b)

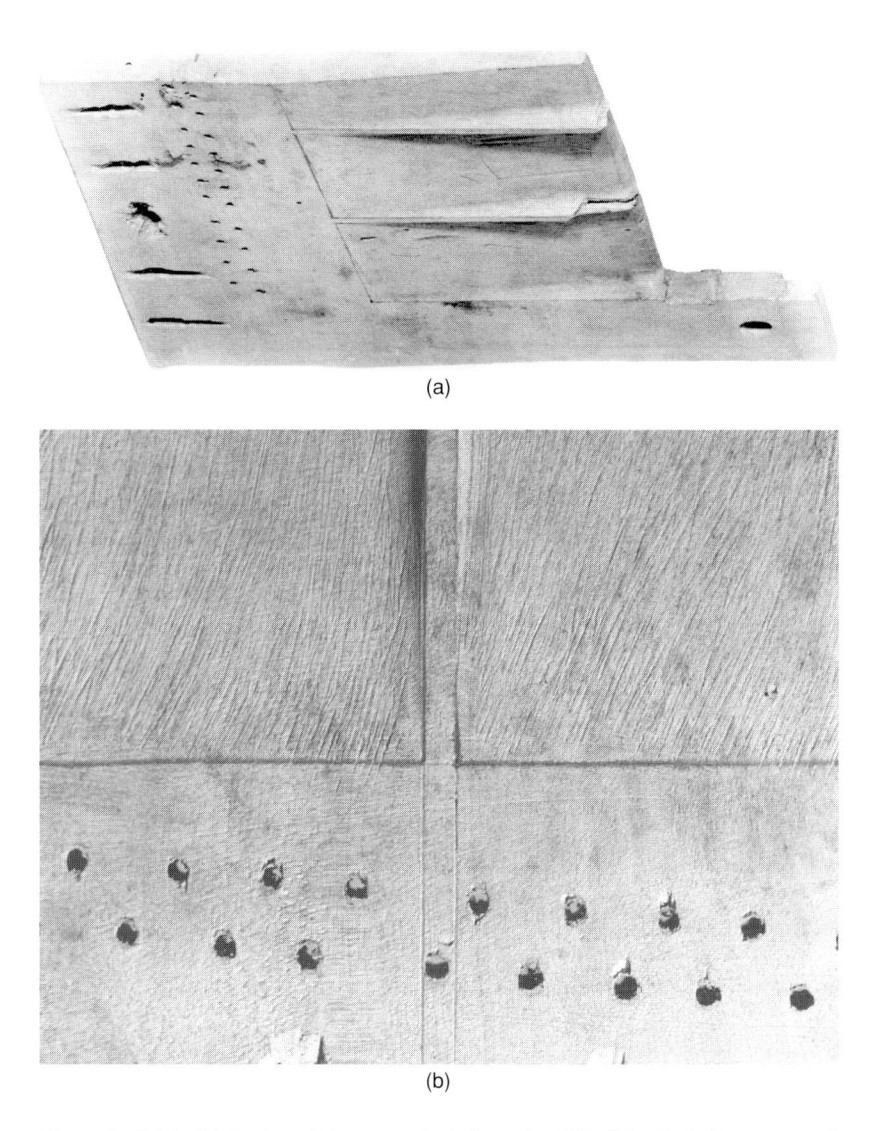

Figure 3.34 (a), (b) Section of the wrestplank from the 1720 Cristofori piano removed during the 1938 restoration. Note the taper, and the carved struts that connected with the belly rail. In 3.34b, note the marks of the rasp used to hollow out the areas between the struts.

soundboard. While examining the 1720 pianoforte using a fiber-optic viewing device and X-ray photography (Figure 3.36), the author discovered two features that he confirmed are also found in the 1722 and 1726 pianos, as well as Cristofori's harpsichords of the same dates: first, the hitchpin rail is attached to a heavy, kerf-bent liner (19 mm thick) that is

Figure 3.35 Gap spacer running from wrestplank to belly rail of the 1726 Cristofori piano.

glued against the inner surface of the bentside and extends from the case bottom to a point above the soundboard; second, a thin internal bentside (approximately 4 mm thick) and a delicate liner glued to it, separated from the outer case and its liner by a narrow spacer (around 4 mm thick), support the soundboard (Figure 3.37).[47]

The diagonal structural braces running from the spine and belly rail to the bentside (Figures 3.38(a) and 3.38(b)) taper into dowel-like projections that pass through (but do not touch) holes of larger diameter drilled in the inner bentside.

The dowel-like projections then lodge in holes drilled in the bentside liner (Figure 3.39). This unusual system of joining the braces to the outer

---

[47] Stewart Pollens, "The Pianos of Bartolomeo Cristofori."

Figure 3.36 X-ray of the 1720 Cristofori piano showing the gap between the inner and outer bentsides. X-ray courtesy of the Objects Conservation Department, The Metropolitan Museum of Art.

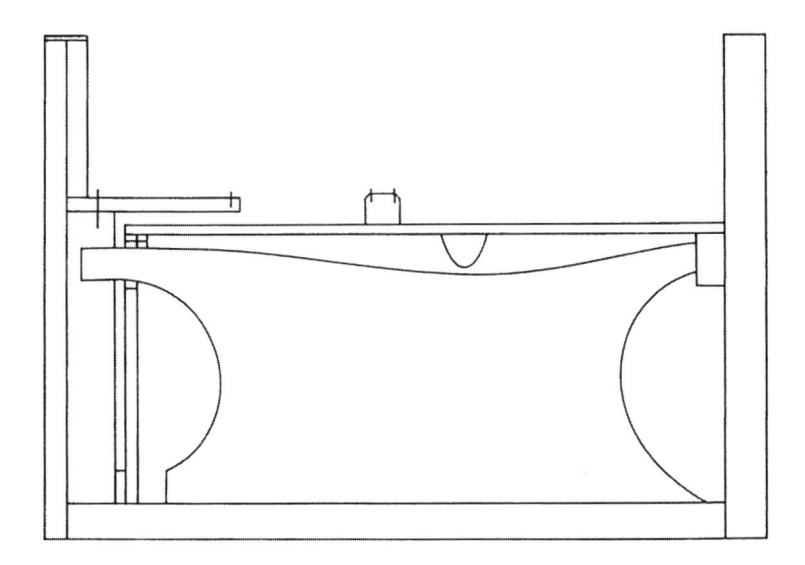

Figure 3.37 Schematic drawing of a cross-section of the 1720 Cristofori piano case showing the hitchpin rail suspended over the soundboard, the internal bentside that supports the soundboard, and a case brace that bypasses the internal bentside and "plugs" into the heavy liner.

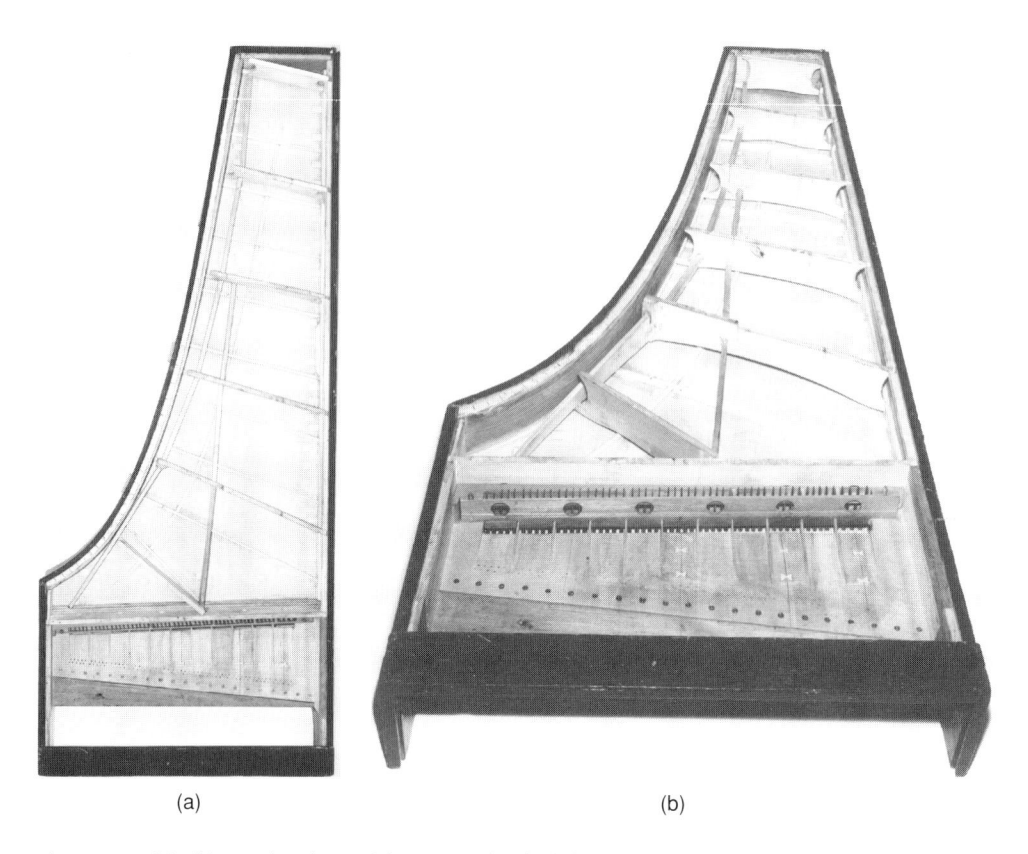

Figure 3.38 (a), (b) Interior views of the 1720 Cristofori piano.

case sides recalls the architectural "flying buttress," as can be seen in the accompanying photographs (Figures 3.38(a), 3.38(b), 3.39, 3.41(a) and 3.41(b)).

The 1720 piano employs six such braces; an X-ray photograph of the 1726 piano reveals nine (Figure 3.40); and the 1722 piano uses seven (see Figures 3.41(a) and 3.41(b)).

In the 1726 piano, the second, third, fourth, sixth, and eighth braces (taken from the treble) resemble those found in the 1720 piano in that they make full contact with the bottom over their entire length, while the fifth, seventh, and ninth braces are similar to those found in the 1722 piano in that they are cut away from the bottom over much of their length.[48] The first brace of the 1726 piano (which may be a modern replacement or

---

[48] I would like to thank Klaus Gernhardt, Universität Leipzig, for sending me copies of the X-ray photographs as well as a drawing of the case interior by Ute Singer made during his 1993 examination of the piano.

Figure 3.39 Detail of interior of 1720 Cristofori piano showing a case brace.

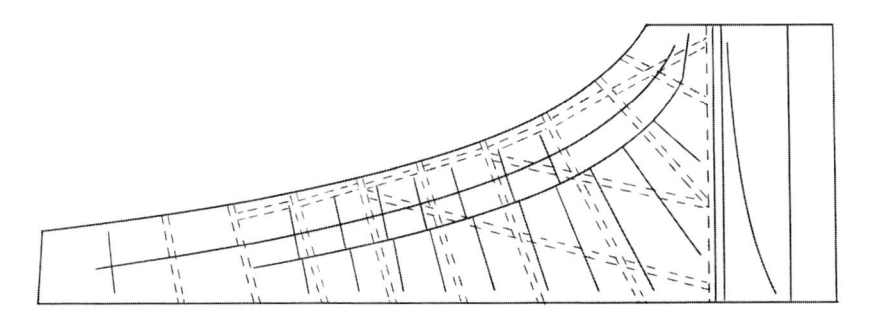

Figure 3.40 Schematic drawing of the bridge, nut, soundboard ribs, cutoff bar (solid lines), case braces and belly rail (dashed lines) of the 1726 Cristofori piano.

(a)

(b)

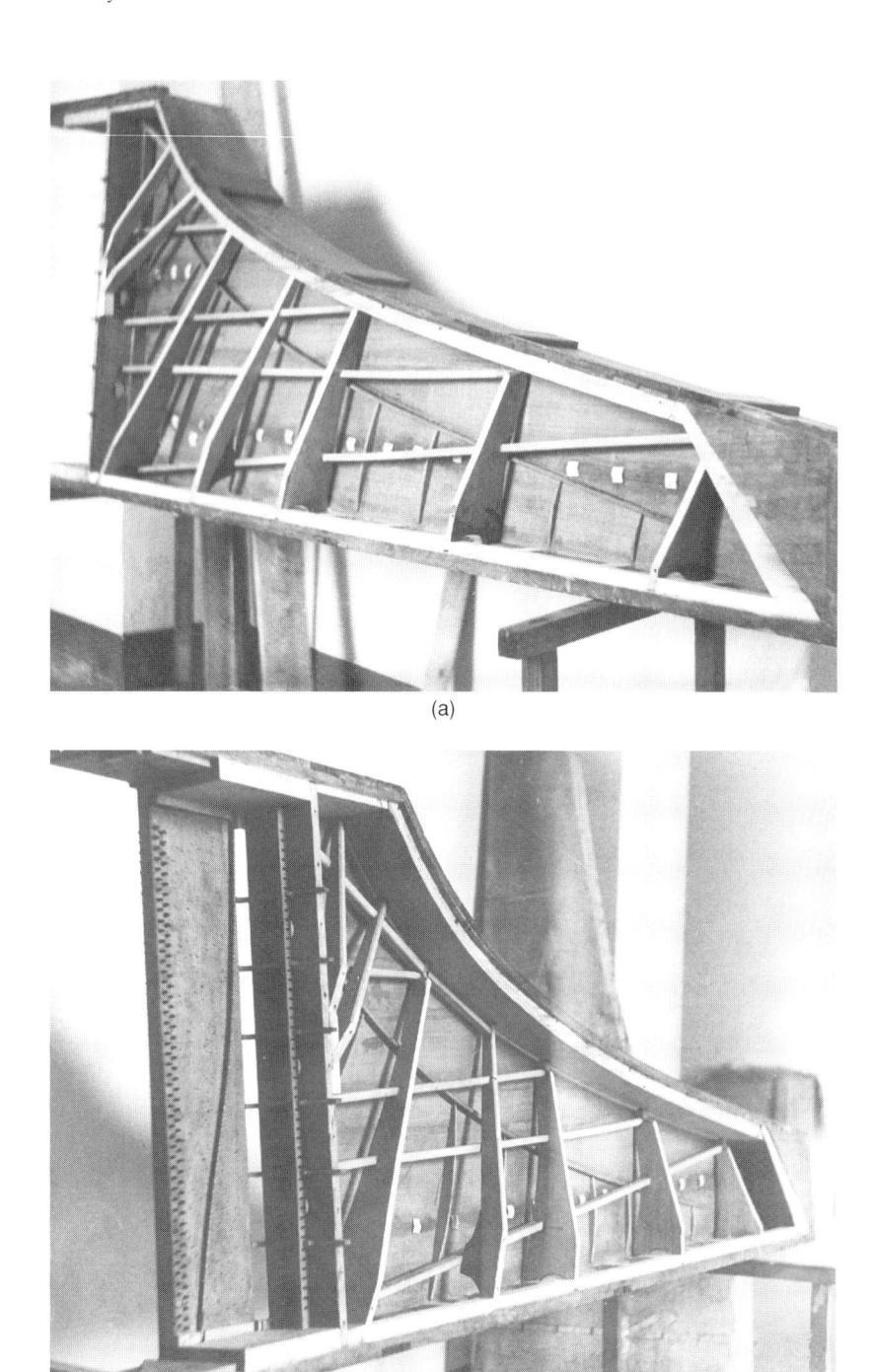

Figure 3.41 (a), (b) Interior views of the 1722 Cristofori piano. Photographs courtesy of the Museo Nazionale degli Strumenti Musicali, Rome.

addition) does not touch the bottom.[49] The 1720 and 1726 pianos use a series of straight stabilizing struts linking the diagonal braces and running essentially parallel to the bentside. Although the outer bentsides appear to be about 12 mm thick above the soundboard, they are actually only around 6 mm thick across their entire breadth, but have a 6 mm lamination glued above the hitchpin rail; a veneer cap conceals this lamination. Below the soundboard, the bentside assembly is quite massive, as it is reinforced by the 19 mm-thick, kerf-bent poplar liner that extends from the broad, overhanging hitchpin rail down to the case bottom. Clearly, the purpose of this unusual construction is to isolate the soundboard (and the delicate bentside supporting it) from the stress-bearing hitchpin rail and outer case. This preserved the properties of the thin-walled bentside that was traditionally used in Italian harpsichords. The overhanging hitchpin rail (which in some respects resembles the cast-iron hitchpin plate in the modern piano) broadens considerably towards the bass, and in addition to the hitchpins, there is a set of bearing pins positioned along its free edge. Maffei states that Cristofori used heavier strings (see discussion below), and so Cristofori cleverly devised this new and extremely complex structure to prevent the case distortion that is so injurious to soundboards.

Maffei, as we may recall, indicated that Cristofori employed some new technique to reduce the elasticity of wood and thus improve the tonal quality of his instruments:

It must not be forgotten that, the universal opinion being that new *gravecembali* are always imperfect, and that they acquire perfection only by age, this maker claims that he can make them in such a manner that they immediately give a sound no less sonorous than old instruments. He asserts that the lack of resonance in new [instruments] arises principally from the property of elasticity, which is retained by the bentside and the bridge; for while these apply force upon the soundboard to retain their shape, the sound remains imperfect, and if this elasticity were to be entirely taken from them before putting them into operation, this defect would immediately be removed, as he finds by practical experience.

Cristofori often used lamination in constructing the outer bentside and case moldings, as well as transverse saw kerfs to facilitate the bending of bridges, cutoff bars, liners, and moldings. Lamination lent shape stability

---

[49] The author observed this fresh-looking brace (as well as a replaced section of the cutoff bar in the treble) after removing a small section of the bottom, which had previously been cut away and loosely replaced. A restoration carried out at the museum is signed inside the piano: Marx/Leipzig/1932. More recently, a continuation of the treble soundboard rib extending from the cutoff bar to the bentside was deemed non-original (it is possibly the work of the 1932 restorer) and was removed.

Figure 3.42 Acoustic holes in the belly rail of the 1720 Cristofori piano.

to curved structures that were traditionally bent by steam or simply held in position by glue, and kerf-bending reduced the stiffness of certain parts that normally bore upon the soundboard and thereby impeded its vibration. These woodworking techniques were not typically employed by other Italian harpsichord makers of the period. Chemical analyses (carried out at the Opificio delle Pietre Dure di Firenze) of the adhesive used in the laminated case sides of the 1690 oval spinet revealed that casein glue was employed in the laminated parts of the case.[50] Casein glue, which is formulated with milk curds and quicklime or potash, has the advantage of being used cold, unlike animal hide glue, which is used hot and must not be allowed to chill while parts are being assembled. Casein glue would have been useful in laminating the broad, curved case sides of the oval spinets, for example, which would have taken considerable time to align and clamp together.

All of the surviving pianofortes have circular openings in the belly rail rather than soundboard roses, confirming Maffei's comments about providing access for air flow beneath the soundboard, as Cristofori believed that an enclosed body of air would stifle soundboard vibration. Such openings would in fact facilitate the soundboard's fundamental vibrational mode and also contribute to lowering the Helmholtz resonance of the instrument's case. The 1720 piano has six openings (Figure 3.42); the 1722 piano, three; and the 1726 piano, four.

The idea of placing openings in the case instead of in the soundboard may not have been an invention of Cristofori's but rather of Girolamo Zenti, as the 1700 Medici musical instrument inventory lists "Un cimbalo di Girolamo Zenti, levatoro di cassa, a due registri principali unison, con fascie e fondo di cipresso, con traversa e scornatura simile con filetto

---

[50] Giancarlo Lanterna and Maria Rizzi, "Adesivi ed elementi metallici," in *Bartolomeo Cristofori: La spinetta ovale del 1690*, p. 92.

d'ebano, senza rosa ma con un solo buchetto nel fondo" (A cembalo by Girolamo Zenti, removable from its case, with two registers at principal unison pitch, with sides and *fondo* of cypress, with jack rail and molding of similar wood with inlaid strips of ebony, without rose but with a single opening in the *fondo*). Here, the term *fondo* may be used in two ways: to denote the soundboard (in this instance a cypress one lacking a decorative rose) and perhaps the case bottom (having a simple acoustical opening), though this may simply be a reference to a harpsichord that was made without a rose, or perhaps that had lost it.[51] It should be mentioned that Maffei refers in passing to a piano made by Cristofori that had a simpler shape, but that was less successful; however, no details were revealed, and no such instrument has come down to us.

In 2000, Kerstin Schwarz (then a restorer at the Musikinstrumenten-Museum der Universität Leipzig – now the Grassi Museum) published a report of her examination of the 1720 piano in which she asserted that this instrument had been shortened at the tail end by approximately 225 mm.[52] She came to this conclusion because of the close proximity to the case's tail of a lid hinge, a vertical brace on the bentside, and an internal buttress. She also noted that the tail angle was square rather than at the 84–86° angle found on the other two Cristofori pianos. However, the critical point of her argument was what she believed to be the uncharacteristic construction of the instrument's tail, which she reported consisted of a single plank of wood, rather than of two pieces with the bass section of the suspended hitchpin rail sandwiched between the upper and lower pieces. A single plank of wood, she posited, was not characteristic of Cristofori's work and therefore must be a replacement, which lent credence to her conclusion that the instrument had been shortened.[53] However, the tail, in fact, is constructed in precisely the same manner as the 1722 and 1726 pianos; that is, it is of two parts with the bass section of the hitchpin rail sandwiched between them. This construction can be readily observed in the unpainted cases of the 1722 piano in Rome and the *spinettone* in

---

[51] In the Medici musical instrument inventories, the term *fondo* is generally used to denote the soundboard of keyboard instruments, though today the soundboard is often referred to as the *tavola armonica* (harmonic table). In Cristofori's day, violin makers such as Stradivari referred to the front, or top, plate of the violin as the *coperto* (cover) and the back plate as the *fondo* (which seems appropriate as this word means "bottom" in Italian). Today, Italian violin makers still use the term *fondo* to denote the back but often use the term *piano armonico* when referring to the front, or table, of the violin.

[52] Kerstin Schwarz, "Bartolomeo Cristofori: Hammerflügel und Cembali im Vergleich," *Scripta Artium* 2 (Leipzig: Fall, 2001), pp. 33–46.

[53] Schwarz, ibid., pp. 35–36.

Leipzig, but the 1720 piano is painted black, and perhaps because of the paint Schwarz failed to observe the exposed edge of the hitchpin rail and incorrectly concluded that the tail consisted of a single plank of wood. As noted above, the 1720 piano is unique among Cristofori's extant pianos in that it was originally made with a compass that extended down to FF, while the other two pianos have four-octave compasses extending down to C. Because of her familiarity with the narrow tails of the C–c^3 compass 1722 and 1726 pianos, Schwarz may have been thrown off by the greater width of the 1720 piano's tail, which was designed to accommodate the five extra bass notes. As can be seen in Table 3.4, the 1720 piano is longer than the 1722 piano, which again runs counter to her argument that the 1720 piano is uncharacteristically short.

What would have been the rationale for shortening the 1720 piano by such a small amount, as Schwarz contends? The most obvious reason would have been the compass shift, which eliminated the five lowest pitched (and presumably, the longest) courses of strings. However, if we consider another of Cristofori's extant instruments that has an extended bass compass – the *spinettone* in Leipzig – we find that the five lowest courses of strings are not mounted on the main bridge but are arranged on three short sections of bridge that run parallel to the end of the main bridge. One of these short bridges supports the BB♭ and BB strings, the next the GG and AA strings, and the last the FF strings. The 1722 piano also uses a short section of bridge running parallel to the main bridge that supports the two bottom courses. Thus, these strings do not extend beyond the C strings mounted on the main bridge. If Cristofori originally mounted the lowest strings of the 1720 piano in a similar fashion, there would have been no need for the case to be any longer than it is today, and consequently no reason to shorten it once the lowest five notes were eliminated. Unfortunately, the replacement of the original soundboard, bridge, wrestplank, and bottom of the 1720 piano in the course of the restoration carried out at The Metropolitan Museum of Art in 1938 (see below) deprives us of the physical evidence needed to resolve this issue.

Soundboard

The soundboards of Cristofori's pianos are of slab-sawn cypress with bridges of rectangular section, double pinned throughout (a feature not generally seen in bridges made prior to those by Cristofori). The bridges of the 1722 and 1726 pianos are of cypress wood and consist of two side-to-side laminations. The 1720 bridge is not authentic, though its kerf-bent

Figure 3.43 Detail of the bass bridge of the 1722 Cristofori piano.

treble section may have been copied from the original. The present bridge is around 15.8 mm high in the bass, 12.5 mm high in the treble, and 9.5 mm wide throughout. As indicated above, the 1722 piano employs a separate bass bridge that runs parallel to the main bridge and carries the bottom two courses (Figure 3.43). The main bridge is 12 mm high by 9 mm wide in the bass and 10 mm high by 9 mm wide in the treble.

The 1726 bridge is 12 mm high by 8 mm wide in the bass, and 11 mm high by 8.5 mm wide in the treble. Where it terminates in the bass, there is a 13 mm-wide lamination that carries the last string. Short bass bridges running parallel to the main bridge and terminal laminations are once again innovations of Cristofori, and can also be found in several of his harpsichords (see above). The mitered bass section of the 1720 piano is probably not an original feature, as it is not found in any original bridges of Cristofori's harpsichords and pianos (the mitered bridge in the ebony harpsichord described above is not original). The 1720 piano's mitered section may have been added when the compass was altered.

Although the soundboard, ribs, cutoff bar, and bridge of the 1720 piano were replaced in the restoration carried out in 1938, a 180 × 362 mm section of the soundboard was preserved.[54] That section was originally glued to the belly rail and shows glue marks of the first treble rib. From evidence provided by glue marks, it is clear that the new treble-most rib mounted on the new soundboard does not lie in the proper angular relationship with the belly rail. The old section of soundboard varies in thickness from 3.2 to 3.7 mm. Soundboard thickness of the 1726 piano varies between 2.9 mm in the treble and 4.0 mm in the middle of the soundboard to the left of the bridge; at the edge it is around 3.5 mm.[55]

Soundboard ribbing differs in the three surviving pianofortes, though all three make use of diagonally oriented ribs and a curved, or segmented, cutoff bar. The 1720 piano has nine stout ribs running parallel to the diagonal case braces (see Figure 3.38a). They are notched and pass over a slender, curved cutoff bar. The 1722 piano has ten ribs (see Figures 3.41a and 3.41b), again running parallel to the case braces, though only up to the cutoff bar. The X-ray photograph of the 1726 piano reveals eleven ribs, ten of which are positioned similarly to those of the 1722 instrument (there is some question whether the eleventh rib in the extreme bass is original). In the 1726 piano seven of the ribs presently have extensions that run from the cutoff bar to the inner bentside. In 1978, the author was permitted to detach the treble section of the 1726 piano's bottom, which had been removed in a restoration carried out around 1970 and then loosely reattached, and he observed that extensions of the three treble-most ribs had been removed because they were believed to be later additions.[56] It was not clear whether the other seven extensions, which were difficult to see, might also be later additions and were left in place because they were inaccessible. From glue marks it was clear

---

[54] Pollens, "The Pianos of Bartolomeo Cristofori," pp. 32–68; and "Curt Sachs and Musical Instrument Restoration," *The Musical Times* 130/1760 (1989), pp. 589–594.

[55] Schwarz, "Bartolomeo Cristofori: Hammerflügel und Cembali," p. 48; and *Erfand Bartolomeo Cristofori mit dem Hammerflügel ein neues Instrument?* (Halle, 1996), p. 19.

[56] Hubert Henkel, personal communication, 1978. Parts (such as sections of soundboard ribs and part of the cutoff bar referred to in the text) that were removed in the *c.* 1970 restoration were unfortunately not saved.

that the removed sections had been lapped against the surviving sections where they fit through notches in the cutoff bar. Unfortunately, the two earlier Cristofori pianos provide conflicting evidence as to whether the rib extensions of the 1726 instrument are original, as the ribs of the 1722 piano do not extend past the cutoff bar, while they do in the 1720 piano (see Figures 3.38(a), 3.38(b), 3.41(a), and 3.41(b); though keep in mind that the 1720 piano's soundboard, ribs, and cutoff bar are modern replacements and may not be accurate copies of the originals). Figure 3.40 shows the soundboard ribbing of the 1726 piano in its present configuration. During the c. 1970 restoration of the 1726 piano, a straight section was added to extend the cutoff bar in the treble. It was not clear whether this awkward strip of wood replaces an original section that may have been removed in the course of an earlier restoration carried out in 1932 by Otto Marx (1871–1964).

While examining the interior of the 1726 piano through the bottom opening, the author noted free-hand marks made with red chalk (*sanguina*) that had evidently been used to lay out the shapes of braces as well as to position notches where case members intersected. Red chalk marks were not observed in the 1720 piano when the author removed the bottom for repairs in the 1980s.

Evidence of Original Stringing

Cristofori evidently recognized that a piano's struck strings must be under greater tension than a harpsichord's plucked strings. This is due to the fact that even a fairly light hammer delivers more energy to a string than does a conventionally voiced plectrum in a harpsichord. This also means that the strings must not be too close to the breaking point, as hammer impact during heavy playing might cause string breakage. To achieve higher tension, Cristofori elected to maintain the scaling that he generally employed in his harpsichords (see Table 3.2) but used heavier gauges of wire, which is noted by Maffei, who wrote that "le corde sono più grosse delle ordinarie" (the strings are thicker than ordinary).

None of the Cristofori pianofortes had original strings when the author examined them in the late 1970s. No gauge markings could be seen on the 1720 and 1722 pianos; however, two marks were visible on the 1726 piano's wrestplank: a "4" at G and what appeared to be a "2" at f#^{2}.[57] It is possible that these were added at a later date because they are not consistent with

---

[57] Kerstin Schwarz, however, interprets the second number as ½ rather than as 2. Schwarz, *Erfand Bartolomeo Cristofori mit dem Hammerflügel ein neues Instrument?*, p. 22.

gauge markings found on Cristofori's harpsichords (see above), which follow the continental style of string gauge numbering in which gauge numbers increase as the wire diameters decrease. An interesting remark on the stringing of the 1720 piano was made by Edward Krehbiel in 1911:

> Seven or eight thicknesses of strings were used in the clavichords, spinets, and harpsichords of the seventeenth century, but the Cristofori pianoforte discloses but three diameters. The evidence adduced by this instrument, however, is not unimpeachable in this respect, since Signor Ponsicchi may have found it necessary, or thought it wise, to alter the stringing so far as diameters were concerned, when he restored it in 1875.[58]

According to Metropolitan Museum of Art records, four diameters of wire were present on the 1720 piano in 1970 when it was restrung in brass by Edwin Ripin, whereas five and seven gauges were measured on the 1722 and 1726 pianos by the author in 1978 (see Table 3.3 below). These gauge transitions may reflect the original string schedule.

Another source, an anonymous manuscript musical dictionary dating from the second half of the eighteenth century, indicates that the Cristofori piano dated 1720 that was then owned by the dictionary's author (which may be the very piano now in the collection of The Metropolitan Museum of Art) was tuned at a low pitch – perhaps an indication that the safety margin provided for Cristofori's harpsichords was insufficient for the needs of his pianos:

> Affinchè la corda che lo esprime si trovi nella sua giusta tensione, se ella è di metallo, deve essere lunga piedi 1., e pollici 6.; ma nel mio gravecembalo co' martellini fatto da Bartolomeo Christofori nell'anno 1720, ed in tuono alquanto grave, la corda predetta di ambedue i registri è lunga piedi 1. pollici 8, e linee fra 6., e 10... Si è inteso del piede di Parigi diviso un 12 pollici, e ogni pollici 12 linee.[59]

(In order that the string rendering it [c^1] has its correct tension, it must, if it is of metal, have the length of one foot six inches; but in my *gravecembalo* with hammers made by Bartolomeo Cristofori in the year 1720, tuned rather low, the aforementioned string in both registers has the length of one foot, eight inches, and between six and ten lines... Here the Parisian foot is meant, divided in twelve inches, and each inch divided in twelve lines.)

As the author of the dictionary states that he had measured Cristofori's pianoforte strings in the old Parisian foot (1 *pied du roi* equals 324.8 mm), the length of c^1 would be 557 mm. This is close to the c^1 string lengths

---

[58] Henry Edward Krehbiel, *The Pianoforte and its Music* (New York, 1911), p. 40.
[59] Bologna, Civico Museo Bibliografico Musicale, H 62; Cervelli, "Noterelle Cristoforiane," p. 164.

found in the three surviving pianos (1720, 567 mm; 1722, 567 mm; 1726, 568 mm).

Provenance of the 1720 Pianoforte

As indicated above, it is possible that the 1720 piano in The Metropolitan Museum of Art in New York is the very same instrument that was owned by the author of the anonymous musical dictionary, for considering the complexity of Cristofori's pianos, it is unlikely that he made more than one in a given year.[60]

In 1889, Mrs. John Crosby Brown, the wife of a wealthy banker and trustee of The Metropolitan Museum of Art, presented her collection of approximately 280 instruments to that institution. She continued to collect and donate instruments to the museum until 1904.[61] In 1894 she asked a cousin, Mrs. Launt Thompson, who was living in Florence, to procure a Cristofori piano for her collection. A group of letters addressed to Mrs. Brown from her cousin describes her attempts to locate one.[62] A letter dated August 5, 1894 mentions that she had found such an instrument and was about to purchase it for 800 francs. Her last-minute reservations, and the dealer's refusal to issue her a certificate of authenticity, caused her to resume her search. We learn from later correspondence that the dealer Leopoldo Franciolini had tried to sell her a fake Cristofori piano, and so it can be assumed that the unnamed dealer in the letter of August 5 was in fact that unscrupulous individual.[63] A letter dated December 7, 1894 mentions a fruitless search in Siena. By June 11, 1895 Mrs. Thompson had located an authentic piano owned by a private party, later revealed as the Martelli family of Florence. The instrument was guaranteed authentic by the Museo del Bargello, where it had been displayed. The letter of June 11 mentions that the piano was valued at 20,000 francs, but that the owner

---

[60] Hubert Henkel's overly optimistic assertion that Cristofori made 400 instruments during his lifetime is clearly at odds with the evidence presented in Cristofori's bills to court, the Medici inventories, and the surviving instruments, which provide corroborating evidence of Cristofori's rather limited production. Henkel, "Cristofori as Harpsichord Maker," p. 15.

[61] For a history of The Metropolitan Museum of Art's Crosby Brown Collection see Emanuel Winternitz, "The Crosby Brown Collection: Its Origin and Development," *Metropolitan Museum Journal* 3 (1970), pp. 337–356; Mary E. Brown and William Adams Brown, *Musical Instruments and their Homes* (New York, 1888); John A. Kouwenhoven, *Partners in Banking* (New York, 1968), pp. 142–154.

[62] These letters are preserved in the Archives Department of The Metropolitan Museum of Art.

[63] For an account of the dealings of Leopoldo Franciolini, and his trial, see Edwin M. Ripin, *The Instrument Catalogs of Leopoldo Franciolini*, Music Indexes and Bibliographies No. 9, ed. George R. Hill (Hackensack, NJ, 1974), pp. 181–199.

was offering it for sale at 8000 francs. Letters dated June 19, July 7, and July 24 deal with matters of payment and shipping. In a document dated November 23, 1895, Diego Martelli reveals how his family came to possess the 1720 Cristofori piano. He states:

This piano was bought by my maternal grandfather, Dr. Fabio Mocenni, years ago, when my mother was about five years old. My mother was born in 1814, and her father must have acquired the piano between 1819 and 1820. It remained always in my grandfather's house until his daughter married my father (the engineer, Charles Martelli). Then she brought that piano into my family and always preserved it, not because of its great value, as she knew nothing of it until very lately, but in memory of her dead father, and because on that piano, when still a child, she learned the first rudiments of music. My mother, by family tradition, knew that this piano had been purchased by her father at a public sale which took place in the Grand Ducal Palace in Siena, by order of the Minister of the Household, of all such things as he considered as worthless and of no use. The discovery that this piano is very valuable was as follows: For the sake of economy during the time that Florence was the Capital of Italy, we rented the first floor of our house, No. 3 Via del Melarancio, and occupied the second floor. In 1872, Signora Martelli (my mother) again changed her apartments from the second to the first floor, and at the moment the transfer of our furniture was taking place from one floor to the other, Prof. Cosimo Conti, a scholar and an intimate friend of ours, came to visit us. The professor was in close correspondence with Cavaliere L. Puliti, who was spending a great deal of his time in trying to discover the origin of the piano, and discovered on it, to his great surprise, an inscription which attested that it had been made by Bartolomeo de Cristoforis. He immediately informed his friend, Cavaliere L. Puliti, of this fact, and he came at once to examine it. Then it was ascertained that it was one of the rarest and most valuable pianos in existence. We at once sent for a tuner and had it put in good condition, and the most distinguished pianists of Italy have since played on it.

Cavaliere L. Puliti published a book on the life of Ferdinando de' Medici, Grand Duke of Tuscany, and in it he treated of the origin of the piano. In this learned book, on page 31, he mentions the piano in possession of my mother [Signora Martelli], which is now your property.

In 1876, Signor Cesare Ponsicchi published a work entitled *Il Pianoforte, sua origine e sviluppo*. In his monograph, Signor Ponsicchi, on pages 26 and 27, speaks at length of this piano and illustrates it at the end of the volume.

I believe that the above information will satisfy your legitimate curiosity, and by indicating to you the above published works to which you may refer for more detailed information, I have complied with your wishes in the matter. I remain, very truly [signed] Diego Martelli, Only son and heir of Ernesta Mocenni, Widow Martelli.[64]

---

[64] The Metropolitan Museum of Art: *The Crosby Brown Collection of Musical Instruments of All Nations – Catalogue of the Keyboard Instruments* (New York, 1903), pp. 305–306.

The keyboard historian A. J. Hipkins reported that Dr. Fabio Mocenni, the grandfather of Diego Martelli, obtained the piano from a tuner in Siena in exchange for wine.[65] The source of Hipkins' statement may well have been Puliti, who mentioned the exchange for wine in 1874.[66] According to Diego Martelli's letter of November 23, 1895, Puliti first saw the 1720 piano in 1872 when it was in the possession of Ernesta Mocenni, Diego Martelli's mother. The story of the piano's acquisition may have been relayed to Puliti by Ernesta Mocenni, and as she was only a generation removed from its purchaser (her father) the detail concerning the exchange for wine may not be apocryphal.[67] Nonetheless, there is the discrepancy between purchasing the instrument at a sale of household items at the ducal palace in Siena and obtaining it from a piano tuner in Siena in exchange for wine. Puliti noted that Violante Beatrice di Baviera (1673–1731), the widow of Grand Prince Ferdinando, was appointed Governatrice della Città e dello Stato di Siena (Governess of the City and State of Siena) by Grand Duke Cosimo III in 1717. This might account for the presence of a Cristofori pianoforte in the ducal palace in Siena, though it would have been commissioned after her departure from Florence. If The Metropolitan Museum of Art's 1720 piano was purchased in the mid-nineteenth century from the ducal palace in Siena, then it may not be the same piano owned by the author of the anonymous, eighteenth-century musical dictionary cited above.

Alterations and Restorations of the 1720 Cristofori Pianoforte

The history of the 1720 piano's restorations is complex. The compass of the instrument has been altered from FF–c^3 (with FF# and GG# omitted) to its present range of C–f^3. That alteration involved shortening the bottom five key levers (FF, GG, AA, $BB^\flat$, BB) and moving them up to the treble (thereby becoming $c\#^3$, d^3, $e^{\flat 3}$, e^3, and f^3), cutting down the trapezoidal key frame in the bass and extending it in the treble, and extending the distal end of all the key levers. When reinstalled in the piano, the keyboard was thereby shifted to the left (the lowest key is now C and occupies the pin numbered "6" on the balance rail). Because most of the keys would then have activated strings a fourth lower than originally intended, the rebuilder made an effort to re-establish the original scaling. This was accomplished by moving the bridge closer to the nut. As can be seen in

---

[65] *Grove's Dictionary of Music and Musicians*, 5th edn (London, 1954), s.v. "Cristofori."
[66] Puliti, *Della vita del Ser.^{mo} Ferdinando dei Medici*, p. 209.
[67] These letters are preserved in the files of the Department of Musical Instruments, The Metropolitan Museum of Art, New York.

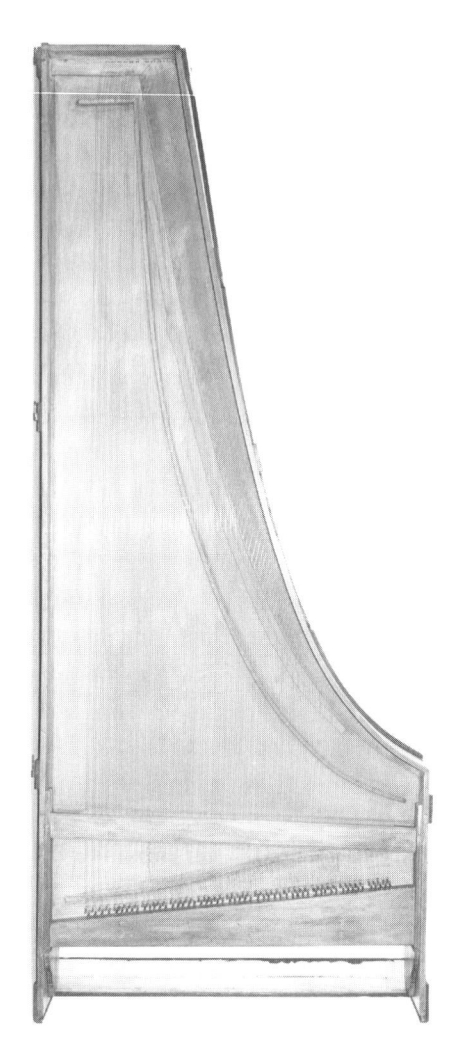

Figure 3.44 Plan view of the 1720 Cristofori piano showing present non-original position of the bridge, which veers away from the bentside.

Table 3.2, this operation appears to have been relatively successful, as the string lengths of the 1720 piano are fairly consistent with the 1722 and 1726 pianos, though the bridge of the piano now awkwardly veers away from the bentside rather than following its curve (Figure 3.44).

Because the re-establishment of the original string lengths involved moving only the bridge, the ratio of striking point to string length is not as Cristofori intended: the striking points are now further from the nut. Another problem resulting from the compass alteration can be observed in an X-ray photograph of the soundboard, in which one can see that the newly positioned bridge intersects the cutoff bar. This compass alteration might have taken place in the latter part of the eighteenth century, when a top note of c^3 would have become restrictive, though compasses extending to f^3 were used as far back as the early sixteenth century.

Glued to the underside of the hammer rack is what appears to be an old balance rail that has a peculiar compass of FF, GG, AA–b^2. The inexplicable lack of c^3 suggests that this structure may have nothing to do with the history of the 1720 piano.

The Cristofori piano of 1720 bears the following inscription on the hammer rack: Restaurato l'Anno 1875 / da Cesare Ponsicchi / Firenze (Restored in the year 1875 by Cesare Ponsicchi in Florence). The extent of this restoration is not known, though the marginally earlier date of publication (1874) of a drawing by Puliti – which shows the replacement wood hammer tops, leather hammer hinges, metal screw plates, and screws – would suggest that Ponsicchi was not responsible for those alterations.[68] These changes were apparently influenced by the design of late-eighteenth-century English or French square pianos, which used leather-hinged hammers. It is possible that these hinges were installed when the compass was altered.

The 1720 piano underwent an unfortunate restoration at The Metropolitan Museum of Art in 1938. Having fled the Nazis, and living in New York at the time, the eminent musicologist and museum curator Curt Sachs was called in by the museum as a consultant, and under his direction a piano technician named Wolfgang Staub undertook the work.[69] In the course of this restoration, the following parts were removed and replaced with new ones: soundboard (Figure 3.45), lower section of the wrestplank (Figures 3.34(a) and 3.34(b)), nut, bridge, case bottom, strings, hammer coverings, and damper material. Photographs made prior to this intervention reveal an essentially intact soundboard with a few long cracks that were certainly repairable. Museum officials unfortunately fell prey to the typical modern piano technician's rebuilding recommendation calling for the installation of a "new block and board." As indicated above, a small section of the soundboard (Figure 3.45) and the original lower section of the wrestplank were saved.

In 1970 Edwin Ripin, Assistant Curator of Musical Instruments, restrung the piano entirely in brass (in accordance with the theory that short-scaled Italian keyboard instruments were intended for brass) and

---

[68] Puliti, "Allegato F.: Descrizione di un clavicembalo a piano e forte," pl. 2.
[69] Pollens, "Curt Sachs," pp. 589–594.

Figure 3.45 Fragment of the original soundboard that was removed from the 1720 Cristofori piano in the 1938 restoration.

replaced the leather on the damper register. Repairs to certain action parts were made as well.[70] With brass wire, the piano cannot be tuned much above a minor third below A = 440 without encountering string breakage. This breakage may be due to unintended changes in scaling below c that occurred during the eighteenth-century compass alteration or the more recent replacement of the bridge and soundboard, though it could also indicate that the piano was originally strung in iron wire through most of its compass. It may not be a coincidence that all three Cristofori pianos were discovered strung with similar gauges of iron wire (with brass in the bass). Though most of Cristofori's harpsichords and pianofortes exhibit the same "short" scaling (in fact, the approx. 285 mm c^2 string length found in most of Cristofori's instruments is close to the theoretical transition point between ferrous and brass scaling), his bills to court indicate that he ordered *aciero* (steel) wire on two occasions in 1690, and *ottone* (brass) wire once in 1693, though none of the bills in which the wire is listed deals specifically with payment for the construction of a new harpsichord, spinet, or pianoforte.

During my tenure as conservator of musical instruments at The Metropolitan Museum of Art (1976–2006), I was responsible for maintaining the 1720 Cristofori piano in playing condition for use in numerous concerts, gallery demonstrations, and recordings. Among the first of these events that I was involved with was a sequence of LP recordings of sonatas

---

[70] White epoxy glue, presumably used by Mr. Ripin, can be seen in certain repairs to hammer heads and shanks.

by Lodovico Giustini (the first music composed expressly for the newly invented piano; see Chapter 4) performed by Mieczysław Horszowski in 1977–1978 and 1979–1980.[71] For these recordings I made minor repairs, regulated the action, and tuned, as I did on innumerable occasions in the years that followed. In the 1980s, the Spanish harpsichordist and organist Antonio Baciero played several gallery concerts on the Cristofori piano and was involved in a recording project that unfortunately was never issued. In the late 1990s, Eva and Paul Badura-Skoda made a ninety-minute video entitled *The History of the Pianoforte: A Documentary in Sound* that includes a Scarlatti sonata played on the Cristofori piano by maestro Badura-Skoda.[72] Following the filming, Badura-Skoda played a recital at the museum on the Cristofori piano and several other early pianos in the collection. For that grueling event, which involved many hours of rehearsals, filming, and performance, I made a replica keyboard and action for the Cristofori piano, not only to relieve the original mechanism of stress and wear, but also to restore (in the copy) some of the features that had been altered in the original parts. As indicated above, the shape of the hammer butts had been changed to accommodate individual leather hinges rather than the original pivot rods. With this alteration, the hammers were positioned further from the points of contact with the intermediate levers than they had been with their original pivot points. This required the application of greater force on the keys in order to propel the hammers towards the strings. Furthermore, the back quadrants of the semicircular hammer butts that had originally served to counterbalance the weight of the hammer shanks and heads now contributed to the effective mass of the hammers, further increasing the touch weight. In addition to restoring the original pivot rods and hammer-butt shape in the replica action, I replaced the later ovoid wood hammer-head tops covered with multiple layers of leather with rolled paper cylinders topped with a single layer of leather, as found in the 1726 piano (Figure 3.46).

These freshly made parts worked very well – the action was lighter, and the tone brighter and more harpsichord-like. Unfortunately, all of this work was in vain, as Badura-Skoda preferred the mellower tone of the original, and the greater key weight rendered the "original" more

---

[71] These historic LP recordings were unfortunately never transferred to CD format. The first of the Giustini recordings was issued in 1978 by The Metropolitan Museum of Art (MMA L1803); this recording was subsequently reissued by Titanic Records in 1980 (TI/78, vol. 1) along with a second volume (TI/78, vol. 2).

[72] Eva Badura-Skoda, *The History of the Pianoforte: A Documentary in Sound*. Video tape (Bloomington, Ind.: 1999).

Figure 3.46 Reconstruction of a hammer for the 1720 Cristofori piano made by the author showing the original shape of the hammer butt, the leather bushing for the pivot rod, and the cylindrical hammer head. Compare against Figure 3.28, which shows alterations, including the leather hinge (rather than use of a pivot rod) and the replaced top of the hammer head, with multiple layers of leather.

conducive to his style of playing. In 1999, I prepared and tuned the Cristofori piano for a CD recording made by Martin Souter, who played music by Carlos de Seixas, Antonio Soler, and Domenico Scarlatti.[73] The last recording that I worked on was Susan Alexander-Max's CD recording of Domenico Zipoli's *Sonate d' Intavolatura per Organo e Cimbalo*, which were recorded in 2002, again using the original action.[74] As indicated above, the low pitch used in the recordings is due to the brass wire stringing that was installed around 1970 and scaling anomalies (perhaps due to alterations and restoration work carried out in the past) that prevent the pitch from being raised much above a minor third below modern pitch (the low pitch is not maintained for conservation purposes).

The Gatti-Kraus Action

During the late eighteenth and nineteenth centuries, the public sales of household materials from the former ducal residences in Florence provided tremendous opportunities for private collectors. One such collector was Baron Alessandro Kraus, a Florentine who amassed an important group of musical instruments. His collection, sold to Wilhelm Heyer of Cologne in 1908, became part of the University of Leipzig's instrument collection in 1926. The Kraus collection included five of the ten extant keyboard instruments made by Bartolomeo Cristofori: the 1726

---

[73] Martin Souter, *Keyboard Classics: The 1720 Cristofori Pianoforte*, issued in 1999 by Classical Communications (CCL CD005).

[74] Susan Alexander-Max, *Sonate d' Intavolatura per Organo e Cimbalo* by Domenico Zipoli, issued in 2004 by Albany Records (Troy 669).

Figure 3.47 The "Gatti-Kraus" Cristofori piano action. Museo degli Strumenti Musicali del Conservatorio "Luigi Cherubini" di Firenze.

pianoforte, 1726 harpsichord, 1722 harpsichord, *cembalo traverso*, and 1693 oval spinet. In 1997, a direct relation of Alessandro Kraus, Baron Giulio Gatti-Kraus, presented a pianoforte action, said to have been made by Bartolomeo Cristofori, to the Museo degli Strumenti Musicali del Conservatorio "Luigi Cherubini" di Firenze (it had previously been offered for sale to The Metropolitan Museum of Art, but was turned down). In Florence, the action was promptly put on display at the Galleria dell' Accademia with many of the important instruments from the "Cherubini" collection, including Cristofori's ebony harpsichord, and the subsequent addition of the 1690 oval spinet that was "rediscovered" in 2000.

The "Gatti-Kraus" pianoforte action (Figure 3.47) is not listed in Alessandro Kraus' *Catalogo della collezione etnografico-musicale Kraus in Firenze* (1901), so we may assume that it was acquired after publication of that comprehensive catalog.[75]

The catalog does include such sundries as a collection of spinet, psaltery and harpsichord strings, tuning wrenches, a model of the 1711 Cristofori piano action, a group of piano hammers demonstrating the process of applying felt to the striking surface, as well as models of an upright piano action made by Carlo Perotti of Turin and a model of the *Melopiano* by Caldera.[76] Most of these miscellaneous parts, tools, and models were transferred with the Kraus collection when it was sold to Wilhelm Heyer,

---

[75] Baron Giulio Gatti-Kraus did not provide any documentation regarding the provenance of the Cristofori action.
[76] A. Kraus, Jr., *Catalogo della collezione etnografico-musicale Kraus in Firenze* (Florence, 1901), p. 20.

though one of the action models listed by Kraus does not appear in Georg Kinsky's 1910 catalog of the Heyer collection.[77]

In 1932, an exhibition was held in Florence honoring the life of Bartolomeo Cristofori. An article by A. Parrini published in 1934 indicates that the 1932 exhibition included a group of action models illustrating the development of the piano mechanism as well as "an original keyboard of the celebrated maker" ("una tastiera originale del celebre costruttore").[78] The action models, bearing the stamp of Cesare Ponsicchi, were probably those that are today part of the Florence conservatory collection and presently exhibited alongside the Gatti-Kraus action attributed to Cristofori in the Galleria dell'Accademia in Florence. Though the Parrini article is somewhat vague, "the keyboard of the celebrated maker" may be the first mention of the Gatti-Kraus Cristofori piano action.

The dating of the design of the Gatti-Kraus piano action is fairly straightforward, as there are three extant pianos dated 1720, 1722, and 1726, as well as a diagram and description of an earlier action configuration published in 1711. The lost portrait of Cristofori, signed with the initials A. T. F. and dated 1726, shows him holding a sketch of a hammer action, which provides additional evidence for dating the Gatti-Kraus action design.

As indicated above, the drawing of Cristofori's piano action published by Scipione Maffei in the *Giornale de' letterati d'Italia* 1711 shows a massive, intermediate lever pivoted about one-third from its far end and a jaw-bone shaped projection at the near end of the intermediate lever that supports a spring-loaded escapement jack. This system is not found in the actions of the three surviving pianos or the Gatti-Kraus action. In the surviving actions, the massive intermediate lever is replaced by a thin strip of wood that is hinged at its far end. The spring-loaded escapement jack is mounted in a mortise in the key lever, and the return spring is positioned on the underside of the key. When the key is pressed, the escapement jack raises the intermediate lever, which in turn lifts the hammer, and the damper is raised directly by the back end of the key. In the 1711 action drawing, as well as the actions of the 1720, 1722, and 1726 pianos, the escapement occurs when the jack slips off a stepped contact point on either the hammer butt (1711) or the intermediate lever (1720–1726). The

---

[77] Kinsky, *Musikhistorisches Museum*, vol. I, p. 199.
[78] A. Parrini, "Nel secondo centenario della morte di Bartolomeo Cristofori," *Atti dell' Accademia del Regio Conservatorio di Musica Luigi Cherubini* 58 (Florence, 1934), p. 44, cited in Gai, *Gli strumenti musicali della corte medicea*, p. 170, n. 26.

light action of the escapement spring allows the jack to glide past the fallen hammer or intermediate lever as the key returns. Thus, sometime between the writing of Maffei's article and the making of the 1720 piano, Cristofori redesigned his piano action. The Gatti-Kraus action is clearly of the later type, using the light, hinged intermediate lever and an escapement jack mounted in the key mortise.

Cristofori also experimented with two different wrestplank configurations. In Maffei's 1711 article, he states that "it should be observed that the plank in which the pegs, or iron pins that hold the strings are fixed, and which, in other *gravecembali*, is under the strings themselves, is here above, and the pins come through it, and the strings are attached to them below, there being more need of space underneath to admit the whole of the mechanism of the key action." This type of wrestplank, which I have termed an "inverted" wrestplank (see above), is used in the 1722 and 1726 pianos. In the 1720 piano and the action pictured in Cristofori's portrait, the wrestplank is in the conventional position.

There is a difference in the design of the hammers in pianos made with the two types of wrestplank. In pianos with inverted wrestplanks (1722 and 1726), the hammer heads are short, varying in height between 12 mm and 24.5 mm (the variation principally depending upon whether the hammer heads consist of simple, leather-faced blocks of wood or leathered paper cylinders poised on top of wood blocks). In the piano with non-inverted wrestplank (1720), the hammer heads must be considerably taller, between 46.5 mm and 49.5 mm, in order to clear the wrestplank. The Gatti-Kraus action has the shorter hammer heads (22.5 mm), consisting of leathered paper cylinders glued to wood blocks, similar to those found in the 1726 piano. Therefore, it appears that the Gatti-Kraus action was designed for use in a piano with an inverted wrestplank. This conclusion is supported by the presence of notches in the hammer frame that would have provided clearance for a nut glued to the underside of the wrestplank.

The escapement jacks and most other action parts of the Gatti-Kraus action are more similar in detail to those employed in the 1726 action than to the earlier examples. In fact, the only significant dimensional difference between the 1726 action and the Gatti-Kraus action is the length of the intermediate lever: the Gatti-Kraus intermediate levers are about 4 mm shorter than those in the 1726 piano.

Between the years 1720 and 1726, Cristofori altered certain aspects of case design that had direct bearing on key-lever length. The 1722 piano case is somewhat shorter and considerably narrower at the tail than that of the 1720 piano; this is principally due to the reduced compass of the 1722 piano. Like the 1722 piano, the 1726 piano had a four-octave compass, though the 1726 piano had a considerably longer case (2366 mm, as opposed to 2257 mm and 2224 mm for the 1720 and 1722 pianos, respectively). Though the string lengths of the 1720, 1722, and 1726 pianos are similar through most of the keyboard range, the 1726 piano exhibits less foreshortening in the lowest octave, requiring the longer case. Other structural matters, such as the front-to-back dimensions of the wrestplank and position of the nut, and the depth of the key well, are reflected in the length of the keys. The key levers of the 1720 piano are considerably longer than those of the 1722 and 1726 pianos due to the presence of the stiffening plank mounted on the wrestplank, which increases the wrestplank's overall depth. The 1720 piano keys range in length from 443 to 407 mm, whereas the 1722 keys are 332–320 mm and the 1726 keys are 344–336 mm in length. The key levers of the Gatti-Kraus action are 343–333 mm – almost identical in length to those of the 1726 piano. Thus, from the configuration and measurements of the action parts, the Gatti-Kraus action appears to have been designed to fit into an instrument with key-well dimensions similar to those of the 1726 piano.

Regarding the workmanship quality of the mechanical parts found in Cristofori's pianos, there is considerable variability from one instrument to another. The marked differences in the details of construction strongly suggest that different hands were at work. From archival records preserved in Florence, we know that Cristofori employed assistants and cabinetmakers to help with the construction of new instruments. These assistants and cabinetmakers are unnamed in his bills to the Medici court, so we do not know whether he employed the same individuals on each occasion. Furthermore, as the piano action was very much under development throughout his working life, Cristofori apparently never standardized the dimensions of the action's mechanical parts or constructed jigs to ease their fabrication. Even in his last-known piano, the outlines, sawn and cut incisions, and positions of drilled holes in each action part are marked out with a scratch gauge. Though the use of a scratch gauge guaranteed uniformity in these parts, evidence of its use demonstrates the laborious task of fabricating the hundreds of parts that comprised each piano action. Considering Cristofori's position in the Medici court, it is unlikely that he had to make all of these parts himself, though oddly, no bill from Cristofori survives for the construction of a pianoforte. Nevertheless, we must assume that he employed assistants in their construction, just as he did for the harpsichords he made for the court. One assistant, Giovanni Ferrini, went on to make pianos himself (see below), so we may conclude that he assisted Cristofori in this work. Thus, in evaluating the authenticity of Cristofori's piano action parts, we must relax our critical standards somewhat.

Despite the dimensional variability and different standards of craftsmanship evident in the actions of the three surviving Cristofori pianos, it would appear that the Gatti-Kraus action is essentially a reconstruction fabricated around a few authentic parts. Even before disassembling the Gatti-Kraus action, the author noted that the two sections of the action frame do not fit together properly. There are positioning dowels projecting from the cheeks of the key frame that are intended to fit into holes in the frame that supports the intermediate levers and hammers (henceforth referred to as the hammer frame). Though the dowels engage the holes, the lower projecting edge of the front rail of the hammer frame interferes with the seating of the frame. The hammer frame does not sit squarely on the key frame, as it does in the three actions of the surviving pianofortes. More importantly, the escapement jacks are not in proper alignment with the padded contact points on the intermediate levers; consequently, this action was never functional. Superficially, the hammer and key frames themselves are convincing, as they have all of the requisite construction points required for them to fit into the case of a Cristofori piano. For example, the cheeks of the hammer frame have two sets of notches at their far upper ends. These would have been needed to clear the damper register (which was mounted up against the belly rail) and the nut (which was mounted to the underside of the wrestplank in the 1722 and 1726 examples). The key frame also has two mortises cut in the front rail that were used in the *una corda* mechanism. One might think that a copyist fabricating an action independently of a piano case would have neglected to make these notches and mortises. However, other important details suggest that the maker of this action was oblivious to one important feature found in all of Cristofori's pianos: the presence of six to ten gap spacers located between the wrestplank and belly rail. In the 1722 and 1726 pianos, these gap spacers interrupt the string band slightly and require the hammers to be spaced accordingly in the hammer rack. It is clear that the Gatti-Kraus hammer rack was never designed to accommodate such gap spacers.

On the lowest key lever of the Gatti-Kraus action, there are score lines marking out the key heads, mortises for the escapement jacks, holes for the escapement springs, holes for the back checks, balance pin mortises, etc. However, none of the other keys has these score marks, which is unusual, as such marks were generally scribed across the entire plank used to make the keyboard. By scribing clear across the plank, the balance pins

Figure 3.48 Two key levers from the Gatti-Kraus action showing score lines on one key and their absence on the other.

and various mortises and drilled holes would line up nicely after the keys were sawn from the plank. Such scribe lines are found running across the key levers of all of Cristofori's pianofortes. The lack of the scribe lines on forty-eight of the forty-nine keys comprising the Gatti-Kraus keyboard strongly suggests that all but one key (the lowest one) are not authentic (Figure 3.48).

The ebonized key block at the bass end of the keyboard exhibits chatter marks more closely resembling those made by a motorized thickness planer or jointer than a hand plane, which would indicate that that part could not have been made in the eighteenth century. There was no evidence of the use of power machinery in the fabrication of the other parts.

Upon closer examination, many other discrepancies were discovered between the lowest key and all of the others: the boxwood key coverings of the upper forty-eight keys are not neatly made, and the arcades are poorly cut in comparison to the finely cut arcade of the lowest key. The hole for the escapement spring of the lowest key passes completely through the key (as in the actions of the three surviving pianos); however, in the top forty-eight keys, the holes do not extend through the top surface. The little blocks of wood used to retain the escapement jacks of the top forty-eight keys are crudely formed with a file or rasp, whereas the retaining block mounted on the lowest key is more carefully fabricated. Furthermore, the top forty-eight blocks have been stained to match the color of the block mounted on the lowest key – a sure sign that they are not original. Though the top forty-eight escapement jacks are closely modeled after the jack mounted in the lowest key lever, there are slight differences in shape and tool marks as well as in the color of the wood (Figure 3.49).

As can be seen in Figure 3.50, the back check and escapement-jack stop wires of the top forty-eight keys are slightly smaller in diameter (1.6 mm) than those mounted on the bottom one (1.7 mm). The diameter of the back check wire of the lowest key of the Gatti-Kraus action is similar to that of the three extant pianos.

The hammer-head cylinders of the first and last hammers of the Gatti-Kraus action differ from the others in that they are composed of many layers of diagonally rolled and glued paper, whereas the other hammer-head cylinders are made up of only two layers of pre-laminated paper without the diagonal-ply construction (Figure 3.51).

The diagonal-ply construction is found in the Leipzig Cristofori piano, and thus it would appear that only the top and bottom hammer heads of the Gatti-Kraus action are original. Furthermore, the leather facing on these two hammer heads is consistent in terms of thickness and grain orientation (flesh side out) with that of the surviving instruments. The middle forty-seven hammer heads of the Gatti-Kraus action have the hair side out, which is uncharacteristic.

The hammer butts of the Gatti-Kraus action lack the circular score marks that are observed in the butts of the three surviving pianos. These score marks were probably made to facilitate the uniform shaping of these parts. In addition, the hammer butts lack the leather pivot-wire bearings found in all of the other Cristofori actions.

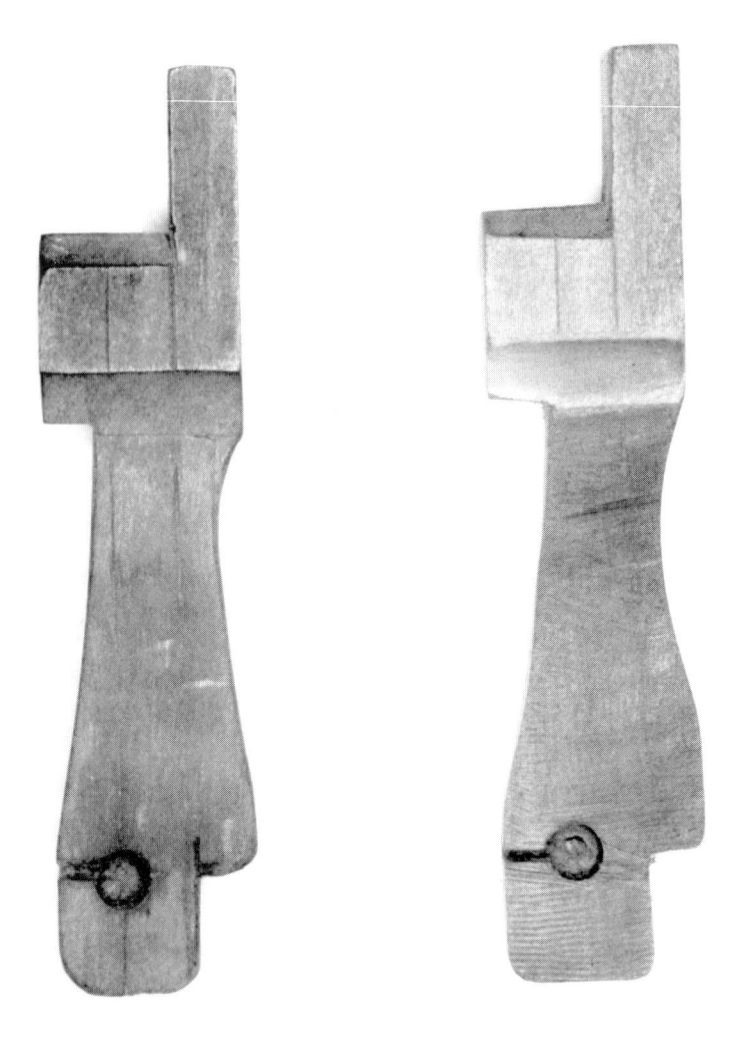

Figure 3.49 Two escapement jacks from the Gatti-Kraus action showing discrepancies in workmanship and tool marks.

The damper rack is not original, and perhaps only four of the dampers are original (Figure 3.52). These four were likely treble dampers, as Cristofori used wider dampers in the bass.

It is therefore reasonable to conclude that this action is either a "reconstruction" employing unrelated action frames, one original key lever, two original hammer heads, and four original dampers, or a fake. As we do not know the intention of the maker of the non-original parts or of the individual who commissioned or sold it, it is impossible to say. Who might the maker have been? We know that Cesare Ponsicchi was making action models in 1875 and later, but his models on display at the Galleria dell'

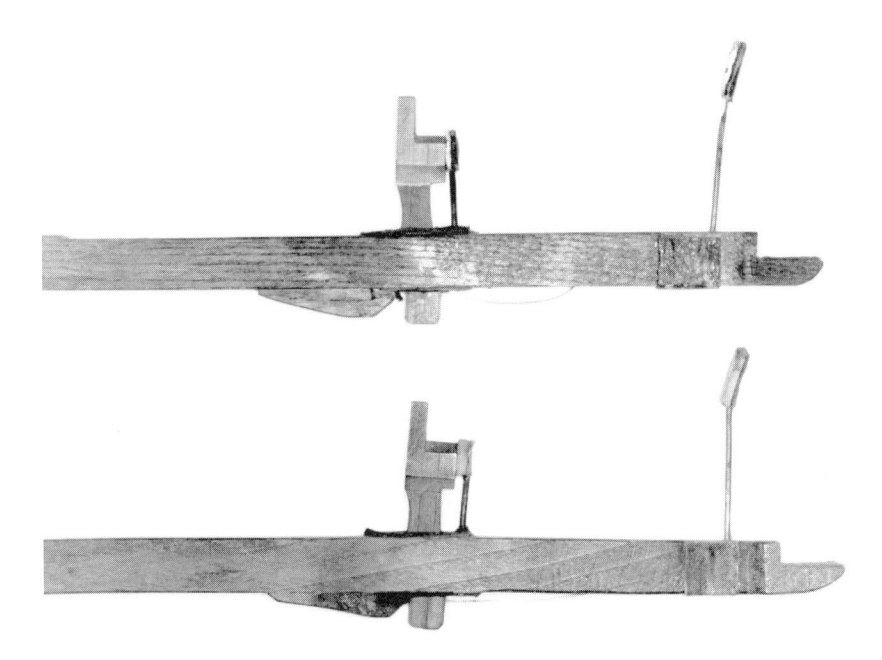

Figure 3.50 Two escapement mechanisms from the Gatti-Kraus action showing discrepancies in workmanship and tool marks.

Figure 3.51 Two hammer heads from the Gatti-Kraus action showing discrepancies in workmanship. Note differences in the cylindrical hammer head and leather covering.

Figure 3.52 Two dampers from the Gatti-Kraus action showing discrepancies in workmanship.

Accademia appear much cruder than the later parts in the Gatti-Kraus action. The 1711 piano action model mentioned in the 1901 Kraus catalog may be the one first exhibited in Florence in 1876 and listed in the exposition catalog written in that year.[79] In 1897, the Regio Istituto Musicale di Firenze also ordered such a model, along with several others, and this commission is mentioned in an article on the *pianoforte verticale*,

---

[79] Cesare Ponsicchi, *Il Pianoforte – sua origine e sviluppo – (con tavole) e rassegna dell'esposizione storica fatta nello stabilimento musicale Brizzi e Niccolai nell'occasione delle onoranze a Bartolommeo Cristofori inventore del pianoforte* (Florence, 1876).

which was written the same year by Cesare Ponsicchi.[80] It is not known whether these three publications are describing the same 1711 model, but the fact that this model is not listed in Georg Kinsky's 1910 catalog of the Heyer collection suggests that it was not included with the rest of the Kraus collection and thus remained in Florence.

Cesare Ponsicchi (a piano tuner and restorer working for the Regio Istituto Musicale di Firenze) restored the 1720 piano in 1875, just prior to its exhibition in 1876 at the Stabilimento Musicale Brizzi e Niccolai in Florence. His close familiarity with the 1720 piano enabled him to make what appears from a photograph in the Kinsky catalog to have been a faithful working model of that action. This model (catalog no. 215, Heyer collection[81]) is not a model of the action of the 1726 piano from the Kraus collection (as stated by Kinsky); rather, it is a model of the action found in the 1720 Cristofori piano now in The Metropolitan Museum of Art. The exhibition at the Brizzi and Niccolai piano showroom consisted of approximately thirty-three objects (mostly pianos), including both the 1720 pianoforte (then privately owned by Mrs. Ernesta Mocenni) and the 1726 pianoforte from the Kraus collection. We know that Ponsicchi restored the 1720 Cristofori piano, as he states so in an inscription on the instrument's hammer rail; however, it is not clear what work he did, and much of it may be obscured by a later restoration undertaken at The Metropolitan Museum under the direction of Curt Sachs in 1938. The gross alteration of the hammer action, which involved removal of a section of wood from each hammer butt, removal of the hammer pivot rods, and the independent suspension of each hammer from leather hinges, appears to have been carried out earlier than 1875, as the hinges, hand-made brass screws, and brass retaining plates appear in an earlier engraving published by Leto Puliti in 1874.[82]

Seven action models made by Cesare Ponsicchi are owned by the Florence conservatory collection and are described by Vinicio Gai in his 1969 catalog.[83] These action models are critical in establishing whether Ponsicchi fabricated parts of the Gatti-Kraus action. Some have voiced the opinion that the hammer leathers in the Gatti-Kraus action are the same as those used in the models. The author does not share this opinion.

---

[80] Cesare Ponsicchi, "Il primo pianoforte verticale," *La nuova musica – pubblicazione musicale – mensile* 11/24 (1897), pp. 3–4. A later edition of this article, published as a booklet in Florence in 1898 entitled *Il primo pianoforte-verticale*, neglects to mention this commission.
[81] Kinsky, *Musikhistorisches Museum*, vol. I.
[82] Puliti, "Della vita del Ser.^{mo} Ferdinando dei Medici," pp. 210–214, table 2.
[83] Gai, *Gli strumenti musicali della corte medicea*, p. 20.

178   *Cristofori's Extant Instruments*

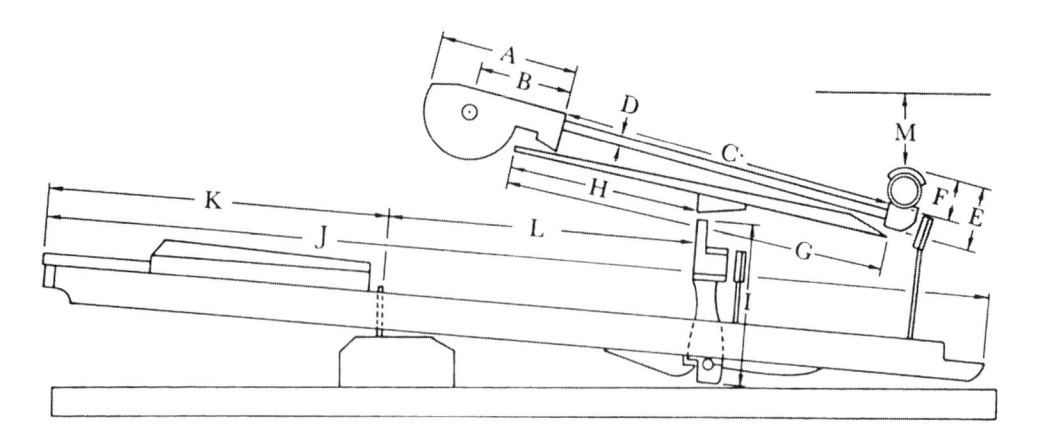

Figure 3.53 Schematic drawing of Cristofori's hammer action.

Table 3.1 Measurements of Cristofori's hammer actions (all measurements in millimeters)

Part	1720 piano	1722 piano	Gatti-Kraus*	1726 piano
A	52	48	49	48.5
B	34	33	33	32.5
C Bottom note	123.5	116	118	121
C Top note	112.5	115	118	117.5
D	4	4	4	4
E Bottom note	49.5	12	22.5	24.5
E Top note	46.5	13.5	22.5	19.5
F Bottom note	19	4†	15	18.5
F Top note	16	3.5†	15	12
G	113	130	131	135.5
H	54	68	70	69.5
I	62	59	57	56.5
J Bottom note	443	332	343	344.5
J Top note	407	320	333	336
K Bottom note	165	124	121	123.5
K Top note	159	123	122	125
L Bottom note	148	110	113	116
L Top note	135	110	108	111
M (approx.)	31–35	35–36		22–23

* See discussion of the Gatti-Kraus action below.
† Denotes thickness of leather.

Table 3.2 String lengths/striking points of Cristofori's pianos (all measurements in millimeters)

Note	1720	1722	1726
C	1885/163.5	1816/121	1961/133
F	1879/151.5	1585/110	1608/108
c	1100/134.5	1120/89	1125/73
f	838/118.5	849/71	841/57
c^1	567/91.5	565/43	568/38
f^1	429/73	412/31	422/29
c^2	286/51	281/21	280/17
f^2	214/39	210/14	213/13
c^3	151/26	141/8	142/7
f^3	122/19		

Table 3.3 Wire diameters found in Cristofori's pianos

1720 piano*

C–B	Brass	.020″ (.51 mm)
c–b^1	Ferrous	.0175 – .018″ (.44 –. 46 mm)
c^2–b^2	Ferrous	.0125″ (.32 mm)
c^3–f^3	Ferrous	.010″ (.25 mm)

1722 piano[†]

C–C#	Brass	.55 mm
D–A	Brass	.50 mm
A#–e	Ferrous	.40 mm
f–e^1	Ferrous	.35 mm
f^1–c^3	Ferrous	.306 mm – .31mm

1726 piano[‡]

C–F#	Brass	.456 mm – .50 mm
G–A#	Ferrous	.42 mm
B–d	Ferrous	.40 mm
d#–a#	Ferrous	.372 mm
b–$a\#^1$	Ferrous	.34 mm
b^1–$f\#^2$	Ferrous	.326 mm
g^2–c^3	Ferrous	.278 mm

* Wire measured by Edwin Ripin in 1970 prior to his restringing in brass. Original measurements are in thousandths of an inch.
[†] Wire measured by the author in 1978.
[‡] Wire measured by the author in 1978.

Table 3.4 Case and keyboard measurements of Cristofori's pianos (all measurements in millimeters)

Piano	Length	Width	Height	Three-octave span
1720	2286	956	235	496
1722	2257	813	215	497
1726	2390	801	205	491

Inscriptions Found on the Pianos

BARTHOLOMÆVS CRISTOPHORI PATAVINVS FACIEBAT FLORENTIÆ [plus the Roman numeral for the date]

The 1722 piano lacks the N in PATAVINVS, but has a line drawn above and bridging the I and final V.

One must also consider the fact that Ponsicchi worked on the 1720 piano and had first-hand knowledge of the 1726 piano. The author brought small samples of the hammer and damper leathers from the 1720 piano to Florence for comparison with the action models and the Gatti-Kraus action. Those samples bear no similarity to the leathers employed in the models or the Gatti-Kraus hammers and dampers, and thus they provide no evidence that Ponsicchi constructed the non-original action parts of the Gatti-Kraus action. Curiously, the hammer leathers of the Gatti-Kraus action appear to show impact marks from string pairs. This is inexplicable, as the action does not appear to have ever functioned due to the lack of coordination between key frame and hammer frame. However, there remains the distinct possibility that at some point these upper and lower sections belonged to two separate actions that differed slightly in their overall dimensions, and were once installed in pianofortes.

Cristofori's Assistants

Certainly the first makers to fully understand the construction of Cristofori's pianofortes were those who assisted him: Giovanni Ferrini (*c.* 1700–1758), and at the end of his life, Anna and Margherita del Mela. An entry in an anonymous eighteenth-century manuscript dictionary from the library of Padre Giovanni Battista Martini (1706–1784) contains a fortuitous entry about Cristofori's primary assistant, Giovanni Ferrini:

Ferrini Giovanni morto in Fiorenza sua Patria nell'anno 1758. Fu celebre artefice di gravecembali, ne fu ottimo resarcitore, fu il migliore de' due scolari di Bartolomeo Cristofori da Padova; costruì gravecembali a martelli sulla norma, e invenzione del suo maestro con aggiungervi in più il poterli suonare ancora a penne, e fu il primo a costruire gravecembali con le corde di minugia mosse dal suolo posto ne' saltarelli invece della penna, e producenti una qualità di voce simile a quella dell'arpa.[84]

(Ferrini Giovanni died in Florence, the city of his birth, in the year 1758. He was a celebrated maker of harpsichords, and also an excellent restorer, and the best of two students of Bartolomeo Cristofori of Padua; he constructed *gravecembali* with hammers in the conventional way, according to the invention of his teacher, to which was added the possibility of playing with quills, and was the first to construct keyboard instruments with gut strings and sole leather in the jacks rather than quills, that produce a sound quality similar to that of the harp.)

The *Encyclopédie méthodique* (Paris, 1791) contains a short passage on Ferrini confirming that he made gut-strung harpsichords.[85]

Giovenale Sacchi's biography (1784) of the famed *castrato* Farinelli (Carlo Broschi, 1705–1782) indicates that one of his keyboard instruments was a pianoforte made by "Ferrini Fiorentino, allievo del Bortolo Padovano, primo inventore del piano, e forte."[86] (Ferrini of Florence, pupil of Bartolo[meo Cristofori] of Padua, first inventor of the pianoforte.) Eleven years earlier, Charles Burney reported having heard Farinelli play that very same instrument and gave its date as 1730.[87] In fact, the first item listed in a posthumous inventory of Farinelli's musical instruments (dated May 2, 1783) is

Un Cembalo a martellini con suo piede torlito, e copertoro di badana rosa; detti martellini servono per piani, e forti; il detto Cembalo denominato Raffaele d'Urbino hà per Autore Giovanni Ferrini Fiorentino, firmato ... L 1000.[88]

(A *cembalo* with little hammers with its turned stand, and cover of red fabric; the said hammers serve for soft and loud; the said *cembalo* named "Raffaele d'Urbino" is signed by its maker Giovanni Ferrini *Fiorentino* [of Florence] ... 1000 *lire*.)

---

[84] Civico Museo Bibliografico Musicale di Bologna, collection H 62, miscellaneous writings of Padre Martini, vol. c; also cited in Luigi Ferdinando Tagliavini and John Henry van der Meer, *Clavicembali e spinette dal XVI al XIX secolo: Collezione Luigi Ferdinando Tagliavini* (Bologna, 1986), pp. 186–200; Luigi Ferdinando Tagliavini, "Giovanni Ferrini and his Harpsichord 'a penne e a martelletti'," *Early Music* 19/3 (1991), pp. 399–408.
[85] *Encyclopédie méthodique: Musique*, vol. I (Paris, 1791), p. 286.
[86] Giovenale Sacchi, *Vita del cavaliere Don Carlo Broschi* (Venice, 1784), p. 47.
[87] Charles Burney, *The Present State of Music in France and Italy* (London, 1773; facs. repr. New York, 1969; repr. Cambridge, 2014), p. 210.
[88] Sandro Cappelletto, *La voce perduta: vita di Farinelli, evirato cantore* (Turin, 1995), p. 209.

In these passing references, important information is revealed about the eighteenth-century Florentine keyboard instrument maker Giovanni Ferrini. We learn that he made pianofortes after the design of his master, and if the date of Farinelli's instrument is correctly given by Burney, Ferrini was signing instruments prior to the death of Bartolomeo Cristofori, implying that he had become a fully capable and independent instrument maker within the lifetime of his teacher. Furthermore, we discover that Ferrini was the better of two students of Bartolomeo Cristofori, though unfortunately the second individual is not named. Rosario Profeta suggested that the other of Cristofori's two students was either "Geronimo da Firenze" or "Gherardo of Padua"[89] (though virtually nothing is known of these makers), but it is more likely that Cristofori's second pupil was a member of the del Mela family (see below).

As we have learned in Chapter 2, Giovanni Ferrini was mentioned as a major beneficiary in Cristofori's first will, drawn up in 1729. In that will, Cristofori bequeathed all of his tools to him; however, a new will made in 1730 granted a greater share (including his tools and instruments) to Anna and Margherita del Mela and only a perfunctory sum of money to Ferrini. This might indicate that the relationship between the two men had deteriorated in the year that transpired between the drawing up of the first and second versions of the will, a period in which Cristofori was ill and had come to rely upon members of the del Mela family for assistance (see below). During that time, Ferrini may have asserted his independence and begun to support himself through commissions for new instruments, including the piano that he constructed in 1730, which came into the possession of the Queen of Spain and ultimately Farinelli (see below).

As mentioned earlier, Cristofori never joined the instrument makers' guild, the Università di Por San Piero e dei Fabbricanti, nor did Giovanni Ferrini until 1736 (he remained on the guild's rolls until 1749).[90] Ferrini's sons Giuseppe and Filippo carried on their father's profession as instrument makers and restorers. Ducal archives indicate that the sons primarily worked on harpsichords, and it is not until 1784 that there is a record that they worked on a piano – one that was situated at the Casino di San Marco, formerly a Medici residence once occupied by Francesco Maria de' Medici, the younger brother of Grand Duke Cosimo III.[91]

---

[89] Rosario Profeta, *Storia e letteratura degli strumenti musicali* (Florence, 1924), p. 272.
[90] ASF Università di Por San Piero e dei Fabbricanti, no. 208, fols. 184r–184v; no. 209, fols. 214r–214v.
[91] Ferrari and Montanari, "Giovanni, Giuseppe e Filippo Ferrini," pp. 29–47.

During the last years of Cristofori's life, and following his death, Giovanni Ferrini continued to make the pianos and the large *spinettoni* with multiple registers that had been invented by his master. In the surviving signed works of Ferrini, it is clear that they retained many of Cristofori's mechanical and structural innovations. Since the last-known instrument bearing Ferrini's inscription is dated 1755, his activity is documented to within three years of his death in 1758. It is also probable that Ferrini had assisted Cristofori in fabricating the myriad parts that constituted the piano's hammer action, and so knew the mechanism intimately. Cristofori had well-formulated ideas about acoustics, which were manifested in unusually designed case and soundboard structures (see Chapter 3). Ferrini evidently took no shortcuts in constructing instruments based upon Cristofori's designs, and his few surviving instruments retain the action and case designs of his master. Ferrini's combination pianoforte/harpsichord (described below) exhibits several clever mechanical features that testify to his own ingenuity.

Giovanni Ferrini's Combination Pianoforte/Harpsichord

This extraordinary double-manual keyboard instrument (Figure 3.54) is inscribed IOANNES FERRINI FLORENTINVS FECIT ANNO MDCCXLVI.

It is probable that this is the same combination pianoforte/harpsichord that is referred to in the anonymous eighteenth-century dictionary cited above, as it is unlikely that Ferrini made many instruments of such enormous complexity. The combination pianoforte/harpsichord has a compass of 57 keys, GG–e^3 with GG# omitted, and two manuals. The three-octave span is 492 mm; natural key length is 120 mm, and accidental length 83.5 mm; natural score-line spacing is 4.2mm. Natural key plating is boxwood; accidentals are black-stained wood with ebony overlay.

The lower manual controls two registers of harpsichord jacks and the upper manual operates a piano mechanism similar in design to that of Cristofori. Both the harpsichord jacks and the piano hammers activate the same pairs of strings, and thus the harpsichord jacks must be oriented on either side of the paired unisons with the front register of jacks plucking to the left, and the back register plucking to the right. This requires the back sections of the harpsichord's key levers to make an abrupt S-curve to accommodate the far row of jacks. In order for the piano hammers to function independently of the harpsichord's jacks, the jacks are not fitted with dampers; separate damper "jacks" are mounted in a register situated

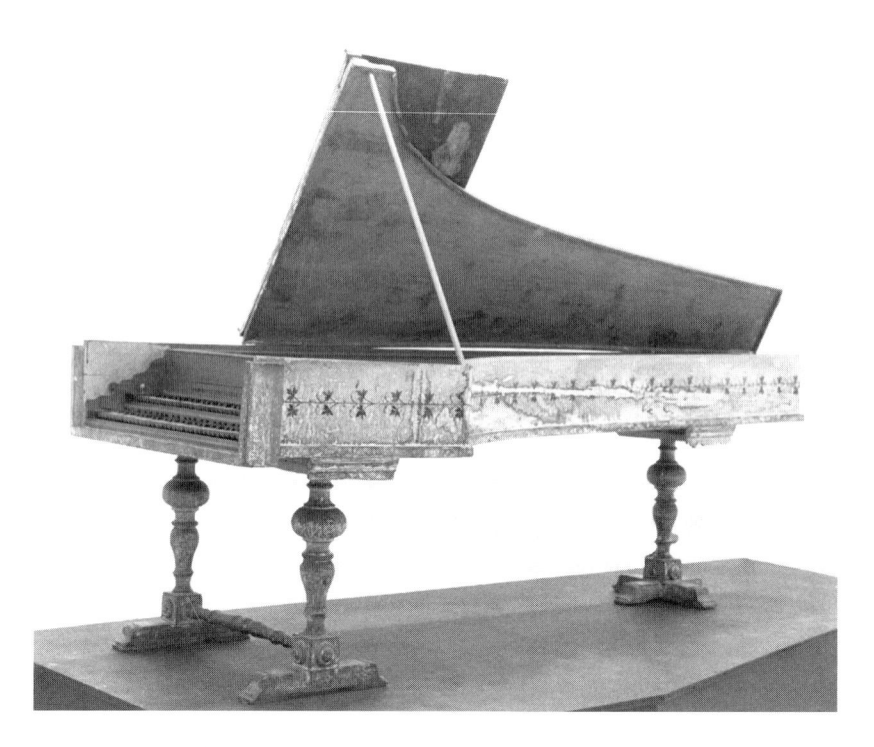

Figure 3.54 Pianoforte/harpsichord by Giovanni Ferrini, Florence, 1746; collection of Luigi Ferdinando Tagliavini, Bologna.

between the hammer strike line and the harpsichord jack registers. The manuals of the Ferrini pianoforte/harpsichord are positioned slightly out of alignment; this is due to the fact that the hammers must be aligned directly under the strings, while the right row of jacks (plucking to the left) stands to the side of the strings, as do its respective key levers.

The harpsichord jack registers are immovable in this instrument, and registration changes are made by sliding the keyboard toward or away from the player, a method similar to that found in Cristofori's *cembali traversi* and oval spinets. In Ferrini's pianoforte/harpsichord, the harpsichord keyboard locks in either position by spring-loaded catches in the form of accidental keys located in the keyboard end blocks; again, a feature borrowed from Cristofori's spinets. Once these catches are pressed, metal flaps are lifted, grasped, and used to slide the keyboard forward or backward. When the lower keyboard is pulled towards the player, both 8′ registers are activated; when it is pushed away from the player, the front row of jacks aligns with grooves cut in the backs of the keys so they are not lifted when the keys are pressed. In that position, only the back 8′

jacks operate. As with the *cembali traversi*, this clever, though awkward system requires two hands to operate it, and thus it was probably used to isolate choirs of strings for tuning rather than for changing harpsichord registration while playing. Because the jacks are not fitted with dampers, the front row of jacks cannot hang from damper cloths when they are disengaged and are thus suspended over grooves in the key levers; instead, leather pads glued to the sides of these jacks prevent them from slipping into the grooves when the keyboard is pushed back. The fixed upper and lower jack slides are not leathered (in contrast to the damper guides). The walnut harpsichord jacks have brass leaf springs positioned in front of the tongues in the style of Cristofori (i.e., they push back on extensions of the tongues that rest below the pivot points, rather than pushing forward on the backs of the tongues above the pivot points). Like Cristiofori's, the fronts of the jacks are routed to provide recesses for the leaf springs so that they do not project and interfere with the jacks' up and down motion. The jacks' tongues are mortised for quill plectra.

There is no coupling arrangement between the upper keyboard (which operates the hammers) and the lower keyboard (which operates the harpsichord jacks), so the combined effect of striking and plucking the strings was not an option for the player, though the player did have the option of shifting from one manual to the other for contrast. From their appearance, the front row of jacks (Figure 3.55) would appear to dog-leg, but they do not function that way – they narrow at the bottom so that they can align with the grooves in the keys.

The damper jacks are racked between the paired unisons in upper and lower leathered slides, and they are dog-legged to operate from either keyboard. The damper material is a ribbon of leather running through a narrow slot and up across blocks mounted on top of the thin jack, a system similar to that employed in the 1726 Cristofori piano (Figures 3.32 and 3.56).

The hammer action of the Ferrini pianoforte/harpsichord is very much like that found in Cristofori's pianofortes (see Table 3.7), though it has been compressed in order to share space with the harpsichord keyboard beneath it – in a case that is only about one centimeter deeper than the 1720 piano. Consequently, action parts such as the escapement jacks and back checks have been reduced in height (Figure 3.57). Sections of the key levers beyond the escapement jack mortises have also been cut down to provide a recess for the intermediate levers.

Like Cristofori's 1720 piano, Ferrini's pianoforte/harpsichord employs a wrestplank in the conventional, non-inverted position (see above), and

Figure 3.55 Jack from the pianoforte/harpsichord by Giovanni Ferrini. Note the leaf spring positioned at the front of the jack, an unusual feature borrowed from Bartolomeo Cristofori. This jack is not dog-legged to the upper manual – the narrow section at the bottom sits on a platform on the back of the key when the rank of jacks is on, and aligns with a notch in the key when the rank is off.

Figure 3.56 Damper from the pianoforte/harpsichord by Giovanni Ferrini. The dampers dog-leg and operate from both the harpsichord and piano keyboards.

Figure 3.57 Detail of key lever from the piano keyboard of Ferrini's pianoforte/harpsichord showing the vertically attenuated escapement jack and the cutout area that allows the intermediate levers to sit lower and more compactly.

consequently these two instruments have similarly configured hammer heads, which consist of two parts: a tall, lower section (needed to clear the non-inverted wrestplank) and an upper section consisting of a rolled cylinder of paper (replaced with wood in the 1720 Cristofori piano though preserved in his 1726 piano) or parchment (used in Ferrini's 1746 combination instrument) that is leathered on top. The hammer heads of the Ferrini instrument have been altered at some point: wooden cores were inserted within the parchment cylinders (Figure 3.58), most likely to restore their shape or to provide greater strength or mass to produce a stronger tone.[92]

There are many other similarities between Cristofori's and Ferrini's hammer actions. For example, Ferrini's hammer butts closely resemble the semicircular design developed by Cristofori; these hammer butts have leather bearings inset on one side of the pivot holes and beveled depressions on the opposite side to facilitate insertion of the pivot rod. Both makers positioned the escapement-jack spring below the key lever, used leather-hinged intermediate levers of similar design, and constructed their back checks in a similar fashion (they consist of a narrow metal rod padded with leather). Clearly, Ferrini closely modeled these and other parts after those designed by Cristorfori.

---

[92] The wooden cores, observed by the author when he examined the instrument in 1989, were subsequently removed during a restoration, according to the instrument's owner, Luigi Ferdinando Tagliavini. Tagliavini, "Giovanni Ferrini and his Harpsichord 'a penne e a martelletti'," pp. 399–408.

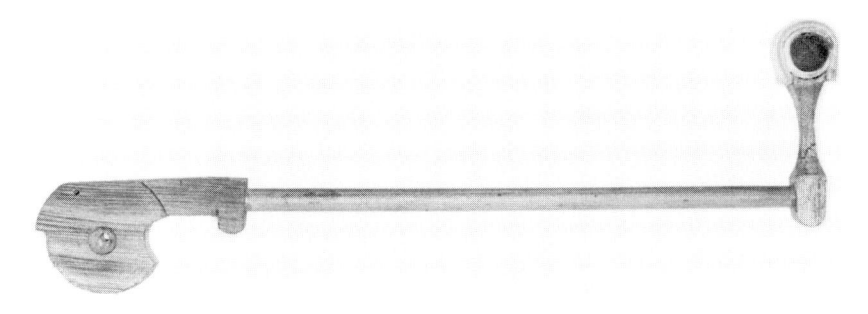

Figure 3.58 Hammer from the Ferrini pianoforte/harpsichord. The wooden core of the cylindrical hammer head shown here is not original and was removed during a recent restoration.

The string-gauge markings found on the 1746 combination pianoforte/harpsichord may be original and appear to be about three gauges heavier than those found on a typical Cristofori harpsichord (Table 3.9).[93] (See also pp. 157–159 and Table 3.3.) Ferrini's heavy stringing in his pianoforte/harpsichord thus accommodates the hammer action rather than the harpsichord's quilled jacks.

Cristofori evidently realized from the outset that while there is considerable leeway in the positioning of the plucking point of a harpsichord jack (registration changes exploit the various tone colors created by differing plucking points), the optimal hammer position in a pianoforte is much more restricted, as hammers work best, particularly in the treble, when they strike close to the nut. In designing his combination pianoforte/harpsichord, Ferrini was able to preserve, to a remarkable degree, the strike line and plucking points established by Cristofori in both his pianos and harpsichords. He accomplished this by positioning the hammers close to the nut, racking the dog-legged dampers behind the hammer lines, and arranging the harpsichord jacks beyond the dampers. (See Table 3.8 for a comparison of string lengths, striking points, and plucking points of the 1746 Ferrini pianoforte/harpsichord, 1722 Cristofori harpsichord, and 1739 del Mela pianoforte.)

Externally, the Ferrini pianoforte/harpsichord is very similar to Cristofori's pianos. The thick-walled outer case design is simple in conception, with a lower case molding of rectangular section. Like the moldings in

---

[93] In 1978 the author discovered two marks on the 1726 piano that appear to be string gauge numbers: a 4 at G and a 2 at f#^{2}. Kirsten Schwarz, however, interpreted the second number as a ½, rather than a 2. In either case, these numbers do not appear to be original. Schwarz, *Erfand Bartolomeo Cristofori mit dem Hammerflügel ein neues Instrument?*, p. 22.

Figure 3.59 Detail of the bottom of the Ferrini pianoforte/
harpsichord showing kerf-bending of the molding and case side – a
wood-bending technique employed by Cristofori and used in most
of his instruments.

Cristofori's pianofortes, the bending of this molding was assisted through lamination and the use of transverse saw cuts. Ferrini's bentside is also curved through the use of deep transverse saw cuts (Figure 3.59).

While Cristofori made little attempt to preserve the illusion of "false inner-outer" construction in his thick-walled pianos and harpsichords, Ferrini took greater pains and succeeded in this respect. The cypress keywell, inner case walls, and cap moldings run the full length of the

Figure 3.60 Keywell bracket of the Ferrini pianoforte/harpsichord. The design of the upper section is derived from Cristofori's bracket. Note the extra "accidental" key and hinged plate on the end block of the lower manual. Accidentals on both sides of the keyboard operate catches that allow the lower keyboard to be pushed in and out to change registration.

instrument, providing a convincing impression of a case within a case (Figure 3.60; note how Ferrini has "quoted" Cristofori's signature bracket design [stepped cove, reverse cyma, stepped quarter-round] for the upper manual, and improvised his own extension for the lower manual).

Though some of the moldings on Ferrini's instrument are more complex than those found on Cristofori's instruments, a comparison of certain elements suggests that Ferrini copied the molding scrapers of his teacher, or perhaps made use of them (even though Cristofori's last will stipulated that all of his instrument-making tools were to go to the del Mela family rather than to Ferrini).

The internal construction of this instrument follows the complex design developed by Cristofori, which employs a light, inner bentside as a support for the soundboard edge. As in the Cristofori pianos, the inner bentside is isolated from the internal struts and outer case. This is accomplished by carving down projections of the diagonal braces to form dowel-like extensions. Oversized holes in the inner bentside allow these extensions to pass through to the heavy outer case, where they are inserted and glued into holes. In Cristofori's pianos, the inner bentside (which supports the

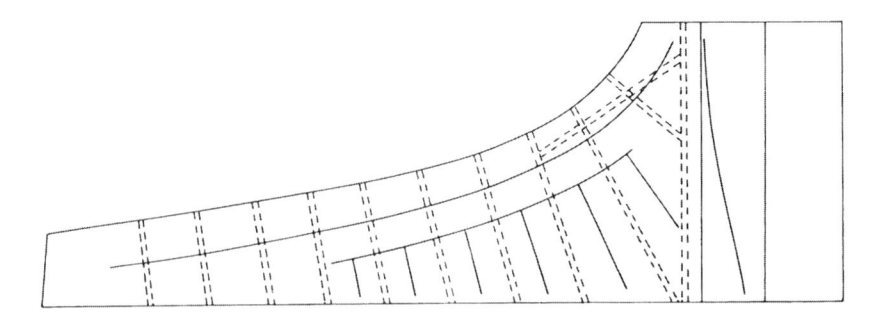

Figure 3.61 Schematic drawing of the Ferrini pianoforte/harpsichord. Nut, bridge, soundboard ribs, and cutoff bar are solid lines; case braces are dashed lines.

soundboard) extends to the bottom of the outer case; however, in Ferrini's pianoforte/harpsichord, the inner bentside does not extend fully to the case bottom, as does the massive liner glued to the inner surface of the outer case wall. As in Cristofori's pianos, Ferrini's broad hitchpin rail is glued on top of the outer case liner. A thin lamination of cypress, which forms the wall of the mock inner case, is glued over the hitchpin rail and may serve to prevent the hitchpin rail from lifting off the liner. As in the Cristofori pianos, the hitchpin rail extends over the soundboard but does not touch it. This suspended structure carries the hitchpins and a set of bearing pins.

Ferrini employed a system of diagonal bracing similar to that of Cristofori. In Ferrini's instrument there are ten diagonal braces, whereas Cristofori used nine in his 1726 piano (Figures 3.61 and 3.40), seven in the 1722 piano (Figures 3.41(a) and 3.41(b)) and six in the one dated 1720 (Figures 3.38(a) and 3.38(b)).

There are presently four iron gap spacers in the Ferrini combination harpsichord/pianoforte, but the wooden blocks that form the grid of the hammer frame indicate that the hammers were originally grouped to accommodate seven gap spacers (the same number used in Cristofori's 1726 piano.) Thus there is a disparity between the number of gap spacers and the spacing of the hammers. Apparently, Ferrini first intended to employ seven spacers (perhaps of wood as in the Cristofori pianos) and laid out his keyboard and action parts accordingly, but later decided to use only four spacers (the instrument does not show evidence of having been modified at a later date to accommodate a reduced number of spacers). Perhaps a mid-course decision to use metal gap spacers instead of wood led Ferrini to reduce their number.

The Ferrini pianoforte/harpsichord makes use of a wrestplank in the conventional, non-inverted configuration, like the 1720 Cristofori

Figure 3.62 Posts with metal pins used as the "nut" of Ferrrini's pianoforte/harpsichord. Because the strings pass under the pins, the pins prevent the strings from lifting during impact from the hammers.

pianoforte. In the 1720 piano, the plank is beveled from below to provide clearance for the hammer shanks; in the Ferrini instrument, the plank is inclined along the top edge to lower the strings at the gap. "Up-bearing" is provided by a series of metal pins driven horizontally through hardwood posts that extend vertically from the wrestplank (Figure 3.62). Because the strings pass beneath the pins, they cannot be lifted off the pins due to the impact of the hammers. Cristofori solved this problem by using an inverted wrestplank in his 1722 and 1726 pianos (see Chapter 3). Ferrini's wooden posts also act as spacers for the unison string pairs.

Soundboard ribbing consists of a curved cutoff bar with six ribs perpendicular to it (Figure 3.61). The soundboard is of cypress, as is the bridge, which is rectangular in section and double-pinned throughout, in the manner of Cristofori's pianos. As in Cristofori's pianos and his large harpsichords, there is no soundboard rosette; apertures in the belly rail serve as acoustic case openings.

Ferrini's was not the last combination pianoforte/harpsichord, as instruments of this kind were made by Johann Andreas Stein, Joseph Merlin, and Diego Fernández later in the eighteenth century. While hammer and harpsichord actions might seem to produce incompatible timbres, the common strings, soundboard, and case provide a unifying resonant structure. Nevertheless, the rationale for constructing these complex instruments may have been to console customers who were undecided as to which type of keyboard instrument to invest in. When the Ferrini pianoforte/harpsichord was examined by the author in 1987, only a few keys were functional. In playing these few notes, it seemed that the component mechanisms were well integrated and, in fact, complemented each other.[94] Ferrini's combination pianoforte/harpsichord should thus be viewed as more than an elaborate exercise in combining two diverse instruments in one case (see Table 3.10 for measurements). While the combination pianoforte/harpsichord could indeed be used as two discrete instruments, when approached as a two-manual instrument, it would certainly provide fascinating tonal and dynamic contrasts. In conclusion, though Ferrini followed the basic action geometry developed by Cristofori, he dealt imaginatively with many new problems encountered in executing this complex design. Limited space required him to reduce the overall height of the upper keyboard assembly, and he cleverly employed Cristofori's push–pull system of changing harpsichord registration (as seen in Cristofori's and Ferrini's *cembali traversi*) to adapt the jacks to closely paired unisons.

Giovanni Ferrini's *cembalo traverso*

In addition to making pianos patterned after Cristofori's design, Giovanni Ferrini also copied Cristofori's *spinettone da orchestra*, the special *cembalo traverso* that was originally designed for use in the opera orchestra (see Chapters 2 and 4). One such instrument (Figure 3.63), signed IOANNES FERRINI FACTO AN[NO] 1731, is presently preserved in the Museo Clemente Rospigliosi in Pistoia, Italy. It has a 49-note compass of C–c^3.

Like the *cembalo traverso* by Cristofori preserved in the collection of the Grassi Museum für Musikinstrumente der Universität Leipzig, it has two choirs of strings, one at 8′ pitch and the other at 4′ pitch. Because of the compressed string band and alternating plucking directions of neighboring jacks in these spinets, it is impossible to change registration by shifting jack guides. Instead, registration changes are made by sliding the keyboard in and out.

The backs of the key levers of Ferrini's *cembalo traverso* have wide slots bridged by padded platforms. The rear key guide consists of strips of wood that project from the back rail of the key frame and fit through the slots in the keys. Thus, the jacks rest either upon the padded platform or

---

[94] Professor Luigi Ferdinando Tagliavini had this instrument restored in 1990, and it is now in full working order.

Figure 3.63 Ferrini *cembalo traverso*, Florence, 1731. Museo Clemente Rospigliosi, Pistoia.

the key guide, depending upon the position of the keyboard. The Ferrini instrument offers the use of the 8′ alone when the the keyboard is pulled out, or the 8′ and 4′ together when the keyboard is pushed in. The keyboard is locked into position by two extra spring-loaded "accidentals" that are mounted on the keyboard end blocks (Figure 3.64). These are depressed on both sides to unlock the keyboard, little knobs in front of the "accidentals" are then grasped and the keyboard shoved or pulled into position.

As indicated above, Cristofori's *cembalo traverso* in Leipzig employs a somewhat different system in that a third position permits the 4′ to be played alone. Instead of using a slotted key guide, raised platforms are used to support the jacks, while gaps provide clearance for them when the stop is inactive. It should be noted that the apparent lack of provision for the 4′ to be played alone in the Ferrini spinet may be due to changes made in the past or to recent restorations (due to the fragility of the instrument, which was in tenuous playing condition when the author examined it in 1989, its owner, Professor G. Pineschi, would not allow the keyboard to be removed in order to study the registration mechanism more closely).

An interesting feature of the Ferrini *cembalo traverso* that is also seen in several instruments made by Cristofori is the divided 4′ bridge and nut (see above). In Ferrini's *cembalo traverso* the top twelve notes are supported by a bridge and nut that are stepped back from the main sections in order to provide longer scaling. String lengths of the 4′ up to c^2 are almost precisely

Figure 3.64 Detail of keyboard and stop mechanism of Ferrini *cembalo traverso*.

half the length of the 8′ strings; however, the 4′ f² is 0.62 × the length of its 8′ counterpart. Because there are no physical obstructions that would have interfered with the curves of the bridge and nut at the break, it is likely that the discontinuity reflects either a change in string material from brass to iron or perhaps a recognition that wire becomes progressively stronger due to the phenomenon of "tensile pickup," which occurs as wire makes successive passes through successively smaller drawing dies. Mounting the bridge further from the edge of the soundboard and onto a more acoustically active region of the soundboard might have been the rationale for partitioning the bridge. The curve of the 8′ bridge also changes abruptly (in fact, it is a separate, mitered section; see Figure 3.65) to accommodate the top octave of strings.

Cristofori's *cembalo traverso* in Leipzig uses divided nuts and bridges in the treble for both the 8′ and 4′ choirs, and this technique is also found in his 1726 harpsichord (see above). A feature of the Ferrini *cembalo traverso* in Pistoia that is seen in Cristofori's 1722 harpsichord (also preserved in Leipzig) is the short section of wood glued along the bass end of the bridge that carries a single string.

The original jacks of the Pistoia *cembalo traverso* are of beech with brass leaf springs located in front of the tongue that push back on extensions

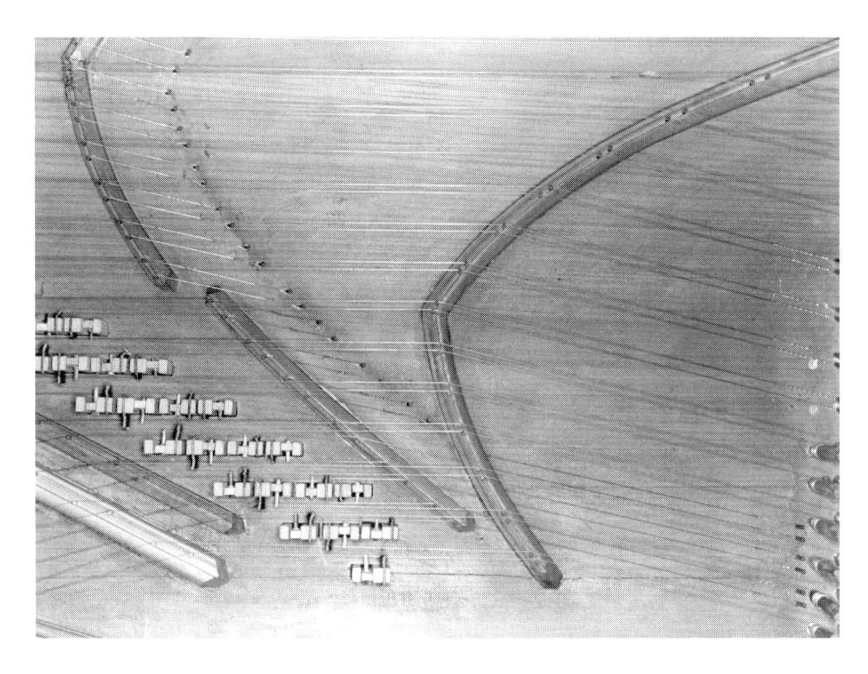

Figure 3.65 Detail of the treble sections of the 4′ and 8′ bridges of the Ferrini *cembalo traverso*. Note stepped-back treble section of 4′ bridge and mitered 8′ bridge.

of the tongue below their pivot points. This is a feature copied from Cristofori's jacks.

The soundboard of the Pistoia instrument is of cypress. X-ray photographs reveal that there are two soundboard ribs, both roughly perpendicular to the belly rail. One rib is to the left of the rose, the other to the right. The case construction resembles Cristofori's in its use of heavy walls (in this case approximately 12 mm thick) and lack of decorative cap moldings. The case sides are of poplar, and it is unusual in that only the spine and two of the front case pieces (including the long right-hand section) overlap the bottom. The other case walls, including the projecting key-well, rest on top of the case bottom, and no attempt was made to conceal this unsightly joint with a molding. (It is a characteristic of Italian harpsichords, including those of Cristofori, for the case sides to overlap the bottom.) A feature of both the Ferrini and Cristofori *cembali traversi* is the lack of a distinctly curved case side. The use of a case side following the curve of the bridge is a logical and attractive feature generally found in "bentside" spinets, as well as conventional harpsichords. While the long, right case side of the Ferrini example does arc slightly by use of lamination and multiple transverse saw cuts, it does not mirror the curve of the bridge. The use of lamination (in this instance, two thin sections are glued against

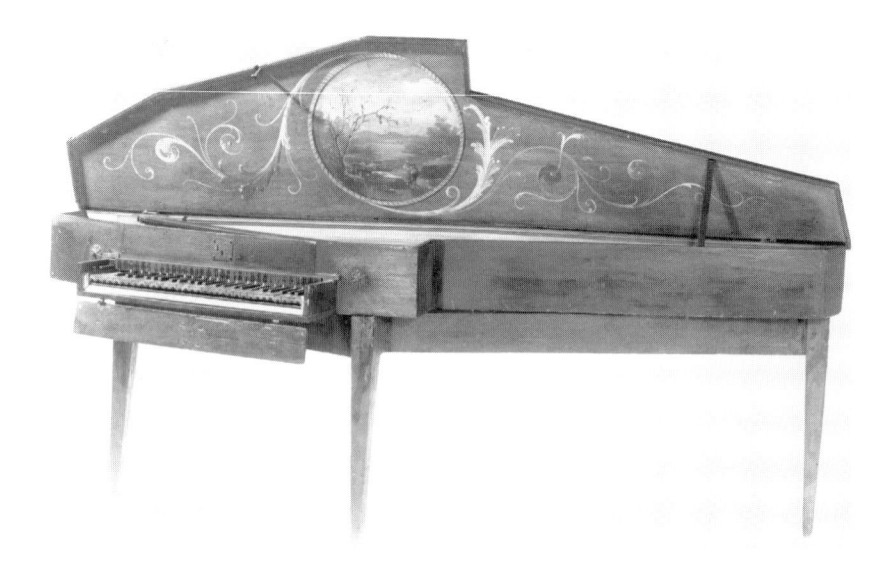

Figure 3.66 *Cembalo traverso* attributed to Giovanni Solfanelli, 1704. Photograph courtesy of the Smithsonian Institution, National Museum of American History, Washington, DC.

each other) and transverse saw cuts to create curved surfaces (rather than steam-bending) were techniques developed by Cristofori and found in many of his instruments (see above). The front section of the case behind the keyboard is also arched, but this crude "curve" is awkwardly simulated by three mitered straight sections; a similar technique is employed in the Leipzig example, though in that instrument this section of the case consists of four mitered sections. In Ferrini's *cembalo traverso*, internal bracing consists of four struts running from the bentside to the spine and positioned nearly perpendicularly to the bentside. The case pieces that extend from the case to form the keyboard console run back to the spine, thereby providing additional structural support.

A similar *spinettone* in the collection of the Smithsonian Institution in Washington, DC (Figures 3.66 and 3.67), once tentatively attributed to Bartolomeo Cristofori or Giovanni Ferrini, is inscribed GS/1704 on the lowest key lever.[95] This instrument has now been ascribed to Giovanni Solfanelli on the basis of molding profiles and the inscribed initials.[96]

---

[95] I would like to acknowledge the late William Dowd for bringing this instrument to my attention and for inviting me to examine it with him in Washington. The inscription on the key was previously mistakenly reported to me as "G. F." See Pollens, "Three Keyboard Instruments Signed by Cristofori's Assistant, Giovanni Ferrrini," pp. 77–93.

[96] Denzil Wraight, "Cristofori's Instruments," p. 701.

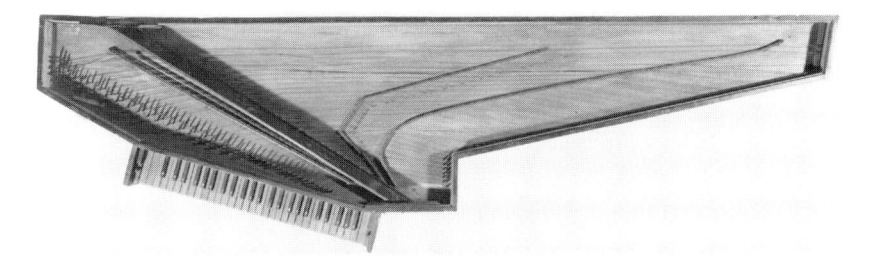

Figure 3.67 Plan view of the *cembalo traverso* attributed to Giovanni Solfanelli showing mitered (rather than curved) bridges. Photograph courtesy of the Smithsonian Institution, National Museum of American History, Washington, DC.

Table 3.5 String lengths/plucking points of *cembali traversi* (*spinettone*) (all measurements in millimeters)

		FF	C	c	c^1	c^2	c^3
Cristofori	8′	2045/170	1965/174	1106/149	557/124	335/112	166/73
	4′	1355/106	1054/111	551/86	276/67	165/53	82/41
Solfanelli	8′	2067/171	1833/162	1118/135	553/108	265/88	131/68
(attrib.)	4′	1242/86	999/82	503/66	261/50	155/35	76/25
Ferrini	8′		1861/163	1056/137	540/111	257/88	125/63
	4′		1118/138	555/113	265/88	132/65	83/55

Table 3.6 Case measurements of *cembali traversi* (*spinettone*) (all measurements in millimeters)

	Length	Width	Case Depth
Ferrini, Pistoia	2200	509*	204
Cristofori, Leipzig	2435	550†/675‡	202
Solfanelli, Washington, DC	2445	720§	199

Measurements exclude case moldings and lid.
* Measured from front to spine, excluding keyboard console.
† Original dimension before compass enlargement, measured front to spine, excluding keyboard console.
‡ Present width including extended keyboard console.
§ Present width including keyboard console.

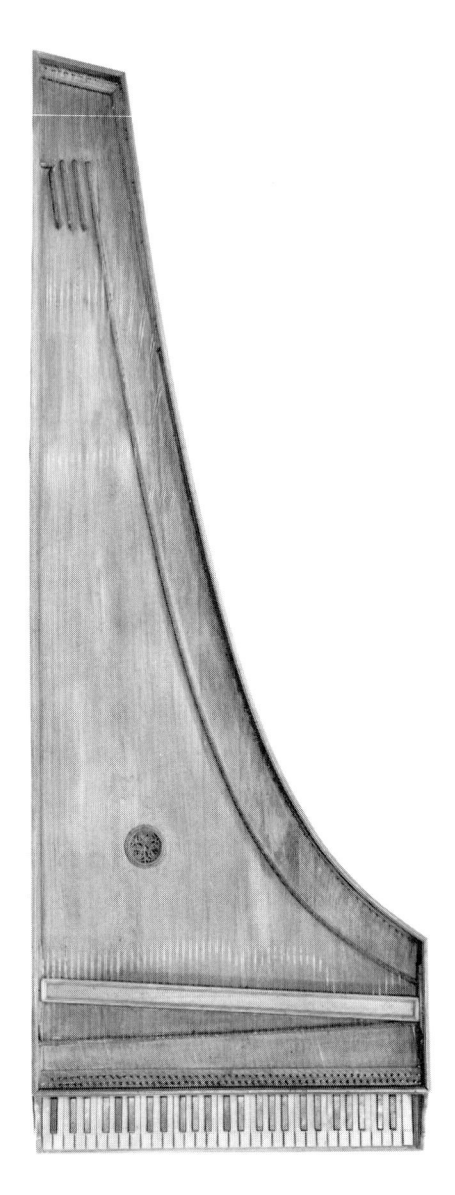

Figure 3.68 Plan view of a harpsichord by Girolamo Zenti, Rome, 1666. The Metropolitan Museum of Art, Crosby Brown Collection, 89.4.1220.

Giovanni Ferrini's Restoration Work

Cristofori's influence can also be seen in his rebuilding of a harpsichord made in 1666 by Girolamo Zenti (Figure 3.68) that is preserved in The Metropolitan Museum of Art in New York. The nameboard of that harpsichord bears two inscriptions:

HIERONYMVS ZENTI FECIT ROMAE A. S. MDCLXVI

And beneath it:

IOANNES FERRINI FLORENTINVS RESTAVRAVIT MDCCLV

The Zenti harpsichord originally had a 53-note keyboard and a compass of GG–c^3 with GG# omitted. It is presently 57 notes with a range of AA–f^3, though it is unclear whether Ferrini was responsible for creating this final range, as comparatively crude extensions of the nut, the treble end of the bridge, and one of three parallel sections forming the bass end of the bridge (Figure 3.69) were clearly not made by the same individual who fashioned the main bridge, nut, and the other two parallel sections, which are presumably the handiwork of Ferrini. The use of short, parallel sections of bridge at the bass end is a feature borrowed from Cristofori (for example, it was used in his 1726 harpsichord; see above).

The main bridge and nut now in the Zenti harpsichord were undoubtedly made by Ferrini as they achieve their requisite curves by use of Cristofori's signature technique of kerf-bending. The present scaling ($c^2 = 290$ mm) is similar to that of Cristofori's instruments.[97]

The Domenico del Mela Upright Pianoforte

Very little has come to light about the del Mela family or Domenico del Mela, the priest who made the upright piano described below. He was born in Vico Val d'Elsa on July 30, 1683, entered a seminary in 1696, and was ordained on September 22, 1708. He resided in the town of Galliano (spelled Gagliano on the nameboard of his upright piano), which lies in an outlying region of Florence known as the Mugello, and he died there in 1755.[98] In addition to his sacerdotal duties at the Compagnia della Santissima Annunziata, he built and repaired organs for local churches in the Mugello, and constructed other instruments and machines.[99] Though there is no documented working association between Domenico del Mela and Cristofori, two members of the del Mela family (their relationship to Domenico del Mela has yet to be determined) are mentioned in Cristofori's will:

---

[97] A more thorough discussion of the restoration work carried out on this instrument can be found in Pollens, "Three Keyboard Instruments Signed by Cristofori's Assistant, Giovanni Ferrrini," pp. 77–93.

[98] Paolo Romagnoli, "Domenico Del Mela (1683–1755) autore del primo pianoforte vertical: figura, biografia" (Ph.D. diss., University of Pavia, 2006); Lino Chini, *Storia antica e moderna del Mugello* (Florence, 1875), pp. 378–379; Ponsicchi, "Il primo pianoforte verticale," pp. 3–4.

[99] Giuseppe Maria Brocchi, *Descrizione della provincia del Mugello* (Florence, 1748), p. 17.

Figure 3.69 Detail of Girolamo Zenti harpsichord showing separate parallel bass bridges, two of which (those closest to the main bridge) are likely the work of Giovanni Ferrini, who restored the harpsichord (and extended the compass) in 1755. Short, parallel bass bridges were sometimes used by Ferrini's master, Bartolomeo Cristofori, for example in the 1726 harpsichord. The Metropolitan Museum of Art, Crosby Brown Collection, 89.4.1220.

To the said Del Mela ladies, sister and daughter of the late Gio. Del Mela... in repayment primarily for their continued assistance lent to him during his illnesses and indispositions, but also in the name of charity, all that belongs to him at his death: the furniture, household goods, clothes and linens, instruments of all sorts, and tools for making such instruments, as well as 200 *scudi* in cash... For legal reasons, and in such recognition for the good service lent by Gio. Ferrini, his assistant, he leaves five *scudi* this one time only.[100]

Cristofori's virtual disinheritance of Ferrini and the bestowment of his possessions acquired in Florence, including the means of production and a sizable amount of cash, to members of the del Mela family is inexplicable. Perhaps this change of heart was due to his protracted illness and gratitude owed to the del Mela ladies, who may have assisted him not only with household chores but in the workshop as well. This might explain why he willed them his tools for making instruments. Nothing is known about the occupation of their relative Giovanni del Mela, who is mentioned in the will, nor their connection with Domenico del Mela, the maker of the upright piano described below. Domenico del Mela would seem to have been well set up with regard to tools and workshop materials, for according to a contemporary account, he had an excellent reputation as an organ restorer as well as an instrument and clock maker.[101]

In 1898, the piano historian and musicologist Cesare Ponsicchi asserted that the earliest known upright piano is an instrument dated 1739 that is today preserved in the collection of the Museo degli Strumenti Musicali del Conservatorio "Luigi Cherubini" di Firenze (no. 103 in Vinicio Gai's *Catalogo descrittivo*; Figure 3.70).[102]

This instrument bears the following inscription: P. Dominicus del Mela de Gagliano invent'r: fecit anno: MDCCXXXIX.[103] (Figure 3.71).

At least one anonymous upright pianoforte (Grassi Museum für Musikinstrumente der Universität Leipzig, no. 106) has been cited as having a marginally earlier date (1735) inscribed on its uppermost key.[104] This date, however, was questioned as early as 1910 by Kinsky, who thought 1765 or 1785 was more reasonable.[105] Other early upright pianos include that by Christian Ernst Friederici of Gera, *c.* 1745 (see below). The purpose here is not to prove or disprove del Mela's claim as inventor, as indicated in the nameboard inscription, but simply to document the early piano-making activity of a maker influenced by Cristofori. Indeed, *invent'r* (inventor) in this instance could well refer to the instrument's unusually

---

[100] ASF, Notarile Moderno, 23370, testamenti 1728–1733, 5091/8, fol. 39v.
[101] Brocchi, *Descrizione*, p. 17.
[102] Gai, *Gli strumenti musicali della corte medicea*, pp. 181–185.
[103] The inscription is incorrectly transcribed as "D. Dominicus Del Mela inventor fecit anno 1739" in Arnaldo Bonaventura, "Domenico Del Mela e il primo pianoforte verticale," *Bollettino della Società Mugellana di studi storici* 4/1 (1928), p. 8.
[104] Kinsky, *Musikhistorisches Museum*, vol. I, p. 127.   [105] Ibid.

Figure 3.70 Upright pianoforte by Domenico del Mela, Gagliano, 1739. Photograph courtesy of the Museo degli Strumenti Musicali del Conservatorio "Luigi Cherubini" di Firenze.

shaped case or to the particular design of the hammer action, rather than to the broader notion of an upright pianoforte.

The outer form of the del Mela pianoforte is quite unusual. It owes its general features to the *clavicytherium*, or upright harpsichord, although the case is peculiarly shaped in that its bentside does not follow the curve of the present bridge; rather, it bulges outward at the top of the

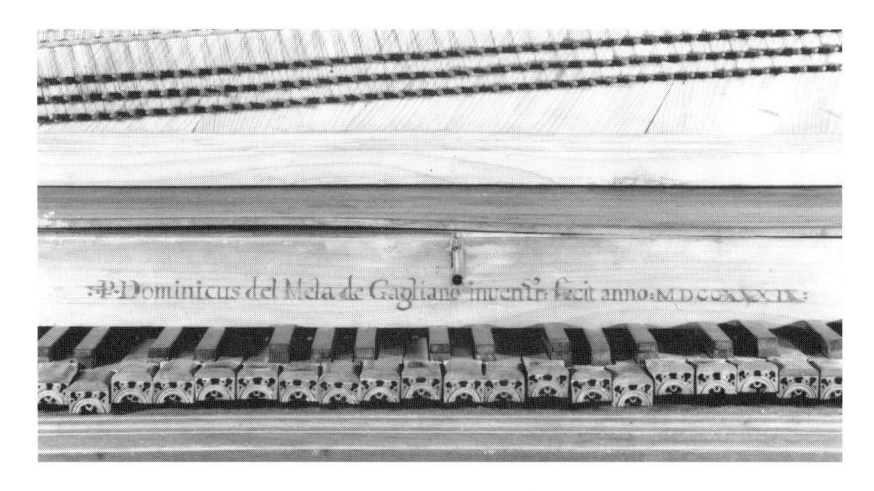

Figure 3.71 Nameboard inscription of the del Mela upright pianoforte. Note decorative key-front arcades.

case so that the bridge sits almost centrally on the soundboard through much of its length. There is a series of plugged holes in the soundboard positioned close to the bentside, and which follows its sinuous curve; it is possible that these holes represent an earlier bridge position, though their location would imply much longer string lengths. Unlike in most keyboard instruments, the soundboard is not inset within the case, but is glued over its front edge. This design may owe its inspiration to Cristofori's upright harpsichord listed in the 1700 inventory that is described as *senza fascie*, that is, "without sides" (see Chapter 2).

The del Mela upright piano is ornate, though it is not particularly well crafted. Its decorative features include a fretwork "gap cover", elaborately configured keyboard brackets, and pierced key arcades backed with red leather. A carved cypress and parchment rose (approximately 60 mm in diameter) is mounted in the soundboard.[106] None of the case moldings of the del Mela upright matches any of those found on Cristofori's or Ferrini's instruments.

The instrument's compass is C/E–c^3. Natural key platings are of heavy boxwood (113 mm long, 4.8 mm thick), with black-stained sharps (75 mm long, 12.2–12.3 mm wide). There are double score lines (4 mm spacing) running across the natural key tops. A peculiarity of the keyboard is the width of the natural tails. Italian keyboards, including those of Cristofori

---

[106] For photographs of decorative elements of the del Mela upright see Pollens, *The Early Pianoforte*, pp. 109–110.

and Ferrini, typically have wide D tails. In the del Mela upright, the B, C, E, and F tails are wide (15 mm), while the G and A tails are 12 mm, and the Ds 13.5 mm. This suggests the maker was not well versed in the Italian tradition of keyboard instrument making. Curiously, the back sections of the key levers are carved (as in clavichords), although the carving is hidden from view by a cover. The three-octave span is 498 mm.

The sides of the thin-walled case are of slab-sawn cypress, as are the bridge and nut. The soundboard appears to be of quartered cedar, with grain running diagonally and nearly perpendicular to the bridge. The soundboard continues beyond the gap and serves as a facing for the wrestplank. Although internal case construction could not be observed, it was evident that Cristofori's complex case design, consisting of an internal bentside that both supports the soundboard and isolates it from the stress-bearing portions of the case, is not employed in this instrument. There is, however, considerable stress on the case, as the piano is triple strung throughout (Cristofori's three known pianos and the pianoforte/harpsichord of Ferrini described above are double strung throughout). String lengths of the del Mela upright differ considerably from those employed by Bartolomeo Cristofori and Giovanni Ferrini (see Table 3.8), though the upright is similarly short-scaled ($c^2 = 275$ mm). As indicated above, a series of plugged holes in the soundboard suggests that the bridge may have been moved to shorten the string length.

The heart of a piano is its hammer action. The action found within the del Mela upright is quite unusual and bears little similarity to the action developed by Cristofori, which employs a spring-assisted escapement jack that lifts an intermediate lever, which in turn raises the hammer. The rudiments of this design could in fact be used in an upright action (see discussion of the Friederici *Pyramide* piano in the Goethe-Museum in Frankfurt, Chapter 5), though no elements of Cristofori's system are evident in the action developed by del Mela. In del Mela's upright action (Figure 3.72), a vertical sticker (about 130 mm in length) rests on the back of the key lever. The sticker is connected via a brass staple to an intermediate lever (120 mm long), which shares a pivot rod with its hammer. The hammer consists of two long sections attached at nearly right angles. The section bearing the pivot rod is about 116 mm long, the other section, which might be termed the hammer head, is 137 mm long.

The long, turned hammer head terminates in a flat striking surface that does not appear to have had a leather covering (Figure 3.73). The principal hammer parts (vertical sticker, intermediate lever, and hammer) appear to be of pear wood.

Figure 3.72 Hammer action of the del Mela upright pianoforte.

Mounted on the back of the intermediate lever is a cloth-padded hammer rest, about 24 mm long, and a 1.4 mm diameter brass rod that is bent into an arc and passes through a mortise in the pivoted section of the hammer. The rod serves to align and direct the motion of the hammer. In its resting position, the section of the hammer bearing the pivot rod is inclined at about thirty degrees from the horizontal. Because of the massive joint between the two sections of the hammer, and the

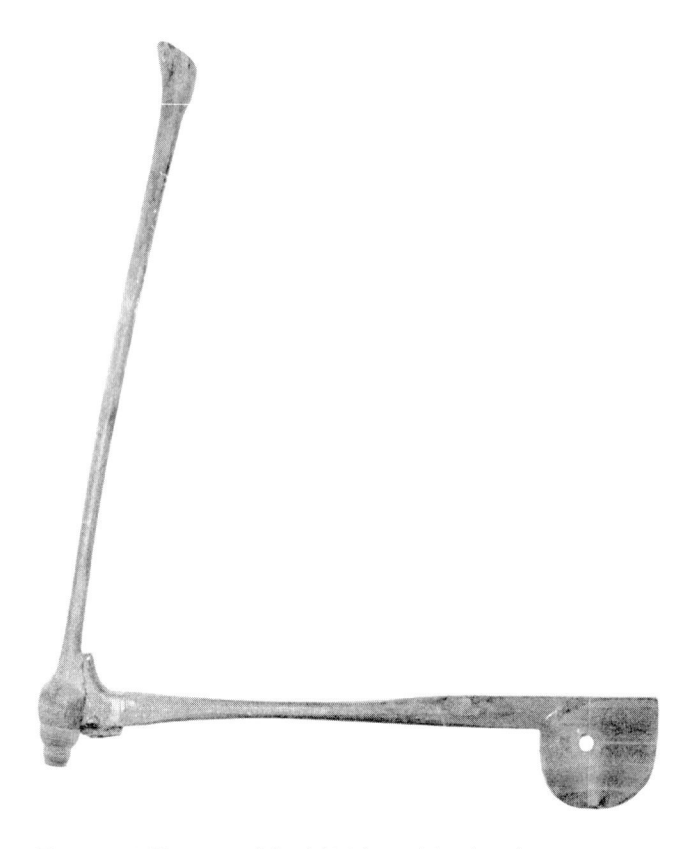

Figure 3.73 Hammer of the del Mela upright pianoforte.

weight of the intermediate lever, the hammer's return is amply assisted by gravity. A brass wire spring (0.93 mm diameter) connects the vertical sticker and the intermediate lever. In some previously published drawings, this wire spring is either not present or looks like a slack cord.[107] In fact, the spring is tensioned to push outwards, and thus acts to support or stabilize the intermediate lever upon the hammer's return. In del Mela's action, there is no escapement mechanism; rather, the hammer is initially lifted by the intermediate lever and is carried to the string by momentum. Upon rebounding off the string, the hammer is cushioned by the hammer rest and the supporting spring, rather than being actively snared by the clever back check developed by Cristofori. A wire hook at the end of the intermediate lever couples with the bottom loop of a long, narrow U-shaped vertical wire linkage to retract the damper.

[107] Ponsicchi, *Il primo pianoforte-verticale*, p. 10; Rosamund Harding, *The Pianoforte: Its History Traced to the Great Exhibition of 1851* (Cambridge, 1933; facs. repr. Cambridge, 2014), p. 31; Gai, *Gli strumenti musicali della corte medicea*, p. 181.

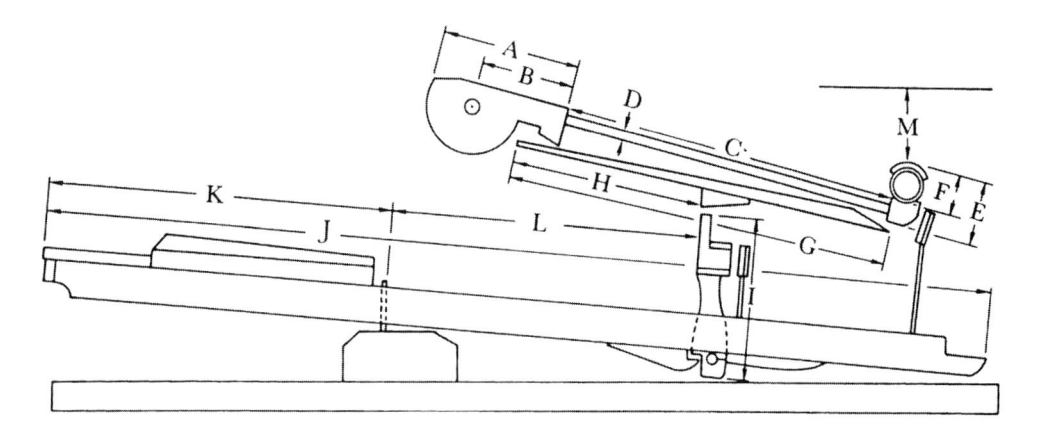

Figure 3.74 Schematic drawing of the Ferrini pianoforte hammer action.

Table 3.7 Comparative measurements of hammer actions of Cristofori and Ferrini pianos (all measurements in millimeters)

		1720 Cristofori	1726 Cristofori	1746 Ferrini
A		52	48.5	43
B		34	32.5	29
C	Bottom hammer	123.5	121	115.5
C	Top hammer	112.5	117.5	112.5
D		4	4	5
E	Bottom hammer	49.5	24.5	43.5
E	Top hammer	46.5	19.5	42
F	Bottom hammer	19	18.5	12.5
F	Top hammer	16	12	11
G		113	135.5	125
H		54	69.5	68
I		62	56.5	44.5
J	Bottom hammer	443	344.5	359
J	Top hammer	407	336	358.5
K	Bottom hammer	165	123.5	146
K	Top hammer	159	125	146
L	Bottom hammer	148	116	126
L	Top hammer	135	111	128
M	(Approximate)	31–35	22–23	32–37

Small springs (perhaps modern replacements for earlier ones) assist in returning the metal damper lever. This metal lever is pinned to a wooden support and guided at the back by a pin. The pivoted ends of the hammers and intermediate levers are semicircular, a shape evidently borrowed

Table 3.8 String lengths/striking points/plucking points of del Mela, Ferrini, and Cristofori instruments (all measurements in millimeters)

Note	del Mela 1739 (pianoforte)	Ferrini 1746 (pianoforte)	Ferrini 1746 (harpsichord)*	Cristofori 1722 (harpsichord)*
GG		2217/137	2217/182	
C		2030/125	2030/172	1981/165
C/E	1617/105			
F	1570/103	1616/106	1616/152	1619/156
c	1075/95	1112/78	1112/122	1131/145
f	782/89	838/58	838/103	849/134
c¹	517/80	546/37	546/81	569/120
f¹	405/73	406/30	406/74	427/109
c²	275/69	272/22	272/67	285/93
f²	211/56	204/18	204/64	215/81
c³	139/55	141/16	141/65	141/65
e³		119/15	119/62	

* Measurements given are of longer strings of each pair and the more distant plucking point.[108]

Table 3.9 String-gauge markings of Ferrini/Cristofori instruments

| Ferrini pianoforte/harpsichord 1746 || Cristofori harpsichord 1726 ||
Key	Gauge number	Key	Gauge number
GG	1		
D	2	D	5
G#	3	G#	6
		e♭	7
e	4		
		a#	8
c¹	5		
		f#¹	9
g#¹	6		
		d#²	10
f²	7		
c³	8		

[108] Discrepancies between the above measurements and those published in the 2008 catalog of the Tagliavini collection may reflect repairs that were made to the instrument's soundboard in a major restoration that postdated the author's 1987 examination. These repairs may have altered (or perhaps corrected) the position of the bridge and nut, and thus the string lengths, plucking, and striking points. John Henry van der Meer and Luigi Ferdinando Tagliavini, *Collezione Tagliavini: catalogo degli strumenti musicali 1* (Bologna, 2008), p. 358.

Table 3.10 Case measurements of Ferrini pianoforte/harpsichord (all measurements are in millimeters and exclude moldings, external braces, stand, and lid)

Length	2842
Width	961
Height	247
Three-octave span	492

Table 3.11 Case measurements of del Mela upright pianoforte (all measurements in millimeters)

Width	816
Width of stand with moldings	930
Depth (keyboard bracket to back of case)	574
Depth (including front case molding)	586
Height (excluding stand)	2010
Stand height	695

from the design of Cristofori's hammer butts. Like Cristofori's hammers, those of the del Mela upright fit into a rack, though unlike Cristofori's action frame, each hammer assembly is held in place by two pins that support a short, independent pivot rod. By withdrawing these pins, the hammers can be lifted out individually. This provides an advantage over the system employed by Cristofori, in which the entire set of hammers is supported by two long pivot rods that meet in the center. When removing one of Cristofori's hammers, other hammers tumble free as the pivot rod is withdrawn.

Very little can be surmised about the tonal qualities of the del Mela upright from its present condition. Restoration of this instrument would be extremely problematic, in part because the action is complex and fragile. Little helper springs have been added to facilitate the return of hammers, though wear and dirt may not have been the major factors leading to the installation of the extra springs; it seems likely that basic problems with the action geometry may have been the cause. The del Mela upright piano exhibits a complex though perhaps flawed design. Although its hammer action owes little to Cristofori's conception, its development was undoubtedly inspired by Cristofori's pioneering work.

4 | Musical Life in Florence in Cristofori's Time

Sacred and secular music flourished in the Medici court under the patronage of Grand Prince Ferdinando, who came to be known as "l'Orfeo dei Prìncipi" ("The Orpheus of Princes"; Orpheus was a Greek mythological figure associated with music). The court was served by such Florentine-based and Florentine-born composers as Martino Bitti (1655 or 1666–1743), Giovanni Maria Casini (1652–1719), Lorenzo Conti (c. 1680–1740), Francesco de Castris (c. 1650–1724), Giuseppe Maria Orlandini (1675–1760), Giovanni Maria Pagliardi (1637–1702), and Antonio Veracini (1659–1733), as well as by composers native to or principally engaged in other cities, notably Giuseppe Maria Buini (1680–1739), Antonio Caldera (c. 1670–1736), Francesco Gasparini (1668–1727), George Frideric Handel (1685–1759), Giovanni Legrenzi (1626–1690), Jacopo and Alessandro Melani (1623–1676; 1639–1703), Giacomo Antonio Perti (1661–1756), Carlo Francesco Pollarolo (1653–1723), Niccolò Porpora (1686–1768), Alessandro Scarlatti (1660–1725), Antonio Vivaldi (1678–1741), and Giovanni Carlo Maria Clari (1677–1754). A year after Ferdinando's death, a eulogy was published in the *Giornale de' letterati d'Italia* (1714) that summarized his educational background and listed his tutors, who included Marchese Luca degli Albizzi, who served as his *maestro di camera* until 1689, Bernardo Benvenuti, Padre Jacopo Morigia (1633–1708; humane letters), Vincenzio Viviani (1622–1703; geometry and mathematics), Francesco Redi (1626–1699; philosophy and natural science), Baron Boudnausen (ethics), Filippo Sengher (fl. 1675–1704) (an artisan who taught him the "gentleman's hobby" of ivory turning), Padre Giovanni Maria Pagliardi (1637–1702; who taught him to play the cembalo, instructed him in counterpoint and general musical studies, and who was later appointed *maestro di tasti*), and Piero Salvetti (1675–1741; who instructed him in playing bowed-string instruments).[1]

Ferdinando maintained numerous keyboard instruments in his living quarters within the Pitti Palace (see below), and was evidently sufficiently

[1] *Giornale de' letterati d'Italia* 17 (1714), p. 5.

skilled to rehearse and even direct operas from the keyboard, serving on occasion as *primo maestro al cembalo*.[2] Ferdinando's wife, Grand Princess Violante Beatrice (1673–1731), had use of a *cembalo* made in 1547 by Alessandro Trasuntino, according to an inventory loan notation dated 1693.[3] In 1699 the organist and church musician Giovanni Maria Casini was appointed Ferdinando's chaplain; he became Violante Beatrice's *maestro di cappella* in 1708, and later served as organist to Grand Duke Cosimo III.

Ferdinando's younger brother Prince Gian Gastone (1671–1737) was evidently an accomplished keyboard player as well. Like his brother, he appointed musicians to court, the most notable being the prolific composer of operas Giuseppe Maria Orlandini (1676–1760), who received the title of *maestro di cappella* around 1711, though did not formally enter the Medici *ruolo* until 1732. Gian Gastone also engaged Piero di Jacopo Mazzetti (d. 1744), an instrument maker who joined the *ruolo* as *strumentaio* in 1732, shortly after the death of Cristofori. Mazzetti prepared a musical instrument inventory in that year. Gian Gastone maintained musical activities at court after Ferdinando's death on October 30, 1713 (at which time Gian Gastone's title changed from Prince to Grand Prince), and he ultimately became the last Medici Grand Duke after the death of his father, Cosimo III, in 1723; Gian Gastone reigned until his death in 1737.

A memorandum dated May 3, 1714 filed with the 1700 musical instrument inventory indicates that Gian Gastone signed out "un cimbalo di cipresso, opera di Bartolomeo Cristofori, con cassa d'albero e sopra coperta di corame rosso orlate di nastrino d'oro" (a keyboard instrument of cypress wood, work of Bartolomeo Cristofori, with a case of poplar and outer cover of red leather hemmed in gold ribbon). Just below it is another memorandum dated July 13th (no year or borrower's name is given, though the year is presumably 1714 and the borrower Gian Gastone) that makes note of the loan of "un cimbalo di cipresso di piano e forte, con tastatura di bossolo, opera di Bartolomeo Cristofori, con suoi piedi d'albero dorati et ombrati e sopra coperta di corame rosso foderata di taffeta verde, guarnita a torno di nostrino d'oro" (a keyboard instrument of cypress wood with soft and loud [i.e., a pianoforte], with keyboard of boxwood, work of Bartolomeo Cristofori, with its legs of poplar gilded and shaded and an outer cover of red leather lined with green taffeta,

---

[2] *The New Grove Dictionary of Opera* (London and New York, 1998), s.v. "Florence."
[3] ASF GM 1005, "Inventario di strumenti."

hemmed all around with gold ribbon).[4] It is not clear whether these memoranda refer to a pair of keyboard instruments made by Cristofori, consisting of a conventional harpsichord and a pianoforte, or to a single instrument variously described that was borrowed twice. In any case, the July 13th loan memorandum may explain why the Cristofori pianoforte that is described in detail in the inventory of 1700 is not listed in the inventory of 1716. As indicated in Chapter 2, Princess Eleonora de Medici (the wife of Cosimo's younger brother Francesco Maria) is recorded as having borrowed an archlute from the collection. She was served by a gentleman in waiting named Antonio Citerni, who borrowed a harpsichord that had been adjusted by Cristofori. Clearly, the Medici princes and princesses were skilled musicians.

Though not as devoted to music as were his sons, the titular head of the Medici, Grand Duke Cosimo III (1642–1723), officially appointed and paid many of the court's virtuosi directly. As indicated in Chapter 2, when Cristofori's monthly stipends terminated around 1698 and he no longer submitted bills to *La Camera del Ser.^{mo} Prin.^{e} Ferdinando* (The Chamber of The Most Serene Prince Ferdinando), he continued to be paid for piecework, as it were, though out of the ducal treasury. Between 1704 and 1713 (the year of Ferdinando's death) Cristofori's court income amounted to a few *scudi* for occasional keyboard tunings, as opposed to the 10–12 *scudi* monthly stipend plus additional payments for tuning and keyboard maintenance at Pratolino, major keyboard restorations, and the construction of new instruments that he had received on a regular basis from Ferdinando (see Chapter 2).[5] Though Cristofori was appointed the official *custode* (custodian) of the Medici collection of instruments three years after Ferdinando's death, no record has come to light that he was paid for this administrative post, nor for compiling an inventory in 1716 (see Chapter 2). Perhaps the lack of remuneration is responsible for the perfunctory nature of this inventory and its relative lack of technical detail when compared to the one drawn up in 1700. As indicated in Chapter 2, it is possible that Cristofori was also the author of the 1700 inventory, for whoever compiled it was knowledgeable about the terminology associated with keyboard instrument design, such as keyboard range, the use of split sharps and short octaves, registration, stop-action mechanisms, as well as the materials used in their construction. If Cristofori was not the official author of that inventory, it is entirely possible that he supplied the technical information on the keyboard instruments, for not only had he made seven

---

[4] ASF GM 1117, f. 1c; Gai, *Gli strumenti musicali della corte medicea*, p. 22.
[5] Michael Kent O'Brien, "Bartolomeo Cristofori at Court," pp. 88–89.

of them (including the newly invented pianoforte), but he maintained and restored others and was thus capable of describing them.

Opera

Opera was the most popular form of musical entertainment for the Medici and members of Florence's nobility. During Cristofori's years there, a number of theaters served as venues for opera, the most notable being the Cocomero, Pergola, and Sorgenti theaters. Construction of the Teatro di via del Cocomero began in 1650 under the auspices of the Accademia degli Immobili. It had around 15 boxes as well as a *platea* (the seating and standing area for the audience) that could accommodate an audience of about 500, and was available to the Medici, other academies, and traveling opera companies.[6] The Teatro di via della Pergola was founded in 1656 by elite members of the Accademia degli Immobili with the financial assistance and support of Cardinal Giovanni Carlo de' Medici. Construction of the theater was completed in 1657, and it was used by the Medici court and the faction of the Accademia degli Immobili that had split away from its other members, who continued to use the Cocomero theater under the guise of a new academy called the Infuocati. The Pergola theater had 47 boxes and a *platea* that could accommodate an audience about double the size of the Cocomero theater's.[7] It served as a venue for numerous Medici court musical events, including the 1661 performance of the opera *Ercole in Tebe* composed by Antonio Boretti, which was staged in celebration of the wedding of Cosimo III de' Medici and Marguerite d'Orleans. The theater closed in 1663 but was briefly reopened at Medici expense for a production of Giovanni Maria Pagliardi's opera *Il Greco in Troia*, which was performed as part of the wedding celebrations for Grand Prince Ferdinando de' Medici and Princess Violante Beatrice of Bavaria in 1689. That event, which took place shortly after Cristofori arrived in Florence, was presumably one of the first to test his abilities as the newly appointed court keyboard restorer and tuner. After the closing of the Teatro della Pergola (it eventually reopened in 1718 and is still active today), the Teatro del Cocomero continued as the chief venue for opera in Florence. Though the non-aristocratic Sorgenti academy members assisted Immobili and Infuocati members in their performances at the Cocomero theater, the

---

[6] James Samuel Leve, "Humor and Intrigue: A Comparative Study of Comic Opera in Florence and Rome during the Late Seventeenth Century" (Ph.D. diss., Yale University, 1998), vol. 1, p. 37.
[7] Ibid., p. 36.

Sorgenti built their own theater in 1679.[8] A host of other Florentine academies also produced operas, including the Cadenti, Efimeri, Illuminati, Innominati, Irresoluti, Nascenti, Oscuri, and Saggiati academies.

Various genres of opera were performed in Florence, including dramatic works (generally on mythological or historical subjects such as *Il Greco in Troia* and *Il Marco Aurelio*), pastoral dramas (*Il sospetto senza fondamento*), and comic operas (*Trespolo tutore* and *L'ipocondriaco*). Staging was complex, with many scenes and complex machinery for changing sets. A number of seventeenth-century treatises on perspective deal with stage and set design employed during that period, including Giulio Troili's *Paradossi per pratticare la prospettiva* (Bologna, 1672), Andrea Pozzo's *Prospettiva de' pittori e architetti* (Rome, 1693), and Ferdinando Galli-Bibiena's *L'architettura civile* (Parma, 1711).[9] These works include detailed technical renderings of stage and scenery construction employing flat-wing design, as well as instructions for drafting painted scenery in multi-point perspective, which encouraged the viewer's eye to wander from side to side rather than to focus on a single vanishing point. Then in use was Giacomo Torelli's "wheeled pole and carriage" device for quickly introducing and changing scenery through slots in the stage floor (in fact, these slots are represented in an engraving of the third floor theater constructed in the Medici villa at Pratolino; Figure 4.1).[10] Dramatic operas invariably included comedic characters and intermezzi to enliven performances, as well as ballet interludes.

In addition to the Cocomero, Pergola, and Sorgenti theaters, another major performance venue for opera was the Casino di San Marco, a Medici palace presided over by Cosimo III's younger brother, Francesco Maria. In 1686, when Francesco Maria was appointed cardinal and relocated to Rome, his nephew Grand Prince Ferdinando took up the mantle and carried on as the Medici's principal patron of opera. With Ferdinando's financial support and under his close supervision, operas were performed yearly at the Medici villa at Pratolino, generally in the month of September, and libretti published on those occasions bear the official Medici seal. The villa, in the countryside around twelve kilometers north of Florence, had been built by Grand Duke Francesco I de' Medici on land acquired in

---

[8] Ibid., pp. 31–39.
[9] Dunbar H. Ogden, trans. and commentary, *The Italian Baroque Stage: Documents by Giulio Troili, Andrea Pozzo, Ferdinando Galli-Bibiena, Baldassare Orsini* (Berkeley, Los Angeles, and London, 1978).
[10] Bernardo Sansone Sgrilli, *Descrizione della regia villa, fontane, e fabriche di Pratolino* (Florence, 1742).

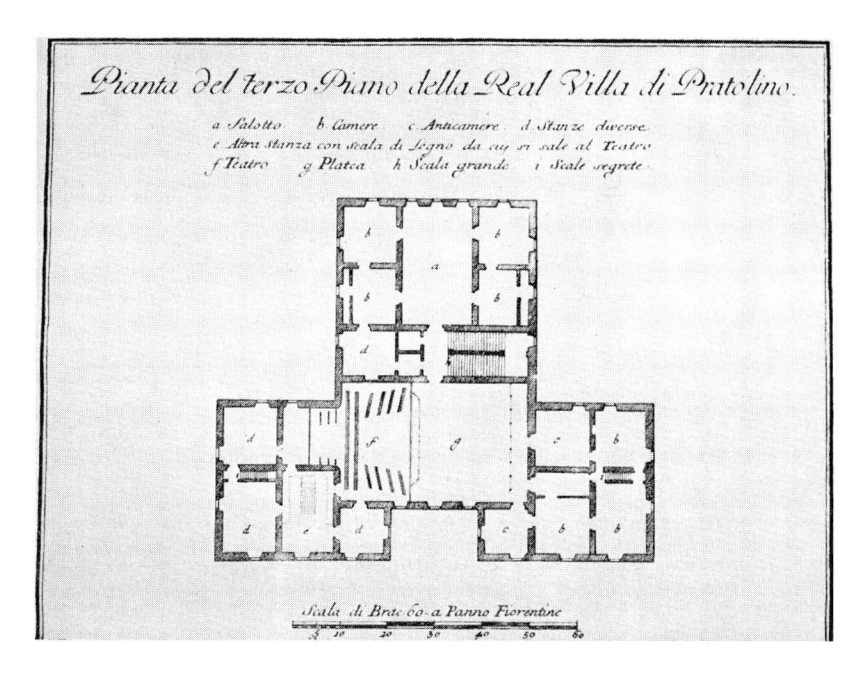

Figure 4.1 Engraving of the third floor of the Medici Villa di Pratolino showing the theater (marked "f") and the *platea*, or area for the audience (marked "g"). From Bernardo Sansone Sgrilli's *Descrizione della regia villa, fontane, e fabriche di Pratolino* (Florence, 1742).

1568. It was completed in 1581 and though it originally featured a theater, in 1696 Ferdinando added a more intimate one designed by Antonio Maria Ferri on the third floor.[11] Ferdinando staged operas at Pratolino between 1679 and 1710; however, performances ceased there in 1711 due to his illness and did not resume after his death in 1713. According to the architectural rendering of the third floor of the villa (Figure 4.1), the stage area was around 25 *braccia* (approx. 13.78 meters) in width and 22 *braccia* deep (12.1 meters), and the *platea* was about 25 × 25 *braccia* (13.78 × 13.78 meters). A grand staircase led up to the *platea*, while a smaller staircase served the backstage area. There were also two "secret" staircases, one behind the *platea*, which perhaps served the royal box, and another leading backstage. Unfortunately, the villa was demolished in 1820 and the surrounding gardens reconfigured.

The Archivio di Stato Firenze, Depositeria Generale records payments made to court musicians involved in these yearly performances. Payments were generally made in late September or early October. For example, on

---

[11] Holmes, *Opera Observed*, pp. 23–24.

Operas performed at the Villa di Pratolino during the years of
Cristofori's service to Ferdinando de' Medici

Year	Opera Title or Work	Composer	Librettist
1688[‡]	Il tiranno di Colco	G. M. Pagliardi	G. A. Moniglia
1689	La serva favorita	A. Scarlatti (?)	C. Villifranchi
1690	Name of opera unknown	Possibly A. Scarlatti	
1691[‡]	Il Marco Aurelio	G. M. Pagliardi	Apostolo Zeno
1692[*]	Trespolo oste	Ricciardi (?)	C. Villifranchi
1693[*]	Attilio Regolo	G. M. Pagliardi	M. Noris
1694	No opera performed that year		
1695	L'ipocondriaco	G. B. Benini	C. Villifranchi
1696	Tito Manlio	C. F. Pollarolo	M. Noris
1697	Name of opera unknown		
1698[§]	L' Anacreonte tiranno	M. Bitti, F. de Castris, A. Scarlatti	F. Bussani
1699[*]	Faramondo	C. F. Pollarolo	A. Zeno
1700[†]	Lucio Vero	M. Bitti; G. A. Perti	A. Zeno
1701[*]	Astianatte	G. A. Perti	A. Salvi
1702[‡]	Il Flavio Cuniberto	A. Scarlatti	M. Noris
1703[*]	Arminio	A. Scarlatti	A. Salvi
1704[*]	Turno Aricino	A. Scarlatti	S. Stampaglia
1705[*]	Lucio Manlio l'imperioso	A. Scarlatti	S. Stampaglia
1706[*]	Il Gran Tamerlano	A. Scarlatti	A. Salvi
1707[*]	Dionisio Re di Portogallo	G. A. Perti	A. Salvi
1708[*]	Ginevra Principessa di Scozia	G. A. Perti	A. Salvi
1709[*]	Berenice Regina di Egitto	G. A. Perti	A. Salvi
1710[*]	Rodelinda Regina dei Longobardi	G. A. Perti	A. Salvi

[*] Composers and dates given by Puliti.[12]
[†] Composers and dates suggested by Puliti and Kirkendale.[13]
[‡] Composer according to a copy of the libretto cited by Kirkendale.[14]
[§] A copy of the libretto for the performance at Pratolino on September 25, 1698 has a handwritten notation indicating that Martino Bitti, Alessandro Scarlatti, and F. de Castris composed the score.[15]

September 24, 1688 – the year that Cristofori began working at the Medici court, he and the following singers and musicians were paid for their contributions to performances of a *commedia* at the Medici villa at Pratolino:

[12] Puliti, "Della vita del Ser.mo Ferdinando dei Medici," p. 165.
[13] Puliti, ibid; Kirkendale, *The Court Musicians in Florence*, p. 435.
[14] Kirkendale, ibid., pp. 427, 430, 439; see also Edward Joseph Dent, *Alessandro Scarlatti: His Life and Works* (London, 1905), p. 72.
[15] Kirkendale, ibid., p. 435.

Giovan Maria Pagliardi, *compositore*	S. 142.6
Fran.o de Castro	S. 142.6
Carlo Antonio Zanardi	S. 142.6
Giuseppo Canavese	S. 114.6
Marcantonio	S. 142.6
Gio. Dom.o Graziani	S. 50
Bartolomeo Brischi	S. 20
Giovani Taglia	S. 20
Gio. B.ta Gigli	S. 25
Fran.o Assolani	S.25
Martino Bitti	S. 25
Pietro Salvetti	S. 25
Giovani Figli	S. 25
Prete Jacopucci	S. 5.5
Franco Peri	S. 2.6
Student of Monsu' Agniolo	S. 11.3
Bartolomeo Cristofori	S. 25
Prete Gio. Maria	S. 25
(ASF DG 434, 80r)	

The most highly paid members of this production were Giovanni Maria Pagliardi (member of the Medici *ruolo* from 1681 to 1702), listed as the composer (his *Il tiranno di Colco* was performed that year at Pratolino), and singers Fran.o de Castro (Francesco di Castris), Carlo Antonio Zanardi, Giuseppe Canavese, and Marcantonio (Marc'Antonio da Palermo), who had been borrowed for this production from the ducal court in Modena.

Prior to Giovanni Maria Pagliardi's involvement with the Medici, he served as the *maestro di cappella del Giesù* in Genoa. His first major success came in 1672 with his opera *Caligula delirante*, with libretto by Domenico Gisberti, first performed in Venice (followed by a revival there in 1680). This work was also performed in Naples (1673), Rome (1674), Bologna (1674), Ferrara (1675), Milan (1675), Palermo (1675), Pesaro (1675), Vicenza (1675), Palermo (1678), Verona (1680), Florence (1685), Genoa (1688), Crema (1689), and Lucca (1696). Pagliardi's association with the Medici court began sometime between 1668 and 1670, and a 1672 libretto of *Caligula delirante* identifies him as the *maestro di cappella del sereniss. Gran Duca di Toscana*. However, his name first appears in the official court *ruolo* of Cosimo III on February 1, 1681 (where he is listed until the year of his death), though his title in Cosimo's court was not *maestro di cappella*, but rather the more modest *maestro di tasti* (master of the keyboard) at a salary of 20 *scudi*, far short of the payment he received from Ferdinando's treasury in 1688 for work as composer at Pratolino, cited above – 142.6 *scudi*, the same amount he received on four subsequent occasions through 1695. His opera *Il Greco in Troia* was performed in 1689 at the Pergola theater in Florence as part of the celebration of Prince Ferdinando's marriage to Violante Beatrice of Bavaria. Pagliardi is recorded as having borrowed a harpsichord from the court collection in November of 1680, and on October 30, 1695 Cristofori submitted a bill of 30 *lire* to Prince Ferdinando as reimbursement for expenses involved in the purchase of a *spineta* from the Florentine maker Niccolò Berti by Ferdinando and its delivery to Pagliardi. As indicated in the 1714 eulogy for Ferdinando published in the *Giornale de' letterati d'Italia*, Pagliardi taught the young Ferdinando musical theory and was his harpsichord instructor. He later became involved in a legal dispute with the castrato Francesco de Castris, who himself fell afoul of the court and was exiled from Florence in 1703.

As was often the case, the libretti of Pagliardi's operas were published for use by those attending performances (often numbering in the hundreds, depending upon the venue), and thus numerous copies are preserved. Some operas had repeat performances, so many copies of the libretti were required. When a particular opera was revived or performed in other cities, the various editions of the libretti often reveal changes; for instance, it was not uncommon for the score of one act or another to be replaced with one by another composer. An example is the opera *L'Anacreonte tiranno*, which is generally ascribed to Alessandro Scarlatti, though in its 1698 performance at Pratolino the music of the first and third acts was replaced by Martino Bitti's, and various arias were composed or rewritten by de Castris.[16] The libretto for the historical drama *Il Greco in Troia* published in Florence in 1688 (under the imprint Sua Altezza Serenissima) is notable in that it features seventeen engraved illustrations by Arnold Westerhout and Robert van Audenaerd. Scores, unfortunately, were not published (the reason being that fewer than a dozen or so musicians typically took part in these performances, and their parts were probably just written out or perhaps even improvised); consequently, manuscript scores are rare. Robert Lamar Weaver lists no extant scores for operas performed at Pratolino.[17] However, the Biblioteca Nazionale Marciana in Venice and the Biblioteca de Conservatorio di Musica S. Pietro a Majella

---

[16] Ibid., p. 435.
[17] Robert Lamar Weaver and Norma Wright Weaver, *A Chronology of Music in the Florentine Theater 1590–1750* (Detroit, 1978), pp. 162–223.

in Naples have scores of Pagliardi's *Caligula delirante*, which Warren Kirkendale argues may have been performed at Pratolino in 1685.[18] Scores of other popular operas by Pagliardi, *Il Numa Pompilio* (performed in Florence in 1674, though not at Pratolino) and *Il Lisamaco*, are preserved in the Biblioteca Nazionale Marciana (a score of *Il Numa Pompilio* is also located in the Österreichische Nationalbibliothek). A score for Alessandro Melani's pastoral drama *Il sospetto senza fondamento*, performed in Florence in 1691 and 1699, is preserved in the Biblioteca Apostolica Vaticana, and arias from Pollarolo's *Tito Manlio*, first performed in Florence in 1696, can be found in the library of the Naples Conservatory. Though no complete scores of Alessandro Scarlatti's *Il Flavio Cuniberto* (performed in Florence in 1702) are known, a collection of arias from that opera is preserved in the Bibliothek des Priesterseminars in Münster. In the scores examined by the author, only the vocal line and a rudimentary keyboard part are provided, and all of the keyboard parts could have been executed on a C–c^3 keyboard. Cristofori's instruments that have extended bass compasses (including his special *spinettone* designed for use in the theater and the 1720 pianoforte with its original compass) could have been used improvisationally to double the diapasons of the theorbo, especially when accompanying arias (full orchestral playing during this period was generally restricted to non-singing passages).[19]

The *castrato* Francesco de Castris (also known as de' Massimi, Cecchino, and Checchino; *c.* 1650–1724) first performed Pagliardi's *Caligula delirante* in Pratolini in 1685, though his name was not officially entered in the court *ruolo* until the next year. In his early years he had made his mark in performances in Bologna, Ferrara, and Venice before coming to the Medici court. He served the Medici until 1703, when he was dismissed due to court intrigue and resettled in Rome, where he continued to receive a Medici stipend and was involved in diplomatic functions on behalf of the Medici court. He was on occasion called upon by Grand Duke Cosimo to intervene in matters involving Ferdinando.[20] The *castrati* Carlo Antonio Zanardi (1657–1704) and Giuseppe Canavese (active in Florence between 1693 and 1705) were not formally associated with the court (that is, they were not listed on the *ruolo*), though they sang various roles in operas performed at Pratolino, and their names appear in numerous libretti and payment records. In a testament registered in Bologna on May 22, 1704,

---

[18] Kirkendale, *The Court Musicians in Florence*, p. 423.
[19] *The New Grove Dictionary of Opera* (London and New York, 1998), s.v. "orchestra."
[20] Kirkendale, *The Court Musicians in Florence*, pp. 437–446.

Zanardi bequeathed a keyboard instrument (possibly a pianoforte) made by Cristofori to de Castris.[21] On June 15, 1709, Cardinal Pietro Ottoboni (1667–1740) wrote to Ferdinando from Rome that "Il Sig.ʳ Francesco di Castris ha sentito il raro cembalo, che me ha favorite V.A." (Signor Francesco di Castris has heard the rare *cembalo* with which Your Lordship has favored me.).[22] The *raro cembalo* referred to here is certainly the Cristofori pianoforte that Scipione Maffei indicated had been given to Cardinal Ottoboni (see Chapter 3). Strangely, the 4000-page inventory of Ottoboni's possessions that was compiled after his death in 1740 lists an organ, fourteen harpsichords, and a small spinet, though no piano.[23] The harpsichords in the inventory are described in considerable technical detail (the number of registers, keyboard ranges, etc. are given), so it is unlikely that the rare piano that Cardinal Ottoboni had received as a gift in 1709 was misidentified as a harpsichord.

The instrumentalists listed in the 1688 payment record cited above are Bartolomeo Brischi (spelled Bruschi in later opera payment accounts) and Giovanni Taglia, who were freelance violists (neither is listed in the Medici *ruolo* as an appointed court musician). Giovanni Battista Gigli ("Il Tedeschino") was a theorbo player who entered the Medici *ruolo* in 1684 and served the court until his death in 1703. Francesco Assolani (Giovanni Francesco di Pietro Assolani) and Martino Bitti were court violinists; Assolani is listed in the *ruolo* between 1646 and 1706, while Bitti (Martino di Cristofano Bitti) entered the *ruolo* in 1685 and served the court through 1741. Bitti was well regarded as a violinist and also composed several operas, including *L'Anacreonte tiranno* and *Lucio Vero*, numerous oratorios, a violin concerto, sonatas, and chamber works. Pietro Salvetti (who joined the *ruolo* in 1664 and served through 1695) was a versatile string player who played the violin, viola, and *violone*. In the 1688 performance at Pratolino, he probably played the *violone*. The eulogy for Grand Prince Ferdinando published in the *Giornale de' letterati d'Italia* (1714) states that Salvetti taught the prince to play bowed instruments. Giovani Figli (most likely Fuga, as it is spelled in later Pratolino payment records) was a keyboard player. Also listed in the 1688 payment record are Father Jacopucci, for performing a lament, Franco Peri, for turning pages,

---

[21] Vitali, "Un cantante legrenziano e la biographia Francesco de Castris 'musico politico,'" in *Giovanni Legrenzi e la cappella ducale di San Marco*, p. 584.

[22] Puliti, "Della vita del Ser.ᵐᵒ Ferdinando dei Medici," p. 148. Corrected citation given in Kirkendale, *The Court Musicians in Florence*, p. 446. Archivio Mediceo, file 5899, no. 47.

[23] Rome, Archivio di Stato, prot. 1838, fols., 88v, 125v, 134r, 175v, 182r, 298v, 698r, 704r, 723r. Kirkpatrick, *Domenico Scarlatti*, p. 360; Alberto Cametti, "I cembali del Cardinale Ottoboni," *Musica d'Oggi* 8 (1926), pp. 339–341.

Figure 4.2 Group portrait of Medici court musicians by Anton Domenico Gabbiani, 1685–1686. The musicians depicted are likely (from left to right) Pietro Salveti (cello), Giovanni Fuga (keyboard), Giovanni Gigli (mandolin), Bartolomeo Bruschi and Giovanni Taglia (violas), and Francesco Assolani and Martino Bitti (violins). Courtesy of the Palazzo Pitti, Appartamenti Monumentali, inventory no. 1890/2805.[24]

a student of Monsu' Agniolo for work on the ballet, the priest Giovanni Maria for staying to play the *cimbalo*, and of course, Bartolomeo Cristofori, who was most likely paid for tuning and adjusting keyboard instruments used in these performances. Separate bills (see Chapter 2) were generally submitted by him for moving *cembali* back and forth between Florence and Pratolino.

A number of the musicians listed above may be identified in group portraits by Anton Domenico Gabbiani that are presently at the collection of the Palazzo Pitti in Florence. For example, a painting entitled *I musici del Gran Principe Ferdinando*, c. 1685–1686 (Figure 4.2), depicts seven musicians arranged around a *cembalo*.

[24] Hill, "Antonio Veracini in Context," pp. 545–546. In this article, Hill proposes that the two violinists on the right of Gabbiani's painting are Antonio Veracini (1659–1733) and his father Francesco Veracini (1638–1720), though as Hill notes, Antonio was "peripheral to music-making at the Medici grand ducal court," and both he and Francesco "lost their preferred position upon Bitti's arrival in 1685." (Neither of the Veracinis ever held formal appointments in the Medici court.) In light of the Veracinis' distant relationship with the Medici, the date ascribed to the painting (1685–1686), and the inconclusive facial resemblance between known portraits of the Veracinis and the two musicians represented in the Gabbiani painting, it is more likely that the violinists in the painting are courtiers Assolani and Bitti.

The instruments they are holding (a large theorbo or lute would probably have presented compositional difficulty for Gabbiani, hence the diminutive mandolin held by Gigli) are presumably from the Medici collection. Because it is likely that the painting dates from before the delivery of all five of the instruments ordered from Stradivari in 1684 (the last of which, the two violas, were delivered in 1690), the bowed-string instruments listed in the 1700 inventory that might be those depicted in the Gabbiano painting include violins by Nicolò, and Antonio & Hieronymus, Amati as well as Jacob Stainer, violas by the Amatis, and cellos by the Amatis, Antonio Catini, Fabritius Senta, and P. Roccus. Though the stringed instruments depicted in the Gabbiani painting are not rendered with sufficient detail to identify their makers, the harpsichord features Girolamo Zenti's signature key bracket, and the red exterior with decorative border may be one of the leather covers hemmed with gold ribbon that are described in the Medici inventories.[25]

Another musical venue for the Medici was their villa in Poggio a Caiano. The court generally resettled there in the spring to enjoy the gardens and various forms of entertainment. Though opera was not often performed there, in 1694 the *Commedia I tre fratelli rivali per la sorella* was staged there. The 1697 inventory of the villa lists two keyboard instruments:

Un Zimbalo di Bar.o Cristoffori lungo braccia 4 2/5 di cipresso con cassa di cipresso simile bianca e tastatura di bossolo e pero tinto di nero, con tre piedi a balaustro intagliati in alto, vernicati di nero e dorati in parte, con sua coparta di corame.

(A *cembalo* by Bartolomeo Cristofori 4 2/5 *braccia* [approx. 2425 mm] in length of cypress wood with an outer case of cypress wood similarly white [i.e. natural color, or "unfinished"] and a keyboard of boxwood and pear wood tinted black, with three baluster [turned] legs carved at the top, varnished black and parcel gilt with a cover of leather.)

Un organo che fa cimbalo, organo e tiorba con tastatura d'avorio e ebano con cassa di cipresso e contracassa tutta tinta di turchino e rabescata d'oro, anzi verde antico e rabescata d'oro con suo piede che fa cassa davanti et i mantici, tinta di verde antico e rabescata d'oro con fiancate dipintovi a olio paese con figure et il restante di taffetà turchino inquartatovi la tutti dorati retto da piede da un balaustro tutto intagliato tinto di turchino e dorato parte, con la sua sopracoperta di corame turchino con nastro per legare.

(An organ made with *cembalo* [a clavi-organ], organ and *tiorba* [thus, possibly an organ combined with a gut-string harpsichord] with keyboard of ivory and ebony

---

[25] Hill, in "Antonio Veracini in Context," misidentifies this keyboard instrument as having been made by Cristorori. The upper part of Cristofori's signature key bracket is similar to Zenti's, but it lacks the half-round element at the bottom, which is visible in the painting.

with a case of cypress wood and outer case tinted entirely dark blue with arabesques of gold, rather antique green with arabesques of gold, with its base that forms the front of the case and the bellows painted antique green with arabesques of gold with sides painted in oil depicting a country scene with figures, and the remaining of dark blue taffeta, a quarter of the whole gilded, standing upright on a baluster fully carved and painted dark blue and partially gilded, with its cover of dark blue leather with a ribbon for tying it.)

The latter instrument appears to have been moved to Grand Prince Ferdinando's apartment in the Pitti Palace, for it fits the description of an instrument in the inventory made shortly after the prince's death in 1713 (see below).

Oratorios

The oratorio during Cristofori's time was a sacred musical work generally involving three to five vocal soloists, a small ensemble of musicians, and sometimes a chorus. Instrumental accompaniment might be limited to a single keyboard instrument, though two or three stringed instruments may also have joined in. At the end of the eighteenth century, larger instrumental ensembles began to be employed. Known for his piety (and anti-Semitism), Grand Duke Cosimo III favored this genre over opera, which tended to feature secular themes.[26] Oratorios were not usually performed in private residences but in churches, such as that of S. Firenze. They were also sponsored by certain learned societies equipped with halls (oratories) designed for delivering speeches, such as the Congregazione dell'Oratorio, the Compagnia dell'Arcangelo Raffaello detta la Scala, the Compagnia di San Sebastiano, the Compagnia della Purificazione di Maria Vergine e di San Zenobi detta di San Marco, and the Compagnia di San Jacopo detta del Nicchio.

An example of an oratorio involving a more substantial assembly of musicians is related in an account (dated March 27, 1712) of an event performed at the Compagnia di San Jacopo:

Some of our loving brothers having decided to present, in our venerable company of S. Jacopo Apostolo detta del Nicchio, a noble oratorio with 4 voices entitled *Il figliuol prodigo* to be sung solemnly the evening of Easter, an invitation was first sent to the Most Serene Prince Gian Gastone, and then to Monsignor Girolamo

---

[26] Howard E. Smither, *A History of the Oratorio*, vol. 1 (Chapel Hill, NC, 1977), p. 285.

Archinto, Papal Nuncio, and to Monsignor the Bishop of Fiesole; and the news of such a celebration having spread throughout the city, at 20 hours some of the brothers began to arrive to take their places. On this day the Vespers gathering was put aside, and although the great door of the company [i.e., of the church of the company] was kept locked, many people were admitted privately through the exit from the sacristy past the small cross; and the great door of the company having been opened at 22½ hours, there was such a crowd of people that they not only filled the whole company, but also the cloak room and the outer corridor, beyond which it was filled with people right up to the musicians' stage; and many of the nobility had to sit above it. The said stage occupied the presbytery from one side to the other, right up to the cornice of the altar, of which it was in front and was movable. The [number of] people continually growing, they had to stand in the sacristy and above it on the balconies at the main altar; in sum there was such a crowd of people that one cannot clearly explain it. It was so big that [though] it had been decided to sing Compline, it was not possible to sing it. Thus at 24 hours the said oratorio was begun with great triumph, the parts of which were distributed to the following performers:

First soprano: Sig. Stefano Frilli, virtuoso musician, who played the part of the Prodigal Son.
Second soprano: Sig. Morasi, Florentine musician as is the soprano above, who played the part of the Brother of the Prodigal.
Contralto: Sig. Domenico Tempesti, excellent Florentine musician, who played the part of the Mother of the Prodigal.
Bass: Rev. Father Ferdinando Paolucci, Servite, favorite musician of Most Serene Prince Ferdinando of Tuscany, who played the part of the Father of the Prodigal.

In sum, everything was greeted by general applause; the said voices were accompanied by a great quantity of instruments, as follows: Three harpsichords, two contrabasses, and in place of the 3rd contrabass, a bassoon was played by a German; then three bass viols, the first among which was played by Sig. Dr.... Salucci, celebrated player; the theorbo was played by Gio. Filippo Palafuti, our brother; and beside there were 16 violins, including violas, the first of which was played by Sig. Martino Bitti, Genovese, favorite of Most Serene Prince Ferdinando, a most celebrated player and famous throughout the world; and beside the oboe was played by Sig.___[Lodovico Erdtman?] and in fact he also was a celebrated performer; since a fine ensemble was created with such a quantity of instruments a smooth sound greeted the ears. When, in the course of the said oratorio Sig. Martino Bitti, the first violinist, as well as the said Sig. [Lodovico Erdtman?], oboe player, played things to arouse admiration, the people responded by crying *viva* in loud voices... the said oratorio was finished; it was set by Giuseppe Maria Orlandini, Florentine, *maestro di cappella* of Most Serene Prince Gian Gastone, and composer to the same prince;

it was dedicated to Most Illustrious Sig.ra Marchese Teresa Tornaquinci, Borboni del Monte.[27]

Lodovico Erdtmann (also spelled Erdmann and Etman; d. 1759), the celebrated German-born oboist referred to above, joined the Medici court *ruolo* in 1709. He may have been responsible for the court's acquisition of woodwind instruments by such makers as Amsterdam-based Richard Haka (a set of sixteen *flauti o zufoli*, recorders) and I. C. Denner of Nuremburg (*fagotto*, bassoon).

Alessandro Scarlatti

Much has been written about Alessandro Scarlatti's involvement at the Medici court (see Fabbri, Dent, and Fitzpatrick).[28] His voluminous correspondence with Grand Prince Ferdinando de' Medici reveals dissatisfaction with his positions in Rome and Naples, as well as his concern for the future of his son Domenico, whom he characterized in a letter to Ferdinando as "an eagle whose wings have grown... he must not remain idle in the nest, and I must not hinder his flight."[29] In 1702 Alessandro applied to the court in Naples for leave from his position as *maestro di cappella* (he had been appointed to that post in 1684). He was granted four months' leave, and both he and Domenico set out for Florence, though neither was offered a court appointment. Consequently, Domenico returned to Naples, where he resumed his post in the royal chapel as organist and composer, and Alessandro left for Rome, where he was appointed assistant *maestro di cappella* at the church of S. Maria Maggiore in 1703. Despite Alessandro's brief stay in Florence, numerous operas of his were performed there, before his arrival, during his visit and after. The first, *Il figlio delle Selve*, was performed in 1688 at the Teatro della Pergola, which had just been refurbished by Ferdinando in preparation for celebratory musical events surrounding his marriage in 1689. There was voluminous correspondence between Scarlatti and Ferdinando, and much of it is preserved in the Medici archives. In these letters, Scarlatti responds to Ferdinando's criticisms of his work – that his operas could be more cheerful, less melancholy, and more melodic.[30] In June of 1705,

---

[27] Ibid., pp. 286–288. A few very minor adjustments to the translation have been made here.
[28] Dent, *Alessandro Scarlatti*; Mario Fabbri, *Alessandro Scarlatti e il principe Ferdinando de' Medici* (Florence, 1961); Kirkpatrick, *Domenico Scarlatti*.
[29] Kirkpatrick, ibid., p. 21.   [30] Dent, *Alessandro Scarlatti*, pp. 102–103, 114.

Ferdinando suggested that Scarlatti compose a new opera based upon a drama by Silvio Stampiglia, entitled *Lucio Manlio*, the text of which was dispatched to Scarlatti in Rome and the score completed within a few weeks. This collaboration mirrors Ferdinando's close involvement with court painters, such as Giovanni Antonio Fumiani and Anton Domenico Gabbiani (both were sent to Venice in order to "improve their color" under the tutelage of Niccolò Cassana), and the suggestions he often made with regard to subject matter and composition when commissioning works from Sebastiano Ricci and Giuseppe Maria Crespi.[31] After 1706, Grand Prince Ferdinando turned his attention away from Scarlatti and toward Bologna-based Giacomo Antonio Perti, who composed the final operas staged at Pratolino.[32]

George Frideric Handel

George Frideric Handel is another composer who is often associated with the Medici court, though like Scarlatti he never achieved an official appointment there. His introduction to the court may have come about from a propitious meeting with Prince Gian Gastone in Hamburg in 1703–1704; however, his first visit to Florence was not until the fall of 1706. Handel's opera *Vincer se stesso è la maggior vittoria*, more popularly known as *Rodrigo*, was performed at the Cocomero theater in 1707. He returned intermittently to Florence through 1709.

Grand Prince Ferdinando "at home"

During Grand Prince Ferdinando's time, the Pitti Palace had a keyboard room on the ground floor that was not only used to store many of the keyboard instruments owned by the Medici, but was also used for performances. Prince Ferdinando's private apartment in the Pitti Palace also contained numerous harpsichords, as well as several flutes, and a few books and librettos. An inventory made shortly after his death in 1713 entitled *Inventario dei mobili e masserizie della proprietà del Serenissimo Signor Principe Ferdinando di Gloriosa ricordanza. Ritrovate doppo da di*

---

[31] Haskell, *Patrons and Painters*, pp. 232–240.
[32] Francesco Lora, "I drammi per musica di Giacomo Antonio Perti per il teatro della villa medicea Pratolino (1700–01; 1707–10)" (Ph.D. diss., University of Bologna, 2012).

lui morte nel suo appartamento nel Palazzo de' Pitti, e sono l'appresso cioè (Inventory of furniture and goods that were property of the Serene Lord Prince Ferdinando of glorious memory. Found after his death in his apartment in the Pitti Palace and nearby) lists the following:[33]

Un organo con canne di legno e tastatura di bossolo et ebano, con concerto di campanelli di bronzo d'Inghilterra, con sua tonda davanti d'ermisino bianca tutta dipinta a rabeschi, fiori e uccelli di più sorte, ferma sopra un telaio.

(An organ with wood pipes and keyboard of boxwood and ebony, with a set of bells made of English bronze, with its front trimmed in white *sarsenet* [a light-weight silk] all painted with arabesques, flowers and birds of all sorts, set on a stand.)

Un cimbalo di cipresso con tastatura d'avorio, fatto da Girolamo Zonti [*sic*] romano, con cassa tutta coperta di dommasco alla cataluffa, opera piccolo rossa e dorata, confitta di bottoncini dorati, guarnita di nastrino d'oro e seta con suo piede tutto intagliato di tre sirene, e tutto dorato.

(A *cembalo* of cypress wood with a keyboard of ivory, made by the Roman Girolamo Zenti, with case all covered with damask, with fine red and gold embroidery, studded with little gilded buttons, garnished with gold ribbons and silk with its legs totally carved in the form of three sirens, and all gilded.)

Una sopracoperta per detto cimbalo di corame, foderata di ermisino rosso, orlata di nastrino e seta rossa.

(An outer cover of leather for the above cembalo, lined with red sarsenet, hemmed with red silk ribbons.)

Un cimbalo di cipresso, con tastatura di bossolo, fatto da Domenico Pesarese, con cassa tinta di rosso, rabescata d'oro e vernicata, dipintovi nello sportello che si alza femmine che ballano e veduta di paese, con suo piede tutto intagliato a scartocci e rabeschi tutti dorati.

(A *cembalo* of cypress wood, with keyboard of boxwood, made by Domenico of Pesaro, with case colored red, arabesques of gold and varnished, the lid painting depicting women dancing in the countryside, with its stand all carved with cartouches and arabesques, all gilded.)

Una sopracoperta per il suddetto cimbalo di corame, orlata di nastrino di oro, foderata di taffetà giallo.

(An outer cover of leather for the above *cembalo*, hemmed with gold ribbon, lined with yellow taffeta.)

---

[33] ASF, GM 1222.

Un organo con canne di cipresso quadre, fermo dentro nella grossezza del muro della camera de' cimbali, con tastatura di cipresso, con un'asse avanti a dette canne tinta di verde rabescata d'oro, fermovi due viticci d'ottone dorato, con suoi mantici et alter applicazione.

(An organ with square cypress wood pipes, mounted in the wall of the keyboard room, with keyboard of cypress, with a plank in front of the said pipes colored green with gold arabesques, stabilized by two lattice works of gilded brass, with its bellows and other accessories.)

Un cimbalo di cipresso, con tastatura di bossolo et ebano, opera di Girolamo Zonti [sic] romano, con cassa coperta di drappetto opera piccolo verde e dorato con poco d'oro, guarnito di nastrino d'oro e seta verde, confitto di bullette d'ottone dorate a rosette.

(A *cembalo* of cypress wood, with keyboard of boxwood and ebony, work of the Roman Girolamo Zenti, with case cover of draped work light green and gilded with a little gold, garnished with gold ribbon and green silk, studded with gilded brass upholsterer's tacks, and one rosette.)

Un sopracoperta per detto cimbalo di corame, orlata di nastrino d'oro, foderata di taffetà verde.

(An outer cover of leather for the said *cembalo*, hemmed with gold ribbon, lined with green taffeta.)

Un cimbalo simile con tastatura d'avorio et ebano, con traversa et il davanti sopra la tastatura di ebano e granatiglio filettato e rabescato d'avorio, con cassa d'abeto.

(A similar *cembalo* with keyboard of ivory and ebony, with cross-piece and the front above the keyboard of ebony and granadilla wood, edged and arabesqued with ivory, with a case of softwood.)

Una sopracoperta per detto cimbalo di corame, orlata di nastrino d'oro e seta rossa, foderata d'ermisino rosso.

(An outer cover of leather for the named *cembalo*, hemmed with gold ribbon and red silk, lined with red sarsenet [light silk].)

Uno spinettone di cipresso, filattato di ebano, fatto da Bartolommeo Cristofori, con testate d'angolo acuti e tastatura di bossolo et ebano, con cassa d'abeto.

(A large spinet of cypress wood, edged with ebony, made by Bartolomeo Cristofori, with acutely angled ends and keyboard of boxwood and ebony, with a case of softwood.)

Una sopracoperta per detta spinetta di corame, orlata di nastrino d'oro e seta, foderata di taffetà rosso.

(An outer cover of leather for the named spinet, hemmed with gold ribbon and silk, lined with red taffeta.)

Uno spinettone fatto da Bartolommeo Cristofori di cipresso, con tastatura di avorio, impiallacciato di granatiglio, con corniccette di ebano con testate ad angoli acuti, con cassa d'abeto.

(A large spinet made of cypress wood by Bartolomeo Cristofori, with keyboard of ivory, veneered with grenadilla, framed with ebony with acutely angled ends, with case of softwood.)

Una sopracoperta per detto di corame rosso, orlata di nastrino d'oro, foderata di taffetà rosso.

(An outer cover of red leather for the above, hemmed with gold ribbon, lined with red taffeta.)

Un graviorgano con tastatura d'avorio et ebano, fermo nella sua cassa d'albero tinta di turchino tutta dipinta a fiori, mostri marini et altro, con corniccette che lo ricorrono attorno tutte dorate e per di sopra tutto rabescato d'oro lumeggiato, con fondo verde, posa sopra altra cassa, ove vi è l'organo, tinta di verde rappresentatovi rabeschi di legno dorato, tramezzati di corniccette simili e sotto a detta vi è altra cassa quadra per i mantici, tutta dipinta per davanti, entrovi due femmine e satiri et altri bacccanti, con veduta di paese e dall'altre parti tinto di verde e rabescato d'oro, lumeggiato, con un piede tornito a balaustro, tutto dorato.

(A clavi-organ [see below] with keyboard of ivory and ebony, mounted on its case of softwood colored deep blue painted throughout with flowers, sea creatures, and others, with molding all around completely gilded and above with arabesques illuminated with gold, with bottom green, set above another case where there is the organ, tinted green representing arabesques of gilded wood, divided by similar molding and below the said another square case for the bellows, all painted as before, depicting two women and satyrs and other bacchants, with country landscape and the other parts painted green with arabesques illuminated with gold, with a turned baluster stand, all gilded.)

Una sopracoperta per il suddetto graviorgano di corame turchino, foderato di frustagno.

(An outer cover of dark blue leather for the above large organ [or clavi-organ], lined with fustian cloth.)

Un cimbalo con tastatura d'avorio et ebano, con sua cassa d'albero, posa sopra due piedi d'albero torniti, con sopracoperta di corame giallo.

(A *cembalo* with keyboard of ivory and ebony, with its case of softwood, resting on two turned stands, with an outer cover of yellow leather.)

Una spinetta con cassa tinta di color di noce, filettata di giallo, con tastatura di cipresso e contracassa d'albero, con sopracoperta di corame rosso, con suoi piedi d'albero torniti, tinti di color di noce e filettati d'oro.

(A spinet with case tinted the color of walnut, edged in yellow, with keyboard of cypress and outer case of softwood, with outer cover of red leather, with its turned softwood stand painted the color of walnut and edged with gold.)

Un flauto impiallacciato di tartaruga, con bocchetta et annodature di avorio.

(A flute veneered with tortoiseshell, with mouthpiece and mounts of ivory.)

Due flauti simili d'avorio alla francese piccolo, con sua custodia di sacri nero.

(Two similar flutes of ivory in the small French style [perhaps flageolets or bird flutes], with their case of black cloth.)

Un instrumento o cimbalo di cipresso lungo nel più braccia 4 1/3 con tastatura simile, con piedi intagliati, tinti di rosso e dorati in parte, con sopracoperta da levare e porre di corame rosso, guarnita attorno e su le cuciture di nastro di seta rossa et oro, foderata di taffetà color simile.

(An instrument or *cembalo* of cypress wood in length over 4 1/3 *braccia* with keyboard similar, with carved stand, colored red and partially gilded, with outer cover of red leather that can be lifted and put aside, trimmed over the stitching with a ribbon of red silk and gold, lined with similarly colored taffeta.)

This inventory, which lists thousands of *objets*, including furniture, paintings, sculpture, silver, crystal, porcelain, clocks, and scientific instruments, focuses on the decorative aspects of the musical instruments rather than their technical features, such as keyboard range, number of registers, and physical dimensions. Thus, it is difficult to establish concordances with the musical instrument inventories of 1700 and 1716 (the 1700 inventory, in particular, is strong with regard to technical aspects, though the 1716 inventory that is signed by Cristofori himself is surprisingly weak in this regard and focuses instead on decorative aspects). Several of the instruments can be tentatively identified; for example, the two spinets by Bartolomeo Cristofori with "acutely angled ends" in the 1713 inventory may be the spinets "in the form of ovals" dated 1690 and 1693 in the 1700 Medici musical instrument inventory (though both are absent in the 1716 inventory). The Zenti harpsichord with the ivory keys and cover studded with little gilded buttons in the 1713 inventory may be the three-register harpsichord dated 1658 in the 1700 inventory; however the decoration of the harpsichord by Domenico da Pesaro in the 1713 inventory does not match any by that maker listed in the 1700 and 1716 inventories. The instrument in the 1713 inventory termed a *graviorgano* (a term that might refer to a large organ) is very likely the "cimbalo con' il gran organo, con' sua cassa dipintovi baccanali diversi intagliato, e straforato in parte in alcuni luoghi, tinta d.ª cassa di verde, e rabescata d'oro, con' sua sopracopta di corame turchino fod.ᵗᵃ di fustagno" (*cembalo* [harpsichord] with a large organ [thus, a clavi-organ], with its case painted with bacchanals, variously carved and worked in part in some places, the case painted green, and arabesqued in gold, with its dark blue leather outer cover lined with fustian) that is listed in both the 1716 inventory and an inventory compiled in 1697 at the Medici villa in Poggio a Caiano. The organ with the set of bells made of English bronze listed in 1713 is nowhere to be found in the 1700 and 1716 inventories. The organ described as having wooden pipes may be the one that Cristofori made for the court in 1693; the fact that it was installed in the wall of the keyboard room might explain why it was not listed in the 1700 and 1716 inventories of "portable" instruments.

Ferdinando's music library was apparently never catalogued, though the inventory of his personal belongings compiled in 1713 lists several untitled volumes in five separate entries:

due libri in foglio entrovi stampe diverse di uomini e donne di diverse nazioni, che alcune miniate di diversi colori, coperti di corame rosso, filettati d'oro

(two books in folio, within printed pages by a variety of men and women from different nations, with some miniatures of diverse colors, covered in red leather, bordered in gold)

otto libretti stampatovi commedie diverse, con sopracoperte di tartaruga, fermovi alcuni rabeschi di fil di grana d'argento

(eight printed librettos of diverse comedies, having an outer cover of tortoiseshell with arabesques of gold filigree)

una coperta per libro alta braccia ¼ incirca di tartaruga simile alle suddette

(a cover for a book approximately ¼ *braccia* [137.8 mm] of tortoiseshell similar to the above)

un libretto braccia 1/6 incirca, stampatovi il settenario di S. Niccola da Tolentino, con sopracoperta di velluto rosso con fibbie d'argento

(a libretto [or small book] about 1/6 *braccia* [91.8 mm], printed on the seventieth anniversary of S. Niccola da Tolentino, with outer cover of red velvet with a silver clasp)

un libro in foglio entrovi attaccate più e diverse erbe e fiori al naturale, con sua sopracoperta di cartapecora (a book in folio, within many and diverse natural herbs and flowers, with its outer cover of sheepskin parchment).

The nine libretti listed above might very well have been those published in Florence for operas and oratorios performed in Florence by various court composers, such as: Pagliardi's *Caligula delirante*, 1685; *Il pazzo per forza*, 1687; *Il tiranno di colco*, 1688; *Il Greco in Troia*, 1689; *Lisamaco*, 1690; *Il Marco Aurelio*, 1691; *Attilio Regolo*, 1693; also Gigli's *La libertà prodigiosa: rappresentazione sacra*, 1692; and Bitti's *Il martirio di S. Agata a cinque voci*, 1693; *L'accademia festeggiante nel giorno natalizio del Ser.^{mo} Principe Ferdinando di Toscana*, 1695; *L'Anacreonte tiranno*, 1698; *Lucio Vero*, 1700; *I trionfi di Giosue: oratorio a cinque voci*, 1703; *Sara in Egitto: oratorio a quattro voci*, 1703; and *Dal trionfo le perdite ovvero Jefte, che sagrifica la sua figlia: oratorio a quattro voci*, 1716. The libretto described as "stampatovi il settenario di S. Niccola da Tolentino" (published on the seventieth anniversary of S. Niccola da Tolentino) may refer to a performance of a sacred work in celebration of the foundation of the church of S. Niccola da Tolentino in Naples in the year 1618.

An inventory of music books and scores compiled at court in 1771 unfortunately contains musical works mostly composed after the deaths of Cristofori, Grand Duke Cosimo III, Grand Prince Ferdinando, and Grand Duke Gian Gastone.[34] That inventory better reflects the musical tastes of the Lorraine regime, which assumed control of Tuscany after the demise of the Medici. Opera was evidently still at the forefront, with many operatic works of Galuppi, García Fajer, Gassmann, Gluck, Guglielmi, and Piccinni appearing in the list. Though a few of the listed works might have been in the possession of the late Medici, such as the *concerti grossi* of Corelli and Geminiani, Veracini's *Te Deum*, mandolin sonatas by Melli, and perhaps Gottlieb Muffat's *Componimenti musicali per il cembalo*, conspicuously absent from this inventory are the works of the earlier Medici court composers and musicians (notably Bitti, Pagliardi, Perti, Orlandini, and A. Scarlatti) who composed pieces while in the employ of Ferdinando and Gian Gastone, as well as Cosimo III. Handel's oratorios *Messiah* and *Acis and Galatea*, as well as his *Elogio del Re d'Inghilterra* (presumably composed upon the death of George I in 1727), are listed, and these scores or libretti might have been acquired by the Medici, though numerous performances of Handel's works took place in Florence between 1768 and 1772, in part due to the importation of scores by an

---

[34] Stefania Gitto, "La collezione musicale di Palazzo Pitti (1): il catalogo del 1771," *Fonti Musicali Italiane* 17 (2012), pp. 175–192.

English expatriate residing in Florence named George Nassau Clavering, Third Earl Cowper, as well as the patronage of the Lorraine dynasty that replaced the Medici, in particular Grand Duke Pietro Leopoldo (ruled 1765–1790), who arranged for performances of *Alexander's Feast* and *The Messiah* at the Pitti Palace.[35] Libretti of these works were translated into Italian and published in Florence. The disinterest in, and thus absence – or perhaps more properly "purge" – of a previous generation's musical works is mirrored in the Spanish court, where a catalog of the music library of the *Infante* Gabriel de Borbón (whose keyboard tutor, Antonio Soler, was a pupil of Domenico Scarlatti) does not list a single work by Scarlatti – just one generation removed from his lifelong involvement with the Spanish court.[36]

As indicated above, both Ferdinando and Gian Gastone were accomplished keyboard players. With their predilection for opera, one can well imagine one of them, or perhaps court *sonatore di tasti* Federigo di Antonio Meccoli, accompanying court singers – such as the *castrati* Vincenzo di Pietro Olivicciani, Domenico Melani, and Francesco de Castris – in private rehearsals or concerts. An anonymous collection of fifteen keyboard works bound in gold-tooled red morocco, emblazoned with the Medici arms (Figure 4.3), is preserved in the Biblioteca del Conservatorio di Musica "Luigi Cherubini" di Firenze (D.2358). These pieces, entitled "Alemanda," "Aria alla Francese" (Figure 4.4), "Passagagli," "Passagagli Pastorali," "Preludio," "Preludio di Botte, Acciachature, e Ligature," "Preludio Cantabile con Ligature," and "Tochata" appear to date from the late seventeenth century. This may be a notebook of works composed for Ferdinando or Gian Gastone, perhaps by Giovanni Francesco Pagliardi, who served as *maestro di tasti* (keyboard tutor) of Ferdinando. Various court musicians, such as violinist Martino Bitti and *tiorbo* player Giovanni Battista Gigli, wrote violin sonatas and chamber music that featured various combinations of instruments, as well as solo works for harpsichord.

Though published after the death of Cristofori and Grand Prince Ferdinando, Lodovico Giustini's solo keyboard works entitled *Sonate da Cimbalo di piano, e forte detto volgarmente di martelletti* (*Sonatas for cembalo with soft and loud, commonly called the "little hammers"*) are considered

---

[35] John A. Rice, "An Early Handel Revival in Florence," *Early Music* 18/1 (1990), pp. 63–71.
[36] Laura Cuervo, "La biblioteca musical del Infante Gabriel de Borbón y Sajonia (1752–1788)," in *Nuevas perspectivas sobre la música para tecla de Antonio Soler* (Series FIMTE, Garrucha, 2016), pp. 147–162.

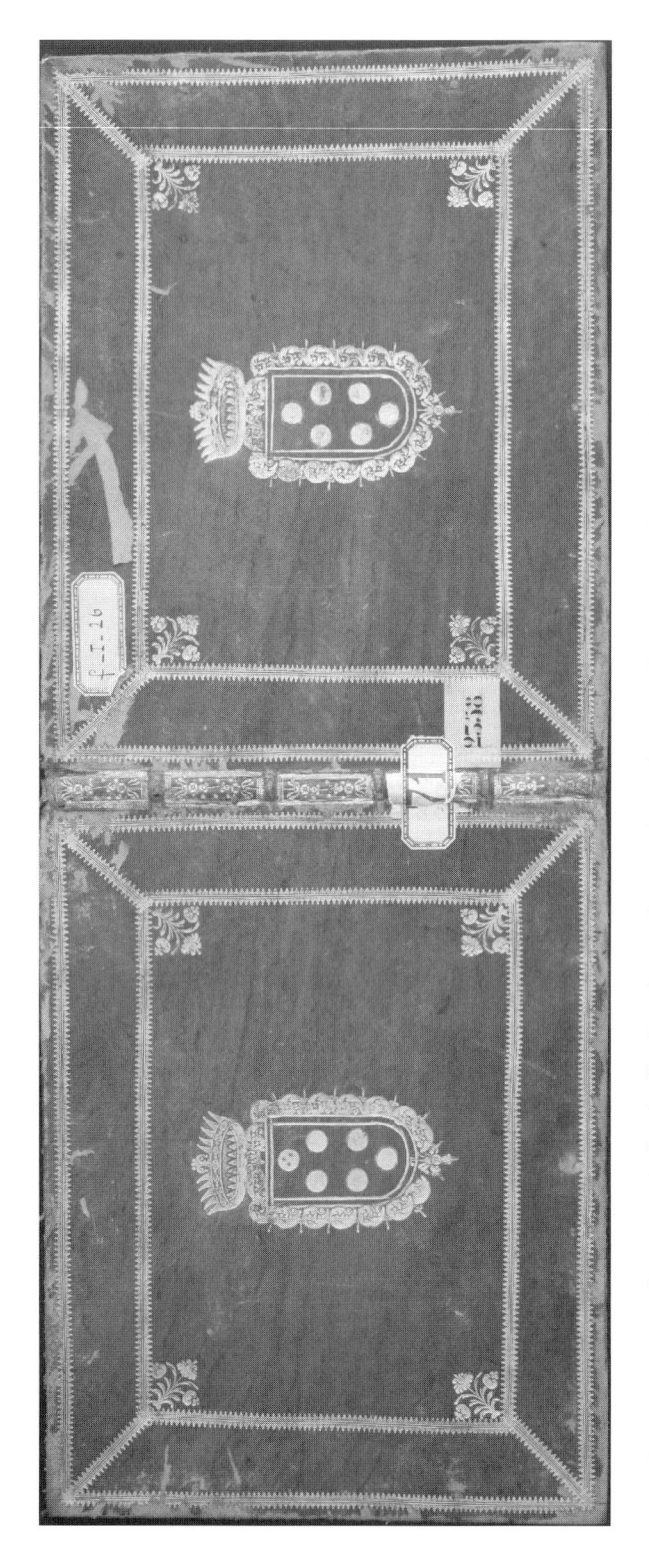

Figure 4.3 Cover of a manuscript book of keyboard music bearing the Medici arms that is preserved in the Biblioteca del Conservatorio di Musica "Luigi Cherubini" di Firenze, catalog number D.2358. Courtesy of the Biblioteca del Conservatorio di Musica "Luigi Cherubini" di Firenze.

Figure 4.4 "Aria alla Francese" from the Medici keyboard book. Courtesy of the Biblioteca del Conservatorio di Musica "Luigi Cherubini" di Firenze.

the first works specifically intended for Cristofori's newly invented piano. The title page indicates that these twelve sonatas were dedicated to the *Infante* of Portugal, Don Antonio, and that these first works (*opera prima*) of D. Lodovico Giustini of Pistoia were published in Florence in 1732.[37] In his dedication of this published work, D. Giovanni de Seixas remarks: "Queste sonate, udite già da me con particolare soddisfazione nel mio soggiorno in Italia, e da quelli Intendenti di tal Professione giudicate di molto buon gusto." (These sonatas, heard by me with particular satisfaction during my sojourn in Italy, [were] judged by the experts of the profession to be very good.) This indicates that Giustini's sonatas predate the date of publication and may have been familiar to and perhaps played by Ferdinando, who was not only surrounded by expert court musicians and composers, but was a connoisseur himself, and at that time one of the very few owners of a keyboard instrument fitted with hammers. These sonatas range from BB to c^3, though the low B appears only once, in Sonata 12, as the final note in an unresolved cadence in a movement in e minor entitled *Siciliano*. Though marked *Affettuoso* in the first measure, curiously there are no dynamic markings in this movement. *Forte*, *piano*, *più piano*, and *più forte* are found elsewhere in this edition – the first of such markings to appear in keyboard literature. Giustini appears to have inserted dynamic markings (Figure 4.5) for purposes of contrast (and in a manner that would have been virtually impossible to execute on the harpsichord through the manipulation of hand stops), rather than to indicate *crescendi* and *diminuendi*.

The 1720 Cristofori piano at The Metropolitan Museum of Art originally had a compass extending down to FF, and thus could have accommodated the low BB found in Giustini's sonatas; however, the Cristofori piano listed in the 1700 Medici inventory only extended to C, as do the extant Cristofori pianos of 1722 and 1726 (see Chapter 3).

A Keyboard Temperament Possibly Favored by Cristofori

In Chapter 3 we examined Scipione Maffei's article entitled "Nuova invenzione d' un gravecembalo col piano, e forte" published in the *Giornale de' letterati d'Italia* in 1711. Clearly, some of the general remarks that Cristofori made about keyboard temperament in the course of his interview did

---

[37] A facsimile edition with a preface by Rosamund Harding was published in 1933 by Cambridge University Press.

Figure 4.5 Page from Lodovico Giustini's *Sonate da Cimbalo di piano, e forte*, showing dynamic markings.

not refer only to his pianofortes; for example, there is no evidence that he ever made pianofortes with split sharps, though his 1690 oval spinet did have them. In the 1711 article, Maffei mentions another "rare *gravecembalo*" owned by the *maestro di cappella* Sig. Casini, which had five sets of keys (enharmonic keyboard) so that "one can circulate through all the keys without hitting any dissonance at all." Perhaps this was the instrument made in 1548 for Gioseffo Zarlino by Dominicus Pisaurensis, which was examined by Charles Burney during his visit to Florence in 1770.[38] Maffei's reference to this instrument does not relate to Cristofori's comments on temperament, and its inclusion appears to have been an afterthought on the part of Maffei.[39]

The notes Maffei made in connection with the writing of the 1711 article are miraculously preserved and shed additional light on Cristofori's ideas regarding temperament (see Appendix 1).[40] It is clear that he did not fully understand Cristofori's comments, and in the translation below no attempt has been made to clarify or correct Maffei's notations:

---

[38] Burney, *The Present State of Music in France and Italy*, pp. 262–263.
[39] Gioseffo Zarlino, *Le istitutioni harmoniche* (Venice, 1558; facs. repr. Bologna, 2008), p. 140.
[40] Verona, Biblioteca Capitolare, cod. DCCCCLX, fasc. VI, no. 1.

That the violin is the only perfect instrument, because it does not have keys and one finds in the whole perfect harmony, that is the flats and sharps each in its place... That on the violin, you can transpose where you want in any sort of key, without hearing an unpleasant effect, because it has equal fifths, and all just, and it does not fall into false and bad sound, like in other instruments...

That *l'armonia* [the harmony] is divided into five *quinti*, from one note to the other. That from the sharp of *Gesolreut* [g#] to the flat of *Alamire* [a♭] there must be one [*quinto*] difference; but the black keys are split, otherwise it is not in tune. That it is easy to tune the split keys by fifths, tuning the split key of *Alamire* with the flat of *elami* [e♭]. That in tuning an ordinary instrument the octave should be perfect, the fifth must drop, otherwise the instrument will not be tuned. The fourth must be higher, the major third higher. That a spinet or theorbo will never be in tune with a violin (and this can be seen when the scales are played together, not sounding in concert) because we do not have the fifths correct, because the *quinti* are not observed and are not distinct. That one realises in hearing the instrument played that something is displaced or that the instrument is out of tune, because one hears a drop in pitch in those black keys that do not have the fifth, and they are false. But music is not composed using these keys, and when they are used, it is sparingly, and the good masters use them when the text is suited to a false and unpleasant note. (Note that it could be that the system of tones is formed on this, that is, as many are made as there are strings that have a good fifth and good consonance, or are at least passable.)

He says that making [...] the division of the notes, with a circle divided into 42 parts, or with a square lined and then cut across, in one way they coincide, in another they do not. That this is theoretical music. That in practice one does bother [...] to find the reason for this, and whether this is musical science.

Cristofori here seems to be describing, or perhaps advocating, fifth-comma meantone temperament, which has narrow fifths, wide fourths and thirds, and in which the notes comprising the scale fall close to 43 (not 42 as Maffei recalls) equal divisions of the octave. Other divisions of the octave that were proposed historically include 17, 19, 22, 24, 31, 34, 41, 53, and 55.[41] The French acoustician Joseph Sauveur (1653–1716) proposed the division of the octave into 43 parts in 1701.[42] The "square lined and then cut across" may refer to the *mesolabium*, a mathematical device for finding mean proportionals mechanically, which was employed by such theorists as Zarlino in establishing intervals for various meantone temperaments.

---

[41] J. Murray Barbour, *Tuning and Temperament: A Historical Survey* (New York, 1972), pp. 107–132.

[42] Joseph Sauveur, "Système général des intervalles des sons," *Mémoires de l'académie royale des sciences* (Paris, 1701), p. 445f.

The Use of Cristofori's Keyboard Instruments in Florence

Grand Prince Ferdinando de' Medici's preoccupation with opera may have provided him with little opportunity to explore the resources of Cristofori's newly invented pianoforte as a solo instrument, though he is said to have been an accomplished keyboard player and certainly supported the development of this new invention. As indicated above, Ferdinando's music library was apparently never cataloged, so we have no sense of his taste or interest in solo keyboard repertoire, nor are there any references to keyboard scores composed by Florentine *maestro de capella* Girolamo Frescobaldi, who was on the Medici *ruolo* from 1631 through 1634, and in his day was the highest paid musician at the Medici court.[43] One of his pupils, the harpsichordist Lucia di Francesco Coppa, was on the Medici *ruolo* between 1664 and 1698, though she may not have lived to see the development of the piano. Preoccupied with their *commedie* and other operatic productions, it is unlikely that the Medici princes cared much for Frescobaldi's more cerebral toccatas and canzonas, or even his *Arie musicali* composed in Florence in 1630.[44]

With regard to Cristofori's pianoforte, as we have noted, Scipione Maffei indicated in 1711 that it was properly a chamber instrument that could be used in a moderate ensemble, though it was not suited for church music or for a large orchestra. Large orchestras were not then employed in the production of operas in such venues as the villa at Pratolino (seven or eight musicians – two violinists, two violists, a bass viol player or cellist, a theorbo player, and one or two keyboard players – constituted the typical ensemble), though it is unlikely that Cristofori's soft-voiced piano would have been used in such performances; his *spinettone da orchestra* (as it is referred to in the 1700 inventory), which had two registers at principal and octave pitches and an extended range of GG–c^3, would have been the keyboard instrument of choice.

As documented in Chapters 2 and 3, Cristofori not only made new keyboard instruments for the court, he was also paid for "moving," "restoring," "remaking," "resetting," and presumably "tuning" others. Medici musical instrument inventory memoranda indicate that numerous court musicians borrowed instruments. For example, composer and *maestro di tasti* Giovanni Maria Pagliardi (*ruolo* 1681–1702) is recorded as having borrowed a harpsichord and a *spinetina* by Niccolò Berti; the contralto

---

[43] Kirkendale, *The Court Musicians in Florence*, pp. 377–380.
[44] Frederick Hammond, *Girolamo Frescobaldi* (Cambridge, Mass., 1983), pp. 70–78.

Raffaello Baldi (*ruolo* 1737–1738) borrowed a *spinetta* by Domenico da Pesaro; violinist Pietro Salvetti (*ruolo* 1664–1695) borrowed harpsichords; oboist Lodovico Erdtmann (*ruolo* 1709–1736) borrowed a harpsichord by Domenico da Pesaro; keyboard player Federigo Meccoli (*ruolo* 1664–1710) borrowed a spinet and a harpsichord; and the *castrato* Vincenzo Olivicciani (*ruolo* 1664–1724) borrowed harpsichords. Cristofori billed the court for working on keyboard instruments for others tangentially involved with the court as well, such as Princess Eleonora's "gentleman in waiting," Antonio Citerni.

5 | Cristofori's Influence

In part due to the 1711 publication of Scipione Maffei's illustrated article in the *Giornale de' letterati d'Italia* announcing Cristofori's invention of the piano, its republication in his compilation of literary works in *Rime e prose* in 1719, then its translation into German by Johann Ulrich König and publication in 1725 in Mattheson's *Critica Musica*,[1] not only did the idea of a new type of keyboard instrument featuring dynamic flexibility become widely known, but the mechanical details of how this new capability was achieved were revealed. In addition to these published accounts, the mobility of courtiers and musicians helped spread the word of Cristofori's invention throughout Europe, and as a result, not only were pianos ordered directly from him and his principal assistant, Giovanni Ferrini, but keyboard instrument makers in Portugal, Spain, Germany, and France began making copies of these exciting new instruments shortly after their arrival.

The Iberian Pianoforte

During the reign of João V, it has been estimated that the Portuguese extracted approximately five hundred tons of gold and diamonds from mines in Brazil,[2] and that around one-fifth of this went directly into the king's coffers.[3] With this newfound wealth augmenting an already profitable trade in the re-export of South American tobacco, sugar, and rare hardwoods, João was able to undertake extravagant building projects and pursue his taste for French and Italian art – acquiring and commissioning

---

[1] Johann Ulrich König, "Musicalische Merckwürdigkeiten des Marchese, Scipio Maffei, Beschreibung eines neuerfundenen Claviceins, auf welchem das piano und forte zu haben, nebst einigen Betrachtungen über die Musicalische Instrumente, aus dem Welschen ins Teutsche übersetzt," in Johann Mattheson, *Critica Musica*, vol. II (Hamburg, 1725; facs. repr. Laaber, 2003), pp. 335–342.

[2] A. J. R. Russell-Wood, "Portugal and the World in the Age of Dom João V," in *The Age of the Baroque in Portugal*, ed. Jay A. Levenson (Washington, DC, 1993), p. 28.

[3] Leonor d'Orey, "The Silver Table Service of Dom José I of Portugal," in *The Age of the Baroque in Portugal*, ibid., p. 168.

great quantities of paintings, sculptures, objects of silver and gold, coaches, furniture, musical instruments, and other luxury items. The vibrant musical activity of his court, including the construction and staffing of an opera house, drew a great number of Italian musicians to Portugal. Walther's *Musicalisches Lexicon* (1732) names at least nine Italian musicians in the royal orchestra and indicates that the principal singers employed at the court were also Italian.[4] Considering the influx of Italian musicians, it is not surprising that news of the newly invented piano made its way to Portugal. The diary of Medici court theorbo player Niccolò Susier (see Chapter 2) contains an entry marking Bartolomeo Cristofori's death that indicates the King of Portugal (João V) paid two hundred gold *louis d'or* each for Cristofori's pianos.[5] (The pre-French Revolution old *louis d'or* was approximately equivalent to 28 Florentine *lire* or 4 *scudi*.) Such a sum was four to five times what might have been paid for an antique Ruckers harpsichord that had undergone a *grand ravalement* in Paris, and the value of around thirty new Stradivari violins. The price paid by João V for these early Florentine pianos (Susier refers to them in the plural – *detti istrumenti*) indicates that they were highly valued and did not casually find their way onto Portuguese shores. Unfortunately, no date is given for the purchases, though it is likely that the first Florentine pianos arrived in Portugal and Spain in the 1720s (that is, after the development of Cristofori's later hammer action, which is first seen in the piano dated 1720, and which served as the model for pianos made by Portuguese and Spanish harpsichord makers).

While it is widely assumed that the Florentine piano was introduced to Spain by way of Portugal through Maria Bárbara and her harpsichord tutor Domenico Scarlatti, who followed her to Spain after her marriage to that country's crown prince in 1729, it is possible that it may also have come to Spain by way of Charles, then Duke of Parma and Piacenza (1716–1788), who later, as Charles III, reigned as king of Spain between 1759 and 1788. Charles was a cousin of Grand Duke Gian Gastone de' Medici (the last of the Medici dukes) and visited Florence in 1732. That year, Giovanni Ferrini adjusted a harpsichord for Charles' use while he was residing at the Pitti Palace as Gian Gastone's guest.[6] Thus, Charles may have become familiar with the piano while in Florence, perhaps even the one made by Ferrini in 1730 that was destined for Maria Bárbara and was ultimately

---

[4] Johann Georg Walther, *Musicalisches Lexicon* (Leipzig, 1732; repr. Kassel and Basel, 1953), p. 489.
[5] Florence, Biblioteca Moreniana, Acquisti diversi 54, ff. 73r, 73v.   [6] ASF GM 1373, n. 504.

bequeathed by her to court castrato Farinelli (see below). Charles III was the father of the *Infante* Don Gabriel (1752–1788), whose keyboard tutor was Antonio Soler, himself a student of Domenico Scarlatti.

Domenico Scarlatti (b. Naples, 1685; d. Madrid, 1757) was esteemed as a keyboard virtuoso early in his career, though most of his highly idiomatic keyboard compositions (over 520 in number) were written in the latter half of his life while he was serving royal patrons in Portugal and Spain. It is unclear whether Scarlatti first encountered the pianoforte in his native Italy or upon his arrival in Portugal in 1719.[7] It has been established that he traveled to Florence in 1702 and 1705, which would have presented early opportunities to become acquainted with Cristofori's newly invented pianoforte. In 1702 and 1705, however, Cristofori's hammer action was then in a rudimentary state of development (see Chapter 3) and is unlikely to have impressed a brilliant artist accustomed to the harpsichord's quick action. Domenico Scarlatti later served as *maestro di cappella* to the exiled Queen Maria Casimira of Poland in Rome between 1709 and 1714, and during this period he might have come in contact with the Cristofori pianoforte that had been given to Cardinal Ottoboni by Grand Prince Ferdinando de' Medici in 1709, though again, that instrument would have had the earlier type of action pictured by Maffei in 1711. Scarlatti traveled to Italy twice during the years he was engaged in Portugal, once in 1724 and again in 1728, and these trips would have provided opportunities to test the more sophisticated action design that had been developed by Cristofori around 1720. This improved hammer action might well have suited Scarlatti. As his primary duty in the Portuguese court was the keyboard instruction of King João V's musically gifted younger brother, Don Antonio, and daughter, Maria Bárbara, the inevitable question arises as to whether he might have played a role in informing his pupils of this newly invented keyboard instrument and induced them to acquire one. As João craved all that was fashionable in Italy, it is little wonder that Cristofori was ultimately commissioned to build pianofortes for the court.

Maria Bárbara was just eight years old when Scarlatti took up his post as director of music at the Portuguese court in 1719. He became her keyboard tutor and held that position until his death in 1757. In 1729 she married the Spanish crown prince, and Scarlatti followed her to the Spanish court, where in 1746 she became queen consort. An inventory of her possessions made after her death in 1758 lists twelve keyboard instruments, including

---

[7] Gerhard Doderer, "Remarks on Domenico Scarlatti's Portuguese Period (1719–1729)," in *Domenico Scarlatti en España*, ed. Luisa Morales (Garrucha, 2009), pp. 161–183.

five pianofortes, four of them Florentine.[8] The inventory indicates that two of the latter had been converted into harpsichords. The Florentine pianofortes might have been ordered by the Portuguese court when Scarlatti was employed there and then sent on to Maria Bárbara after her move to Spain, though one of the pianos listed in the inventory was apparently made by Giovanni Ferrini in 1730, that is, after her arrival in Spain.[9]

Interest in the Florentine pianoforte evidently continued in the Portuguese court after Maria Bárbara's departure for Spain in 1729, as evidenced by the dedication, in 1732, of Lodovico Giustini's pianoforte sonatas to Don Antonio, then the *Infante* of Portugal (the younger brother of João V) and a keyboard student of Domenico Scarlatti (see Chapter 4).[10] This collection of twelve sonatas is believed to be the first music written specifically for the pianoforte. The king's daughter, Maria Bárbara, however, remained Scarlatti's most devoted student, and "Domingo" Scarlatti (as the firmly entrenched Domenico signed his name in Spain in later years) continued in service to her for the rest of his life. Aside from thirty sonatas comprising the *Essercizi per gravicembalo* (dedicated to João V in 1738, shortly after Scarlatti's knighting), nearly all of his later keyboard compositions are dedicated to the Spanish queen.

The five pianofortes listed in Queen Maria Bárbara's inventory are described as follows:

"1. Un clavicordio de Piano echo en Florencia todo lo interior de Zipres; la Cassa de chopo dada de color de palosanto, teclado de Vox, y ebano, con cinquenta y seis teclas, y pie torneado de aya.
2. Otro clabicordio de pluma que antes fue de piano echo en Florencia, lo interior de Zipres y lo esterior dado de color verde con cinquenta y seis teclas de ebano y hueso en pie torneado de aya.
3. Otro clavicordio de la misma manera y color verde echo tambien en Florencia que fue de piano, y aora es de pluma con cinquenta teclas de ebano y hueso en pie torneado de aya.
4. Un clavicordio de Piano echo en Florencia de cipres dado de color encarnado teclado de vox y ebano con quarenta y nueba teclas en pie torneado de aya, que esta en Aranjuez.

---

[8] Madrid, Biblioteca del Palacio Royal, ms. VII E 4 305, fols. 228r–331r; appended in 1758 to the testament of 1756. The inventory is transcribed in Kirkpatrick, *Domenico Scarlatti*, p. 361, and discussed on pp. 175–186. See also Michael Latcham, "Pianos and Harpsichords for Their Majesties," *Early Music* 36/3 (2008), pp. 359–396.
[9] Cappelletto, *La voce perduta*, pp. 209–210.
[10] Lodovico Giustini, *Sonate da Cimbalo di piano, e forte detto volgarmente di martelletti* (Florence, 1732; facs. repr. Cambridge, 2015).

5. Otro Clavicordio de Piano de Zipres color verde teclado de Box y ebano con cinquenta y quattro teclas y pie torneado de Aya el qual se halla en el Real sitio de San Lorenzo."[11]

1. A keyboard instrument [in the form] of piano made in Florence, the entire interior of cypress wood; the case of black poplar given the color of palosanto;[12] keyboard of boxwood and ebony, with fifty-six keys; and a stand turned of beech.
2. Another keyboard instrument with quills that was previously [constructed] as a piano made in Florence, the interior of cypress wood and the exterior given the color green; with fifty-six keys of ebony and bone; on a stand of turned beech.
3. Another keyboard instrument of the same sort and colored green; also made in Florence as a piano and now with quills; with fifty keys of ebony and bone; on a stand of turned beech.
4. A keyboard instrument [in the form] of piano made in Florence of cypress wood given the color red; keyboard of boxwood and ebony, with forty-nine keys; on a stand of turned beech; situated in Aranjuez.
5. Another keyboard instrument [in the form] of piano of cypress wood colored green; keyboard of boxwood and ebony, with fifty-four keys; and a stand of turned beech; that you find in the royal residence in San Lorenzo.

Unfortunately, the keyboard compasses of these instruments are not specified in the inventory, though some of the possible ranges include: FF–c^3, FF–d^3 with FF# and GG# omitted, GG–d^3, GG–e^3 with GG# and $d\#^3$ omitted,[13] GG/BB–g^3 with $f\#^3$ omitted, C–g^3 or AA–e^3 (56 keys); FF–c^3 with FF# and GG# omitted, GG–c^3, C–f^3, AA–d^3, and GG/BB–e^3 (54 keys); GG/BB–c^3, C/E–f^3, or C–d^3 with C# omitted (50 keys); and C–c^3 (49 keys).[14] The most likely of these are GG–d^3 (56 keys), FF–c^3 with FF# and GG# omitted (54 keys), GG/BB–c^3 (50 keys), and C–c^3 (49 keys). It is

---

[11] Kirkpatrick, *Domenico Scarlatti*, p. 361.
[12] Palo santo wood is variously identified as *Bulnesia sarmienti* or Guaiac wood (*Guaiacum officinale*). Guaiac wood, also known as lignum vitae, may be golden with dark green or brown streaks or principally dark brownish-green (especially the heartwood), having a mottled, striated appearance. It is not inconceivable that the color palosanto may be dark green.
[13] The unusual compass of GG–e^3 with GG# and $d\#^3$ omitted was proposed by John Henry van der Meer in "Queen Maria Barbara's Florentine Keyboard Instruments," an unpublished paper delivered at the fourteenth congress of the International Musicological Society, Bologna, 1987. An abstract of this paper was published in *Atti del XIV Congresso della Società Internazionale di Musicologia* (Bologna, Ferrara, and Parma, 1987), pp. 292–293.
[14] Several of the less than ordinary compasses listed here are derived from Spanish, Portuguese, and Florentine harpsichords, clavichords, and pianofortes. See Gerhard Doderer, *Clavicórdios portugueses do século dezoito* (Lisbon, 1971); Macario Santiago Kastner, "Portugiesische und spanische Clavichorde des 18. Jahrhunderts," *Acta Musicologica* 24/1–2 (1952), pp. 52–61;

interesting to compare these compasses with surviving early pianofortes: of the four surviving Cristofori pianoforte actions (dating from 1720 to 1726), three have C–c^3 compasses (49 keys), and one was originally made with an extended compass of FF–c^3 (with FF# and GG# omitted, 54 keys); Ferrini's combination pianoforte/harpsichord of 1746 has a 57-note compass of GG–e^3 with GG# omitted; Gottfried Silbermann's pianos had 58- and 60-note compasses of FF–d^3 and FF–e^3; the three early Portuguese pianos have 51-note compasses of C–d^3; and the two intact Spanish pianos have 56-note (GG–d^3) and 61-note (GG–g^3) compasses.

Four of the five anonymous pianos listed in Maria Bárbara's inventory are specified as having been made in Florence (three were probably made by Cristofori, and at least one was made by Ferrini); presumably the fifth was made in Spain or Portugal.[15] Iberian court archives and other documents list numerous indigenous keyboard instrument makers who were active between the 1720s and 1775.[16] These include: Diego Fernández (b. Vera [Granada], December 26, 1703; d. February 15, 1775; harpsichord maker and tuner in the Spanish royal court between 1722 and 1775),[17] Julián Fernández (b. Madrid; d. 1780; nephew of Diego; Spanish court tuner and instrument maker), Pedro Manuel de Liborna Echavarría (appointed Royal Chapel organ builder in 1724; d. 1771), Pedro de Liborna Echavarría (father of Pedro Manuel; tuner of the Royal Chapel organs and harpsichords from 1703; d. 1724), Andrés Fernández Santos (Valladolid; maker, active 1728–1754), Augustin de Puertas (tuner, c. 1730), and Phelipe Gaular (harpsichord tuner for the Buen Retiro theater and at Aranjuez palace during the reign of Fernando VI). Francisco Pérez Mirabal (active Seville, 1745–1773) was a harpsichord maker who also

---

Beryl Kenyon de Pascual, "Two Features of Early Spanish Keyboard Instruments," *The Galpin Society Journal* 44 (1991), pp. 94–102.

[15] Kirkpatrick, *Domenico Scarlatti*, pp. 175–178, 361–363; Michael Latcham, "The Twelve *Clavicordios* owned by Queen Maria Barbara of Spain and the Seven *Cembali* owned by Carlo Broschi, known as Farinelli: Facts and Speculation," *Five Centuries of Spanish Keyboard Music: Proceedings of the FIMTE Conferences 2002–2004* (Garrucha, 2007), pp. 255–281.

[16] Beryl Kenyon de Pascual, "Diego Fernández – Harpsichord-Maker to the Spanish Royal Family from 1722 to 1775 – and his Nephew Julián Fernández," *The Galpin Society Journal* 38 (1985), pp. 35–47; "Notes and Queries: Queen Maria Barbara's Harpsichords," *Galpin Society Journal* 39 (1986), pp. 125–128; and "Correspondence/Spanish Pianos," *Early Music* 14/3 (1986), pp. 469–470.

[17] Diego Fernández submitted bills in 1743 and 1744 for replacing the keyboards, registers, and jacks of two harpsichords owned by the Duchess of Osuna; he may have added a "registro de mazos" (register of clubs, i.e. hammers) to a harpsichord. Kenyon de Pascual, "Diego Fernández," ibid., p. 45.

constructed pianofortes. Manuel Antunes is known to have constructed harpsichords and pianofortes (*cravos con martelos*) from 1760, the year in which he received a royal "privilege" that gave him sole authority to manufacture pianos with his improved action for a ten-year period (see discussion below). Joachim Jozé Antunes, probably the son of the preceding maker, carried on the family instrument-making tradition (active dates 1758–1789). A maker hailing from Tournai, Henrique van Casteel (b. Tournai, 1722; d. Brussels, 1790), was active in pianoforte making in Lisbon between 1757 and 1767. Mathias Bostem was a German-born keyboard-instrument maker living in Lisbon around 1786. Late-eighteenth-century makers, such as Juan del Marmol (b. Seville, 1737; active through 1780s), constructed square pianos with English-style cases and actions. Work of these later makers is, however, beyond the scope of this study.

It is surprising that two of the pianofortes listed in Queen Maria Bárbara's inventory were converted into harpsichords (numbers 2 and 3), as these early examples were extremely rare and expensive instruments. The conversions suggest that either their escapement mechanisms did not work properly, or were too unfamiliar or complex for local harpsichord makers to regulate or repair; another explanation is that there was greater need or preference for the harpsichord. The removal of hammer actions and the installation of conventional registers and jacks would have been a fairly straightforward procedure for local harpsichord makers. One should not rule out the possibility that the inventory descriptions of the converted pianos may reflect changed or enlarged compasses.

It is unfortunate that only a few Spanish and Portuguese keyboard instruments have survived. Because their number is so small, it is difficult to establish typical compasses, dispositions, and structural characteristics. This problem has been especially vexing to Scarlatti scholars. Ralph Kirkpatrick noted that "the only instruments in the Queen's possession on which the full five-octave sonatas of Scarlatti could have been played were the three Spanish harpsichords with sixty-one notes and two registers." (One sonata, K. 485, extends beyond five octaves and requires a compass of FF to g^3, or 63 notes.) Kirkpatrick's observation suggests that Scarlatti preferred the harpsichord, and Spanish ones in particular, as they had wider compasses than the typical Florentine four-octave piano; however, his point may be misleading, as only nineteen sonatas require the 61-note compass of GG–g^3. Though the actual compasses of the pianofortes are not known, even the most limited (i.e. 49 notes, C–c^3) can accommodate ninety-one of Scarlatti's sonatas, and a 54-note pianoforte with a short-octave compass of GG–d^3 can manage 438 of his sonatas.[18] Kirkpatrick observed that sonatas K. 148–155 appear to be of a different character and are perhaps more suited to the early pianoforte; he also noted that the compass of these sonatas falls within the range of the Queen's pianofortes.[19] On stylistic grounds, Joel Sheveloff more generously concluded that perhaps "two-hundred Scarlatti sonatas will come to be associated with the pianoforte."[20]

Like Scarlatti, the Italian *castrato* Farinelli (Carlo Broschi, b. Andria, Apulia, 1705; d. Bologna, 1782) spent much of his career in the Spanish court (1739–1759); despite his cloistered existence in Spain, he remained perhaps the most famous singer in Europe. He retired from the Spanish court shortly after the death of Maria Bárbara and returned to his native Italy. Visiting Farinelli at his *palazzo* outside Bologna in 1771, Charles Burney recounted that Farinelli had given up singing, but continued to play the *viola d'amore* and keyboard instruments. He had amassed a large collection of keyboard instruments made in different countries, of which Burney writes:

His first favourite is a *piano forte*, made at Florence in the year 1730, on which is written in gold letters, *Rafael d'Urbino*...he played a considerable time upon his Raphael, with great judgement and delicacy, and has composed several elegant pieces for that instrument. The next in favour is a harpsichord given him by the late queen of Spain, who was Scarlatti's scholar, both in Portugal and Spain; it was for this princess that Scarlatti made his two first books of lessons, and to her the first edition, printed at Venice, was dedicated, when she was princess of Asturias; this harpsichord, which was made in Spain, has more tone than any of the others. His third favourite is one made likewise in Spain, under his own direction; it has moveable keys, by which, like that of Count Taxis, at Venice, the player can transpose a composition either higher or lower. Of these Spanish harpsichords the natural keys are black, and the flats and sharps are covered with mother of pearl, all the wood is cedar, except the bellies, and they are put into a second case.[21]

This account differs in one important detail from Farinelli's will, which includes his Italian translation of a provision in Queen Maria Bárbara's will that bequeathed the following to him:

---

[18] Joel Sheveloff, "The Keyboard Music of Domenico Scarlatti: A Re-evaluation of the Present State of Knowledge in the Light of the Sources" (Ph.D. diss., Brandeis University, 1970), pp. 538–541. My figures are derived from Sheveloff's tabulation of the sonatas' ranges.
[19] Kirkpatrick, *Domenico Scarlatti*, p. 184.
[20] Joel Sheveloff, "Domenico Scarlatti: Tercentenary Frustrations (Part II)," *The Musical Quarterly* 72/1 (1986), p. 94.
[21] Burney, *The Present State of Music in France and Italy*, pp. 211–212.

Item Comando che à Dn Carlo Broschi Farineli [sic], il quale me hà servito sempre con molto zelo è fedeltà se li dia l'anello di diamante grande rotondo giallo, e tutti li miei libri e carte di musica, e trè cembali, uno di registro, altro à martellino, ed altro a penna, li migliori . . . [22]

(Item [I] Command that Don Carlo Broschi Farineli, who has always served me with much zeal and faithfulness, be given the ring with the large, round canary diamond, and all my books and music, and three cembali, one with register [perhaps the Spanish one with the transposing device], another with little hammers [Ferrini's piano], and another with quill [the Spanish harpsichord with "more tone than any of the others"], the best . . .)

According to Farinelli, all three of the keyboard instruments that Burney saw had been given to him by the queen, not just one of the Spanish-made harpsichords.[23] The fact that this famed singer's favorite keyboard instrument was a pianoforte made by Ferrini provides strong evidence that the early Florentine piano was especially appreciated for vocal accompaniment. As noted in Chapters 3 and 4, the Italian *castrati* Zanardi and de Castris also may have owned Florentine pianos.

When comparing the hammer actions of the surviving Spanish and Portuguese pianos with those of Florentine makers, it becomes clear that the Iberian versions were modeled after the improved action design developed by Cristofori around the year 1720 and kept in production by Ferrini through at least 1746. The 1732 diary entry of Niccolò Susier cited above and in Chapter 3 does not provide a date for the transactions between King João and Cristofori, though it is possible that Florentine pianos were purchased over an extended period.

Unfortunately, and surprisingly, not one of the instruments associated with Scarlatti, Maria Bárbara, and Farinelli has been preserved; however, several mid-eighteenth-century Portuguese and Spanish pianofortes with actions closely modeled after Cristofori's later design are extant. Although their case and soundboard structures differ from those of Cristofori, the similarities of the small escapement parts demonstrate that local Iberian makers had access to and carefully studied Florentine originals. The Iberian-made instruments represent a fusion of the Florentine hammer action (with minor changes in dimensions and mechanical details) and

---

[22] Bologna, Archivio Notarile. Testamento di mè, d. Carlo Broschi detto Farineli consegnato al Sigr Notaro Dn Lorenzo Gamarini – questo di 20 Febraio, 1782, pp. 20–22. Transcribed from Kirkpatrick, *Domenico Scarlatti*, p. 362.

[23] Burney, *The Present State of Music in France and Italy*, pp. 210–211; Latcham, "The Twelve Clavicordios," pp. 255–281.

a more conventional case design influenced by north German models. String lengths and striking points do not follow Cristofori's design closely. Though Spanish and Portuguese makers outwardly mimicked certain features of Florentine case structure (such as the suspended hitchpin rail; see Chapter 3), they were either ignorant of their complex internal construction or decided not to make use of the inner bentside that supported the soundboard and isolated it from the stress-bearing parts of the case. Such labyrinthine construction could only have been discovered by disassembling the case (candle or lamp light directed through a soundhole in the belly rail would not have revealed the existence of the double bentside, for example), and such an opportunity perhaps did not arise. Instead, Iberian makers made a well-crafted case of simplified design, and of more than adequate strength. There was no internal bentside supporting the soundboard, though the broad, overhanging hitchpin rail found in Cristofori's and Ferrini's pianofortes was evidently deemed an indispensable element and was retained, but only superficially. In the surviving Portuguese and Spanish pianos, the hitchpin rails are glued directly on top of the soundboards, though they are undercut so that they appear to be suspended over the soundboard as in the Florentine instruments. Because the undercutting extends nearly to the soundboard liners, the soundboards are, in fact, relatively unencumbered by these broad planks of wood.

Two Spanish Pianofortes[24]

It is likely that Florentine pianofortes were introduced to Portugal before they were brought to Spain, and that copies may have been made first in Portugal as well. Unfortunately, the earliest Portuguese pianofortes seem to have perished in the devastating 1755 earthquake, and thus, the earliest dated Portuguese pianos are rather late and date from the 1760s. The oldest surviving Iberian pianos therefore appear to be two anonymous and undated instruments that are attributed to the Spaniard Francisco Pérez Mirabal (active in Seville, 1745–1773) dating from about

---

[24] In addition to the four instruments discussed in this chapter, remnants of another Iberian pianoforte are reported by Raymond Russell (*The Harpsichord and Clavichord*, pl. 102a). This instrument is said to have had a piano action; however, Arnold Dolmetsch, believing this was a later modification, discarded the action and converted the instrument into a harpsichord. There is evidence that this instrument was fitted with a Cristofori-style action, as there are mortises in the key levers. See Beryl Kenyon de Pascual and David Law, "Another Early Iberian Grand Piano," *The Galpin Society Journal* 47 (1995), pp. 68–93.

Figure 5.1 Spanish piano attributed to Francisco Pérez Mirabal, Seville, 1745. Collection of the late Bartolomé March, Madrid.

1745, one in the collection of the late Bartolomé March of Madrid (Figure 5.1) and the other in the Museo Provincial de Bellas Artes in Seville.

The March piano (probably the earlier of the two because of the shorter keyboard range and simplified wrestplank bracing) has a compass of GG–d^3, whereas the piano in Seville extends from GG to g^3 (see Table 5.6). Though these instruments are unsigned and undated (at least on external surfaces), the March pianoforte is undoubtedly the instrument previously in the possession of the artist Gonzalo Bilboa (d. 1938) and pictured in *Spanish Interiors and Furniture* (1922) by Arthur Byne and Mildred Stapley.[25] The instrument in the illustration is described in the text as a piano, and the following inscription is given: "Me fecit Francisco Pérez Mirabal en Sevilla, 1745." Oddly, this inscription presently cannot be located on the March pianoforte, either on the front or back of the nameboard, any exposed surface of the case, or the action.[26] The date given in the Byne and Stapley book thus remains a mystery, though

---

[25] A. Byne and M. Stapley, *Spanish Interiors and Furniture* (New York, 1922; repr. 1969), pl. 129; Kenyon de Pascual, "Francisco Pérez Mirabal's Harpsichord and the Early Spanish Piano," *Early Music* (November, 1987), pp. 503–513.

[26] Kenyon de Pascual, ibid., p. 503.

perhaps the inscription was washed off in the course of a recent superficial cleaning, or the part bearing the inscription has been misplaced.

From its external appearance, the March piano is very similar to north German harpsichords: the double-curved bentside, the stand (notably the faceted, baluster legs, floor-height stretcher, bun feet, and the profile of the apron), as well as the *chinoiserie* decoration recall several of Hieronymus Albrecht Hass' instruments made in the early 1730s. Gottfried Silbermann employed a similar case and stand design in one of his pianos of the 1740s, though no example by him has survived with *chinoiserie* decoration. Indeed, if the presence of early Florentine pianos in Spain were not documented, one might conclude that the Spanish pianos discussed here were patterned after an instrument made by Gottfried Silbermann in the 1740s (see below). Though Francisco Pérez Mirabal's pianos date from the same period as the ones Silbermann made for Frederick the Great (see below), it is likely that Mirabal had already adopted north German harpsichord case design, and, like Silbermann, rejected the complex case structure employed by the Florentine builders, choosing instead to adapt the hammer action to the simpler style of case. However, as will be shown, certain idiosyncrasies of the action indicate that Pérez Mirabal copied a Florentine action rather than one made by Silbermann.

Contemporary documentation provides further evidence of this maker's work. There is an advertisement for a used *clave piano* by Pérez Mirabal appearing in the *Diario Historico y Politico de Sevilla* of 1792.[27] Tax records for the city of Seville list Francisco Pérez Mirabal as an "organ builder" in 1762, a generic designation that does not rule out the building of other types of keyboard instruments. An account book of the Colegiata de Antequera mentions a harpsichord ordered from Pérez Mirabal in 1773. The entry states that he was "a harpsichord maker from Seville who gives the greatest satisfaction." The instrument in question was said to have cost 3,400 *reales*.[28]

Both of the Spanish pianofortes discussed below appear to have been made by the same maker and have in common a number of highly unusual characteristics. The most notable are the use of paired, short-scaled strings (March, c^2 = 256 mm/striking point 52 mm; Seville, c^2 = 251 mm/striking point 46 mm; see Table 5.3) and a third choir of longer-scaled

---

[27] Ibid., p. 506.
[28] A. Llorden, "Maestros Organistas de la Colegiata de Antequera," *Anuario Musical* 33–35 (1978–1980), p. 76; Kenyon de Pascual, ibid., p. 503.

Figure 5.2 Third-choir mutation batten (located beyond the damper rack) of Spanish piano; collection of the late Bartolomé March, Madrid.

strings using the same bridge but running across a separate nut up to e^{b2} (March, $c^2 = 293$ mm/striking point 85 mm; Seville, $c^2 = 297$ mm/striking point 84 mm; see Table 5.3). Both instruments have a batten fitted with soft leather pads that can be brought to bear against the third set of strings (Figure 5.2).

This batten is not located at the nut, where it might function as a buff stop, but beyond the damper rack, so that its only apparent function would be to dampen the strings (either partially or entirely) rather than to modify their tone. The batten is brought into position by turning large winged wooden bolts at either end. (The wooden bolts have been removed in the Seville piano and replaced with metal ones.) This threaded mechanism permits sensitive adjustment of the batten's position relative to the strings, though as indicated above, it is unlikely that it could have served as a mutation stop no matter how carefully it was adjusted.

The instrument in the March collection exhibits extraordinarily fine and highly ornate *chinoiserie* decoration on case, lid, and stand. Similar, though somewhat simplified decoration is found on the interior of the lid of the pianoforte in the Museo Provincial de Bellas Artes in Seville, but it is lacking from the outer case sides. There are some unsolved problems with the instrument in Seville; for example, the stand is considerably longer (recess for instrument 2445 mm) than the case of the piano (length 2393 mm). The stand could have accommodated an instrument as long as the piano in the March collection (2440 mm); however, the Seville piano is wider (1030 mm) than the March instrument (956 mm) because of its larger compass, and the stand of the Seville piano is properly configured for this greater width. The Seville stand has been altered in several ways: the lower stretcher frame is lost and the legs have either been cut down or replaced. The absence of the raised *chinoiserie* on the outer case sides and the presence of gold leaf banding and heavy varnish suggest that the outer case may have been stripped of its original decoration, possibly because it was extensively damaged, and given a perfunctory gold banding and varnished. The case sides were cursorily examined using ultraviolet fluorescence to check for residue of animal glue and gesso that might have been used to build up the raised areas of *chinoiserie*, but traces of such decoration, as is found on the March piano, were not discovered.

The most important and distinguishing mechanical structure of the pianoforte is the hammer and escapement mechanism. Both of the Spanish actions are very similar to those used in the Cristofori pianos. The actions of the two Spanish pianos are nicely constructed, and that of the March instrument is particularly well preserved. The key levers of these Spanish pianos are of chestnut and are finely carved and notched beyond the playing surfaces. It is surprising that the maker went to the effort to carve the backs of the key levers, as they are completely hidden from view unless the actions are removed for adjustment or repair. The levers are considerably longer than those in the Cristofori instruments, and balance

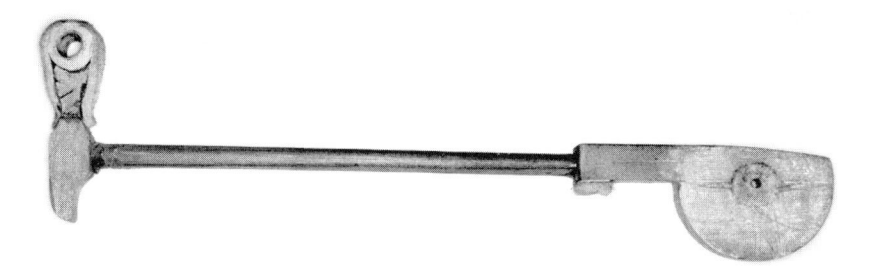

Figure 5.3 Hammer of Spanish piano; collection of the late Bartolomé March, Madrid.

points do not provide the same leverage (see Table 5.1). Cristofori used wooden posts to space and guide the keys at the distal end, whereas the Spanish pianofortes employ a rack fitted with projecting wood slips that simultaneously space and guide the keys. The key levers are cranked to the left and right to make way for one iron gap spacer located between a# and b. Interruptions in the hammer line are also found between G# and A, and c^2 and $c\#^2$, but there is no corresponding metalwork. The piano in Seville has one metal gap spacer and seven additional spacers of wood. Splaying of the keys indicates that these wooden spacers were part of the original design. Key length decreases from bass to treble, providing a slightly skewed hammer line, similar to that of Cristofori's 1726 piano (the angle is greater in the Portuguese pianos described below). The lengths of the key levers of Gottfried Silbermann's pianos are the same from bass to treble (similar to those of the 1722 Cristofori piano; see Chapter 3 and below), and thus their strike lines are not skewed but virtually perpendicular to the spine of the case. This is evidence that Pérez Mirabal did not copy a Silbermann piano, but rather one of Florentine origin. Lead weights are set into the backs of the key levers of both Spanish pianos, and the fronts are undercut below the key covers. Natural key platings are of bone, their lengths being 132 mm in the March piano and 134 mm in the Seville instrument. The skunk-tail accidentals are of rosewood with an inlaid bone strip; their lengths are 89 mm (March) and 91 mm (Seville). The three-octave span of both instruments is 488 mm.

The hammer butts of the Spanish pianos have a cork pivot bearing inlaid on one side (Spain and Portugal remain the world's principal sources of cork used in the bottling of wine), and a countersunk depression on the other side to help guide the pivot rods during assembly (Figures 5.3 and 5.4). These details are also present in Cristofori's hammers (see Chapter 3), though leather is used as a bushing material rather than cork.

Figure 5.4 Hammer of Spanish piano; collection of the Museo Provincial de Bellas Artes, Seville.

An interesting refinement seen in the Spanish instruments is the graded width of the hammer butts, which are 10 mm wide in the bass, diminishing to 8 mm in the treble. This grading required special care in constructing the hammer rack, as the spacers had to be appropriately graded and spaced. The hammer shanks are of cedar in the March instrument; the spruce shanks of the Seville piano are replacements. The shanks are approximately 5 mm in diameter, slightly stouter than those used by Cristofori (which are approximately 4 mm in diameter). In the Spanish pianos, the pivot points are perpendicular to the spine of the case, and there is a marked reduction in shank length as one moves from bass to treble (see Table 5.1), which contributes to the skewed hammer line.

The hammer heads are of two pieces: a lower part fitted to the shank, and a rolled parchment cylinder approximately 10 mm in diameter and 2 mm thick (almost twice as thick as those made by Cristofori) glued into a depression in the lower section and topped with soft leather. The hammer heads of the March piano are made of very thin parchment, rolled in many layers. The Seville piano has replacement heads made of rolled paper. Neither piano appears to have its original leather hammer coverings. The hammers of the March instrument are presently fitted with one layer of chamois; the Seville instrument's hammers are covered with a single layer of tanned leather, nicely skived around the wooden molding, but strangely with the finished (hair) side exposed.

The escapement jacks of the Spanish pianos are quite similar to those of Cristofori; they work in neatly cut mortises (Figure 5.5) that extend from the key lever into blocks of wood glued to the top and bottom of each key.

The method of pivoting the jacks is actually better designed in the Spanish pianos. In Cristofori's action, the jacks have a notch cut at their lower end, and this notch rocks against a padded block of wood glued to the bottom of the key (see Chapter 3). Because of this design feature, the jacks can be lifted out of the key only after the jack spring is unhitched,

Figure 5.5 Escapement mechanism of Spanish piano; collection of the Museo Provincial de Bellas Artes, Seville.

which requires removal of the entire key lever from the key frame. The Spanish pianos, in contrast, use a staple driven up through the bottom of the key to support the jack (Figure 5.6).

The horizontal section of the staple passes through a leather bearing in the jack and provides a true pivot rod. The jack can be pulled free of the staple for repair and simply pressed back down to re-seat it. The brass wire spring, as in Cristofori's design, is located below the key and projects from a block of wood glued to the underside of the key. The spring acts

Figure 5.6 Staple and escapement spring of Spanish piano; collection of the Museo Provincial de Bellas Artes, Seville.

Figure 5.7 Back section of key levers of Spanish piano; collection of the Museo Provincial de Bellas Artes, Seville.

by pushing downward, slightly behind the pivot point. This somewhat indirect method of applying pressure provides a short lever arm for the spring to act upon, and consequently the spring supplies a very light force for the return of the jack. The jack stop is similar in design to that of Cristofori and consists of a thin metal rod with a loop at the top faced with leather to prevent noise (Figure 5.7). To regulate the position of the escapement jack, the jack stop is bent back and forth by a probe inserted between the intermediate levers.

The intermediate levers are again closely modeled after those of Cristofori, even to the point of having their leather hinges sewn to the wood support rail for reinforcement (rather than simply glued). Lever lengths tend to be shorter than those used by Cristofori, and the contact point with the jack is closer to the lever's free end, thereby increasing the mechanical advantage of the lever, but reducing the speed and displacement of the hammer in comparison to Cristofori's geometry.

Dampers rest on the back end of the key levers and consist of a thin strip of wood positioned between the unisons, with the paired strings on the right and the longer-scaled string on the left. Upper and lower registers guide the damper jacks, and flat pads of leather are used as a damping material. Dampers run up to the top treble string. The original damper mechanism has been removed from the Seville piano and a set of racked over-dampers installed in its place. This is undoubtedly a mid- to late-nineteenth-century modification.

String lengths and striking points represent departures from Cristofori's design. As indicated above, both of the Spanish pianos described here employ a set of paired strings along with a third set of strings having a longer scale. The three sets of strings share the same bridge, but employ different nuts. This is most unusual, especially as there is no way of shifting the hammers from one set of strings to another. The nut for the paired strings is not continuous, but consists of a series of shallow blocks (approximately 2 mm high). Gaps between the blocks permit the longer, third set of strings to pass through. The strings are double-pinned at their respective nuts; however, the pins do not actually pass through the nuts but are driven into the wrestplank immediately in front of and behind them. At e^{b2} the nut for the short-scaled strings terminates, and from e^2 to the top note, all three sets of strings are pinned to the nut that is closer to the player, so string lengths and striking points for the unisons become more or less equivalent. All three strings are struck simultaneously, though as mentioned earlier, it might have been possible to soften the effect of or completely dampen the third, longer-scaled set of strings by raising the muting batten. Until one of these Spanish pianos is restored or copied, the function of the third set of strings and its mutation device will remain unclear. The strings do not appear to be original on either of the Spanish pianos, and the Seville instrument is presently strung with what appears to be uncharacteristically heavy wire. The bottom nine trichords of the March piano are of brass, the rest are iron.

Because these instruments lack soundboard and belly rail openings and are fully enclosed, soundboard ribbing and internal construction could not be determined. The outer cases are of walnut with double-curved bentsides (March, 14 mm thick; Seville, 11.5 mm thick). The case sides (March cheekpiece, 11.5 mm thick; Seville cheekpiece, 15 mm thick; March spine, 14 mm thick; Seville spine, 12.5 mm thick) overlap the bottom and are fixed to it with wood trenails. The wrestplanks are similar to the 1720 Cristofori piano in several respects: they are in the conventional non-inverted orientation, they taper towards the gap, and have heavy yokes mounted in front of the tuning pins for structural support.

The soundboards of these two pianos are of quartered spruce with chamfered, double-pinned bridges of approximately square section, tapering from 15 mm (width) × 15 mm (height) in the bass to 12 mm (width) × 12 mm (height) in the treble. The bridges of the Spanish instruments are

Figure 5.8 Treble section of soundboard of Spanish piano showing broad hitchpin rail; collection of the Museo Provincial de Bellas Artes, Seville.

continuous (that is, there is no separate bass section). The broad, walnut hitchpin rails bear a hitchpin and a bearing pin for each string, and there is little in the way of side draft after the string leaves the bridge (Figure 5.8).

The March piano's hitchpin rail is 88 mm wide at the treble and 79 mm wide in the bass, while the Seville's is somewhat narrower (68 mm) in the treble. As mentioned earlier, both hitchpin rails are deeply undercut, though they are not suspended over the soundboards as in the Cristofori and Ferrini pianos, which employ a separate internal bentside (see above and Chapter 3). In the March piano the chamfering extends to about 25–30 mm from the bentside, suggesting that the hitchpin rail may be undercut as far back as the soundboard liner.

Three Portuguese Pianofortes

Of three eighteenth-century Portuguese pianos that are known, only two are signed and dated. (Another "Antunes school" instrument in the collection of the Museu da Música – examined by the author in the 1990s while it was in storage at the Royal Palace-Convent, Mafra – previously thought to be another early piano, is actually a harpsichord converted to a piano at a rather late date.) The earliest of the dated instruments, which is

The Iberian Pianoforte 263

Figure 5.9 Piano by Henrique Van Casteel. Museu da Música, Lisbon.

also preserved in the collection of the Museu da Música (Figure 5.9), bears the mark "HENRIQUE VAN CASTEEL 1763" stamped on the action frame (Figure 5.10) and the signature "Henrique Van Casteel" on the top key lever (Figure 5.11).

Little is known about the maker Henrique Van Casteel: he was baptized Henri-Joseph Van Casteel in Tournai (Belgium) on November 19, 1722 and died in Brussels in 1790; his period of activity as an instrument maker

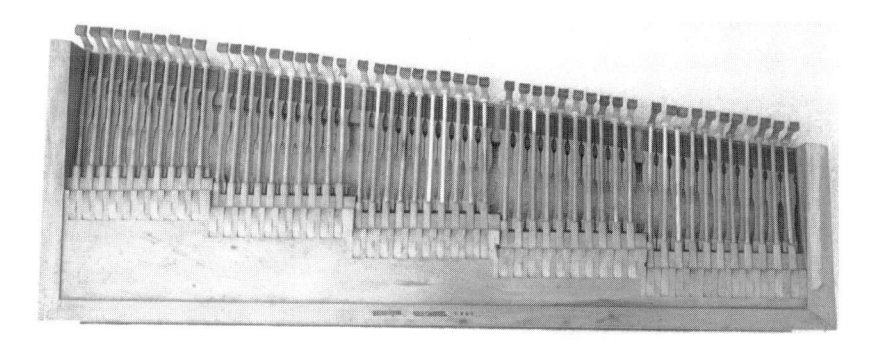

Figure 5.10 Action frame of the piano by Henrique Van Casteel; note maker's name and date stamped on frame.

Figure 5.11 Detail of key levers of Van Casteel piano showing maker's inscription "Henrique [partially missing] Van Casteel."

in Lisbon extended between 1757 and 1767, though he settled in Brussels in 1769 and was active as a maker in that city through the late 1770s.[29] Other than the pianoforte discussed below, two instruments by Van Casteel are known. He constructed a *Pyramide* piano in Brussels in 1771 (Kaufmann Collection), and the Muziekinstrumentenmuseum in Brussels has a square-piano nameboard bearing the inscription "HENRICUS VAN-CASTEEL, FECIT BRUXELLIS 1778."[30]

The second Portuguese piano (Figure 5.12) was in the collection of Harold Lester in London, and is now owned by a private collector in Switzerland. This instrument is unsigned, but certain aspects of the action design bear a strong resemblance to the Van Casteel instrument.

The third instrument (Figure 5.13), now in the National Music Museum in Vermillion, South Dakota, is inscribed "1767 ANTUNES" on the top key (Figure 5.14).

It is not known whether this instrument was made by Manuel Antunes or Joachim Jozé Antunes (possibly the son of Manuel). According to the late Dr. Macario Santiago Kastner, Manuel Antunes signed his instruments with only his surname, never adding "Manuel," while Joachim Jozé Antunes inscribed his full name either on the nameboard, key, or jack.

---

[29] P. Raspé, personal communication, 1985.
[30] Victor-Charles Mahillon, *Catalogue descriptif & analytique du Musee instrumental du Conservatoire royal de musique de Bruxelles*, vol. IV (Brussels, 1912), p. 450; Malou Haine and Nicolas Meeùs, *Dictionnaire des facteurs d'instruments de musique en Wallonie et à Bruxelles du 9e siècle à nos jours* (Brussels, 1986), pp. 414–415, and *Instruments de musique anciens à Bruxelles et en Wallonie – 17ᵉ–20ᵉ siècles* (Brussels, 1985), no. 21.

Figure 5.12 Anonymous Portuguese piano. Private collection, Switzerland.

Kastner's conclusion was, however, derived from just a few examples. As the Vermillion piano is simply signed "Antunes," Kastner's rule suggests that it was constructed by Manuel; however, this instrument is actually more similar in structure to a harpsichord signed by Joachim Jozé formerly in the collection of Richard Burnett (Finchcocks, Kent) than to a harpsichord by Manuel in the collection of the Conservatório de Música, Mafra.[31] On these grounds, the pianoforte in Vermillion is tentatively attributed to Joachim Jozé Antunes. We should keep in mind that Manuel and Joachim Jozé were very likely related and may have worked together; thus, there may be no reliable way of distinguishing their work on stylistic grounds.

[31] This is the opinion of Christopher Nobbs as reported to me in 1993.

Figure 5.13 Portuguese piano by Antunes. National Music Museum, Vermillion, South Dakota.

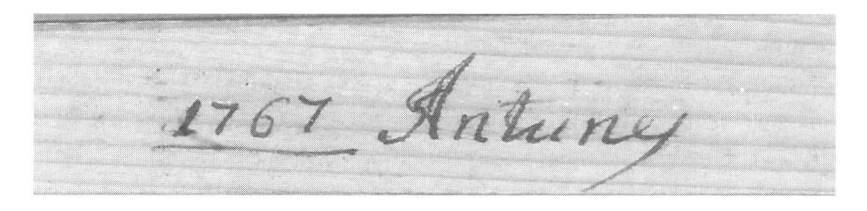

Figure 5.14 Inscription on a key lever of the Antunes piano. National Music Museum, Vermillion, South Dakota.

Of interest is Manuel Antunes' involvement in piano making, as attested by his application in 1760 for a royal privilege to be the sole manufacturer of "hammer-operated harpsichords" for a period of ten years. His petition, forwarded by the Board of Trade and dated April 21, 1760, states:

SIR: May your majesty be notified, by the Secretary of State for Trade of the Kingdom, that on the first day of the month this Board has been requested to issue an opinion on an application made by Manuel Antunes.

The petitioner, who is a Master Artisan in the manufacture of harpsichords and musical instruments, desires to make public a new invention which avoids the problems regularly encountered in the most up-to-date manufacture of harpsichords, which is the tardiness of the mechanism, and because of which, the delicacy of the *sol fa* cannot be perceived due to the noise of the keys, which becomes mixed up and clashes with the sound produced, thus creating a confused lack of harmony.

In order for him to take advantage of this new invention he desires the exclusive privilege for a period of ten years and promises that the price of the same will be much lower than hammer-operated harpsichords that are regularly sold.

Our experience of the petitioner in his manufactured articles leads us to conclude that he is capable of introducing new, improved ideas, and the concession of this favor causes us no loss but will rather be of benefit to the Kingdom.

It is the opinion of this Board of Trade that it is in your best interest to grant the above-named Manuel Antunes this exclusive privilege for a period of ten years for the new invention of harpsichords, and that a prohibition order should be issued on similar instruments coming from abroad of the same type discovered by Officials of the Foreign Ministry.[32]

On October 18, 1760 a privilege was issued with the proviso that Antunes' instruments not sell for more than 120,000 *reis*. Apparently this privilege was not scrupulously obeyed by other makers, as Van Casteel's piano was made in 1763, well before the ban on the construction of pianofortes by other makers had expired. It is possible, however, that Van Casteel's return to his native country in 1769 may have been the result of the restrictions imposed upon his livelihood by the royal order.

All of the extant Portuguese instruments have 51-note compasses of C–d^3 and relatively short scales (Van Casteel, $c^2 = 254$ mm, striking point 27 mm; Antunes, $c^2 = 273$ mm, striking point 43 mm; unsigned, $c^2 = 279$ mm, striking point 48 mm; see Table 5.4). The keyboards of all three Portuguese pianofortes have boxwood natural key platings, although the

---

[32] Translation by José Manuel Borges de Azevedo.

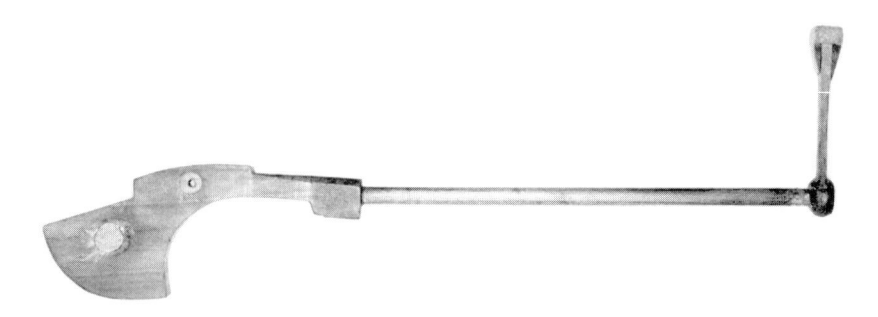

Figure 5.15 Hammer of the piano by Van Casteel; collection of the Museu da Música, Lisbon.

transverse scoring differs in each case. The Van Casteel piano has double score lines separated by 4.5 mm; the anonymous instrument has three score lines, the first two lines separated by 3.6 mm, and the rear line 1.8 mm behind the central scoring. The Antunes also has three score lines; however, the front two are separated by 2.5 mm and the back line is spaced 4.5 mm behind the central line. The boxwood key platings of the Antunes' keys (length 123 mm) are quite thick, approximately 4 mm at the playing surface tapering to 3 mm at the end of the tail. The Van Casteel and anonymous pianos have solid ebony accidentals (lengths 80 mm, 74 mm) while the Antunes has heavy ebony slips over rosewood blocks (length 83 mm). The three-octave span of the Van Casteel piano is 498 mm, that of the Swiss collector's anonymous piano 492 mm, while that of the Antunes is 490 mm.

The hammer butts of the three Portuguese pianos bear close resemblance to those of the 1722 Cristofori piano in that they do not have the full semicircular outline, but have a segment removed thus effectively lightening the hammer (Figure 5.15).

The Portuguese hammer butts are leaded behind the pivot point, which serves as a counterweight to further lighten the touch. Boxwood is used for the hammer butts of the anonymous piano, pear wood for the butts of the Antunes. Considering its ready availability in Portugal, it is not surprising that cork was selected as the bushing material in the pivot bearings of all three instruments. The hammer heads of the three Portuguese pianos are tall, like those of the 1720 Cristofori piano. This is necessary because the piano has the conventional wrestplank configuration with strings hitched to the top surface. (The Cristofori pianos of 1722 and 1726, whose nuts and strings are fixed to the underside, have short hammer heads, as do the Silbermann pianos; see below and Chapter 3.) Common to the hammer heads of all three Portuguese pianos is the flat striking surface, a feature also found in the 1722 Cristofori hammer heads. The Antunes piano is the only Portuguese instrument that may have its original hammer leather, which consists of a single layer of golden-colored leather, 3.5–4 mm thick, glued to the flat top of the wooden hammer head. Though most of the Van Casteel hammer heads appear to be original, the original leather surface has been replaced in recent times with a layer of leather over an underlayer of felt. When examined in 1984, the unsigned piano in the Harold Lester collection (now owned by a Swiss collector) had a thin, woolly layer of leather stretched over a harder, rounded leather pad. The wooden heads of the Lester piano appeared to be rather recent replacements. (See Table 5.2 for comparative measurements.)

One of the most interesting features of the Portuguese pianos is the design of the hammer rack and the mounting of the hammers in parallel sections. The Cristofori pianos use a single pivot line, with two pivot rods inserted from either end of the rack. Blocks of wood, which space and align the hammers, are drilled to admit the pivot rods. A problem with this system arises when a hammer must be removed for repair: one rod must be pulled out, and thus all the hammers between the midpoint and the impaired hammer then tumble free. The Portuguese makers arranged the hammers in four groups and set them in stepped configuration (Figure 5.10), creating a sharply angled strike line, a feature not found in Cristofori's pianos, which employ strike lines that are either slightly angled or nearly perpendicular to the case's spine, the angle being achieved in the 1720 and 1726 pianos by progressively shortening the hammer shank length from bass to treble (the shanks of the 1722 piano are essentially the same length from bass to treble). In the Portuguese pianos, each group of hammers has its own short pivot rod, which makes hammer removal more convenient; nevertheless, there would appear to be a great disadvantage to this system as it creates a discontinuity in the lengths of the hammer shanks at the transition points. For example: in the Van Casteel piano, the first group of hammers has progressively shorter shank lengths ranging from 122 mm to 107 mm; the first hammer shank of the second section then increases in length to 119 mm, and the next nine shanks progressively decrease to 107 mm; the first hammer shank of the third section then increases to 119 mm, and so the pattern continues. Surprisingly, there do not appear to be unacceptable variations in touch or volume at these transition points. Of course, the simplest method of achieving a sharply angled strike line while preserving uniform hammer shank length would have been to hinge the hammers individually – though

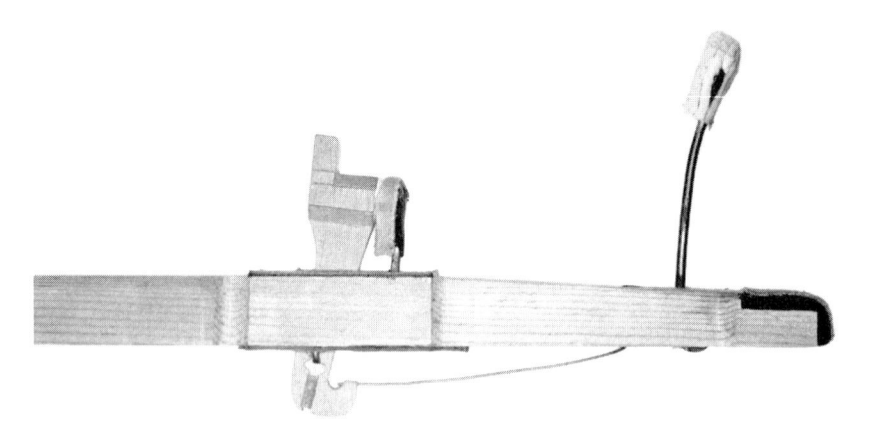

Figure 5.16 Detail of escapement mechanism of the Van Casteel piano; collection of the Museu da Música, Lisbon.

that idea evidently did not occur to the Iberian makers or their Florentine forebears.

In the Van Casteel and anonymous pianos, the escapement jacks pass through mortises in the key levers (Figure 5.16). The mortises are oversize, and leather guides are used (above and below in both the Van Casteel and Antunes instruments, and at the top surface only in the anonymous piano).

The anonymous piano uses a pivot pin driven through the key lever, while the Van Casteel piano employs a staple very much like the type used in the Spanish pianos attributed to Pérez Mirabal. In the anonymous instrument, the jack is slotted at the bottom. To assemble the escapement, the jack was pressed down over the staple. A leather pad was then inserted as a bearing surface and the jack secured by a wooden slip pressed up into the slot. The system used in the anonymous piano preserves the long lever arm of the escapement jack in Cristofori's design. The Antunes escapement jack represents a novel approach, though it recalls the tongue of a harpsichord jack in many respects (Figure 5.17). A 33 mm tall, slotted pivot block is mounted to the vertical-grained spruce key lever via a thin brass rod. The rod passes through a brass plaque, inlaid in the top surface of the key, which acts as a wear plate so that the pivot block can be bent back and forth for regulation without damaging the hole in the key lever. A pivot hole is drilled 6 mm from the top of the pivot block, and mounted in the slot is the 21 mm long escapement jack of walnut, with its pivot hole drilled 13 mm from the top. Except for a T-shaped extension that projects above the pivot block, this jack, together with its spring, resembles

Figure 5.17 Detail of escapement mechanism of the Antunes piano; collection of the National Music Museum, Vermillion, South Dakota.

a harpsichord tongue. The wire spring is mounted in the pivot block and presses directly against the front edge of the jack. The jack thus has a very short effective length of 13 mm, so it must subtend a rather large angle to disengage the intermediate lever. Nevertheless, the action is surprisingly quick and secure, perhaps because the wire spring works directly against the jack rather than indirectly from below (as in the Florentine design).

In the Portuguese pianos, the intermediate levers are glued and secured with stitching, just as in the Cristofori and Ferrini pianos. The leather hinges of the Antunes' intermediate levers are of the same pinkish morocco-grained leather that is found on the damper guides and the supporting layer of the back checks, and thus all leather appears to be original. The soft, woolly front layers of the back checks are very likely cut from the same skin as the hammer coverings.

Key cloths in all three Portuguese instruments are replacements; therefore, it was not possible to determine the original key dip. The key levers of the Van Casteel and anonymous piano are guided and spaced in the back by wooden posts, as in the Cristofori pianos. During the first of two recent restorations of the anonymous piano, a pin rack was installed (although the original wood posts were left in place). In a subsequent restoration (predating 1991) the original key guiding system was reinstated. The Antunes pianoforte uses a pin rack to guide the back ends of the keys. The rack is a laminate consisting of two layers of cross-grained

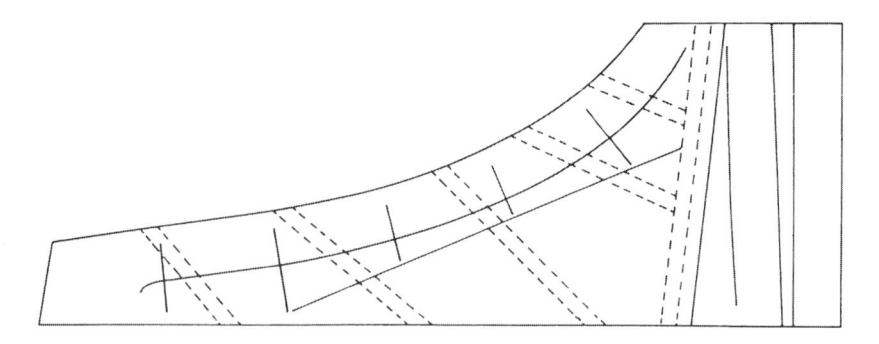

Figure 5.18 Schematic drawing of the bridge, nut, soundboard ribs, cutoff bar (solid lines), and case braces (dashed lines) of the anonymous Portuguese piano, private collection, Switzerland. (After a drawing by Christopher Nobbs.)

spruce, with the vertically oriented section positioned at the forward, narrow end of the slot to reduce pin friction.

The damper action of the Portuguese pianos is similar to that of Cristofori's pianos in that the damper jacks consist of a thin slip of wood that passes between the bichords and runs in upper and lower guides. In the Portuguese pianos, both the upper and lower guides are leathered. The dampers are lifted by the leather-padded back ends of the key levers. Damper material in the Portuguese pianos consists of a leather band that passes through a horizontal slot in the damper jack (as in the 1726 Cristofori piano); most of the original damper material has been replaced in the three instruments.

The Van Casteel and anonymous pianos have three holes in their belly rails, the Antunes piano has none (these are similar to those employed for acoustical purposes by Cristofori; see Chapter 3). The apertures in the belly rails of two of the Portuguese pianos permit the case and soundboard structure to be seen, though not with great clarity. It appears that the Portuguese makers did not follow the complex case design of Cristofori, as there is no separate, internal bentside supporting the soundboard, isolating it from the stress-bearing parts of the case. Casework of the Portuguese pianofortes is quite massive, undoubtedly designed to support the heavier stringing. The anonymous piano employs dovetailed case joints. Unlike the Spanish pianos, the Portuguese instruments have square tails rather than double-curved bentsides.

The anonymous piano has five braces mounted diagonally from bentside to the spine and belly rail (Figure 5.18), while the Van Casteel has four (Figure 5.19).

The Iberian Pianoforte 273

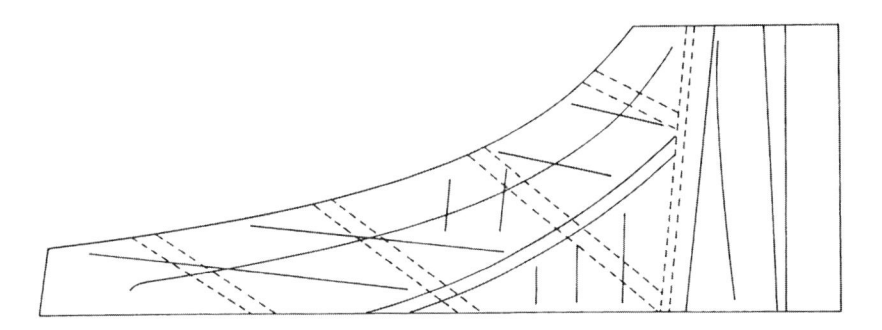

Figure 5.19 Schematic drawing of the bridge, nut, soundboard ribs, cutoff bar (solid lines), and case braces (dashed lines) of the Van Casteel piano, Museu da Música, Lisbon.

The anonymous piano has a strip of iron, perhaps original, that links the bentside, cheek, and belly rail.[33] The internal bracing of the Antunes piano was observed through cracks in the case bottom (Figure 5.20) and consists of three equi-spaced braces (43–49 mm high) running perpendicularly from spine to bentside.[34] Two diagonal struts run from the belly rail to the case bottom, while another two run from bentside liner to bottom; one of these wedges up against a bottom brace, while the other wedges up against the belly rail. Another brace is located between the bentside and belly rail in the extreme treble.

The arrangement of the diagonal braces in the Portuguese pianos is reminiscent of the buttressing found in the Cristofori and Ferrini pianos, and it is possible that Portuguese makers adopted this system after peering through the bellyrail holes of a Florentine piano. While the broad, diagonal braces could have been observed in this way, it would have been impossible to distinguish the separate internal bentside found in Cristofori's pianos with such limited visual access. The soundboard liner of the anonymous Portuguese piano extends to the case bottom, resulting in a very thick case wall. That of the Van Casteel piano is quite stout (approximately 30 mm wide) but does not extend to the case bottom (it extends approximately 80 mm below the soundboard). The cases of the Portuguese pianos exhibit some traits of northern-European-style construction. Most notably, the case walls are built upon the bottom, and a lower case molding conceals the edge of the bottom board. In the Antunes instrument, trenails pass from the bottom up into the case sides.

---

[33] Christopher Nobbs, personal communication, 1991.
[34] John Koster kindly allowed me to examine his drawing of the case interior and ribbing.

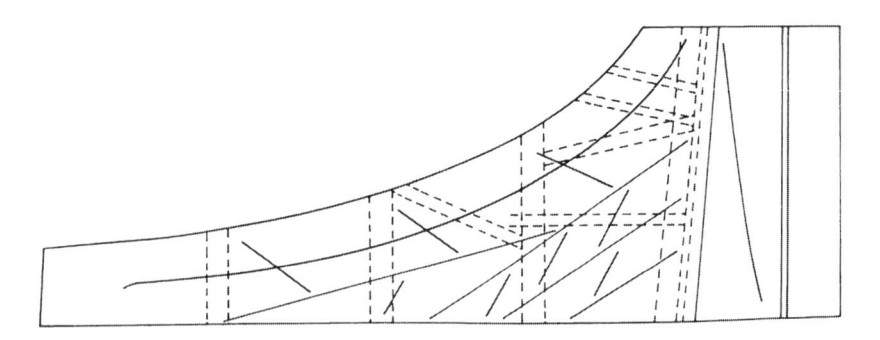

Figure 5.20 Schematic drawing of the bridge, nut, soundboard ribs, cutoff bar (solid lines), and case braces (dashed lines) of the Antunes piano, National Music Museum, Vermillion, South Dakota. (After a drawing by John Koster.)

The Van Casteel piano has very unusual soundboard ribbing (Figure 5.19). Owing to limited visual access, it was not possible to determine whether all of the ribs are original, though as the bottom shows evidence of having been removed, it is possible that the ribbing has been altered. In this instrument, the cutoff bar is curved and is so massive that it resembles a harpsichord's four-foot hitchpin rail. In the non-active portion of the soundboard (to the left of the cutoff bar) there are three ribs mounted perpendicularly to the spine. These three short ribs are steeply curved along their lower edges, extending to a depth of approximately 50 mm at the center. If one discounts the massiveness of the hitchpin rail and the contour of the three short ribs, this cutoff bar and group of ribs comprise the familiar north-European-style ribbing configuration, consistent with Van Casteel's origins (Tournai) and presumed training. Four additional ribs, and the glue line of a fifth, are present in the acoustically "active" area of the soundboard between the cutoff bar and bentside. These are again deeply profiled (approximately 50–60 mm deep at their midpoints) and run nearly parallel to the strings. They are undercut where they intersect the bridge. Also, there are two shorter ribs (again, having similarly deep profiles) running between and perpendicularly to the second and third ribs. There is a possibility that these unusually shaped ribs were fitted during a restoration in order to flatten the soundboard.[35] Until the ribbing can be examined more carefully, it will be impossible to tell if the present arrangement of ribs is original.

The soundboard ribbing of the anonymous Portuguese piano consists of a straight cutoff bar with five ribs in the acoustically active region

---

[35] Christopher Nobbs, "Two Portuguese Pianos and a Harpsichord" (unpublished paper, 1990).

mounted perpendicularly to the bentside, four of which abut the cutoff bar, and one being located beyond the cutoff bar in the bass (Figure 5.18).[36]

The Antunes ribbing consists of a principal cutoff bar and three parallel bars mounted at an angle to it (Figure 5.20). The closest of these three parallel bars forms a continuation of the principal cutoff bar. Five short ribs are mounted between these four bars, and three ribs run under the bridge between the bentside and the cutoff bars (the ribs are undercut where they intersect the bridge). The positions of these ribs and cutoff bars are reminiscent of those found in the 1785 Joachim Jozé Antunes harpsichord formerly in the collection of Richard Burnett.

The bridges of the three Portuguese pianos are similar in that they are double-pinned throughout, just as in Cristofori's and Ferrini's pianos. Their dimensions, construction, and materials differ, however. The Van Casteel piano has a sawn bridge of jacaranda (or possibly stained walnut) measuring 22 mm high and 23.5 mm wide in the bass, and 15.5 mm high and 15.5 mm wide in the treble. The anonymous piano has a bent bridge of beech (treble section replaced) of slighter dimensions: 19 mm high and 16 mm wide in the bass, and 14.5 mm high and 10 mm wide in the treble. This bridge has a simple, rounded top. The Antunes bridge is walnut, nearly square in section, with chamfered corners. It is 15 mm high and 22 mm wide in the bass, and 12 mm high and 9 mm wide in the treble.

All of the Portuguese pianos have a wide, undercut hitchpin rail in imitation of those found in the Cristofori and Ferrini pianos. Again, the Florentine hitchpin rails are actually fixed to the outer case liner and suspended over the soundboard, which is fixed to a separate, internal bentside. In the Portuguese pianos there is no internal bentside supporting the soundboard, and the hitchpin rails are glued directly on top of the soundboard. Undercutting of the Portuguese hitchpin rails extends nearly to the soundboard liners, so the soundboards are relatively unencumbered by these broad plates of wood. This form of case construction is similar to that of the Spanish pianos discussed earlier. The pinning of the hitchpin rails varies in each instrument: the Antunes piano uses a bearing pin and a hitchpin (as in the Cristofori pianos); the anonymous piano has just a single hitchpin; and the Van Casteel piano uses two bearing pins and a hitchpin, except for the top eleven notes, which employ only a hitchpin.

---

[36] Rib positions were derived from a full scale drawing of Harold Lester's anonymous piano made during its restoration by Christopher Nobbs, 1989. I would like to thank Mr. Nobbs for supplying me with a copy of his drawing. The piano is now owned by a collector in Switzerland.

The stringing of the anonymous and Van Casteel pianos is unusual in that the bichords are not paired, but form an evenly spaced string band (similar to that found in the Gottfried Silbermann pianos; see below). The string band is broken only in the Van Casteel piano by four iron hoops extending from the wrestplank to the belly rail that bridge the gap. This discontinuity is mirrored by gaps in the keyboard and hammer line. (Iron gap spacers are also found in the Ferrini pianoforte/harpsichord; see above.) The strings of the Antunes piano are paired. All of the Portuguese examples exhibit considerable foreshortening of string lengths in the bass (as compared to Cristofori), and striking points are significantly further away from the nut. The anonymous piano exhibits greater similarity in string lengths and striking points to the Antunes piano than to those of the Van Casteel instrument. In general, the Portuguese and Spanish pianos exhibit similar scalings and striking points that distinguish them from the Florentine instruments (see Tables 5.3 and 5.4).

String-gauge markings are found on the anonymous and Antunes pianofortes (see Table 5.5). The repetition of the last marked gauge in the anonymous piano could indicate a transition point from brass to iron, whereas the upper and lower markings of the Antunes piano may have been repeated to prevent confusion that can occur when it is unclear whether gauges are associated with tuning pins to the left or right of the mark. There is evidence that the Antunes piano was at some time strung completely in brass.[37] It is clear that the stringing schedules of these instruments are considerably heavier than those typically employed in harpsichord building. Possible metric equivalents are provided in Table 5.5.

The Van Casteel and Antunes pianos have provision for *una corda*, whereas the anonymous piano appears to have been modified to provide this feature (the bass key block has been crudely reduced in width, thus permitting lateral displacement of the action). It is likely that the facility for *una corda* was intended to isolate a single choir of strings for tuning, rather than for use as a mutation stop, as these very early pianos were quiet enough to begin with, and their innate dynamic flexibility placed the ability to play softly at the player's fingertips.

The three Portuguese pianos have similar case decoration. All have two-piece trestle stands with fret-sawn, inverted hearts (a decorative feature frequently seen in Portuguese clavichord stands and furniture;

---

[37] John Koster informed me that he had observed copper corrosion products on bridge pins throughout the compass of the instrument. This would be consistent with brass (an alloy of copper and zinc) wire coming in contact with the pins.

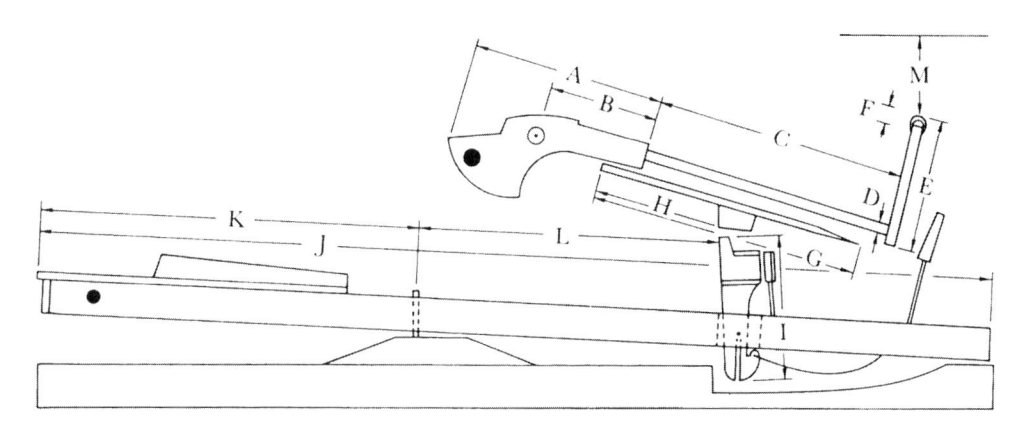

Figure 5.21 Schematic drawing of Spanish and Portuguese hammer actions.

Table 5.1 Comparative measurements of hammer actions of Cristofori and Spanish pianos (all measurements in millimeters)

	Cristofori piano		Spanish piano	
	1720	1726	March Collection	Museo – Seville
A	52	48.5	56	56
B	34	32.5	39	37
C Bottom	123.5	121	115	112
C Top	112.5	117.5	106	104
D	4	4	5–5.25	5
E Bottom	49.5	24.5	43	43
E Top	46.5	19.5	43	44
F Bottom	19	18.5	11	12
F Top	16	12	11	13
G	113	135.5	95	108
H	54	69.5	43	40
I	62	56.5	61	60
J Bottom	443	344.5	479	474
J Top	407	336	471	466
K Bottom	165	123.5	211	351
K Top	159	125	211.5	360
L Bottom	148	116	145	143
L Top	135	111	144	151
M (approx.)	31–35	22–23	32	36

see Figures 5.9, 5.12, and 5.13). The stand of the anonymous piano is a composite, the rear section possibly having been used to support a clavichord. Macacauba wood (*Platymiscium pinnatum*) veneer (often used in Portuguese furniture) lines the keyboard consoles and soundboard wells.

Table 5.2 Comparative measurements of hammer actions of Cristofori and Portuguese pianos (all measurements in millimeters)

	Cristofori 1720	Cristofori 1722	Cristofori 1726	Van Casteel	Antunes	Anonymous
A	52	48	48.5	68–71	72	73
B	34	33	32.5	39.5–41	38	42
C Bottom	123.5	116	121	122	117	116
C Top	112.5	115	117.5	101	102	96
D	4	4	4	3.3–4	4.25	4
E Bottom	49.5	12	24.5	41	39	49
E Top	46.5	13.5	19.5	41	39	49
F Bottom	19	4*	18.5		4*	
F Top	16	3.5*	12		3.5*	
G	113	130	135.5	130–104	129–113	106–95
H	54	68	69.5	64–56	69–62	51–40
I	62	59	56.5	57.5	21	56
J Bottom	443	332	344.5	437	443	444
J Top	407	320	336	343	367	363
K Bottom	165	124	123.5	170	175	178
K Top	159	123	125	138	139	145
L Bottom	148	110	116	160	170	
L Top	135	110	111	119	144	
M (approx.)	31–35	35–36	22–23	45–37	42	41–35

* Denotes thickness of leather.

Carved projections on the key blocks assist in withdrawing the action or shifting it for *una corda*. The external case walls of the anonymous and Van Casteel pianos are painted a dark green. The Van Casteel lid interior is painted in *faux bois* to match the macacauba console; the anonymous lid interior has been repainted vermilion. The painted decoration of the Antunes – consisting of light-blue panels with flowers, dark blue borders, and gilt scrolls – may be a later addition.

Table 5.3 String lengths/striking points of Cristofori and Spanish pianos (all measurements in millimeters)

Note	Cristofori 1720	Cristofori 1726	Mirabal March Collection	Mirabal Museo – Seville
GG		1810/113	1835/123	
			1856/155*	1886/165
C	1885/163	1961/133	1693/110	1705/120
			1747/155	1758/160
F	1879/151	1608/108	1488/107	1443/117
			1548/152	1503/155
c	1100/134	1125/73	1013/100	968/105
			1073/144	1026/148
f	838/118	841/57	767/93	724/96
			824/139	777/136
c^1	567/91	568/38	507/78	499/79
			559/123	548/120
f^1	429/73	422/29	385/67	387/67
			431/105	435/108
c^2	286/51	280/17	256/52	251/46
			293/85	297/84
f^2	214/39	213/13	207/60	211/63
			212/60	214/64
c^3	151/26	142/7	133/30	137/38
			136/30	138/39
d^3			120/25	
			121/25	
f^3	122/19			101/25
				103/25
g^3				93/20
				94/20

* Lower sets of figures are for third choir of long-scaled strings (see text).

Table 5.4 String lengths/striking points of Cristofori and Portuguese pianos (all measurements in millimeters)

	Cristofori				
Note	1720	1726	Van Casteel 1763	Antunes 1767	Anonymous
C	1885/163	1961/133	1684/123	1776/138	1677/125
F	1879/151	1608/108	1431/110	1486/123	1415/115
C	1100/134	1125/73	981/87	1047/101	961/100
F	838/118	841/57	744/73	791/88	748/90
c^1	567/91	568/38	492/55	530/71	532/75
f^1	429/73	422/29	381/42	396/58	406/65
c^2	286/51	280/17	254/27	273/43	279/48
f^2	214/39	213/13	184/20	202/35	218/37
c^3	151/26	142/7	127/14	132/23	143/23
d^3			110/10	118/21	129/18
f^3	122/19				

Table 5.5 String-gauge markings of Portuguese pianos

Anonymous	Gauge	Antunes	Gauge	Possible equivalents (Antunes)
C	I	C	00	.68 mm
		D	00	.68 mm
		D#	01	.60 mm
F#	II			
		e	1	.54 mm
		f	2	.48 mm
a	III			
		$d\#^1$	3	.43 mm
b^1	IIII			
$c\#^2$	IIII			
		d^2	4	.38 mm
		d^3	4	.38 mm

Table 5.6 Case measurements of Portuguese and Spanish pianos* (all measurements in millimeters)

	Anonymous	Van Casteel	Antunes	March	Seville
Length	2293	2268	2267	2440	2393
Width	810	870	822	956	1030
Height	227	217	227	234	224

* All measurements exclude moldings, external braces, stands, and lids.

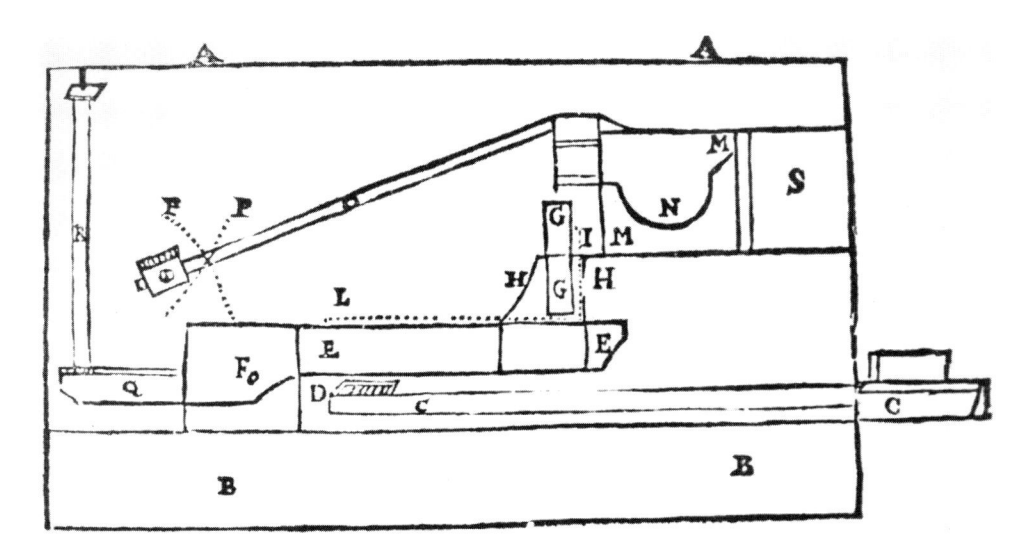

Figure 5.22 Cristofori's hammer action as it appeared in Johann Ulrich König's "Musicalische Merckwürdigkeiten des Marchese, Scipio Maffei," in Johann Mattheson, *Critica Musica* (Hamburg, 1725).

The Pianoforte in Germany

Scipione Maffei's "Nuova invenzione d'un Gravecembalo col piano, e forte," which appeared first in 1711 in the *Giornale de' letterati d'Italia* and again in 1719 in *Rime e prose*, was soon translated into German by Johann Ulrich König, court poet in Dresden. This complete and accurate translation, which includes a facsimile of Maffei's drawing of Cristofori's hammer action (Figure 5.22), was published in Mattheson's *Critica musica* in 1725.[38]

Surprisingly, not a single instrument from the first half of the eighteenth century survives that employs an action modeled after Maffei's or König's drawings. One action that vaguely resembles the drawing is found in late-eighteenth-century square pianos made by Ignace Joseph Senft of Augsburg (Figure 5.23).

This action has a pivoted secondary lever with a block of wood mounted upon it that bears resemblance to the jawbone-shaped piece pictured by Maffei and König. Despite this superficial similarity, Senft's mechanism works on an entirely different principle, utilizing a *Prelleiste* (rebound rail) and a hammer mounted on the key lever via a *Kapsel* (a fork-shaped bearing mounted on a metal rod) similar to that employed in the German and Viennese actions.

[38] Johann Ulrich König, "Musicalische Merckwürdigkeiten des Marchese, Scipio Maffei," in Mattheson, *Critica Musica*, vol. II, pp. 335–342.

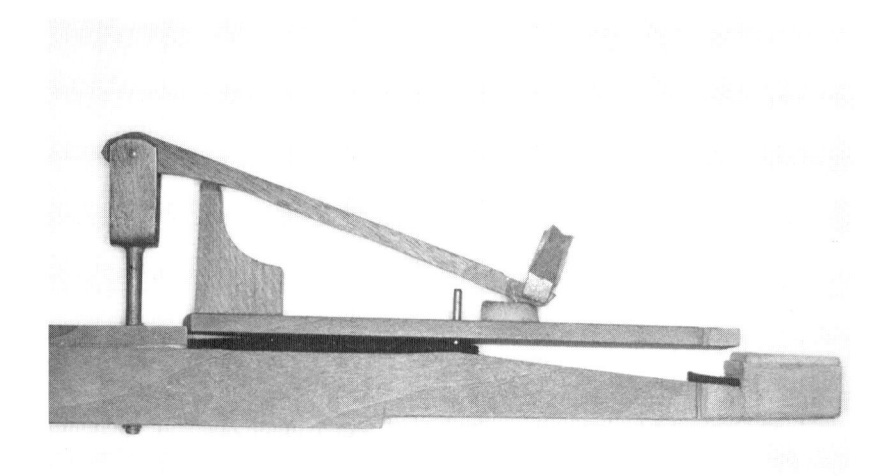

Figure 5.23 Hammer action, Ignace Joseph Senft; Crosby Brown Collection, The Metropolitan Museum of Art. Note the similarity to the drawing of Cristofori's early action pictured in Figure 5.22.

Though König's translation of Maffei's article may have alerted German builders to the idea of the pianoforte, they were apparently unable to successfully meet the challenge of making such instruments until the arrival in Germany of a piano by Cristofori with his later style of action (see Chapter 3). Among the earliest pianofortes built in Germany were those of Gottfried Silbermann (b. Klein Bobritzsch, Saxony, 1683; d. Freiberg, 1753), whose extant instruments have hammer actions that are virtual replicas of the type used in the 1726 Cristofori piano (see Chapter 3). In 1733 Johann Heinrich Zedler wrote that:

Dieser berühmte Herr Silbermann [hat] nur vor kurzem wiederum ein neues Instrument erfunden, so er Piano Fort nennet, und in vorigem Jahre Ihro Königl. Hoheit dem Cron-Prinzen von Pohlen und Littauen u. auch Churfürsten in Sachsen übergeben, und soil dasselbe wegen seines ausserordentlichen angenehmen Klanges sehr gnädig aufgenommen worden seyn.[39]

(This famous Mr. Silbermann has only recently invented a new instrument called the Piano Fort, and in the previous year delivered one to His Royal Highness, the Crown Prince of Poland and Lithuania, and also Elector of Saxony [Frederick Augustus I], which was well received on account of its extraordinarily pleasant sound.)

---

[39] Johann Heinrich Zedler, *Grosses vollständiges Universal-Lexicon*, 64 vols. (Halle and Leipzig, 1732–1750), vol. v (1733), s.v. "Cembalo d'Amour."

The idea that Silbermann invented the piano persisted in Germany through the early nineteenth century. For example, Christian Friedrich Daniel Schubart's *Ideen zu einer Aesthetik der Tonkunst* (Vienna, 1806) states that "dieses vortreffliche Instrument ist – Heilung! wieder eine Erfindung der Deutschen. Silbermann fühlte die Unart des Flügels, der entweder ganz und gar das Kolorit nicht ausdrücken konnte" (this admirable instrument is – hurrah! again an invention of the Germans. Silbermann perceived the failing of the harpsichord, which could not express color at all).[40]

Other early makers of the pianoforte in Germany include Wahl Friedrich Ficker (Zeitz), who advertised a *Cymbal-Clavir* with cloth-covered hammers in the *Leipziger Post-Zeitungen* on October 23, 1731; Christian Ernst Friederici (b. Meerane, Saxony, 1709; d. Gera, 1780); and Franz Jacob Späth (or Spath) of Regensburg (1714–1786), who, Ernst Ludwig Gerber claimed, had "presented by 1751 to the Elector of Bonn a *Tangenten-Flügel* with thirty varieties of tone" (überreichte schon 1751 dem Churfürsten zu Bonn einen Tangenten-Flügel mit 30 Veränderungen).[41] The surviving pianos ascribed to Silbermann and Friederici will be examined below.

Christoph Gottlieb Schröter

Perhaps developed somewhat earlier than the working instruments made by Silbermann and Friederici were two experimental hammer-action models designed by Christoph Gottlieb Schröter (1699–1782). The versatile Schröter – organist, composer, and theoretician – claimed to have invented the hammer action in 1717 in an announcement dated September 22, 1738 (though not published until 1747, in Mizler's *Musikalische Bibliothek*).[42] In this account, Schröter admits that he learned of Cristofori's hammer action through König's translation of Maffei's article. However, he was apparently unaware of the date of publication of the original article by Maffei, perhaps because the lengthy title of König's version lacks the date: "Musicalische Merckwürdigkeiten. Des Marchese, Scipio Maffei, Beschreibung eines neuerfundenen *Claviceins*, auf welchem das *piano* und *forte* zu haben, nebst einigen Betrachtungen über die Musicalische Instrumente, aus dem Welschen ins Teutsche übersetzt" ("Musical

---

[40] Christian Friedrich Daniel Schubart, *Ideen zu einer Aesthetik der Tonkunst* (Vienna, 1806), p. 142.
[41] Ernst Ludwig Gerber, *Neues historisches-biographisches Lexicon der Tonkünstler* (Leipzig, 1812), p. 225.
[42] Lorenz Mizler, *Neu eröffnete musikalische Bibliothek*, 4 vols. (Leipzig, 1739–1754), vol. III (1747), pp. 474–475.

curiosities. The Marquis Scipio Maffei's description of a newly discovered clavier, which has soft and loud, along with an account of musical instruments, translated from the Italian into German"). Because Maffei's article was first published in 1711, Schröter's claim of being the inventor of the hammer action does not hold up chronologically (furthermore, Cristofori had actually developed the piano by the year 1700; see Chapter 3). Schröter's announcement in Mizler's *Musikalische Bibliothek* is as follows:

To be sure, some of these craftsmen, who for several years were bold enough to pass off one of my inventions as their own, do not deserve to be dealt with as fairly as will actually be the case: I did, in fact, in 1717 in Dresden, after much consideration, have a model made of a new keyboard instrument with hammers, partly with, and partly without intermediate levers [see discussion below], on which one could play as one desired, softly or loudly, always in a singing and refined manner. Not long thereafter, I was greatly privileged to present this model twice to His Royal Majesty [Frederick Augustus I], of most blessed memory, in the presence of Count Vizthum, as well as a few chamberlains, and the highly esteemed Capellmeister, Mr. Schmied, all [of whom] found it to their approval. Consequently, it was decided to find a capable craftsman to develop and perfect it.

I will, to avoid excessive length, not name other distinguished people, most of them according to trustworthy report still alive, who have also seen and heard this model with their own eyes and ears. Also I will not say for certain whether the person who carried out this praiseworthy undertaking, to my great cost and his greatest disgrace, and after my departure from Saxony popularized this invention within and outside of Germany, was an honorable builder. But this much is certain, that Signor Bartolomeo Christofali, who is mentioned in the second volume of Mattheson's *Musikalische Critik*, covered on page 336, can only be the second inventor, so that I, according to the correct chronology, am in fact the first; it would, then, be evident that two different people at different times invented the same thing with the same intention. I am obliged to add that with the invention of the printing press a similar dispute erupted.

Now, I might also name those who copied my invention in Germany. Some changed it one way, others in another in minor details; only out of pity for their failed results do I now withhold their well-known names. Anyway, I have long been certain that not one was able to give this instrument the necessary strength so that at least it could be distinctly perceived in chamber music. Consequently, they have not done anything further than to confirm the saying: "It is easier to copy a good thing in a mediocre way than to invent a good thing well oneself."

Schröter elaborated on his claim in a letter published some years later in Friedrich Wilhelm Marpurg's *Kritische Briefe über die Tonkunst*.[43]

---

[43] Friedrich Wilhelm Marpurg, *Kritische Briefe über die Tonkunst*, 3 vols. (Berlin, 1760–1764), vol. III, pt 1 (1763), pp. 81–104.

The title of this twenty-three-page letter dated August 20, 1763 is "A detailed description by Mr. Christoph Gottlieb Schröter, organist of the *Hauptkirche* in Nordhausen, of his keyboard instrument invented in 1717, upon which one can play in discernible gradations of loud and soft, and as easy to play as a clavichord. Including two diagrams."[44] In his defensive and often bitter account, Schröter describes in detail how he attempted to present his action models to the Elector of Saxony in Dresden on February 11, 1721. He repeats his account published by Mizler of the presentation to the Elector and various members of the court, and adds that he was invited back to the royal residence the following week to perform on the harpsichord and clavichord. According to Schröter's account, the Elector and other members of the court were impressed with his playing, and he claims that there was even talk of offering him a position at court. Schröter then relates an odd incident regarding the princess' Austrian chief lady-in-waiting, alleging that she asked him some peculiar questions, the last being an indelicate one that, being a "born Saxon," he felt he could not answer in the affirmative. Apparently embarrassed by this episode, he took his leave. As a result of this event, he states that he decided to leave Dresden, though despite polite and repeated attempts, he was never able to recover the action models before his departure. To his consternation, instruments bearing his hammer action shortly began to appear in Germany as well as other countries, though he was never properly credited as the inventor.

In the sixteen years that separated Schröter's two published letters, it is clear that the pianoforte had begun to gain popularity in Germany. Schröter reports in Marpurg's *Kritische Briefe* that "in more than twenty cities and towns known to me, the manufacture of the common harpsichord was replaced, after 1721, with keyboard instruments having hammers or tangents," and that "if you ask any of the builders of such instruments who the inventor is, the answer in practically every case is that he [the builder] is the inventor." He adds, "who cannot be aware here of the scores of sheer lies?" The indignant Schröter, evidently still unaware of the date of publication of Maffei's article on Cristofori, even goes so far as to accuse Bartolomeo Cristofori and an "ingenious man in Dresden" (most likely Gottfried Silbermann) of deliberately neglecting to include his "steel pressure bar" (*Widerstandseisen*; see below) in their instruments as a stratagem to "convince the world that no one by the name of Schröter had ever busied himself with the invention of such a keyboard instrument."

---

[44] For a full transcription and translation of Schröter's *Briefe*, see Pollens, *The Early Pianoforte*, pp. 162–168, 246–264.

Though history has demonstrated that Cristofori preceded Schröter in designing a hammer action, Schröter's claim was accepted as fact by some: Heinrich Christoph Koch's *Musikalisches Lexicon* (Frankfurt, 1802) states that the "Fortepiano ist das bekannte Lieblingsinstrument der jetzigen Clavierspielenden Welt, welches im Jahre 1717 von Christoph Gottlieb Schröter, einer Kreuzschüler in Dresden, der in der Folge die Organistenstelle in der Hauptkirche zu Nordhausen bekleidete, erfunden worden ist"[45] (fortepiano is the well-known, favored instrument of the modern keyboard-playing world, which was invented in the year 1717 by Christoph Gottlieb Schröter, a student of the Kreuzschule in Dresden, who subsequently occupied the post of organist in the principal church in Nordhausen). German encyclopedists reiterated this claim well into the nineteenth century.

Though taken seriously in some quarters, how credible are the details of Schröter's account? Can it be that he lost his action models as the result of fleeing an indiscreet question posed to him? If the models ever existed, did they bear any resemblance to the drawings appearing in Marpurg's *Kritische Briefe*? Though Schröter's two actions do differ considerably from those of Cristofori, there are some similarities. For example, it is possible that the pivoting hammer and intermediate lever in Schröter's first action (Figure 5.24) were derived from Cristofori's design.

As in Cristofori's action, the hammer faces away from the player and is suspended from an independent rail. Also, Schröter's tangent is shaped the same and is positionally analogous to *das bewegliche Zünglein* (the little, movable tongue) pictured in König's engraving of Cristofori's action (Figure 5.22), though unlike Cristofori's tongue, Schröter's tangent does not work as an escapement by rocking back and forth, but travels straight up and down like a harpsichord jack and simply transfers motion from the intermediate lever and the hammer. In his second design (Figure 5.25), the tangent is the striking element itself. The shapes of parts and their positional similarities suggest that Schröter's first design was derived from the drawing and description published by Maffei or König, and thus cast doubt upon his claim as an independent inventor.

An element common to both Schröter's action designs is a device for applying pressure on the strings from above to prevent the strings from lifting off the nut as a result of the hammer's impact. Such a device is not specified in Maffei's description, nor is one depicted in the action

---

[45] Heinrich Christoph Koch, *Musikalisches Lexicon*, 2 vols. (Frankfurt, 1802; repr. Kassel, 2000), vol. I, s.v. "Fortepiano."

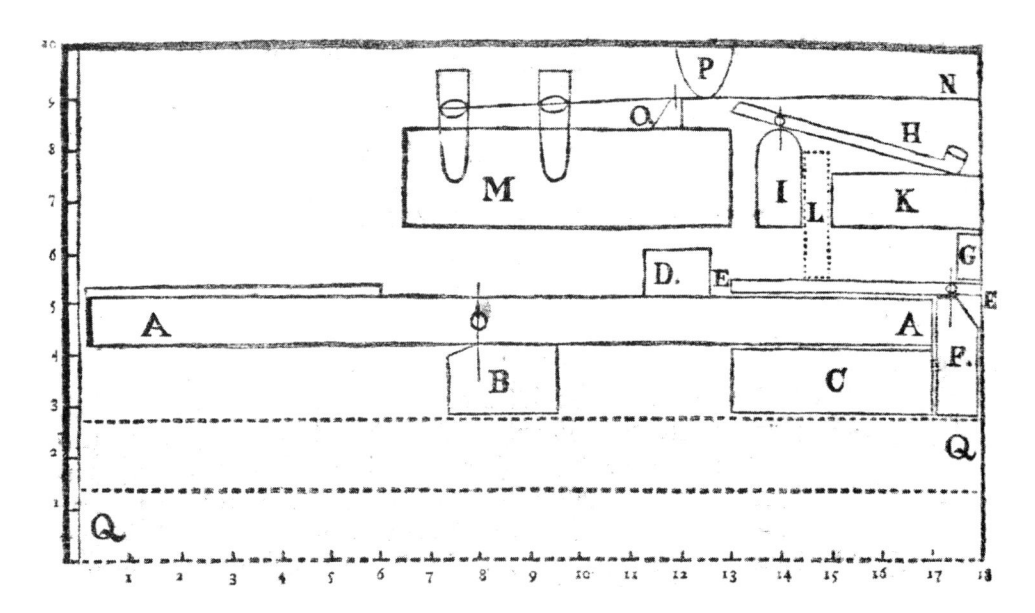

Figure 5.24 Christoph Gottlieb Schröter's first hammer action, from Marpurg's *Kritische Briefe über die Tonkunst* (Berlin, 1763).

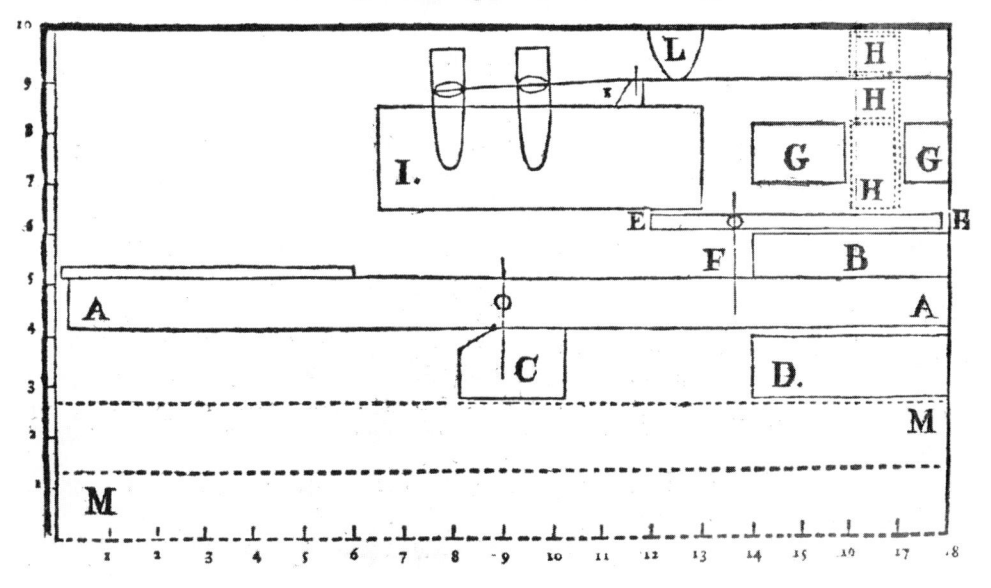

Figure 5.25 Christoph Gottlieb Schröter's second hammer action, from Marpurg's *Kritische Briefe über die Tonkunst* (Berlin, 1763).

drawing that accompanies his article; however, it is implied by his allusion to the use of an inverted wrestplank, which places the nut above the strings (see Chapter 3). It should be noted that Cristofori indicated that he employed an inverted wrestplank in order to create more room for the hammer action – he made no mention of its preventing the strings from lifting during impact. Schröter's actions feature an iron "pressure bar," which would have performed the same function as Cristofori's inverted wrestplank and nut (the latter being fitted with a metal bearing rod rather than with individual pins). It is unlikely that the need of such a pressure bar would have occurred to someone who had merely constructed hammer action models and had not encountered acoustical problems arising from strings lifting off of nut pins in a working piano. It is thus likely that Schröter had come across an actual piano before making his belated claim of having invented the piano action.

According to Schröter, his designs were immediately taken up by other German makers, though tangible evidence of this cannot be found until the emergence of tangent actions made by Franz Jacob Späth (1714–1796) and Christoph Friedrich Schmahl (a partner of Späth from 1774 to 1793) in the 1770s. Instruments by Späth and Schmahl employ striking tangents and intermediate levers, a system apparently derived from Schröter's second design. Gottfried Silbermann is known to have constructed a pianoforte for the Prince of Schwarzburg-Rudolstadt (see Johann Friedrich Agricola's remark below); ironically, Schröter visited the Prince at the royal residence in Frankenhausen in 1753 and played upon this very piano, but according to his account, he was simply told that it had been made by an "ingenious man in Dresden." Schröter remarked that the action was heavy and required great effort to play, though it was apparently one of Silbermann's later, more refined mechanisms derived from Cristofori's *c.* 1726 action (see discussion below).

Schröter indicates that his inspiration for developing a hammer action for a keyboard instrument derived from having heard the virtuoso hammered-dulcimer player, Pantaleon Hebenstreit (1669–1750).[46] Schröter states that pianos with down-striking actions were referred to as *Pantalons*, though a corruption of this term (*Bandlony*) was applied somewhat later (*c.* 1790) by Johann Christoph Jeckel and Christian Jeckel of Worms to their square pianofortes with up-striking actions. Christian Friedrich Daniel Schubart (1739–1791) was utterly disdainful of the *Pantalon* piano, which he characterized as *ein Zwerg vom Fortepiano* (a dwarf of a fortepiano). Criticizing its tinny, poorly sustaining sound and

[46] Marpurg, *Kritische Briefe*, vol. III, pt 1, p. 85.

incapacity for nuance, he predicted its early demise.[47] Until 1727, the large hammered dulcimers (termed *Pantaleons*) used by Hebenstreit were in fact constructed by Gottfried Silbermann. In that year, Silbermann and Hebenstreit had a dispute and Hebenstreit applied for and received a royal writ preventing Silbermann from constructing *Pantaleons* without Hebenstreit's consent.[48] Hebenstreit performed widely throughout Europe and was appointed court *Pantaleonist* in Dresden in 1714. He is credited with having designed his large concert dulcimer, which was said to have been approximately nine feet in length and to have had a double soundboard. It was fitted with two sets of strings, one of metal and one of gut. After hearing Hebenstreit during a tour of France in 1705, Louis XIV is reported to have suggested that his hammered dulcimer be renamed the *Pantaleon*.[49] Charles Burney saw this *Pantaleon* during his visit to Dresden in 1772 and provides a good description of it:

> At night I went to M. Binder's house to see the ruins of the famous *Pantaleone*. This instrument, and the performance upon it, at Paris, in 1705, gave birth to a very ingenious little work, under the title of *Dialogue sur la Musique des Anciens*, by the Abbé Chateauneuf: the inventor went by the name of his instrument ever after; it is more than nine feet long, and had, when in order, 186 strings of catgut. The tone was produced by two *baguettes*, or sticks, like the dulcimer; it must have been extremely difficult to the performer, but seems capable of great effects. The strings were now almost all broken, the present Elector will not be at the charge of furnishing new ones, though it had ever been thought a court instrument in former reigns, and was kept in order at the expense of the prince. M. Binder lamented, that he could not possibly afford to string it himself, as it was an instrument upon which he had formerly employed so much of his time.[50]

Gottfried Silbermann

Although Gottfried Silbermann (1683–1753) is primarily known as an organ builder (in 1723 he was appointed court and provincial organ builder by Frederick Augustus I, the Elector of Saxony), he also constructed a variety of stringed keyboard instruments. These included clavichords (one of which was owned by C. P. E. Bach and alluded to in his keyboard composition *Abschied von meinem Silbermannischen Claviere* [1781]) and a new form of clavichord termed the *Cembal d'amour* (designed before

---

[47] Schubart, *Ideen zu einer Aesthetik der Tonkunst*, pp. 174–175.
[48] Flade, *Der Orgelbauer Gottfried Silbermann*, p. 253.
[49] *The New Grove Dictionary of Musical Instruments* (London and New York, 1984), s.v. "Pantaleon."
[50] Charles Burney, *The Present State of Music in Germany, the Netherlands, and United Provinces*, 2 vols. (London, 1775), vol. II, pp. 57–58.

1721), which used centrally activated strings.[51] As with Schröter, Silbermann's fascination with the hammered dulcimer may have stimulated his interest in making keyboard instruments with hammers.

It would be surprising if Gottfried Silbermann and the Dresden court poet and librettist Johann Ulrich König were not acquainted, as König wrote technical descriptions of several of Silbermann's newly constructed organs, his *Cembal d'amour*, and even a poem about the *Pantalon*.[52] It is thus likely that Silbermann was aware of König's translation of Maffei's article on Cristofori. The article may have provided Silbermann with the impetus to experiment with this new form of keyboard instrument, though if we believe Schröter's claim, the inspiration came from his unrecovered models. In any case, we can deduce from Johann Heinrich Zedler's *Universal-Lexicon* that Silbermann constructed his first pianos as early as 1732.[53]

In Jacob Adlung's *Musica mechanica organoedi* (1768), Johann Friedrich Agricola writes:

Herr Gottfr. Silbermann hatte dieser Instrumente im Anfange zwey verfertiget. Eins davon hatte der sel. Kapelm. Hr. Joh. Sebastian Bach gesehen und bespielet. Er hatte den Klang desselben gerühmet, ja bewundert: Aber dabey getadelt, daß es in der Höhe zu schwach lautete, und gar zu schwer zu spielen sey. Dieses hatte Hr. Silbermann, der gar keinen Tadel an seinen Ausarbeitungen leiden konnte, höchst übel aufgenommen. Er zürnte deswegen lange mit dem Hrn. Bach. Und dennoch sagte ihm sein Gewissen, daß Hr. Bach nicht unrecht hätte. Er hielt also, und das sey zu seinem großen Ruhme gesagt, fur das beste nichts weiter von diesen Instrumenten auszugeben; dagegen aber desto fleißiger auf Verbesserung der vom Hrn. J. S. Bach bemerkten Fehler zu denken. Hieran arbeitete er viele Jahre. Und daß dies die wahre Ursache dieses Verzugs sey, zweifele ich um so viel weniger: da ich sie selbst vom Hrn. Silbermann aufrichtig habe bekennen horen. Endlich, da Hr. Silbermann wirklich viele Verbesserungen, sonderlich in Ansehung des Tractaments gefunden hatte, verkaufte er wieder eins an den Fürstlichen Hof zu Rudolstadt. Dies ist vermuthlich eben dasselbe dessen Hr. Schröter im listen Krit. Briefe, S. 102. gedenkt. Kurz darauf liessen des Königs von Preussen Maj. eines dieser Instrumente, und als dies Dero allerhöchsten Beyfall fand, noch verschiedene mehr, vom Hrn. Silbermann verschreiben. An alien diesen Instrumenten sahen und hörten sonderlich die, welche, so wie auch ich, eines der beyden Alten gesehen hatten, sehr

---

[51] *Sammlung von Natur und Medicin – wie auch hierzu gehörigen Kunst und Literatur – Geschichten*, ed. Johann Kanold, *et al.* (Leipzig and Budissin, 1723); Johann Friedrich Agricola in Jacob Adlung, *Musica mechanica organoedi*, 2 vols., vol. II (Berlin, 1768), pp. 123–126.

[52] Werner Müller, *Gottfried Silbermann: Persönlichkeit und Werk* (Frankfurt, 1982), pp. 48, 168; Flade, *Der Orgelbauer Gottfried Silbermann*, p. 251.

[53] Zedler, *Universal-Lexicon*, vol. v, pp. 135–140.

leicht, wie fleißig Hr. Silbermann an deren Verbesserung gearbeitet haben mußte. Hr. Silbermann hatte auch den loblichen Ehrgeiz gehabt, eines dieser Instrumente, seiner neuern Arbeit, dem seel. Hrn. Kapellmeister Bach zu zeigen und von ihm untersuchen zu lassen; und dagegen von ihm völlige Gutheißung erlanget.[54]

(Mr. Gottfried Silbermann had at first built two of these instruments. One of them was seen and played by the late Kapellmeister, Mr. Joh. Sebastian Bach. He praised, indeed admired, its tone, but complained that it was too weak in the high register, and was too hard to play. This was taken greatly amiss by Mr. Silbermann, who could not bear to have any fault found in his handiwork. He was therefore angry at Mr. Bach for a long time. And yet, his conscience told him that Mr. Bach was not wrong. He therefore decided, and greatly to his credit be it said, not to deliver any more of these instruments, but instead to think all the harder about how to eliminate the faults Mr. J. S. Bach had observed. He worked for many years on this. And that this was the real cause of the postponement I do not doubt since I myself heard it frankly acknowledged by Mr. Silbermann. Finally, when Mr. Silbermann had really achieved many improvements, notably in respect to the action, he sold one again to the Court of the Prince of Rudolstadt. This is presumably the same as that mentioned by Schröter in the *Kritische Briefe*, no. 141, page 102. Shortly thereafter, His Majesty the King of Prussia had one of these instruments ordered, and, when it met with His Majesty's most gracious approval, he had several more ordered from Mr. Silbermann. It could be very easily seen and heard from all these new instruments, particularly by those (including myself) who had seen one of the two earlier ones, how diligently Mr. Silbermann had worked on improving them. Mr. Silbermann also had the laudable ambition to show one of these instruments of his later workmanship to the late Kapellmeister Bach and have it examined by him, and he received, in turn, complete approval from him.)[55]

It is possible that Silbermann's earliest hammer actions (predating 1733, the date of Zedler's publication cited above) were based upon the models constructed by Schröter. Johann Sebastian Bach's complaint that Silbermann's early pianos were too hard to play might also indicate that the instruments were fitted with the massive secondary lever employed in the early version of Cristofori's action – the design pictured by Maffei and König. Such a structure might have made the action heavy and unresponsive. It is also possible that Bach was critical of an instrument fitted with Cristofori's later-style action (which had been developed by 1720), but that some refinement was required to lighten the key touch and strengthen the tone of the treble (perhaps by paring down heavy parts,

---

[54] Adlung, *Musica mechanica organoedi*, vol. II, pp. 116–117.
[55] This translation is from Hans Theodore David and Arthur Mendel, *The Bach Reader* (New York, 1966), p. 259.

easing or relocating pivot and bearing points, and experimenting with different leather hammer coverings). Agricola indicates that a number of years transpired between Silbermann's early experiments and his later, more successful attempts. Because all of the surviving Silbermann pianos (dating from 1746–1749) have actions that are closely modeled after the later action developed by Cristofori, it is clear that Silbermann had one of the later Cristofori pianos at his disposal sometime prior to 1746.

How did Gottfried Silbermann come in contact with an instrument by Cristofori? There is little chance that Silbermann ever communicated with Cristofori directly, as he is not known to have traveled to Italy, nor is Cristofori known to have ever left Italy. Furthermore, Cristofori died in 1731, one or two years prior to Silbermann's earliest documented interest in the piano. It has been suggested that Silbermann may have learned of the work of Cristofori through the organ builder Eugen Casparini (who worked for some years in Cristofori's home town of Padua and later worked with Gottfried's brother Andreas around 1697; see Chapter 1).[56] However, Cristofori probably invented the piano after both he and Casparini had left Padua, so Casparini probably did not have first-hand knowledge of the piano's mechanism, even if he had become acquainted with Cristofori during his years in Padua. Gottfried Silbermann's presence in Freiberg (after 1710), in close proximity to Dresden, may have introduced him to the large community of Italian musicians and singers employed in the court opera. It has been suggested that the singer, organist, and composer Antonio Lotti (b. Venice? *c.* 1667, d. Venice, 1740; active in Dresden between 1717 and 1719) might have informed Silbermann of Cristofori's work.[57] However, this is unlikely to have provided an immediate impetus, as Silbermann probably had not got involved in constructing pianos as early as 1719. (Perhaps it is not coincidental that Schröter served as Lotti's copyist in 1717, the same year he claimed to have invented the hammer action.) It is worth noting that the earliest documented owners of Cristofori's and Ferrini's pianos were singers (see Chapters 3 and 4), and at least one, Farinelli, favored his piano made by Giovanni Ferrini in 1730 over the harpsichords in his possession. As has been demonstrated above, Florentine pianos made by either Cristofori or his pupil Ferrini were not sequestered in the Medici court, but made their way to Rome, Portugal, and Spain shortly after they were constructed; the

---

[56] Flade, *Der Orgelbauer Gottfried Silbermann*, pp. 7, 255–256.
[57] Hubert Henkel, "Bach und das Hammerklavier," in *Beiträge zur Bachforschung*, ed. Werner Felix, Winfried Hoffmann, and Armin Schneiderheinze (Leipzig, 1983), vol. II, p. 58.

King of Portugal, for example, purchased pianos directly from Cristofori. When Frederick the Great appointed Karl Heinrich Graun *Kapellmeister* in 1740, Graun's first major task was to journey to Italy in order to enlist singers for the opera house that was to open in Berlin in 1742. Perhaps he or one of the Italians forming the principal singers of Frederick's newly formed Berlin Opera brought a Florentine pianoforte to Germany, which was then closely examined and scrupulously copied by Gottfried Silbermann.[58]

In the 1740s, Frederick the Great (1712–1786; reigned as King of Prussia from 1740–1786) commissioned a number of pianos from Gottfried Silbermann. Johann Nikolaus Forkel claimed in 1802 that Frederick owned fifteen such instruments, though this is very likely an exaggerated number.[59] Burney mentions but one piano in his visit (1775) to Sanssouci and the Neues Palais.[60] Prior to World War II, three of the Silbermann pianos were still to be found in the Potsdam palaces, though one was apparently destroyed in the war.[61] Of the two that survive, one presently located in the Sanssouci palace (Figure 5.26) bears the date of 1746 (written on the underside of the soundboard; see transcription below). The second piano (date unknown, *c.* 1746) is located in the Neues Palais (Figure 5.27). A third Silbermann piano, dated 1749, is in the collection of the Germanisches Nationalmuseum in Nuremberg, though there is no documentation linking it with the court of Frederick II.

Frederick loved music and was an accomplished flautist. Johann Joachim Quantz (1697–1773), the flautist, composer, and flute maker, was his teacher, and he composed over 300 works for that instrument that Frederick performed in rotation in nightly court concerts. In 1754 there were over fifty musicians plus chorus members at court, and by 1756 the Berlin opera was producing two new operas a season, most of which were written by *Kapellmeister* Graun in the Italian style featuring a cast of Italian soloists.[62] Also serving the king was Carl Philipp Emanuel Bach (1714–1788), who received a court appointment in 1740. Through Carl Philipp Emanuel, Frederick the Great extended an invitation to Johann

---

[58] Friedrich Wilhelm Marpurg, *Historische-kritische Beyträge zur Aufnahme der Musik*, 5 vols. (Berlin, 1754–1778; facs. repr. Hildesheim, 1970), vol. I, pp. 76–79.
[59] Johann Nikolaus Forkel, *Johann Sebastian Bach: His Life, Art, and Work*, trans. and ed. Charles Sanford Terry (New York, 1974), p. 25 (Forkel's note).
[60] Burney, *The Present State of Music in Germany, the Netherlands, and the United Provinces*, vol. II, p. 145.
[61] Forkel, *Johann Sebastian Bach*, p. 25 (editor's note).
[62] Marpurg, *Historische-Kritische Beyträge*, vol. I (1754), pp. 76–79.

Figure 5.26 Piano by Gottfried Silbermann, 1746. Stiftung Preußische Schlösser und Gärten Berlin-Brandenburg, Potsdam, Sanssouci.

Figure 5.27 Piano by Gottfried Silbermann, *c.* 1746. Stiftung Preußische Schlösser und Gärten Berlin-Brandenburg, Potsdam, Neues Palais.

Sebastian Bach to visit Potsdam, though the elder Bach did not arrive until May of 1747. The events surrounding this visit are recounted by Johann Nikolaus Forkel:

Der König hatte um diese Zeit alle Abende ein Cammerconcert, worin er meistens selbst einige Concerte auf der Flöte blies. Eines Abends wurde ihm, als er eben seine Flöte zurecht machte, und seine Musiker schon versammelt waren, durch einen Officier der geschriebene Rapport von angekommenen Fremden gebracht. Mit der Flöte in der Hand übersah er das Papier, drehte sich aber sogleich gegen die versammelten Capellisten und sagte mit einer Art von Unruhe: Meine Herren, der alte Bach ist gekommen! Die Flöte wurde hierauf weggelegt, und der alte Bach, der in der Wohnung seines Sohns abgetreten war, sogleich auf das Schloss beordert. Wilh. Friedemann, der seinen Vater begleitete, hat mir diese Geschichte erzählt, und ich muß sagen, daß ich noch heute mit Vergnügen an die Art denke, wie er sie mir erzählt hat. Es wurden in jener Zeit noch etwas weitläuftige Complimente gemacht. Die erste Erscheinung Joh. Seb. Bachs vor einem so großen Könige, der ihm nicht einmahl Zeit ließ, sein Reisekleid mit einem schwarzen Cantor-Rock zu verwechseln, mußte also nothwendig mit vielen Entschuldigungen verknüpft seyn. Ich will die Art dieser Entschuldigungen hier nicht anführen, sondern bloß bemerken, daß sie in Wilh. Friedemanns Munde ein förmlicher Dialog zwischen dem König und die Entschuldiger waren.

Aber was wichtiger als dieß alles ist, der König gab für diesen Abend sein Flötenconcert auf, nöthigte aber den damahls schon sogenannten alten Bach, seine in mehrern Zimmern des Schlosses herumstehende Silbermannische Fortepiano zu probiren.* Die Capellisten gingen von Zimmer zu Zimmer mit, und Bach mußte überall probiren und fantasiren. Nachdem er einige Zeit probirt und fantasirt hatte, bat er sich vom König en Fugenthema aus, um es sogleich ohne alle Vorbereitung auszuführen. Der König bewunderte die gelehrte Art, mit welcher sein Thema so aus dem Stegreif durchgeführt wurde, und äußerte nun, vermuthlich um zu sehen, wie weit eine solche Kunst getrieben werden könne, den Wunsch, auch eine Fuge mit 6 obligaten Stimmen zu hören. Weil aber nicht jedes Thema zu einer solchen Vollstimmigkeit geeignet ist, so wählte sich Bach selbst eines dazu, und fuhrte es sogleich zur größten Verwunderung aller Anwesenden auf eine eben prachtvolle und gelehrte Art aus, wie er vorher mit dem Thema des Königs gethan hatte. Auch seine Orgelkunst wollte der König kennen lernen. Bach wurde daher an den folgenden Tagen von ihm eben so zu allen in Potsdam befindlichen Orgeln geführt, wie er vorher zu allen Silbermannischen Fortepianos geführt worden war. Nach seiner Zurückkunft nach Leipzig arbeitete er das vom König erhaltene Thema 3 und 6stimmig aus, fügte verschiedene kanonische Kunststücke darüber hinzu, ließ es unter dem Titel: Musikalisches Opfer, in Kupfer stechen, und dedicirte es dem Erfinder desselben.

*Die Pianoforte's des Freyberger Silbermann gefielen dem König so sehr, daß er sich vornahm, sie alle aufkaufen zu lassen. Er brachte ihrer 15 zusammen. Jetzt sollen sie alle als unbrauchbar in verschiedenen Winkeln des Königl. Schloß umher stehen.[63]

(At this time the King used to have a private concert every evening, in which he himself generally performed some concertos on the flute. One evening, just as he was getting his flute ready and his musicians assembled, an officer brought him the written list of the strangers who had arrived. With his flute in his hand, he ran over the list, but immediately turned to the assembled musicians and said, with a kind of agitation: "Gentlemen, old Bach is come." The flute was now laid aside; and old Bach, who had alighted at his son's lodgings, was immediately summoned to the Palace. William Friedemann, who accompanied his father, told me this story, and I must say that I still think with pleasure on the manner in which he related it. At that time it was the fashion to make rather effusive compliments. The first appearance of J. S. Bach before so great a King, who did not even give him time to change his traveling dress for a black cantor's coat, must necessarily have been attended with many apologies. I will not here dwell on these, but merely observe that according to William Friedemann, there was a formal dialogue between the King and the apologist.

But what is more important than this is that the King gave up his concert for the evening and invited Bach, then already called Old Bach, to test his fortepianos, made by Silbermann, which stood in several rooms of the Palace.* The musicians went with him from room to room, and Bach was invited to play extemporaneously upon them at each location. After he had gone on for some time, he asked the King to give him a subject for a fugue in order to execute it immediately without any preparation. The King admired the skillful manner in which his subject was developed; and, probably to see how far such art could be carried, expressed a wish to hear also a fugue with six *obbligato* parts. But as not every subject is fit for such full harmony, Bach chose one himself and immediately executed it to the astonishment of all present in the same magnificent and learned manner as he had done that of the King. His Majesty desired also to hear his performance on the organ. The next day, therefore, Bach was taken to all the organs in Potsdam as he had before been to Silbermann's fortepianos. After he returned to Leipzig, he composed the subject which he had received from the King in three and six parts, added several intricate pieces in strict canon on the subject, had it engraved under the title of *Musicalisches Opfer*, and dedicated it to the inventor.

*The pianofortes manufactured by Silbermann, of Freiberg, pleased the King so much that he resolved to buy them all up. He collected fifteen. I hear that they all now stand, unfit for use, in various corners of the Royal Palace.)

The use of the term *probiren* (*probieren*, or "test") is especially relevant, as Bach was often called upon to examine newly constructed organs

---

[63] Johann Nikolaus Forkel, *Ueber Johann Sebastian Bachs Leben, Kunst und Kunstwerke* (Leipzig, 1802), pp. 9–10.

The Pianoforte in Germany   297

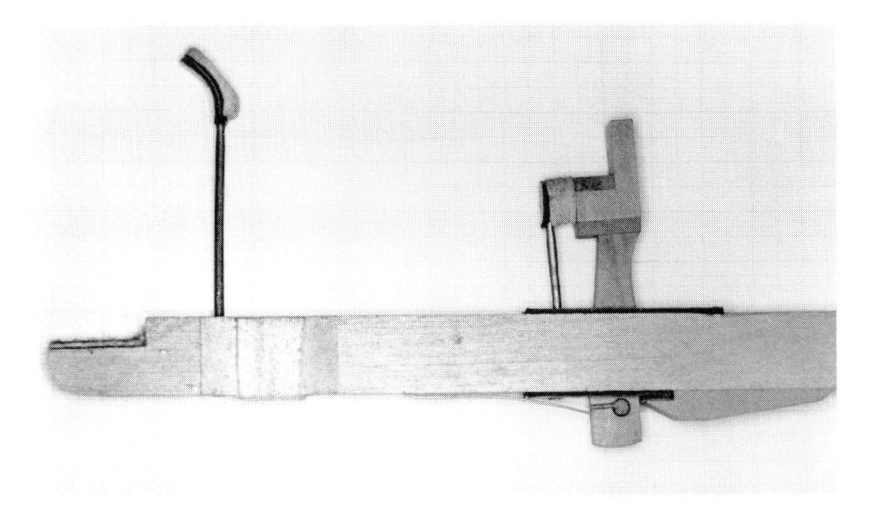

Figure 5.28 Escapement mechanism of Gottfried Silbermann piano, 1746; Sanssouci, Potsdam.

(Andreas Werckmeister published a treatise entitled *Orgel-Probe* in 1698 that listed the various tests that could be applied in evaluating an organ). Despite Johann Sebastian Bach's negative asessment of Silbermann's earliest pianos, his experience with Frederick II's pianos in Potsdam appears to have been more positive. It is interesting that Bach served as Gottfried Silbermann's intermediary in the sale of a piano to Count Branitzky of Bialystok on May 9, 1749, perhaps indicating that Bach had become a supporter of this new form of keyboard instrument.[64]

Gottfried Silbermann's Pianofortes

One can see from the escapement mechanism, the escapement lever, and hammer (Figures 5.28, 5.29, 5.30, and Table 5.7) that Silbermann's hammer actions share more than a passing resemblance to that employed in Cristofori's 1726 piano (see Chapter 3).

In addition to this basic design, one can see many similarities in the way the complex parts are constructed. Whereas Cristofori's hammer actions often betray the fact that they are experimental (they differ from one another in design and in their dimensions, and workmanship is decidedly rough in places), Silbermann's surviving actions are very consistent

---

[64] Christoph Wolff, "New Research on Bach's *Musical Offering*," *The Musical Quarterly* 57/3 (1971), p. 403.

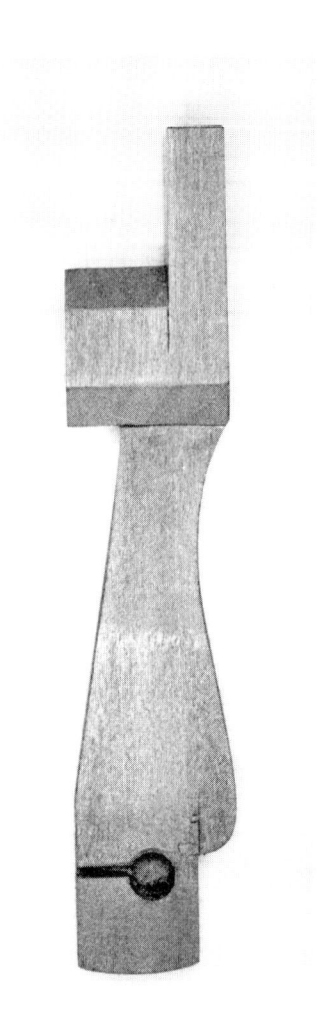

Figure 5.29 Escapement jack of Gottfried Silbermann piano, 1746; Sanssouci, Potsdam.

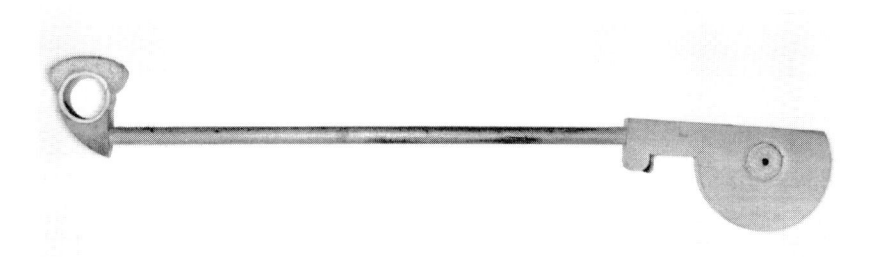

Figure 5.30 Hammer of Gottfried Silbermann piano, 1746; Sanssouci, Potsdam.

dimensionally (see Table 5.7), and the workmanship is extraordinarily refined. One could scarcely make cleaner or more accurate parts with the benefit of a room full of modern woodworking machinery.

Crucial to the tone of the instrument is the structure of the hammers. The 1726 Cristofori piano hammer heads (and most likely the original hammer heads of the 1720 piano) are made up of two sections, a lower part of wood and an upper part consisting of a cylinder made of around seven diagonal-ply layers of paper held together with glue that is capped with a strip of woolly leather (see Figure 3.28). This design is found in the Silbermann pianos as well (Figure 5.30), though as can be seen in the photographs, Silbermann employed a much thicker piece of leather. The hammer butts of the Silbermann and 1720 and 1726 Cristofori pianos have a similar semicircular shape and projecting beak. Both makers made use of an unusual leather pivot bearing that extends only partially through the hammer butt. Other similarities are the grid of wood spacers that aligns the hammers, and the independent rack that supports both the hammers and intermediate levers. While Cristofori used two brass rods as hammer pivots (the rods meet between the two central hammers), Silbermann used a single rod. The complex escapement jacks of the Cristofori and Silbermann pianos are also nearly identical (Figures 3.25 and 5.29), and both are notched to rest and pivot on a similarly shaped ledge glued to the bottom of the key lever. As in the Cristofori pianos, the escapement springs in the Silbermann pianos are mounted below the key levers and fit into slotted recesses drilled and sawn into the sides of the jacks. Both makers hinged the intermediate levers with leather, and for extra support, sewed the hinges to a wooden rail.

The key levers in Cristofori's and Silbermann's pianos are guided at the back by stout, turned wooden pins, a method not generally employed by other makers, who typically used nails or slips of wood, horn, or whalebone projecting from the back ends of the key levers that ran in a slotted rack located at the back of the key frame. There are slight differences in the back checks of the Cristofori and Silbermann pianos (Figures 3.24 and 5.28): the top edges of Silbermann's checks are turned back, while Cristofori's checks are simply angled to receive the hammer head. Cristofori's checks trap the hammer upon its return from the string, whereas Silbermann's merely cushion the hammer. This departure may indicate that Silbermann misunderstood how Cristofori's back check functioned, or perhaps he felt that cushioning the hammer, rather than trapping it, was sufficient to prevent it from rebounding, and that it was unnecessary to delay its return to provide an opportunity for the escapement mechanism to re-engage.

It should be pointed out that Cristofori's back check required careful adjustment, for if the check was positioned too close to the hammer it would snag it and prevent it from striking, and if it was too far away it would fail to catch the hammer upon its return; Silbermann's back check did not require such careful adjustment.

The keyboards in Silbermann's pianos show certain idiosyncrasies of the organ builder. The keys are unsplayed, which accounts for the string band and keyboard width being identical; the natural key platings consist of especially thick sections of ebony, and the accidentals are heavily capped with ivory (2.1–2.5 mm thick), providing the type of robust, long-wearing surface that is typical of North European organ keyboards. Cristofori used the more delicately proportioned boxwood naturals and ebony-plated accidentals that are commonly found on Italian stringed keyboard instruments. Silbermann's three-octave spans are 481–482 mm; natural key lengths are about 119 mm, accidental key lengths 79 mm. An important difference between the actions of the two makers is that Cristofori's hammers, keys, and intermediate levers decrease in length from bass to treble, whereas Silbermann kept these parts consistent in length. This results in a slightly angled strike line in Cristofori's pianos, though one that is virtually perpendicular to the case spine in Gottfried Silbermann's. The angling of the strike line can have an important effect upon the ratios of string lengths to striking points, though nut placement can compensate somewhat for the presence or lack of an angled strike line (to compare these ratios, see Table 6.1).

While Silbermann fastidiously copied Cristofori's action parts, he disregarded most aspects of Cristofori's case structure. He did, however, adopt the "inverted" wrestplank as found in the 1722 and 1726 Cristofori pianos (Figures 3.33 and 5.31). By employing a wrestplank with a nut glued to its underside and strings hitched to tuning pins that protrude below the plank, the hammer heads could be kept short and lightweight.

Cristofori's piano cases utilize a light internal bentside to support the soundboard (see Chapter 3). This bentside runs parallel to the heavy external bentside that forms part of the outer, structural case of the instrument, and it is completely isolated from internal frame members. Strings are hitched to an overhanging hitchpin rail mounted on a liner glued to the heavy outer bentside, a precaution further insuring that the soundboard remains isolated from the stress-bearing parts of the case. Silbermann's case is more conventional in design and employs a single bentside buttressed by a system of triangular knees alternating with diagonal braces running from bentside to spine and belly rail (Figure 5.32). Silbermann's

Figure 5.31 Keywell of piano by Gottfried Silbermann, *c.* 1746; Neues Palais, Potsdam. Note how the tuning pins protrude below the wrestplank, which is mounted in the inverted position like those of the 1722 and 1726 Cristofori pianos. The lever, which normally protrudes from the nameboard (removed in this photo), is used to raise the dampers, no doubt to create the effect of a hammered dulcimer, or *Pantalon*. One of the knobs on the keyboard end block is raised and lowered to unlock and lock the transposing keyboard in position, while the other knob is used to shift the keyboard.

instruments are soundly constructed; their oak and hardwood-reinforced softwood braces are pegged to thick (23 mm, Sanssouci piano) softwood bottoms.

String lengths of the Silbermann pianos are fairly consistent among the three pianos measured, and it is clear that Silbermann did not copy Cristofori's scalings (Table 5.8). Compared with Cristofori's, Silbermann's strings are longer in the treble down to c. Below c, Cristofori's strings are longer. The keyboard compasses are also different: his pianos of 1722 and 1726 range from C to c^3; the 1720 piano's original compass was GG–c^3. Two of Silbermann's pianos have a range of FF–e^3 (1749, Germanisches Nationalmuseum, Nuremberg; undated, *c.* 1746, Neues Palais, Potsdam), while one has a more limited compass of FF–d^3 (1746, Sanssouci, Potsdam). Both the Cristofori and Silbermann pianos are double strung throughout, and though Cristofori's strings are just perceptibly paired,

Figure 5.32 X-ray view of Gottfried Silbermann piano, 1749; collection of the Germanisches Nationalmuseum, Nuremberg. Note the alternating knees and diagonal buttresses. Bridge, cutoff bar, and ribs are somewhat darker than the more X-ray opaque case bracing.

those of Silbermann's pianos are virtually equally spaced throughout the string band. While the wire of the three Cristofori pianos is not original, and that of the two Potsdam pianos has also been replaced, much of the wire of the Silbermann piano now in Nuremberg may be old, if not original. While there is some disorder in the progression of gauges in the Nuremberg Silbermann, a stringing schedule has been reconstructed and is given below (Table 5.9). Also, there is a close correlation between the wire gauges found in that instrument and the replacement stringing of the other two pianos in Potsdam. In comparing the Cristofori and Silbermann stringing schedules (see Tables 3.4, 5.8), it appears that Silbermann strung his pianos more heavily than did Cristofori.

Silbermann's sawn-out bridges are considerably stouter than the kerf-bent or laminated bridges of Cristofori. While both makers used double pinning, Silbermann's bridges have a rounded and chamfered profile, and are tapered in height and width from bass to treble. Cristofori's bridges are essentially rectangular in profile, though tapered from bass to treble (see pages 154–156 and Figure 3.43 above) and just slightly beveled along the top edges.

Silbermann's soundboards are of quartered spruce with grain running parallel to the spine. Measurements made at a crack in the bass section and at the rosette of the piano in the Neues Palais revealed that the soundboards are fairly thin at those points (1.8 mm and 2.0 mm). Cristofori's soundboards are made of slab-sawn cypress 3.2–3.5 mm in thickness (measured near the belly rail on an original fragment of 1720 soundboard). Silbermann used a curved cutoff bar (as did Cristofori), but the ribs of his pianos run perpendicularly to the spine and are positioned between the cutoff bar and spine (see Figure 5.32 and Chapter 3 for a discussion of Cristofori's soundboard ribbing). The soundholes in the soundboards of the Silbermann pianos are fitted with virtually identical, laminated paper rosettes (Figure 5.33). Cristofori's pianos lack soundboard rosettes and employ a series of small holes in the belly rail for acoustical purposes (see Chapter 3).

Silbermann's pianos are equipped with a damper-raising mechanism operated by levers projecting from the nameboard, as well as an unusual mutation stop that consists (in the pianos in the Neues Palais and Nuremberg collection) of a row of flat ivory plates mounted over the strings just above the strike line of the hammers (Figure 5.34).

In the piano in Nuremberg, the row of five ivory plates is tapered in width from 6 mm in the bass to 0.9 mm in the treble. The Sanssouci piano's mutation stop is similar, but uses a brass plate in the extreme treble rather than one of ivory (though it is possible that the brass plate is a replacement installed during a restoration by Adolf Hartmann prior to 1943). The plates are spring loaded, and small screws (turned with a pocket-watch winding key) at the ends of each plate can be used to precisely adjust the position of the plates relative to the strings. When

Figure 5.33 Rosette of Gottfried Silbermann piano, *c.* 1746; Neues Palais, Potsdam.

engaged by stop knobs mounted to the left and right of the mutation batten, this stop produces a bright tonal quality.

Two of the pianos, the Nuremberg instrument and the piano at Sanssouci, have transposing keyboards (allowing transposition of a semitone). To shift the keyboard, a knob is pulled out of one of the keyboard end blocks and the keyboard shifted by grasping other knobs at either end of the keyboard. The first knob is then inserted in the other end block to secure the keyboard (Figure 5.31).

In the Silbermann pianos, the mutation stops (including the damper-raising mechanism) are controlled by levers that must be operated simultaneously by both hands. Thus, it is not possible to operate the stops in the midst of playing, but only at pauses. Silbermann's pianos were the first to feature a damper-raising mechanism, and when used with the ivory mutation stop, the piano would produce an undamped tonal

Figure 5.34 Detail of mutation batten showing springs, ivory plates, and adjustment screws. Gottfried Silbermann piano, *c.* 1746; Neues Palais, Potsdam.

quality reminiscent of the hammered dulcimer, or *Pantalon*. There was a fondness for this type of sound in Germany through the late eighteenth century, and damperless pianos with bare-wood hammers, referred to as the *Pantalon* or *Bandlony*, were enormously popular. (Christoph Gottlieb Schröter used the term *Pantalon* to denote a piano with down-striking action.) Through the 1760s, unfretted clavichords were also constructed with a stop that could isolate the vibrating portion of the string from the damping cloth – Adlung termed this the *Pantalon* stop.[65] Silbermann undoubtedly took great pleasure in constructing pianos with the damper-raising mechanism and ivory mutation stop, as he was thereby able, in spirit, to evade the royal writ that had been successfully applied for by Hebenstreit that prevented him from constructing the large *Pantaleons* played by hand-held mallets.

The case decoration of the three Silbermann pianos is quite simple. The two instruments in Potsdam have plain, varnished oak cases while

[65] Jacob Adlung, *Anleitung zu der musikalischen Gelahrtheit* (Erfurt, 1758), p. 568.

the piano in Nuremberg is of walnut. It is safe to say that the cases of the two Potsdam pianos were the most austere-looking objects in the royal residences. However, the stand of the piano in the Neues Palais is ornately carved and gilded, and was probably made under the supervision of Peter Schwizer, the craftsman responsible for much of the ornamental carving in the concert room in which the piano still sits. The stand and the concert room were clearly made *en suite*, though as the Neues Palais was still being designed in 1755 (actual construction took place between 1762 and 1769), the stand was undoubtedly made some years after the piano was completed. The simpler stand of the piano in Sanssouci consists of five turned and faceted legs with lower stretchers and bun feet; it was possibly constructed by Matthäus Daniel Pöppelmann or an assistant.

The 1746 piano in Sanssouci was somewhat playable when examined by the author in 1985, and the tonal quality was similar to that of the Cristofori piano in New York. While the sound was quite lovely, the piano did not produce much volume and the soft attack and mellow timbre (no doubt due to the rather thick leather covering the hammer heads) lacked clarity in the live acoustical environment of the Sanssouci concert room. The mutation stop gave the instrument more brilliance, but diminished the sweetness created by the thick, woolly leather hammer coverings. Silbermann's pianos would have provided discreet accompaniment for the baroque flute or the human voice. Frederick II's flute tutor, Johann Joachim Quantz, wrote:

Auf einem Clavicymbal mit einem Claviere, kann das Piano durch einen gemäßigten Anschlag, und durch die Verminderung der Stimmen, das Mezzo forte durch Verdoppelung der Octaven im Basse, das Forte durch eben dieses, und wenn man noch in der linken Hand einige zum Accorde gehörige Consonanzen mitnimmt, das Fortissimo aber, durch geschwinde Brechungen der Accorde von unten herauf, durch eben diese Verdoppelung der Octaven, und der Consonanzen, in der linken Hand, und durch einen heftigern und stärkern Anschlag, hervor gebracht werden. Auf einem Clavicymbal mit zweyen Clavieren, hat man über dieses noch den Vortheil, zum Pianissimo sich des obersten Claviers bedienen zu können. Auf einem Pianoforte aber, kann alles erforderliche am allerbequemsten bewerkstelliget werden: denn dieses Instrument hat vor allem, was man Clavier nennet, die zum guten Accompagnement *nöthigen* Eigenschaften am meisten in sich: und kömmt dabey blos auf den Spieler und seine Beurtheilung an. Auf einem guten Clavichord hat es zwar eben dieselbe Beschaffenheit im Spielen, nicht aber in Ansehung der Wirkung, weil das Fortissimo mangelt.[66]

[66] Johann Joachim Quantz, *Versuch einer Anweisung die Flöte traversiere zu spielen* (Berlin, 1752; repr. Kassel, 2000), p. 175.

(On a harpsichord with one keyboard, passages marked *piano* may be produced by a moderate touch and by diminishing the number of parts, those marked *mezzo forte* by doubling the bass in octaves, those marked *forte* in the same manner and also by taking some consonances belonging to the chord into the left hand, and those marked *fortissimo* by quick arpeggiations of the chords from below upwards, by the same doubling of the octaves and the consonances in the left hand, and by a more vehement and forceful touch. On a harpsichord with two keyboards, you have the additional advantage of being able to use the upper keyboard for the *pianissimo*. But on a pianoforte everything required may be accomplished with the greatest convenience, for this instrument, of all those that are designated by the word keyboard, has the greatest number of qualities necessary for good accompaniment, and depends for its effect only upon the player and his judgement. The same is true of a good clavichord with regard to playing, but not with regard to effect, since it lacks the *fortissimo*.)[67]

Despite his musical conservatism, it is clear that Frederick concurred with Quantz and favored these new keyboard instruments for their dynamic flexibility and their ability to concert with his soft-timbred flute. (See below for a description of similar pianos patterned after Cristofori made by Gottfried Silbermann's nephew Johann Heinrich [Jean-Henri] Silbermann.)

Christian Ernst Friederici

Christian Ernst Friederici (b. Meerane, 1709; d. Gera, 1780) was the first of a distinguished family of keyboard instrument makers that remained active through the end of the nineteenth century. The *Meeraner Chronik* states that C. E. Friederici apprenticed in organ building with Gottfried Silbermann in Freiberg in 1730.[68] In 1736 he assisted the organ builder Tobias Heinrich Gottfried Trost in Altenburg. In 1737 he settled in Gera, and in 1744 his brother Christian Gottfried (1714–1777) joined him. Between 1744 and Christian Gottfried's death, the two collaborated in making keyboard instruments. Christian Gottfried's son, Christian Gottlob (1750–1805), joined the firm upon his father's death, assisting his uncle, Christian Ernst. After the death of Christian Ernst, Christian Gottlob continued the family enterprise. A claviorganum (*c.* 1800) and a square piano built over a chest of drawers (1804) by Christian Gottlob are preserved in the Grassi Museum für Musikinstrumente der Universität Leipzig.

---

[67] Translation from Johann Joachim Quantz, *On Playing the Flute*, trans. Edward R. Reilly (New York, 1966), p. 259.

[68] *Die Musik in Geschichte und Gegenwart*, ed. Friedrich Blume (Kassel and Basel, 1955), s.v. "Friederici."

The name "Friederici" appears in numerous literary sources. In a letter to a friend written on November 10, 1773, Carl Philipp Emanuel Bach states that "die Friedericischen Clavicorde haben bey mir einen grösseren Vorzug vor den Fritzischen und Hassischen wegen des Tractaments und wegen des Basses ohne Octave, welche ich nicht leiden kann."[69] (The Friederici clavichords are much to be preferred to those of Fritz and Hass because of their workmanship and because the bass is made without octave strings, which I dislike.) Wolfgang Amadeus Mozart warned his father in 1777 that "wenn Du mit Herrn [Johann Andreas] Stein sprichst, so musst Du all Gelegenheit vermeiden, von unseren Instrumenten von Gera eine Meldung zu machen, denn er ist eifersüchtig mit dem Friederici."[70] (When you speak with Mr. Johann Andreas Stein, you must in any event avoid mentioning our instruments from Gera, for he is jealous of Friederici.)

Writing of Friederici in his *Historisch-biographisches Lexicon der Tonkünstler*, Ernst Ludwig Gerber stated that "Seine Klaviere und Fortepianos, in Gestalt der Klaviere, die er Fortbien nannte, sind in der halben Welt berühmt und zerstreut."[71] (His *Klaviere* and pianofortes, in the form of *Klaviere*, which he termed *Fortbien*, are famous and scattered over half the world.) This is repeated by Heinrich Christoph Koch in his *Musikalisches Lexicon* (1802), where *Fortbien* is defined as "Eine Art von Fortepiano in Clavierform, die von dem Orgelbauer Friederici in Gera ums Jahr 1758 erfunden worden ist."[72] (A type of fortepiano in the shape of a keyboard instrument invented by the organ builder Friederici of Gera around the year 1758.) Though *Klavier* and *Clavierform* are ambiguous terms, the word *Clavier* (or *Klavier*) was sometimes used in eighteenth-century Germany to denote the clavichord, so later writers took Koch's statement to mean that Friederici had invented the square piano.

Johann Wolfgang von Goethe mentioned in his autobiography, *Dichtung und Wahrheit*, that "Auch für uns ward ein großer Friedericischer Flügel angeschafft, den ich, bei meinem Klavier verweilend, wenig berührte, der aber meiner Schwester zu desto größerer Qual gedieh, weil sie, um das neue Instrument gehörig zu ehren, täglich noch einige Zeit

---

[69] C. H. Bitter, *Carl Philipp Emanuel und Wilhelm Friedemann Bach und deren Brüder* (Berlin, 1868), p. 336.

[70] *Leopold Mozart: Briefe und Aufzeichnungen*, selected and with commentary by Wilhelm A. Bauer and Otto Erich Deutsch, vol. II: 1777–1779 (Kassel, Basel, London, and New York, 1962), pp. 41–43.

[71] Ernst Ludwig Gerber, *Historisch-biographisches Lexicon der Tonkunstler*, 2 vols. (Leipzig, 1790–1792; repr. Graz, 1977), vol. I, pp. 443–444.

[72] Koch, *Musikalisches Lexicon*, s.v. "Fortbien."

mehr auf ihre Übungen zu verwenden hatte."[73] (Also purchased for us was a large *Flügel* of Friederici, which I, sticking to my *Klavier*, hardly touched, but which so much increased my sister's troubles, as, to properly honor the new instrument, she had to spend more time practicing every day.) It is unclear whether this new instrument was a piano or a harpsichord; nevertheless, it was clearly not a *Pyramide*, but a *Flügel*, or wing-shaped instrument. It should be emphasized that there is no documentation indicating that the *Pyramide* piano now in Goethe's house in Frankfurt (discussed below) ever belonged to his family. In his later years, while living in Weimar, Goethe is known to have owned a pianoforte by Streicher.[74]

Of passing interest is a report of the existence of receipts from Friederici for supplying unspecified instruments to the Moravian community in Bethlehem, Pennsylvania.[75] Thus, there is a remote possibility that pianos from Germany arrived in the New World shortly after they were developed.

In 1745 Johann Christian Müller of Gera published an engraving of an upright pianoforte termed a *Pyramide* (Figure 5.35) accompanied by the following text:

Abbildung eines Musicalischen Instruments, genannt die Pyramide, eigentlich ein stehendes Forte piano welches vor andern drey vorzüge, 1:) ein sehr leichtes Tractament 2.) braucht man keines bekielens, 3.) hat es nicht mehr als einen Platz von drey schuen nothig. Solches hat erfunden, und fertiget. Christian Ernst Friederici. Orgelbauer und instrument Macher in Gera. Anno 1.7.45.

(Picture of a musical instrument called the *Pyramide*, properly a vertical fortepiano with the following three properties: (1) a very light action; (2) it does not need quilling; (3) it does not require more than three feet of space. Such has been invented and made by Christian Ernst Friederici, organ and instrument maker in Gera, in the year 1745.)

The term *Pyramide* refers to the shape of the symmetrically tapered upright case. Its outward design recalls the late-seventeenth-century "bishop's mitre" *clavicytherium* (an upright harpsichord) made by Martin Kaiser (presently in the Kunsthistorisches Museum, Vienna). In Kaiser's instrument, however, the bass strings are mounted in the center of the soundboard, and the treble strings alternate on either side (rollers are used to couple the keys to the jacks). In the three *Pyramide* pianos described below,

---

[73] Johann Wolfgang von Goethe, *Dichtung und Wahrheit* (Oxford, 1894), p. 132.
[74] Eric Werner, *Mendelssohn: Leben und Werk in neuer Sicht* (Zürich and Freiburg, 1980), p. 45.
[75] Laurence Libin, "Nazareth Piano may be Among America's First," *Moravian Music Journal* 33/1 (Spring, 1988), p. 2.

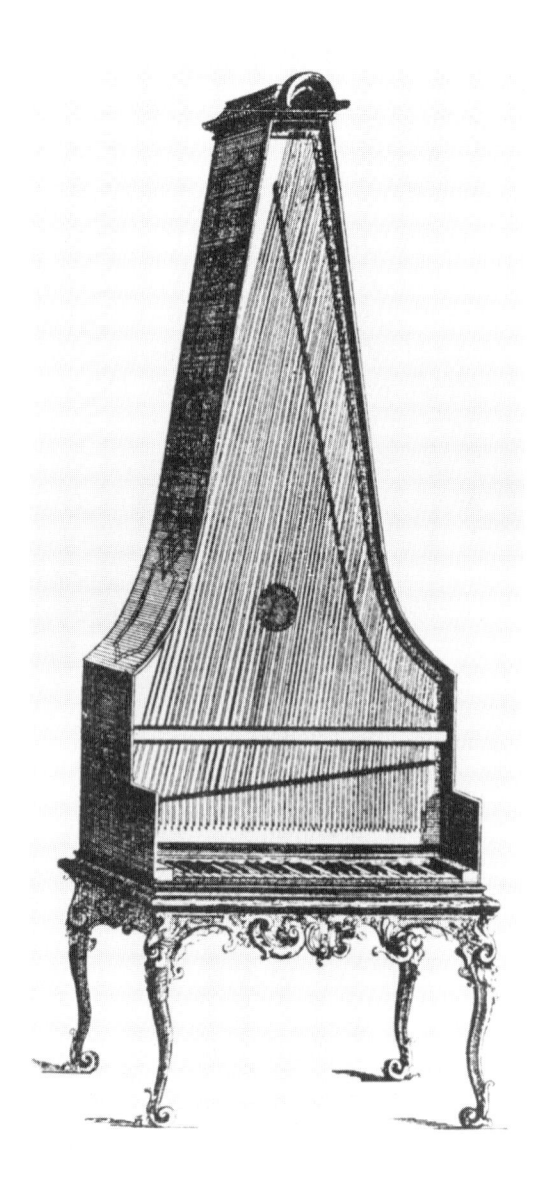

Figure 5.35 *Pyramide* piano by Christian Ernst Friederici. Engraving, Johann Christian Müller, Gera, 1745.

the stringing follows the conventional scheme of bass strings on the left and treble strings on the right, though the string band is inclined so that the longest strings are hitched near the center of the case. Unfortunately, the similarity between the three instruments ends at this point. The pianos in the Muziekinstrumentenmuseum, Brussels, the Frankfurter Goethe-Haus, and the Germanisches Nationalmuseum in Nuremberg

Figure 5.36 *Pyramide* piano by Christian Ernst Friederici, c. 1745; Frankfurter Goethe-Haus.

display dissimilar action and case designs, different string lengths, striking points, compasses, octave spans, and bridge designs. Even the scoring patterns on the natural keys differ. It is therefore likely that at least two of these instruments were not made by Christian Ernst Friederici. Only the *Pyramide* piano in the Frankfurter Goethe-Haus (Figure 5.36) bears an outward similarity to the 1745 engraving (Figure 5.35).

Some of the original features of these instruments may have been obscured in recent restorations and by the replacement of important parts. Labels glued inside the case of the piano in Frankfurt state that it was restored in 1901 by Hermann Seyffartt; in 1934 by J. C. Neupert (on this occasion the soundboard and wrestplank were replaced); again in 1972 by J. C. Neupert; and once again in 1986 by Wolf Dieter Neupert.[76] Because the restoration labels are glued to the inside surface of the back of the instrument, the soundboard or back must have been removed on each of these occasions. The soundboard of the Nuremberg *Pyramide* is also a replacement. In the Brussels piano, the wrestplank is new (replaced *c.* 1970), and a stain applied to the soundboard in order to conceal shims makes it difficult to determine the soundboard's age, though there is evidence that the present soundboard has been removed at least once to make repairs. Because of the replacement of soundboards and wrestplanks of these instruments, the string lengths and striking points given below (Table 5.11) may differ from the originals. When the author examined the Brussels and Nuremberg pianos in 1993, these instruments were in such a poor state that they could not be fully assembled or even stood upright. Measurements of case height, width, and depth (see Table 5.13) therefore had to be estimated. Regarding the Nuremberg piano, parts of the action frame could not be located during the author's visit, and thus it was not possible to assemble the action completely. In this instance, a drawing of the action found in Walter Pfeiffer's *Der Hammer* (though inaccurate in some respects) was used to determine the essential action geometry of that piano.[77] A similar problem existed with the *Pyramide* piano in Brussels. The case of that instrument was so weakened that it could not be moved for a detailed examination, and the action could not be assembled within it. An action drawing published by Rosamond Harding shows the hammers striking away from the player;[78] this is, however, incorrect. As in the Frankfurt piano, the damper mechanism and hammer action were positioned behind the strings so that the hammers strike in the direction of the player.

It is important to note that of the three *Pyramide* pianos, only the example in Brussels bears a signature. An ink inscription on a paper label

---

[76] Photographs of the interior of the Frankfurt Friederici piano were lent to the author for examination by Mr. Wolf Dieter Neupert. These photographs show various repair labels glued inside the instrument. Unfortunately, the photographs had been badly damaged and could not be reproduced here. I would like to thank Mr. Neupert for kindly lending me these photographs.

[77] Walter Pfeiffer, *Der Hammer* (Stuttgart, 1948), p. 41.   [78] Harding, *The Pianoforte*, p. 33.

(glued to a thin block of wood mounted on the inside surface of the back, and observable through perforations in the soundboard rosette) reads: "Dieße Pyramite hat gefertiget und Erfunden, Christian Ernst Friederici Orgelbauer in Gera in Monats [*sic*] 7br: Ao 1745. S.D.G." ("This *Pyramide* was finished and invented by Christian Ernst Friederici, organ builder in Gera in the month of September, 1745. S.D.G. [Soli Deo Gloria.]") Close examination of this label was not possible. It is conceivable, however, that it is not original and was placed inside long after the instrument was constructed – the wording on the label having been inspired by the well-known 1745 copperplate engraving that was printed and circulated by Friederici. The only inscription on the instrument in Frankfurt is the date "Ao 1745" engraved on the back of the brass lock plate; again, this may have been added later and could be a reference to the date on the copperplate engraving.

Both the Frankfurt and Nuremberg *Pyramide* pianos have been attributed to Friederici primarily on the basis of their superficial similarity to the Brussels piano and the 1745 engraving. The soundboard rose in the Frankfurt piano (Figure 5.37) is similar to Gottfried Silbermann's pianoforte roses (Figure 5.33) as well as those of Christian Ernst Friederici's brother, Christian Gottfried.

If it is not a copy, it may have been transferred from the original soundboard, which has not been preserved. The rose in the Brussels *Pyramide* bears no resemblance to those of the Silbermann/Friederici school.

Despite the fact that these three pianos can all be classified as *Pyramides*, their case structures differ considerably. The Frankfurt case is of solid oak with panel-and-frame shutters; the Brussels piano has a veneered case with well-executed marquetry; and the Nuremberg piano has a walnut case of simplified design without shutters (a framed, cloth panel protects the soundboard). The new soundboard installed in the Frankfurt *Pyramide* in 1934 by J. C. Neupert has ten diagonally oriented ribs, though it is not known whether they replicate the original ribbing pattern. The case bracing of this piano consists of five diagonally oriented buttresses, each having large rectangular openings that permit three vertical struts (running from top to belly rail and right bentside to belly rail) to pass through them. In addition, three horizontal struts pass from one bentside to the other. These are notched where they intersect the diagonal braces and are pegged at the points of intersection and where they cross the vertical struts.[79] The case of the Nuremberg *Pyramide* is fitted with four braces

---

[79] This information is derived from photographs lent to the author by Mr. Wolf Dieter Neupert.

Figure 5.37 Soundboard rose of the Friederici *Pyramide* piano; Frankfurter Goethe-Haus.

running parallel to the belly rail. Pierced buttresses run perpendicularly between the four horizontal braces and are let into grooves. The only similarity between the bracing of the Frankfurt and Nuremberg pianos is the presence of apertures in the principal buttresses. In the Nuremberg piano, the apertures seem to have been made to reduce mass, as no struts pass through them. Because the Nuremberg's soundboard ribs do not align with notches in the soundboard liner, and there is no evidence that earlier ribs were mounted on the soundboard, it is clear that it is not original.

The compasses of the three instruments differ: the Brussels piano extends from FF to d^3; the Frankfurt piano from FF to f^3; and the Nuremberg piano from FF to g^3. The Frankfurt and Nuremberg pianos have ebony naturals and stained pear wood accidentals with ivory plating. Consistent with its elaborately decorated case, the Brussels piano has ivory naturals

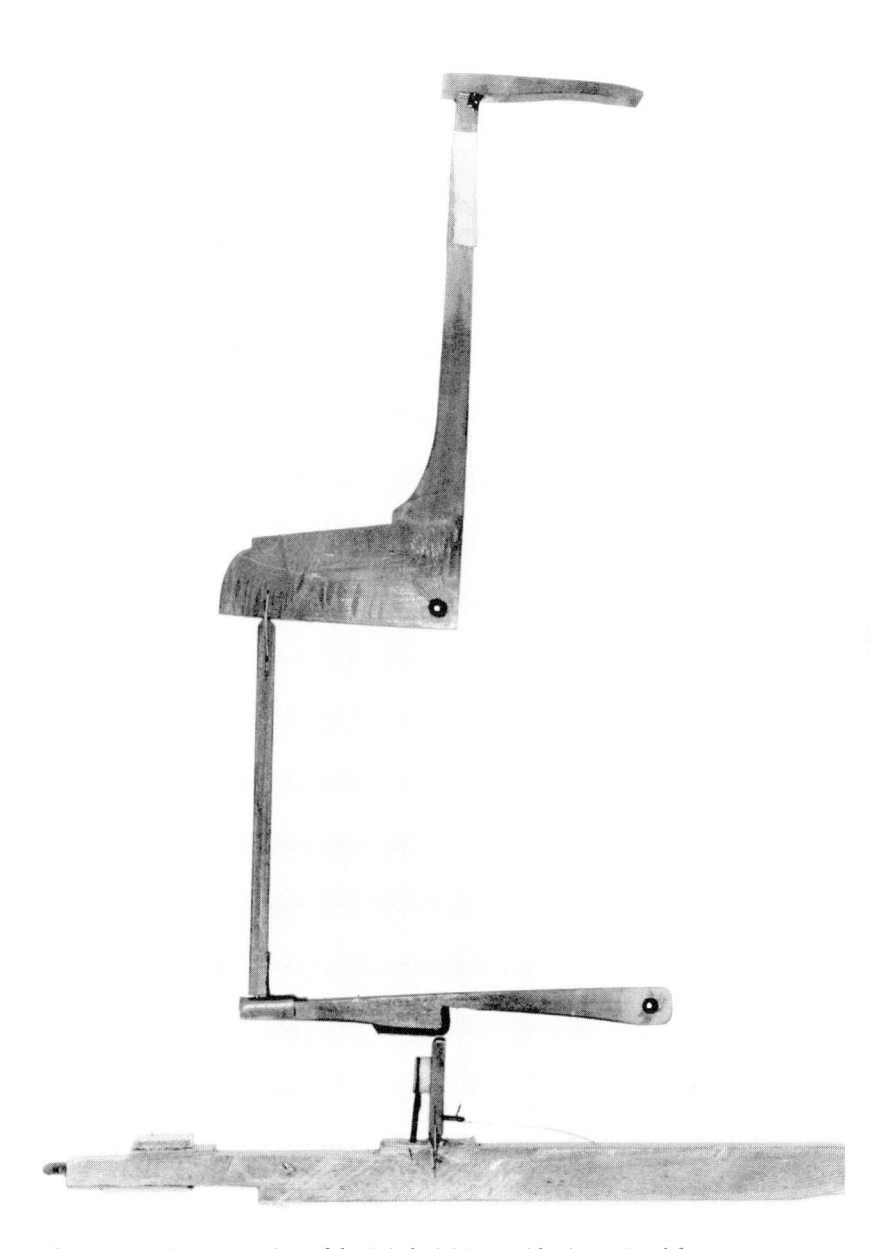

Figure 5.38 Hammer action of the Friederici *Pyramide* piano; Frankfurter Goethe-Haus.

with ebony sharps. The natural key fronts of all three pianos have four scribe lines, although the spacing of these lines differs. The three-octave spans of the keyboards are inconsistent as well (see Table 5.13).

The actions of the three instruments (see Figures 5.38, 5.39, 5.40, 5.41, 5.43, 5.44, and 5.45) also differ considerably. That of the Frankfurt piano

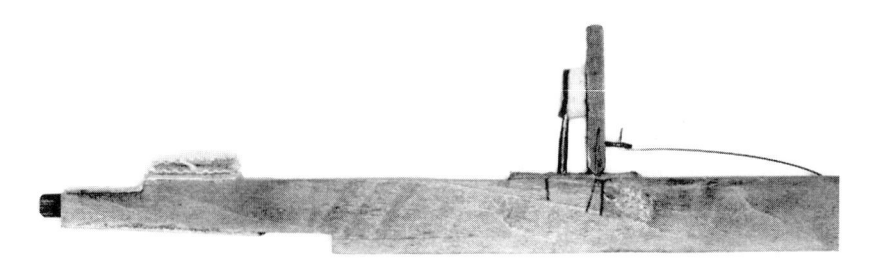

Figure 5.39 Detail of the escapement lever of the Friederici *Pyramide* piano; Frankfurter Goethe-Haus.

(Figure 5.38) is the most sophisticated, and despite its "upright" orientation is homologous to the actions found in Cristofori's pianos, as well as those of Gottfried Silbermann (see Table 5.12).

Mounted on the key lever is a spring-assisted escapement jack which interacts with a projection on a pivoted intermediate lever (Figure 5.39).

The intermediate lever is hinged to a sticker that in turn is hinged to an elongated hammer butt. The hammers, which are mounted behind the strings and strike towards the player, rotate on a pivot rod. They, as well as the intermediate levers, have pivot holes that are bushed with leather. The motion of the hammer is very much like that of the "square" used in organ key actions, in that the upward motion of the sticker causes the hammer head to rotate forward towards the string. The hammer heads up to $c\#^1$ are bare wood and are rather sharply profiled. From d^1 up, the hammer heads are tipped with ivory, giving the sound an even brighter, more percussive character.

The Frankfurt *Pyramide* has several handstops. The dampers, which extend to the highest note, are activated by a sticker mounted at the back of the key, and by a rocker, which rotates the damper away from the string when the key is pressed. The dampers are leather (modern replacements). The entire damper mechanism can be disengaged by two knobs, one on each side of the case. To operate, both of the knobs have to be activated simultaneously, just as in Gottfried Silbermann's pianofortes. There is a moderator (cloth strip; modern replacement) operated by a knob on the right. It is probable that an instrument built with bare wood and ivory hammers, such as this *Pyramide* piano, was originally fitted with such a mutation apparatus. A bassoon stop (extending up to c^1) is rotated into position from the left side. Since all of the wooden parts of the Friederici piano have been stripped of their original finish and revarnished, it is difficult to judge the relative age of the bassoon mechanism, though it was

Figure 5.40 Hammer action of the *Pyramide* piano in the Germanisches Nationalmuseum, Nuremberg.

most likely added at the turn of the nineteenth century when such stops became fashionable.

The action of the Nuremberg *Pyramide* consists of a short, vertical sticker firmly mounted on the back of the key lever, which pushes up on a projection of the hammer butt (Figure 5.40).

As can be seen in the photograph, there is a thin kerf sawn transversely in the key just in front of this sticker. Several of the kerfs in the key levers have slivers of parchment in them, from which we may deduce that the Nuremberg *Pyramide* originally had a hinged escapement, perhaps like that in the Frankfurt piano. There are also holes that may have supported a jack stop and spring, again similar to those in the Frankfurt *Pyramide*. The hammers consist of a brass wire (1.1 mm diameter) extending from a pear wood shank and a two-part wooden head. A section of dowel (6.2 mm diameter, treble; 9.8 mm diameter, bass), mounted cross-wise and covered with leather, forms the striking surface. The hammers strike

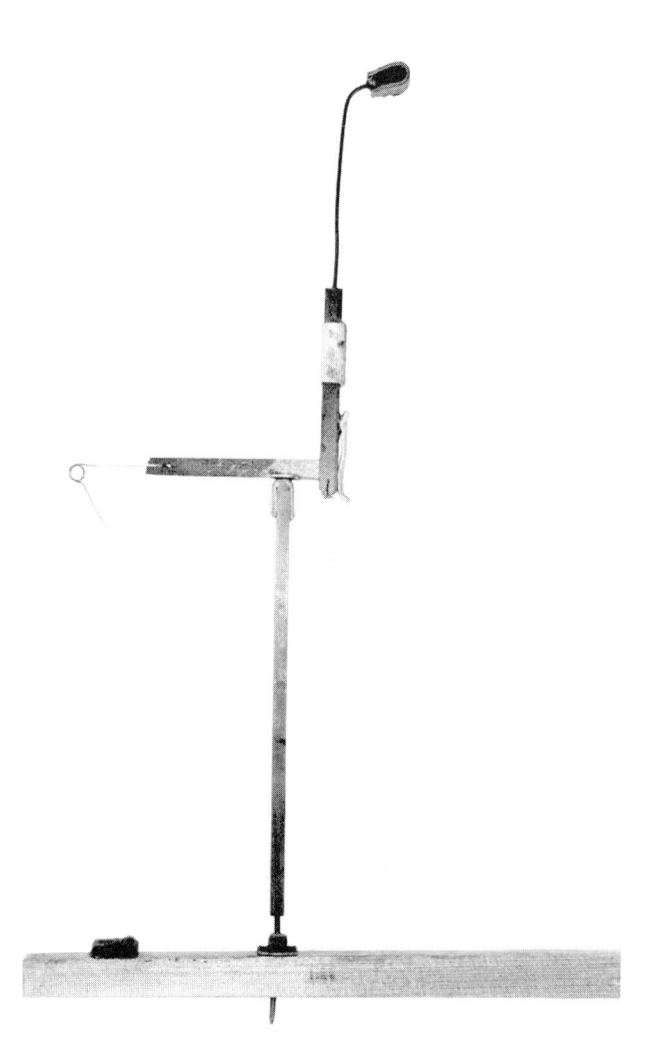

Figure 5.41 Hammer action of the *Pyramide* piano, Muziekinstrumentenmuseum, Brussels.

from behind the strings, in the direction of the player. In the drawing by Pfeiffer referred to above, an L-shaped assembly may have been part of the damper mechanism. This piece was apparently pressed against the strings with a wire spring. The long arm of the L-shaped part is capped by a thin, firm disc of leather, whose diameter was slightly greater than the diameter of the shaft. The function of the disc could not be determined. The rest of the damper assembly is lost, and unfortunately Pfeiffer's drawing is a bit schematic with regard to it.

The action of the Brussels *Pyramide* uses a vertical sticker that rests on the back of the key lever and conveys motion to the hammer (Figure 5.41).

A wood rack and a threaded brass pin that passes through a hole in the key keep the sticker in alignment and flexible. The height of the sticker, and thus the hammer's let-off, is adjusted with a leather nut. The hammer is L-shaped, and hinged from a strip of parchment. A wire spring bears upon the far end of the tenoned arm, assisting the hammer's return. The hammer shank consists of the vertical section and a brass rod extension (1.42 mm diameter) that is bent towards the strings at the top. The wire supports a short, leathered, solid-wood hammer head. The damper mechanism again employs stickers and parchment-hinged "squares" that draw the dampers away from the strings when the keys are pressed.

When the author examined the Nuremberg *Pyramide*, the soundboard and wrestplank were not glued into position; consequently, it was not possible to measure string lengths and striking points. As stated earlier, the soundboard and wrestplank of the Frankfurt piano and the wrestplank of the Brussels piano are replacements, and so the string lengths and striking points given in Table 5.11 may differ from those established by the original parts. Today, the two instruments appear to have quite different scaling (Brussels $c^2 = 34.3$ cm; Frankfurt $c^2 = 29.5$ cm). Owing to the fact that the action could not be installed in the Brussels piano, striking points of that instrument could not be assessed. There is only a vague similarity between the scaling of the Gottfried Silbermann pianos and that of the Brussels *Pyramide*. The Nuremberg and Frankfurt *Pyramides* are bichord up to b^1, and trichord from c^2 to g^3 and f^3, respectively. The Brussels piano is bichord up to a, shifting to trichord at a#.

In conclusion, the gross disparities among these three instruments suggest that they were made by different makers. Of the three pianos discussed here, the instrument in Frankfurt bears the closest resemblance to the 1745 engraving of a Friederici *Pyramide*. The action of that instrument is also the most sophisticated, and its escapement mechanism is clearly derived from the later action used in the pianofortes of Cristofori, possibly by way of Gottfried Silbermann. The actions in the Brussels and Nuremberg *Pyramides* do not employ an escapement, and are relatively primitive in comparison to that of the Frankfurt example.

These three instruments provide evidence of early interest in the upright piano in Germany, though only the example in Frankfurt is likely the work of Christian Ernst Friederici. *Pyramide* pianos were made well into the nineteenth century by such makers as Johann Schmid of Salzburg and Dieudonné & Schiedmayer of Stuttgart. Two anonymous *Pyramides* superficially resembling the Nuremberg instrument (Deutsches Museum,

Munich;[80] Musée instrumental, Paris[81]) are thought to date from the late eighteenth and early nineteenth centuries. Both of these instruments have framed cloth panels like the Nuremberg *Pyramide*. Because of the stylistic similarity to these later instruments, it is very possible that the Nuremberg *Pyramide* also dates from the end of the eighteenth century. It should be noted that the actions in these *Pyramides* differ considerably from that in the 1739 del Mela upright described above, so there is little likelihood that the del Mela upright served as a model for them.

Two other early upright pianos (Grassi Museum für Musikinstrumente der Universität Leipzig;[82] another formerly in the Schloss-Museum, Berlin)[83] are not discussed here because they are of uncertain date and make: the rather crude upright presently in Leipzig dates from about 1765 (a date of 1735 is erroneously given in some sources); the upright that had been in Berlin was lost in World War II.

---

[80] Fritz Thomas and Peter Kunze, *Alte Musik aus vier Jahrhunderten: Tasteninstrumente im Deutschen Museum* (Munich, 1980), p. 12.
[81] Ghislaine Juramie, *Histoire du Piano* (Paris, 1947), p. 103.
[82] Kinsky, *Musikhistorisches Museum*, vol. I, p. 127.   [83] Harding, *The Pianoforte*, pp. 30–34.

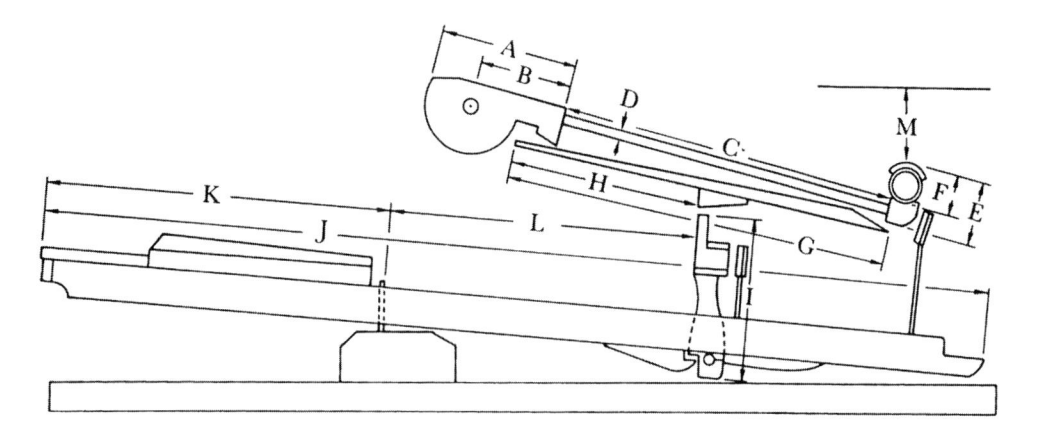

Figure 5.42 Schematic drawing of the Gottfried Silbermann hammer action.

Table 5.7 Comparative measurements of hammer actions of Cristofori and Silbermann pianos (all measurements in millimeters)

	Cristofori			Gottfried Silbermann		
	1720	1722	1726	Sanssouci	Neues Palais	Nuremberg
A	52	48	48.5	47.5	47.5	47.5
B	34	33	32.5	32.8	33	33.4
C bottom	123.5	116	121	123	122.5	122
C top	112.5	115	117.5	123	122.5	122.5
D	4	4	4	4	4	4
E bottom	49.5	12	24.5	24	23	23.5
E top	46.5	13.5	19.5	21	21	20.5
F bottom	19	4	18.5	17.5	15	16.5
F top	16	3.5	12	13	13	12.5
G	113	130	135.5	138	138	139
H	54	68	69.5	70	70	70.5
I	62	59	56.5	63.5	65.5	63
J bottom	443	332	344.5	352	352	352
J top	407	320	336	352	352	352
K bottom	165	124	123.5	124	124	123
K top	159	123	125	123.5	124	123
L bottom	148	110	116	114	116	115
L top	135	110	111	115	116	115
M	31–35	35–36	22–23	42–43	41–42	43–47

Table 5.8 String lengths/striking points of Cristofori and Silbermann pianos (all measurements in millimeters)

Note	Cristofori 1726	Gottfried Silbermann Sanssouci	Neues Palais	Nuremberg
FF		1841/147	1852/150	1846/152
C	1961/133	1590/134	1603/133	1597/137
F	1608/108	1371/118	1384/121	1378/122
c	1125/73	1067/94	1078/95	1072/98
f	841/57	859/78	874/76	854/81
c^1	568/38	609/56	619/59	614/60
f^1	422/29	461/45	472/47	467/47
c^2	280/17	310/31	320/33	313/33
f^2	213/13	231/24	230/24	228/25
c^3	142/7	152/16	160/16	155/15
d^3		134/15		
e^3			129/12	122/12

All measurements are of the longer string of each pair. The Neues Palais and Nuremberg piano strings were measured in non-transposing position.

Table 5.9 String diameters of Silbermann pianos (all measurements in millimeters)

	Material	Diameter
Silbermann piano of 1749		
FF–FF#	Brass	.90
GG–AA	Brass	.85
AA#–D#	Brass	.75
E–G	Brass	.68
G#–A	Brass	.59
A#–c#	Ferrous	.63
d–f	Ferrous	.58
f#–g#	Ferrous	.53
a–c^1	Ferrous	.48
c#^{1}–c^2	Ferrous	.39
c#^{2}–f^2	Ferrous	.36
f#^{2}–e^3	Ferrous	.33
Silbermann piano, Neues Palais		
FF–A	Brass	.85–.60
A#–e^3	Ferrous	.60–.275

Table 5.10 Cristofori and Silbermann piano-case dimensions* (all measurements in millimeters)

	Cristofori	Silbermann		
	1726	Neues Palais	Sanssouci	Nuremberg
Length	2390	2304	2304	2303
Width	801	949	923	962
Height	205	237	236	236

* Case measurements exclude moldings, stands, and lids.

Table 5.11 String lengths/striking points of Friederici *Pyramide* pianos* (all measurements in millimeters)

Note	Frankfurt[†]	Brussels[‡]
FF	1646/63	1744
C	1380/57	1499
F	1195/52	1320
c	955/48	1073
f	791/46	897
c^1	581/42	651
f^1	450/39	498
c^2	295/38	343
f^2	222/30	262
c^3	151/28	167
d^3		145
f^3	118/26	

* String lengths of the *Pyramide* piano in Nuremberg could not be measured directly owing to the condition of the piano.
[†] The soundboard and wrestplank of the *Pyramide* piano in Frankfurt are not original.
[‡] Striking points of the *Pyramide* piano in Brussels could not be measured directly because of the condition of the piano.

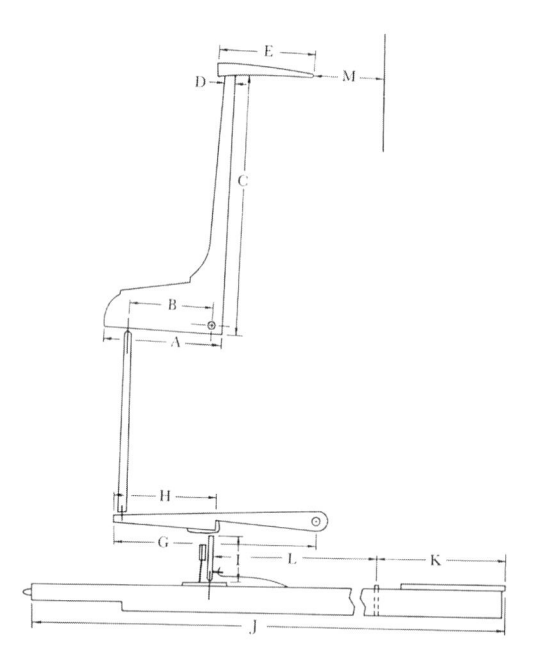

Figure 5.43 Schematic drawing of the Friederici *Pyramide* hammer action; Frankfurter Goethe-Haus.

Table 5.12 Hammer-action measurements of Friederici *Pyramide* (Frankfurt) and Silbermann pianos (all measurements in millimeters)

	Pyramide, Frankfurt	Silbermann, Sanssouci
A	69	47.5
B	49	32.8
C	140	123
D	4	4
E bottom	57.5	24
E top	59	21
F bottom	—	17.5
F top	—	13
G	117	138
H	57	70
I	29	63.5
J	405	352
K	162	124
L bottom	138	114
L top	141	115
M	27.5–31.5	42–43

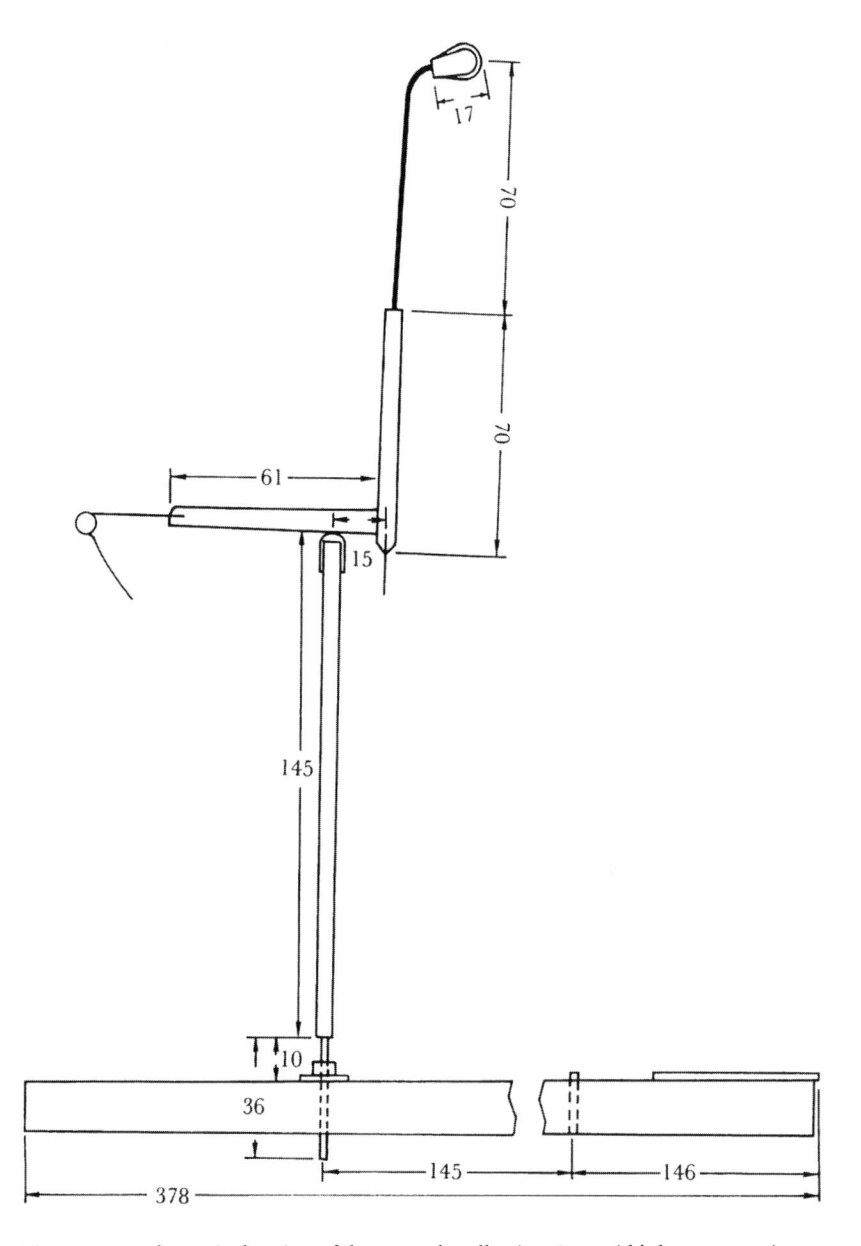

Figure 5.44 Schematic drawing of the Brussels collection *Pyramide*'s hammer action.

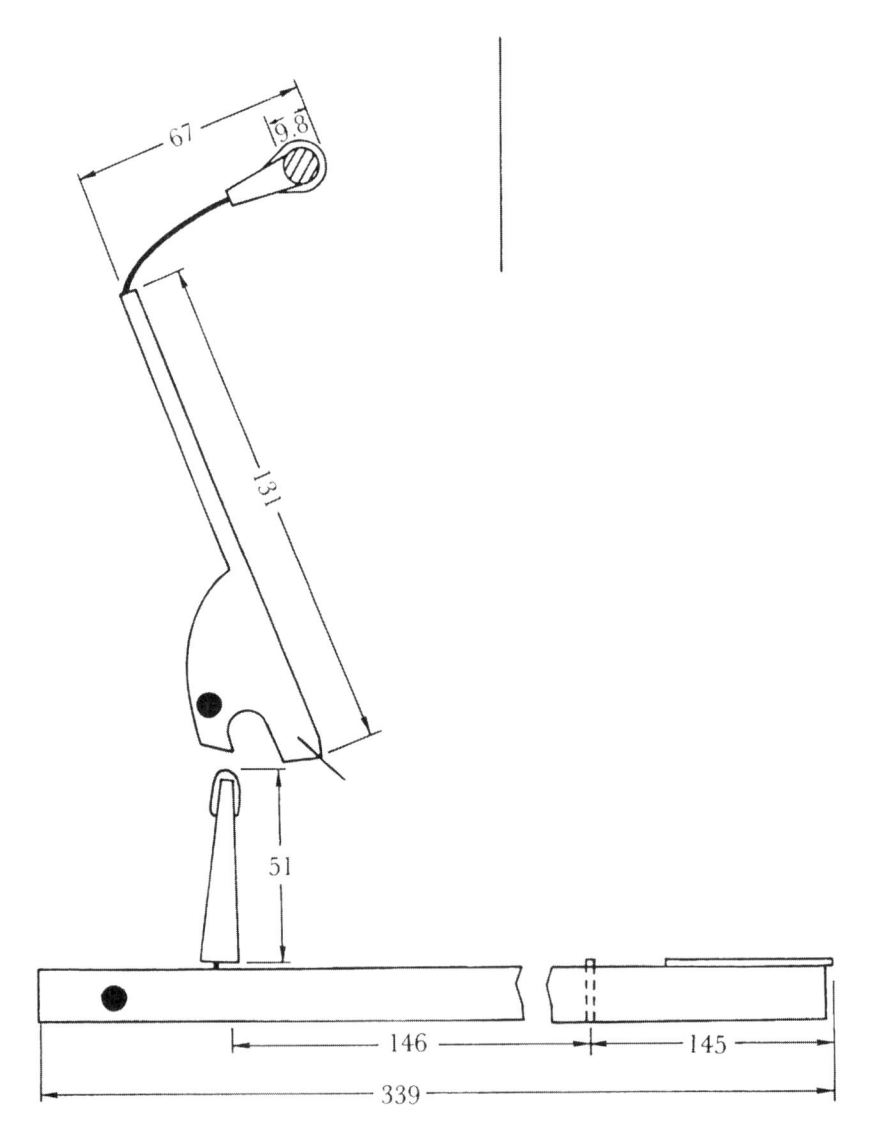

Figure 5.45 Schematic drawing of the Nuremberg collection *Pyramide*'s hammer action.

Table 5.13 Case and keyboard dimensions of *Pyramide* pianos (all measurements in millimeters)

	Frankfurt	Nuremberg	Brussels
Overall height	2690	2270*	2830*
Case height	2050	1620	2220
Case width†	974	914	945
Case depth; at soundboard	253	200	234
Case depth; at keyboard†	496	391	430
Three-octave span	481	452	493

* Estimated (case disassembled when measured).
† Measurement excluding case molding.

Inscriptions

On the underside of the soundboard of the Gottfried Silbermann piano in Sanssouci, Potsdam:

Dieß Instrument: Piano et Forte genandt, ist von den Königl. Pohlnischen, und Churfl. Sächsischen / Hof und Landt Orgel, und Instrument macher, in Freyberg von Herrn, Gottfried / Silbermann, verfertiget worden, Datum Freyberg in Meißen den 11. Junij / Ano: Christi 1746

On the underside of the soundboard of the Gottfried Silbermann piano in the Germanisches Nationalmuseum, Nuremberg:

Heut dato ist dieser boden den 22 7bris 1749 ein geleimet worden verfertiget / von H. Gottfried Silbermann, kögl Pohl. Churfl. Sächsischen Hoff und Landorgel / und Instrument Macher wohnhafft in Freyberg im Meissischen Creuss / Piano et Forte genandt

In ink on a paper label glued to the inside of the back of the *Pyramide* piano in Brussels:

Dieße Pyramite hat geferti / get und Erfunden, Christian / Ernst Friederici Orgelbauer / in Gera in Monats 7br: / Ao 1745. S.D.G.

Engraved on the back of the brass lock of the *Pyramide* piano in Frankfurt:

Ao / 1745

Engraved on brass plate pinned to back of right shutter, *Pyramide* piano, Frankfurt:

Geschenk des Herrn Major / Karl v. Portatius / Weinachten 1902

The Pianoforte in France

In 1716, five years after the publication of Maffei's announcement of Cristofori's invention of the piano, Jean Marius of Paris made a belated claim that he had invented a *clavecin à maillets* (keyboard instrument with hammers). A lawyer by training, Marius was a clever and extremely versatile inventor: he designed a collapsible tent, a machine to sow seeds, a water pump, a method of waterproofing cloth, an improved pocket watch, a system of harpsichord pedals controlling dynamics, a bowed keyboard instrument, and a portable organ.[84] His engineering skills led to his appointment as adjunct mechanician of the Académie royale des sciences on July 9, 1718. In 1707 Jean Marius' address was rue de Richelieu, à porte cochère, vis à vis du Lion Ferré. An individual named Marius, living in 1715 on the rue des Fossés St. Germain "aux trois Entonnoirs," advertised a newly invented folding umbrella; it is likely that this individual and the inventor of the *clavecin à maillets* are one and the same.[85] Marius died on April 6, 1720.[86]

What prompted Jean Marius to pursue his experiments with the striking mechanisms and to submit drawings of his actions to the Académie royale des sciences is unknown. In 1713, none other than François Couperin wrote (in the preface to his first volume of *Pièces de clavecin*) that "le Clavecin est parfait quant à son etendue, et brillant par luy même; mais, comme on ne peut enfler ny diminuer ses sons, je sçauray toûjours gré à ceux qui, par un art infini soutenu par le goût, pourront ariver à rendre cet instrument susceptible d'expression."[87] (The *clavecin* is perfect as to its range, and brilliant in itself, but as it is impossible to swell or diminish the volume of sound, I would be forever grateful to anyone who, by infinite art sustained by taste, is able to render the instrument capable of expression.) Such a provocative challenge may have inspired Marius to develop a hammer action, though there may have been direct communication between him and the Medici court, and possibly with Cristofori himself, for an instrument described as "un Cimbalo da ripiegare, lavoro fatto in Francia, con' il fondo dipinto à rabeschi, con' tastatura d'avorio, et ebano in tre

---

[84] Albert Cohen, *Music in the French Royal Academy of Sciences: A Study in the Evolution of Musical Thought* (Princeton, 1981), pp. 49–52.

[85] G. Thibault, J. Jenkins, and J. Bran-Ricci, *Eighteenth Century Musical Instruments: France and Britain* (London, 1973), pp. 8–9.

[86] Cohen, *Music in the French Royal Academy of Sciences*, pp. 50–51.

[87] François Couperin, *Pièces de clavecin*, Book 1 (Paris, 1713; facs. repr. New York, 2010), pp. 10–11.

pezzi, con' invenzione per poterlo accordare di uno Strumento d'ottone" (a cembalo that folds up, made in France, with its soundboard painted with arabesques, with keys of ivory and ebony, in three sections, with an invention that allows tuning by an instrument of brass) is listed in the 1716 Medici musical instrument inventory drawn up by Cristofori. Such a folding harpsichord, with a built-in monochord for tuning meantone temperament, was invented by Marius in 1700. Though such an instrument did not arrive in time to be listed in the 1700 Medici musical instrument inventory, its inclusion in the very next inventory is indicative of the speedy exchange of ideas and inventions at that time. Another of these cleverly designed folding harpsichords was owned by Frederick the Great.

The earliest official reference to Jean Marius is a certificate of approbation dated December 18, 1699, signed by four court organists, Guillaume-Gabriel Nivers, François Couperin, Nicolas-Antoine Lebègue, and Jean-Baptiste Buterne, attesting to the merits of Marius' *clavecin brisé*, the French term for his harpsichord made in three hinged sections that could be folded for transport. On January 16, 1700, Marius presented his plans for this instrument to the Académie royale des sciences and received its certificate of approval on January 24, 1700. He then petitioned for a royal *privilège*, which was issued on September 18, 1700, entitling him to sole production rights for a period of twenty years. Marius was not a member of the Communauté des maîtres faiseurs d'instruments de musique (Paris's guild of master instrument makers), and in retaliation the guild challenged his *privilège* in the courts. Though his *privilège* for the *clavecin brisé* was upheld, a successful challenge by the Communauté prevented Marius from receiving a *privilège* to produce his newly invented *clavecin à maillets*, plans for which were submitted to the Académie royale des sciences on March 21, 1716. Details of Marius' legal struggle to win this *privilège*, which extended through 1718, are preserved in the *Dossier Marius* in the archives of the Académie.[88]

Drawings and descriptions of Jean Marius' hammer actions, which evidently never went into production, were published posthumously in an article in *Machines et inventions approuvées par l'Académie royale des sciences*, vol. III (Paris, 1735). The article consists of four engravings and accompanying descriptions of different types of striking mechanisms. In the first mechanism, the hammer faces away from the player and rests

---

[88] Albert Cohen, "Jean Marius' *Clavecin brisé* and *Clavecin à maillets* Revisited: The 'Dossier Marius' at the Paris Academy of Sciences," *Journal of the American Musical Instrument Society* 13 (1987), pp. 23–38.

on top of the back end of the key lever. It is free to move independently of the key, and made heavier so that it descends promptly after striking the string. Marius' second figure shows three different mechanisms: two that have hammers that strike down on the strings, and another in which the hammer strikes upwards. The third figure illustrates an upright piano with a striking element that consists of a conventional harpsichord jack with its quill replaced by a rigid striking element. His fourth system is essentially a reiteration of the third (though illustrated with a harpsichord in the more conventional, non-upright orientation), with the addition of a rank of harpsichord jacks that can be operated independently or in conjunction with the hammers – an idea that anticipated Giovanni Ferrini's combination pianoforte/harpsichord.[89]

As indicated above, Jean Marius lost his legal battle with the Communauté des maîtres faiseurs d'instruments de musique. Without the protection of a royal *privilège*, he elected not to produce his *clavecin à maillets*.

In 1759, Weltman (possibly Andries Veltman, b. Amsterdam, 1730; d. Amsterdam, 1796) submitted plans to the Académie royale des sciences in Paris for *un nouveau clavessin susceptible d'un grand nombre de changements* (a new harpsichord capable of a great many effects), having "marteaux; espèce de sautereaux qui, au lieu de pincer les cordes, les frappent en dessous" (hammers; a kind of jack that instead of plucking the strings, strikes from below). One year earlier, an advertisement appeared for a "*Clavecin*, new and very curious, designed by Sr Wittman, which gives, by means of an encased mechanism, diverse modulations of sounds from *pianissimo* up to *fortissimo*." It is possible that Weltman and Wittman were the same person, and that this *clavecin* of curious design was one of the first pianos made in France.

Though some pianoforte making was undertaken in Paris in the 1760s, no examples from that decade survive. However, evidence of piano making can be found in an inventory dated 1763 made by the wife of Claude-Bénigne Balbastre (1729–1799), which lists a "clavecin à marteau à ravallement à un seul clavier et tirace dans son etuy de bois peint, le clavecin fait par Blanchet" (*Clavecin* with hammers of enlarged compass with one keyboard and pull-downs in a painted wood case, the *clavecin* made by Blanchet).[90] This is one of the earliest references to piano making (or

---

[89] For a full transcription, translation, and illustration of Marius' hammer action drawings, see Pollens, *The Early Pianoforte*, pp. 214–220, 265–267.

[90] Paris, Archives Nationales, Minutier central des notaires parisiens, XLVI 392; William Dowd, "The Surviving Instruments of the Blanchet Workshop," *The Historical Harpsichord* 1 (1984), p. 89n.

possibly the conversion of a harpsichord into a piano) in France. Balbastre was a noted composer and organist, and it is understandable that his pianoforte was equipped with a pull-down pedal board. While a "clavecin à marteau avec son pied verni en noir commun" (keyboard instrument with hammers and its stand, both painted black) appears in the posthumous, 1766 inventory of the workshop of François-Étienne Blanchet II, there is no indication of the instrument's origin.[91] It may have been made in France, perhaps by Blanchet, as cases and stands were commonly painted in that country, though it is possible that the instrument was Italian. Through the 1760s, French newspaper articles increasingly report news of pianos being made and played in France, a clear sign of growing interest in this "new" keyboard instrument.[92]

Johann Kilian Mercken (1743–1819) may be considered the first Parisian maker dedicated to the manufacture of pianos, as a square piano (with a simple sticker action) of his is dated 1770 (Musée des arts et métiers, Paris), with many other pianos of his in existence dating to 1809.[93] Another Parisian maker, Adrien de l'Épine (b. Toulouse, 1735, d. c. 1780), was constructing organized pianos as early as 1772.[94]

Through the third quarter of the eighteenth century, the harpsichord continued its glorious reign in France, and, for the most part, the piano was viewed suspiciously as a foreign instrument. Among the earliest pianos made in eighteenth-century France were those of Jean-Henri (Johann Heinrich) Silbermann (1727–1799) of Strasbourg, a grandson of the organ builder Andreas Silbermann and nephew of Gottfried Silbermann. Jean-Henri's pianos (made around 1775) were closely modeled after those of his uncle: his cases had inverted wrestplanks (Figure 5.46) but were made with mitered instead of curved tails, the actions retained leather-covered cylindrical hammer heads (Figure 5.47) but lacked individual back checks and employed a padded hammer rest instead (Figure 5.48), and the compasses were extended to five octaves. *L'Avantcoureur* announced Jean-Henri's construction of this type of instrument in 1761,[95] though the

---

[91] Hubbard, *Three Centuries of Harpsichord Making*, p. 293.
[92] Eugène de Bricqueville, *Les ventes d'instruments de musique au XVIIIe siècle* (Paris, 1908), passim.
[93] Constant Pierre, *Les facteurs d'instruments de musique. Les luthiers et la facture instrumentale. Précis historique* (Paris, 1893; facs. Geneva, 1976), pp. 139–140; Marie-Christine Weber and Jean-François Weber, *J. K. Mercken: Premier facteur parisien de forte-pianos* (Paris, 2008).
[94] Albert Cohen, *Music in the French Royal Academy of Sciences*, p. 59; Adélaïde de Place, *Le Piano-forte à Paris entre 1760 et 1822* (Paris, 1986).
[95] *L'Avantcoureur* (April 6, 1761), pp. 219–220; de Place, ibid., pp. 21–22.

Figure 5.46 Jean-Henri Silbermann piano, detail of the inverted wrestplank. Photograph courtesy of Alan Curtis.

earliest known examples are dated 1776. By 1783, he was also producing pedal pianos.[96]

Surprisingly, in 1785, *L'Encyclopédie méthodique* stated:

Forté-piano, ou Clavecin à marteau; Ce clavecin a été inventé, il y a environ 25 ans, à Freyberg en Saxe, par M. Silbermann; de la Saxe l'invention a pénétré a Londres, d'où viennent presque tous ceux qui se vendent en France.[97]

(Fortepiano, or keyboard instrument with hammers; this instrument was invented around twenty-five years ago in Freiberg, Saxony, by Mr. Silbermann; the Saxon invention made its way to London, which is the source of almost all such instruments sold in France.)

While the first part of this statement regarding Jean-Henri's Silbermann's uncle Gottfried is clearly false, the comment about England being the source of most of the pianos in France at that time is largely correct. For example, many Broadwood square pianos made in the late eighteenth century bear bilingual (English and French) labels (Figure 5.49) that indicate how to regulate the action and prevent the dampers from rattling.

[96] *Strassburger Gelehrte Nachrichten* (Strassburg, 1783), p. 255; Donald Boalch, *Makers of the Harpsichord and Clavichord 1440–1840*, 2nd edn (London, 1974), s.v. "Johann Heinrich Silbermann."
[97] *Art du faiseur d'instruments de musique et lutherie: Extrait de L'Encyclopédie méthodique, arts et métiers mécaniques* (Paris, 1785; repr. Geneva, 1972), p. 8.

Figure 5.47 Jean-Henri Silbermann piano, detail of hammer showing leathered cylindrical hammer head. Photograph courtesy of Alan Curtis.

Most French musicians and writers, however, remained disdainful of the newcomer, despite its growing popularity. Upon hearing an English piano being played at the Tuileries in 1774, Balbastre is reported to have remarked to the noted Parisian harpsichord maker Pascal Taskin (1723–1793): "jamais ce nouveau venu ne détrônera le majestueux clavecin" (never will the newcomer dethrone the majestic harpsichord).[98] This comment is ironic, as the inventory cited above suggests that Balbastre owned a pianoforte, and within a few years of making this comment, he was composing pieces for the instrument. In 1775, Voltaire referred to the pianoforte as "un instrument de chaudronnier en comparaison du clavecin" (a cauldron maker's instrument in comparison to the harpsichord).[99] Pierre-Antoine-Augustin, Chevalier de Piis characterized it as follows:

Fier de ses sons moelleux qu'il enfante sans peine / Avec un flegme anglais le piano se traîne / Et nargue, fils ingrat, le grêle clavecin.[100]

(Proud of its velvety sounds that are born without effort with English reserve the piano drags itself along and defies, ungrateful child, the frail harpsichord.)

Further criticism was voiced by Canon Trouflaut in 1773:

---

[98] René Brancour, *Histoire des instruments de musique* (Paris, 1921), p. 92.
[99] Letter to Marquise du Deffand, December 8, 1774; Brancour, ibid.
[100] Brancour, ibid., p. 93.

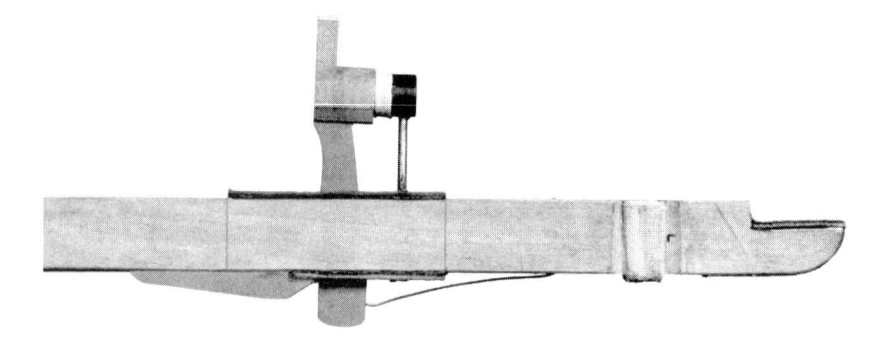

Figure 5.48 Jean-Henri Silbermann piano, detail of escapement mechanism; note lack of back check. Photograph courtesy of Alan Curtis.

J'ose ajouter, avec confiance, que le clavecin à buffles est très-supérieur aux piano-forté... Placés chez le vendeur, ils ont de quoi plaire & séduire; mais si l'on porte un coup-d'oeil attentif sur l'intérieur de leur construction, leur complication effraye à l'instant. Si les dessus en sont charmans, les basses dures, sourdes & fausses, semblent donner la consomption à nos oreilles françoises.[101]

(I dare to add with confidence that the harpsichord with *buffles* [*peau de buffle*, soft, buffalo-hide plectra invented by Pascal Taskin] is much superior to the pianoforte... At the dealer they may please and seduce; but if one takes a close look at their internal construction, their complexity will instantly cause alarm. If the treble is charming, the bass is hard, dull and false, seeming to give consumption to our French ears.)

In the 1777 inventory of Pascal Taskin's workshop, six finished pianos are listed, one of which was of foreign make.[102] A finely veneered pianoforte by this maker dated 1788 (clearly in the English style) survives (Musée de la musique, Paris; inventory no. 10298). It incorporates a fixed jack, an intermediate lever, and a sticker hinged to the hammer. The overhanging hitchpin rail – similar in outward appearance to that employed by Cristofori, though not mounted to an internal bentside – is used. Louis Bas of Villeneuve Lès Avignon made a pianoforte in 1781 (Figures 5.50 and 5.51; National Music Museum, Vermillion, South Dakota, inventory no. 4653) with a hammer action loosely modeled on that of either Cristofori or Silbermann – certainly the swan song for this type of action.[103] At this point piano making had firmly established itself in France.

---

[101] *Art du faiseur d'instruments de musique et lutherie*, pp. 9–10.
[102] Pierre J. Hardouin and Frank Hubbard, "Harpsichord Making in Paris: Part I, Eighteenth Century," *The Galpin Society Journal* 10 (1957), p. 19.
[103] John Koster, "Two Early French Grand Pianos," *Early Keyboard Journal* 12 (1994), pp. 7–37.

Figure 5.49 Label in English and French in a late-eighteenth-century Broadwood square piano, providing instructions for regulating the action.

Figure 5.50 Piano by Louis Bas, 1781. National Music Museum, Vermillion, South Dakota.

Figure 5.51 Rose of Louis Bas piano, 1781. National Music Museum, Vermillion, South Dakota.

Sébastien Erard's Repetition Action

Sébastien Erard is credited with having invented the modern piano action, which is variously referred to as the "repetition action" and "double escapement action"; however, it would appear that the engraving of Cristofori's early hammer action published by Maffei in 1711 and 1719 (as well as by König in 1725) may have been the direct inspiration for the action patented by Erard in 1821. If this is the case, we must link Cristofori even more closely with the development of the modern piano.

The noted French piano maker Sébastien Erard (1752–1831) was originally trained as a draftsman and surveyor, though in 1768 he arrived in Paris and found work with a harpsichord maker. In that year he was employed by the Duchess of Villeroy, and in 1777 he constructed a pianoforte for her in workshop facilities set up in her château on the rue de Bourbon.[104] Some sources refer to this as the first piano constructed in France, though this is clearly not the case.

In 1781, Erard established a manufacturing and sales facility at nos. 13 and 21 rue du Mail in Paris, where he was assisted by his brother, Jean-Baptiste. In 1785 Louis XVI issued Sébastien a *Brevet* (license) that exempted him from membership of the fan-makers' guild, to which Parisian musical instrument makers then belonged. Many French aristocrats were patrons of Erard, and he is also known to have designed and built a special transposing piano for Queen Marie Antoinette in 1787. Because he was suspected of royalist leanings, he fled France in 1792 to avoid the guillotine and opened a manufacturing facility in London. A London post office record indicates that he had an address there as early as 1786, but this would appear to have been a sales room rather than a factory. In 1802, the Erard shop moved from 18 Great Marlborough Street to 189 Regent Street, and in 1804 to 158a New Bond Street. Sébastien Erard returned to Paris in 1796 but maintained the workshop in London. The firm began taking out English patents on pianos and harps in 1794 – first under Sébastien's name, and under his nephew Pierre's in 1821; it began registering French patents in 1809.[105]

Sébastien Erard evidently preferred the so-called English action to the German or Viennese actions, though he did on occasion make use of the principles of the Viennese action (most notably in the up-striking hammers for the bass strings in his 1808 patent drawing for the *mécanisme à étrier*). Americus Backers is believed to have first developed the English grand action in 1771.[106] This action may be seen as a simplified version of Cristofori's design in which the intermediate lever has been eliminated and the escapement jack placed in direct contact with the hammer butt. To achieve the requisite leverage, the escapement jack was mounted closer to the pivot point of the hammer than in Cristofori's design. In both the English and Erard action (which is similar to the English action but with a few subtle differences), the escapement jack did not passively slide off the hammer butt (as in Cristofori's early design), but was actively displaced by an adjustable stop. As the jack was pushed off the hammer butt, it

---

[104] A. Grangier, *A Genius of France: A Short Sketch of the Famous Inventor, Sébastien Erard, and the Firm he Founded in Paris, 1780*, trans. Jean Fouqueville (Paris, 1924), p. 2.

[105] Barrie Heaton, *A History of Sébastien Erard, Piano and Harp Maker* (UK Piano Page, 2006), pp. 1–8.

[106] See Warwick Henry Cole, "Americus Backers: Original Forte Piano Maker," *Harpsichord & Fortepiano Magazine* 4/4 (1987), pp. 79–85.

gradually slid away from the pivot point of the hammer, thereby creating a subtle decelerating effect similar to that produced in Cristofori's hammer action.

Around 1790, Erard built square pianos with an action termed "*à double pilotes*," which interposed a short, hinged intermediate lever between the sticker and the hammer. This action, which was developed by Johann Christoph (Johannes) Zumpe around 1788, provided an inclined point of contact between the lower "pilot" and the intermediate lever that served to decelerate the hammer as the key was pressed. This would appear to have been Erard's first practical experience with the use of an intermediate lever, an element that was to become an important part of his so-called "repetition action."[107]

Prior to Erard's invention of his repetition action, the mechanisms of many keyboard instruments required the key to return completely before it could reactivate the hammer. Only the clavichord and pianos fitted with simple sticker or tangent actions enabled the player to re-strike the note before the key had returned to rest.[108] This was not a great problem with instruments having a shallow key dip, but English-action grand pianos tended to have a greater key dip than grand pianos fitted with a German or a Viennese action. The greater depth of touch appears to have proved uncomfortable to some pianists accustomed to the shallower action. Evidence of this can be found in Beethoven's Erard piano made in 1803, the action of which had been modified twice in Vienna by 1805 and again in 1813, most likely by Matthäus Andreas Stein, apparently in an effort to render the touch shallower and lighter.[109]

Sébastien Erard set his inventive mind to solving the repetition problem and arrived at a new action design that was patented in England in 1808 (patent no. 3170). This action was termed the *mécanisme à étrier* (stirrup mechanism) because of a stirrup-shaped escapement jack that pulled down upon a projection of the hammer. This projection, or "beak," was clearly borrowed from German or Viennese action design. Curiously, the patent drawing and description of this action call for the bass strings to be

---

[107] "Repetition action" is the term used in Rosamond Harding's *The Pianoforte*, though Erard's 1821 patent merely refers to the action as an "improvement" and gives no special name for it. Montal refers to Erard's action as the *mécanisme à double échappement* – see Claude Montal, *L'Art d'accorder soi-même son piano* (Paris, 1836; facs. Geneva, 1976), p. 221.

[108] Any lost motion between the beak and the escapement jack in the German or Viennese action provides some leeway, however.

[109] Alfons Huber, "Beethovens Erard-Flügel: Überlegungen zu seiner Restaurierung," *Restauro* 3 (1990), pp. 181–188; Tilman Skowroneck, *Beethoven the Pianist* (Gothenburg, 2007), pp. 141–154.

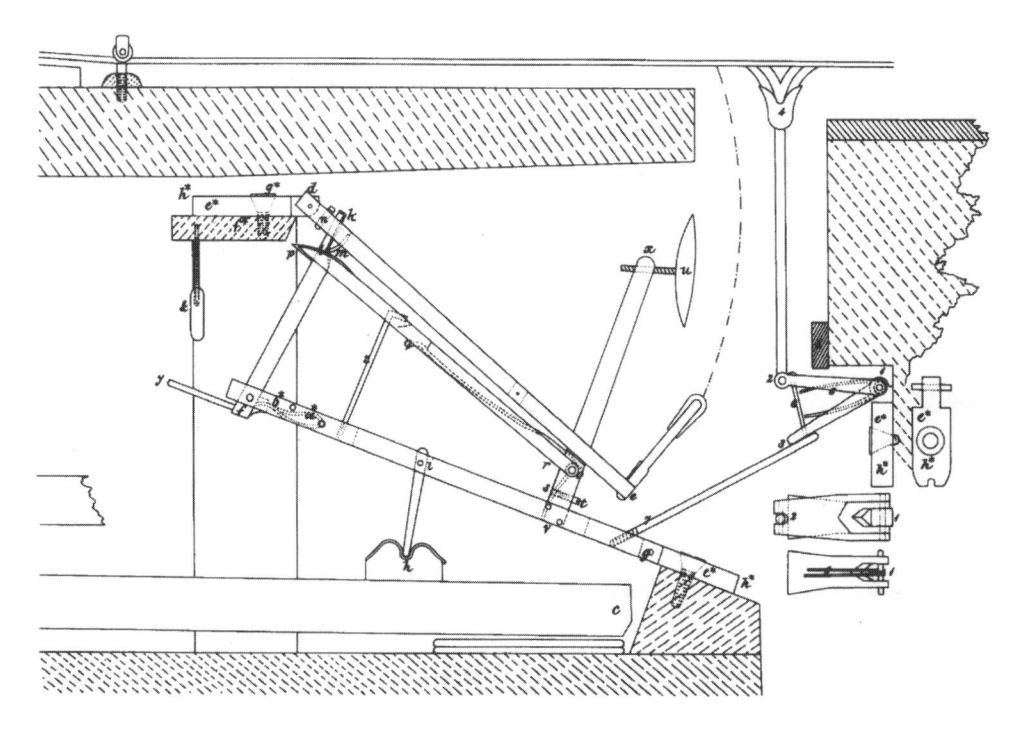

Figure 5.52 Erard 1821 patent drawing for the repetition action.

mounted below the soundboard, where they are struck using a modified form of the action in which the stirrup extends from the underside of the key front and pushes down on the hammer beak. In the *mécanisme à étrier* proper, the stirrup was designed to advance under spring tension so that it could re-engage the hammer beak before the key had fully returned. Jan Ladislav Dussek is said to have played on an Erard piano fitted with this action in 1810. Some disadvantages were later reported however; Claude Montal, a professor of piano tuning at the Paris Conservatoire, wrote in 1836 that after some use the *mécanisme à étrier* became shaky and noisy.[110]

The Erard firm persevered and in 1821 they developed the repetition action, patented in London on December 22nd of that year (English patent no. 4631; Figure 5.52) by Sébastien's nephew and business partner Pierre.

This action was patented in France in August of 1822 (French patent no. 3512), and in the same year the firm completed its first piano with the repetition action in its Paris workshop (serial no. 12055). Franz Liszt,

---

[110] Montal, *L'Art d'accorder*, p. 217.

then twelve years old, made his sensational debut in Paris in 1823 on an Erard piano fitted with the newly invented action; in his subsequent tour of Europe Liszt helped popularize this radically new design. Other virtuosi were not immediately impressed with the new action, which Ignaz Moscheles found heavy (though he prophesied that it would revolutionize the piano).[111]

The repetition action enabled the player to repeat notes without the full return of the key, thereby providing greater playing speed and dynamic control. The rather lengthy text of Pierre Erard's original patent is reprinted in Rosamond Harding's *The Pianoforte*, though the action can be more briefly described as follows: the escapement jack and auxiliary lever are supported by a pivoted intermediate lever that extends beyond the back of the key.[112] The auxiliary lever is maintained in position by a strong spring so that it travels together with the intermediate lever and the hammer as the back of the key rises. Just before the hammer strikes, the auxiliary lever is depressed slightly so that the escapement jack makes direct contact with the hammer butt and trips it, but as the front of the key begins to rise and the back check releases the hammer, the auxiliary lever, which was depressed, rises and lifts the hammer slightly, enabling the escapement jack to slip back under the hammer butt and re-engage it. Like the escapement jacks in the English grand action, the escapement jacks of Erard's repetition action are actively pushed off the hammer butt, though in Erard's design the jack is rotated off the hammer butt by a projecting arm that comes in contact with an adjustable stop. Unlike the back checks used in Cristofori's later action and in the English grand action, those employed in Erard's repetition action do not extend from the back end of the keys but project from the intermediate levers and pass through slots in the hammer shanks, thereby catching the hammer heads in front rather than from behind. The Erard firm continued to use these unusually positioned back checks through the 1890s.

Though Erard's repetition action may be viewed as a development of the English grand action, it can also be seen as a re-introduction of the design Cristofori employed in his early action, pictured in Maffei's 1711 article, in which the escapement lever is mounted on the intermediate lever. If Maffei's 1711 drawing of Cristofori's action is rotated 20° and

---

[111] Charlotte Moscheles, *Life of Moscheles*, 2 vols. (London, 1873; facs. repr. Cambridge, 2014), vol. I, p. 59.
[112] Harding, *The Pianoforte*, pp. 172–174.

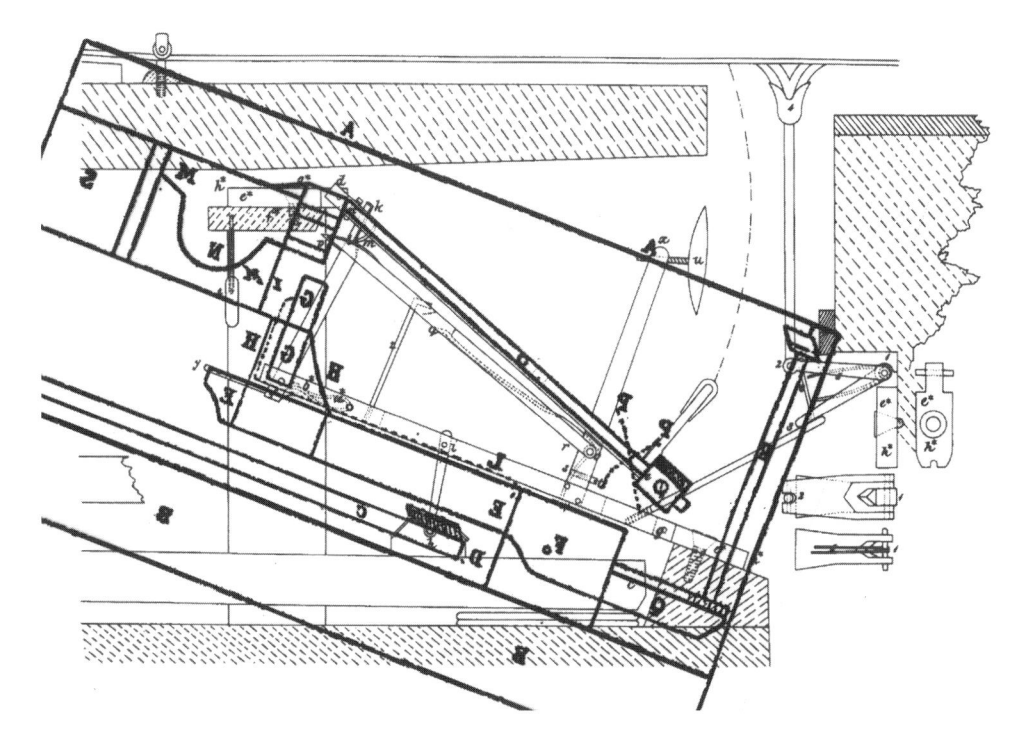

Figure 5.53 Superimposition of the 1821 patent drawing of Sébastien Erard's "repetition action" (from Rosamund Harding's *The Pianoforte*) and a version of Maffei's drawing of Cristofori's hammer action. Note that the hammers, intermediate levers, and escapement jacks of the actions are similarly positioned and proportioned.

superimposed upon the 1821 patent drawing of Erard's repetition action (Figure 5.53), a stunning similarity is revealed.

As one can see, not only are the levers and escapement jacks arranged in the same fashion, but they are proportionally similar. Another feature that Erard appears to have borrowed from Cristofori's design is the under-damper. In the 1711 drawing, the back of the intermediate lever causes the damper to retract from the strings as the key is depressed. Prior to the development of this system, dampers were generally mounted above the strings and were lifted off them when the keys were depressed (the so-called "peacock" under-damper used in English square pianos of the late eighteenth and early nineteenth centuries is a notable exception). In the 1821 patent, Erard made use of dampers that were lowered away from the strings by extensions at the backs of the intermediate levers.

Today's grand-piano hammer action retains all of the salient features of Erard's repetition action, though in the modern action the so-called "wippen" is sturdier, more compact, and has additional points of adjustment (such as the "drop" screw, a screw for adjusting the position of the jack, and screws for adjusting the tension of the springs). Furthermore, the intermediate lever does not extend beyond the back of the key, as it does in Erard's design, and the back check is mounted on the key and grabs the hammer from behind, just as in Cristofori's design.

Erard's repetition action may thus have been inspired by Cristofori's action design as published in 1711. Though no examples of this early style of action by Cristofori are known to have survived in Erard's day, the availability of Maffei's published drawing could very well have provided the inspiration for the development of the repetition action that is used in the modern piano.

Conclusion

At the outset, the pianoforte was not universally accepted, and those who appreciated its unique qualities did not necessarily agree that it was compatible with all genres of keyboard music. In Cristofori's day, members of the musical establishment in Florence argued over the pianoforte's merits and shortcomings, though most admitted that it was best suited for the chamber, rather than for the larger settings of church or opera orchestra. Scipione Maffei, the noted poet, dramatist, and essayist who wrote about Cristofori's piano in 1711, was an ardent admirer of the instrument and recognized its value as a solo instrument. He likened it to the lute, harp, and viol because of its expressive capability. Nevertheless, the early Florentine piano was most successful as an instrument of accompaniment (it became the preferred keyboard instrument of some of eighteenth-century Europe's most famous singers, including the *castrati* Carlo Broschi [Farinelli], Carl' Antonio Zanardi, and Francesco de Castris).

In his *Versuch über die wahre Art das Clavier zu spielen* (Berlin, 1759), Carl Philipp Emanuel Bach admitted that the piano (most likely Gottfried Silbermann's copies of Florentine originals) sounded well alone but thought it was better suited for use in small ensembles and in accompaniment. In France, faithful devotees of the harpsichord railed against the pianoforte as a "cauldron maker's instrument," calling its sound "muddled."

The first music written expressly for the piano is Lodovico Giustini's *Sonate da Cimbalo di piano, e forte detto volgarmente di martelletti*, published in Florence in 1732. These twelve sonatas were dedicated to the Portuguese *Infante*, Don Antonio, at about the time a few Florentine pianos appeared in the courts of Portugal and Spain. Domenico Scarlatti was undoubtedly familiar with the early Florentine piano and with Portuguese and Spanish copies, as were indigenous composers and cembalists of the Iberian peninsula, such as Carlos Seixas and Padre Antonio Soler, and there is documentary evidence that Bartolomeo Cristofori sold an instrument directly to King João V of Portugal.

In the early 1730s, Gottfried Silbermann showed his first efforts in piano making to Johann Sebastian Bach, from whom they received a mixed response. Silbermann refined these instruments over the next few years, and in 1747 Bach was taken for a tour of Frederick the Great's collection of Silbermann pianos, at least one of which had been made just the previous year. Seated at one of these improved instruments, Bach improvised upon a theme presented to him by the king. That theme, and the elaborations that spontaneously poured forth, became the *Musical Offering*. Through the mid-eighteenth century, however, the pianoforte remained a curiosity primarily enjoyed by privileged court composers and musicians.

Before the 1760s there was apparently no piano making in England. Charles Burney's article on the "Harpsichord" in Abraham Rees' *The Cyclopædia; or Universal Dictionary of Arts, Sciences, and Literature*, vol. XVII (London, 1819) provides a concise history of piano making in England.

> In the beginning of the last century, hammer harpsichords were invented at Florence, of which there is a description in the Giornale d'Italia, 1711. The invention made but a slow progress. The first that was brought to England was made by an English monk at Rome, Father Wood, for an English friend (the late Samuel Crisp, esq. of Chesington, author of Virginia, a tragedy), a man of learning, and of exquisite taste in all the fine arts.
>
> The tone of this instrument was so superior to that produced by quills, with the additional power of producing all the shades of *piano* and *forte* by the finger, that though the touch and mechanism were so imperfect that nothing quick could be executed upon it, yet the dead march in Saul, and other solemn and pathetic strains, when executed with taste and feeling by a master a little accustomed to the touch, excited equal wonder and delight to the hearers. Fulk Greville, esq. purchased this instrument of Mr. Crisp for 100 guineas, and it remained *unique* in this country for several years, till Plenius, the maker of the lyrichord, tuned by weights, and the tone produced by wheels, made a piano-forte in imitation of that of Mr. Greville. Of this instrument the touch was better, but the tone very much inferior.
>
> Backers, a harpsichord maker of the second rank, constructed several piano-fortes, and improved the mechanism in some particulars, but the tone, with all the delicacy of Schroeter's touch, lost the spirit of the harpsichord, and gained nothing in sweetness.
>
> After the arrival of John Chr. Bach in this country, and the establishment of his concert, in connection with Abel, all the harpsichord makers tried their mechanical powers at piano-fortes, but the first attempts were always on the large size, till Zumpé, a German, who had long worked under Schudi, constructed small piano-fortes of the shape and size of the virginal, of which the tone was very sweet, and the touch, with a little use, equal to any degree of

rapidity. These, from their low price, and the convenience of their form, as well as power of expression, suddenly grew into such favour, that there was scarcely a house in the kingdom where a keyed-instrument had ever had admission, but was supplied with one of Zumpé's piano-fortes, for which there was nearly as great a call in France as in England. In short, he could not make them fast enough to gratify the craving of the public. Pohlman, whose instruments were very inferior in tone, fabricated an almost infinite number for such as Zumpé was unable to supply. Large piano-fortes afterwards receiving great improvement in the mechanism by Merlin, and in the tone by Broadwood and Stoddard, the harsh scratching of the quills of a harpsichord can now no longer be borne.[1]

Burney's account provides a concise summary of the piano's introduction in England. Aside from this article, little is known of Father Wood's piano made in Rome, which may have been inspired by one of Cristofori's instruments, perhaps the one owned by Cardinal Ottoboni. Unfortunately, no instruments by the inventive Roger Plenius have survived (b. Orsoy, 1696; d. 1774, London).

As Burney indicates, the earliest pianos made in England were those of Johannes Zumpe and Johannes Pohlmann, both of German birth. The turmoil brought about by the Seven Years War (1756–1763) caused a group of keyboard instrument makers that had been active in Germany to emigrate to England and settle in London. Known today as the "Twelve Apostles" (though this group was comprised of more than twelve keyboard instrument makers), they included: Americus Backers, Frederick Beck, Adam Beyer, Gabriel Buntebart, Christopher Ganer, George Garcka, John Geib, Meincke Meyer, Johannes Pohlmann, George Schoene, Christoph Sievers, and Johannes Zumpe. Several had been associated with Gottfried Silbermann and were familiar with piano construction, and these German craftsmen were responsible for the major impetus in piano making in England. Burney remarked that "the Germans work much better out of their own country than they do in it, if we may judge by the harpsichords of Kirkman and Shudi; the piano fortes of Backers; and the organs of Snetzler; which far surpass, in goodness, all the keyed instruments that I met with, in my tour through Germany."[2] As discussed by Burney above, one German émigré, Johannes Zumpe, constructed small square

---

[1] Abraham Rees, *The Cyclopædia; or Universal Dictionary of Arts, Sciences, and Literature*, vol. XVII (London, 1819), s.v. "Harpsichord."
[2] Burney, *The Present State of Music in Germany, the Netherlands and the United Provinces*, vol. II, p. 147.

pianos from 1767; another, Americus Backers, working with Stodart and Broadwood, is believed to have made his first "grand" in 1772.

In England, the pianoforte was first used in a public concert (for vocal accompaniment) in 1767,[3] though as a solo instrument it is first mentioned in the *Public Advertiser* of June 2, 1768. An advertisement states:

For the benefit of Mr. Fisher. At the Large Room, Thatch'd House, St. James's-street. This Day, June the 2nd, will be performed a Grand Concert of Vocal and Instrumental Music. First Violin and Concerto by Sig. Pugnani. Concerto on the German Flute, Mr. Tacet. Concerto on the Hautbois by Mr. Fisher. Songs by Sig. Guarducci. Solo on the Viola di Gamba by Mr. Abel. Solo on the Piano Forte by Mr. Bach.

It was J. C. Bach's interest in the piano that led Nicholas Hullmandel to deduce that the piano's star was rising. Writing of the harpsichord, Hullmandel remarks that:

(its) music has been given the type of harmony and performance, the grace and lightness which is suitable to it. Alberti, Scarlatti, Rameau, Mütel, Wagenseil, then Schobert have wrought this revolution almost simultaneously. The different styles of these composers have served for more than twenty-five years as models for those who have composed for the harpsichord after them. Perhaps Emanuel Bach, for his learned, agreeable and piquant music, has merited the first place among original artists, but since he composed for the piano-forte, in use in Germany before being known elsewhere, he must not be confused with them. He is one of various composers who in giving their music the graduated nuances, oppositions, and a melody suitable to the sound and resources of the piano-forte, have prepared or decided the downfall of the harpsichord.[4]

In his biography of the musician William Babel (*c.* 1690–1723) in *A General History of Music* (1782), Charles Burney revealed his growing appreciation for the new piano vis-à-vis the harpsichord. Burney states:

[He] seems to have been the first, in this country at least, who thinned, simplified, and divested the Music of keyed-instruments of the crouded and complicated harmony, and which, from the convenience of the clavier, and passion for full and elaborate Music, it had been embarassed from its earliest cultivation. This author acquired great celebrity by wire-drawing the favourite songs of the opera of Rinaldo, and others of the same period, into *showy* and brilliant lessons, which by

---

[3] Charles Burney, *A General History of Music*, 2 vols. (London, 1776–1789; repr. New York, 1957), vol. II, p. 874 (editor's note).

[4] *Encyclopédie méthodique: Musique*, vol. I (Paris, 1791), s.v. "Clavecin"; Hubbard, *Three Centuries of Harpsichord Making*, p. 260.

mere rapidity of finger in playing single sounds, without assistance of taste, expression, harmony, or modulation, enabled the performer to astonish ignorance, and acquire the reputation of a great player at a small expence. There is no instrument so favourable to such frothy and unmeaning Music as the harpsichord. Arpeggios, which lie under the fingers, and running up and down the scales of easy keys with velocity, are not difficult, on an instrument of which neither the tone nor tuning depends on the player; as neither his breath nor bow-hand is requisite to give existence or sweetness to its sounds. And Mr. Babel by avoiding its chief difficulties of full harmony, and dissimilar motion of the parts, at once gratified idleness and vanity. I remember well in the early part of my life being a dupe to the glare and glitter of this kind of tinsel; this *poussiere dans les yeux*, which Mr. Felton continued, and other dealers in *notes, et rien que des notes*, till Jozzi, the singer, by his neat and elegant manner of executing the brilliant, graceful, and pleasing lessons of Alberti, rendered them the objects of imitation. At length, on the arrival of the late Mr. Bach, and construction of piano-fortes in this country, the performers on keyed-instruments were obliged wholly to change their ground; and instead of surprising by the *seeming* labour and dexterity of execution, had the real and more useful difficulties of taste, expression, and light and shade, to encounter.[5]

Indeed, musical taste was being reshaped by the expressive capabilities afforded by the newly invented piano. Changing taste and the growing popularity of inexpensive square pianos (made in great number both in England and Germany during the final quarter of the eighteenth century) not only placed the piano on firm popular footing, but ultimately led to the demise of the harpsichord. Despite Burney's recognition of the piano's musical advantages, he was apparently unconvinced of its impending dominance, for in 1788 he acquired a majestic Jacob and Abraham Kirckman two-manual harpsichord, replete with lute register, machine stop, Venetian swell, and an inlaid keyboard console.[6]

English-made pianos began to be exported to the continent around 1760 – the French at first disparaged the piano as an "English" instrument, though by around 1780 were producing pianos in significant numbers. While the French were late to accept and produce pianofortes, piano making was adopted quite early in Germany. Writing in 1742, Christoph Gottlieb Schröter stated that after 1721 he knew of "more than twenty towns and villages in which the usual manufacture of harpsichords has been replaced with the manufacture of keyboard instruments equipped with hammers or striking tangents."[7] This may have been an

---

[5] Burney, *A General History of Music*, vol. II, pp. 996–997.
[6] Burney's harpsichord is now in a private collection in New York and regularly tuned and looked after by the author.
[7] Marpurg, *Kritische Briefe*, vol. III, pt 1, p. 83.

exaggeration at such an early date, though by the end of the century "German" and "Viennese" action instruments were ubiquitous. Even Italian makers (seemingly oblivious of the details of Cristofori's work) were almost exclusively using *kapsel* mounted hammers in their square and grand pianos. Many late-eighteenth and early-nineteenth-century Italian pianos are anonymous, and some of the extant instruments bear false inscriptions or are misattributed to Viennese makers – an ironic postscript to the inventive work that began in Italy just one hundred years earlier.

Piano Making in Italy in the Late Eighteenth Century

The two surviving pianofortes made by Giovanni Ferrini and Domenico del Mela described in Chapter 3 represent the known remains of the "Cristofori School" of pianoforte building. The hammer actions and case construction of later Florentine pianos, such as those of Vincenzo Sodi (fl. 1780–1790), bear little resemblance to those of Cristofori.

References to piano making in Italy can be found in a series of letters exchanged in 1766 between Padre G. B. Martini and Antonio Loccatelli of Vicenza (not to be confused with the composer Pietro Locatelli). In these letters, mention is made of a *cembalo á martellino* that was constructed for Martini by Paolo Morellati of Bologna on a model supplied by Carlo Broschi (Farinelli). Farinelli, the famed *castrato* whose involvement with and ownership of a pianoforte made by Ferrini is documented above, retired in 1759 to a *palazzo* just outside Bologna after having spent twenty-five years in service to the Spanish court. Little is known of Morellati, though the correspondence reveals that the *cembalo á martellino* made for Martini was constructed from the body of an old harpsichord. Morellati is credited with having made two other pianos, in 1770 and 1773; these had actions and cases made by him.[8] The whereabouts of Morellati's instruments are unknown.

There was a brief revival of piano making in late-eighteenth-century Italy by such makers as Giuseppe Zannetti, Francesco Spighi, Vicenzio Sodi, Luigi Vignoli,[9] and Errico Gustadt.[10] Pianos by these makers bear little resemblance to the works of Cristofori and Ferrini; rather, they are more closely modeled after later English and Viennese instruments. Van

---

[8] Anne Schnoebelen, *Padre Martini's Collection of Letters in the Civico Museo Bibliografico Musicale in Bologna* (New York, 1979), pp. 338, 357, 409, 410–411.
[9] John A. Rice, "The Tuscan Piano in the 1780s," *Early Music* 21/1 (1993), pp. 5–26.
[10] An instrument signed by Errico Gustadt is preserved in The Metropolitan Museum of Art in New York. This pianoforte, dated 1798, has a Viennese action.

der Meer cites an anonymous tangent-action piano from the last third or quarter of the eighteenth century, possibly from Catania.[11] Again, this instrument derived little inspiration from the early Florentine school. Another unsigned piano with a tangent action is in a private collection in Verona. This instrument is said to have been brought by the present owner's family from Sicily and, like the instrument from Catania, may represent a little-known tradition in late-eighteenth-century Sicily of building damperless tangent pianos (perhaps derived from German models).

---

[11] John Henry van der Meer, "A Curious Instrument with a Five-Octave Compass," *Early Music* 14/3 (1986), pp. 397–400. This instrument appears to be referred to in *Art du faiseur d'instruments de musique et lutherie*, p. 10.

Appendix 1

Verona, Biblioteca Capitolare, cod. DCCCCLX, fasc. VI, no.1

The following is a translation and transcription of Scipione Maffei's notes made in connection with his interview with Bartolomeo Cristofori in preparation for publication of his article entitled "Nuova invenzione d'un Gravecembalo col piano, e forte," in the *Giornale de' letterati d'Italia* 5 (Venice, 1711), pp. 144–159 (full text below). For a critical explication of this text, see the discussion of Maffei's writings in Chapters 2 and 3.

The ellipses in square brackets denote illegible text.

Musical instruments

Christofori [crossed out] Bortolo Cristofali of Padua salaried by the Serene Prince has invented on his own the cembalo with piano and forte; he has made three so far, two sold in Florence, one to Cardinal Ottoboni.

That the violin is the only perfect instrument, because it does not have keys and one finds in the whole perfect harmony, that is, the flats and sharps each in its place, etc.

That only bowed stringed instruments have the sound-post; that by moving this slightly and pulling it here and there varies the harmony of the strings; one becomes more sonorous, the other duller, etc.

That in harpsichords or spinets a hole or outlet is needed; not necessarily a rose, nor so large, but a smaller hole is sufficient, and it can be located anywhere in the body, as long as the case has it. The spinets can do without, because they have the hole in the front, where it rises above the keyboard. But harpsichords which have another type of case and remain closed, cannot do without. True, instead of a rose, two or three small holes can be made in the front closure, which remain hidden and protected from dust.

This opening is necessary because otherwise (he says) the air that is inside remains fixed, not being able to yield and to flow out when it is impelled; and the soundboard does not move and does not yield downward as it should do (that this happens is seen from the trembling of anything that you might place upon it when you play). Thus the sound remains dull and brief and not resonant. This is contrary to the opinion of some recent [makers], that instruments are better without holes.

The perfection of instruments is found in their dimensions and above all in not having a soundboard that is too thick, nor too thin, and in having first removed the elasticity in their curvature and the bridge. Because as long as these push on the soundboard to restore their shape, the instrument does not sound well (this is one of the reasons why the old ones are good: because there is hardly any [pressure on the] soundboard).

As for the squeaking which my [Maffei's?] instrument makes, one needs to find what sort of squeaking it is, which cannot be distinguished except by the ear. It could occur because the end of the string touches the soundboard; it could occur because there is a fissure that has opened up due to damp or dry weather, which causes stress in the wood, and thus is . . .

That in winter when it is always humid the instruments rise a tone above the norm.

To make instruments, Pesaro began to disassemble grain crates in Padua and Venice that were made of cypress wood from Cyprus and Candia.

That the harmony [= temperament] is divided into five *quinti*, from one note to the other. That from the sharp of *Gesolreut* to the flat of *Alamire* there must be one [*quinto*] difference; but the black keys are split, otherwise it is not in tune. That it is easy to tune the split keys by fifths, tuning the split key of *Alamire* with the flat of *elami*. That in tuning an ordinary instrument the octave should be perfect, the fifth must drop, otherwise the instrument will not be tuned. The fourth must be higher, the major third higher. That a spinet or theorbo will never be in tune with a violin (and this can be seen when the scales are played together, not sounding in concert) because we do not have the fifths correct, because the *quinti* are not observed and are not distinct. That one realises in hearing the instrument played that something is displaced or that the instrument is out of tune, because one hears a drop in pitch in those black keys that do not have the fifth, and they are false. But music is not composed using these keys, and when they are used, it is sparingly, and the good masters use them when the text is suited to a false and unpleasant note. (Note that it could be that the system of tones is formed on this, that is, as many are made as there are strings that have a good fifth and good consonance, or are at least passable.)

He says that making [. . .] the division of the notes, with a circle divided into 42 parts, or with a square lined and then cut across, in one way they coincide, in another they do not. That this is theoretical music. That in practice one does bother ([. . .] to find the reason for this, and whether this is musical science).

Returning to the hole. That having made one instrument without a hole, it sounded dull; that once the hole is made, one immediately sees the soundboard lower by half a finger, the string remain higher and sound stronger. This lowering shows that the outflow of air gives place to [. . .]. The holes made in front and hidden [. . .], by putting your fingers near the hole, you will feel a breeze and the air come out.

That on the violin, you can transpose where you want in any sort of key, without hearing an unpleasant effect, because it has the fifths equal and the right tone, and does not fall into false and bad sound, like in other instruments.

Another instrument maker argues that without the hole, excellently, etc.

Spinet harpsichord soundboard/top/plan of lower part/front and back/sides/jacks; that [. . .] they have a cavity on the bottom on one side; hollowed out; beveled. The fabric serves to damp the sound, because when it is lowered, it touches the string and stops it.

To attribute the invention of the pianoforte to Bortolo. For he learned very much from the others after coming here. That at the beginning it was very tiring for him to be in the large room with this deafening noise. That he told the prince that he did not want it so; the latter responded, he will do it, I wish it. He [received] ten *scudi* a month.

The opening on the front of the spinet, little door.

where the strings stand, bridges, or little bridges.

the space between the two, partition.

the jack pointed below, beveled.

the wooden case, tongue.

quill front, quill in back.

where the red fabric enters, a hollow.

the irons that are on the bridges, pins.

To ask and find out why a good player does not play well for dancing; what playing for dancing consists of.

[Two lines are crossed out.]

When I return, I will have Cavalier Albisi, relative of Buonarroti, describe the cembalo and note all the terminology.

To have the instrument maker write a report noting the substance of the invention, wherein lies its strengths and wherein its greatest difficulties.

It is in having observed the difference of the motion of engagement of [...] toward the center, and [...] near the circumference. When it is pushed upwards near the center every smallest impulse makes it go up, and if it is pushed with force it goes up with much pressure, etc.

Original text

Istromenti da suonare

Christofori [crossed out] Bortolo Cristofali padovano stipendiato dal s. principe, ha inventato senza motivo avuto da altra cosa il cimbalo col piano e forte; ne ha fatti tre fin ora, due venduti in Firenze, uno al card. Ottoboni.

Che il violino è l'istromento unicamente perfetto, perché non ha tasti e si trova in tutti l'armonia perfetta, cioè i bmolli e diesis in suo luogo, ecc.

Che i soli stromenti da arco han l'anima; che questa mossa un poco e tirata piú in là varia l'armonia delle corde: una ne diventa piú sonora, l'altra piú ottusa, ecc.

Che ne' cembali o spinette è necessario un buco, o sia sfogatoio; non già rosa, né sí grande, ma basta assai piú piccolo, e può essere in qualsiasi sito del corpo, pur che il casso lo abbia. Le spinette pon far senza, perché già lo hanno davanti, dove si leva sopra la tastatura. Ma i cembali, che hanno un'altra incassatura e restano chiusi, non posson far senza. Ben in vece di rosa si posson fare due o tre piccoli buchi nel chiudimento davanti, che restano occulti e guardati da polivere.

V'è necessario questo sfogo perché altrimenti (dice egli) l'aria ch'è dentro resta dura, non potendo cedere e andar fuori quando è impulsa; e però il fondo non si move e non cede in giú come deve fare (che lo faccia si vede dal tremare ciò che vi porrai sopra quando suoni). Quindi il suono resta ottuso e breve e non risonante. Contro l'opinione d'alcuni recenti, che senza buchi gli stromenti sian migliori.

La perfezione degli stromenti sta nelle misure e sopra tutto in non essere il fondo né troppo grosso, né troppo sottile, e nell'aver primo tolto la virtú elastica al loro incurvato ed al ponte. Perché sin che questi fan forza nel fondo per restituirsi l'istromento non suona bene (quest'è una delle ragioni che i vecchi son buoni: perché non v'è piú quasi fondo).

Il cisolare che fa il mio bisogna veder che sorte è di cisolamento, che non si può distinguere se non dall'orecchio. Può venire perché la coda della corda tocchi il fondo; può venire perché il primo de' salterelli tocchi la corda; può venire perché vi sia qualche fessura, che nel tempo viscido o secco si apra nel far forza dal legno, e quindi è [...].

Che nell'inverno quando fa sempre umido gli stromenti crescono un tuono dall'usato.

Che il Pesaro cominciò a disfare i cassoni de' granaj in Padova e Venezia per fare istromenti, trovabili di cipresso di Cipro e di Candia.

Che l'armonia si divide in 5 quinti, da una voce all'altra. Che dal diesis di Gesolreut al b molle d'Alamire dee esservene uno di differenza; però si tagliano i negri, altrimenti non accorda. Che per accordar i tagliati è facile per 5ª accordando il tagliato d'Alamire col b molle elami. Che nell'accordare un'istromento ordinario la ottava dee essere perfetta, la quinta dee calare, altramente non si accorderà l'istromento. La quarta dee crescere, la terza maggiore crescere. Che una spinetta o tiorba col violino non sarà accordata mai (e se ne accorgerà facendo insieme la scala, non suonando in concerto) perchè non abbiamo le 5e giuste, per i quinti non osservati e non distinti. Che uno s'accorge in sentir suonare che una cosa è spostata o che l'istromento è scordato, perché sente cadere in que' negri che non hanno 5^a e far falsità di voce. Però non si compone in quelli, e quando vi si va è con riserva, e si fanno cadere da buoni maestri, dove alla parola ben conviene il falso e 'l disgustoso della voce. (Nota che può esser che su questo sia stato formato il sistema de' tuoni, cioè fatti tanti quante sono le corde che han buona quinta e buone consonanze, o almeno passabili.)

Dice che facendo [...] la partizione delle voci, con un circolo diviso in 42 parti, o con un quadrato lineato e poi tagliato di traverso, in un modo tornano, in un altro no. Che questa è la musica teorica. Che in prattica non si affà ([...] per trovare il fondo di ciò, e se questa sia la scienza musica.)

Tornando al buco. Che avendone fatto uno senza era ottuso; che fatto il buco si vide subito dar giú il fondo mezzo deto, restar la corda piú alta e prender la voce. Il dar giú mostra che l'uscita dell'aria fece luogo al [. . .] Fatti i buchi davanti occulti [. . .], accostando i deti nel suonare, sentirai far vento, e uscir l'aria.

Che sul violino si può trasportare dove un vuole in ogni sorte di tuono, senza che se ne senta cattivo effetto, perché hanno le 5e eguali e tuon giusto, e non si cade in false o cattive come negli altri stromenti.

Altro artefice che senza buco ottimamente, ecc.

Spinetta cimbalo fondo/il di sopra/pianta il di sotto/sponde/i lati/salterelli; quel [. . .] che hanno in fondo da una parte lo scavo; scavato; smussato. Il panno serve per ammorzar il suono, perché ne far giú tocca la corda e la ferma.

Accordar a Bortolo l'invenzione del piano e forte. Che molto ha imparato qua dopo venuto da gli altri. Che da principio durava fatica ad andare nello stanzone in questo strepito. Che fu detto al principe, che non voleva [underlined in MS]; rispos'egli il farò volere io. Gli da dieci scudi al mese.

L'apertura davanti d.^{e} spinette, portella.

dove stanno sù le corde, ponti, o ponticelli.

lo spazio fra lor due, spartimento.

il salterello oghiviso sotto, smussato.

il legnetto mobile, linguetta.

penna davanti, penna di dietro.

dov'entra il panno rosso scavatura, incavatura.

i ferretti che son sui ponti, punte.

Dimandare e cercare perché un suonator buono non sona ben da ballo; in che consiste il suonar da ballo.

[Two lines are crossed out.]

Quando tornerò farsi ancora descrivere dal cav. Albisi, nepote di Buonarroti, il cimbalo, e notarsi tutti i termini.

Far che l'artefice ne stenda una relazione notando la sostanza dell' invenzione, dove ne consiste la forza e dove le maggiori difficoltà. Sta nell'aver osservato la differenza del moto d'ingaggio di [. . .] verso il centro, e [. . .] vicino la circonferenza. Quando è spinto in su vicino al centro ogni piccolissimo impulso lo fa salire e se è spinto con forza va su con moltissima impennata, ecc.[1]

---

[1] Och, "Bartolomeo Cristofori, Scipione Maffei e la prima descrizione del 'gravicembalo col piano e forte'," pp. 16–23.

Appendix 2

Transcription of Scipione Maffei's "Nuova invenzione d'un Gravecembalo col piano, e forte; aggiunte alcune considerazioni sopra gli strumenti musicali," *Giornale de' letterati d'Italia* 5 (Venice, 1711). See Chapter 3 for the translation.

Se il pregio delle invenzioni dee misurarsi dalla novità, e dalla difficoltà, quella, di cui siamo al presente per dar ragguaglio, non è certamente inferiore a qualunque altra da gran tempo in qua si sia veduta. Egli è noto a chiunque gode della musica, che uno de' principali fonti, da' quali traggano i periti di quest'arte il segreto di singolarmente dilettar chi ascolta, è il piano, e'l forte; o sia nelle proposte, e risposte, o sia quando con artifiziosa dagradazione lasciandosi a poco a poco mancar la voce, si ripiglia poi ad un tratto strepitosamente: il quale artifizio è usato frequentemente, ed a maraviglia ne' gran concerti di Roma con diletto incredibile di chi gusta la perfezion dell'arte. Ora di questa diversità, ed alterazione di voce, nella quale eccellenti sono fra gli altri gli strumenti da arco, affatto privo è il gravecembalo; e sarebbe da chi che sia stata riputata una vanissima immaginazione il proporre di fabbricarlo in modo, che avesse questa dote. Con tutto ciò una sì ardita invenzione è stata non meno felicemente pensata, che eseguita in Firenze dal Sig. Bartolommeo Cristofali, Padovano, Cembalista stipédiato dal Serenissimo Principe di Toscana. Egli ne ha finora fatti tre della grandezza ordinaria degli altri gravecembali, e son tutti riusciti perfettamente. Il cavare da questi maggiore, o minor suono dipende dalla diversa forza, con cui dal sonatore vengono premuti i tasti, regolando la quale, si viene a sentire non solo il piano, e il forte, ma la degradazione, e diversità della voce, qual sarebbe in un violoncello. Alcuni professori non hanno fatto a quest'invenzione tutto l'applauso ch'ella merita; prima, perchè non hanno inteso, quanto ingegno si richiedesse a superarne le difficoltà, e qual maravigliosa delicatezza di mano per compirne con tanta aggiustatezza il lavoro: in secondo luogo, perchè è paruto loro, che la voce di tale strumento, come differente dall' ordinaria, sia troppo molle, e ottusa; ma questo è un sentimento, che si produce nel primo porvi su le mani per l'assuefazione, che abbiamo all'argentino degli altri gravecembali; per altro in breve tempo vi si adatta l'orecchio, e vi si affeziona talmente, che non sa staccarsene, e non gradisce più i gravecembali comuni; e bisogna avvertire, che riesce ancor più soave l'udirlo in qualche distanza. E' stata altresì opposta eccezione di non avere questo strumento gran voce, e di non avere tutto il forte degli altri gravecembali. Al che si risponde prima, che ha però assai più voce, ch'essi non credono, quando altri voglia, e sappia cavarla, premendo il tasto con impeto; e secondariamente, che bisogna saper prendere le cose per lo suo verso, e non considerare in riguardo ad un fine ciò ch'è fatto per un'altro. Questo è propriamente strumento da camera, e non è però adattabile a una musica di Chiesa, o ad una grand'orchestra. Quanti strumenti vi sono, che non si usano in tali occasioni, e che non pertanto si stimano de' più dilettevoli? Egli è certo, che per accompagnare un cantante, e per secondare uno strumento, ed anche per un moderato concerto riesce perfettamente: benchè non sia però questa l'intenzion sua principale, ma si quella d'esser sonato a solo, come il leuto, l'arpa, le viole da sei corde, ed altri strumenti de' più soavi. Ma veramente la maggior opposizione, che abbia patito questo nuovo strumento, si è il non sapersi universalmente a primo incontro sonare, perchè non basta il sonar perfettamente gli ordinarj strumenti da tasto, ma essendo strumento nuovo, ricerca persona, che intendendone la forza vi abbia fatto sopra alquanto di studio particolare, così per regolare la misura del diverso impulso, che dee darsi a' tasti, e la graziosa degradazione a tempo e luogo, come per iscegliere cose a proposito, e delicate, e massimamente spezzando, e facendo camminar le parti, e sentire i soggetti in più luoghi.

Ma venendo alla struttura particolare di questo strumento, se l'artefice, che l'ha inventato, avesse così saputo descriverlo, come ha saputo perfettamente fabbricarlo, non sarebbe malagevole il farne comprendere a' lettori l'artifizio: ma poichè egli non è in ciò riuscito, anzi ha giudicato impossibile il rappresentarlo in modo, che se ne possa concepire l'idea, è forza, ch'altri si ponga all'impresa, benchè senza aver più lo strumento davanti agli occhi, e solamente sopra alcune memorie fattesi già nell' esaminarlo, e sopra un disegno rozzamente da prima disteso. Diremo adunque primieramente, che in luogo degli usati salterelli, che suonano con la penna, si pone qui un registro di martelletti, che vanno a percuotere la corda per di sotto, avendo la cima, con cui percuotono, coperta di dante. Ogni martello dipende nel suo principio da una rotella, che lo rende mobile, e le rotelle stanno nascoste in un pettine, nel quale sono infilate. Vicino alla rotella, e sotto il principio dell' asta del martello vi è un sostegno, o prominenza, che ricevendo colpo per di sotto, alza il martello, e lo spinge a percuoter la corda con quella misura d'impulsione, e con quel grado di forza, che vien dato dalla mano; e quindi viene il maggiore, o minor suono a piacere del sonatore; essendo agevole anche il farlo percuotere con molta violenza, a cagione, che il martello riceve l'urto vicino alla sua imperniatura, che vuol dire, vicino al centro del giro, ch'egli descrive; nel qual caso ogni mediocre impulso fa salire con impeto un raggio di ruota. Ciò che dà il colpo al martello sotto l'estremità della prominenza suddetta, è una linguetta di legno, posta sopra una leva, che viene all'incontro del tasto, e ch'è alzata da esso, quando vien premuto dal sonatore. Questa linguetta non posa però sopra la leva, ma n'è alquanto sollevata, e si sta infilzata in due ganasce sottili, che le son poste a questo effetto una per parte. Ma perchè bisognava, che il martello percossa la corda subito la lasciasse, staccandosene, benchè non ancóra abbandonato il tasto dal sonatore; ed era però necessario, che il detto martello restasse subito in libertà di ricadere al suo luogo; perciò la linguetta, che gli dà il colpo, è mobile, ed è in tal maniera congegnata, che va in su, e percuote ferma, ma dato il colpo subito scatta, cioè passa; e quando lasciato il tutto ella torna giù, cede, e rientra, riponendosi ancóra sotto il martello. Questo effetto ha conseguito l'artefice con una molla di filo d'ottone, che ha fermata nella leva, e che distendendosi viene a battere con la punta sotto la linguetta, e facendo alquanto di forza la spinge, e la tiene appoggiata a un altro filo d'ottone, che ritto, e fermo le sta dal lato opposto. Per questo appoggio stabile, che ha la linguetta, e per la molla, che ha sotto, e per l'imperniatura, che ha dalle parti, ella si rende ora ferma, ed ora pieghevole, secondo il bisogno. Perchè i martelli ricadendo dopo la percossa non risalissero, e ribattessero nella corda, si fanno cadere, e posare sopra una incrociatura di cordoncini di seta, che quetamente li raccoglie. Ma perchè in questa sorte di strumenti è necessario spegnere, cioè fermare il suono, che continuando confonderebbe le note, che seguono, al qual effetto hanno le spinette il panno nelle cime de' salterelli; essendo anche necessario in questo nuovo strumento l'ammorzarlo affatto, e subito; perciò ciascheduna delle nominate leve ha una codetta, e sopra queste codette è posto un filare, o sia un registro di salterelli, che dal loro ufizio potrebbero dirsi spegnitoj. Quando la tastatura è in quiete, toccano questi la corda con panno, che han su la cima, ed impediscono il tremolare, ch'essa farebbe al vibrarsi dell'altre sonando: ma compresso il tasto, ed alzata da esso la punta della leva, viene per conseguenza ad abbassarsi la coda, ed insieme lo spegnitojo, con lasciar libera la corda al suono, che poi s'ammorza lasciato il tasto, rialzandosi lo spegnitojo stesso a toccar la corda. Ma per conoscere più chiaramente ogni movimento di questa macchina, e l'interno suo artifizio, si prenda per mano il disegno, e si osservi a parte a parte la denominazione di esso.

Spiegazione del disegno

A. corda.
B. telajo, o sia pianta della tastatura.
C. tasto ordinario, o sia prima leva, che col zoccoletto alza la seconda.
D. zoccoletto del tasto.
E. seconda leva, alla quale sono attaccate una per parte le ganasce, che tengono la linguetta.
F. perno della seconda leva.
G. linguetta mobile, che alzandosi la seconda leva, urta, e spinge in su il martello.
H. ganasce sottili, nelle quali è imperniata la linguetta.
I. filo fermo d'ottone schiacciato in cima, che tien ferma la linguetta.
L. molla di fil d'ottone, che va sotto la linguetta, e la tiene spinta verso il filo fermo, che ha dietro.
M. pettine, nel quale sono seguitamente infilati tutti i martelletti.
N. rotella del martello, che sta nascosta dentro al pettine.
O. martello, che spinto per di sotto dalla linguetta va a percuoter la corda col dante, che ha su la cima.
P. incrociatura di cordoncini di seta, fra' quali posano l'aste de' martelli.
Q. coda della seconda leva, che si abbassa nell'alzarsi la punta.
R. registro di salterelli, o spegnitoj, che premuto il tasto si abbassano, e lasciano libera la corda, tornando subito a suo luogo per fermare il suono.
S. regolo pieno per fortezza del pettine.

Dopo di tutto questo è da avvertire, che il pancone, dove si piantano i bischeri, o piroli di ferro, che tengono le corde, dove negli altri gravecembali è sotto le corde stesse, qui è sopra, e i bischeri passano, e le corde vi si attaccano per di sotto, essendovi bisogno di più sito nel basso, affinchè v'entri tutta la macchina della tastatura. Le corde sono più grosse delle ordinarie, e perchè il peso non nocesse al fondo, non sono raccomandate ad esso, ma alquanto più alto. In tutti i contatti, che vale a dire in tutti i luoghi, dove si potrebbe generar rumore, è impedito con cuojo, o con panno; specialmente ne' fori, dove passano perni, è posto da per tutto con singolar maestría del dante, e il perno passa per esso. Quest'invenzione è stata dall'artefice ridotta ad effetto anche in altra forma, avendo fatto un altro gravecembalo pur col piano e forte con differente, e alquanto più facile struttura, ma nondimeno è stata più applaudita la prima.

Essendo questo ingegnoso uomo eccellente anche nel lavorare gravecembali ordinarj, merita di notarsi, com'egli non sente co' moderni artefici, che per lo più gli fabbricano non solo senza rosa, ma ancóra senza sfogo alcuno in tutto il casso. Non già ch'egli creda necessario un sì gran foro, come erano le rose fattevi dagli antichi, ne che stimi opportuno il forargli in quel sito, ch'è sì esposto a ricever la polvere; ma suol'egli farvi due piccoli buchi nella fronte, o sia nel chiudimento davanti, che restano occulti, e difesi: ed afferma esser necessario in alcuna parte dello strumento un tale sfogatojo, perchè nel sonare il fondo dee muoversi, e cedere; e che il faccia, si conosce dal tremare che farà ciò che vi porrai sopra, quando altri suona: ma se il corpo non avrà foro alcuno, non potendo l'aria ch'è dentro cedere, e uscire, ma standosi dura, e forte, il fondo non si muove, e quindi il suono ne viene alquanto ottuso, e breve, e non risonante. Là dove fattovi un buco, vedrai tosto dar giù il fondo, e restar la corda più alta, e sentirai maggior voce, e accostando le dita al predetto foro, quando altri suona, sentirai far vento, e uscirne l'aria. A questo proposito non vogliamo lasciar di dire, che ricavandosi, come è noto, bellissimi lumi per la Filosofía naturale dall'indagare le affezioni, e gli effetti dell'aria, e del moto; un fonte grandissimo, benchè finora affatto sconosciuto, di scoprimenti, e di cognizioni intorno a ciò esser potrebbe l'osservar sottilmente le diverse, e mirabili operazioni dell' aria impulsa negli strumenti musicali; esaminando la fabbrica loro, e riflettendo da che nasca in essi la perfezione, o'l difetto, e da che se ne alteri la costituzione: come, a cagion d'esempio, la variazion del suono, che succede negli strumenti, che hanno l'anima, quai son quelli da arco, se questa un pocolino si muove di sito; divenendone tosto l'una corda più sonora, l'altra più ottusa; l'alterazione, e la diversità delle armoníe, che ricevono gli strumenti dalle diverse misure, e singolarmente i gravecembali dall'essere il loro fondo alquanto più grosso, e alquanto più sottile, e così di mill'altre considerazioni. Non è anche da tralasciare, che tenendosi universalmente, che siano sempre imperfetti i gravecembali nuovi, e che acquistino perfezione solamente col lungo tempo; pretende questo artefice, che si possa la vorargli in modo, che rendano subito sonora voce non meno degli stromenti vecchi. Afferma egli, che il non risonar bene de' nuovi nasca principalmente dalla virtù elastica, che per qualche tempo conservano la sponda incurvata, ed il ponte; perchè, finchè questi fanno forza sul fondo per restituirsi, la voce non vien perfetta: che però se questa virtù elastica sarà loro tolta interamente prima di porgli in opera, verrà subito a levarsi questo difetto, com'egli in pratica esperimenta. Contribuirà ancóra la buona qualità del legno: onde il Pesaro si cominciò a servire de' cassoni vecchi, che trovava sopra i granaj di Venezia, e di Padova, e ch'erano per lo più di cipresso di Candia, o di Cipro.

Non sarà qui discaro agli amatori della musica, che alcuna cosa si dica anche d'un altro raro gravecembalo, che si trova pure in Firenze in mano del Sig. Casini, Maestro lodatissimo di Cappella. Ha questo cinque tastami, cioè cinque interi ordini di tasti, l'uno sopra l'altro gradatamente; e si può però dire strumento perfetto, essendovi divisa ogni voce ne' suoi cinque quinti: ond'è, che si può in esso far la circolazione, e scorrere per tutti i tuoni senza urtare in dissonanza alcuna, e trovando sempre tutti gli accompagnamenti perfetti, come fa sentire il suo posseditore, che lo ricerca eccellentemente. Gli ordinarj gravecembali, come tutti gli strumenti, che hanno tasti, sono molto imperfetti, a cagione, che non essendo le voci divise nelle sue parti, molte corde vi sono, che non hanno Quinta giusta, e bisogna servirsi degli stessi tasti per diesis, e per b molli; per ischivare in parte il quale errore alcune vecchie spinette si vedono, massimamente dell'Undeo, con alcuni de' neri tagliati, e divisi in due, del che non comprendono la cagione molti professori; ed è veramente, perchè dovendo per modo d'esempio dal diesis di Gesolreut, al b molle d'Alamirè corrervi almeno un quinto di voce di differenza, v'è necessità di due corde. Ma nasce dall'imperfezione accennata, che un gravecembalo, o tiorba non si può interamente accordare con un violino, benchè sonando in concerto l'orecchio non se n'avvegga; e ne nasce parimente, che ne i più de' neri non si compone, e solo vi si va con riserva, e da alcuni Maestri solamente, quando alla parola ben conviene il falso, e'l disgustoso della voce. Questa imperfezione degli strumenti, che hanno tasti, cagiona altresi, che nell'udir sonare s'accorgeremo molte volte, quando il componimento è spostato, come parla il dialetto Fiorentino, o come dice la lingua comune, trasportato: perchè venendo a cadere in quelle corde, che non hanno Quinta, la falsità del suono offende l'orecchio. Non così avverrà nel violino, che non avendo tasti, può trovar tutto a suo luogo, e in qualsisia tuono far sentir le voci perfette. Il gravecembalo adunque, di cui parliamo, oltre al diletto del perfetto suono, può esser utile a molte speculazioni su la teorica della musica: ne si credesse, che troppo difficile fosse la sua accordatura, mentre anzi è più facile, atteso chè procede sempre per Quinte perfette; là dove ne gli strumenti ordinarj, bisogna aver attenzione di far che cali la Quinta, che crescano la Quarta, e la Terza maggiore, con più altre avvertenze.

Bibliography

Note that many early works are now available in facsimile as print-on-demand copies.

Abbiati, F. *Storia della musica* (Milan, 1939–1946), 3 (1941).
Acton, Harold. *The Last Medici* (London, 1980).
Adlung, Jacob. *Anleitung zu der musikalischen Gelahrtheit* (Erfurt, 1758).
   Musica mechanica organoedi, 2 vols. (Berlin, 1768; repr. Kassel, 1961).
Art du faiseur d'instruments de musique et lutherie: Extrait de L'Encyclopédie méthodique, arts et métiers mécaniques (Paris, 1785; repr. Geneva, 1972).
Badura-Skoda, Eva. *The History of the Pianoforte: A Documentary in Sound* (Bloomington, Indiana, 1999); video tape.
Baldinucci, Filippo. *Vocabolario toscano dell' arte del disegno* (Florence, 1631).
Banchieri, Adriano. *Conclusioni nel suono dell' organo* (Bologna, 1609; repr. New York, 1975).
Barbieri, Patrizio. "Cembalaro, organaro, chittararo e fabbricatore di corde armoniche nella *Polyanthea technica* di Pinaroli (1718–32)," *Ricercare* 1 (1989), pp. 123–210.
   "Gold- and Silver-Stringed Musical Instruments: Modern Physics vs. Aristotelianism in the Scientific Revolution," *Journal of the American Musical Instrument Society* 26 (2010), pp. 118–154.
Barbour, J. Murray. *Tuning and Temperament: A Historical Survey* (New York, 1972).
Behrends, Rainer. "Zum Stil und zu den Vorlagen für die Lackdekorationen des Cembalos und des Hammerklavieres von Bartolomeo Cristofori aus dem Jahre 1726," *Scripta Artium* 2 (Leipzig: Fall, 2001), pp. 7–12.
Belt, Philip R., Maribel Meisel, Derek Adlam, *et al*. *The New Grove Piano* (New York, London, 1988).
Birsak, Kurt. *Klaviere im Salzburger Museum Carolino Augusteum* (Salzburg, 1988).
Bitter, C. H. *Carl Philipp Emanuel und Wilhelm Friedemann Bach und deren Brüder* (Berlin, 1868).
   Johann Sebastian Bach (Berlin, 1881).
Blume, Friedrich (ed.), *Die Musik in Geschichte und Gegenwart* (Kassel and Basel, 1955).
Boalch, Donald. *Makers of the Harpsichord and Clavichord 1440–1840*, 2nd edn (London, 1974).
Bonaventura, Arnaldo. "Domenico Del Mela e il primo pianoforte verticale," *Bollettino della Società Mugellana di studi storici* 4/1 (1928), pp. 1–10.

Brancour, René. *Histoire des instruments de musique* (Paris, 1921).

Breidenstein, Irmela. "Dass nichts in der Welt, das ewig dauret … Zur Lackfassung der Instrumentenkästen und ihrer Restaurierung," *Scripta Artium* 2 (Leipzig: Fall, 2001), pp. 13–17.

Brocchi, Giuseppe Maria. *Descrizione della provincia del Mugello* (Florence, 1748).

Brown, Clifford M. *Isabella d'Este and Lorenzo da Pavia* (Geneva, 1982).

Brown, Mary E. and William Adams Brown, *Musical Instruments and their Homes* (New York, 1888).

Brunelli Bonetti, Bruno. "Bartolomeo Cristofori e il mondo musicale padovano," in *Bartolomeo Cristofori, inventore del pianoforte, nel terzo centenario dalla nascita* (Padua, 1955), pp. 13–41.

Burney, Charles. *A General History of Music* (London, 1776–1789; repr. New York, 1957).

The Present State of Music in France and Italy (London, 1773; facs. repr. New York, 1969; repr. Cambridge 2014).

The Present State of Music in Germany, the Netherlands, and United Provinces, 2 vols. (London, 1775).

Byne, A. and M. Stapley. *Spanish Interiors and Furniture* (New York, 1922; repr. 1969).

Cametti, Alberto. "I cembali del Cardinale Ottoboni," *Musica d'Oggi* 8 (1926), pp. 339–341.

Campbell, Margaret. *Dolmetsch: The Man and His Work* (Seattle, 1975).

Cappelletto, Sandro. *La voce perduta: vita di Farinelli, evirato cantore* (Turin, 1995).

Casaglia, Ferdinando. *Bartolommeo Cristofori, inventore del pianoforte* (Florence, 1894).

Per le onoranze a Bartolommeo Cristofori (Florence, 1876).

Casella, A. *Il pianoforte* (Milan, 1937).

Cassell's Italian Dictionary (New York, 1967).

Ceballos, Sara Gross. "Keyboard Portraits: Performing Character in the Eighteenth Century," Ph.D. diss., University of California Los Angeles, 2008.

Cervelli, Luisa. *La galleria armonica: catalogo del Museo degli strumenti musicali di Roma* (Rome, 1994).

"Noterelle Cristoforiane," *Quadrivium* 22/1 (1981), pp. 157–167.

"Un prezioso organo del '400: alla ricerca della sua voce perduta," *Bollettino dei Musei Civici Veneziani* 4 (1969), pp. 21–36.

Chiarini, Marco. "Gli Appartamenti Reali al tempo dei Medici," in *Gli Appartamenti Reali di Palazzo Pitti*, ed. Marco Chiarini and Serena Padovani (Florence, 1993), pp. 45–60.

Chiesa, Carlo and Duane Rosengard, *The Stradivari Legacy* (London, 1998).

Chini, Lino. *Storia antica e moderna del Mugello* (Florence, 1875).

Chinnery, Tony. "A Celestini Harpsichord Rediscovered," *Recercare* 11 (1999), pp. 51–73.

"The Measurements," in *Bartolomeo Cristofori: La spinetta ovale del 1690*, ed. Gabriele Rossi-Rognoni (Florence, 2002), p. 83.

Chinnery, Tony and Kerstin Schwarz. "La creazione di un nuovo strumento: la spinetta ovale vista da un costruttore," in *Bartolomeo Cristofori: La spinetta ovale del 1690*, ed. Gabriele Rossi-Rognoni (Florence, 2002), pp. 44–61.

Closson, Ernest. *Histoire du piano* (Brussels, 1944).

History of the Piano, trans. Delano Ames, ed. and rev. Robin Golding (London, 1976).

Cohen, Albert. *Music in the French Royal Academy of Sciences: A Study in the Evolution of Musical Thought* (Princeton, 1981).

"Jean Marius' *Clavecin brisé* and *Clavecin à maillets* Revisited: The 'Dossier Marius' at the Paris Academy of Sciences," *Journal of the American Musical Instrument Society* 13 (1987), pp. 23–38.

Cole, Warwick Henry. "Americus Backers: Original Forte Piano Maker," *Harpsichord & Fortepiano Magazine* 4/4 (1987), pp. 79–85.

Couperin, François. *L'art de toucher le clavecin* (Paris, 1717; facs. repr. Geneva, 1986).

Pièces de clavecin, Book 1 (Paris, 1713; facs. repr. New York, 2010).

Cuervo, Laura. "La biblioteca musical del Infante Gabriel de Borbón y Sajonia (1752–1788)," in *Nuevas perspectivas sobre la música para tecla de Antonio Soler* (Series FIMTE, Garrucha, 2016), pp. 147–162.

Damerini, A. "Verità storica sull' invenzione di Bartolomeo Cristofori," *Bartolomeo Cristofori, inventore del pianoforte, nel terzo centenario dalla nascita* (Padua, 1955), pp. 43-86.

David, Hans Theodore. *J. S. Bach's Musical Offering* (New York, 1972).

David, Hans Theodore and Arthur Mendel. *The Bach Reader* (New York, 1966).

de Bricqueville, Eugène. *Les ventes d'instruments de musique au XVIIIe siècle* (Paris, 1908).

de La Lande, Jérôme. *Voyage d'un françois en Italie*, vol. III (Venice, Paris, 1769).

dell'Acqua, Carlo. *Lorenzo Gusnasco e i Lingiardi da Pavia* (Milan, 1886).

Denis, Valentin. *De Muziekinstrumenten in de Nederlanden en in Italié naar hun afbeelding in de 15c-eeuwsche Kunst* (Antwerp, 1944).

Dent, Edward Joseph. *Alessandro Scarlatti: His Life and Works* (London, 1905).

de Place, Adélaïde. *Le Piano-forte à Paris entre 1760 et 1822* (Paris, 1986).

de Wit, Paul. "Ein aufrechtes Hammerklavier von Friederici," *Zeitschrift für Instrumentenbau*, no. 27 (June 21, 1900), pp. 700–703.

"Ein Hammerklavier in Tafelform aus dem Jahre 1742," *Zeitschrift für Musikinstrumentenbau*, no. 1 (October 1, 1925), pp. 4–5.

Dilworth, John. "Two-part Invention," *The Strad* 95/1136 (1985), pp. 668–670.

Di Pasquale, Marco and Giuliana Montanari. "Le collezioni di strumenti musicali dei Medici e dei Lorena: modalità e vicende della dispersione," in *Il museo degli strumenti musicali del Conservatorio "Luigi Cherubini"* (Livorno, 1999), pp. 90–101.

Doderer, Gerhard. *Clavicórdios portugueses do século dezoito* (Lisbon, 1971).
  "Remarks on Domenico Scarlatti's Portuguese Period (1719–1729)," in *Domenico Scarlatti en España*, ed. Luisa Morales (Garrucha, 2009), pp. 161–183.
Dolge, Alfred. *Pianos and their Makers* 2 vols. (Covina, Calif., 1911, 1913; repr. New York, 2012).
d'Orey, Leonor. "The Silver Table Service of Dom José I of Portugal," in *The Age of the Baroque in Portugal*, ed. Jay A. Levenson (Washington, DC, 1993).
Dowd, William. "The Surviving Instruments of the Blanchet Workshop," *The Historical Harpsichord* 1 (1984), pp. 17–108.
"Elogio del fu serenissimo Ferdinando de' Medici, principe di Toscana," *Giornale de' Letterati d'Italia* 17 (Venice, 1714), pp. 1–27.
Encyclopédie méthodique: Musique, vol. 1 (Paris, 1791).
Ernst, Friedrich. *Der Flügel Johann Sebastian Bachs* (Frankfurt, 1966).
Fabbri, Mario. *L'alba del pianoforte* (Milan, 1964).
  Alessandro Scarlatti e il principe Ferdinando de' Medici (Florence, 1961).
  "L'alba del pianoforte," in *Dal clavicembalo al pianoforte* (Brescia, 1968), pp. 35–53.
  "Nuova luce sull'attività fiorentina di Giacomo Antonio Perti, Bartolomeo Cristofori e Giorgio F. Haendel: valore storico e critico di una 'Memoria' di Francesco M. Mannucci," *Chigiana* 21 (1964), pp. 143–190.
Fabbri, Mario, Vinicio Gai, and Leonardo Pinzauti, *Conservatorio di Musica Luigi Cherubini: Antichi strumenti* (Florence, 1980).
Falletti, Franca, Renato Meucci, and Gabriele Rossi-Rognoni. *La musica e i suoi strumenti: La Collezione Granducale del Conservatorio Cherubini*, ed. Franca Falletti (Florence, 2001).
Ferrari, Pierluigi. "Ancora sulla collezione medicea di strumenti musicali: gli inventari inediti del 1670 e 1691," in *Studi in onore di Giulio Cattin* (Rome, 1990), pp. 242–244.
Ferrari, Pierluigi and Giuliana Montanari. "Giovanni, Giuseppe e Filippo Ferrini cembalari della corte del Granducato di Toscana – uno studio documentario," in *Musicus perfectus – studi in onore di L. F. Tagliavini "prattico e speculativo"*, ed. Pio Pellizzari (Bologna, 1995), pp. 29–47.
Fioravanti, Marco and Francesca Ciattini. "Le specie legnose," in *Bartolomeo Cristofori: La spinetta ovale del 1690*, ed. Gabriele Rossi-Rognoni (Florence, 2002), pp. 87–90.
Flade, Ernst. *Der Orgelbauer Gottfried Silbermann* (Leipzig, 1952).
Forkel, Johann Nikolaus. *Johann Sebastian Bach: His Life, Art, and Work*, trans. and ed. Charles Sanford Terry (New York, 1974).
  Ueber Johann Sebastian Bachs Leben, Kunst und Kunstwerke (Leipzig, 1802).
Freitas, Roger. *Portrait of a Castrato: Politics, Patronage, and Music in the Life of Atto Melani* (Cambridge, 2009).

Gai, Vinicio. *Gli strumenti musicali della corte medicea e il Museo del Conservatorio Luigi Cherubini di Firenze, cenni storici e catalogo descrittivo* (Florence and Licosa, 1969).

Gallini, Natale and Franco. *Museo degli strumenti musicali: Catalogo* (Milan, 1963).

Galpin, Francis W. *Old English Instruments of Music* (London, 1910; rev. repr., 1978).

Garrett, Lee R. "The Contributions of Adriano Banchieri," *The Organ Yearbook* 13 (1982), pp. 46–59.

Gerber, Ernst Ludwig. *Historisch-biographisches Lexicon der Tonkünstler*, 2 vols. (Leipzig, 1790–1792; repr. Graz, 1977).

Neues historisches-biographisches Lexicon der Tonkünstler (Leipzig, 1812; repr. Graz, 1966).

Gernhardt, Klaus. "Ergänzende Bemerkungen zu den Kästen des Hammerflügels (Inv.-Nr. 170) und des Cembalos (Inv.-Nr. 85)," *Scripta Artium* 2 (Leipzig: Fall, 2001), pp. 19–22.

Gitto, Stefania. "Le carte da musica del Gran Principe Ferdinando," in *Il Gran Principe Ferdinando de' Medici (1663–1713)*, ed. Riccardo Spinelli (Florence, 2013), pp. 127–133.

"La collezione musicale di Palazzo Pitti (1): il catalogo del 1771," *Fonti Musicali Italiane* 17 (2012), pp. 175–192.

Giustini, Lodovico. *Sonate da Cimbalo di piano, e forte detto volgarmente di martelletti* (Florence, 1732; facs. repr. Cambridge, 2015).

Goethe, Johann Wolfgang von. *Dichtung und Wahrheit* (Oxford, 1894).

Goodway, Martha and Jay Scott Odell. *The Metallurgy of 17th- and 18th-Century Music Wire – The Historical Harpsichord* 2, ed. Howard Schott (Stuyvesant, NY, 1987).

Grangier, A. *A Genius of France: A Short Sketch of the Famous Inventor, Sébastien Erard, and the Firm he Founded in Paris, 1780*, trans. Jean Fouqueville (Paris, 1924).

Grove's Dictionary of Music and Musicians, 5th edn (London, 1954).

The Grove Dictionary of Opera (London and New York, 1998).

Haine, Malou and Nicolas Meeùs. *Dictionnaire des facteurs d'instruments de musique en Wallonie et à Bruxelles du 9ᵉ siècle à nos jours* (Brussels, 1986).

Instruments de musique anciens à Bruxelles et en Wallonie – 17ᵉ–20ᵉ siècles (Brussels, 1985).

Hammond, Frederick. *Girolamo Frescobaldi* (Cambridge, Mass., 1983).

"Musical Instruments at the Medici Court in the Mid-Seventeenth Century," in *Analecta Musicologica* 15: *Studien zur Italienisch-Deutschen Musikgeschichte* 10 (Cologne, 1975), pp. 202–219.

"Some Notes on Giovanni Battista Boni da Cortona, Girolamo Zenti, and Others," *The Galpin Society Journal* 40 (1987), pp. 37–47.

Hanks, Sarah E. "Pantaleon's Pantalon: An 18th-Century Musical Fashion," *The Musical Quarterly* 55/2 (1969), pp. 215–227.

Harding, Rosamund. *The Pianoforte: Its History Traced to the Great Exhibition of 1851* (Cambridge, 1933; facs. repr. Cambridge, 2014).

Hardouin, Pierre J. and Frank Hubbard. "Harpsichord Making in Paris: Part I, Eighteenth Century," *The Galpin Society Journal* 10 (1957), pp. 10–29.

Haskell, Francis. *Patrons and Painters: Art and Society in Baroque Italy* (New York, 1971).

Heaton, Barrie. *A History of Sébastien Erard, Piano and Harp Maker* (UK Piano Page, 2006), pp. 1–8.

Hellwig, Friedemann. "The Single-Strung Italian Harpsichord," in *Keyboard Instruments: Studies in Keyboard Organology*, ed. Edwin M. Ripin (Edinburgh, 1971), pp. 27–36.

Henkel, Hubert. *Musikinstrumenten-Museum der Karl-Marx-Universität Leipzig, Katalog, Band 2: Kielinstrumente* (Leipzig, 1979).

"Bach und das Hammerklavier," in *Beiträge zur Bachforschung*, ed. Werner Felix, Winfried Hoffmann, and Armin Schneiderheinze (Leipzig, 1983), vol. II, pp. 56–63.

"Cristofori as Harpsichord Maker," *The Historical Harpsichord* 3 (Stuyvesant, NY, 1992), pp. 1–58.

"Sechszehnfuss-Register im Italienischen Cembalobau," *Das Musikinstrument* 39 (1990), pp. 6–10.

Hildebrandt, Dieter. *Pianoforte: A Social History of the Piano*, trans. Harriet Goodman (London, Melbourne, Auckland, and Johannesburg, 1985).

Hill, John Walter. "Antonio Veracini in Context: New Perspectives from Documents, Analysis and Style," *Early Music* 18/4 (1990), pp. 545–562.

Hill, W. H. and A. E. Hill. *The Violin Makers of the Guarneri Family* (London, 1931; repr. New York, 2016).

Hipkins, Alfred James. *A Description and History of the Pianoforte and of the Older Keyboard Stringed Instruments* (London, 1896).

Hirt, Franz Joseph. *Stringed Keyboard Instruments 1440–1880*, trans. M. Boehme-Brown (Boston, 1968).

Holmes, William C. *Opera Observed: Views of a Florentine Impresario in the Early Eighteenth Century* (Chicago, 1993).

Hornbostel, E. M. and C. Sachs. "Systematik der Musikinstrumente," *Zeitschrift für Ethnologie* 46 (1914), pp. 553–590.

Howell, Standley. "Medical Astrologers and the Invention of Stringed Keyboard Instruments," *Journal of Musicological Research* 10/1–2 (1990), pp. 1–17.

Hubbard, Frank. *Three Centuries of Harpsichord Making* (Cambridge, Mass., 1965).

Huber, Alfons. "Beethovens Erard-Flügel: Überlegungen zu seiner Restaurierung," *Restauro* 3 (1990), pp. 181–188.

James, Philip. *Early Keyboard Instruments from their Beginnings to the Year 1820* (London, 1930).

Junghanns, Herbert. *Der Piano und Flügelbau* (Berlin, 1952).

Juramie, Ghislaine. *Histoire du Piano* (Paris, 1947).
Kanold, Johann, *et al. Sammlung von Natur und Medicin – wie auch hierzu gehörigen Kunst und Literatur – Geschichten* (Leipzig and Budissin, 1723).
Kastner, Macario Santiago. "Portugiesische und spanische Clavichorde des 18. Jahrhunderts," *Acta Musicologica* 24/1–2 (1952), pp. 52–61.
Kenyon de Pascual, Beryl. "Correspondence/Spanish Pianos," *Early Music* (1986), pp. 469–470.
"Diego Fernández – Harpsichord-Maker to the Spanish Royal Family from 1722 to 1775 – and his Nephew Julián Fernández," *The Galpin Society Journal* 38 (1985), pp. 35–47.
"Francisco Perez Mirabal's Harpsichord and the Early Spanish Piano," *Early Music* (1987), pp. 503–513.
"Harpsichords, Clavichords, and Similar Instruments in Madrid in the Second Half of the Eighteenth Century," *Research Chronicle of the Royal Musical Association* 18 (1982).
"Notes and Queries: Queen Maria Barbara's Harpsichords," *The Galpin Society Journal* 39 (1986), pp. 125–128.
"Two Features of Early Spanish Keyboard Instruments," *The Galpin Society Journal* 44 (1991), pp. 94–102.
Kenyon de Pascual, Beryl and David Law, "Another Early Iberian Grand Piano," *The Galpin Society Journal* 47 (1995), pp. 68–93.
Keyssler, Johann Georg. *Neueste Reisen*, vol. I (Hanover, 1751).
Kinsky, Georg. *Musikhistorisches Museum von Wilhelm Heyer in Cöln*, 4 vols., (Cologne, 1910–1916).
Kirkendale, Warren. *The Court Musicians in Florence during the Principate of the Medici* (Florence, 1993).
Kirkpatrick, Ralph. *Domenico Scarlatti* (Princeton, 1953).
Kisch, Bruno. *Scales and Weights: A Historical Outline* (New Haven, 1965).
Koch, Heinrich Christoph. *Musikalisches Lexicon*, 2 vols. (Frankfurt, 1802; repr. Kassel, 2000).
König, Johann Ulrich. "Musicalische Merckwürdigkeiten des Marchese, Scipio Maffei, Beschreibung eines neuerfundenen *Claviceins*, auf welchem das *piano* und *forte* zu haben, nebst einigen Betrachtungen über die Musicalische Instrumente, aus dem Welschen ins Teutsche übersetzt," in Johann Mattheson, *Critica Musica*, vol. II (Hamburg, 1725), pp. 335–342.
Koster, John. "Three Grand Pianos in the Florentine Tradition," *Musique, Images, Instruments* 4 (Paris, 1999), pp. 95–116.
"Two Early French Grand Pianos," *Early Keyboard Journal* 12 (1994), pp. 7–37.
Kouwenhoven, John A. *Partners in Banking* (New York, 1968), pp. 142–154.
Kraus, A, Jr. *Catalogo della collezione etnografico-musicale Kraus in Firenze* (Florence, 1901).
Krehbiel, Henry Edward. *The Pianoforte and its Music* (New York, 1911).
Krickeberg, Dieter. *"Meine Herren, der alte Bach is gekommen!"* (Berlin, 1976).

Lanterna, Giancarlo and Maria Rizzi. "Adesivi ed elementi metallici," in *Bartolomeo Cristofori: La spinetta ovale del 1690*, ed. Gabriele Rossi-Rognoni (Florence, 2002), pp. 91–94.

Latcham, Michael. "Pianos and Harpsichords for Their Majesties," *Early Music* 36/3 (2008), pp. 359–396.

"The Twelve Clavicordios owned by Queen Maria Barbara of Spain and the Seven Cembali Owned by Carlo Broschi, known as Farinelli: Facts and Speculation," *Five Centuries of Spanish Keyboard Music: Proceedings of the FIMTE Conferences 2002–2004* (Garrucha, 2007), pp. 255–281.

Leve, James Samuel. "Humor and Intrigue: A Comparative Study of Comic Opera in Florence and Rome during the Late Seventeenth Century" (Ph.D. diss., Yale University, 1998).

Levenson, Jay. *The Age of the Baroque in Portugal* (Washington, 1993).

Libin, Laurence. "Nazareth Piano may be Among America's First," *Moravian Music Journal* 33/1 (1988), p. 2.

Llorden, A. "Maestros organistas de la Colegiata de Antequera," *Anuario Musical* 33–35 (1978–1980), pp. 51–80.

Loesser, Arthur. *Men, Women and Pianos: A Social History* (New York, 1954).

Lora, Francesco. "I drammi per musica di Giacomo Antonio Perti per il teatro della villa medicea Pratolino (1700–01; 1707–10)" (Ph.D. diss., University of Bologna, 2012).

Mabbett, Margaret. "Italian Musicians in Restoration England (1660–90)," *Music & Letters* 67/3 (1986), pp. 237–247.

Mace, Thomas. *Musick's Monument* (London, 1676; repr. New York, 1966).

Machines et inventions approuvées par l'Académie royale des sciences, 7 vols. (Paris, 1735–1777).

Maffei, Scipione. "Nuova invenzione d'un Gravecembalo col piano, e forte; aggiunte alcune considerazioni sopra gli strumenti musicali," *Giornale de' letterati d'Italia* 5 (Venice, 1711), pp. 144–159.

Rime e prose del Sig. Marchese Scipione Maffei, parte raccolte da varij libri, e parte non più stampate (Venice, 1719), pp. 309–315.

Mahillon, Victor-Charles. *Catalogue descriptif & analytique du Musée instrumental du Conservatoire royal de musique de Bruxelles*, vol. IV (Brussels, 1912).

Marpurg, Friedrich Wilhelm. *Historische-kritische Beyträge zur Aufnahme der Musik*, 5 vols. (Berlin, 1754–1778; facs. repr. Hildesheim, 1970).

Kritische Briefe über die Tonkunst, 3 vols. (Berlin, 1760–1764; facs. repr. Hildesheim, 1974 (vols. I and II).

Martini, Angelo. *Manuale di metrologia* (Turin, 1883).

Massinelli, Anna Maria and Filippo Tuena. *Treasures of the Medici* (New York, 1992).

Mathias, F. X., Paul Smets, and Josef Wörsching. *Die Orgelbauer-Familie Silbermann in Strassburg i.E* (Mainz, 1959).

Matthéson, Johann. *Critica Musica* (Hamburg, 1725; facs. repr. Laaber, 2003).

Meeùs, Nicolas. "Keyboard Scholarship," *Early Music* 8/2 (1980), pp. 222–226.

Mersenne, Marin. *Harmonie Universelle* (Paris, 1636).
The Metropolitan Museum of Art: The Crosby Brown Collection of Musical Instruments of All Nations – Catalogue of the Keyboard Instruments (New York, 1903).
Mischiati, O. "Un elenco romano di cembalari redatto nel 1741," *L'Organo* 10/1 (1972), pp. 105–106.
Mizler, Lorenz. *Neu eröffnete musikalische Bibliothek*, 4 vols. (Leipzig, 1739–1754).
Mola, C. *Elementi di tecnica del clavicembalo e pianoforte* (Milan, 1941).
Montal, Claude. *L'Art d'accorder soi-même son piano* (Paris, 1836; facs. Geneva, 1976).
Montanari, Giuliana. "Le spinette ovali e la collezione di strumenti a penna del Granprincipe Ferdinando de' Medici," in *Bartolomeo Cristofori: La spinetta ovale del 1690*, ed. Gabriele Rossi-Rognoni (Florence, 2002), pp. 32–40.
 "Bartolomeo Cristofori: A List and Historical Survey of his Instruments," *Early Music* 19 (1991), pp. 383–396.
 "Florentine Claviorgans (1492–1900)," *The Galpin Society Journal* 58 (2005), pp. 242–243.
 "The Keyboard Instrument Collection of Grand Prince Ferdinando de' Medici at the Time of Alessandro and Domenico Scarlatti's Journeys to Florence, 1702–1705," in *Domenico Scarlatti en España: actas de los Symposia FIMTE, 2006–2007* (Garrucha, 2009), pp. 117–142.
Moscheles, Charlotte. *Life of Moscheles*, 2 vols. (London, 1873; facs. repr. Cambridge, 2014).
Mosconi, Andrea and Carlo Torresani. *Il Museo stradivariano di Cremona* (Milan, 1987).
Mozart, Leopold. *Leopold Mozart: Briefe und Aufzeichnungen*, selected and with commentary by Wilhelm A. Bauer and Otto Erich Deutsch, 7 vols. (Kassel, Basel, London, and New York, 1962–1975).
Müller, Werner. *Gottfried Silbermann: Persönlichkeit und Werk* (Frankfurt, 1982).
Neupert, Hanns. *Vom Musikstab zum Modernen Klavier* (Berlin, 1960).
New Grove Dictionary of Music and Musicians (London and New York, 1980).
New Grove Dictionary of Musical Instruments (London and New York, 1984).
New Grove Dictionary of Opera (London, 1997, 1998).
Nisoli, Michele. "Bartolomeo Cristofori (1655–1732): Rassegna bibliografica con alcune aggiunte biografiche sugli anni padovani" (Ph.D. diss., University of Florence, 2011).
Nobbs, Christopher. "Two Portuguese Pianos and a Harpsichord" (unpublished paper, 1990).
O'Brien, Grant. "Il percorso di un' idea: dal progetto allo strumento," in *Bartolomeo Cristofori: La spinetta ovale del 1690*, ed. Gabriele Rossi-Rognoni (Florence, 2002), pp. 62–80.
 "Some Principles of Eighteenth Century Harpsichord Stringing and their Application," *The Organ Yearbook* 12 (1981).

O'Brien, Grant and Francesco Nocerino. "The Tiorbino: An Unrecognised Instrument Type Built by Harpsichord Makers with Possible Evidence for a Surviving Instrument," *The Galpin Society Journal* 58 (2005), pp. 184–208.

O'Brien, Michael Kent. "Bartolomeo Cristofori at Court in Late Medici Florence" (Ph.D. diss., The Catholic University of America, 1994).

"Dark Shadows Across the 'Nuova Luce' of Mario Fabbri," paper delivered at the 1991 meeting of the American Musical Instrument Society, Bethlehem, Penn.

Och, Laura. "Interessi e conoscenze musicali di Scipione Maffei," in proceedings of the conference *Scipione Maffei nell'Europa del Settecento, Verona, 23–25 settembre 1996*, ed. Gian Paolo Romagnani (1998), pp. 551–577.

"Bartolomeo Cristofori, Scipione Maffei e la prima descrizione del 'gravicembalo col piano e forte'," *Il Flauto Dolce* 14–15 (1986), pp. 16–23.

Ogden, Dunbar H. *The Italian Baroque Stage: Documents by Giulio Troili, Andrea Pozzo, Ferdinando Galli-Bibiena, Baldassare Orsini* (Berkeley, Los Angeles, and London, 1978).

Parrini, A. "Nel secondo centenario della morte di Bartolomeo Cristofori," *Atti dell' Accademia del Regio Conservatorio di Musica Luigi Cherubini* 58 (Florence, 1934), pp. 39–65.

Parrish, Carl. "Criticisms of the Piano when it was New," *The Musical Quarterly* 30/4 (1944), pp. 428–440.

Paul, Oscar. *Geschichte des Klaviers* (Leipzig, 1868).

Pedrell, Felipe. *Organografía musical antiqua española* (Barcelona, 1901).

Pfeiffer, Walter. *Der Hammer* (Stuttgart, 1948).

Taste und Hebeglied des Klaviers (Leipzig, 1920).

Pierre, Constant. *Les facteurs d'instruments de musique. Les luthiers et la facture instrumentale. Précis historique* (Paris, 1893; facs. Geneva, 1976).

Pollens, Stewart. *The Early Pianoforte* (Cambridge, 1995; repr. 2009).

The Manual of Musical Instrument Conservation (Cambridge, 2015).

Stradivari (Cambridge, 2010).

The Violin Forms of Antonio Stradivari (London, 1992).

"The Bonafinis Spinet," in *Atti del XIV Congresso della Società Internazionale di Musicologia, Study Session: Cembali, e cembali che fanno il piano e il forte*, ed. Eva Badura-Skoda (1987), pp. 286–287.

"The Bonafinis Spinet: An Early Harpsichord converted into a Tangent Piano," *Journal of the American Musical Instrument Society* 13 (1987), pp. 5–22.

"Cristofori and Erard," *Le pianoforte en France 1780–1820: Musique, Images, Instruments* 11 (Paris, 2009), pp. 75–81.

"Curt Sachs and Musical Instrument Restoration," *The Musical Times* 130/1760 (1989), pp. 589–594.

"Early Nineteenth-Century German Language Works on Piano Maintenance," *Early Keyboard Journal* 8 (1990), pp. 91–109.

"The Early Portuguese Piano," *Early Music* 13 (1985), pp. 18–27.

"The Gatti-Kraus Piano Action Ascribed to Bartolomeo Cristofori," *The Galpin Society Journal* 55 (2002), pp. 269–278.

"Gottfried Silbermann's Pianos," *The Organ Yearbook* 17 (1986), pp. 103–121.

"Historical Metrology in the Service of Organology: Some Caveats," in *Unisonus: Musikinstrumente erforschen, bewahren, sammeln* (Vienna, 2014), pp. 510–537.

"Michele Todini's Golden Harpsichord: An Examination of the Machine of Galatea and Polyphemus," *Metropolitan Museum Journal* 25 (1990), pp. 33–47.

"The Pianoforte in the Performance of Scarlatti's Sonatas," in *Domenico Scarlatti en España: actas de los Symposia FIMTE, 2006–2007* (Garrucha, 2009), pp. 301–311.

"The Pianos of Bartolomeo Cristofori," *Journal of the American Musical Instrument Society* 10 (1984), pp. 32–68.

"Soler's Temperament and his *Acordante*," in *Nuevas perspectivas sobre la música para tecla de Antonio Soler* (Series FIMTE, Garrucha, 2016), pp. 17–38.

"Three Keyboard Instruments Signed by Cristofori's Assistant, Giovanni Ferrini," *The Galpin Society Journal* 44 (1991), pp. 77–93.

"An Upright Pianoforte by Domenico Del Mela," *The Galpin Society Journal* 45 (1992), pp. 22–28.

Ponsicchi, Cesare. *Il Pianoforte – sua origine e sviluppo – (con tavole) e rassegna dell' esposizione storica fatta nello stabilimento musicale Brizzi e Niccolai nell' occasione delle onoranze a Bartolommeo Cristofori inventore del pianoforte* (Florence, 1876).

Il primo pianoforte-verticale (Florence, 1898).

"Il primo pianoforte verticale," *La Nuova Musica – pubblicazione musicale – mensile* 11/24 (1897), pp. 3–4.

Praetorius, Michael. *Syntagma Musicum*, vol. II (Wolfenbüttel, 1619; facs. repr. Kassel, 1985).

Printz, Wolfgang Caspar. *Historische Beschreibung* (Dresden, 1690).

Profeta, Rosario. *Storia e letteratura degli strumenti musicali* (Florence, 1924).

Puliti, Leto. "Allegato F.: Descrizione di un clavicembalo a piano e forte fabbricato in Firenze nell' anno 1720," *Atti dell' Accademia del R. Istituto Musicale di Firenze* 12 (1874), pp. 207–216.

"Della vita del Ser.mo Ferdinando dei Medici Granprincipe di Toscana e della origine del pianoforte," *Atti dell' Accademia del R. Istituto Musicale di Firenze* 12 (1874), pp. 92–240.

"Lettere tratte dal Carteggio di S. Alt.za Ser.ma Ferdinando dei Medici, Granprincipe di Toscana," *Atti dell' Accademia del R. Istituto Musicale di Firenze* 12 (1874), pp. 137–152.

Quantz, Johann Joachim. *Versuch einer Anweisung die Flöte traversiere zu spielen* (Berlin, 1752; repr. Kassel, 2000 (reduced format)).

On Playing the Flute, trans. Edward R. Reilly (New York, 1966).

Rees, Abraham. *The Cyclopædia; or Universal Dictionary of Arts, Sciences, and Literature*, vol. XVII (London, 1819).

Restle, Konstantin. *Bartolomeo Cristofori und die Anfänge des Hammerclaviers* (Munich, 1991).

Rice, John A. "An Early Handel Revival in Florence," *Early Music* 18/1 (1990), pp. 63–71.

"The Tuscan Piano in the 1780s," *Early Music* 21/1 (1993), pp. 5–26.

Rimbault, Edward Francis. *The Pianoforte: Its Origin, Progress, and Construction* (London, 1860).

Rinaldi, Mario. "Modernità del clavicembalo," *La Tribuna* (Rome, February 11, 1942).

Ripin, Edwin M. *The Instrument Catalogs of Leopoldo Franciolini*, Music Indexes and Bibliographies No. 9, ed. George R. Hill (Hackensack, NJ, 1974).

(ed.) *Keyboard Instruments: Studies in Keyboard Organology* (Edinburgh, 1971).

"The Surviving Oeuvre of Girolamo Zenti," *Metropolitan Museum Journal* 7 (1973), pp. 71–87.

Romagnoli, Paolo. "Domenico Del Mela (1683–1755) autore del primo pianoforte verticale: figura, biografia" (Ph.D. diss., University of Pavia, 2006).

Rossi, Lemmi. *Sistema musico* (Perugia, 1666).

Russell, Raymond. *The Harpsichord and Clavichord: An Introductory Study*, 2nd edn., rev. Howard Schott (London, 1973).

Russell-Wood, A. J. R. "Portugal and the World in the Age of Dom João V," in *The Age of the Baroque in Portugal*, ed. Jay A. Levenson (Washington, DC, 1993).

Sacchi, Giovenale. *Vita del cavaliere Don Carlo Broschi* (Venice, 1784).

Sachs, Curt. *Handbuch der Musikinstrumentenkunde* (Leipzig, 1920).

Das Klavier (Berlin, 1923).

Samoyault-Verlet, Colombe. *Les Facteurs de clavecins parisiens: Notices biographiques et documents (1550–1793)* (Paris, 1966).

Sauveur, Joseph. "Système général des intervalles des sons," *Mémoires de l'académie royale des sciences* (Paris, 1701), pp. 403–498.

Schnoebelen, Anne. *Padre Martini's Collection of Letters in the Civico Museo Bibliografico Musicale in Bologna* (New York, 1979).

Schubart, Christian Friedrich Daniel. *Ideen zu einer Aesthetik der Tonkunst* (Vienna, 1806; repr. Leipzig, 1924).

Schünemann, Georg. "Ein Bildnis Bartolomeo Cristoforis," *Zeitschrift für Musikwissenschaft* 16/11–12 (1934), pp. 534–536.

Schwarz, Kerstin. *Erfand Bartolomeo Cristofori mit dem Hammerflügel ein neues Instrument?* (Halle, 1996).

"Bartolomeo Cristofori: Hammerflügel und Cembali im Vergleich," *Scripta Artium* 2 (Leipzig: Fall, 2001), pp. 23–68.

Sgrilli, Bernardo Sansone. *Descrizione della regia villa, fontane, e fabriche di Pratolino* (Florence, 1742).

Sheveloff, Joel Leonard. "Domenico Scarlatti: Tercentenary Frustrations," *The Musical Quarterly* 71/4 (1985), pp. 399–436.

"Domenico Scarlatti: Tercentenary Frustrations (Part II)," *The Musical Quarterly* 72/1 (1986), pp. 90–117.

"The Keyboard Music of Domenico Scarlatti: A Re-evaluation of the Present State of Knowledge in the Light of the Sources" (Ph.D. diss., Brandeis University, 1970).

Skowroneck, Tilman. *Beethoven the Pianist* (Gothenburg, 2007).

Smither, Howard E. *A History of the Oratorio*, vol. 1 (Chapel Hill, NC, 1977).

Spinelli, Lorenzo. "Le esperienze veneziane del principe Ferdinando de' Medici e le influenze sulla politica spettacolare e dinastica toscana (1688–1696)," *Medioevo e Rinascimento* 19/16 (2005), pp. 159–199.

Spinelli, Riccardo (ed.). *Il Gran Principe Ferdinando de' Medici (1663–1713): Collezionista e mecenate* (Florence, 2013).

Sumner, William Leslie. *The Pianoforte* (London, 1966).

Sutherland, David. "Bartolomeo Cristofori's Paired Cembalos of 1726," *Journal of the American Musical Instrument Society* 26 (2000), pp. 5–56.

Tagliavini, Luigi Ferdinando. "Giovanni Ferrini and his Harpsichord 'a penne e a martelletti'," *Early Music* 19/3 (1991), pp. 399–408.

and John Henry van der Meer. *Clavicembali e spinetti dal XVI al XIX secolo: Collezione Luigi Ferdinando Tagliavini* (Bologna, 1986).

Terry, Charles Sanford. *Johann Sebastian Bach: A Biography* (London, 1933).

Thibault, G., J. Jenkins, and J. Bran-Ricci. *Eighteenth Century Musical Instruments: France and Britain* (London, 1973).

Thomas, Fritz and Peter Kunze. *Alte Musik aus vier Jahrhunderten: Tasteninstrumente im Deutschen Museum* (Munich, 1980).

Thomas, Michael. "The Tunings and Pitch of Early Clavichords," *The English Harpsichord Magazine* 1/6 (1976), ed. Edgar Hunt, pp. 175–180.

Tiella, Marco. "The Positive Organ of Lorenzo da Pavia (1494)," *The Organ Yearbook* 7 (1976), pp. 4–15.

Todini, Michele. *Dichiaratione della Galleria armonica* (Rome, 1676; repr. Lucca, 1988).

Toffolo, Stefano. *Antichi strumenti veneziani – 1500–1800: quattro secoli di liuteria e cembalaria* (Venice, 1987).

Türk, Daniel Gottlob. *Klavierschule* (Leipzig and Halle, 1789; facs. repr. Kassel, 1997).

van der Meer, John Henry. *Collezione Tagliavini: catalogo degli strumenti musicali* 1 (Bologna, 2008).

"A Curious Instrument with a Five-Octave Compass," *Early Music* 14/3 (1986), pp. 397–400.

"Das Florentiner 'Ebenholzcembalo': Eine Arbeit von Bartolomeo Cristofori," in *Festschrift für Gerhard Bott zum 60. Geburtstag*, ed. Ulrich Schneider (Darmstadt, 1987), pp. 227–235.

"Queen Maria Barbara's Florentine Keyboard Instruments," unpublished paper delivered at the fourteenth congress of the International Musicological Society, Bologna, 1987. Abstract of this paper published in *Atti del XIV Congresso della*

Società Internazionale di Musicologia (Bologna, Ferrara, and Parma, 1987), pp. 292–293.

van der Meer, John Henry and Luigi Ferdinando Tagliavini. *Clavicembali e spinette dal XVI al XIX secolo: Collezione Luigi Ferdinando Tagliavini* (Bologna, 1986).

Vita del Gran Principe Ferdinando di Toscana (Florence, 1887).

Vitali, Carlo. "Un cantante legrenziano e la biographia Francesco de Castris 'musico politico'," in *Giovanni Legrenzi e la Cappella ducale di San Marco: Atti del convegno internazionale di studi*, ed. Francesco Passadore and Franco Rossi (Florence, 1994), pp. 567–603.

Vitali, Carlo and Antonello Furnari. "Händels Italienreise – neue Dokumente, Hypothesen und Interpretationen," *Göttinger Händel-Beiträge im Auftrag der Göttinger Händel-Gesellschaft herausgegeben von Hans Joachim Marx* 4 (Kassel, 1991), pp. 64–65.

von Essen, Bertha. *Bouwen Geschiedenis van het Klavier* (Rotterdam, 1948).

von Gonterhausen, H. Welcker. *Der Flügel* (Frankfurt, 1856).

Der Klavierbau (Frankfurt, 1870).

Wainwright, David. *Broadwood by Appointment* (London, 1982).

Walther, Johann Georg. *Musicalisches Lexicon* (Leipzig, 1732; repr. Kassel and Basel, 1953).

Weaver, Robert Lamar. "Florentine Comic Operas of the Seventeenth Century," Ph.D. diss., University of North Carolina, 1958.

Weaver, Robert Lamar and Norma Wright Weaver. *A Chronology of Music in the Florentine Theater 1590–1750* (Detroit, 1978).

Weber, Marie-Christine and Jean-François Weber. *J. K. Mercken: Premier facteur parisien de forte-pianos* (Paris, 2008).

Wells, Elizabeth. "An Early Stringed Keyboard Instrument: The Clavicytherium in the Royal College of Music, London," *Early Music* 6/4 (1978), pp. 568–571.

Werner, Eric. *Mendelssohn: Leben und Werk in neuer Sicht* (Zürich and Freiburg, 1980).

Wilkes, John (compiler). *Encyclopaedia Londinensis, or Universal Dictionary of Arts, Sciences, and Literature* (London, 1810).

Williams, Peter. *The European Organ 1450–1850* (London, 1966).

A New History of the Organ (Bloomington and London, 1980).

Williams, Peter and Barbara Owen. *The New Grove Organ* (New York, London, 1988).

Winternitz, Emanuel. "The Crosby Brown Collection: Its Origin and Development," *Metropolitan Museum Journal* 3 (1970), pp. 337–356.

"A Spinettina for the Duchess of Urbino," *Metropolitan Museum Journal* 1 (1968), pp. 95–108.

Wolff, Christoph. "New Research on Bach's *Musical Offering*," *The Musical Quarterly* 57/3 (1971), pp. 379–408.

Wraight, Ralph Denzil. "Cristofori's Instruments," *Early Music* 20/4 (1992), p. 701.
    "Differences between Maffei's Article on Cristofori's Piano in its 1711 and 1719 Versions, their Subsequent Transmission and the Implications," www.denzilwraight.com (2015).
    "The Stringing of Italian Keyboard Instruments c. 1500–c.1650," Ph.D. diss., The Queen's University of Belfast, 1996.
    "A Zenti Harpsichord Rediscovered," *Early Music* 19/1 (1991), pp. 99–102.
Zarlino, Gioseffo. *Le istitutioni harmoniche* (Venice, 1558; facs. repr. Bologna, 2008).
Zedler, Johann Heinrich. *Grosses vollständiges Universal-Lexicon*, 64 vols. (Halle and Leipzig, 1732–1750), vol. v (1733).
Zelter, Christian Friedrich. *Briefwechsel Goethe-Zelter*, ed. M. Hecker (Leipzig, 1913).
Zingarelli, Nicola. *Vocabolario della lingua Italiana*, 12th edn (Bologna, 1998).
Zupko, Ronald Edward. *Italian Weights and Measures from the Middle Ages to the Nineteenth Century* (Philadelphia, 1981).

Index

Académie royale des sciences, 328, 329, 330
Accademia Patavina, 9
Adlung, Jakob, 290, 291, 305, 363
Agricola, Johann Friedrich, 288, 290
Agricola, Martin, 292
Alberti, Domenico, 346
Albizzi, Luca Casimiro degli, 28
Albizzi, Rinaldo degli, 28
Amati, family of violin makers, 224
Amati, Nicolò, 10
Antonius Patavinus, 13
Antunes, 262, 265, 266, 267, 268, 270, 271, 272, 273, 274, 275, 276, 278, 280
Antunes, Joachim Jozé, 249, 264, 265, 275
Antunes, Manuel, 249, 264, 267
Aranjuez, Palace at, 246, 247, 248
Arpicimbalo . . . che fa' il piano, e il forte, 15, 66, 72, 119, 120
Art du faiseur d'instruments de musique et lutherie, 334
Assolani, Francesco, 24, 219, 222, 223, 224
Augustus I, Frederick, 284

Babel, William, 346
Bach, Carl Philipp Emanuel, 289, 293, 308, 343, 346
Bach, Johann Christian, 344
Bach, Johann Sebastian, 290, 291, 295, 296, 344
  Musical Offering, 57
Bach, Wilhelm Friedemann, 295, 296
Backers, Americus, 337, 345, 346
Badura-Skoda, Paul and Eva, 165
Baffo, Giovanni Antonio, 30
Balbastre, Claude-Bénigne, 330
Bárbara, Maria, Queen of Spain, 244, 245, 246, 248, 249, 250, 251
  inventory of her keyboard instruments, 246–248
Bartolomei, Christofaro, 10
Bas, Louis, 334
Basilica of S. Antonio, Padua, 12
Basilica of S. Giustina, Padua, 12
Bassilichi, Luigi, 18

Beck, Frederick, 345
Beethoven, Ludwig van, 338
Berni, Agnolo, 24
Berti, Antonfrancesco, 18
Berti, Niccolò, 18, 30, 40, 57, 58, 220, 241
Beyer, Adam, 345
Biblioteca Apostolica Vaticana, 73, 221
Biblioteca Capitolare, Verona, 350
Biblioteca del Conservatorio di Musica "Luigi Cherubini", 235
Biblioteca Nazionale Marciana, 220, 221
Bibliothek des Priesterseminars, 221
Bitter, Carl Hermann, 308
Bitti, Martino, 24, 32, 68, 212, 218, 219, 220, 222, 223, 224, 226, 234, 235
Blanchet, François-Étienne II, 331
Boalch, Donald H., 332, 363
Bolgioni, Antonio, 16
Brancour, René, 333
Broadwood, John, 346
Brown, Mrs. John Crosby, 159
Bruschi (Brischi), Bartolommeo, 24, 219, 222
Buechenberg, Matheus, 33
Buen Retiro theater, 248
Buini, Giuseppe Maria, 57, 212
Buntebart, Gabriel, 345
Buoni, Giuseppe, 30, 39
Burnett, Richard, 265
Burney, Charles, 181, 182, 239, 250, 251, 289, 293, 344, 345, 346, 347, 364
Buterne, Jean-Baptiste, 329

Caldera, Antonio, 212
Caligula delirante, 219, 221, 234
Canavese, Giuseppe, 23, 219, 221
Canovese, Giosefo, 48
Casella, Antonio, 30, 364
Casini, Giovanni Maria, 212
Caspar, Adam, 12
Casparini, Eugen, 5, 12, 13, 292
Cassana, Niccolò, 228
castrati, 23, 69, 181, 220, 221, 242, 245, 250, 348

Castris, Francesco de, 23, 69, 70, 212, 218, 219, 220, 221, 222, 235, 251, 343, 376
Castro, Francesco de, 219
Catini, Antonio, 224
Cazzati, Mauritio, 45
Celestini, Giovanni, 48, 55
cemballo of Cortona, 39
Ceroti, Giuseppo, 24
Challis, John, 5
Charles II, King, 28
Chevalier de Piis, Pierre-Antoine-Augustin, 333
chinoiserie, 254, 256
Church of S. Luca, Padua, 8
Church of S. Maria Maggiore, Rome, 227
Church of S. Maria Nuova, Florence, 17
Ciampi, Sabatino, 12
Citerni, Antonio, 63, 214, 242
Clari, Giovanni Carlo Maria, 212
Clavering, George Nasau, Third Earl Cowper, 235
clavichord, 2, 5, 6, 29, 40, 67, 72, 77, 95, 97, 99, 112, 113, 114, 115, 116, 119, 252, 276, 285, 289, 306, 307, 308, 338, 363, 374
claviorgano, 57
Cocomero theater, 215, 216, 228
Compagnia de San Sebastiano, 225
Compagnia dell'Arcangelo Raffaello detta la Scala, 225
Compagnia della Purificazione di Maria Vergine e di San Zenobi detta de San Marco, 225
Compagnia di San Jacopo detta del Nicchio, 225
Congregazione dell'Oratorio, 225
Conservatório de Música, Mafra, 265
Conti, Cosimo, 160
Coppa, Luzia di Francesco, 57
Cosimo III de' Medici, Grand Duke, 19
Couperin, François, 329
Crespi, Giuseppe Maria, 228
Crisp, Samuel, 344
Cristofori, Bartolomeo
  address in Florence, 22
  alternate spellings of his surname, 8
  appointed keeper of Medici instrument collection, 64–66
  assistants, 180–211
  bill of 1690 for a spineta, 33–35
  bill of 1692 for a cembalo, 40–41
  bill of 1692 for cembalo for the theater, 42–43
  bill of 1693 for an organ, 46–47
  bill of 1693 for oval spinet, 49–52
  bill of 1697 for upright harpsichord, 59–61
  bill of 1698 for a cembalo, 61–62
  birth, 8
  cemballo of 1692, 40–41
  cembalo with tiorbino stop, 47–48
  cited in Pratolino opera payment records, 219
  clavichord of 1719, 77–78, 119
  critical reception of the piano, 67–68
  death in 1732, 73–74
  ebony harpsichord, 79–88
  fakes, 79
  final itemized bill to court, 64
  first impression of Florence, 18–19
  first record of payment in Medici court, 16
  first work for Medici court, 22–24
  Gatti-Kraus action, 166–180
  harpsichord of 1722, 100–105
  harpsichord of 1726, 105–112
  household supplies provided by Medici court, 20–22
  how many instruments he made, 68–73
  interviewed by Maffei, 121–129, 350–355
  invention of the piano, 66–67
  invitation to work in Medici court, 14
  last bill for constructing a harpsichord, 61–62
  last will and testament, 74–76
  nicknames, 9
  no record of apprenticeship, 9–12
  organ of 1693, 46–47
  oval spinet of 1690, 33–38
  oval spinet of 1693, 49–52
  oval spinets compared, 88–93
  piano of 1720, alterations, 161–166
  piano, earliest formal documentation, 119–121
  pianos compared, 129–157
  pianos, evidence of original stringing, 157–159
  pianos, keyboard ranges, 129
  portrait, 76–77
  provenance of 1720 piano, 159–161
  spinettone da orchestra or *da teatro*, 42, 43, 45, 94, 100
  supplemental bills submitted to court, 24–27
  upright harpsichord of 1697, 59–61
  use of his instruments in Florence, 241–242
  workshop in Florence, 22
Curtis, Alan, 4, 332, 333, 334

da Palermo, Marcantonio, 219
de Bricqueville, Eugène, 331

de l'Épine, Adrien, 331
de Piis, Chevalier, 333
del Mela, Domenico, 61, 75, 201, 203, 204, 348
    female relations mentioned in Cristofori's will, 202–203
    lack of evidence he assisted Cristofori, 201
    upright pianoforte, 201–211
Denner, Johann Christoph, 29, 33, 227
Dieffopruchar, Magno, 33
Dolmetsch, Arnold, 112, 113, 252
Don Antonio, Infante of Portugal, 343
Dowd, William, 330
Dussek, Jan Ladislav, 339

ebony harpsichord, 14, 31, 41, 66, 74, 80, 81, 82, 83, 84, 85, 86, 93, 156, 167
Echavarría, Pedro de Liborna, 248
Encyclopédie méthodique, 181
Erard, Jean-Baptiste, 337
Erard, Pierre, 337, 339
Erard, Sébastien, 5, 336, 337, 338
Erdtmann, Ludovico, 226, 227

Fabbri, Mario, 11, 67, 227, 372
Falconi, Giuseppe, 18
Farinelli (Carlo Broschi), 181, 182, 245, 248, 250, 251, 292, 343, 348, 364, 370
Fernández, Diego, 193, 248, 369
Fernández, Julian, 248
Feroci, Michele, 18
Ferrini, Giovanni, 22, 56, 74, 75, 78, 81, 83, 84, 85, 96, 110, 170, 180, 181, 182, 183, 184, 186, 187, 188, 194, 195, 196, 197, 198, 200, 202, 206, 243, 244, 246, 292, 330, 348, 373, 375
    cembalo traverso of 1731, 194–198
    combination pianoforte/harpsichord of 1746, 183–194
    documentary references, 180–182
    restoration of Zenti harpsichord, 201
    virtual disinheritance in Cristofori's will, 203
Ferrini, Giuseppe, 56, 81, 83, 87
Ficker, Wahl Friedrich, 283
Figli, Giovanni (probably misspelling of Giovanni Fuga), 219, 222
Flade, Ernst, 12, 13, 289, 290, 292
Florentine currency, 7
Floriani, Benedetto, 78
Forkel, Johann Nikolaus, 293, 295, 296, 366
Francesco of Padua ("Il Ongaro"), 13, 30
Franciolini, Leopoldo, 112, 116, 159, 374
Franciscus Patavinus (Francesco of Padua), 13, 30

Frederick II "the Great" of Prussia, 290, 293, 295, 296, 344
Frescobaldi, Girolamo, 57, 241, 367
Friederici, Christian Ernst, 203, 206, 283, 307, 308, 309, 310, 311, 312, 313, 315, 316, 319, 323, 324, 327, 365
Friederici, Christian Gottfried, 307
Friederici, Christian Gottlob, 307
Fritz, Barthold, 308
Fuga, Giovanni, 24, 32, 222, 223, 224
Fumiani, Giovanni Antonio, 228
Furnari, Antonello, 67, 376

Gabbiani, Anton Domencio, 19, 24, 99, 223, 224, 228
Gabriel de Borbón, Infante, 235
Galleria dell' Accademia, 4, 66, 72, 88, 168, 176
Ganer, Christopher, 345
Ganzaga, Princess Eleonora, 63, 64, 214, 242
Garcka, George, 345
Gasparini, Francesco, 212
Gaular, Phelipe, 248
Geib, John, 345
George I, King, 234
Gerber, Ernst Ludwig, 283, 308
German action, 338
Germanisches Nationalmuseum, Nuremberg, 4, 293, 301, 302, 305, 310, 317, 327
Gigli, Giovanni, 24, 68, 219, 222, 223, 224, 234, 235
Giornale de' letterati d'Italia, 8, 18, 121, 122, 123, 168, 212, 220, 222, 243, 281, 344
Gisberti, Domenico, 219
Giustini, Lodovico, 235, 343
Goethe-Haus, Frankfurt, 311
gold strings, 54
Grantorto, 9
Grassi Museum, Leipzig, 94
Grassi Museum für Musikinstrumente der Universität Leipzig, 14, 29, 44, 51, 77, 88, 89, 94, 101, 104, 106, 107, 114, 115, 153
Graun, Karl Heinrich, 293
gravecembalo, 68, 125, 127, 128, 151, 169, 181, 356, 357, 359, 360, 361
Graziani, Domenico, 219
Gustadt, Errico, 348

Haka, Richard, 29, 33, 227
Handel, George Frideric, 67, 212, 228, 376
Harding, Rosamund, 6, 208, 238, 312, 320, 338, 340, 341, 368
Hardouin, Pierre J., 334

Hass family, 308
Hebenstreit, Pantaleon, 288, 289, 305
Henkel, Hubert, 48, 68, 71, 72, 93, 94, 95, 109, 156, 159, 292, 368
Henley, William, 79
Heyer, Wilhelm, 166, 167
Hill, William Henry, Arthur, and Alfred Ebsworth, 79
Hipkins, A. J., 161
Hubbard, Frank, 28, 38, 331, 334, 346, 368
Hullmandel, Nicholas, 346

Il figlio delle Selve, 227
Il Greco in Troia, 215, 216, 220, 234
Il Lisamaco, 221
Il Numa Pompilio, 221
in sesta, 32, 36, 49, 54, 55

Jeckel, Christian, 288
Jeckel, Johann Christoph, 288
João V, King of Portugal, 73, 243, 244, 245, 246, 343, 374

Kaufmann Collection, 264
Kenyon de Pascual, Beryl, 248, 252, 253, 254, 369
Kinsky, Georg, 168
Kirckman, Jacob and Abraham, 347
Kirkman, family of harpsichord makers, 345
Kirkpatrick, Ralph, 69, 222, 227, 246, 248, 249, 250, 251, 369
Koch, Heinrich Christoph, 286, 308
König, Johann Ulrich, 243, 281, 282, 283, 286, 290, 291, 295, 336, 369
Kraus, Alessandro, 166
Kreuzschule, Dresden, 286

L'Avantcoureur, 331
L'Encyclopédie méthodique, 332
L'Ipocondriaco, 57
"L'Ongaro," 13, 30
Landi, Agostino, 18
Lassagnini, Giovanni Battista, 17, 66
Lebègue, Nicolas-Antoine, 329
Legrenzi, Giovanni, 212
Leipzig University, 166
Lester, Harold, 264
Liszt, Franz, 339
Loccatelli, Antonio, 348
Longo, Magno, 33
Lorenzo da Pavia, 13
Louis XVI, King of France, 337

Lucio Manlio, 228
Lütgendorff, Willibald Leo Freiherrn von, 79
lute register, 347

machine stop, 347
Maffei, Marchese Francesco Scipione, 4, 8, 12, 14, 18, 19, 26, 67, 69, 77, 102, 116, 118, 121, 122, 123, 124, 130, 131, 132, 133, 134, 135, 138, 140, 142, 144, 151, 152, 153, 157, 168, 169, 222, 238, 239, 240, 241, 243, 245, 281, 282, 283, 284, 285, 286, 290, 291, 328, 336, 340, 341, 342, 343, 350, 351, 356, 369, 370, 372, 377
Magnelli, Giovanni Battista, 30
Mahillon, Victor-Charles, 264, 370
Mannucci, Franceso Maria, 67
Marcantonio (*see* Marcantonio da Palermo), 23, 219
Marie Antoinette, Queen of France, 337
Marius, Jean, 5, 29, 328, 329, 330, 365
Marmol, Juan del, 249
Marpurg, Friedrich Wilhelm, 284, 285, 286, 287, 288, 293, 347, 370
Martelli, Diego, 160, 161
Martini, Angelo, 7
Martini, Giovanni Battista, 180, 348
Mattheson, Johann, 243, 281, 284, 369, 370
meantone temperament, fifth comma, 240
Measurement
    Florentine units, 7
Meccoli, Federigo, 66, 242
Medici
    archives, 11
    changes in court billing procedure, 62–63
    court musicians, 8
    court pays for repairs to Cristofori's house, 58
    inventories of musical instruments, 31–66
    musical instrument collection, 27–31
    musical instrument inventories, 31–33
Medici, Anna Maria Luisa de', 42, 64
Medici, Ferdinando de', 3, 9, 12, 15, 16, 22, 32, 33, 39, 53, 62, 77, 121, 122, 215, 218, 227, 245, 366, 367, 371, 375
    as a keyboard player, 228–235
    communication with Cardinal Pietro Ottoboni, 222
    travels to Padua in 1688, 15
Medici, Ferdinando II de', 57
Medici, Francesco Maria de', 64, 182
Medici, Gian Gastone de', 42, 64, 70, 71, 123, 213, 225, 226, 228, 234, 235, 244

Medici, Grand Duke Cosimo III de', 19, 39, 42, 57, 59, 62, 161, 182, 212, 213, 214, 221, 225, 234
Medici, Violante Beatrice de', Grand Princess (formerly Violante Beatrice of Bavaria), 17, 39, 161, 213, 215, 220
Melani, Alessandro, 212, 221
Melani, Domenico, 235
Melani, Niccolò, 75
Mercken, Johann Kilian, 331
Metropolitan Museum of Art, 1, 3, 4, 11, 29, 78, 79, 81, 84, 102, 121, 129, 130, 147, 154, 158, 159, 160, 161, 163, 164, 165, 167, 177, 200, 202, 238, 282, 348, 370, 371
Meyer, Meincke, 345
Migliai, Antonio, 18
Mizler, Lorenz, 283
Mocenni, Ernesta, 161
Mocenni, Dr. Fabio, 160, 161
Mondini, Giuseppe, 30, 48, 58
Montal, Claude, 339
Morellati, Paolo, 348
Moscheles, Charlotte, 340
Moscheles, Ignaz, 340
Mozart, Leopold, 308
Mozart, Wolfgang Amadeus, 308
Musée des arts et métiers, Paris, 331
Muziekinstrumentenmuseum, Brussels, 264
Museo Bardini, 14, 35
Museo Correr, 13
Museo degli Strumenti Musicali del Conservatorio "Luigi Cherubini," Florence, 14, 35, 61, 79, 80, 88, 167, 203, 204
Museo degli Strumenti Musicali, Milan, 43
Musical Offering, Johann Sebastian Bach, 344
Müthel, Johann Gottfried, 346

Nacchianti, Christofano, 74
National Music Museum, Vermillion, 266, 271, 334, 335, 336
Neues Palais, 293, 294, 301, 303, 304, 306, 321, 322, 323
Neupert, Johann Christian, 312
Neupert, Wolf Dieter, 312
Nivers, Guillaume-Gabriel, 329

O'Brien, Grant, 7
Olivicciani, Vincenzo di Pietro, 235
Onofri, Nicola, 60
Opera, 215–225
Oratorio, 225–227

Orlandini, Giuseppe Maria, 212, 213, 226, 234
Österreichische Nationalbibliothek, 221
ottava bassa, 47, 61
ottava stesa, 32, 41, 43, 47, 49, 51, 60, 61, 80, 119, 121
Ottoboni, Cardinal Pietro, 69, 70, 121, 222, 245, 345, 350, 353, 364

Padua
    Cristofori's place of birth, 8
    Drio Domo, 9
Pagliardi, Giovanni Francesco, 19, 23, 53, 57, 67, 212, 215, 218, 219, 220, 221, 234, 235, 241
Pagliardi, Giovanni Maria, 23, 24
Palazzo Pitti, 223
Palermo, Marcantonio da, 23
Pantaleon/Pantalon, 288, 290, 301, 305, 367
Papafava, 9
    Laura, 9
    Roberto, 9, 18
Papi, Iacopo, 18
peau de buffle, 334
Pérez Mirabal, Francisco, 248, 252, 253, 254, 257, 270
Pergola theater, 39, 215, 216, 220
Peri, Francesco, 219
Perotti, Carlo, 167
Perti, Giacomo Antonio, 67, 212, 218, 228, 234, 366, 370
Pertici, Giovanni, 18
Pesaro, Domenico da, 30, 32, 49, 57, 78, 114, 115, 128, 219, 229, 232, 242, 351, 354, 361
Pfeiffer, Walter, 312
Pianoforte (*see also* Cristofori, Bartolomeo)
    English, 346
    First mention in Medici documents, 15
    French, 328–342
    German, 281–327
    Portuguese, 262–277
    Spanish, 252–262
Pichileri, Giovanni, 18
Pierre, Constant, 331
Pini, Bartolomeo, 18
Pisauriensis, Dominicus (*see* Pesaro, Domenico da), 28
Pitti Palace, 19, 26, 46, 47, 212, 225, 228, 235, 244
Plenius, Roger, 344
Poggi, Francesco, 18
Poggio a Caiano, 59, 224, 233
Pohlmann, Johannes, 345
Pollarolo, Carlo Francesco, 212, 218

Ponsicchi, Cesare, 4, 136, 158, 160, 163, 168, 174, 176, 177, 180, 201, 203, 208, 373
Porpora, Niccolò, 212
Pratolino, 17, 22, 24, 25, 39, 45, 49, 52, 57, 58, 59, 60, 68, 77, 214, 216, 217, 218, 219, 220, 221, 222, 228, 241, 370, 374
"Prete da Imola" (Giuseppe Mondini), 30
Public Advertiser, 346
Pucini (or Puccini), Signor, 59
Puertas, Augustin de, 248
Puliti, Leto, 16, 160, 161, 163
Pyramide piano, 206, 264, 309, 310, 311, 312, 313, 314, 315, 316, 317, 318, 319, 320, 323, 324, 325, 326, 327

Querci, Vincenzio, 18

Rameau, Jean Philippe, 346
Redi, Francesco, 212
Rees, Abraham, 344
Ricci, Sebastiano, 228
Ricevuti, Aurelio, 18
Ripin, Edwin, 1, 163
Royal College of Music, 61
Russell, Raymond, 252

Sachs, Curt, 156, 163, 177, 372
Salvetti, Pietro, 24, 32, 212, 219, 222, 242
Sanssouci, 293, 294, 298, 301, 303, 304, 306, 321, 322, 323, 324, 327
Santiago Kastner, Dr. Macario, 264
Santos, Andrés Fernández, 248
Sauveur, Joseph, 240
Scarlatti, Alessandro, 212, 218, 221, 227–228
Scarlatti, Domenico, 6, 57, 69, 165, 166, 218, 220, 222, 227, 234, 235, 244, 245, 246, 248, 249, 250, 251, 343, 346, 365, 366, 369, 371, 373, 374, 375
Schmahl, Christoph Friedrich, 288
Schobert, Johann, 346
Schoene, George, 345
Schröter, Christoph Gottlieb, 5, 283, 284, 285, 286, 287, 288, 290, 291, 292, 305, 347
Schubart, Christian Friedrich Daniel, 283, 288, 289
Schünemann, Georg, 76, 136, 137
Seixas, Carlos de, 166
Seixas, Giovanni de, 238
Sengher, Filippo, 212
Senta, Fabritius, 224
senza spezzati, 41, 43, 48, 49, 51, 54, 60, 80, 119
Seven Years War, 345
Seyffartt, Hermann, 312

Sheveloff, Joel Leonard, 250, 374
Shudi, Burkat, 345
Sievers, Christoph 345
Silbermann, Andreas, 13
Silbermann, Gottfried, 12, 13, 248, 254, 257, 276, 282, 285, 288, 289, 290, 291, 292, 293, 294, 297, 298, 300, 301, 302, 304, 305, 307, 313, 316, 319, 321, 322, 327, 331, 343, 345, 366, 371, 373
Silbermann, Jean-Henri, 331
Sodi, Vincenzo, 348
Soldini, Agostino, 18
Soler, Antonio, 55, 166, 235
Sorgenti theater, 215, 216
Spada, Laura, 18
Späth, Franz Jacob, 283, 288
Spighi, Francesco, 348
Spinettina with strings of gold, 54–55
spinettone da orchestra, 2, 30, 31, 43, 44, 45, 52, 68, 72, 77, 78, 94, 95, 97, 99, 100, 108, 110, 114, 153, 154, 194, 198, 221, 230, 231, 241
Stampiglia, Silvio, 228
Stein, Matthäus Andreas, 338
Stodart, Robert, 346
Stradivari, Antonio, 3, 10, 35, 53, 65, 66, 74, 153, 224, 244, 364, 372
Susier, Niccolò, 8, 73, 244, 251

Taglia, Giovanni, 219, 224
Taskin, Pascal, 333, 334
Taxis, Count, 250
theorbo, 68, 73, 129, 136, 221, 222, 224, 226, 240, 241, 244, 351
Thompson, Mrs. Launt, 159
tiorbino, 48, 61
Tito Manlio, 221
Transcription of Scipione Maffei's "Nuova invenzione d'un Gravecembalo col piano, e forte; aggiunte alcune considerazioni sopra gli strumenti musicali," *Giornale de' letterati d'Italia* 5 (Venice, 1711), Appendix 2. *See* Chapter 3 for the translation, 124–129
Trost, Tobias Heinrich Gottfried, 307
"Twelve Apostles," 345

Università di Por San Piero e dei Fabbricanti, 18, 20, 58, 182

van Audenaerd, Robert, 220
Van Casteel, Henrique, 263, 264, 267, 268, 269, 270, 271, 272, 273, 274, 275, 276, 278, 280
Van der Meer, John Henry, 349

Veltman, Andries, 330
Venetian swell, 347
Veracini, Antonio, 24, 212, 223, 368
Viennese action, 338
Vignoli, Luigi, 348
Vincenti, Ferdinando, 18
Violante Beatrice de' Medici, Grand Princess, 17, 39, 161, 213, 215, 220
Vitali, Carlo, 67, 70, 222
Vivaldi, Antonio, 212
Viviani, Vincenzio, 212
Volpini, Bastiano, 71
Voltaire, 333

Wagenseil, Georg Christoph, 346
Walther, Johann Georg, 244, 376

Weaver, Robert Lamar, 220
Westerhout, Arnold, 220
Wise, Christopher, 29

Zanardi, Carlo Antonio, 23, 69, 70, 219, 221, 222, 251, 343
Zannetti, Giuseppe, 348
Zarlino, Gioseffo, 66, 239, 240
Zenti Girolamo, and instruments made by him, 16, 28, 29, 45, 47, 48, 55, 56, 61, 81, 84, 152, 200, 201, 202, 224, 229, 230, 232, 367, 374
Zipoli, Domenico, 166
Zolfanelli, Giuseppe, 18
Zumpe, Johann Christoph (Johannes), 338, 344